Understanding the

LINUX
KERNEL

Understanding the
LINUX
KERNEL

DANIEL P. BOVET & MARCO CESATI

O'REILLY®

Beijing • Cambridge • Farnham • Köln • Paris • Sebastopol • Taipei • Tokyo

Understanding the Linux Kernel
by Daniel P. Bovet and Marco Cesati

Published by O'Reilly & Associates, Inc., 101 Morris Street, Sebastopol, CA 95472.

Editor: Andy Oram

Production Editor: Catherine Morris

Cover Designer: Edie Freedman

Printing History:

January 2001:   First Edition.

Library of Congress Cataloging-in-Publication Data:

Bovet, D. (Daniel)
    Understanding the Linux kernel / Daniel P. Bovet & Marco Cesati.
        p. cm
    ISBN 0-596-00002-2
    1. Linux. 2. Operating systems (Computers) I. Cesati, Marco. II. Title.

QA76.76.O63 B665 2000
005.4'32--dc21   00-053027

0-596-00002-2
[M]   [9/01]

TABLE OF CONTENTS

PREFACE

In the spring semester of 1997, we taught a course on operating systems based on Linux 2.0. The idea was to encourage students to read the source code. To achieve this, we assigned term projects consisting of making changes to the kernel and performing tests on the modified version. We also wrote course notes for our students about a few critical features of Linux like task switching and task scheduling.

We continued along this line in the spring semester of 1998, but we moved on to the Linux 2.1 development version. Our course notes were becoming larger and larger. In July, 1998 we contacted O'Reilly & Associates, suggesting they publish a whole book on the Linux kernel. The real work started in the fall of 1998 and lasted about a year and a half. We read thousands of lines of code, trying to make sense of them. After all this work, we can say that it was worth the effort. We learned a lot of things you don't find in books, and we hope we have succeeded in conveying some of this information in the following pages.

The Audience for This Book

All people curious about how Linux works and why it is so efficient will find answers here. After reading the book, you will find your way through the many thousands of lines of code, distinguishing between crucial data structures and secondary ones—in short, becoming a true Linux hacker.

Our work might be considered a guided tour of the Linux kernel: most of the significant data structures and many algorithms and programming tricks used in the kernel are discussed; in many cases, the relevant fragments of code are discussed line by line. Of course, you should have the Linux source code on hand and should be willing to spend some effort deciphering some of the functions that are not, for sake of brevity, fully described.

On another level, the book will give valuable insights to people who want to know more about the critical design issues in a modern operating system. It is not specifically addressed to system administrators or programmers; it is mostly for people who want to understand how things really work inside the machine! Like any good guide, we try to go beyond superficial features. We offer background, such as the history of major features and the reasons they were used.

Organization of the Material

When starting to write this book, we were faced with a critical decision: should we refer to a specific hardware platform or skip the hardware-dependent details and concentrate on the pure hardware-independent parts of the kernel?

Others books on Linux kernel internals have chosen the latter approach; we decided to adopt the former one for the following reasons:

*   Efficient kernels take advantage of most available hardware features, such as addressing techniques, caches, processor exceptions, special instructions, processor control registers, and so on. If we want to convince you that the kernel indeed does quite a good job in performing a specific task, we must first tell what kind of support comes from the hardware.

*   Even if a large portion of a Unix kernel source code is processor-independent and coded in C language, a small and critical part is coded in assembly language. A thorough knowledge of the kernel thus requires the study of a few assembly language fragments that interact with the hardware.

When covering hardware features, our strategy will be quite simple: just sketch the features that are totally hardware-driven while detailing those that need some software support. In fact, we are interested in kernel design rather than in computer architecture.

The next step consisted of selecting the computer system to be described: although Linux is now running on several kinds of personal computers and workstations, we decided to concentrate on the very popular and cheap IBM-compatible personal computers—thus, on the Intel 80x86 microprocessors and on some support chips included in these personal computers. The term *Intel 80x86 microprocessor* will be used in the forthcoming chapters to denote the Intel 80386, 80486, Pentium, Pentium Pro, Pentium II, and Pentium III microprocessors or compatible models. In a few cases, explicit references will be made to specific models.

One more choice was the order followed in studying Linux components. We tried to follow a bottom-up approach: start with topics that are hardware-dependent and end with those that are totally hardware-independent. In fact, we'll make many references to the Intel 80x86 microprocessors in the first part of the book, while the rest of it is relatively hardware-independent. Two significant exceptions are made in Chapter 11, *Kernel Synchronization*, and Chapter 13, *Managing I/O Devices*. In practice, following a bottom-up approach is not as simple as it looks, since the areas of memory management, process management, and filesystem are intertwined; a few forward references—that is, references to topics yet to be explained—are unavoidable.

Each chapter starts with a theoretical overview of the topics covered. The material is then presented according to the bottom-up approach. We start with the data structures needed to support the functionalities described in the chapter. Then we usually move from the lowest level of functions to higher levels, often ending by showing how system calls issued by user applications are supported.

Level of Description

Linux source code for all supported architectures is contained in about 4500 C and Assembly files stored in about 270 subdirectories; it consists of about 2 million lines of code, which occupy more than 58 megabytes of disk space. Of course, this book can cover a very small portion of that code. Just to figure out how big the Linux source is, consider that the whole source code of the book you are reading occupies less than 2 megabytes of disk space. Therefore, in order to list all code, without commenting on it, we would need more than 25 books like this!*

So we had to make some choices about the parts to be described. This is a rough assessment of our decisions:

- We describe process and memory management fairly thoroughly.

- We cover the Virtual Filesystem and the Ext2 filesystem, although many functions are just mentioned without detailing the code; we do not discuss other filesystems supported by Linux.

- We describe device drivers, which account for a good part of the kernel, as far as the kernel interface is concerned, but do not attempt analysis of any specific driver, including the terminal drivers.

- We do not cover networking, since this area would deserve a whole new book by itself.

In many cases, the original code has been rewritten in an easier to read but less efficient way. This occurs at time-critical points at which sections of programs are often written in a mixture of hand-optimized C and Assembly code. Once again, our aim is to provide some help in studying the original Linux code.

While discussing kernel code, we often end up describing the underpinnings of many familiar features that Unix programmers have heard of and about which they may be curious (shared and mapped memory, signals, pipes, symbolic links).

---

* Nevertheless, Linux is a tiny operating system when compared with other commercial giants. Microsoft Windows 2000, for example, reportedly has more than 30 million lines of code. Linux is also small when compared to some popular applications; Netscape Communicator 5 browser, for example, has about 17 million lines of code.

Overview of the Book

To make life easier, Chapter 1, *Introduction*, presents a general picture of what is inside a Unix kernel and how Linux competes against other well-known Unix systems.

The heart of any Unix kernel is memory management. Chapter 2, *Memory Addressing*, explains how Intel 80x86 processors include special circuits to address data in memory and how Linux exploits them.

Processes are a fundamental abstraction offered by Linux and are introduced in Chapter 3, *Processes*. Here we also explain how each process runs either in an unprivileged User Mode or in a privileged Kernel Mode. Transitions between User Mode and Kernel Mode happen only through well-established hardware mechanisms called *interrupts* and *exceptions*, which are introduced in Chapter 4, *Interrupts and Exceptions*. One type of interrupt is crucial for allowing Linux to take care of elapsed time; further details can be found in Chapter 5, *Timing Measurements*.

Next we focus again on memory: Chapter 6, *Memory Management*, describes the sophisticated techniques required to handle the most precious resource in the system (besides the processors, of course), that is, available memory. This resource must be granted both to the Linux kernel and to the user applications. Chapter 7, *Process Address Space*, shows how the kernel copes with the requests for memory issued by greedy application programs.

Chapter 8, *System Calls*, explains how a process running in User Mode makes requests to the kernel, while Chapter 9, *Signals*, describes how a process may send synchronization signals to other processes. Chapter 10, *Process Scheduling*, explains how Linux executes, in turn, every active process in the system so that all of them can progress toward their completions. Synchronization mechanisms are needed by the kernel too: they are discussed in Chapter 11, *Kernel Synchronization*, for both uniprocessor and multiprocessor systems.

Now we are ready to move on to another essential topic, that is, how Linux implements the filesystem. A series of chapters covers this topic: Chapter 12, *The Virtual Filesystem*, introduces a general layer that supports many different filesystems. Some Linux files are special because they provide trapdoors to reach hardware devices; Chapter 13, *Managing I/O Devices* offers insights on these special files and on the corresponding hardware device drivers. Another issue to be considered is disk access time; Chapter 14, *Disk Caches*, shows how a clever use of RAM reduces disk accesses and thus improves system performance significantly. Building on the material covered in these last chapters, we can now explain in Chapter 15, *Accessing Regular Files*, how user applications access normal files. Chapter 16, *Swapping: Methods for Freeing Memory*, completes our discussion of Linux memory management and explains the techniques used by Linux to ensure that enough memory is always available. The last chapter dealing with files is Chapter 17, *The Ext2 Filesystem*, which illustrates the most-used Linux filesystem, namely Ext2.

The last two chapters end our detailed tour of the Linux kernel: Chapter 18, *Process Communication*, introduces communication mechanisms other than signals available to User Mode processes; Chapter 19, *Program Execution*, explains how user applications are started.

Last but not least are the appendixes: Appendix A, *System Startup*, sketches out how Linux is booted, while Appendix B, *Modules*, describes how to dynamically reconfigure the running kernel, adding and removing functionalities as needed. Appendix C, *Source Code Structure*, is just a list of the directories that contain the Linux source code. The Source Code Index includes all the Linux symbols referenced in the book; you will find here the name of the Linux file defining each symbol and the book's page number where it is explained. We think you'll find it quite handy.

Background Information

No prerequisites are required, except some skill in C programming language and perhaps some knowledge of Assembly language.

Conventions in This Book

The following is a list of typographical conventions used in this book:

Constant Width
> Is used to show the contents of code files or the output from commands, and to indicate source code keywords that appear in code.

Italic
> Is used for file and directory names, program and command names, command-line options, URLs, and for emphasizing new terms.

How to Contact Us

We have tested and verified all the information in this book to the best of our abilities, but you may find that features have changed or that we have let errors slip through the production of the book. Please let us know of any errors that you find, as well as suggestions for future editions, by writing to:

O'Reilly & Associates, Inc.
101 Morris St.
Sebastopol, CA 95472
(800) 998-9938 (in the U.S. or Canada)
(707) 829-0515 (international/local)
(707) 829-0104 (fax)

You can also send messages electronically. To be put on our mailing list or to request a catalog, send email to:

> *info@oreilly.com*

To ask technical questions or to comment on the book, send email to:

> *bookquestions@oreilly.com*

We have a web site for the book, where we'll list reader reviews, errata, and any plans for future editions. You can access this page at:

> *http://www.oreilly.com/catalog/linuxkernel/*

We also have an additional web site where you will find material written by the authors about the new features of Linux 2.4. Hopefully, this material will be used for a future edition of this book. You can access this page at:

> *http://www.oreilly.com/catalog/linuxkernel/updates/*

For more information about this book and others, see the O'Reilly web site:

> *http://www.oreilly.com*

Acknowledgments

This book would not have been written without the precious help of the many students of the school of engineering at the University of Rome "Tor Vergata" who took our course and tried to decipher the lecture notes about the Linux kernel. Their strenuous efforts to grasp the meaning of the source code led us to improve our presentation and to correct many mistakes.

Andy Oram, our wonderful editor at O'Reilly & Associates, deserves a lot of credit. He was the first at O'Reilly to believe in this project, and he spent a lot of time and energy deciphering our preliminary drafts. He also suggested many ways to make the book more readable, and he wrote several excellent introductory paragraphs.

Many thanks also to the O'Reilly staff, especially Rob Romano, the technical illustrator, and Lenny Muellner, for tools support.

We had some prestigious reviewers who read our text quite carefully (in alphabetical order by first name): Alan Cox, Michael Kerrisk, Paul Kinzelman, Raph Levien, and Rik van Riel. Their comments helped us to remove several errors and inaccuracies and have made this book stronger.

—Daniel P. Bovet
Marco Cesati
September 2000

CHAPTER ONE

INTRODUCTION

Linux is a member of the large family of Unix-like operating systems. A relative new-comer experiencing sudden spectacular popularity starting in the late 1990s, Linux joins such well-known commercial Unix operating systems as System V Release 4 (SVR4) developed by AT&T, which is now owned by Santa Cruz Operation, Inc.; the 4.4 BSD release from the University of California at Berkeley (4.4BSD), Digital Unix from Digital Equipment Corporation (now Compaq); AIX from IBM; HP-UX from Hewlett-Packard; and Solaris from Sun Microsystems.

Linux was initially developed by Linus Torvalds in 1991 as an operating system for IBM-compatible personal computers based on the Intel 80386 microprocessor. Linus remains deeply involved with improving Linux, keeping it up-to-date with various hardware developments and coordinating the activity of hundreds of Linux developers around the world. Over the years, developers have worked to make Linux available on other architectures, including Alpha, SPARC, Motorola MC680x0, PowerPC, and IBM System/390.

One of the more appealing benefits to Linux is that it isn't a commercial operating system: its source code under the GNU General Public License* is open and available to anyone to study, as we will in this book; if you download the code (the official site is *http://www.kernel.org/*) or check the sources on a Linux CD, you will be able to explore from top to bottom one of the most successful, modern operating systems. This book, in fact, assumes you have the source code on hand and can apply what we say to your own explorations.

---

* The GNU project is coordinated by the Free Software Foundation, Inc. (*http://www.gnu.org/*); its aim is to implement a whole operating system freely usable by everyone. The availability of a GNU C compiler has been essential for the success of the Linux project.

Technically speaking, Linux is a true Unix kernel, although it is not a full Unix operating system, because it does not include all the applications such as filesystem utilities, windowing systems and graphical desktops, system administrator commands, text editors, compilers, and so on. However, since most of these programs are freely available under the GNU General Public License, they can be installed into one of the filesystems supported by Linux.

Since Linux is a kernel, many Linux users prefer to rely on commercial distributions, available on CD-ROM, to get the code included in a standard Unix system. Alternatively, the code may be obtained from several different FTP sites. The Linux source code is usually installed in the */usr/src/linux* directory. In the rest of this book, all file pathnames will refer implicitly to that directory.

Linux Versus Other Unix-Like Kernels

The various Unix-like systems on the market, some of which have a long history and may show signs of archaic practices, differ in many important respects. All commercial variants were derived from either SVR4 or 4.4BSD; all of them tend to agree on some common standards like IEEE's POSIX (Portable Operating Systems based on Unix) and X/Open's CAE (Common Applications Environment).

The current standards specify only an application programming interface (API)—that is, a well-defined environment in which user programs should run. Therefore, the standards do not impose any restriction on internal design choices of a compliant kernel.*

In order to define a common user interface, Unix-like kernels often share fundamental design ideas and features. In this respect, Linux is comparable with the other Unix-like operating systems. What you read in this book and see in the Linux kernel, therefore, may help you understand the other Unix variants too.

The 2.2 version of the Linux kernel aims to be compliant with the IEEE POSIX standard. This, of course, means that most existing Unix programs can be compiled and executed on a Linux system with very little effort or even without the need for patches to the source code. Moreover, Linux includes all the features of a modern Unix operating system, like virtual memory, a virtual filesystem, lightweight processes, reliable signals, SVR4 interprocess communications, support for Symmetric Multiprocessor (SMP) systems, and so on.

By itself, the Linux kernel is not very innovative. When Linus Torvalds wrote the first kernel, he referred to some classical books on Unix internals, like Maurice Bach's *The Design of the Unix Operating System* (Prentice Hall, 1986). Actually, Linux still has some bias toward the Unix baseline described in Bach's book (i.e., System V). However,

---

* As a matter of fact, several non-Unix operating systems like Windows NT are POSIX-compliant.

Linux doesn't stick to any particular variant. Instead, it tries to adopt good features and design choices of several different Unix kernels.

Here is an assessment of how Linux competes against some well-known commercial Unix kernels:

- The Linux kernel is monolithic. It is a large, complex do-it-yourself program, composed of several logically different components. In this, it is quite conventional; most commercial Unix variants are monolithic. A notable exception is Carnegie-Mellon's Mach 3.0, which follows a microkernel approach.

- Traditional Unix kernels are compiled and linked statically. Most modern kernels can dynamically load and unload some portions of the kernel code (typically, device drivers), which are usually called *modules*. Linux's support for modules is very good, since it is able to automatically load and unload modules on demand. Among the main commercial Unix variants, only the SVR4.2 kernel has a similar feature.

- Kernel threading. Some modern Unix kernels, like Solaris 2.x and SVR4.2/MP, are organized as a set of *kernel threads*. A kernel thread is an execution context that can be independently scheduled; it may be associated with a user program, or it may run only some kernel functions. Context switches between kernel threads are usually much less expensive than context switches between ordinary processes, since the former usually operate on a common address space. Linux uses kernel threads in a very limited way to execute a few kernel functions periodically; since Linux kernel threads cannot execute user programs, they do not represent the basic execution context abstraction. (That's the topic of the next item.)

- Multithreaded application support. Most modern operating systems have some kind of support for multithreaded applications, that is, user programs that are well designed in terms of many relatively independent execution flows sharing a large portion of the application data structures. A multithreaded user application could be composed of many *lightweight processes* (LWP), or processes that can operate on a common address space, common physical memory pages, common opened files, and so on. Linux defines its own version of lightweight processes, which is different from the types used on other systems such as SVR4 and Solaris. While all the commercial Unix variants of LWP are based on kernel threads, Linux regards lightweight processes as the basic execution context and handles them via the nonstandard `clone()` system call.

- Linux is a nonpreemptive kernel. This means that Linux cannot arbitrarily interleave execution flows while they are in privileged mode. Several sections of kernel code assume they can run and modify data structures without fear of being interrupted and having another thread alter those data structures. Usually, fully preemptive kernels are associated with special real-time operating systems. Currently, among conventional, general-purpose Unix systems, only Solaris 2.x and Mach 3.0 are fully preemptive kernels. SVR4.2/MP introduces some *fixed preemption points* as a method to get limited preemption capability.

- Multiprocessor support. Several Unix kernel variants take advantage of multiprocessor systems. Linux 2.2 offers an evolving kind of support for symmetric multiprocessing (SMP), which means not only that the system can use multiple processors but also that any processor can handle any task; there is no discrimination among them. However, Linux 2.2 does not make optimal use of SMP. Several kernel activities that could be executed concurrently—like filesystem handling and networking—must now be executed sequentially.

- Filesystem. Linux's standard filesystem lacks some advanced features, such as journaling. However, more advanced filesystems for Linux are available, although not included in the Linux source code; among them, IBM AIX's Journaling File System (JFS), and Silicon Graphics Irix's XFS filesystem. Thanks to a powerful object-oriented Virtual File System technology (inspired by Solaris and SVR4), porting a foreign filesystem to Linux is a relatively easy task.

- STREAMS. Linux has no analog to the STREAMS I/O subsystem introduced in SVR4, although it is included nowadays in most Unix kernels and it has become the preferred interface for writing device drivers, terminal drivers, and network protocols.

This somewhat disappointing assessment does not depict, however, the whole truth. Several features make Linux a wonderfully unique operating system. Commercial Unix kernels often introduce new features in order to gain a larger slice of the market, but these features are not necessarily useful, stable, or productive. As a matter of fact, modern Unix kernels tend to be quite bloated. By contrast, Linux doesn't suffer from the restrictions and the conditioning imposed by the market, hence it can freely evolve according to the ideas of its designers (mainly Linus Torvalds). Specifically, Linux offers the following advantages over its commercial competitors:

Linux is free.
    You can install a complete Unix system at no expense other than the hardware (of course).

Linux is fully customizable in all its components.
    Thanks to the General Public License (GPL), you are allowed to freely read and modify the source code of the kernel and of all system programs.[*]

Linux runs on low-end, cheap hardware platforms.
    You can even build a network server using an old Intel 80386 system with 4 MB of RAM.

Linux is powerful.
    Linux systems are very fast, since they fully exploit the features of the hardware components. The main Linux target is efficiency, and indeed many design choices

---

[*] Several commercial companies have started to support their products under Linux, most of which aren't distributed under a GNU Public License. Therefore, you may not be allowed to read or modify their source code.

of commercial variants, like the STREAMS I/O subsystem, have been rejected by Linus because of their implied performance penalty.

Linux has a high standard for source code quality.

Linux systems are usually very stable; they have a very low failure rate and system maintenance time.

The Linux kernel can be very small and compact.

Indeed, it is possible to fit both a kernel image and full root filesystem, including all fundamental system programs, on just one 1.4 MB floppy disk! As far as we know, none of the commercial Unix variants is able to boot from a single floppy disk.

Linux is highly compatible with many common operating systems.

It lets you directly mount filesystems for all versions of MS-DOS and MS Windows, SVR4, OS/2, Mac OS, Solaris, SunOS, NeXTSTEP, many BSD variants, and so on. Linux is also able to operate with many network layers like Ethernet, Fiber Distributed Data Interface (FDDI), High Performance Parallel Interface (HIPPI), IBM's Token Ring, AT&T WaveLAN, DEC RoamAbout DS, and so forth. By using suitable libraries, Linux systems are even able to directly run programs written for other operating systems. For example, Linux is able to execute applications written for MS-DOS, MS Windows, SVR3 and R4, 4.4BSD, SCO Unix, XENIX, and others on the Intel 80x86 platform.

Linux is well supported.

Believe it or not, it may be a lot easier to get patches and updates for Linux than for any proprietary operating system! The answer to a problem often comes back within a few hours after sending a message to some newsgroup or mailing list. Moreover, drivers for Linux are usually available a few weeks after new hardware products have been introduced on the market. By contrast, hardware manufacturers release device drivers for only a few commercial operating systems, usually the Microsoft ones. Therefore, all commercial Unix variants run on a restricted subset of hardware components.

With an estimated installed base of more than 12 million and growing, people who are used to certain creature features that are standard under other operating systems are starting to expect the same from Linux. As such, the demand on Linux developers is also increasing. Luckily, though, Linux has evolved under the close direction of Linus over the years, to accommodate the needs of the masses.

Hardware Dependency

Linux tries to maintain a neat distinction between hardware-dependent and hardware-independent source code. To that end, both the *arch* and the *include* directories include nine subdirectories corresponding to the nine hardware platforms supported. The standard names of the platforms are:

arm
> Acorn personal computers

alpha
> Compaq Alpha workstations

i386
> IBM-compatible personal computers based on Intel 80x86 or Intel 80x86-compatible microprocessors

m68k
> Personal computers based on Motorola MC680x0 microprocessors

mips
> Workstations based on Silicon Graphics MIPS microprocessors

ppc
> Workstations based on Motorola-IBM PowerPC microprocessors

sparc
> Workstations based on Sun Microsystems SPARC microprocessors

sparc64
> Workstations based on Sun Microsystems 64-bit Ultra SPARC microprocessors

s390
> IBM System/390 mainframes

Linux Versions

Linux distinguishes stable kernels from development kernels through a simple numbering scheme. Each version is characterized by three numbers, separated by periods. The first two numbers are used to identify the version; the third number identifies the release.

As shown in Figure 1-1, if the second number is even, it denotes a stable kernel; otherwise, it denotes a development kernel. At the time of this writing, the current stable version of the Linux kernel is 2.2.14, and the current development version is 2.3.51. The 2.2 kernel, which is the basis for this book, was first released in January 1999, and it differs considerably from the 2.0 kernel, particularly with respect to memory management. Work on the 2.3 development version started in May 1999.

New releases of a stable version come out mostly to fix bugs reported by users. The main algorithms and data structures used to implement the kernel are left unchanged.

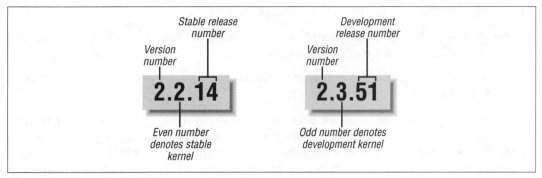

Figure 1-1. Numbering Linux versions

Development versions, on the other hand, may differ quite significantly from one another; kernel developers are free to experiment with different solutions that occasionally lead to drastic kernel changes. Users who rely on development versions for running applications may experience unpleasant surprises when upgrading their kernel to a newer release. This book concentrates on the most recent stable kernel that we had available because, among all the new features being tried in experimental kernels, there's no way of telling which will ultimately be accepted and what they'll look like in their final form.

At the time of this writing, Linux 2.4 has not officially come out. We tried to anticipate the forthcoming features and the main kernel changes with respect to the 2.2 version by looking at the Linux 2.3.99-pre8 prerelease. Linux 2.4 inherits a good deal from Linux 2.2: many concepts, design choices, algorithms, and data structures remain the same. For that reason, we conclude each chapter by sketching how Linux 2.4 differs from Linux 2.2 with respect to the topics just discussed. As you'll notice, the new Linux is gleaming and shining; it should appear more appealing to large corporations and, more generally, to the whole business community.

Basic Operating System Concepts

Any computer system includes a basic set of programs called the *operating system*. The most important program in the set is called the *kernel*. It is loaded into RAM when the system boots and contains many critical procedures that are needed for the system to operate. The other programs are less crucial utilities; they can provide a wide variety of interactive experiences for the user—as well as doing all the jobs the user bought the computer for—but the essential shape and capabilities of the system are determined by the kernel. The kernel, then, is where we fix our attention in this book. Hence, we'll often use the term "operating system" as a synonym for "kernel."

The operating system must fulfill two main objectives:

- Interact with the hardware components servicing all low-level programmable elements included in the hardware platform.

- Provide an execution environment to the applications that run on the computer system (the so-called user programs).

Some operating systems allow all user programs to directly play with the hardware components (a typical example is MS-DOS). In contrast, a Unix-like operating system hides all low-level details concerning the physical organization of the computer from applications run by the user. When a program wants to make use of a hardware resource, it must issue a request to the operating system. The kernel evaluates the request and, if it chooses to grant the resource, interacts with the relative hardware components on behalf of the user program.

In order to enforce this mechanism, modern operating systems rely on the availability of specific hardware features that forbid user programs to directly interact with low-level hardware components or to access arbitrary memory locations. In particular, the hardware introduces at least two different execution modes for the CPU: a nonprivileged mode for user programs and a privileged mode for the kernel. Unix calls these User Mode and Kernel Mode, respectively.

In the rest of this chapter, we introduce the basic concepts that have motivated the design of Unix over the past two decades, as well as Linux and other operating systems. While the concepts are probably familiar to you as a Linux user, these sections try to delve into them a bit more deeply than usual to explain the requirements they place on an operating system kernel. These broad considerations refer to Unix-like systems, thus also to Linux. The other chapters of this book will hopefully help you to understand the Linux kernel internals.

Multiuser Systems

A *multiuser system* is a computer that is able to concurrently and independently execute several applications belonging to two or more users. "Concurrently" means that applications can be active at the same time and contend for the various resources such as CPU, memory, hard disks, and so on. "Independently" means that each application can perform its task with no concern for what the applications of the other users are doing. Switching from one application to another, of course, slows down each of them and affects the response time seen by the users. Many of the complexities of modern operating system kernels, which we will examine in this book, are present to minimize the delays enforced on each program and to provide the user with responses that are as fast as possible.

Multiuser operating systems must include several features:

- An authentication mechanism for verifying the user identity

- A protection mechanism against buggy user programs that could block other applications running in the system

- A protection mechanism against malicious user programs that could interfere with, or spy on, the activity of other users

- An accounting mechanism that limits the amount of resource units assigned to each user

In order to ensure safe protection mechanisms, operating systems must make use of the hardware protection associated with the CPU privileged mode. Otherwise, a user program would be able to directly access the system circuitry and overcome the imposed bounds. Unix is a multiuser system that enforces the hardware protection of system resources.

Users and Groups

In a multiuser system, each user has a private space on the machine: typically, he owns some quota of the disk space to store files, receives private mail messages, and so on. The operating system must ensure that the private portion of a user space is visible only to its owner. In particular, it must ensure that no user can exploit a system application for the purpose of violating the private space of another user.

All users are identified by a unique number called the *User ID*, or UID. Usually only a restricted number of persons are allowed to make use of a computer system. When one of these users starts a working session, the operating system asks for a *login name* and a *password*. If the user does not input a valid pair, the system denies access. Since the password is assumed to be secret, the user's privacy is ensured.

In order to selectively share material with other users, each user is a member of one or more *groups*, which are identified by a unique number called a *Group ID*, or GID. Each file is also associated with exactly one group. For example, access could be set so that the user owning the file has read and write privileges, the group has read-only privileges, and other users on the system are denied access to the file.

Any Unix-like operating system has a special user called *root*, *superuser*, or *supervisor*. The system administrator must log in as root in order to handle user accounts, perform maintenance tasks like system backups and program upgrades, and so on. The root user can do almost everything, since the operating system does not apply the usual protection mechanisms to her. In particular, the root user can access every file on the system and can interfere with the activity of every running user program.

Processes

All operating systems make use of one fundamental abstraction: the *process*. A process can be defined either as "an instance of a program in execution," or as the "execution context" of a running program. In traditional operating systems, a process executes a single sequence of instructions in an *address space*; the address space is the set of memory addresses that the process is allowed to reference. Modern operating systems allow processes with multiple execution flows, that is, multiple sequences of instructions executed in the same address space.

Multiuser systems must enforce an execution environment in which several processes can be active concurrently and contend for system resources, mainly the CPU. Systems that allow concurrent active processes are said to be *multiprogramming* or *multiprocessing*.* It is important to distinguish programs from processes: several processes can execute the same program concurrently, while the same process can execute several programs sequentially.

On uniprocessor systems, just one process can hold the CPU, and hence just one execution flow can progress at a time. In general, the number of CPUs is always restricted, and therefore only a few processes can progress at the same time. The choice of the process that can progress is left to an operating system component called the *scheduler*. Some operating systems allow only *nonpreemptive* processes, which means that the scheduler is invoked only when a process voluntarily relinquishes the CPU. But processes of a multiuser system must be *preemptive*; the operating system tracks how long each process holds the CPU and periodically activates the scheduler.

Unix is a multiprocessing operating system with preemptive processes. Indeed, the process abstraction is really fundamental in all Unix systems. Even when no user is logged in and no application is running, several system processes monitor the peripheral devices. In particular, several processes listen at the system terminals waiting for user logins. When a user inputs a login name, the listening process runs a program that validates the user password. If the user identity is acknowledged, the process creates another process that runs a shell into which commands are entered. When a graphical display is activated, one process runs the window manager, and each window on the display is usually run by a separate process. When a user creates a graphics shell, one process runs the graphics windows, and a second process runs the shell into which the user can enter the commands. For each user command, the shell process creates another process that executes the corresponding program.

Unix-like operating systems adopt a *process/kernel* model. Each process has the illusion that it's the only process on the machine and it has exclusive access to the operating system services. Whenever a process makes a *system call* (i.e., a request to the kernel), the hardware changes the privilege mode from User Mode to Kernel Mode, and the process starts the execution of a kernel procedure with a strictly limited purpose. In this way, the operating system acts within the execution context of the process in order to satisfy its request. Whenever the request is fully satisfied, the kernel procedure forces the hardware to return to User Mode and the process continues its execution from the instruction following the system call.

---

* Some multiprocessing operating systems are not multiuser; an example is Microsoft's Windows 98.

Kernel Architecture

As stated before, most Unix kernels are monolithic: each kernel layer is integrated into the whole kernel program and runs in Kernel Mode on behalf of the current process. In contrast, *microkernel* operating systems demand a very small set of functions from the kernel, generally including a few synchronization primitives, a simple scheduler, and an interprocess communication mechanism. Several system processes that run on top of the microkernel implement other operating system–layer functions, like memory allocators, device drivers, system call handlers, and so on.

Although academic research on operating systems is oriented toward microkernels, such operating systems are generally slower than monolithic ones, since the explicit message passing between the different layers of the operating system has a cost. However, microkernel operating systems might have some theoretical advantages over monolithic ones. Microkernels force the system programmers to adopt a modularized approach, since any operating system layer is a relatively independent program that must interact with the other layers through well-defined and clean software interfaces. Moreover, an existing microkernel operating system can be fairly easily ported to other architectures, since all hardware-dependent components are generally encapsulated in the microkernel code. Finally, microkernel operating systems tend to make better use of random access memory (RAM) than monolithic ones, since system processes that aren't implementing needed functionalities might be swapped out or destroyed.

Modules are a kernel feature that effectively achieves many of the theoretical advantages of microkernels without introducing performance penalties. A *module* is an object file whose code can be linked to (and unlinked from) the kernel at runtime. The object code usually consists of a set of functions that implements a filesystem, a device driver, or other features at the kernel's upper layer. The module, unlike the external layers of microkernel operating systems, does not run as a specific process. Instead, it is executed in Kernel Mode on behalf of the current process, like any other statically linked kernel function.

The main advantages of using modules include:

Modularized approach
> Since any module can be linked and unlinked at runtime, system programmers must introduce well-defined software interfaces to access the data structures handled by modules. This makes it easy to develop new modules.

Platform independence
> Even if it may rely on some specific hardware features, a module doesn't depend on a fixed hardware platform. For example, a disk driver module that relies on the SCSI standard works as well on an IBM-compatible PC as it does on Compaq's Alpha.

Frugal main memory usage

A module can be linked to the running kernel when its functionality is required and unlinked when it is no longer useful. This mechanism also can be made transparent to the user, since linking and unlinking can be performed automatically by the kernel.

No performance penalty

Once linked in, the object code of a module is equivalent to the object code of the statically linked kernel. Therefore, no explicit message passing is required when the functions of the module are invoked.*

An Overview of the Unix Filesystem

The Unix operating system design is centered on its filesystem, which has several interesting characteristics. We'll review the most significant ones, since they will be mentioned quite often in forthcoming chapters.

Files

A Unix file is an information container structured as a sequence of bytes; the kernel does not interpret the contents of a file. Many programming libraries implement higher-level abstractions, such as records structured into fields and record addressing based on keys. However, the programs in these libraries must rely on system calls offered by the kernel. From the user's point of view, files are organized in a tree-structured name space as shown in Figure 1-2.

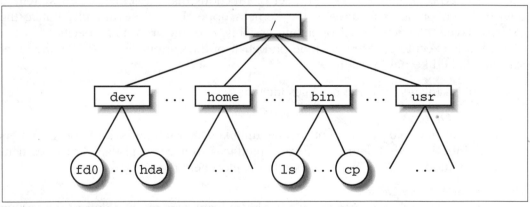

Figure 1-2. An example of a directory tree

---

* A small performance penalty occurs when the module is linked and when it is unlinked. However, this penalty can be compared to the penalty caused by the creation and deletion of system processes in microkernel operating systems.

All the nodes of the tree, except the leaves, denote directory names. A directory node contains information about the files and directories just beneath it. A file or directory name consists of a sequence of arbitrary ASCII characters,* with the exception of / and of the null character \0. Most filesystems place a limit on the length of a filename, typically no more than 255 characters. The directory corresponding to the root of the tree is called the *root directory*. By convention, its name is a slash (/). Names must be different within the same directory, but the same name may be used in different directories.

Unix associates a *current working directory* with each process (see the section "The Process/Kernel Model" later in this chapter); it belongs to the process execution context, and it identifies the directory currently used by the process. In order to identify a specific file, the process uses a *pathname*, which consists of slashes alternating with a sequence of directory names that lead to the file. If the first item in the pathname is a slash, the pathname is said to be a*bsolute*, since its starting point is the root directory. Otherwise, if the first item is a directory name or filename, the pathname is said to be *relative*, since its starting point is the process's current directory.

While specifying filenames, the notations "." and ".." are also used. They denote the current working directory and its parent directory, respectively. If the current working directory is the root directory, "." and ".." coincide.

Hard and Soft Links

A filename included in a directory is called a *file hard link*, or more simply a *link*. The same file may have several links included in the same directory or in different ones, thus several filenames.

The Unix command:

```
$ ln f1 f2
```

is used to create a new hard link that has the pathname f2 for a file identified by the pathname f1.

Hard links have two limitations:

* Users are not allowed to create hard links for directories. This might transform the directory tree into a graph with cycles, thus making it impossible to locate a file according to its name.

* Links can be created only among files included in the same filesystem. This is a serious limitation since modern Unix systems may include several filesystems located on different disks and/or partitions, and users may be unaware of the physical divisions between them.

---

* Some operating systems allow filenames to be expressed in many different alphabets, based on 16-bit extended coding of graphical characters such as Unicode.

In order to overcome these limitations, *soft links* (also called *symbolic links*) have been introduced. Symbolic links are short files that contain an arbitrary pathname of another file. The pathname may refer to any file located in any filesystem; it may even refer to a nonexistent file.

The Unix command:

```
$ ln -s f1 f2
```

creates a new soft link with pathname f2 that refers to pathname f1. When this command is executed, the filesystem creates a soft link and writes into it the f1 pathname. It then inserts—in the proper directory—a new entry containing the last name of the f2 pathname. In this way, any reference to f2 can be translated automatically into a reference to f1.

File Types

Unix files may have one of the following types:

- Regular file
- Directory
- Symbolic link
- Block-oriented device file
- Character-oriented device file
- Pipe and named pipe (also called FIFO)
- Socket

The first three file types are constituents of any Unix filesystem. Their implementation will be described in detail in Chapter 17, *The Ext2 Filesystem*.

Device files are related to I/O devices and device drivers integrated into the kernel. For example, when a program accesses a device file, it acts directly on the I/O device associated with that file (see Chapter 13, *Managing I/O Devices*).

Pipes and sockets are special files used for interprocess communication (see the section "Synchronization and Critical Regions" later in this chapter and Chapter 18, *Process Communication*).

File Descriptor and Inode

Unix makes a clear distinction between a file and a file descriptor. With the exception of device and special files, each file consists of a sequence of characters. The file does not include any control information such as its length, or an End-Of-File (EOF) delimiter.

All information needed by the filesystem to handle a file is included in a data structure called an *inode*. Each file has its own inode, which the filesystem uses to identify the file.

While filesystems and the kernel functions handling them can vary widely from one Unix system to another, they must always provide at least the following attributes, which are specified in the POSIX standard:

- File type (see previous section)

- Number of hard links associated with the file

- File length in bytes

- Device ID (i.e., an identifier of the device containing the file)

- Inode number that identifies the file within the filesystem

- User ID of the file owner

- Group ID of the file

- Several timestamps that specify the inode status change time, the last access time, and the last modify time

- Access rights and file mode (see next section)

Access Rights and File Mode

The potential users of a file fall into three classes:

- The user who is the owner of the file

- The users who belong to the same group as the file, not including the owner

- All remaining users (others)

There are three types of access rights, *Read, Write,* and *Execute,* for each of these three classes. Thus, the set of access rights associated with a file consists of nine different binary flags. Three additional flags, called *suid* (Set User ID), *sgid* (Set Group ID), and *sticky* define the file mode. These flags have the following meanings when applied to executable files:

suid
> A process executing a file normally keeps the User ID (UID) of the process owner. However, if the executable file has the **suid** flag set, the process gets the UID of the file owner.

sgid
> A process executing a file keeps the Group ID (GID) of the process group. However, if the executable file has the **sgid** flag set, the process gets the ID of the file group.

`sticky`

> An executable file with the `sticky` flag set corresponds to a request to the kernel to keep the program in memory after its execution terminates.[*]

When a file is created by a process, its owner ID is the UID of the process. Its owner group ID can be either the GID of the creator process or the GID of the parent directory, depending on the value of the `sgid` flag of the parent directory.

File-Handling System Calls

When a user accesses the contents of either a regular file or a directory, he actually accesses some data stored in a hardware block device. In this sense, a filesystem is a user-level view of the physical organization of a hard disk partition. Since a process in User Mode cannot directly interact with the low-level hardware components, each actual file operation must be performed in Kernel Mode.

Therefore, the Unix operating system defines several system calls related to file handling. Whenever a process wants to perform some operation on a specific file, it uses the proper system call and passes the file pathname as a parameter.

All Unix kernels devote great attention to the efficient handling of hardware block devices in order to achieve good overall system performance. In the chapters that follow, we will describe topics related to file handling in Linux and specifically how the kernel reacts to file-related system calls. In order to understand those descriptions, you will need to know how the main file-handling system calls are used; they are described in the next section.

Opening a file

Processes can access only "opened" files. In order to open a file, the process invokes the system call:

```
fd = open(path, flag, mode)
```

The three parameters have the following meanings:

`path`

> Denotes the pathname (relative or absolute) of the file to be opened.

`flag`

> Specifies how the file must be opened (e.g., read, write, read/write, append). It can also specify whether a nonexisting file should be created.

`mode`

> Specifies the access rights of a newly created file.

---

[*] This flag has become obsolete; other approaches based on sharing of code pages are now used (see Chapter 7, *Process Address Space*).

This system call creates an "open file" object and returns an identifier called *file descriptor*. An open file object contains:

- Some file-handling data structures, like a pointer to the kernel buffer memory area where file data will be copied; an `offset` field that denotes the current position in the file from which the next operation will take place (the so-called *file pointer*); and so on.

- Some pointers to kernel functions that the process is enabled to invoke. The set of permitted functions depends on the value of the `flag` parameter.

We'll discuss open file objects in detail in Chapter 12, *The Virtual Filesystem*. Let's limit ourselves here to describing some general properties specified by the POSIX semantics:

- A file descriptor represents an interaction between a process and an opened file, while an open file object contains data related to that interaction. The same open file object may be identified by several file descriptors.

- Several processes may concurrently open the same file. In this case, the filesystem assigns a separate file descriptor to each file, along with a separate open file object. When this occurs, the Unix filesystem does not provide any kind of synchronization among the I/O operations issued by the processes on the same file. However, several system calls such as `flock()` are available to allow processes to synchronize themselves on the entire file or on portions of it (see Chapter 12).

In order to create a new file, the process may also invoke the `creat()` system call, which is handled by the kernel exactly like `open()`.

Accessing an opened file

Regular Unix files can be addressed either sequentially or randomly, while device files and named pipes are usually accessed sequentially (see Chapter 13). In both kinds of access, the kernel stores the file pointer in the open file object, that is, the current position at which the next read or write operation will take place.

Sequential access is implicitly assumed: the `read()` and `write()` system calls always refer to the position of the current file pointer. In order to modify the value, a program must explicitly invoke the `lseek()` system call. When a file is opened, the kernel sets the file pointer to the position of the first byte in the file (offset 0).

The `lseek()` system call requires the following parameters:

```
newoffset = lseek(fd, offset, whence);
```

which have the following meanings:

`fd`
    Indicates the file descriptor of the opened file

offset
> Specifies a signed integer value that will be used for computing the new position of the file pointer

whence
> Specifies whether the new position should be computed by adding the offset value to the number 0 (offset from the beginning of the file), the current file pointer, or the position of the last byte (offset from the end of the file)

The read() system call requires the following parameters:

```
nread = read(fd, buf, count);
```

which have the following meaning:

fd
> Indicates the file descriptor of the opened file

buf
> Specifies the address of the buffer in the process's address space to which the data will be transferred

count
> Denotes the number of bytes to be read

When handling such a system call, the kernel attempts to read count bytes from the file having the file descriptor fd, starting from the current value of the opened file's offset field. In some cases—end-of-file, empty pipe, and so on—the kernel does not succeed in reading all count bytes. The returned nread value specifies the number of bytes effectively read. The file pointer is also updated by adding nread to its previous value. The write() parameters are similar.

Closing a file

When a process does not need to access the contents of a file anymore, it can invoke the system call:

```
res = close(fd);
```

which releases the open file object corresponding to the file descriptor fd. When a process terminates, the kernel closes all its still opened files.

Renaming and deleting a file

In order to rename or delete a file, a process does not need to open it. Indeed, such operations do not act on the contents of the affected file, but rather on the contents of one or more directories. For example, the system call:

```
res = rename(oldpath, newpath);
```

changes the name of a file link, while the system call:

```
res = unlink(pathname);
```

decrements the file link count and removes the corresponding directory entry. The file is deleted only when the link count assumes the value 0.

An Overview of Unix Kernels

Unix kernels provide an execution environment in which applications may run. Therefore, the kernel must implement a set of services and corresponding interfaces. Applications use those interfaces and do not usually interact directly with hardware resources.

The Process/Kernel Model

As already mentioned, a CPU can run either in User Mode or in Kernel Mode. Actually, some CPUs can have more than two execution states. For instance, the Intel 80x86 microprocessors have four different execution states. But all standard Unix kernels make use of only Kernel Mode and User Mode.

When a program is executed in User Mode, it cannot directly access the kernel data structures or the kernel programs. When an application executes in Kernel Mode, however, these restrictions no longer apply. Each CPU model provides special instructions to switch from User Mode to Kernel Mode and vice versa. A program executes most of the time in User Mode and switches to Kernel Mode only when requesting a service provided by the kernel. When the kernel has satisfied the program's request, it puts the program back in User Mode.

Processes are dynamic entities that usually have a limited life span within the system. The task of creating, eliminating, and synchronizing the existing processes is delegated to a group of routines in the kernel.

The kernel itself is not a process but a process manager. The process/kernel model assumes that processes that require a kernel service make use of specific programming constructs called *system calls*. Each system call sets up the group of parameters that identifies the process request and then executes the hardware-dependent CPU instruction to switch from User Mode to Kernel Mode.

Besides user processes, Unix systems include a few privileged processes called *kernel threads* with the following characteristics:

*   They run in Kernel Mode in the kernel address space.

*   They do not interact with users, and thus do not require terminal devices.

*   They are usually created during system startup and remain alive until the system is shut down.

Notice how the process/kernel model is somewhat orthogonal to the CPU state: on a uniprocessor system, only one process is running at any time and it may run either in User or in Kernel Mode. If it runs in Kernel Mode, the processor is executing some kernel routine. Figure 1-3 illustrates examples of transitions between User and Kernel Mode. Process 1 in User Mode issues a system call, after which the process switches to Kernel Mode and the system call is serviced. Process 1 then resumes execution in User Mode until a timer interrupt occurs and the scheduler is activated in Kernel Mode. A process switch takes place, and Process 2 starts its execution in User Mode until a hardware device raises an interrupt. As a consequence of the interrupt, Process 2 switches to Kernel Mode and services the interrupt.

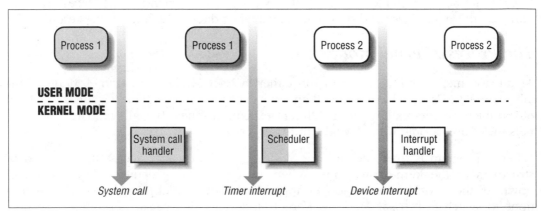

Figure 1-3. Transitions between User and Kernel Mode

Unix kernels do much more than handle system calls; in fact, kernel routines can be activated in several ways:

- A process invokes a system call.

- The CPU executing the process signals an *exception*, which is some unusual condition such as an invalid instruction. The kernel handles the exception on behalf of the process that caused it.

- A peripheral device issues an *interrupt signal* to the CPU to notify it of an event such as a request for attention, a status change, or the completion of an I/O operation. Each interrupt signal is dealt by a kernel program called an *interrupt handler*. Since peripheral devices operate asynchronously with respect to the CPU, interrupts occur at unpredictable times.

- A kernel thread is executed; since it runs in Kernel Mode, the corresponding program must be considered part of the kernel, albeit encapsulated in a process.

Process Implementation

To let the kernel manage processes, each process is represented by a *process descriptor* that includes information about the current state of the process.

When the kernel stops the execution of a process, it saves the current contents of several processor registers in the process descriptor. These include:

*   The program counter (PC) and stack pointer (SP) registers

*   The general-purpose registers

*   The floating point registers

*   The processor control registers (Processor Status Word) containing information about the CPU state

*   The memory management registers used to keep track of the RAM accessed by the process

When the kernel decides to resume executing a process, it uses the proper process descriptor fields to load the CPU registers. Since the stored value of the program counter points to the instruction following the last instruction executed, the process resumes execution from where it was stopped.

When a process is not executing on the CPU, it is waiting for some event. Unix kernels distinguish many wait states, which are usually implemented by queues of process descriptors; each (possibly empty) queue corresponds to the set of processes waiting for a specific event.

Reentrant Kernels

All Unix kernels are *reentrant*: this means that several processes may be executing in Kernel Mode at the same time. Of course, on uniprocessor systems only one process can progress, but many of them can be blocked in Kernel Mode waiting for the CPU or the completion of some I/O operation. For instance, after issuing a read to a disk on behalf of some process, the kernel will let the disk controller handle it and will resume executing other processes. An interrupt notifies the kernel when the device has satisfied the read, so the former process can resume the execution.

One way to provide reentrancy is to write functions so that they modify only local variables and do not alter global data structures. Such functions are called *reentrant functions*. But a reentrant kernel is not limited just to such reentrant functions (although that is how some real-time kernels are implemented). Instead, the kernel can include nonreentrant functions and use locking mechanisms to ensure that only one process can execute a nonreentrant function at a time. Every process in Kernel Mode acts on its own set of memory locations and cannot interfere with the others.

If a hardware interrupt occurs, a reentrant kernel is able to suspend the current running process even if that process is in Kernel Mode. This capability is very important, since it improves the throughput of the device controllers that issue interrupts. Once a device has issued an interrupt, it waits until the CPU acknowledges it. If the kernel is able to answer quickly, the device controller will be able to perform other tasks while the CPU handles the interrupt.

Now let's look at kernel reentrancy and its impact on the organization of the kernel. A *kernel control path* denotes the sequence of instructions executed by the kernel to handle a system call, an exception, or an interrupt.

In the simplest case, the CPU executes a kernel control path sequentially from the first instruction to the last. When one of the following events occurs, however, the CPU interleaves the kernel control paths:

- A process executing in User Mode invokes a system call and the corresponding kernel control path verifies that the request cannot be satisfied immediately; it then invokes the scheduler to select a new process to run. As a result, a process switch occurs. The first kernel control path is left unfinished and the CPU resumes the execution of some other kernel control path. In this case, the two control paths are executed on behalf of two different processes.

- The CPU detects an exception—for example, an access to a page not present in RAM—while running a kernel control path. The first control path is suspended, and the CPU starts the execution of a suitable procedure. In our example, this type of procedure could allocate a new page for the process and read its contents from disk. When the procedure terminates, the first control path can be resumed. In this case, the two control paths are executed on behalf of the same process.

- A hardware interrupt occurs while the CPU is running a kernel control path with the interrupts enabled. The first kernel control path is left unfinished and the CPU starts processing another kernel control path to handle the interrupt. The first kernel control path resumes when the interrupt handler terminates. In this case the two kernel control paths run in the execution context of the same process and the total elapsed system time is accounted to it. However, the interrupt handler doesn't necessarily operate on behalf of the process.

Figure 1-4 illustrates a few examples of noninterleaved and interleaved kernel control paths. Three different CPU states are considered:

- Running a process in User Mode (User)

- Running an exception or a system call handler (Excp)

- Running an interrupt handler (Intr)

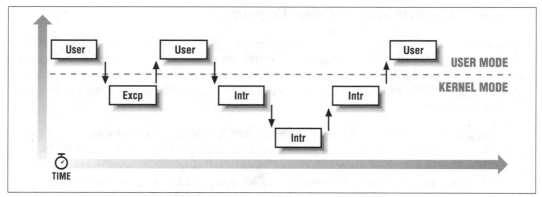

Figure 1-4. Interleaving of kernel control paths

Process Address Space

Each process runs in its private address space. A process running in User Mode refers to private stack, data, and code areas. When running in Kernel Mode, the process addresses the kernel data and code area and makes use of another stack.

Since the kernel is reentrant, several kernel control paths—each related to a different process—may be executed in turn. In this case, each kernel control path refers to its own private kernel stack.

While it appears to each process that it has access to a private address space, there are times when part of the address space is shared among processes. In some cases this sharing is explicitly requested by processes; in others it is done automatically by the kernel to reduce memory usage.

If the same program, say an editor, is needed simultaneously by several users, the program will be loaded into memory only once, and its instructions can be shared by all of the users who need it. Its data, of course, must not be shared, because each user will have separate data. This kind of shared address space is done automatically by the kernel to save memory.

Processes can also share parts of their address space as a kind of interprocess communication, using the "shared memory" technique introduced in System V and supported by Linux.

Finally, Linux supports the `mmap()` system call, which allows part of a file or the memory residing on a device to be mapped into a part of a process address space. Memory mapping can provide an alternative to normal reads and writes for transferring data. If the same file is shared by several processes, its memory mapping is included in the address space of each of the processes that share it.

Synchronization and Critical Regions

Implementing a reentrant kernel requires the use of synchronization: if a kernel control path is suspended while acting on a kernel data structure, no other kernel control path will be allowed to act on the same data structure unless it has been reset to a consistent state. Otherwise, the interaction of the two control paths could corrupt the stored information.

For example, let's suppose that a global variable V contains the number of available items of some system resource. A first kernel control path A reads the variable and determines that there is just one available item. At this point, another kernel control path B is activated and reads the same variable, which still contains the value 1. Thus, B decrements V and starts using the resource item. Then A resumes the execution; because it has already read the value of V, it assumes that it can decrement V and take the resource item, which B already uses. As a final result, V contains -1, and two kernel control paths are using the same resource item with potentially disastrous effects.

When the outcome of some computation depends on how two or more processes are scheduled, the code is incorrect: we say that there is a *race condition.*

In general, safe access to a global variable is ensured by using *atomic operations.* In the previous example, data corruption would not be possible if the two control paths read and decrement V with a single, noninterruptible operation. However, kernels contain many data structures that cannot be accessed with a single operation. For example, it usually isn't possible to remove an element from a linked list with a single operation, because the kernel needs to access at least two pointers at once. Any section of code that should be finished by each process that begins it before another process can enter it is called a *critical region.**

These problems occur not only among kernel control paths but also among processes sharing common data. Several synchronization techniques have been adopted. The following section will concentrate on how to synchronize kernel control paths.

Nonpreemptive kernels

In search of a drastically simple solution to synchronization problems, most traditional Unix kernels are nonpreemptive: when a process executes in Kernel Mode, it cannot be arbitrarily suspended and substituted with another process. Therefore, on a uniprocessor system all kernel data structures that are not updated by interrupts or exception handlers are safe for the kernel to access.

---

* Synchronization problems have been fully described in other works; we refer the interested reader to books on the Unix operating systems (see the bibliography near the end of the book).

Of course, a process in Kernel Mode can voluntarily relinquish the CPU, but in this case it must ensure that all data structures are left in a consistent state. Moreover, when it resumes its execution, it must recheck the value of any previously accessed data structures that could be changed.

Nonpreemptability is ineffective in multiprocessor systems, since two kernel control paths running on different CPUs could concurrently access the same data structure.

Interrupt disabling

Another synchronization mechanism for uniprocessor systems consists of disabling all hardware interrupts before entering a critical region and reenabling them right after leaving it. This mechanism, while simple, is far from optimal. If the critical region is large, interrupts can remain disabled for a relatively long time, potentially causing all hardware activities to freeze.

Moreover, on a multiprocessor system this mechanism doesn't work at all. There is no way to ensure that no other CPU can access the same data structures updated in the protected critical region.

Semaphores

A widely used mechanism, effective in both uniprocessor and multiprocessor systems, relies on the use of *semaphores*. A semaphore is simply a counter associated with a data structure; the semaphore is checked by all kernel threads before they try to access the data structure. Each semaphore may be viewed as an object composed of:

* An integer variable
* A list of waiting processes
* Two atomic methods: down( ) and up( )

The down( ) method decrements the value of the semaphore. If the new value is less than 0, the method adds the running process to the semaphore list and then blocks (i.e., invokes the scheduler). The up( ) method increments the value of the semaphore and, if its new value is greater than or equal to 0, reactivates one or more processes in the semaphore list.

Each data structure to be protected has its own semaphore, which is initialized to 1. When a kernel control path wishes to access the data structure, it executes the down( ) method on the proper semaphore. If the value of the new semaphore isn't negative, access to the data structure is granted. Otherwise, the process that is executing the kernel control path is added to the semaphore list and blocked. When another process executes the up( ) method on that semaphore, one of the processes in the semaphore list is allowed to proceed.

Spin locks

In multiprocessor systems, semaphores are not always the best solution to the synchronization problems. Some kernel data structures should be protected from being concurrently accessed by kernel control paths that run on different CPUs. In this case, if the time required to update the data structure is short, a semaphore could be very inefficient. To check a semaphore, the kernel must insert a process in the semaphore list and then suspend it. Since both operations are relatively expensive, in the time it takes to complete them, the other kernel control path could have already released the semaphore.

In these cases, multiprocessor operating systems make use of *spin locks.* A spin lock is very similar to a semaphore, but it has no process list: when a process finds the lock closed by another process, it "spins" around repeatedly, executing a tight instruction loop until the lock becomes open.

Of course, spin locks are useless in a uniprocessor environment. When a kernel control path tries to access a locked data structure, it starts an endless loop. Therefore, the kernel control path that is updating the protected data structure would not have a chance to continue the execution and release the spin lock. The final result is that the system hangs.

Avoiding deadlocks

Processes or kernel control paths that synchronize with other control paths may easily enter in a *deadlocked* state. The simplest case of deadlock occurs when process *p1* gains access to data structure *a* and process *p2* gains access to *b,* but *p1* then waits for *b* and *p2* waits for *a.* Other more complex cyclic waitings among groups of processes may also occur. Of course, a deadlock condition causes a complete freeze of the affected processes or kernel control paths.

As far as kernel design is concerned, deadlock becomes an issue when the number of kernel semaphore types used is high. In this case, it may be quite difficult to ensure that no deadlock state will ever be reached for all possible ways to interleave kernel control paths. Several operating systems, including Linux, avoid this problem by introducing a very limited number of semaphore types and by requesting semaphores in an ascending order.

Signals and Interprocess Communication

Unix signals provide a mechanism for notifying processes of system events. Each event has its own signal number, which is usually referred to by a symbolic constant such as `SIGTERM`. There are two kinds of system events:

Asynchronous notifications
> For instance, a user can send the interrupt signal `SIGINT` to a foreground process by pressing the interrupt keycode (usually, CTRL-C) at the terminal.

Synchronous errors or exceptions

For instance, the kernel sends the signal SIGSEGV to a process when it accesses a memory location at an illegal address.

The POSIX standard defines about 20 different signals, two of which are user-definable and may be used as a primitive mechanism for communication and synchronization among processes in User Mode. In general, a process may react to a signal reception in two possible ways:

- Ignore the signal.

- Asynchronously execute a specified procedure (the signal handler).

If the process does not specify one of these alternatives, the kernel performs a *default action* that depends on the signal number. The five possible default actions are:

- Terminate the process.

- Write the execution context and the contents of the address space in a file (*core dump*) and terminate the process.

- Ignore the signal.

- Suspend the process.

- Resume the process's execution, if it was stopped.

Kernel signal handling is rather elaborate since the POSIX semantics allows processes to temporarily block signals. Moreover, a few signals such as SIGKILL cannot be directly handled by the process and cannot be ignored.

AT&T's Unix System V introduced other kinds of interprocess communication among processes in User Mode, which have been adopted by many Unix kernels: *semaphores*, *message queues*, and *shared memory*. They are collectively known as *System V IPC*.

The kernel implements these constructs as *IPC resources*: a process acquires a resource by invoking a shmget(), semget(), or msgget() system call. Just like files, IPC resources are persistent: they must be explicitly deallocated by the creator process, by the current owner, or by a superuser process.

Semaphores are similar to those described in the section "Synchronization and Critical Regions" earlier in this chapter, except that they are reserved for processes in User Mode. Message queues allow processes to exchange messages by making use of the msgsnd() and msgget() system calls, which respectively insert a message into a specific message queue and extract a message from it.

Shared memory provides the fastest way for processes to exchange and share data. A process starts by issuing a shmget() system call to create a new shared memory having a required size. After obtaining the IPC resource identifier, the process invokes the shmat() system call, which returns the starting address of the new region within the process address space. When the process wishes to detach the shared memory from its address space, it invokes the shmdt() system call. The implementation of shared memory depends on how the kernel implements process address spaces.

Process Management

Unix makes a neat distinction between the process and the program it is executing. To that end, the fork() and exit() system calls are used respectively to create a new process and to terminate it, while an exec()-like system call is invoked to load a new program. After such a system call has been executed, the process resumes execution with a brand new address space containing the loaded program.

The process that invokes a fork() is the *parent* while the new process is its *child*. Parents and children can find each other because the data structure describing each process includes a pointer to its immediate parent and pointers to all its immediate children.

A naive implementation of the fork() would require both the parent's data and the parent's code to be duplicated and assign the copies to the child. This would be quite time-consuming. Current kernels that can rely on hardware paging units follow the Copy-On-Write approach, which defers page duplication until the last moment (i.e., until the parent or the child is required to write into a page). We shall describe how Linux implements this technique in the section "Copy On Write" in Chapter 7.

The exit() system call terminates a process. The kernel handles this system call by releasing the resources owned by the process and sending the parent process a SIGCHLD signal, which is ignored by default.

Zombie processes

How can a parent process inquire about termination of its children? The wait() system call allows a process to wait until one of its children terminates; it returns the process ID (PID) of the terminated child.

When executing this system call, the kernel checks whether a child has already terminated. A special *zombie* process state is introduced to represent terminated processes: a process remains in that state until its parent process executes a wait() system call on it. The system call handler extracts some data about resource usage from the process descriptor fields; the process descriptor may be released once the data has been collected. If no child process has already terminated when the wait() system call is executed, the kernel usually puts the process in a wait state until a child terminates.

Many kernels also implement a waitpid() system call, which allows a process to wait for a specific child process. Other variants of wait() system calls are also quite common.

It's a good practice for the kernel to keep around information on a child process until the parent issues its `wait()` call, but suppose the parent process terminates without issuing that call? The information takes up valuable memory slots that could be used to serve living processes. For example, many shells allow the user to start a command in the background and then log out. The process that is running the command shell terminates, but its children continue their execution.

The solution lies in a special system process called *init* that is created during system initialization. When a process terminates, the kernel changes the appropriate process descriptor pointers of all the existing children of the terminated process to make them become children of *init*. This process monitors the execution of all its children and routinely issues `wait()` system calls, whose side effect is to get rid of all zombies.

Process groups and login sessions

Modern Unix operating systems introduce the notion of *process groups* to represent a "job" abstraction. For example, in order to execute the command line:

```
$ ls | sort | more
```

a shell that supports process groups, such as `bash`, creates a new group for the three processes corresponding to `ls`, `sort`, and `more`. In this way, the shell acts on the three processes as if they were a single entity (the job, to be precise). Each process descriptor includes a *process group ID* field. Each group of processes may have a *group leader*, which is the process whose PID coincides with the process group ID. A newly created process is initially inserted into the process group of its parent.

Modern Unix kernels also introduce *login sessions*. Informally, a login session contains all processes that are descendants of the process that has started a working session on a specific terminal—usually, the first command shell process created for the user. All processes in a process group must be in the same login session. A login session may have several process groups active simultaneously; one of these process groups is always in the foreground, which means that it has access to the terminal. The other active process groups are in the background. When a background process tries to access the terminal, it receives a `SIGTTIN` or `SIGTTOUT` signal. In many command shells the internal commands `bg` and `fg` can be used to put a process group in either the background or the foreground.

Memory Management

Memory management is by far the most complex activity in a Unix kernel. We shall dedicate more than a third of this book just to describing how Linux does it. This section illustrates some of the main issues related to memory management.

Virtual memory

All recent Unix systems provide a useful abstraction called *virtual memory*. Virtual memory acts as a logical layer between the application memory requests and the hardware Memory Management Unit (MMU). Virtual memory has many purposes and advantages:

- Several processes can be executed concurrently.

- It is possible to run applications whose memory needs are larger than the available physical memory.

- Processes can execute a program whose code is only partially loaded in memory.

- Each process is allowed to access a subset of the available physical memory.

- Processes can share a single memory image of a library or program.

- Programs can be relocatable, that is, they can be placed anywhere in physical memory.

- Programmers can write machine-independent code, since they do not need to be concerned about physical memory organization.

The main ingredient of a virtual memory subsystem is the notion of *virtual address space*. The set of memory references that a process can use is different from physical memory addresses. When a process uses a virtual address,* the kernel and the MMU cooperate to locate the actual physical location of the requested memory item.

Today's CPUs include hardware circuits that automatically translate the virtual addresses into physical ones. To that end, the available RAM is partitioned into *page frames* 4 or 8 KB in length, and a set of page tables is introduced to specify the correspondence between virtual and physical addresses. These circuits make memory allocation simpler, since a request for a block of contiguous virtual addresses can be satisfied by allocating a group of page frames having noncontiguous physical addresses.

Random access memory usage

All Unix operating systems clearly distinguish two portions of the random access memory (RAM). A few megabytes are dedicated to storing the kernel image (i.e., the kernel code and the kernel static data structures). The remaining portion of RAM is usually handled by the virtual memory system and is used in three possible ways:

- To satisfy kernel requests for buffers, descriptors, and other dynamic kernel data structures

---

* These addresses have different nomenclatures depending on the computer architecture. As we'll see in Chapter 2, *Memory Addressing*, Intel 80x86 manuals refer to them as "logical addresses."

- To satisfy process requests for generic memory areas and for memory mapping of files

- To get better performance from disks and other buffered devices by means of caches

Each request type is valuable. On the other hand, since the available RAM is limited, some balancing among request types must be done, particularly when little available memory is left. Moreover, when some critical threshold of available memory is reached and a page-frame-reclaiming algorithm is invoked to free additional memory, which are the page frames most suitable for reclaiming? As we shall see in Chapter 16, *Swapping: Methods for Freeing Memory,* there is no simple answer to this question and very little support from theory. The only available solution lies in developing carefully tuned empirical algorithms.

One major problem that must be solved by the virtual memory system is *memory fragmentation.* Ideally, a memory request should fail only when the number of free page frames is too small. However, the kernel is often forced to use physically contiguous memory areas, hence the memory request could fail even if there is enough memory available but it is not available as one contiguous chunk.

Kernel Memory Allocator

The Kernel Memory Allocator (KMA) is a subsystem that tries to satisfy the requests for memory areas from all parts of the system. Some of these requests will come from other kernel subsystems needing memory for kernel use, and some requests will come via system calls from user programs to increase their processes' address spaces. A good KMA should have the following features:

- It must be fast. Actually, this is the most crucial attribute, since it is invoked by all kernel subsystems (including the interrupt handlers).

- It should minimize the amount of wasted memory.

- It should try to reduce the memory fragmentation problem.

- It should be able to cooperate with the other memory management subsystems in order to borrow and release page frames from them.

Several kinds of KMAs have been proposed, which are based on a variety of different algorithmic techniques, including:

- Resource map allocator

- Power-of-two free lists

- McKusick-Karels allocator

- Buddy system

- Mach's Zone allocator

- Dynix allocator

- Solaris's Slab allocator

As we shall see in Chapter 6, *Memory Management*, Linux's KMA uses a Slab allocator on top of a Buddy system.

Process virtual address space handling

The address space of a process contains all the virtual memory addresses that the process is allowed to reference. The kernel usually stores a process virtual address space as a list of *memory area descriptors*. For example, when a process starts the execution of some program via an `exec()`-like system call, the kernel assigns to the process a virtual address space that comprises memory areas for:

- The executable code of the program

- The initialized data of the program

- The uninitialized data of the program

- The initial program stack (that is, the User Mode stack)

- The executable code and data of needed shared libraries

- The heap (the memory dynamically requested by the program)

All recent Unix operating systems adopt a memory allocation strategy called *demand paging*. With demand paging, a process can start program execution with none of its pages in physical memory. As it accesses a nonpresent page, the MMU generates an exception; the exception handler finds the affected memory region, allocates a free page, and initializes it with the appropriate data. In a similar fashion, when the process dynamically requires some memory by using `malloc()` or the `brk()` system call (which is invoked internally by `malloc()`), the kernel just updates the size of the heap memory region of the process. A page frame is assigned to the process only when it generates an exception by trying to refer its virtual memory addresses.

Virtual address spaces also allow other efficient strategies, such as the Copy-On-Write strategy mentioned earlier. For example, when a new process is created, the kernel just assigns the parent's page frames to the child address space, but it marks them read only. An exception is raised as soon the parent or the child tries to modify the contents of a page. The exception handler assigns a new page frame to the affected process and initializes it with the contents of the original page.

Swapping and caching

In order to extend the size of the virtual address space usable by the processes, the Unix operating system makes use of *swap areas* on disk. The virtual memory system regards the contents of a page frame as the basic unit for swapping. Whenever some process refers to a swapped-out page, the MMU raises an exception. The exception handler then allocates a new page frame and initializes the page frame with its old contents saved on disk.

On the other hand, physical memory is also used as cache for hard disks and other block devices. This is because hard drives are very slow: a disk access requires several milliseconds, which is a very long time compared with the RAM access time. Therefore, disks are often the bottleneck in system performance. As a general rule, one of the policies already implemented in the earliest Unix system is to defer writing to disk as long as possible by loading into RAM a set of disk buffers corresponding to blocks read from disk. The `sync()` system call forces disk synchronization by writing all of the "dirty" buffers (i.e., all the buffers whose contents differ from that of the corresponding disk blocks) into disk. In order to avoid data loss, all operating systems take care to periodically write dirty buffers back to disk.

Device Drivers

The kernel interacts with I/O devices by means of *device drivers*. Device drivers are included in the kernel and consist of data structures and functions that control one or more devices, such as hard disks, keyboards, mouses, monitors, network interfaces, and devices connected to a SCSI bus. Each driver interacts with the remaining part of the kernel (even with other drivers) through a specific interface. This approach has the following advantages:

- Device-specific code can be encapsulated in a specific module.

- Vendors can add new devices without knowing the kernel source code: only the interface specifications must be known.

- The kernel deals with all devices in a uniform way and accesses them through the same interface.

- It is possible to write a device driver as a module that can be dynamically loaded in the kernel without requiring the system to be rebooted. It is also possible to dynamically unload a module that is no longer needed, thus minimizing the size of the kernel image stored in RAM.

Figure 1-5 illustrates how device drivers interface with the rest of the kernel and with the processes. Some user programs (P) wish to operate on hardware devices. They make requests to the kernel using the usual file-related system calls and the device files normally found in the */dev* directory. Actually, the device files are the user-visible portion of the device driver interface. Each device file refers to a specific device driver, which is invoked by the kernel in order to perform the requested operation on the hardware component.

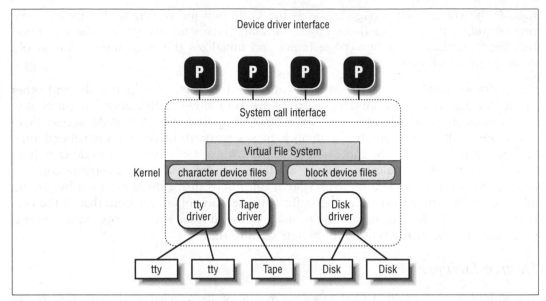

Figure 1-5. Device driver interface

It is worth mentioning that at the time Unix was introduced graphical terminals were uncommon and expensive, and thus only alphanumeric terminals were handled directly by Unix kernels. When graphical terminals became widespread, ad hoc applications such as the X Window System were introduced that ran as standard processes and accessed the I/O ports of the graphics interface and the RAM video area directly. Some recent Unix kernels, such as Linux 2.2, include limited support for some frame buffer devices, thus allowing a program to access the local memory inside a video card through a device file.

CHAPTER TWO

MEMORY ADDRESSING

This chapter deals with addressing techniques. Luckily, an operating system is not forced to keep track of physical memory all by itself; today's microprocessors include several hardware circuits to make memory management both more efficient and more robust in case of programming errors.

As in the rest of this book, we offer details in this chapter on how Intel 80x86 microprocessors address memory chips and how Linux makes use of the available addressing circuits. You will find, we hope, that when you learn the implementation details on Linux's most popular platform you will better understand both the general theory of paging and how to research the implementation on other platforms.

This is the first of three chapters related to memory management: Chapter 6, *Memory Management*, discusses how the kernel allocates main memory to itself, while Chapter 7, *Process Address Space*, considers how linear addresses are assigned to processes.

Memory Addresses

Programmers casually refer to a *memory address* as the way to access the contents of a memory cell. But when dealing with Intel 80x86 microprocessors, we have to distinguish among three kinds of addresses:

Logical address

Included in the machine language instructions to specify the address of an operand or of an instruction. This type of address embodies the well-known Intel segmented architecture that forces MS-DOS and Windows programmers to divide their programs into segments. Each logical address consists of a *segment* and an *offset* (or *displacement*) that denotes the distance from the start of the segment to the actual address.

Linear address

> A single 32-bit unsigned integer that can be used to address up to 4 GB, that is, up to 4,294,967,296 memory cells. Linear addresses are usually represented in hexadecimal notation; their values range from 0x00000000 to 0xffffffff.

Physical address

> Used to address memory cells included in memory chips. They correspond to the electrical signals sent along the address pins of the microprocessor to the memory bus. Physical addresses are represented as 32-bit unsigned integers.

The CPU control unit transforms a logical address into a linear address by means of a hardware circuit called a *segmentation unit*; successively, a second hardware circuit called a *paging unit* transforms the linear address into a physical address (see Figure 2-1).

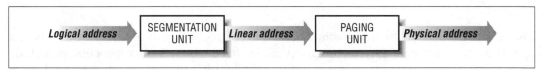

Figure 2-1. Logical address translation

Segmentation in Hardware

Starting with the 80386 model, Intel microprocessors perform address translation in two different ways called *real mode* and *protected mode*. Real mode exists mostly to maintain processor compatibility with older models and to allow the operating system to bootstrap (see Appendix A, *System Startup*, for a short description of real mode). We shall thus focus our attention on protected mode.

Segmentation Registers

A logical address consists of two parts: a segment identifier and an offset that specifies the relative address within the segment. The segment identifier is a 16-bit field called *Segment Selector*, while the offset is a 32-bit field.

To make it easy to retrieve segment selectors quickly, the processor provides *segmentation registers* whose only purpose is to hold Segment Selectors; these registers are called cs, ss, ds, es, fs, and gs. Although there are only six of them, a program can reuse the same segmentation register for different purposes by saving its content in memory and then restoring it later.

Three of the six segmentation registers have specific purposes:

cs

> The code segment register, which points to a segment containing program instructions

ss

> The stack segment register, which points to a segment containing the current program stack

ds

> The data segment register, which points to a segment containing static and external data

The remaining three segmentation registers are general purpose and may refer to arbitrary segments.

The **cs** register has another important function: it includes a 2-bit field that specifies the Current Privilege Level (**CPL**) of the CPU. The value 0 denotes the highest privilege level, while the value 3 denotes the lowest one. Linux uses only levels 0 and 3, which are respectively called Kernel Mode and User Mode.

Segment Descriptors

Each segment is represented by an 8-byte *Segment Descriptor* (see Figure 2-2) that describes the segment characteristics. Segment Descriptors are stored either in the *Global Descriptor Table* (*GDT*) or in the *Local Descriptor Table* (*LDT*).

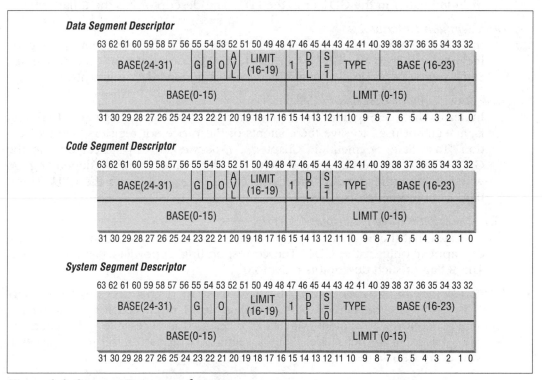

Figure 2-2. Segment Descriptor format

Usually only one GDT is defined, while each process may have its own LDT. The address of the GDT in main memory is contained in the `gdtr` processor register and the address of the currently used LDT is contained in the `ldtr` processor register.

Each Segment Descriptor consists of the following fields:

- A 32-bit `Base` field that contains the linear address of the first byte of the segment.

- A `G` granularity flag: if it is cleared, the segment size is expressed in bytes; otherwise, it is expressed in multiples of 4096 bytes.

- A 20-bit `Limit` field that denotes the segment length in bytes. If `G` is set to 0, the size of a non-null segment may vary between 1 byte and 1 MB; otherwise, it may vary between 4 KB and 4 GB.

- An `S` system flag: if it is cleared, the segment is a system segment that stores kernel data structures; otherwise, it is a normal code or data segment.

- A 4-bit `Type` field that characterizes the segment type and its access rights. The following Segment Descriptor types are widely used:

    Code Segment Descriptor
    Indicates that the Segment Descriptor refers to a code segment; it may be included either in the GDT or in the LDT. The descriptor has the `S` flag set.

    Data Segment Descriptor
    Indicates that the Segment Descriptor refers to a data segment; it may be included either in the GDT or in the LDT. The descriptor has the `S` flag set. Stack segments are implemented by means of generic data segments.

    Task State Segment Descriptor (TSSD)
    Indicates that the Segment Descriptor refers to a Task State Segment (TSS), that is, a segment used to save the contents of the processor registers (see the section "Task State Segment" in Chapter 3, *Processes*); it can appear only in the GDT. The corresponding `Type` field has the value 11 or 9, depending on whether the corresponding process is currently executing on the CPU. The `S` flag of such descriptors is set to 0.

    Local Descriptor Table Descriptor (LDTD)
    Indicates that the Segment Descriptor refers to a segment containing an LDT; it can appear only in the GDT. The corresponding `Type` field has the value 2. The `S` flag of such descriptors is set to 0.

- A `DPL` (*Descriptor Privilege Level*) 2-bit field used to restrict accesses to the segment. It represents the minimal CPU privilege level requested for accessing the segment. Therefore, a segment with its `DPL` set to 0 is accessible only when the `CPL` is 0, that is, in Kernel Mode, while a segment with its `DPL` set to 3 is accessible with every `CPL` value.

- A `Segment-Present` flag that is set to 0 if the segment is currently not stored in main memory. Linux always sets this field to 1, since it never swaps out whole segments to disk.

- An additional flag called `D` or `B` depending on whether the segment contains code or data. Its meaning is slightly different in the two cases, but it is basically set if the addresses used as segment offsets are 32 bits long and it is cleared if they are 16 bits long (see the Intel manual for further details).

- A reserved bit (bit 53) always set to 0.

- An `AVL` flag that may be used by the operating system but is ignored in Linux.

Segment Selectors

To speed up the translation of logical addresses into linear addresses, the Intel processor provides an additional nonprogrammable register—that is, a register that cannot be set by a programmer—for each of the six programmable segmentation registers. Each nonprogrammable register contains the 8-byte Segment Descriptor (described in the previous section) specified by the Segment Selector contained in the corresponding segmentation register. Every time a Segment Selector is loaded in a segmentation register, the corresponding Segment Descriptor is loaded from memory into the matching nonprogrammable CPU register. From then on, translations of logical addresses referring to that segment can be performed without accessing the GDT or LDT stored in main memory; the processor can just refer directly to the CPU register containing the Segment Descriptor. Accesses to the GDT or LDT are necessary only when the contents of the segmentation register change (see Figure 2-3). Each Segment Selector includes the following fields:

- A 13-bit index (described further in the text following this list) that identifies the corresponding Segment Descriptor entry contained in the GDT or in the LDT

- A `TI` (*Table Indicator*) flag that specifies whether the Segment Descriptor is included in the GDT (`TI` = 0) or in the LDT (`TI` = 1)

- An `RPL` (*Requestor Privilege Level*) 2-bit field, which is precisely the Current Privilege Level of the CPU when the corresponding Segment Selector is loaded into the `cs` register[*]

Since a Segment Descriptor is 8 bytes long, its relative address inside the GDT or the LDT is obtained by multiplying the most significant 13 bits of the Segment Selector by 8. For instance, if the GDT is at `0x00020000` (the value stored in the `gdtr` register) and the index specified by the Segment Selector is 2, the address of the corresponding Segment Descriptor is `0x00020000` + (2 × 8), or `0x00020010`.

---

[*] The RPL field may also be used to selectively weaken the processor privilege level when accessing data segments; see Intel documentation for details.

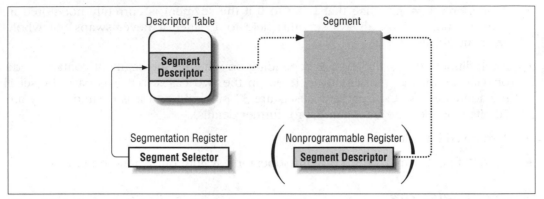

Figure 2-3. Segment Selector and Segment Descriptor

The first entry of the GDT is always set to 0: this ensures that logical addresses with a null Segment Selector will be considered invalid, thus causing a processor exception. The maximum number of Segment Descriptors that can be stored in the GDT is thus 8191, that is, $2^{13}-1$.

Segmentation Unit

Figure 2-4 shows in detail how a logical address is translated into a corresponding linear address. The segmentation unit performs the following operations:

- Examines the **TI** field of the Segment Selector, in order to determine which Descriptor Table stores the Segment Descriptor. This field indicates that the Descriptor is either in the GDT (in which case the segmentation unit gets the base linear address of the GDT from the **gdtr** register) or in the active LDT (in which case the segmentation unit gets the base linear address of that LDT from the **ldtr** register).

- Computes the address of the Segment Descriptor from the **index** field of the Segment Selector. The **index** field is multiplied by 8 (the size of a Segment Descriptor), and the result is added to the content of the **gdtr** or **ldtr** register.

- Adds to the **Base** field of the Segment Descriptor the offset of the logical address, thus obtains the linear address.

Notice that, thanks to the nonprogrammable registers associated with the segmentation registers, the first two operations need to be performed only when a segmentation register has been changed.

Segmentation in Linux

Segmentation has been included in Intel microprocessors to encourage programmers to split their applications in logically related entities, such as subroutines or global and

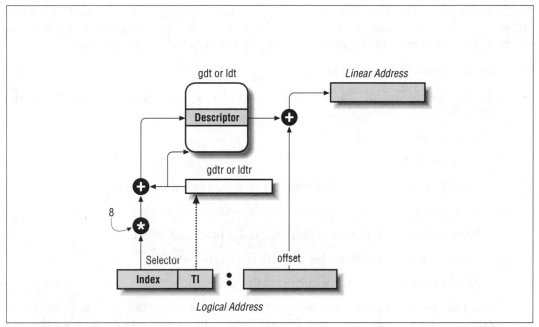

Figure 2-4. Translating a logical address

local data areas. However, Linux uses segmentation in a very limited way. In fact, segmentation and paging are somewhat redundant since both can be used to separate the physical address spaces of processes: segmentation can assign a different linear address space to each process while paging can map the same linear address space into different physical address spaces. Linux prefers paging to segmentation for the following reasons:

- Memory management is simpler when all processes use the same segment register values, that is, when they share the same set of linear addresses.

- One of the design objectives of Linux is portability to the most popular architectures; however, several RISC processors support segmentation in a very limited way.

The 2.2 version of Linux uses segmentation only when required by the Intel 80x86 architecture. In particular, all processes use the same logical addresses, so the total number of segments to be defined is quite limited and it is possible to store all Segment Descriptors in the Global Descriptor Table (GDT). This table is implemented by the array `gdt_table` referred by the `gdt` variable. If you look in the Source Code Index, you can see that these symbols are defined in the file *arch/i386/kernel/head.S*. Every macro, function, and other symbol in this book is listed in the appendix so you can quickly find it in the source code.

Local Descriptor Tables are not used by the kernel, although a system call exists that allows processes to create their own LDTs. This turns out to be useful to applications such as Wine that execute segment-oriented Microsoft Windows applications.

Here are the segments used by Linux:

- A kernel code segment. The fields of the corresponding Segment Descriptor in the GDT have the following values:
  — Base = 0x00000000
  — Limit = 0xfffff
  — G (granularity flag) = 1, for segment size expressed in pages
  — S (system flag) = 1, for normal code or data segment
  — Type = 0xa, for code segment that can be read and executed
  — DPL (Descriptor Privilege Level) = 0, for Kernel Mode
  — D/B (32-bit address flag) = 1, for 32-bit offset addresses

Thus, the linear addresses associated with that segment start at 0 and reach the addressing limit of $2^{32} - 1$. The S and Type fields specify that the segment is a code segment that can be read and executed. Its DPL value is 0, thus it can be accessed only in Kernel Mode. The corresponding Segment Selector is defined by the __KERNEL_CS macro: in order to address the segment, the kernel just loads the value yielded by the macro into the cs register.

- A kernel data segment. The fields of the corresponding Segment Descriptor in the GDT have the following values:
  — Base = 0x00000000
  — Limit = 0xfffff
  — G (granularity flag) = 1, for segment size expressed in pages
  — S (system flag) = 1, for normal code or data segment
  — Type = 2, for data segment that can be read and written
  — DPL (Descriptor Privilege Level) = 0, for Kernel Mode
  — D/B (32-bit address flag) = 1, for 32-bit offset addresses

This segment is identical to the previous one (in fact, they overlap in the linear address space) except for the value of the Type field, which specifies that it is a data segment that can be read and written. The corresponding Segment Selector is defined by the __KERNEL_DS macro.

- A user code segment shared by all processes in User Mode. The fields of the corresponding Segment Descriptor in the GDT have the following values:
  - Base = 0x00000000
  - Limit = 0xfffff
  - G (granularity flag) = 1, for segment size expressed in pages
  - S (system flag) = 1, for normal code or data segment
  - Type = 0xa, for code segment that can be read and executed
  - DPL (Descriptor Privilege Level) = 3, for User Mode
  - D/B (32-bit address flag) = 1, for 32-bit offset addresses

  The S and DPL fields specify that the segment is not a system segment and that its privilege level is equal to 3; it can thus be accessed both in Kernel Mode and in User Mode. The corresponding Segment Selector is defined by the __USER_CS macro.

- A user data segment shared by all processes in User Mode. The fields of the corresponding Segment Descriptor in the GDT have the following values:
  - Base = 0x00000000
  - Limit = 0xfffff
  - G (granularity flag) = 1, for segment size expressed in pages
  - S (system flag) = 1, for normal code or data segment
  - Type = 2, for data segment that can be read and written
  - DPL (Descriptor Privilege Level) = 3, for User Mode
  - D/B (32-bit address flag) = 1, for 32-bit offset addresses

  This segment overlaps the previous one: they are identical, except for the value of Type. The corresponding Segment Selector is defined by the __USER_DS macro.

- A Task State Segment (TSS) segment for each process. The descriptors of these segments are stored in the GDT. The Base field of the TSS descriptor associated with each process contains the address of the tss field of the corresponding process descriptor. The G flag is cleared, while the Limit field is set to 0xeb, since the TSS segment is 236 bytes long. The Type field is set to 9 or 11 (available 32-bit TSS), and the DPL is set to 0, since processes in User Mode are not allowed to access TSS segments.

- A default LDT segment that is usually shared by all processes. This segment is stored in the default_ldt variable. The default LDT includes a single entry consisting of a null Segment Descriptor. Each process has its own LDT Segment Descriptor, which usually points to the common default LDT segment. The Base field is set to the address of `default_ldt` and the `Limit` field is set to 7. If a process requires a real LDT, a new 4096-byte segment is created (it can include up to 511 Segment Descriptors), and the default LDT Segment Descriptor associated with that process is replaced in the GDT with a new descriptor with specific values for the `Base` and `Limit` fields.

For each process, therefore, the GDT contains two different Segment Descriptors: one for the TSS segment and one for the LDT segment. The maximum number of entries allowed in the GDT is 12+2×NR_TASKS, where, in turn, NR_TASKS denotes the maximum number of processes. In the previous list we described the four main Segment Descriptors used by Linux. Four additional Segment Descriptors cover Advanced Power Management (APM) features, and four entries of the GDT are left unused, for a grand total of 12.

As we mentioned before, the GDT can have at most 2^{13} = 8192 entries, of which the first is always null. Since 12 are either unused or filled by the system, NR_TASKS cannot be larger than 8180/2 = 4090.

The TSS and LDT descriptors for each process are added to the GDT as the process is created. As we shall see in the section "Kernel Threads" in Chapter 3, the kernel itself spawns the first process: process 0 running `init_task`. During kernel initialization, the `trap_init()` function inserts the TSS descriptor of this first process into the GDT using the statement:

```
set_tss_desc(0, &init_task.tss);
```

The first process creates others, so that every subsequent process is the child of some existing process. The `copy_thread()` function, which is invoked from the `clone()` and `fork()` system calls to create new processes, executes the same function in order to set the TSS of the new process:

```
set_tss_desc(nr, &(task[nr]->tss));
```

Since each TSS descriptor refers to a different process, of course, each `Base` field has a different value. The `copy_thread()` function also invokes the `set_ldt_desc()` function in order to insert a Segment Descriptor in the GDT relative to the default LDT for the new process.

The kernel data segment includes a process descriptor for each process. Each process descriptor includes its own TSS segment and a pointer to its LDT segment, which is also located inside the kernel data segment.

As stated earlier, the Current Privilege Level of the CPU reflects whether the processor is in User or Kernel Mode and is specified by the `RPL` field of the Segment Selector stored in the `cs` register. Whenever the Current Privilege Level is changed, some segmentation registers must be correspondingly updated. For instance, when the `CPL` is equal to 3 (User Mode), the `ds` register must contain the Segment Selector of the user data segment, but when the CPL is equal to 0, the `ds` register must contain the Segment Selector of the kernel data segment.

A similar situation occurs for the `ss` register: it must refer to a User Mode stack inside the user data segment when the CPL is 3, and it must refer to a Kernel Mode stack inside the kernel data segment when the CPL is 0. When switching from User Mode to Kernel Mode, Linux always makes sure that the `ss` register contains the Segment Selector of the kernel data segment.

Paging in Hardware

The paging unit translates linear addresses into physical ones. It checks the requested access type against the access rights of the linear address. If the memory access is not valid, it generates a page fault exception (see Chapter 4, *Interrupts and Exceptions*, and Chapter 6, *Memory Management*).

For the sake of efficiency, linear addresses are grouped in fixed-length intervals called *pages*; contiguous linear addresses within a page are mapped into contiguous physical addresses. In this way, the kernel can specify the physical address and the access rights of a page instead of those of all the linear addresses included in it. Following the usual convention, we shall use the term "page" to refer both to a set of linear addresses and to the data contained in this group of addresses.

The paging unit thinks of all RAM as partitioned into fixed-length *page frames* (they are sometimes referred to as *physical pages*). Each page frame contains a page, that is, the length of a page frame coincides with that of a page. A page frame is a constituent of main memory, and hence it is a storage area. It is important to distinguish a page from a page frame: the former is just a block of data, which may be stored in any page frame or on disk.

The data structures that map linear to physical addresses are called *page tables*; they are stored in main memory and must be properly initialized by the kernel before enabling the paging unit.

In Intel processors, paging is enabled by setting the PG flag of the `cr0` register. When PG = 0, linear addresses are interpreted as physical addresses.

Regular Paging

Starting with the i80386, the paging unit of Intel processors handles 4 KB pages. The 32 bits of a linear address are divided into three fields:

Directory
    The most significant 10 bits

Table
    The intermediate 10 bits

Offset
    The least significant 12 bits

The translation of linear addresses is accomplished in two steps, each based on a type of translation table. The first translation table is called *Page Directory* and the second is called *Page Table*.

The physical address of the Page Directory in use is stored in the **cr3** processor register. The Directory field within the linear address determines the entry in the Page Directory that points to the proper Page Table. The address's Table field, in turn, determines the entry in the Page Table that contains the physical address of the page frame containing the page. The Offset field determines the relative position within the page frame (see Figure 2-5). Since it is 12 bits long, each page consists of 4096 bytes of data.

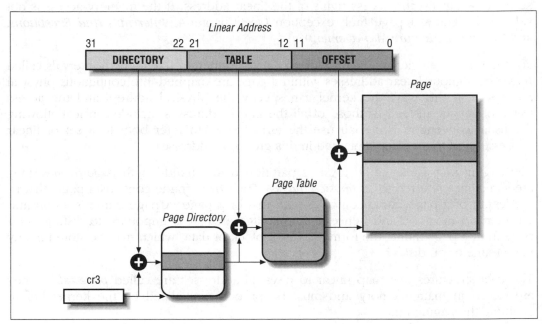

Figure 2-5. Paging by Intel 80x86 processors

Both the Directory and the Table fields are 10 bits long, so Page Directories and Page Tables can include up to 1024 entries. It follows that a Page Directory can address up to $1024 \times 1024 \times 4096 = 2^{32}$ memory cells, as you'd expect in 32-bit addresses.

The entries of Page Directories and Page Tables have the same structure. Each entry includes the following fields:

Present *flag*
    If it is set, the referred page (or Page Table) is contained in main memory; if the flag is 0, the page is not contained in main memory and the remaining entry bits

may be used by the operating system for its own purposes. (We shall see in Chapter 16, *Swapping: Methods for Freeing Memory*, how Linux makes use of this field.)

Field containing the 20 most significant bits of a page frame physical address
Since each page frame has a 4 KB capacity, its physical address must be a multiple of 4096, so the 12 least significant bits of the physical address are always equal to 0. If the field refers to a Page Directory, the page frame contains a Page Table; if it refers to a Page Table, the page frame contains a page of data.

Accessed *flag*
Is set each time the paging unit addresses the corresponding page frame. This flag may be used by the operating system when selecting pages to be swapped out. The paging unit never resets this flag; this must be done by the operating system.

Dirty *flag*
Applies only to the Page Table entries. It is set each time a write operation is performed on the page frame. As in the previous case, this flag may be used by the operating system when selecting pages to be swapped out. The paging unit never resets this flag; this must be done by the operating system.

Read/Write *flag*
Contains the access right (Read/Write or Read) of the page or of the Page Table (see the section "Hardware Protection Scheme" later in this chapter).

User/Supervisor *flag*
Contains the privilege level required to access the page or Page Table (see the later section "Hardware Protection Scheme").

Two flags called PCD *and* PWT
Control the way the page or Page Table is handled by the hardware cache (see the section "Hardware Cache" later in this chapter).

Page Size *flag*
Applies only to Page Directory entries. If it is set, the entry refers to a 4 MB long page frame (see the following section).

If the entry of a Page Table or Page Directory needed to perform an address translation has the Present flag cleared, the paging unit stores the linear address in the cr2 processor register and generates the exception 14, that is, the "Page fault" exception.

Extended Paging

Starting with the Pentium model, Intel 80x86 microprocessors introduce *extended paging*, which allows page frames to be either 4 KB or 4 MB in size (see Figure 2-6).

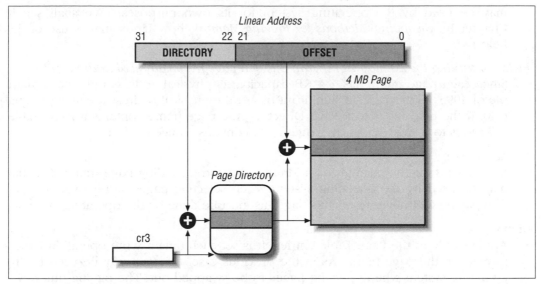

Figure 2-6. Extended paging

As we have seen in the previous section, extended paging is enabled by setting the **Page Size** flag of a Page Directory entry. In this case, the paging unit divides the 32 bits of a linear address into two fields:

Directory
    The most significant 10 bits

Offset
    The remaining 22 bits

Page Directory entries for extended paging are the same as for normal paging, except that:

*   The **Page Size** flag must be set.

*   Only the first 10 most significant bits of the 20-bit physical address field are significant. This is because each physical address is aligned on a 4 MB boundary, so the 22 least significant bits of the address are 0.

Extended paging coexists with regular paging; it is enabled by setting the **PSE** flag of the **cr4** processor register. Extended paging is used to translate large intervals of contiguous linear addresses into corresponding physical ones; in these cases, the kernel can do without intermediate Page Tables and thus save memory.

Hardware Protection Scheme

The paging unit uses a different protection scheme from the segmentation unit. While Intel processors allow four possible privilege levels to a segment, only two privilege levels are associated with pages and Page Tables, because privileges are controlled by the User/Supervisor flag mentioned in the earlier section "Regular Paging." When this flag is 0, the page can be addressed only when the CPL is less than 3 (this means, for Linux, when the processor is in Kernel Mode). When the flag is 1, the page can always be addressed.

Furthermore, instead of the three types of access rights (Read, Write, Execute) associated with segments, only two types of access rights (Read, Write) are associated with pages. If the Read/Write flag of a Page Directory or Page Table entry is equal to 0, the corresponding Page Table or page can only be read; otherwise it can be read and written.

An Example of Paging

A simple example will help in clarifying how paging works.

Let us assume that the kernel has assigned the linear address space between 0x20000000 and 0x2003ffff to a running process. This space consists of exactly 64 pages. We don't care about the physical addresses of the page frames containing the pages; in fact, some of them might not even be in main memory. We are interested only in the remaining fields of the page table entries.

Let us start with the 10 most significant bits of the linear addresses assigned to the process, which are interpreted as the Directory field by the paging unit. The addresses start with a 2 followed by zeros, so the 10 bits all have the same value, namely 0x080 or 128 decimal. Thus the Directory field in all the addresses refers to the 129th entry of the process Page Directory. The corresponding entry must contain the physical address of the Page Table assigned to the process (see Figure 2-7). If no other linear addresses are assigned to the process, all the remaining 1023 entries of the Page Directory are filled with zeros.

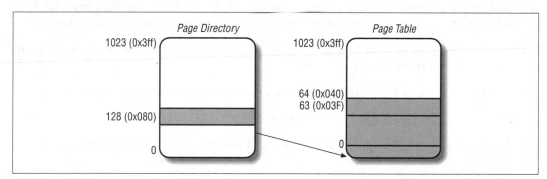

Figure 2-7. An example of paging

The values assumed by the intermediate 10 bits, (that is, the values of the Table field) range from 0 to 0x03f, or from 0 to 63 decimal. Thus, only the first 64 entries of the Page Table are significant. The remaining 960 entries are filled with zeros.

Suppose that the process needs to read the byte at linear address 0x20021406. This address is handled by the paging unit as follows:

1. The Directory field 0x80 is used to select entry 0x80 of the Page Directory, which points to the Page Table associated with the process's pages.

2. The Table field 0x21 is used to select entry 0x21 of the Page Table, which points to the page frame containing the desired page.

3. Finally, the Offset field 0x406 is used to select the byte at offset 0x406 in the desired page frame.

If the **Present** flag of the 0x21 entry of the Page Table is cleared, the page is not present in main memory; in this case, the paging unit issues a page exception while translating the linear address. The same exception is issued whenever the process attempts to access linear addresses outside of the interval delimited by 0x20000000 and 0x2003ffff since the Page Table entries not assigned to the process are filled with zeros; in particular, their **Present** flags are all cleared.

Three-Level Paging

Two-level paging is used by 32-bit microprocessors. But in recent years, several microprocessors (such as Compaq's Alpha, and Sun's UltraSPARC) have adopted a 64-bit architecture. In this case, two-level paging is no longer suitable and it is necessary to move up to three-level paging. Let us use a thought experiment to see why.

Start by assuming about as large a page size as is reasonable (since you have to account for pages being transferred routinely to and from disk). Let's choose 16 KB for the page size. Since 1 KB covers a range of 2^{10} addresses, 16 KB covers 2^{14} addresses, so the Offset field would be 14 bits. This leaves 50 bits of the linear address to be distributed between the Table and the Directory fields. If we now decide to reserve 25 bits for each of these two fields, this means that both the Page Directory and the Page Tables of a process would include 2^{25} entries, that is, more than 32 million entries.

Even if RAM is getting cheaper and cheaper, we cannot afford to waste so much memory space just for storing the page tables.

The solution chosen for Compaq's Alpha microprocessors is the following:

- Page frames are 8 KB long, so the Offset field is 13 bits long.

- Only the least significant 43 bits of an address are used. (The most significant 21 bits are always set 0.)

- Three levels of page tables are introduced so that the remaining 30 bits of the address can be split into three 10-bit fields (see Figure 2-9 later in this chapter). So the Page Tables include $2^{10} = 1024$ entries as in the two-level paging schema examined previously.

As we shall see in the section "Paging in Linux" later in this chapter, Linux's designers decided to implement a paging model inspired by the Alpha architecture.

Hardware Cache

Today's microprocessors have clock rates approaching gigahertz, while dynamic RAM (DRAM) chips have access times in the range of tens of clock cycles. This means that the CPU may be held back considerably while executing instructions that require fetching operands from RAM and/or storing results into RAM.

Hardware cache memories have been introduced to reduce the speed mismatch between CPU and RAM. They are based on the well-known *locality principle*, which holds both for programs and data structures: because of the cyclic structure of programs and the packing of related data into linear arrays, addresses close to the ones most recently used have a high probability of being used in the near future. It thus makes sense to introduce a smaller and faster memory that contains the most recently used code and data. For this purpose, a new unit called the *line* has been introduced into the Intel architecture. It consists of a few dozen contiguous bytes that are transferred in burst mode between the slow DRAM and the fast on-chip static RAM (SRAM) used to implement caches.

The cache is subdivided into subsets of lines. At one extreme the cache can be *direct mapped*, in which case a line in main memory is always stored at the exact same location in the cache. At the other extreme, the cache is *fully associative*, meaning that any line in memory can be stored at any location in the cache. But most caches are to some degree *N-way set associative*, where any line of main memory can be stored in any one of *N* lines of the cache. For instance, a line of memory can be stored in two different lines of a 2-way set associative cache.

As shown in Figure 2-8, the cache unit is inserted between the paging unit and the main memory. It includes both a *hardware cache memory* and a *cache controller*. The cache memory stores the actual lines of memory. The cache controller stores an array of entries, one entry for each line of the cache memory. Each entry includes a *tag* and a few flags that describe the status of the cache line. The tag consists of some bits that allow the cache controller to recognize the memory location currently mapped by the line. The bits of the memory physical address are usually split into three groups: the most significant ones correspond to the tag, the middle ones correspond to the cache controller subset index, the least significant ones to the offset within the line.

When accessing a RAM memory cell, the CPU extracts the subset index from the physical address and compares the tags of all lines in the subset with the high-order bits of the physical address. If a line with the same tag as the high-order bits of the address is found, the CPU has a *cache hit*; otherwise, it has a *cache miss*.

When a cache hit occurs, the cache controller behaves differently depending on access type. For a read operation, the controller selects the data from the cache line and

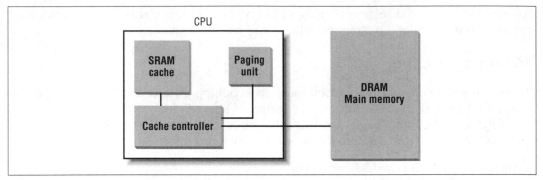

Figure 2-8. Processor hardware cache

transfers it into a CPU register; the RAM is not accessed and the CPU achieves the time saving for which the cache system was invented. For a write operation, the controller may implement one of two basic strategies called *write-through* and *write-back*. In a write-through, the controller always writes into both RAM and the cache line, effectively switching off the cache for write operations. In a write-back, which offers more immediate efficiency, only the cache line is updated, and the contents of the RAM are left unchanged. After a write-back, of course, the RAM must eventually be updated. The cache controller writes the cache line back into RAM only when the CPU executes an instruction requiring a flush of cache entries or when a FLUSH hardware signal occurs (usually after a cache miss).

When a cache miss occurs, the cache line is written to memory, if necessary, and the correct line is fetched from RAM into the cache entry.

Multiprocessor systems have a separate hardware cache for every processor, and therefore they need additional hardware circuitry to synchronize the cache contents. See the section "Hardware Support to Cache Synchronization" in Chapter 11, *Kernel Synchronization*.

Cache technology is rapidly evolving. For example, the first Pentium models included a single on-chip cache called the *L1-cache*. More recent models also include another larger and slower on-chip cache called the *L2-cache*. The consistency between the two cache levels is implemented at the hardware level. Linux ignores these hardware details and assumes there is a single cache.

The CD flag of the cr0 processor register is used to enable or disable the cache circuitry. The NW flag, in the same register, specifies whether the write-through or the write-back strategy is used for the caches.

Another interesting feature of the Pentium cache is that it lets an operating system associate a different cache management policy with each page frame. For that purpose, each Page Directory and each Page Table entry includes two flags: PCD specifies whether the cache must be enabled or disabled while accessing data included in the page frame; PWT specifies whether the write-back or the write-through strategy must be applied while writing data into the page frame. Linux clears the PCD and PWT flags of all Page Directory and Page Table entries: as a result, caching is enabled for all page frames and the write-back strategy is always adopted for writing.

The L1_CACHE_BYTES macro yields the size of a cache line on a Pentium, that is, 32 bytes. In order to optimize the cache hit rate, the kernel adopts the following rules:

- The most frequently used fields of a data structure are placed at the low offset within the data structure so that they can be cached in the same line.

- When allocating a large set of data structures, the kernel tries to store each of them in memory so that all cache lines are uniformly used.

Translation Lookaside Buffers (TLB)

Besides general-purpose hardware caches, Intel 80x86 processors include other caches called *translation lookaside buffers* or *TLB* to speed up linear address translation. When a linear address is used for the first time, the corresponding physical address is computed through slow accesses to the page tables in RAM. The physical address is then stored in a TLB entry, so that further references to the same linear address can be quickly translated.

The invlpg instruction can be used to invalidate (that is, to free) a single entry of a TLB. In order to invalidate all TLB entries, the processor can simply write into the cr3 register that points to the currently used Page Directory.

Since the TLBs serve as caches of page table contents, whenever a Page Table entry is modified, the kernel must invalidate the corresponding TLB entry. To do this, Linux makes use of the flush_tlb_page(addr) function, which invokes __flush_tlb_ one(). The latter function executes the invlpg Assembly instruction:

```
movl $addr,%eax
invlpg (%eax)
```

Sometimes it is necessary to invalidate all TLB entries, such as during kernel initialization. In such cases, the kernel invokes the __flush_tlb() function, which rewrites the current value of cr3 back into it:

```
movl %cr3, %eax
movl %eax, %cr3
```

Paging in Linux

As we explained in the section "Three-Level Paging," Linux adopted a three-level paging model so paging is feasible on 64-bit architectures. Figure 2-9 shows the model, which defines three types of paging tables:

- Page Global Directory

- Page Middle Directory

- Page Table

The Page Global Directory includes the addresses of several Page Middle Directories, which in turn include the addresses of several Page Tables. Each Page Table entry points to a page frame. The linear address is thus split into four parts. Figure 2-9 does not show the bit numbers because the size of each part depends on the computer architecture.

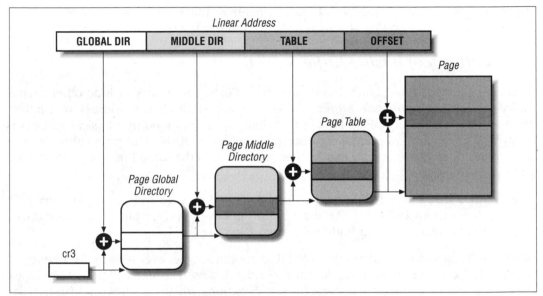

Figure 2-9. The Linux paging model

Linux handling of processes relies heavily on paging. In fact, the automatic translation of linear addresses into physical ones makes the following design objectives feasible:

- Assign a different physical address space to each process, thus ensuring an efficient protection against addressing errors.

- Distinguish pages, that is, groups of data, from page frames, that is, physical addresses in main memory. This allows the same page to be stored in a page frame, then saved to disk, and later reloaded in a different page frame. This is the basic ingredient of the virtual memory mechanism (see Chapter 16).

As we shall see in Chapter 7, each process has its own Page Global Directory and its own set of Page Tables. When a process switching occurs (see the section "Process Switching" in Chapter 3), Linux saves in a TSS segment the contents of the cr3 control register and loads from another TSS segment a new value into cr3. Thus, when the new process resumes its execution on the CPU, the paging unit refers to the correct set of page tables.

What happens when this three-level paging model is applied to the Pentium, which uses only two types of page tables? Linux essentially eliminates the Page Middle Directory field by saying that it contains zero bits. However, the position of the Page Middle Directory in the sequence of pointers is kept so that the same code can work on 32-bit and 64-bit architectures. The kernel keeps a position for the Page Middle Directory by setting the number of entries in it to 1 and mapping this single entry into the proper entry of the Page Global Directory.

Mapping logical to linear addresses now becomes a mechanical task, although somewhat complex. The next few sections of this chapter are thus a rather tedious list of functions and macros that retrieve information the kernel needs to find addresses and manage the tables; most of the functions are one or two lines long. You may want to just skim these sections now, but it is useful to know the role of these functions and macros because you'll see them often in discussions in subsequent chapters.

The Linear Address Fields

The following macros simplify page table handling:

PAGE_SHIFT
> Specifies the length in bits of the Offset field; when applied to Pentium processors it yields the value 12. Since all the addresses in a page must fit in the Offset field, the size of a page on Intel 80x86 systems is 2^{12} or the familiar 4096 bytes; the PAGE_SHIFT of 12 can thus be considered the logarithm base 2 of the total page size. This macro is used by PAGE_SIZE to return the size of the page. Finally, the PAGE_MASK macro is defined as the value 0xfffff000; it is used to mask all the bits of the Offset field.

PMD_SHIFT
> Determines the logarithm of the size of the area a Page Middle Directory entry can map. It yields the value 22 (12 bits from Offset plus 10 bits from Table). The PMD_SIZE macro computes the size of the area mapped by a single entry of the Page Middle Directory, that is, of a Page Table. Thus, PMD_SIZE yields 2^{22} or 4 MB. The PMD_MASK macro yields the value 0xffc00000; it is used to mask all the bits of the Offset and Table fields.

PGDIR_SHIFT
> Determines the logarithm of the size of the area a Page Global Directory entry can map. Since the Middle Directory field has length 0, this macro yields the same value yielded by PMD_SHIFT, which is 22. The PGDIR_SIZE macro computes the size of the area mapped by a single entry of the Page Global Directory, that is, of a Page Directory. PGDIR_SIZE therefore yields 4 MB. The PGDIR_MASK macro yields the value 0xffc00000, the same as PMD_MASK.

PTRS_PER_PTE, PTRS_PER_PMD, *and* PTRS_PER_PGD
> Compute the number of entries in the Page Table, Page Middle Directory, and Page Global Directory; they yield the values 1024, 1, and 1024, respectively.

Page Table Handling

pte_t, pmd_t, and pgd_t are 32-bit data types that describe, respectively, a Page Table, a Page Middle Directory, and a Page Global Directory entry. pgprot_t is another 32-bit data type that represents the protection flags associated with a single entry.

Four type-conversion macros (__pte(), __pmd(), __pgd(), and __pgprot()) cast a 32-bit unsigned integer into the required type. Four other type-conversion macros (pte_val(), pmd_val(), pgd_val(), and pgprot_val()) perform the reverse casting from one of the four previously mentioned specialized types into a 32-bit unsigned integer.

The kernel also provides several macros and functions to read or modify page table entries:

- The pte_none(), pmd_none(), and pgd_none() macros yield the value 1 if the corresponding entry has the value 0; otherwise, they yield the value 0.

- The pte_present(), pmd_present(), and pgd_present() macros yield the value 1 if the Present flag of the corresponding entry is equal to 1, that is, if the corresponding page or Page Table is loaded in main memory.

- The pte_clear(), pmd_clear(), and pgd_clear() macros clear an entry of the corresponding page table.

The macros pmd_bad() and pgd_bad() are used by functions to check Page Global Directory and Page Middle Directory entries passed as input parameters. Each macro yields the value 1 if the entry points to a bad page table, that is, if at least one of the following conditions applies:

- The page is not in main memory (Present flag cleared).

- The page allows only Read access (Read/Write flag cleared).

- Either Accessed or Dirty is cleared (Linux always forces these flags to be set for every existing page table).

No pte_bad() macro is defined because it is legal for a Page Table entry to refer to a page that is not present in main memory, not writable, or not accessible at all. Instead, several functions are offered to query the current value of any of the flags included in a Page Table entry:

pte_read()
> Returns the value of the User/Supervisor flag (indicating whether the page is accessible in User Mode).

pte_write()
> Returns 1 if both the Present and Read/Write flags are set (indicating whether the page is present and writable).

pte_exec()
:   Returns the value of the User/Supervisor flag (indicating whether the page is accessible in User Mode). Notice that pages on the Intel processor cannot be protected against code execution.

pte_dirty()
:   Returns the value of the Dirty flag (indicating whether or not the page has been modified).

pte_young()
:   Returns the value of the Accessed flag (indicating whether the page has been accessed).

Another group of functions sets the value of the flags in a Page Table entry:

pte_wrprotect()
:   Clears the Read/Write flag

pte_rdprotect *and* pte_exprotect()
:   Clear the User/Supervisor flag

pte_mkwrite()
:   Sets the Read/Write flag

pte_mkread() *and* pte_mkexec()
:   Set the User/Supervisor flag

pte_mkdirty() *and* pte_mkclean()
:   Set the Dirty flag to 1 and to 0, respectively, thus marking the page as modified or unmodified

pte_mkyoung() *and* pte_mkold()
:   Set the Accessed flag to 1 and to 0, respectively, thus marking the page as accessed (young) or nonaccessed (old)

pte_modify(p,v)
:   Sets all access rights in a Page Table entry p to a specified value v

set_pte
:   Writes a specified value into a Page Table entry

Now come the macros that combine a page address and a group of protection flags into a 32-bit page entry or perform the reverse operation of extracting the page address from a page table entry:

mk_pte()
:   Combines a linear address and a group of access rights to create a 32-bit Page Table entry.

mk_pte_phys
> Creates a Page Table entry by combining the physical address and the access rights of the page.

pte_page() *and* pmd_page()
> Return the linear address of a page from its Page Table entry, and of a Page Table from its Page Middle Directory entry.

pgd_offset(p,a)
> Receives as parameters a memory descriptor p (see Chapter 6) and a linear address a. The macro yields the address of the entry in a Page Global Directory that corresponds to the address a; the Page Global Directory is found through a pointer within the memory descriptor p. The pgd_offset_k(o) macro is similar, except that it refers to the memory descriptor used by kernel threads (see the section "Kernel Threads" in Chapter 3).

pmd_offset(p,a)
> Receives as parameter a Page Global Directory entry p and a linear address a; it yields the address of the entry corresponding to the address a in the Page Middle Directory referenced by p. The pte_offset(p,a) macro is similar, but p is a Page Middle Directory entry and the macro yields the address of the entry corresponding to a in the Page Table referenced by p.

The last group of functions of this long and rather boring list were introduced to simplify the creation and deletion of page table entries. When two-level paging is used, creating or deleting a Page Middle Directory entry is trivial. As we explained earlier in this section, the Page Middle Directory contains a single entry that points to the subordinate Page Table. Thus, the Page Middle Directory entry *is* the entry within the Page Global Directory too. When dealing with Page Tables, however, creating an entry may be more complex, because the Page Table that is supposed to contain it might not exist. In such cases, it is necessary to allocate a new page frame, fill it with zeros and finally add the entry.

Each page table is stored in one page frame; moreover, each process makes use of several page tables. As we shall see in the section "Page Frame Management" in Chapter 6, the allocations and deallocations of page frames are expensive operations. Therefore, when the kernel destroys a page table, it adds the corresponding page frame to a software cache. When the kernel must allocate a new page table, it takes a page frame contained in the cache; a new page frame is requested from the memory allocator only when the cache is empty.

The Page Table cache is a simple list of page frames. The pte_quicklist macro points to the head of the list, while the first 4 bytes of each page frame in the list are used as a pointer to the next element. The Page Global Directory cache is similar, but the head of the list is yielded by the pgd_quicklist macro. Of course, on Intel architecture there is no Page Middle Directory cache.

Since there is no limit on the size of the page table caches, the kernel must implement a mechanism for shrinking them. Therefore, the kernel introduces high and low *watermarks*, which are stored in the `pgt_cache_water` array; the `check_pgt_cache()` function checks whether the size of each cache is greater than the high watermark and, if so, deallocates page frames until the cache size reaches the low watermark. The `check_pgt_cache()` is invoked either when the system is idle or when the kernel releases all page tables of some process.

Now comes the last round of functions and macros:

`pgd_alloc()`

Allocates a new Page Global Directory by invoking the `get_pgd_fast()` function, which takes a page frame from the Page Global Directory cache; if the cache is empty, the page frame is allocated by invoking the `get_pgd_slow()` function.

`pmd_alloc(p,a)`

Defined so three-level paging systems can allocate a new Page Middle Directory for the linear address a. On Intel 80x86 systems, the function simply returns the input parameter p, that is, the address of the entry in the Page Global Directory.

`pte_alloc(p,a)`

Receives as parameters the address of a Page Middle Directory entry p and a linear address a, and it returns the address of the Page Table entry corresponding to a. If the Page Middle Directory entry is null, the function must allocate a new Page Table. To accomplish this, it looks for a free page frame in the Page Table cache by invoking the `get_pte_fast()` function. If the cache is empty, the page frame is allocated by invoking `get_pte_slow()`. If a new Page Table is allocated, the entry corresponding to a is initialized and the `User/Supervisor` flag is set. `pte_alloc_kernel()` is similar, except that it invokes the `get_pte_kernel_slow()` function instead of `get_pte_slow()` for allocating a new page frame; the `get_pte_kernel_slow()` function clears the `User/Supervisor` flag of the new Page Table.

`pte_free()`, `pte_free_kernel()`, *and* `pgd_free()`

Release a page table and insert the freed page frame in the proper cache. The `pmd_free()` and `pmd_free_kernel()` functions do nothing, since Page Middle Directories do not really exist on Intel 80x86 systems.

`free_one_pmd()`

Invokes `pte_free()` to release a Page Table.

`free_one_pgd()`

Releases all Page Tables of a Page Middle Directory; in the Intel architecture, it just invokes `free_one_pmd()` once. Then it releases the Page Middle Directory by invoking `pmd_free()`.

SET_PAGE_DIR

> Sets the Page Global Directory of a process. This is accomplished by placing the physical address of the Page Global Directory in a field of the TSS segment of the process; this address is loaded in the `cr3` register every time the process starts or resumes its execution on the CPU. Of course, if the affected process is currently in execution, the macro also directly changes the `cr3` register value so that the change takes effect right away.

new_page_tables()

> Allocates the Page Global Directory and all the Page Tables needed to set up a process address space. It also invokes **SET_PAGE_DIR** in order to assign the new Page Global Directory to the process. This topic will be covered in Chapter 7.

clear_page_tables()

> Clears the contents of the page tables of a process by iteratively invoking **free_one_pgd()**.

free_page_tables()

> Is very similar to **clear_page_tables()**, but it also releases the Page Global Directory of the process.

Reserved Page Frames

The kernel's code and data structures are stored in a group of reserved page frames. A page contained in one of these page frames can never be dynamically assigned or swapped to disk.

As a general rule, the Linux kernel is installed in RAM starting from physical address 0x00100000, that is, from the second megabyte. The total number of page frames required depends on how the kernel has been configured: a typical configuration yields a kernel that can be loaded in less than 2 MBs of RAM.

Why isn't the kernel loaded starting with the first available megabyte of RAM? Well, the PC architecture has several peculiarities that must be taken into account:

- Page frame 0 is used by BIOS to store the system hardware configuration detected during the *Power-On Self-Test* (*POST*).

- Physical addresses ranging from 0x000a0000 to 0x000fffff are reserved to BIOS routines and to map the internal memory of ISA graphics cards (the source of the well-known 640 KB addressing limit in the first MS-DOS systems).

- Additional page frames within the first megabyte may be reserved by specific computer models. For example, the IBM ThinkPad maps the 0xa0 page frame into the 0x9f one.

In order to avoid loading the kernel into groups of noncontiguous page frames, Linux prefers to skip the first megabyte of RAM. Clearly, page frames not reserved by the PC architecture will be used by Linux to store dynamically assigned pages.

Figure 2-10 shows how the first 2 MB of RAM are filled by Linux. We have assumed that the kernel requires less than one megabyte of RAM (this is a bit optimistic).

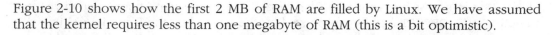

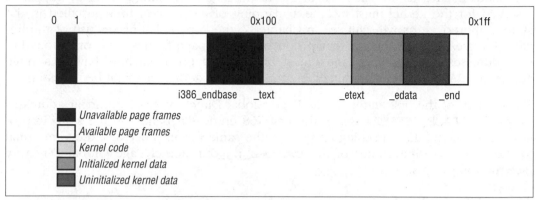

Figure 2-10. The first 512 page frames (2 MB) in Linux 2.2

The symbol **_text**, which corresponds to physical address 0x00100000, denotes the address of the first byte of kernel code. The end of the kernel code is similarly identified by the symbol **_etext**. Kernel data is divided into two groups: initialized and uninitialized. The initialized data starts right after **_etext** and ends at **_edata**. The uninitialized data follows and ends up at **_end**.

The symbols appearing in the figure are not defined in Linux source code; they are produced while compiling the kernel.*

The linear address corresponding to the first physical address reserved to the BIOS or to a hardware device (usually, 0x0009f000) is stored in the **i386_endbase** variable. In most cases, this variable is initialized with a value written by the BIOS during the POST phase.

Process Page Tables

The linear address space of a process is divided into two parts:

*   Linear addresses from 0x00000000 to **PAGE_OFFSET** -1 can be addressed when the process is in either User or Kernel Mode.

*   Linear addresses from **PAGE_OFFSET** to 0xffffffff can be addressed only when the process is in Kernel Mode.

Usually, the **PAGE_OFFSET** macro yields the value 0xc0000000: this means that the fourth gigabyte of linear addresses is reserved for the kernel, while the first three

---

* You can find the linear address of these symbols in the file *System.map*, which is created right after the kernel is compiled.

gigabytes are accessible from both the kernel and the user programs. However, the value of PAGE_OFFSET may be customized by the user when the Linux kernel image is compiled. In fact, as we shall see in the next section, the range of linear addresses reserved for the kernel must include a mapping of all physical RAM installed in the system; moreover, as we shall see in Chapter 7, the kernel also makes use of the linear addresses in this range to remap noncontiguous page frames into contiguous linear addresses. Therefore, if Linux must be installed on a machine having a huge amount of RAM, a different arrangement for the linear addresses might be necessary.

The content of the first entries of the Page Global Directory that map linear addresses lower than PAGE_OFFSET (usually the first 768 entries) depends on the specific process. Conversely, the remaining entries are the same for all processes; they are equal to the corresponding entries of the swapper_pg_dir kernel Page Global Directory (see the following section).

Kernel Page Tables

We now describe how the kernel initializes its own page tables. This is a two-phase activity. In fact, right after the kernel image has been loaded into memory, the CPU is still running in real mode; thus, paging is not enabled.

In the first phase, the kernel creates a limited 4 MB address space, which is enough for it to install itself in RAM.

In the second phase, the kernel takes advantage of all of the existing RAM and sets up the paging tables properly. The next section examines how this plan is executed.

Provisional kernel page tables

Both the Page Global Directory and the Page Table are initialized statically during the kernel compilation. We won't bother mentioning the Page Middle Directories any more since they equate to Page Global Directory entries.

The Page Global Directory is contained in the swapper_pg_dir variable, while the Page Table that spans the first 4 MB of RAM is contained in the pg0 variable.

The objective of this first phase of paging is to allow these 4 MB to be easily addressed in both real mode and protected mode. Therefore, the kernel must create a mapping from both the linear addresses 0x00000000 through 0x003fffff and the linear addresses PAGE_OFFSET through PAGE_OFFSET+0x3fffff into the physical addresses 0x00000000 through 0x003fffff. In other words, the kernel during its first phase of initialization can address the first 4 MB of RAM (0x00000000 through 0x003fffff) either using linear addresses identical to the physical ones or using 4 MB worth of linear addresses starting from PAGE_OFFSET.

Assuming that `PAGE_OFFSET` yields the value `0xc0000000`, the kernel creates the desired mapping by filling all the `swapper_pg_dir` entries with zeros, except for entries 0 and `0x300` (decimal 768); the latter entry spans all linear addresses between `0xc0000000` and `0xc03fffff`. The 0 and `0x300` entries are initialized as follows:

- The address field is set to the address of `pg0`.

- The `Present`, `Read/Write`, and `User/Supervisor` flags are set.

- The `Accessed`, `Dirty`, `PCD`, `PWD`, and `Page Size` flags are cleared.

The single `pg0` Page Table is also statically initialized, so that the ith entry addresses the ith page frame.

The paging unit is enabled by the `startup_32()` Assembly-language function. This is achieved by loading in the `cr3` control register the address of `swapper_pg_dir` and by setting the `PG` flag of the `cr0` control register, as shown in the following excerpt:

```
movl $0x101000,%eax
movl %eax,%cr3        /* set the page table pointer.. */
movl %cr0,%eax
orl $0x80000000,%eax
movl %eax,%cr0        /* ..and set paging (PG) bit */
```

Final kernel page table

The final mapping provided by the kernel page tables must transform linear addresses starting from `PAGE_OFFSET` into physical addresses starting from 0.

The `_pa` macro is used to convert a linear address starting from `PAGE_OFFSET` to the corresponding physical address, while the `_va` macro does the reverse.

The final kernel Page Global Directory is still stored in `swapper_ pg_dir`. It is initialized by the `paging_init()` function. This function acts on two input parameters:

`start_mem`
> The linear address of the first byte of RAM right after the kernel code and data areas.

`end_mem`
> The linear address of the end of memory (this address is computed by the BIOS routines during the POST phase).

Linux exploits the extended paging feature of the Pentium processors, enabling 4 MB page frames: it allows a very efficient mapping from `PAGE_OFFSET` into physical addresses by making kernel Page Tables superfluous.[*]

---

[*] We'll see in the section "Noncontiguous Memory Area Management" in Chapter 6 that the kernel may set additional mappings for its own use based on 4 KB pages; when this happens, it makes use of Page Tables.

The `swapper_pg_dir` Page Global Directory is reinitialized by a cycle equivalent to the following:

```
address = PAGE_OFFSET;
pg_dir = swapper_pg_dir;
pgd_val(pg_dir[0]) = 0;
pg_dir += (PAGE_OFFSET >> PGDIR_SHIFT);
while (address < end_mem) {
    pgd_val(*pg_dir) = _PAGE_PRESENT+_PAGE_RW+_PAGE_ACCESSED
            +_PAGE_DIRTY +_PAGE_4M+_pa(address);
    pg_dir++;
    address += 0x400000;
}
```

As you can see, the first entry of the Page Global Directory is zeroed out, hence removing the mapping between the first 4 MB of linear and physical addresses. The first Page Table is thus available, so User Mode processes can also use the range of linear addresses between 0 and 4194303.

The `User`/`Supervisor` flags in all Page Global Directory entries referencing linear addresses above `PAGE_OFFSET` are cleared, thus denying to processes in User Mode access to the kernel address space.

The `pg0` provisional Page Table is no longer used once `swapper_pg_dir` has been initialized.

Anticipating Linux 2.4

Linux 2.4 introduces two main changes. The TSS Segment Descriptor associated with all existing processes is no longer stored in the Global Descriptor Table. This change removes the hard-coded limit on the number of existing processes. The limit thus becomes the number of available PIDs. In short, you will not find anymore the `NR_TASKS` macro inside the kernel code, and all data structures whose size was depending on it have been replaced or removed.

The other main change is related to physical memory addressing. Recent Intel 80x86 microprocessors include a feature called Physical Address Extension (PAE), which adds four extra bits to the standard 32-bit physical address. Linux 2.4 takes advantage of PAE and supports up to 64 GB of RAM. However, a linear address is still composed by 32 bits, so that only 4 GB of RAM can be "permanently mapped" and accessed at any time. Linux 2.4 thus recognizes three different portions of RAM: the physical memory suitable for ISA Direct Memory Access (DMA), the physical memory not suitable for ISA DMA but permanently mapped by the kernel, and the "high memory," that is, the physical memory that is not permanently mapped by the kernel.

CHAPTER THREE

PROCESSES

The concept of a *process* is fundamental to any multiprogramming operating system. A process is usually defined as an instance of a program in execution; thus, if 16 users are running `vi` at once, there are 16 separate processes (although they can share the same executable code). Processes are often called "tasks" in Linux source code.

In this chapter, we will first discuss static properties of processes and then describe how process switching is performed by the kernel. The last two sections investigate dynamic properties of processes, namely, how processes can be created and destroyed. This chapter also describes how Linux supports multithreaded applications: as mentioned in Chapter 1, *Introduction*, it relies on so-called lightweight processes (LWP).

Process Descriptor

In order to manage processes, the kernel must have a clear picture of what each process is doing. It must know, for instance, the process's priority, whether it is running on the CPU or blocked on some event, what address space has been assigned to it, which files it is allowed to address, and so on. This is the role of the *process descriptor*, that is, of a `task_struct` type structure whose fields contain all the information related to a single process. As the repository of so much information, the process descriptor is rather complex. Not only does it contain many fields itself, but some contain pointers to other data structures that, in turn, contain pointers to other structures. Figure 3-1 describes the Linux process descriptor schematically.

The five data structures on the right side of the figure refer to specific resources owned by the process. These resources will be covered in future chapters. This chapter will focus on two types of fields that refer to the process state and to process parent/child relationships.

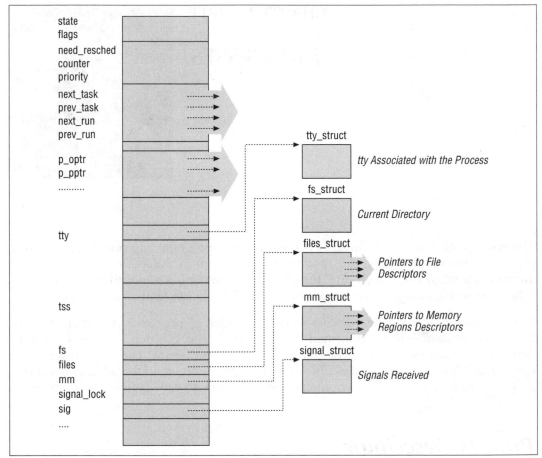

Figure 3-1. The Linux process descriptor

Process State

As its name implies, the `state` field of the process descriptor describes what is currently happening to the process. It consists of an array of flags, each of which describes a possible process state. In the current Linux version these states are mutually exclusive, and hence exactly one flag of `state` is set; the remaining flags are cleared. The following are the possible process states:

TASK_RUNNING
    The process is either executing on the CPU or waiting to be executed.

TASK_INTERRUPTIBLE
    The process is suspended (sleeping) until some condition becomes true. Raising a hardware interrupt, releasing a system resource the process is waiting for, or delivering a signal are examples of conditions that might wake up the process, that is, put its state back to TASK_RUNNING.

TASK_UNINTERRUPTIBLE

Like the previous state, except that delivering a signal to the sleeping process leaves its state unchanged. This process state is seldom used. It is valuable, however, under certain specific conditions in which a process must wait until a given event occurs without being interrupted. For instance, this state may be used when a process opens a device file and the corresponding device driver starts probing for a corresponding hardware device. The device driver must not be interrupted until the probing is complete, or the hardware device could be left in an unpredictable state.

TASK_STOPPED

Process execution has been stopped: the process enters this state after receiving a SIGSTOP, SIGTSTP, SIGTTIN, or SIGTTOU signal. When a process is being monitored by another (such as when a debugger executes a ptrace() system call to monitor a test program), any signal may put the process in the TASK_STOPPED state.

TASK_ZOMBIE

Process execution is terminated, but the parent process has not yet issued a wait()-like system call (wait(), wait3(), wait4(), or waitpid()) to return information about the dead process. Before the wait()-like call is issued, the kernel cannot discard the data contained in the dead process descriptor because the parent could need it. (See the section "Process Removal" near the end of this chapter.)

Identifying a Process

Although Linux processes can share a large portion of their kernel data structures—an efficiency measure known as *lightweight processes*—each process has its own process descriptor. Each execution context that can be independently scheduled must have its own process descriptor.

Lightweight processes should not be confused with user-mode threads, which are different execution flows handled by a user-level library. For instance, older Linux systems implemented *POSIX threads* entirely in user space by means of the *pthread* library; therefore, a multithreaded program was executed as a single Linux process. Currently, the pthread library, which has been merged into the standard C library, takes advantage of lightweight processes.

The very strict one-to-one correspondence between the process and process descriptor makes the 32-bit process descriptor address* a convenient tool to identify processes.

---

* Technically speaking, these 32 bits are only the offset component of a logical address. However, since Linux makes use of a single kernel data segment, we can consider the offset to be equivalent to a whole logical address. Furthermore, since the base addresses of the code and data segments are set to 0, we can treat the offset as a linear address.

These addresses are referred to as *process descriptor pointers.* Most of the references to processes that the kernel makes are through process descriptor pointers.

Any Unix-like operating system, on the other hand, allows users to identify processes by means of a number called the *Process ID* (or *PID*). The PID is a 32-bit unsigned integer stored in the `pid` field of the process descriptor. PIDs are numbered sequentially: the PID of a newly created process is normally the PID of the previously created process incremented by one. However, for compatibility with traditional Unix systems developed for 16-bit hardware platforms, the maximum PID number allowed on Linux is 32767. When the kernel creates the 32768th process in the system, it must start recycling the lower unused PIDs.

At the end of this section, we'll show you how it is possible to derive a process descriptor pointer efficiently from its respective PID. Efficiency is important because many system calls like `kill()` use the PID to denote the affected process.

The task array

Processes are dynamic entities whose lifetimes in the system range from a few milliseconds to months. Thus, the kernel must be able to handle many processes at the same time. In fact, we know from the previous chapter that Linux is able to handle up to NR_TASKS processes. The kernel reserves a global static array of size NR_TASKS called `task` in its own address space. The elements in the array are process descriptor pointers; a null pointer indicates that a process descriptor hasn't been associated with the array entry.

Storing a process descriptor

The `task` array contains only pointers to process descriptors, not the sizable descriptors themselves. Since processes are dynamic entities, process descriptors are stored in dynamic memory rather than in the memory area permanently assigned to the kernel. Linux stores two different data structures for each process in a single 8 KB memory area: the process descriptor and the Kernel Mode process stack.

In the section "Segmentation in Linux" in Chapter 2, *Memory Addressing*, we learned that a process in Kernel Mode accesses a stack contained in the kernel data segment, which is different from the stack used by the process in User Mode. Since kernel control paths make little use of the stack—even taking into account the interleaved execution of multiple kernel control paths on behalf of the same process—only a few thousand bytes of kernel stack are required. Therefore, 8 KB is ample space for the stack and the process descriptor.

Figure 3-2 shows how the two data structures are stored in the memory area. The process descriptor starts from the beginning of the memory area and the stack from the end.

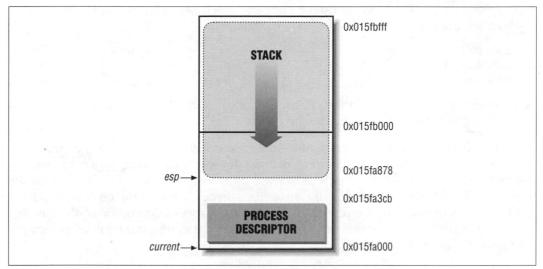

Figure 3-2. Storing the process descriptor and the process kernel stack

The **esp** register is the CPU stack pointer, which is used to address the stack's top location. On Intel systems, the stack starts at the end and grows toward the beginning of the memory area. Right after switching from User Mode to Kernel Mode, the kernel stack of a process is always empty, and therefore the **esp** register points to the byte immediately following the memory area.

The C language allows such a hybrid structure to be conveniently represented by means of the following union construct:

```
union task_union {
    struct task_struct task;
    unsigned long stack[2048];
};
```

After switching from User Mode to Kernel Mode in Figure 3-2, the **esp** register contains the address `0x015fc000`. The process descriptor is stored starting at address `0x015fa000`. The value of the **esp** is decremented as soon as data is written into the stack. Since the process descriptor is less than 1000 bytes long, the kernel stack can expand up to 7200 bytes.

The current macro

The pairing between the process descriptor and the Kernel Mode stack just described offers a key benefit in terms of efficiency: the kernel can easily obtain the process descriptor pointer of the process currently running on the CPU from the value of the **esp** register. In fact, since the memory area is 8 KB (2^{13} bytes) long, all the kernel has to do is mask out the 13 least significant bits of **esp** to obtain the base address of the process descriptor. This is done by the **current** macro, which produces some Assembly instructions like the following:

```
movl $0xffffe000, %ecx
andl %esp, %ecx
movl %ecx, p
```

After executing these three instructions, the local variable **p** contains the process descriptor pointer of the process running on the CPU.*

Another advantage of storing the process descriptor with the stack emerges on multiprocessor systems: the correct current process for each hardware processor can be derived just by checking the stack as shown previously. Linux 2.0 did not store the kernel stack and the process descriptor together. Instead, it was forced to introduce a global static variable called **current** to identify the process descriptor of the running process. On multiprocessor systems, it was necessary to define **current** as an array—one element for each available CPU.

The **current** macro often appears in kernel code as a prefix to fields of the process descriptor. For example, **current->pid** returns the process ID of the process currently running on the CPU.

A small cache consisting of **EXTRA_TASK_STRUCT** memory areas (where the macro is usually set to 16) is used to avoid unnecessarily invoking the memory allocator. To understand the purpose of this cache, assume for instance that some process is destroyed and that, right afterward, a new process is created. Without the cache, the kernel would have to release an 8 KB memory area to the memory allocator and then, immediately afterward, request another memory area of the same size. This is an example of *memory cache*, a software mechanism introduced to bypass the Kernel Memory Allocator. You will find many other examples of memory caches in the following chapters.

The **task_struct_stack** array contains the pointers to the process descriptors in the cache. Its name comes from the fact that process descriptor releases and requests are implemented respectively as "push" and "pop" operations on the array:

free_task_struct()
  This function releases the 8 KB **task_union** memory areas and places them in the cache unless it is full.

alloc_task_struct()
  This function allocates 8 KB **task_union** memory areas. The function takes memory areas from the cache if it is at least half-full or if there isn't a free pair of consecutive page frames available.

---

* One drawback to the shared-storage approach is that, for efficiency reasons, the kernel stores the 8 KB memory area in two consecutive page frames with the first page frame aligned to a multiple of 2^{13}. This may turn out to be a problem when little dynamic memory is available.

The process list

To allow an efficient search through processes of a given type (for instance, all processes in a runnable state) the kernel creates several lists of processes. Each list consists of pointers to process descriptors. A list pointer (that is, the field that each process uses to point to the next process) is embedded right in the process descriptor's data structure. When you look at the C-language declaration of the task_struct structure, the descriptors may seem to turn in on themselves in a complicated recursive manner. However, the concept is no more complicated than any list, which is a data structure containing a pointer to the next instance of itself.

A circular doubly linked list (see Figure 3-3) links together all existing process descriptors; we will call it the *process list*. The prev_task and next_task fields of each process descriptor are used to implement the list. The head of the list is the init_task descriptor referenced by the first element of the task array: it is the ancestor of all processes, and it is called *process 0* or *swapper* (see the section "Kernel Threads" later in this chapter). The prev_task field of init_task points to the process descriptor inserted last in the list.

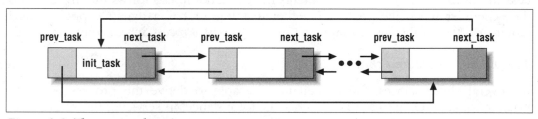

Figure 3-3. The process list

The SET_LINKS and REMOVE_LINKS macros are used to insert and to remove a process descriptor in the process list, respectively. These macros also take care of the parenthood relationship of the process (see the section "Parenthood Relationships Among Processes" later in this chapter).

Another useful macro, called for_each_task, scans the whole process list. It is defined as:

```
#define for_each_task(p) \
    for (p = &init_task ; (p = p->next_task) != &init_task ; )
```

The macro is the loop control statement after which the kernel programmer supplies the loop. Notice how the init_task process descriptor just plays the role of list header. The macro starts by moving past init_task to the next task and continues until it reaches init_task again (thanks to the circularity of the list).

The list of TASK_RUNNING processes

When looking for a new process to run on the CPU, the kernel has to consider only the runnable processes (that is, the processes in the TASK_RUNNING state). Since it would be rather inefficient to scan the whole process list, a doubly linked circular list of TASK_RUNNING processes called *runqueue* has been introduced. The process descriptors include the next_run and prev_run fields to implement the runqueue list. As in the previous case, the init_task process descriptor plays the role of list header. The nr_running variable stores the total number of runnable processes.

The add_to_runqueue() function inserts a process descriptor at the beginning of the list, while del_from_runqueue() removes a process descriptor from the list. For scheduling purposes, two functions, move_first_runqueue() and move_last_runqueue(), are provided to move a process descriptor to the beginning or the end of the runqueue, respectively.

Finally, the wake_up_process() function is used to make a process runnable. It sets the process state to TASK_RUNNING, invokes add_to_runqueue() to insert the process in the runqueue list, and increments nr_running. It also forces the invocation of the scheduler when the process is either real-time or has a dynamic priority much larger than that of the current process (see Chapter 10, *Process Scheduling*).

The pidhash table and chained lists

In several circumstances, the kernel must be able to derive the process descriptor pointer corresponding to a PID. This occurs, for instance, in servicing the kill() system call: when process P1 wishes to send a signal to another process, P2, it invokes the kill() system call specifying the PID of P2 as the parameter. The kernel derives the process descriptor pointer from the PID and then extracts the pointer to the data structure that records the pending signals from P2's process descriptor.

Scanning the process list sequentially and checking the pid fields of the process descriptors would be feasible but rather inefficient. In order to speed up the search, a pidhash hash table consisting of PIDHASH_SZ elements has been introduced (PIDHASH_SZ is usually set to NR_TASKS/4). The table entries contain process descriptor pointers. The PID is transformed into a table index using the pid_hashfn macro:

```
#define pid_hashfn(x) \
    ((((x) >> 8) ^ (x)) & (PIDHASH_SZ - 1))
```

As every basic computer science course explains, a hash function does not always ensure a one-to-one correspondence between PIDs and table indexes. Two different PIDs that hash into the same table index are said to be *colliding*.

Linux uses *chaining* to handle colliding PIDs: each table entry is a doubly linked list of colliding process descriptors. These lists are implemented by means of the `pidhash_next` and `pidhash_pprev` fields in the process descriptor. Figure 3-4 illustrates a `pidhash` table with two lists: the processes having PIDs 228 and 27535 hash into the 101st element of the table, while the process having PID 27536 hashes into the 124th element of the table.

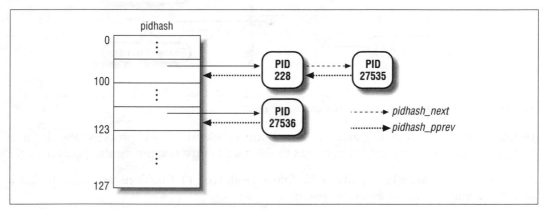

Figure 3-4. The pidhash table and chained lists

Hashing with chaining is preferable to a linear transformation from PIDs to table indexes, because a PID can assume any value between 0 and 32767. Since `NR_TASKS`, the maximum number of processes, is usually set to 512, it would be a waste of storage to define a table consisting of 32768 entries.

The `hash_pid()` and `unhash_pid()` functions are invoked to insert and remove a process in the `pidhash` table, respectively. The `find_task_by_pid()` function searches the hash table and returns the process descriptor pointer of the process with a given PID (or a null pointer if it does not find the process).

The list of task free entries

The `task` array must be updated every time a process is created or destroyed. As with the other lists shown in previous sections, a list is used here to speed additions and deletions. Adding a new entry into the array is done efficiently: instead of searching the array linearly and looking for the first free entry, the kernel maintains a separate doubly linked, noncircular list of free entries. The `tarray_freelist` variable contains the first element of that list; each free entry in the array points to another free entry, while the last element of the list contains a null pointer. When a process is destroyed, the corresponding element in `task` is added to the head of the list.

In Figure 3-5, if the first element is counted as 0, the `tarray_freelist` variable points to element 4 because it is the last freed element. Previously, the processes corresponding to elements 2 and 1 were destroyed, in that order. Element 2 points to another free element of `tasks` not shown in the figure.

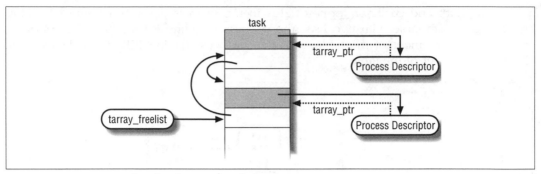

Figure 3-5. An example of task array with free entries

Deleting an entry from the array is also done efficiently. Each process descriptor p includes a `tarray_ptr` field that points to the `task` entry containing the pointer to p.

The `get_free_taskslot()` and `add_free_taskslot()` functions are used to get a free entry and to free an entry, respectively.

Parenthood Relationships Among Processes

Processes created by a program have a parent/child relationship. Since a process can create several children, these have sibling relationships. Several fields must be introduced in a process descriptor to represent these relationships. Processes 0 and 1 are created by the kernel; as we shall see later in the chapter, process 1 (*init*) is the ancestor of all other processes. The descriptor of a process P includes the following fields:

p_opptr *(original parent)*
> Points to the process descriptor of the process that created P or to the descriptor of process 1 (*init*) if the parent process no longer exists. Thus, when a shell user starts a background process and exits the shell, the background process becomes the child of *init*.

p_pptr *(parent)*
> Points to the current parent of P; its value usually coincides with that of p_opptr. It may occasionally differ, such as when another process issues a `ptrace()` system call requesting that it be allowed to monitor P (see the section "Execution Tracing" in Chapter 19, *Program Execution*).

p_cptr *(child)*
> Points to the process descriptor of the youngest child of P, that is, of the process created most recently by it.

p_ysptr *(younger sibling)*
> Points to the process descriptor of the process that has been created immediately after P by P's current parent.

p_osptr *(older sibling)*

    Points to the process descriptor of the process that has been created immediately before P by P's current parent.

Figure 3-6 illustrates the parenthood relationships of a group of processes. Process P0 successively created P1, P2, and P3. Process P3, in turn, created process P4. Starting with **p_cptr** and using the **p_osptr** pointers to siblings, P0 is able to retrieve all its children.

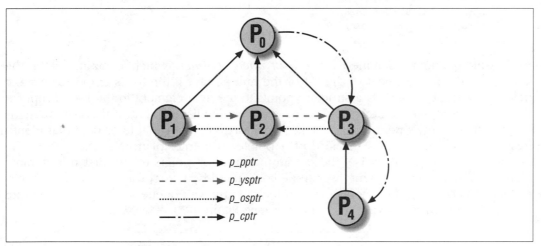

Figure 3-6. Parenthood relationships among five processes

Wait Queues

The runqueue list groups together all processes in a TASK_RUNNING state. When it comes to grouping processes in other states, the various states call for different types of treatment, with Linux opting for one of the following choices:

- Processes in a TASK_STOPPED or in a TASK_ZOMBIE state are not linked in specific lists. There is no need to group them, because either the process PID or the process parenthood relationships may be used by the parent process to retrieve the child process.

- Processes in a TASK_INTERRUPTIBLE or TASK_UNINTERRUPTIBLE state are subdivided into many classes, each of which corresponds to a specific event. In this case, the process state does not provide enough information to retrieve the process quickly, so it is necessary to introduce additional lists of processes. These additional lists are called *wait queues*.

Wait queues have several uses in the kernel, particularly for interrupt handling, process synchronization, and timing. Because these topics are discussed in later chapters, we'll just say here that a process must often wait for some event to occur, such as for a disk operation to terminate, a system resource to be released, or a fixed interval of time to elapse. Wait queues implement conditional waits on events: a process wishing to wait for a specific event places itself in the proper wait queue and relinquishes control. Therefore, a wait queue represents a set of sleeping processes, which are awakened by the kernel when some condition becomes true.

Wait queues are implemented as cyclical lists whose elements include pointers to process descriptors. Each element of a wait queue list is of type `wait_queue`:

```
struct wait_queue {
    struct task_struct * task;
    struct wait_queue * next;
};
```

Each wait queue is identified by a *wait queue pointer*, which contains either the address of the first element of the list or the null pointer if the list is empty. The `next` field of the `wait_queue` data structure points to the next element in the list, except for the last element, whose `next` field points to a dummy list element. If the wait queue is empty, the dummy's `next` field contains the address of the variable or field that identifies the wait queue minus the size of a pointer (on Intel platforms, the size of the pointer is 4 bytes). Otherwise, the dummy's next field points to the first non-dummy element. Thus, the wait queue list can be considered by kernel functions as a truly circular list, since the last element points to the dummy wait queue structure whose `next` field coincides with the wait queue pointer (see Figure 3-7).

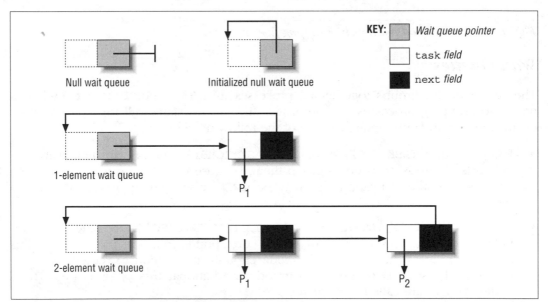

Figure 3-7. The wait queue data structure

The `init_waitqueue()` function initializes an empty wait queue; it receives the address q of a wait queue pointer as its parameter and sets that pointer to q - 4. The `add_wait_queue(q, entry)` function inserts a new element with address `entry` in the wait queue identified by the wait queue pointer q. Since wait queues are modified by interrupt handlers as well as by major kernel functions, the function executes the following operations with disabled interrupts (see Chapter 4, *Interrupts and Exceptions*):

```
if (*q != NULL)
    entry->next = *q;
else
    entry->next = (struct wait_queue *)(q-1);
*q = entry;
```

Since the wait queue pointer is set to **entry**, the new element is placed in the first position of the wait queue list. If the wait queue was not empty, the **next** field of the new element is set to the address of the previous first element. Otherwise, the **next** field is set to the address of the wait queue pointer minus 4, and thus points to the dummy element.

The **remove_wait_queue()** function removes the element pointed to by **entry** from a wait queue. Once again, the function must disable interrupts before executing the following operations:

```
next = entry->next;
head = next;
while ((tmp = head->next) != entry)
    head = tmp;
head->next = next;
```

The function scans the circular list to find the element **head** that precedes **entry**. It then detaches **entry** from the list by letting the **next** field of **head** point to the element that follows **entry**. The peculiar format of the wait queue circular list simplifies the code. Moreover, it is very efficient for the following reasons:

- Most wait queues have just one element, which means that the body of the **while** loop is never executed.

- While scanning the list, there is no need to distinguish the wait queue pointer (the dummy wait queue element) from **wait_queue** data structures.

A process wishing to wait for a specific condition can invoke any of the following functions:

- The **sleep_on()** function operates on the current process, which we'll call P:

```
void sleep_on(struct wait_queue **p)
{
    struct wait_queue wait;
    current->state = TASK_UNINTERRUPTIBLE;
    wait.task = current;
    add_wait_queue(p, &wait);
    schedule();
    remove_wait_queue(p, &wait);
}
```

The function sets P's state to `TASK_UNINTERRUPTIBLE` and inserts P into the wait queue whose pointer was specified as the parameter. Then it invokes the scheduler, which resumes the execution of another process. When P is awakened, the scheduler resumes execution of the `sleep_on()` function, which removes P from the wait queue.

- The `interruptible_sleep_on()` function is identical to `sleep_on()`, except that it sets the state of the current process P to `TASK_INTERRUPTIBLE` instead of `TASK_UNINTERRUPTIBLE` so that P can also be awakened by receiving a signal.

- The `sleep_on_timeout()` and `interruptible_sleep_on_timeout()` functions are similar to the previous ones, but they also allow the caller to define a time interval after which the process will be woken up by the kernel. In order to do this, they invoke the `schedule_timeout()` function instead of `schedule()` (see the section "An Application of Dynamic Timers" in Chapter 5, *Timing Measurements*).

Processes inserted in a wait queue enter the `TASK_RUNNING` state by using either the `wake_up` or the `wake_up_interruptible` macros. Both macros use the `__wake_up()` function, which receives as parameters the address `q` of the wait queue pointer and a bitmask `mode` specifying one or more states. Processes in the specified states will be woken up; others will be left unchanged. The function essentially executes the following instructions:

```
if (q && (next = *q)) {
    head = (struct wait_queue *)(q-1);
    while (next != head) {
        p = next->task;
        next = next->next;
        if (p->state & mode)
            wake_up_process(p);
    }
}
```

The function checks the state `p->state` of each process against `mode` to determine whether the caller wants the process woken up. Only those processes whose state is included in the `mode` bitmask are actually awakened. The `wake_up` macro specifies both the `TASK_INTERRUPTIBLE` and the `TASK_UNINTERRUPTIBLE` flags in `mode`, so it wakes up all sleeping processes. Conversely, the `wake_up_interruptible` macro wakes up only the `TASK_INTERRUPTIBLE` processes by specifying only that flag in `mode`. Notice that awakened processes are not removed from the wait queue. A process that has been awakened does not necessarily imply that the wait condition has become true, so the processes could suspend themselves again.

Process Usage Limits

Processes are associated with sets of *usage limits*, which specify the amount of system resources they can use. Specifically, Linux recognizes the following usage limits:

RLIMIT_CPU

Maximum CPU time for the process. If the process exceeds the limit, the kernel sends it a SIGXCPU signal, and then, if the process doesn't terminate, a SIGKILL signal (see Chapter 9, *Signals*).

RLIMIT_FSIZE

Maximum file size allowed. If the process tries to enlarge a file to a size greater than this value, the kernel sends it a SIGXFSZ signal.

RLIMIT_DATA

Maximum heap size. The kernel checks this value before expanding the heap of the process (see the section "Managing the Heap" in Chapter 7, *Process Address Space*).

RLIMIT_STACK

Maximum stack size. The kernel checks this value before expanding the User Mode stack of the process (see the section "Page Fault Exception Handler" in Chapter 7).

RLIMIT_CORE

Maximum core dump file size. The kernel checks this value when a process is aborted, before creating a **core** file in the current directory of the process (see the section "Actions Performed upon Receiving a Signal" in Chapter 9). If the limit is 0, the kernel won't create the file.

RLIMIT_RSS

Maximum number of page frames owned by the process. Actually, the kernel never checks this value, so this usage limit is not implemented.

RLIMIT_NPROC

Maximum number of processes that the user can own (see the section "The clone( ), fork( ), and vfork( ) System Calls" later in this chapter).

RLIMIT_NOFILE

Maximum number of open files. The kernel checks this value when opening a new file or duplicating a file descriptor (see Chapter 12, *The Virtual Filesystem*).

RLIMIT_MEMLOCK

Maximum size of nonswappable memory. The kernel checks this value when the process tries to lock a page frame in memory using the mlock( ) or mlockall( ) system calls (see the section "Allocating a Linear Address Interval" in Chapter 7).

RLIMIT_AS

Maximum size of process address space. The kernel checks this value when the process uses malloc( ) or a related function to enlarge its address space (see the section "The Process's Address Space" in Chapter 7).

The usage limits are stored in the `rlim` field of the process descriptor. The field is an array of elements of type `struct rlimit`, one for each usage limit:

```
struct rlimit {
    long rlim_cur;
    long rlim_max;
};
```

The `rlim_cur` field is the current usage limit for the resource. For example, `current->rlim[RLIMIT_CPU].rlim_cur` represents the current limit on the CPU time of the running process.

The `rlim_max` field is the maximum allowed value for the resource limit. By using the `getrlimit()` and `setrlimit()` system calls, a user can always increase the `rlim_cur` limit of some resource up to `rlim_max`. However, only the superuser can change the `rlim_max` field or set the `rlim_cur` field to a value greater than the corresponding `rlim_max` field.

Usually, most usage limits contain the value `RLIMIT_INFINITY` (`0x7fffffff`), which means that no limit is imposed on the corresponding resource. However, the system administrator may choose to impose stronger limits on some resources. Whenever a user logs into the system, the kernel creates a process owned by the superuser, which can invoke `setrlimit()` to decrease the `rlim_max` and `rlim_cur` fields for some resource. The same process later executes a login shell and becomes owned by the user. Each new process created by the user inherits the content of the `rlim` array from its parent, and therefore the user cannot override the limits enforced by the system.

Process Switching

In order to control the execution of processes, the kernel must be able to suspend the execution of the process running on the CPU and resume the execution of some other process previously suspended. This activity is called *process switching*, *task switching*, or *context switching*. The following sections describe the elements of process switching in Linux:

- Hardware context
- Hardware support
- Linux code
- Saving the floating point registers

Hardware Context

While each process can have its own address space, all processes have to share the CPU registers. So before resuming the execution of a process, the kernel must ensure that each such register is loaded with the value it had when the process was suspended.

The set of data that must be loaded into the registers before the process resumes its execution on the CPU is called the *hardware context*. The hardware context is a subset of the process execution context, which includes all information needed for the process execution. In Linux, part of the hardware context of a process is stored in the TSS segment, while the remaining part is saved in the Kernel Mode stack. As we learned in the section "Segmentation in Linux" in Chapter 2, the TSS segment coincides with the `tss` field of the process descriptor.

We will assume the `prev` local variable refers to the process descriptor of the process being switched out and `next` refers to the one being switched in to replace it. We can thus define *process switching* as the activity consisting of saving the hardware context of `prev` and replacing it with the hardware context of `next`. Since process switches occur quite often, it is important to minimize the time spent in saving and loading hardware contexts.

Earlier versions of Linux took advantage of the hardware support offered by the Intel architecture and performed process switching through a `far jmp` instruction[*] to the selector of the Task State Segment Descriptor of the `next` process. While executing the instruction, the CPU performs a *hardware context switch* by automatically saving the old hardware context and loading a new one. But for the following reasons, Linux 2.2 uses software to perform process switching:

- Step-by-step switching performed through a sequence of `mov` instructions allows better control over the validity of the data being loaded. In particular, it is possible to check the values of segmentation registers. This type of checking is not possible when using a single `far jmp` instruction.

- The amount of time required by the old approach and the new approach is about the same. However, it is not possible to optimize a hardware context switch, while the current switching code could perhaps be enhanced in the future.

Process switching occurs only in Kernel Mode. The contents of all registers used by a process in User Mode have already been saved before performing process switching (see Chapter 4). This includes the contents of the `ss` and `esp` pair that specifies the User Mode stack pointer address.

Task State Segment

The Intel 80x86 architecture includes a specific segment type called the *Task State Segment* (TSS), to store hardware contexts. As we saw in the section "Segmentation in Linux" in Chapter 2, each process includes its own TSS segment with a minimum length of 104 bytes. Additional bytes are needed by the operating system to store registers that are not automatically saved by the hardware and to store the *I/O Permission bitmap*. That map is needed because the `ioperm()` and `iopl()` system calls may

---

[*] `far jmp` instructions modify both the `cs` and `eip` registers, while simple `jmp` instructions modify only `eip`.

grant a process in User Mode direct access to specific I/O ports. In particular, if the `IOPL` field in the `eflags` register is set to 3, the User Mode process is allowed to access all I/O ports. Otherwise, the User Mode process is allowed to access any of the I/O ports whose corresponding bit in the I/O Permission Bit Map is cleared.

The `thread_struct` structure describes the format of the Linux TSS. An additional area is introduced to store the `tr` and `cr2` registers, the floating point registers, the debug registers, and other miscellaneous information specific to Intel 80x86 processors.

Each TSS has its own 8-byte *Task State Segment Descriptor* (TSSD). This Descriptor includes a 32-bit `Base` field that points to the TSS starting address and a 20-bit `Limit` field whose value cannot be smaller than `0x67` (decimal 103, determined by the minimum TSS segment length mentioned earlier). The `S` flag of a TSSD is cleared to denote the fact that the corresponding TSS is a *System Segment*.

The `Type` field is set to 11 if the TSSD refers to the TSS of the process currently running on the CPU; otherwise it is set to 9.[*] The second least significant bit of the `Type` field is called the *Busy bit* since it discriminates between the values 9 and 11.[†]

The TSSDs created by Linux are stored in the Global Descriptor Table (GDT), whose base address is stored in the `gdtr` register. The `tr` register contains the TSSD Selector of the process currently running on the CPU. It also includes two hidden, nonprogrammable fields: the `Base` and `Limit` fields of the TSSD. In this way, the processor can address the TSS directly without having to retrieve the TSS address from the GDT.

As stated earlier, Linux stores part of the hardware context in the `tss` field of the process descriptor. This means that when the kernel creates a new process, it must also initialize the TSSD so that it refers to the `tss` field. Even though the hardware context is saved via software, the TSS segment still plays an important role because it may contain the I/O Permission Bit Map. In fact, when a process executes an `in` or `out` I/O instruction in User Mode, the control unit performs the following operations:

1. It checks the IOPL field in the `eflags` register. If it is set to 3, the control executes the I/O instruction. Otherwise, it performs the next check.

2. It accesses the `tr` register to determine the current TSS, and thus the proper I/O Permission Bit Map.

3. It checks the bit corresponding to the I/O port specified in the I/O instruction. If it is cleared, the instruction is executed; otherwise, the control unit raises a "General protection error" exception.

---

[*] Linux does not make use of a hardware feature that uses the `Type` field in a peculiar way to allow the automatic reexecution of a previously suspended process. Further details may be found in the Pentium manuals.

[†] Since the processor performs a "bus lock" before modifying this bit, a multitasking operating system may test the bit in order to check whether a CPU is trying to switch to a process that's already executing. However, Linux does not make use of this hardware feature (see Chapter 11, *Kernel Synchronization*).

The switch_to Macro

The switch_to macro performs a process switch. It makes use of two parameters denoted as prev and next: the first is the process descriptor pointer of the process to be suspended, while the second is the process descriptor pointer of the process to be executed on the CPU. The macro is invoked by the schedule() function to schedule a new process on the CPU (see Chapter 10).

The switch_to macro is one of the most hardware-dependent routines of the kernel. Here is a description of what it does on an Intel 80x86 microprocessor:

1. Saves the values of prev and next in the eax and edx registers, respectively (these values were previously stored in ebx and ecx):

   ```
   movl %ebx, %eax
   movl %ecx, %edx
   ```

2. Saves the contents of the esi, edi, and ebp registers in the prev Kernel Mode stack. They must be saved because the compiler assumes that they will stay unchanged until the end of switch_to:

   ```
   pushl %esi
   pushl %edi
   pushl %ebp
   ```

3. Saves the content of esp in prev->tss.esp so that the field points to the top of the prev Kernel Mode stack:

   ```
   movl %esp, 532(%ebx)
   ```

4. Loads next->tss.esp in esp. From now on, the kernel operates on the Kernel Mode stack of next, so this instruction performs the actual context switch from prev to next. Since the address of a process descriptor is closely related to that of the Kernel Mode stack (as explained in the section "Identifying a Process" earlier in this chapter), changing the kernel stack means changing the current process:

   ```
   movl 532(%ecx), %esp
   ```

5. Saves the address labeled 1 (shown later in this section) in prev->tss.eip. When the process being replaced resumes its execution, the process will execute the instruction labeled as 1:

   ```
   movl $1f, 508(%ebx)
   ```

6. On the Kernel Mode stack of next, pushes the next->tss.eip value, in most cases the address labeled 1:

   ```
   pushl 508(%ecx)
   ```

7. Jumps to the __switch_to() C function:

   ```
   jmp __switch_to
   ```

This function acts on the **prev** and **next** parameters that denote the former process and the new process. This function call is different from the average function call, though, because __switch_to() takes the **prev** and **next** parameters from the **eax** and **edx** where we saw earlier they were stored, not from the stack like most functions. To force the function to go to the registers for its parameters, the kernel makes use of __attribute__ and **regparm** keywords, which are nonstandard extensions of the C language implemented by the **gcc** compiler. The __switch_to() function is declared as follows in the *include/asm-i386/system.h* header file:

```
_ _switch_to(struct task_struct *prev,
          struct task_struct *next)
  _ _attribute_ _(regparm(3))
```

The function completes the process switch started by the **switch_to()** macro. It includes extended inline Assembly language code that makes for rather complex reading, because the code refers to registers by means of special symbols. In order to simplify the following discussion, we will describe the Assembly language instructions yielded by the compiler:

a. Saves the contents of the **esi** and **ebx** registers in the Kernel Mode stack of **next**, then loads **ecx** and **ebx** with the parameters **prev** and **next**, respectively:

```
pushl %esi
pushl %ebx
movl %eax, %ecx
movl %edx, %ebx
```

b. Executes the code yielded by the **unlazy_fpu()** macro (see the section "Saving the Floating Point Registers" later in this chapter) to optionally save the contents of the mathematical coprocessor registers. As we shall see later, there is no need to load the floating point registers of **next** while performing the context switch:

```
unlazy_fpu(prev);
```

c. Clears the Busy bit (see the section "Task State Segment" earlier in this chapter) of **next** and load its TSS selector in the **tr** register:

```
movl 712(%ebx), %eax
andb $0xf8, %al
andl $0xfffffdff, gdt_table+4(%eax)
ltr 712(%ebx)
```

The preceding code is fairly dense. It operates on:

The process's TSSD selector, which is copied from **next->tss.tr** to **eax**.

The 8 least significant bits of the selector, which are stored in `al`.* The 3 least significant bits of `al` contain the `RPL` and the `TI` fields of the TSSD.

Clearing the 3 least significant bits of `al` leaves the TSSD index shifted to the left 3 bits (that is, multiplied by 8). Since the TSSDs are 8 bytes long, the index value multiplied by 8 yields the relative address of the TSSD within the GDT. The `gdt_table+4(%eax)` notation refers to the address of the fifth byte of the TSSD. The `andl` instruction clears the `Busy` bit in the fifth byte, while the `ltr` instruction places the `next->tss.tr` selector in the `tr` register and again sets the `Busy` bit.†

d. Stores the contents of the `fs` and `gs` segmentation registers in `prev->tss.fs` and `prev->tss.gs`, respectively:

```
movl %fs,564(%ecx)
movl %gs,568(%ecx)
```

e. Loads the `ldtr` register with the `next->tss.ldt` value. This needs to be done only if the Local Descriptor Table used by `prev` differs from the one used by `next`:

```
    movl 920(%ebx),%edx
    movl 920(%ecx),%eax
    movl 112(%eax),%eax
    cmpl %eax,112(%edx)
    je 2f
    lldt 572(%ebx)
2:
```

In practice, the check is made by referring to the `tss.segments` field (at offset 112 in the process descriptor) instead of the `tss.ldt` field.

f. Loads the `cr3` register with the `next->tss.cr3` value. This can be avoided if `prev` and `next` are lightweight processes that share the same Page Global Directory. Since the PGD address of `prev` is never changed, it doesn't need to be saved.

```
    movl 504(%ebx),%eax
    cmpl %eax,504(%ecx)
    je 3f
    movl %eax,%cr3
3:
```

g. Load the `fs` and `gs` segment registers with the values contained in `next->tss.fs` and `next->tss.gs`, respectively. This step logically complements the actions performed in step 7d.

---

* The `ax` register consists of the 16 least significant bits of `eax`. Moreover, the `al` register consists of the 8 least significant bits of `ax`, while `ah` consists of the 8 most significant bits of `ax`. Similar notations apply to the `ebx`, `ecx`, and `edx` registers. The 13 most significant bits of `ax` specify the TSSD index within the GDT.

† Linux must clear the `Busy` bit before loading the value in `tr`, or the control unit will raise an exception.

```
movl 564(%ebx),%fs
movl 568(%ebx),%gs
```

The code is actually more intricate, as an exception might be raised by the CPU when it detects an invalid segment register value. The code takes this possibility into account by adopting a "fix-up" approach (see the section "Dynamic Address Checking: The Fixup Code" in Chapter 8, *System Calls*).

h. Loads the eight debug registers* with the **next->tss.debugreg[i]** values (0 ≤ i ≤ 7). This is done only if **next** was using the debug registers when it was suspended (that is, field **next->tss.debugreg[7]** is not 0). As we shall see in Chapter 19, these registers are modified only by writing in the TSS, thus there is no need to save them:

```
cmpl $0,760(%ebx)
je 4f
movl 732(%ebx),%esi
movl %esi,%db0
movl 736(%ebx),%esi
movl %esi,%db1
movl 740(%ebx),%esi
movl %esi,%db2
movl 744(%ebx),%esi
movl %esi,%db3
movl 756(%ebx),%esi
movl %esi,%db6
movl 760(%ebx),%ebx
movl %ebx,%db7
4:
```

i. The function ends up by restoring the original values of the **ebx** and **esi** registers, pushed on the stack in step 7a:

```
popl %ebx
popl %esi
ret
```

When the **ret** instruction is executed, the control unit fetches the value to be loaded in the **eip** program counter from the stack. This value is usually the address of the instruction shown in the following item and labeled 1, which was stored in the stack by the **switch_to** macro. If, however, **next** was never suspended before because it is being executed for the first time, the function will find the starting address of the **ret_from_fork()** function (see the section "The clone(), fork(), and vfork() System Calls" later in this chapter).

---

* The Intel 80x86 debug registers allow a process to be monitored by the hardware. Up to four breakpoint areas may be defined. Whenever a monitored process issues a linear address included in one of the breakpoints, an exception occurs.

8. The remaining part of the `switch_to` macro includes a few instructions that restore the contents of the `esi`, `edi`, and `ebp` registers. The first of these three instructions is labeled 1:

```
1:  popl %ebp
    popl %edi
    popl %esi
```

Notice how these `pop` instructions refer to the kernel stack of the `prev` process. They will be executed when the scheduler selects `prev` as the new process to be executed on the CPU, thus invoking `switch_to` with `prev` as second parameter. Therefore, the `esp` register points to the `prev`'s Kernel Mode stack.

Saving the Floating Point Registers

Starting with the Intel 80486, the arithmetic floating point unit (FPU) has been integrated into the CPU. The name *mathematical coprocessor* continues to be used in memory of the days when floating point computations were executed by an expensive special-purpose chip. In order to maintain compatibility with older models, however, floating point arithmetic functions are performed by making use of *ESCAPE instructions*, which are instructions with some prefix byte ranging between 0xd8 and 0xdf. These instructions act on the set of floating point registers included in the CPU. Clearly, if a process is using ESCAPE instructions, the contents of the floating point registers belong to its hardware context.

Recently, Intel introduced a new set of Assembly instructions into its microprocessors. They are called *MMX instructions* and are supposed to speed up the execution of multimedia applications. MMX instructions act on the floating point registers of the FPU. The obvious disadvantage of this architectural choice is that programmers cannot mix floating point instructions and MMX instructions. The advantage is that operating system designers can ignore the new instruction set, since the same facility of the task-switching code for saving the state of the floating point unit can also be relied upon to save the MMX state.

The Intel 80x86 microprocessors do not automatically save the floating point registers in the TSS. However, they include some hardware support that enables kernels to save these registers only when needed. The hardware support consists of a `TS` (Task-Switching) flag in the `cr0` register, which obeys the following rules:

- Every time a hardware context switch is performed, the `TS` flag is set.

- Every time an ESCAPE or an MMX instruction is executed when the `TS` flag is set, the control unit raises a "Device not available" exception (see Chapter 4).

The TS flag allows the kernel to save and restore the floating point registers only when really needed. To illustrate how it works, let's suppose that a process A is using the mathematical coprocessor. When a context switch occurs, the kernel sets the TS flag and saves the floating point registers into the TSS of process A. If the new process B does not make use of the mathematical coprocessor, the kernel won't need to restore the contents of the floating point registers. But as soon as B tries to execute an ESCAPE or MMX instruction, the CPU raises a "Device not available" exception, and the corresponding handler loads the floating point registers with the values saved in the TSS of process B.

Let us now describe the data structures introduced to handle selective saving of floating point registers. They are stored in the `tss.i387` subfield, whose format is described by the `i387_hard_struct` structure. The process descriptor also stores the value of two additional flags:

- The `PF_USEDFPU` flag included in the `flags` field. It specifies whether the process used the floating point registers when it was last executing on the CPU.

- The `used_math` field. This flag specifies whether the contents of the `tss.i387` subfield are significant. The flag is cleared (not significant) in two cases:

  — When the process starts executing a new program by invoking an `execve()` system call (see Chapter 19). Since control will never return to the former program, the data currently stored in `tss.i387` will never be used again.

  — When a process that was executing a program in User Mode starts executing a signal handler procedure (see Chapter 9). Since signal handlers are asynchronous with respect to the program execution flow, the floating point registers could be meaningless to the signal handler. However, the kernel saves the floating point registers in `tss.i387` before starting the handler and restores them after the handler terminates. Therefore, a signal handler is allowed to make use of the mathematical coprocessor, but it cannot carry on a floating point computation started during the normal program execution flow.

As stated earlier, the `__switch_to()` function executes the `unlazy_fpu` macro. This macro yields the following code:

```
if (prev->flags & PF_USEDFPU) {
    /* save the floating point registers  */
    asm("fnsave %0" : "=m" (prev->tss.i387));
    /* wait until all data has been transferred */
    asm("fwait");
    prev->flags &= ~PF_USEDFPU;
    /* set the TS flag of cr0 to 1 */
    stts();
}
```

The `stts()` macro sets the `TS` flag of `cr0`. In practice, it yields the following Assembly language instructions:

```
movl %cr0, %eax
orb $8, %al
movl %eax, %cr0
```

The contents of the floating point registers are not restored right after a process resumes execution. However, the TS flag of cr0 has been set by unlazy_fpu(). Thus, the first time the process tries to execute an ESCAPE or MMX instruction, the control unit raises a "Device not available" exception, and the kernel (more precisely, the exception handler involved by the exception) runs the math_state_restore() function:

```
void math_state_restore(void) {
    asm("clts"); /* clear the TS flag of cr0 */
    if (current->used_math)
        /* load the floating point registers */
        asm("frstor %0": :"m" (current->tss.i387));
    else {
        /* initialize the floating point unit */
        asm("fninit");
        current->used_math = 1;
    }
    current->flags |= PF_USEDFPU;
}
```

Since the process is executing an ESCAPE instruction, this function sets the PF_USEDFPU flag. Moreover, the function clears the TS flag of cr0 so that further ESCAPE or MMX instructions executed by the process won't trigger the "Device not available" exception. If the data stored in the tss.i387 field is valid, the function loads the floating point registers with the proper values. Otherwise, the FPU is reinitialized and all its registers are cleared.

Creating Processes

Unix operating systems rely heavily on process creation to satisfy user requests. As an example, the shell process creates a new process that executes another copy of the shell whenever the user enters a command.

Traditional Unix systems treat all processes in the same way: resources owned by the parent process are duplicated, and a copy is granted to the child process. This approach makes process creation very slow and inefficient, since it requires copying the entire address space of the parent process. The child process rarely needs to read or modify all the resources already owned by the parent; in many cases, it issues an immediate execve() and wipes out the address space so carefully saved.

Modern Unix kernels solve this problem by introducing three different mechanisms:

*   The Copy On Write technique allows both the parent and the child to read the same physical pages. Whenever either one tries to write on a physical page, the kernel copies its contents into a new physical page that is assigned to the writing process. The implementation of this technique in Linux is fully explained in Chapter 7.

- *Lightweight processes* allow both the parent and the child to share many per-process kernel data structures, like the paging tables (and therefore the entire User Mode address space) and the open file tables.

- The `vfork()` system call creates a process that shares the memory address space of its parent. To prevent the parent from overwriting data needed by the child, the parent's execution is blocked until the child exits or executes a new program. We'll learn more about the `vfork()` system call in the following section.

The clone(), fork(), and vfork() System Calls

Lightweight processes are created in Linux by using a function named `__clone()`, which makes use of four parameters:

`fn`
> Specifies a function to be executed by the new process; when the function returns, the child terminates. The function returns an integer, which represents the exit code for the child process.

`arg`
> Pointer to data passed to the `fn()` function.

`flags`
> Miscellaneous information. The low byte specifies the signal number to be sent to the parent process when the child terminates; the `SIGCHLD` signal is generally selected. The remaining 3 bytes encode a group of clone flags, which specify the resources shared between the parent and the child process. The flags, when set, have the following meanings:

> `CLONE_VM`
>> The memory descriptor and all page tables (see Chapter 7).

> `CLONE_FS`:
>> The table that identifies the root directory and the current working directory.

> `CLONE_FILES`:
>> The table that identifies the open files (see Chapter 12).

> `CLONE_SIGHAND`:
>> The table that identifies the signal handlers (see Chapter 9).

> `CLONE_PID`:
>> The PID.[*]

---

[*] As we shall see later, the `CLONE_PID` flag can be used only by a process having a PID of 0; in a uniprocessor system, no two lightweight processes have the same PID.

CLONE_PTRACE:
> If a `ptrace()` system call is causing the parent process to be traced, the child will also be traced.

CLONE_VFORK:
> Used for the `vfork()` system call (see later in this section).

child_stack
> Specifies the User Mode stack pointer to be assigned to the `esp` register of the child process. If it is equal to 0, the kernel assigns to the child the current parent stack pointer. Thus, the parent and child temporarily share the same User Mode stack. But thanks to the Copy On Write mechanism, they usually get separate copies of the User Mode stack as soon as one tries to change the stack. However, this parameter must have a non-null value if the child process shares the same address space as the parent.

`__clone()` is actually a wrapper function defined in the C library (see the section "POSIX APIs and System Calls" in Chapter 8), which in turn makes use of a Linux system call hidden to the programmer, named `clone()`. The `clone()` system call receives only the `flags` and `child_stack` parameters; the new process always starts its execution from the instruction following the system call invocation. When the system call returns to the `__clone()` function, it determines whether it is in the parent or the child and forces the child to execute the `fn()` function.

The traditional `fork()` system call is implemented by Linux as a `clone()` whose first parameter specifies a `SIGCHLD` signal and all the clone flags cleared and whose second parameter is 0.

The old `vfork()` system call, described in the previous section, is implemented by Linux as a `clone()` whose first parameter specifies a `SIGCHLD` signal and the flags `CLONE_VM` and `CLONE_VFORK` and whose second parameter is equal to 0.

When either a `clone()`, `fork()`, or `vfork()` system call is issued, the kernel invokes the `do_fork()` function, which executes the following steps:

1. If the `CLONE_PID` flag has been specified, the `do_fork()` function checks whether the PID of the parent process is not null; if so, it returns an error code. Only the *swapper* process is allowed to set `CLONE_PID`; this is required when initializing a multiprocessor system (see the section "Main SMP Data Structures" in Chapter 11).

2. The `alloc_task_struct()` function is invoked in order to get a new 8 KB `union task_union` memory area to store the process descriptor and the Kernel Mode stack of the new process.

3. The function follows the `current` pointer to obtain the parent process descriptor and copies it into the new process descriptor in the memory area just allocated.

4. A few checks occur to make sure the user has the resources necessary to start a new process. First, the function checks whether `current->rlim[RLIMIT_NPROC]`.

`rlim_cur` is smaller than or equal to the current number of processes owned by the user: if so, an error code is returned. The function gets the current number of processes owned by the user from a per-user data structure named `user_struct`. This data structure can be found through a pointer in the `user` field of the process descriptor.

5. The `find_empty_process()` function is invoked. If the owner of the parent process is not the superuser, this function checks whether `nr_tasks` (the total number of processes in the system) is smaller than `NR_TASKS-MIN_TASKS_LEFT_FOR_ROOT`.* If so, `find_empty_process()` invokes `get_free_taskslot()` to find a free entry in the `task` array. Otherwise, it returns an error.

6. The function writes the new process descriptor pointer into the previously obtained `task` entry and sets the `tarray_ptr` field of the process descriptor to the address of that entry (see the earlier section "Identifying a Process").

7. If the parent process makes use of some kernel modules, the function increments the corresponding reference counters. Each kernel module has its own reference counter, which indicates how many processes are using it. A module cannot be removed unless its reference counter is null (see Appendix B, *Modules*).

8. The function then updates some of the flags included in the `flags` field that have been copied from the parent process:

   a. It clears the `PF_SUPERPRIV` flag, which indicates whether the process has used any of its superuser privileges.

   b. It clears the `PF_USEDFPU` flag.

   c. It clears the `PF_PTRACED` flag unless the `CLONE_PTRACE` parameter flag is set. When set, the `CLONE_PTRACE` flag means that the parent process is being traced with the `ptrace()` function, so the child should be traced too.

   d. It clears `PF_TRACESYS` flag unless, once again, the `CLONE_PTRACE` parameter flag is set.

   e. It sets the `PF_FORKNOEXEC` flag, which indicates that the child process has not yet issued an `execve()` system call.

   f. It sets the `PF_VFORK` flag according to the value of the `CLONE_VFORK` flag. This specifies that the parent process must be woken up whenever the process (the child) issues an `execve()` system call or terminates.

9. Now the function has taken almost everything that it can use from the parent process; the rest of its activities focus on setting up new resources in the child and letting the kernel know that this new process has been born. First, the function

---

* A few processes, usually four, are reserved to the superuser; `MIN_TASKS_LEFT_FOR_ROOT` refers to this number. Thus, even if a user is allowed to overload the system with a "fork bomb" (a one-line program that forks itself forever), the superuser can log in, kill some processes, and start searching for the guilty user.

invokes the `get_pid()` function to obtain a new PID, which will be assigned to the child process (unless the `CLONE_PID` flag is set).

10. The function then updates all the process descriptor fields that cannot be inherited from the parent process, such as the fields that specify the process parenthood relationships.

11. Unless specified differently by the `flags` parameter, it invokes `copy_files()`, `copy_fs()`, `copy_sighand()`, and `copy_mm()` to create new data structures and copy into them the values of the corresponding parent process data structures.

12. It invokes `copy_thread()` to initialize the Kernel Mode stack of the child process with the values contained in the CPU registers when the `clone()` call was issued (these values have been saved in the Kernel Mode stack of the parent, as described in Chapter 8). However, the function forces the value 0 into the field corresponding to the `eax` register. The `tss.esp` field of the TSS of the child process is initialized with the base address of the Kernel Mode stack, and the address of an Assembly language function (`ret_from_fork()`) is stored in the `tss.eip` field.

13. It uses the `SET_LINKS` macro to insert the new process descriptor in the process list.

14. It uses the `hash_pid()` function to insert the new process descriptor in the `pidhash` hash table.

15. It increments the values of `nr_tasks` and `current->user->count`.

16. It sets the `state` field of the child process descriptor to `TASK_RUNNING` and then invokes `wake_up_process()` to insert the child in the runqueue list.

17. If the `CLONE_VFORK` flag has been specified, the function suspends the parent process until the child releases its memory address space (that is, until the child either terminates or executes a new program). In order to do this, the process descriptor includes a kernel semaphore called `vfork_sem` (see the section "Locking Through Kernel Semaphores" in Chapter 11).

18. It returns the PID of the child, which will be eventually be read by the parent process in User Mode.

Now we have a complete child process in the runnable state. But it isn't actually running. It is up to the scheduler to decide when to give the CPU to this child. At some future process switch, the schedule will bestow this favor on the child process by loading a few CPU registers with the values of the `tss` field of the child's process descriptor. In particular, `esp` will be loaded with `tss.esp` (that is, with the address of child's Kernel Mode stack), and `eip` will be loaded with the address of `ret_from_fork()`. This Assembly language function, in turn, invokes the `ret_from_sys_call()` function (see Chapter 8), which reloads all other registers with the values stored in the stack and forces the CPU back to User Mode. The new process will then start its execution right at the end of the `fork()`, `vfork()`, or `clone()` system call. The value returned by the system call is contained in **eax**: the value is 0 for the child and equal to the PID for the child's parent.

The child process will execute the same code as the parent, except that the fork will return a null PID. The developer of the application can exploit this fact, in the manner familiar to Unix programmers, by inserting a conditional statement in the program based on the PID value that forces the child to behave differently from the parent process.

Kernel Threads

Traditional Unix systems delegate some critical tasks to intermittently running processes, including flushing disk caches, swapping out unused page frames, servicing network connections, and so on. Indeed, it is not efficient to perform these tasks in strict linear fashion; both their functions and the end user processes get better response if they are scheduled in the background. Since some of the system processes run only in Kernel Mode, modern operating systems delegate their functions to *kernel threads*, which are not encumbered with the unnecessary User Mode context. In Linux, kernel threads differ from regular processes in the following ways:

* Each kernel thread executes a single specific kernel function, while regular processes execute kernel functions only through system calls.

* Kernel threads run only in Kernel Mode, while regular processes run alternatively in Kernel Mode and in User Mode.

* Since kernel threads run only in Kernel Mode, they use only linear addresses greater than `PAGE_OFFSET`. Regular processes, on the other hand, use all 4 gigabytes of linear addresses, either in User Mode or in Kernel Mode.

Creating a kernel thread

The `kernel_thread()` function creates a new kernel thread and can be executed only by another kernel thread. The function contains mostly inline Assembly language code, but it is somewhat equivalent to the following:

```
int kernel_thread(int (*fn)(void *), void * arg,
             unsigned long flags)
{
    pid_t p;
    p = clone( 0, flags | CLONE_VM );
    if ( p )         /* parent */
        return p;
    else {           /* child */
        fn(arg);
        exit();
    }
}
```

Process 0

The ancestor of all processes, called *process 0* or, for historical reasons, the *swapper process*, is a kernel thread created from scratch during the initialization phase of Linux by the `start_kernel()` function (see Appendix A, *System Startup*). This ancestor process makes use of the following data structures:

- A process descriptor and a Kernel Mode stack stored in the `init_task_union` variable. The `init_task` and `init_stack` macros yield the addresses of the process descriptor and the stack, respectively.

- The following tables, which the process descriptor points to:
  - `init_mm`
  - `init_mmap`
  - `init_fs`
  - `init_files`
  - `init_signals`

  The tables are initialized, respectively, by the following macros:
  - `INIT_MM`
  - `INIT_MMAP`
  - `INIT_FS`
  - `INIT_FILES`
  - `INIT_SIGNALS`

- A TSS segment, initialized by the `INIT_TSS` macro.

- Two Segment Descriptors, namely a TSSD and an LDTD, which are stored in the GDT.

- A Page Global Directory stored in `swapper_pg_dir`, which may be considered as the kernel Page Global Directory since it is used by all kernel threads.

The `start_kernel()` function initializes all the data structures needed by the kernel, enables interrupts, and creates another kernel thread, named *process 1*, more commonly referred to as the *init process*:

```
kernel_thread(init, NULL,
              CLONE_FS | CLONE_FILES | CLONE_SIGHAND);
```

The newly created kernel thread has PID 1 and shares with process 0 all per-process kernel data structures. Moreover, when selected from the scheduler, the *init* process starts executing the `init()` function.

After having created the *init* process, process 0 executes the `cpu_idle()` function, which essentially consists of repeatedly executing the `hlt` Assembly language instruction with the interrupts enabled (see Chapter 4). Process 0 is selected by the scheduler only when there are no other processes in the `TASK_RUNNING` state.

Process 1

The kernel thread created by process 0 executes the `init()` function, which in turn invokes the `kernel_thread()` function four times to initiate four kernel threads needed for routine kernel tasks:

```
kernel_thread(bdflush, NULL,
              CLONE_FS | CLONE_FILES | CLONE_SIGHAND);
kernel_thread(kupdate, NULL,
              CLONE_FS | CLONE_FILES | CLONE_SIGHAND);
kernel_thread(kpiod, NULL,
              CLONE_FS | CLONE_FILES | CLONE_SIGHAND);
kernel_thread(kswapd, NULL,
              CLONE_FS | CLONE_FILES | CLONE_SIGHAND);
```

As a result, four additional kernel threads are created to handle the memory cache and the swapping activity:

kflushd (also bdflush)
Flushes "dirty" buffers to disk to reclaim memory, as described in the section "Writing Dirty Buffers to Disk" in Chapter 14, *Disk Caches*

kupdate
Flushes old "dirty" buffers to disk to reduce risks of filesystem inconsistencies, as described in the section "Writing Dirty Buffers to Disk" in Chapter 14

kpiod
Swaps out pages belonging to shared memory mappings, as described in the section "Swapping Out Pages from Shared Memory Mappings" in Chapter 16, *Swapping: Methods For Freeing Memory*

kswapd
Performs memory reclaiming, as described in the section "The kswapd Kernel Thread" in Chapter 16

Then `init()` invokes the `execve()` system call to load the executable program *init*. As a result, the *init* kernel thread becomes a regular process having its own per-process kernel data structure. The *init* process never terminates, since it creates and monitors the activity of all the processes that implement the outer layers of the operating system.

Destroying Processes

Most processes "die" in the sense that they terminate the execution of the code they were supposed to run. When this occurs, the kernel must be notified so that it can release the resources owned by the process; this includes memory, open files, and any other odds and ends that we will encounter in this book, such as semaphores.

The usual way for a process to terminate is to invoke the `exit()` system call. This system call may be inserted by the programmer explicitly. Additionally, the `exit()` system call is always executed when the control flow reaches the last statement of the main procedure (the `main()` function in C programs).

Alternatively, the kernel may force a process to die. This typically occurs when the process has received a signal that it cannot handle or ignore (see Chapter 9) or when an unrecoverable CPU exception has been raised in Kernel Mode while the kernel was running on behalf of the process (see Chapter 4).

Process Termination

All process terminations are handled by the `do_exit()` function, which removes most references to the terminating process from kernel data structures. The `do_exit()` function executes the following actions:

1. Sets the `PF_EXITING` flag in the `flag` field of the process descriptor to denote that the process is being eliminated.

2. Removes, if necessary, the process descriptor from an IPC semaphore queue via the `sem_exit()` function (see Chapter 18, *Process Communication*) or from a dynamic timer queue via the `del_timer()` function (see Chapter 5).

3. Examines the process's data structures related to paging, filesystem, open file descriptors, and signal handling, respectively, with the `__exit_mm()`, `__exit_files()`, `__exit_fs()`, and `__exit_sighand()` functions. These functions also remove any of these data structures if no other process is sharing it.

4. Sets the `state` field of the process descriptor to `TASK_ZOMBIE`. We shall see what happens to zombie processes in the following section.

5. Sets the `exit_code` field of the process descriptor to the process termination code. This value is either the `exit()` system call parameter (normal termination), or an error code supplied by the kernel (abnormal termination).

6. Invokes the `exit_notify()` function to update the parenthood relationships of both the parent process and the children processes. All children processes created by the terminating process become children of the *init* process.

7. Invokes the `schedule()` function (see Chapter 10) to select a new process to run. Since a process in a `TASK_ZOMBIE` state is ignored by the scheduler, the process will stop executing right after the `switch_to` macro in `schedule()` is invoked.

Process Removal

The Unix operating system allows a process to query the kernel to obtain the PID of its parent process or the execution state for any of its children. A process may, for instance, create a child process to perform a specific task and then invoke a `wait()`-like system call to check whether the child has terminated. If the child has terminated, its termination code will tell the parent process if the task has been carried out successfully.

In order to comply with these design choices, Unix kernels are not allowed to discard data included in a process descriptor field right after the process terminates. They are allowed to do so only after the parent process has issued a `wait()`-like system call that refers to the terminated process. This is why the `TASK_ZOMBIE` state has been introduced: although the process is technically dead, its descriptor must be saved until the parent process is notified.

What happens if parent processes terminate before their children? In such a case, the system might be flooded with zombie processes that might end up using all the available `task` entries. As mentioned earlier, this problem is solved by forcing all orphan processes to become children of the *init* process. In this way, the *init* process will destroy the zombies while checking for the termination of one of its legitimate children through a `wait()`-like system call.

The `release()` function releases the process descriptor of a zombie process by executing the following steps:

1. Invokes the `free_uid()` function to decrement by 1 the number of processes created up to now by the user owner of the terminated process. This value is stored in the `user_struct` structure mentioned earlier in the chapter.

2. Invokes `add_free_taskslot()` to free the entry in `task` that points to the process descriptor to be released.

3. Decrements the value of the `nr_tasks` variable.

4. Invokes `unhash_pid()` to remove the process descriptor from the `pidhash` hash table.

5. Uses the `REMOVE_LINKS` macro to unlink the process descriptor from the process list.

6. Invokes the `free_task_struct()` function to release the 8 KB memory area used to contain the process descriptor and the Kernel Mode stack.

Anticipating Linux 2.4

The new kernel supports a huge number of users and groups, because it makes use of 32-bit UIDs and GIDs.

In order to raise the hardcoded limit on the number of processes, Linux 2.4 removes the `tasks` array, which previously included pointers to all process descriptors.

Moreover, Linux 2.4 no longer includes a Task State Segment for each process. The `tss` field in the process descriptor has thus been replaced by a pointer to a data structure storing the information that was previously in the TSS, namely the register contents and the I/O bitmap. Linux 2.4 makes use of just one TSS for each CPU in the system. When a context switch occurs, the kernel uses the per-process data structures to save and restore the register contents and to fill the I/O bitmap in the TSS of the executing CPU.

Linux 2.4 enhances wait queues. Sleeping processes are now stored in lists implemented through the efficient `list_head` data type. Moreover, the kernel is now able to wake up just a single process that is sleeping in a wait queue, thus greatly improving the efficiency of semaphores.

Finally, Linux 2.4 adds a new flag to the `clone()` system call: `CLONE_PARENT` allows the new lightweight process to have the same parent as the process that invoked the system call.

CHAPTER FOUR

INTERRUPTS AND EXCEPTIONS

An *interrupt* is usually defined as an event that alters the sequence of instructions executed by a processor. Such events correspond to electrical signals generated by hardware circuits both inside and outside of the CPU chip.

Interrupts are often divided into *synchronous* and *asynchronous* interrupts:

* *Synchronous* interrupts are produced by the CPU control unit while executing instructions and are called synchronous because the control unit issues them only after terminating the execution of an instruction.

* *Asynchronous* interrupts are generated by other hardware devices at arbitrary times with respect to the CPU clock signals.

Intel 80x86 microprocessor manuals designate synchronous and asynchronous interrupts as *exceptions* and *interrupts*, respectively. We'll adopt this classification, although we'll occasionally use the term "interrupt signal" to designate both types together (synchronous as well as asynchronous).

Interrupts are issued by interval timers and I/O devices; for instance, the arrival of a keystroke from a user sets off an interrupt. Exceptions, on the other hand, are caused either by programming errors or by anomalous conditions that must be handled by the kernel. In the first case, the kernel handles the exception by delivering to the current process one of the signals familiar to every Unix programmer. In the second case, the kernel performs all the steps needed to recover from the anomalous condition, such as a page fault or a request (via an `int` instruction) for a kernel service.

We start by describing in the section "The Role of Interrupt Signals" the motivation for introducing such signals. We then show how the well-known IRQs (Interrupt ReQuests) issued by I/O devices give rise to interrupts, and we detail how Intel 80x86 processors handle interrupts and exceptions at the hardware level. Next, we illustrate in the section "Initializing the Interrupt Descriptor Table" how Linux initializes all the data structures required by the Intel interrupt architecture. The remaining three sections describe how Linux handles interrupt signals at the software level.

One word of caution before moving on: we cover in this chapter only "classic" interrupts common to all PCs; we do not cover the nonstandard interrupts of some architectures. For instance, laptops generate types of interrupts not discussed here. Other types of interrupts specific to multiprocessor architecture will be briefly described in Chapter 11, *Kernel Synchronization.*

The Role of Interrupt Signals

As the name suggests, interrupt signals provide a way to divert the processor to code outside the normal flow of control. When an interrupt signal arrives, the CPU must stop what it's currently doing and switch to a new activity; it does this by saving the current value of the program counter (i.e., the content of the `eip` and `cs` registers) in the Kernel Mode stack and by placing an address related to the interrupt type into the program counter.

There are some things in this chapter that will remind you of the context switch we described in the previous chapter, carried out when a kernel substitutes one process for another. But there is a key difference between interrupt handling and process switching: the code executed by an interrupt or by an exception handler is not a process. Rather, it is a kernel control path that runs on behalf of the same process that was running when the interrupt occurred (see the section "Nested Execution of Exception and Interrupt Handlers"). As a kernel control path, the interrupt handler is lighter than a process (it has less context and requires less time to set up or tear down).

Interrupt handling is one of the most sensitive tasks performed by the kernel, since it must satisfy the following constraints:

- Interrupts can come at any time, when the kernel may want to finish something else it was trying to do. The kernel's goal is therefore to get the interrupt out of the way as soon as possible and defer as much processing as it can. For instance, suppose a block of data has arrived on a network line. When the hardware interrupts the kernel, it could simply mark the presence of data, give the processor back to whatever was running before, and do the rest of the processing later (like moving the data into a buffer where its recipient process can find it and restarting the process). The activities that the kernel needs to perform in response to an interrupt are thus divided into two parts: a *top half* that the kernel executes right away and a *bottom half* that is left for later. The kernel keeps a queue pointing to all the functions that represent bottom halves waiting to be executed and pulls them off the queue to execute them at particular points in processing.

- Since interrupts can come at any time, the kernel might be handling one of them while another one (of a different type) occurs. This should be allowed as much as possible since it keeps the I/O devices busy (see the section "Nested Execution of Exception and Interrupt Handlers"). As a result, the interrupt handlers must be coded so that the corresponding kernel control paths can be executed in a nested manner. When the last kernel control path terminates, the kernel must be able to resume execution of the interrupted process or switch to another process if the interrupt signal has caused a rescheduling activity.

- Although the kernel may accept a new interrupt signal while handling a previous one, some critical regions exist inside the kernel code where interrupts must be disabled. Such critical regions must be limited as much as possible since, according to the previous requirement, the kernel, and in particular the interrupt handlers, should run most of the time with the interrupts enabled.

Interrupts and Exceptions

The Intel documentation classifies interrupts and exceptions as follows:

- Interrupts:

  Maskable interrupts
  Sent to the INTR pin of the microprocessor. They can be disabled by clearing the IF flag of the `eflags` register. All IRQs issued by I/O devices give rise to maskable interrupts.

  Nonmaskable interrupts
  Sent to the NMI (Nonmaskable Interrupts) pin of the microprocessor. They are not disabled by clearing the IF flag. Only a few critical events, such as hardware failures, give rise to nonmaskable interrupts.

- Exceptions:

  Processor-detected exceptions
  Generated when the CPU detects an anomalous condition while executing an instruction. These are further divided into three groups, depending on the value of the `eip` register that is saved on the Kernel Mode stack when the CPU control unit raises the exception:

  Faults
  The saved value of `eip` is the address of the instruction that caused the fault, and hence that instruction can be resumed when the exception handler terminates. As we shall see in the section "Page Fault Exception Handler" in Chapter 7, *Process Address Space*, resuming the same instruction is

necessary whenever the handler is able to correct the anomalous condition that caused the exception.

Traps

The saved value of `eip` is the address of the instruction that should be executed after the one that caused the trap. A trap is triggered only when there is no need to reexecute the instruction that terminated. The main use of traps is for debugging purposes: the role of the interrupt signal in this case is to notify the debugger that a specific instruction has been executed (for instance, a breakpoint has been reached within a program). Once the user has examined the data provided by the debugger, she may ask that execution of the debugged program resume starting from the next instruction.

Aborts

A serious error occurred; the control unit is in trouble, and it may be unable to store a meaningful value in the `eip` register. Aborts are caused by hardware failures or by invalid values in system tables. The interrupt signal sent by the control unit is an emergency signal used to switch control to the corresponding abort exception handler. This handler has no choice but to force the affected process to terminate.

Programmed exceptions

Occur at the request of the programmer. They are triggered by `int` or `int3` instructions; the `into` (check for overflow) and `bound` (check on address bound) instructions also give rise to a programmed exception when the condition they are checking is not true. Programmed exceptions are handled by the control unit as traps; they are often called *software interrupts*. Such exceptions have two common uses: to implement system calls, and to notify a debugger of a specific event (see Chapter 8, *System Calls*).

Interrupt and Exception Vectors

Each interrupt or exception is identified by a number ranging from 0 to 255; for some unknown reason, Intel calls this 8-bit unsigned number a *vector*. The vectors of nonmaskable interrupts and exceptions are fixed, while those of maskable interrupts can be altered by programming the Interrupt Controller (see the next section, "IRQs and Interrupts").

Linux uses the following vectors:

- Vectors ranging from 0 to 31 correspond to exceptions and nonmaskable interrupts.

- Vectors ranging from 32 to 47 are assigned to maskable interrupts, that is, to interrupts caused by IRQs.

- The remaining vectors ranging from 48 to 255 may be used to identify software interrupts. Linux uses only one of them, namely the 128 or 0x80 vector, which it uses to implement system calls. When an `int` `0x80` Assembly instruction is executed by a process in User Mode, the CPU switches into Kernel Mode and starts executing the `system_call()` kernel function (see Chapter 8).

IRQs and Interrupts

Each hardware device controller capable of issuing interrupt requests has an output line designated as an *IRQ* (Interrupt ReQuest). All existing IRQ lines are connected to the input pins of a hardware circuit called the *Interrupt Controller*, which performs the following actions:

1. Monitors the IRQ lines, checking for raised signals.

2. If a raised signal occurs on an IRQ line:

   a. Converts the raised signal received into a corresponding vector.

   b. Stores the vector in an Interrupt Controller I/O port, thus allowing the CPU to read it via the data bus.

   c. Sends a raised signal to the processor INTR pin—that is, issues an interrupt.

   d. Waits until the CPU acknowledges the interrupt signal by writing into one of the Programmable Interrupt Controllers (PIC) I/O ports; when this occurs, clears the INTR line.

3. Goes back to step 1.

The IRQ lines are sequentially numbered starting from 0; thus, the first IRQ line is usually denoted as IRQ0. Intel's default vector associated with IRQn is $n+32$; as mentioned before, the mapping between IRQs and vectors can be modified by issuing suitable I/O instructions to the Interrupt Controller ports.

Figure 4-1 illustrates a typical connection "in cascade" of two Intel 8259A PICs that can handle up to 15 different IRQ input lines. Notice that the INT output line of the second PIC is connected to the IRQ2 pin of the first PIC: a signal on that line denotes the fact that an IRQ signal on any one of the lines IRQ8–IRQ15 has occurred. The number of available IRQ lines is thus traditionally limited to 15; however, more recent PIC chips are able to handle many more input lines.

Other lines not shown in the figure connect the PICs to the bus: in particular, bidirectional lines D0–D7 connect the I/O port to the data bus, while another input line is connected to the control bus and is used for receiving acknowledgment signals from the CPU.

Since the number of available IRQ lines is limited, it may be necessary to share the same line among several different I/O devices. When this occurs, all the devices connected to the same line will have to be polled sequentially by the software interrupt handler in order to determine which of them has issued an interrupt request. We'll

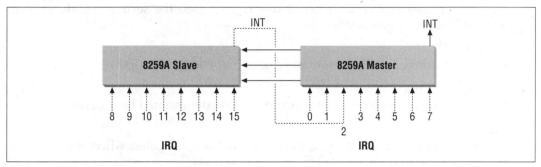

Figure 4-1. Connecting two 8259A PICs in cascade

describe in the section "Interrupt Handling" how Linux handles this kind of hardware limitation.

Each IRQ line can be selectively disabled. Thus, the PIC can be programmed to disable IRQs. That is, the PIC can be told to stop issuing interrupts that refer to a given IRQ line or vice versa to enable them. Disabled interrupts are not lost; the PIC sends them to the CPU as soon as they are enabled again. This feature is used by most interrupt handlers, since it allows them to process IRQs of the same type serially.

Selective enabling/disabling of IRQs is not the same as global masking/unmasking of maskable interrupts. When the **IF** flag of the **eflags** register is clear, any maskable interrupt issued by the PIC is temporarily ignored by the CPU. The **cli** and **sti** Assembly instructions, respectively, clear and set that flag.

Exceptions

The Intel 80x86 microprocessors issue roughly 20 different exceptions.[*] The kernel must provide a dedicated exception handler for each exception type. For some exceptions, the CPU control unit also generates a *hardware error code* and pushes it in the Kernel Mode stack before starting the exception handler.

The following list gives the vector, the name, the type, and a brief description of the exceptions found in a Pentium model. Additional information may be found in the Intel technical documentation.

0 - "Divide error" (fault)
    Raised when a program tries to divide by 0.

1- "Debug" (trap or fault)
    Raised when the T flag of **eflags** is set (quite useful to implement step-by-step execution of a debugged program) or when the address of an instruction or operand

---

[*] The exact number depends on the processor model.

falls within the range of an active debug register (see the section "Hardware Context" in Chapter 3, *Processes*).

2 - Not used
Reserved for nonmaskable interrupts (those that use the NMI pin).

3 - "Breakpoint" (trap)
Caused by an `int3` (breakpoint) instruction (usually inserted by a debugger).

4 - "Overflow" (trap)
An `into` (check for overflow) instruction has been executed when the `OF` (overflow) flag of `eflags` is set.

5 - "Bounds check" (fault)
A `bound` (check on address bound) instruction has been executed with the operand outside of the valid address bounds.

6 - "Invalid opcode" (fault)
The CPU execution unit has detected an invalid opcode (the part of the machine instruction that determines the operation performed).

7 - "Device not available" (fault)
An ESCAPE or MMX instruction has been executed with the `TS` flag of `cr0` set (see the section "Saving the Floating Point Registers" in Chapter 3).

8 - "Double fault" (abort)
Normally, when the CPU detects an exception while trying to call the handler for a prior exception, the two exceptions can be handled serially. In a few cases, however, the processor cannot handle them serially, hence it raises this exception.

9 - "Coprocessor segment overrun" (abort)
Problems with the external mathematical coprocessor (applies only to old 80386 microprocessors).

10 - "Invalid TSS" (fault)
The CPU has attempted a context switch to a process having an invalid Task State Segment.

11 - "Segment not present" (fault)
A reference was made to a segment not present in memory (one in which the `Segment-Present` flag of the Segment Descriptor was cleared).

12 - "Stack segment" (fault)
The instruction attempted to exceed the stack segment limit, or the segment identified by `ss` is not present in memory.

13 - "General protection" (fault)
One of the protection rules in the protected mode of the Intel 80x86 has been violated.

14 - "Page fault" (fault)

The addressed page is not present in memory, the corresponding page table entry is null, or a violation of the paging protection mechanism has occurred.

15 - Reserved by Intel

16 - "Floating point error" (fault)

The floating point unit integrated into the CPU chip has signaled an error condition, such as numeric overflow or division by 0.

17 - "Alignment check" (fault)

The address of an operand is not correctly aligned (for instance, the address of a long integer is not a multiple of 4).

18 to 31

These values are reserved by Intel for future development.

As illustrated in Table 4-1, each exception is handled by a specific exception handler (see the section "Exception Handling" later in this chapter), which usually sends a Unix signal to the process that caused the exception.

Table 4-1. Signals Sent by the Exception Handlers

#	Exception	Exception Handler	Signal
0	"Divide error"	divide_error()	SIGFPE
1	"Debug"	debug()	SIGTRAP
2	NMI	nmi()	None
3	"Breakpoint"	int3()	SIGTRAP
4	"Overflow"	overflow()	SIGSEGV
5	"Bounds check"	bounds()	SIGSEGV
6	"Invalid opcode"	invalid_op()	SIGILL
7	"Device not available"	device_not_available()	SIGSEGV
8	"Double fault"	double_fault()	SIGSEGV
9	"Coprocessor segment overrun"	coprocessor_segment_overrun()	SIGFPE
10	"Invalid TSS"	invalid_tss()	SIGSEGV
11	"Segment not present"	segment_not_present()	SIGBUS
12	"Stack exception"	stack_segment()	SIGBUS
13	"General protection"	general_protection()	SIGSEGV
14	"Page fault"	page_fault()	SIGSEGV
15	Intel reserved	None	None
16	"Floating point error"	coprocessor_error()	SIGFPE
17	"Alignment check"	alignment_check()	SIGSEGV

Interrupt Descriptor Table

A system table called *Interrupt Descriptor Table* (IDT) associates each interrupt or exception vector with the address of the corresponding interrupt or exception handler. The IDT must be properly initialized before the kernel enables interrupts.

The IDT format is similar to that of the GDT and of the LDTs examined in Chapter 2, *Memory Addressing*: each entry corresponds to an interrupt or an exception vector and consists of an 8-byte descriptor. Thus, a maximum of 256× 8=2048 bytes are required to store the IDT.

The `idtr` CPU register allows the IDT to be located anywhere in memory: it specifies both the IDT base physical address and its limit (maximum length). It must be initialized before enabling interrupts by using the `lidt` assembly language instruction.

The IDT may include three types of descriptors; Figure 4-2 illustrates the meaning of the 64 bits included in each of them. In particular, the value of the **Type** field encoded in the bits 40–43 identifies the descriptor type.

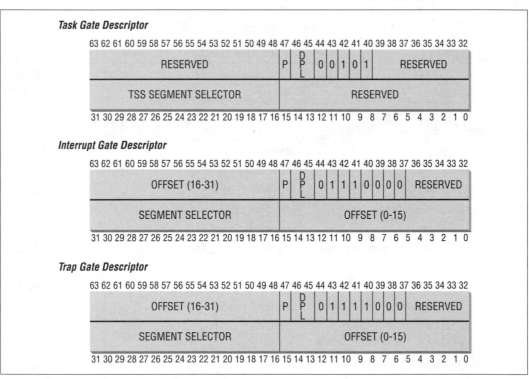

Figure 4-2. Gate descriptors's format

The descriptors are:

Task gate
> Includes the TSS selector of the process that must replace the current one when an interrupt signal occurs. Linux does not use task gates.

Interrupt gate
> Includes the Segment Selector and the offset inside the segment of an interrupt or exception handler. While transferring control to the proper segment, the processor clears the IF flag, thus disabling further maskable interrupts.

Trap gate
> Similar to an interrupt gate, except that while transferring control to the proper segment, the processor does not modify the IF flag.

As we shall see in the section "Interrupt, Trap, and System Gates," Linux uses interrupt gates to handle interrupts and trap gates to handle exceptions.

Hardware Handling of Interrupts and Exceptions

We now describe how the CPU control unit handles interrupts and exceptions. We assume that the kernel has been initialized and thus the CPU is operating in protected mode.

After executing an instruction, the cs and eip pair of registers contain the logical address of the next instruction to be executed. Before dealing with that instruction, the control unit checks whether an interrupt or an exception has occurred while it executed the previous instruction. If one occurred, the control unit:

1. Determines the vector i ($0 \leq i \leq 255$) associated with the interrupt or the exception.

2. Reads the ith entry of the IDT referred by the idtr register (we assume in the following description that the entry contains an interrupt or a trap gate).

3. Gets the base address of the GDT from the gdtr register and looks in the GDT to read the Segment Descriptor identified by the selector in the IDT entry. This descriptor specifies the base address of the segment that includes the interrupt or exception handler.

4. Makes sure the interrupt was issued by an authorized source. First compares the Current Privilege Level (CPL), which is stored in the two least significant bits of the cs register, with the Descriptor Privilege Level (DPL) of the Segment Descriptor included in the GDT. Raises a "General protection" exception if CPL is lower than DPL, because the interrupt handler cannot have a lower privilege than the program that caused the interrupt. For programmed exceptions, makes a further security check: compares the CPL with the DPL of the gate descriptor included in the IDT and raises a "General protection" exception if the DPL is lower than the CPL.

This last check makes it possible to prevent access by user applications to specific trap or interrupt gates.

5. Checks whether a change of privilege level is taking place, that is, if CPL is different from the selected Segment Descriptor's DPL. If so, the control unit must start using the stack that is associated with the new privilege level. It does this by performing the following steps:

    a. Reads the `tr` register to access the TSS segment of the `current` process.

    b. Loads the `ss` and `esp` registers with the proper values for the stack segment and stack pointer relative to the new privilege level. These values are found in the TSS (see the section "Task State Segment" in Chapter 3).

    c. In the new stack, saves the previous values of `ss` and `esp`, which define the logical address of the stack associated with the old privilege level.

6. If a fault has occurred, loads `cs` and `eip` with the logical address of the instruction that caused the exception so that it can be executed again.

7. Saves the contents of `eflags`, `cs`, and `eip` in the stack.

8. If the exception carries a hardware error code, saves it on the stack.

9. Loads `cs` and `eip`, respectively, with the Segment Selector and the Offset fields of the Gate Descriptor stored in the *i*th entry of the IDT. These values define the logical address of the first instruction of the interrupt or exception handler.

The last step performed by the control unit is equivalent to a jump to the interrupt or exception handler. In other words, the instruction processed by the control unit after dealing with the interrupt signal is the first instruction of the selected handler.

After the interrupt or exception has been processed, the corresponding handler must relinquish control to the interrupted process by issuing the `iret` instruction, which forces the control unit to:

1. Load the `cs`, `eip`, and `eflags` registers with the values saved on the stack. If a hardware error code has been pushed in the stack on top of the `eip` contents, it must be popped before executing `iret`.

2. Check whether the CPL of the handler is equal to the value contained in the two least significant bits of `cs` (this means the interrupted process was running at the same privilege level as the handler). If so, `iret` concludes execution; otherwise, go to the next step.

3. Load the `ss` and `esp` registers from the stack, and hence return to the stack associated with the old privilege level.

4. Examine the contents of the `ds`, `es`, `fs`, and `gs` segment registers: if any of them contains a selector that refers to a Segment Descriptor whose DPL value is lower than CPL, clear the corresponding segment register. The control unit does this to

forbid User Mode programs that run with a CPL equal to 3 from making use of segment registers previously used by kernel routines (with a DPL equal to 0). If these registers were not cleared, malicious User Mode programs could exploit them to access the kernel address space.

Nested Execution of Exception and Interrupt Handlers

A *kernel control path* consists of the sequence of instructions executed in Kernel Mode to handle an interrupt or an exception. When a process issues a system call request, for instance, the first instructions of the corresponding kernel control path are those that save the content of the registers in the Kernel Mode stack, while the last instructions are those that restore the content of the registers and put the CPU back into User Mode.

Assuming that the kernel is bug-free, most exceptions can occur only while the CPU is in User Mode. Indeed, they are either caused by programming errors or triggered by debuggers. However, the "Page fault" exception may occur in Kernel Mode: this happens when the process attempts to address a page that belongs to its address space but is not currently in RAM. While handling such an exception, the kernel may suspend the current process and replace it with another one until the requested page is available. The kernel control path that handles the page fault exception will resume execution as soon as the process gets the processor again.

Since the "Page fault" exception handler never gives rise to further exceptions, at most two kernel control paths associated with exceptions may be stacked, one on top of the other.

In contrast to exceptions, interrupts issued by I/O devices do not refer to data structures specific to the current process, although the kernel control paths that handle them run on behalf of that process. As a matter of fact, it is impossible to predict which process will be currently running when a given interrupt occurs.

Linux design does not allow process switching while the CPU is executing a kernel control path associated with an interrupt. However, such kernel control paths may be arbitrarily nested: an interrupt handler may be interrupted by another interrupt handler and so on.

An interrupt handler may also defer an exception handler. Conversely, an exception handler never defers an interrupt handler. The only exception that can be triggered in Kernel Mode is the "Page fault" one just described. But interrupt handlers never perform operations that could induce page faults and thus, potentially, process switching.

Linux interleaves kernel control paths for two major reasons:

- To improve the throughput of programmable interrupt controllers and device controllers. Assume that a device controller issues a signal on an IRQ line: the PIC transforms it into an INTR request, and then both the PIC and the device controller remain blocked until the PIC receives an acknowledgment from the CPU. Thanks to kernel control path interleaving, the kernel is able to send the acknowledgment even when it is handling a previous interrupt.

- To implement an interrupt model without priority levels. Since each interrupt handler may be deferred by another one, there is no need to establish predefined priorities among hardware devices. This simplifies the kernel code and improves its portability.

Initializing the Interrupt Descriptor Table

Now that you understand what the Intel processor does with interrupts and exceptions at the hardware level, we can move on to describe how the Interrupt Descriptor Table is initialized.

Remember that before the kernel enables the interrupts, it must load the initial address of the IDT table into the `idtr` register and initialize all the entries of that table. This activity is done while initializing the system (see Appendix A, *System Startup*).

The `int` instruction allows a User Mode process to issue an interrupt signal having an arbitrary vector ranging from 0 to 255. The initialization of the IDT must thus be done carefully, in order to block illegal interrupts and exceptions simulated by User Mode processes via `int` instructions. This can be achieved by setting the DPL field of the Interrupt or Trap Gate Descriptor to 0. If the process attempts to issue one of such interrupt signals, the control unit will check the CPL value against the DPL field and issue a "General protection" exception.

In a few cases, however, a User Mode process must be able to issue a programmed exception. To allow this, it is sufficient to set the DPL field of the corresponding Interrupt or Trap Gate Descriptors to 3; that is, as high as possible.

Let's now see how Linux implements this strategy.

Interrupt, Trap, and System Gates

As mentioned in the earlier section "Interrupt Descriptor Table," Intel provides three types of interrupt descriptors: Task, Interrupt, and Trap Gate Descriptors. Task Gate Descriptors are irrelevant to Linux, but its Interrupt Descriptor Table contains several

Interrupt and Trap Gate Descriptors. Linux classifies them as follows, using a slightly different breakdown and terminology from Intel:

Interrupt gate
>   An Intel interrupt gate that cannot be accessed by a User Mode process (the gate's DPL field is equal to 0). All Linux interrupt handlers are activated by means of interrupt gates, and all are restricted to Kernel Mode.

System gate
>   An Intel trap gate that can be accessed by a User Mode process (the gate's DPL field is equal to 3). The four Linux exception handlers associated with the vectors 3, 4, 5, and 128 are activated by means of system gates, so the four Assembly instructions int3, into, bound, and int 0x80 can be issued in User Mode.

Trap gate
>   An Intel trap gate that cannot be accessed by a User Mode process (the gate's DPL field is equal to 0). All Linux exception handlers, except the four described in the previous paragraph, are activated by means of trap gates.

The following functions are used to insert gates in the IDT:

set_intr_gate(n,addr)
>   Inserts an interrupt gate in the *n*th IDT entry. The Segment Selector inside the gate is set to the kernel code's Segment Selector. The Offset field is set to addr, which is the address of the interrupt handler. The DPL field is set to 0.

set_system_gate(n,addr)
>   Inserts a trap gate in the *n*th IDT entry. The Segment Selector inside the gate is set to the kernel code's Segment Selector. The Offset field is set to addr, which is the address of the exception handler. The DPL field is set to 3.

set_trap_gate(n,addr)
>   Similar to the previous function, except that the DPL field is set to 0.

Preliminary Initialization of the IDT

The IDT is initialized and used by the BIOS routines when the computer still operates in Real Mode. Once Linux takes over, however, the IDT is moved to another area of RAM and initialized a second time, since Linux does not make use of any BIOS routines (see Appendix A).

The IDT is stored in the idt_table table, which includes 256 entries.[*] The 6-byte idt_descr variable specifies both the size of the IDT and its address; it is used only

---

[*] Some Pentium models have the notorious "f00f" bug, which allows a User Mode program to freeze the system. When executing on such CPUs, Linux uses a workaround based on storing the IDT in a write-protected page frame. The workaround for the bug is offered as an option when the user compiles the kernel.

when the kernel initializes the `idtr` register with the `lidt` Assembly instruction. In all other cases, the kernel refers to the `idt` variable to get the address of the IDT.

During kernel initialization, the `setup_idt()` assembly language function starts by filling all 256 entries of `idt_table` with the same interrupt gate, which refers to the `ignore_int()` interrupt handler:

```
setup_idt:
    lea ignore_int, %edx
    movl $(__KERNEL_CS << 16), %eax
    movw %dx, %ax          /* selector = 0x0010 = cs */
    movw $0x8e00, %dx    /* interrupt gate, dpl=0, present */
    lea idt_table, %edi
    mov $256, %ecx
rp_sidt:
    movl %eax, (%edi)
    movl %edx, 4(%edi)
    addl $8, %edi
    dec %ecx
    jne rp_sidt
    ret
```

The `ignore_int()` interrupt handler, which is in assembly language, may be viewed as a null handler that executes the following actions:

1. Saves the content of some registers in the stack

2. Invokes the **printk()** function to print an "Unknown interrupt" system message

3. Restores the register contents from the stack

4. Executes an `iret` instruction to restart the interrupted program

The `ignore_int()` handler should never be executed: the occurrence of "Unknown interrupt" messages on the console or in the log files denotes either a hardware problem (an I/O device is issuing unforeseen interrupts) or a kernel problem (an interrupt or exception is not being handled properly).

Following this preliminary initialization, the kernel makes a second pass in the IDT to replace some of the null handlers with meaningful trap and interrupt handlers. Once this is done, the IDT will include a specialized trap or system gate for each different exception issued by the control unit, and a specialized interrupt gate for each IRQ recognized by the Programmable Interrupt Controller.

The next two sections illustrate in detail how this is done, respectively, for exceptions and interrupts.

Exception Handling

Linux takes advantage of exceptions to achieve two quite different goals:

- To send a signal to a process to notify an anomalous condition

- To handle demand paging

An example of the first use is if a process performs a division by 0. The CPU raises a "Divide error" exception, and the corresponding exception handler sends a `SIGFPE` signal to the current process, which will then take the necessary steps to recover or (if no signal handler is set for that signal) abort.

Exception handlers have a standard structure consisting of three parts:

1. Save the contents of most registers in the Kernel Mode stack (this part is coded in Assembly language).

2. Handle the exception by means of a high-level C function.

3. Exit from the handler by means of the `ret_from_exception()` function.

In order to take advantage of exceptions, the IDT must be properly initialized with an exception handler function for each recognized exception. It is the job of the `trap_init()` function to insert the final values—that is, the functions that handle the exceptions—into all IDT entries that refer to nonmaskable interrupts and exceptions. This is accomplished through the `set_trap_gate` and `set_system_gate` macros:

```
set_trap_gate(0,&divide_error);
set_trap_gate(1,&debug);
set_trap_gate(2,&nmi);
set_system_gate(3,&int3);
set_system_gate(4,&overflow);
set_system_gate(5,&bounds);
set_trap_gate(6,&invalid_op);
set_trap_gate(7,&device_not_available);
set_trap_gate(8,&double_fault);
set_trap_gate(9,&coprocessor_segment_overrun);
set_trap_gate(10,&invalid_TSS);
set_trap_gate(11,&segment_not_present);
set_trap_gate(12,&stack_segment);
set_trap_gate(13,&general_protection);
set_trap_gate(14,&page_fault);
set_trap_gate(16,&coprocessor_error);
set_trap_gate(17,&alignment_check);
set_system_gate(0x80,&system_call);
```

Now we will look at what a typical exception handler does once it is invoked.

Saving the Registers for the Exception Handler

Let us denote with `handler_name` the name of a generic exception handler. (The actual names of all the exception handlers appear on the list of macros in the previous section.) Each exception handler starts with the following Assembly instructions:

```
handler_name:
    pushl $0 /* only for some exceptions */
    pushl $do_handler_name
    jmp error_code
```

If the control unit is not supposed to automatically insert a hardware error code on the stack when the exception occurs, the corresponding Assembly fragment includes a `pushl $0` instruction to pad the stack with a null value. Then the address of the high-level C function is pushed on the stack; its name consists of the exception handler name prefixed by `do_`.

The Assembly fragment labeled as `error_code` is the same for all exception handlers except the one for the "Device not available" exception (see the section "Saving the Floating Point Registers" in Chapter 3). The code performs the following steps:

1. Saves the registers that might be used by the high-level C function on the stack.

2. Issues a `cld` instruction to clear the direction flag `DF` of `eflags`, thus making sure that autoincrements on the `edi` and `esi` registers will be used with string instructions.

3. Copies the hardware error code saved in the stack at location `esp+36` in `eax`. Stores in the same stack location the value -1: as we shall see in the section "Reexecution of System Calls" in Chapter 9, *Signals*, this value is used to separate `0x80` exceptions from other exceptions.

4. Loads `ecx` with the address of the high-level `do_handler_name()` C function saved in the stack at location `esp+32`; writes the contents of `es` in that stack location.

5. Loads the kernel data Segment Selector into the `ds` and `es` registers, then sets the `ebx` register to the address of the current process descriptor (see the section "Identifying a Process" in Chapter 3).

6. Stores the parameters to be passed to the high-level C function on the stack, namely, the exception hardware error code and the address of the stack location where the contents of User Mode registers was saved.

7. Invokes the high-level C function whose address is now stored in `ecx`.

After the last step is executed, the invoked function will find on the top locations of the stack:

- The return address of the instruction to be executed after the C function terminates (see next section)

- The stack address of the saved User Mode registers

- The hardware error code

Returning from the Exception Handler

When the C function that implements the exception handling terminates, control is transferred to the following assembly language fragment:

```
addl $8, %esp
jmp ret_from_exception
```

The code pops the stack address of the saved User Mode registers and the hardware error code from the stack, then performs a `jmp` instruction to the `ret_from_exception()` function. This function will be described in the later section "Returning from Interrupts and Exceptions."

Invoking the Exception Handler

As already explained, the names of the C functions that implement exception handlers always consist of the prefix `do_` followed by the handler name. Most of these functions store the hardware error code and the exception vector in the process descriptor of `current`, then send to that process a suitable signal. This is done as follows:

```
current->tss.error_code = error_code;
current->tss.trap_no = vector;
force_sig(sig_number, current);
```

When the `ret_from_exception()` function is invoked, it checks whether the process has received a signal. If so, the signal will be handled either by the process's own signal handler (if it exists) or by the kernel; in the latter case, the kernel will usually kill the process (see Chapter 9). The signals sent by the exception handlers have already been illustrated in Table 4-1.

Finally, the handler invokes either `die_if_kernel()` or `die_if_no_fixup()`:

- The `die_if_kernel()` function checks whether the exception occurred in Kernel Mode; in this case, it invokes the `die()` function, which prints the contents of all CPU registers on the console and terminates the `current` process by invoking `do_exit()` (see Chapter 19, *Program Execution*).

- The `die_if_no_fixup()` function is similar, but before invoking `die()` it checks whether the exception was due to an invalid argument of a system call: in the affirmative case, it uses a "fixup" approach, which will be described in the section "Dynamic Address Checking: The Fixup Code" in Chapter 8.

Two exceptions are exploited by the kernel to manage hardware resources more efficiently. The corresponding handlers are more complex because the exception does not necessarily denote an error condition:

- "Device not available": as discussed in the section "Saving the Floating Point Registers" in Chapter 3, this exception is used to defer loading the floating point registers until the last possible moment.

- "Page fault": as we shall see in the section "Page Fault Exception Handler" in Chapter 7, *Process Address Space*, this exception is used to defer allocating new page frames to the process until the last possible fmoment.

Interrupt Handling

As we explained earlier, most exceptions are handled simply by sending a Unix signal to the process that caused the exception. The action to be taken is thus deferred until the process receives the signal; as a result, the kernel is able to process the exception quickly.

This approach does not hold for interrupts, because they frequently arrive long after the process to which they are related (for instance, a process that requested a data transfer) has been suspended and a completely unrelated process is running. So it would make no sense to send a Unix signal to the current process.

Furthermore, due to hardware limitations, several devices may share the same IRQ line. (Remember that PCs supply only a few IRQs.) This means that the interrupt vector alone does not tell the whole story: as an example, some PC configurations may assign the same vector to the network card and to the graphic card. Therefore, an interrupt handler must be flexible enough to service several devices. In order to do this, several *interrupt service routines* (*ISRs*) can be associated with the same interrupt handler; each of them is a function related to a single device sharing the IRQ line. Since it is not possible to know in advance which particular device issued the IRQ, each ISR is executed to verify whether its device needs attention; if so, the ISR performs all the operations that need to be executed when the device raises an interrupt.

Not all actions to be performed when an interrupt occurs have the same urgency. In fact, the interrupt handler itself is not a suitable place for all kind of actions. Long noncritical operations should be deferred, since while an interrupt handler is running, the signals on the corresponding IRQ line are ignored. Most important, the process on behalf of which an interrupt handler is executed must always stay in the TASK_RUNNING state, or a system freeze could occur. Therefore, interrupt handlers cannot perform any blocking procedure such as I/O disk operations. So Linux divides the actions to be performed following an interrupt into three classes:

Critical

Actions such as acknowledging an interrupt to the PIC, reprogramming the PIC or the device controller, or updating data structures accessed by both the device and the processor. These can be executed quickly and are critical because they must be performed as soon as possible. Critical actions are executed within the interrupt handler immediately, with maskable interrupts disabled.

Noncritical

Actions such as updating data structures that are accessed only by the processor (for instance, reading the scan code after a keyboard key has been pushed). These actions can also finish quickly, so they are executed by the interrupt handler immediately, with the interrupts enabled.

Noncritical deferrable

Actions such as copying a buffers contents into the address space of some process (for instance, sending the keyboard line buffer to the terminal handler process). These may be delayed for a long time interval without affecting the kernel operations; the interested process will just keep waiting for the data. Noncritical deferrable actions are performed by means of separate functions called "bottom halves." We shall discuss them in the later section, "Bottom Half."

All interrupt handlers perform the same four basic actions:

1. Save the IRQ value and the registers contents in the Kernel Mode stack.

2. Send an acknowledgment to the PIC that is servicing the IRQ line, thus allowing it to issue further interrupts.

3. Execute the interrupt service routines (ISRs) associated with all the devices that share the IRQ.

4. Terminate by jumping to the `ret_from_intr()` address.

Several descriptors are needed to represent both the state of the IRQ lines and the functions to be executed when an interrupt occurs. Figure 4-3 represents in a schematic way the hardware circuits and the software functions used to handle an interrupt. These functions will be discussed in the following sections.

Interrupt Vectors

As explained in the earlier section "IRQs and Interrupts," the 16 physical IRQs are assigned the vectors 32–47. The IBM-compatible PC architecture requires that some devices must be statically connected to specific IRQ lines. In particular:

- The interval timer device must be connected to the IRQ0 line (see Chapter 5, *Timing Measurements*).

- The slave 8259A PIC must be connected to the IRQ2 line (see Figure 4-1).

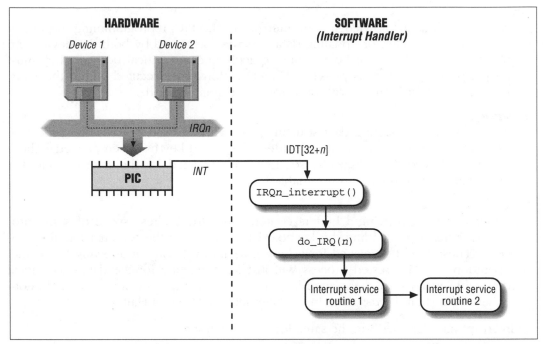

Figure 4-3. Interrupt handling

- The external mathematical coprocessor must be connected to the IRQ13 line (although recent Intel 80x86 processors no longer use such a device, Linux continues to support the venerable 80386 model).

For all remaining IRQs, the kernel must establish a correspondence between IRQ number and I/O device before enabling interrupts. Otherwise, how could the kernel handle a signal from (say) a SCSI disk without knowing which vector corresponds to the device?

Modern I/O devices are able to connect themselves to several IRQ lines. The optimal selection depends on how many devices are on the system and whether any are constrained to respond only to certain IRQs. There are two ways to select a line for each device:

- By a utility program executed when installing the device: such a program may ask the user to select an available IRQ number or determine an available number by itself.

- By a hardware protocol executed at system startup. Under this system, peripheral devices declare which interrupt lines they are ready to use; the final values are then negotiated to reduce conflicts as much as possible. Once this is done, each interrupt handler can read the assigned IRQ by using a function that accesses some I/O ports of the device. For instance, drivers for devices that comply with the Peripheral Component Interconnect (PCI) standard make use of a group of functions such as `pci_read_config_byte()` and `pci_write_config_byte()` to access the device configuration space.

In both cases, the kernel can retrieve the selected IRQ line of a device when initializing the corresponding driver. Table 4-2 shows a fairly arbitrary arrangement of devices and IRQs, such as might be found on one particular PC.

Table 4-2. An Example of IRQ Assignment to I/O Devices

IRQ	INT	Hardware Device
0	32	Timer
1	33	Keyboard
2	34	PIC cascading
3	35	Second serial port
4	36	First serial port
6	38	Floppy disk
8	40	System clock
11	43	Network interface
12	44	PS/2 mouse
13	45	Mathematical coprocessor
14	46	EIDE disk controller's first chain
15	47	EIDE disk controller's second chain

IRQ Data Structures

As always when discussing complicated operations involving state transitions, it helps to understand first where key data is stored. Thus, this section explains the data structures that support interrupt handling and how they are laid out in various descriptors. Figure 4-4 illustrates schematically the relationships between the main descriptors that represent the state of the IRQ lines. (The figure does not illustrate the data structures needed to handle bottom halves; they will be discussed later in this chapter.)

The irq_desc_t descriptor

An `irq_desc` array includes `NR_IRQS` `irq_desc_t` descriptors, which include the following fields:

`status`
    A set of flags describing the IRQ line status.

    `IRQ_INPROGRESS`
        A handler for the IRQ is being executed.

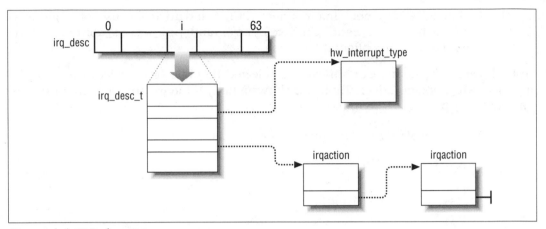

Figure 4-4. IRQ descriptors

IRQ_DISABLED
> The IRQ line has been deliberately disabled by a device driver.

IRQ_PENDING
> An IRQ has occurred on the line; its occurrence has been acknowledged to the PIC, but it has not yet been serviced by the kernel.

IRQ_REPLAY
> The IRQ line has been disabled but the previous IRQ occurrence has not yet been acknowledged to the PIC.

IRQ_AUTODETECT
> The kernel is using the IRQ line while performing a hardware device probe.

IRQ_WAITING
> The kernel is using the IRQ line while performing a hardware device probe; moreover, the corresponding interrupt has not been raised.

`handler`
> Points to the `hw_interrupt_type` descriptor that identifies the PIC circuit servicing the IRQ line.

`action`
> Identifies the interrupt service routines to be invoked when the IRQ occurs. The field points to the first element of the list of `irqaction` descriptors associated with the IRQ. The `irqaction` descriptor is described briefly later in the chapter.

`depth`
> Shows 0 if the IRQ line is enabled and a positive value if it has been disabled at least once. Every time the `disable_irq()` function is invoked, it increments this field; if `depth` was equal to 0, the function disables the IRQ line. Conversely, each invocation of the `enable_irq()` function decrements the field; if `depth` becomes 0, the function enables the IRQ line.

During system initialization, the `init_IRQ()` function sets the `status` field of each IRQ main descriptor to `IRQ_DISABLED` as follows:

```
for (i=0; i<NR_IRQS; i++)
    irq_desc[i].status = IRQ_DISABLED;
```

It then updates the IDT by replacing the provisional interrupt gates with the final ones. This is accomplished through the following statements:

```
for (i = 0; i < NR_IRQS; i++)
    set_intr_gate(0x20+i,interrupt[i]);
```

This code looks in the `interrupt` array to find the interrupt handler addresses that it uses to set up the interrupt gates. The interrupt handler for IRQn is named IRQn_ `interrupt()` (see the later section "Saving the Registers for the Interrupt Handler").

The hw_interrupt_type descriptor

This descriptor includes a group of pointers to the low-level I/O routines that interact with a specific PIC circuit. Linux supports, in addition to the 8259A chip that was mentioned near the beginning of this chapter, several other PIC circuits such as the SMP IO-APIC, PIIX4's internal 8259 PIC, and SGI's Visual Workstation Cobalt (IO-)APIC. But for the sake of simplifying the explanation, we'll assume in this chapter that our computer is a uniprocessor with two 8259A PICs, which provides the 16 standard IRQs discussed earlier. In this case, the `handler` field in each of the 16 `irq_desc_t` descriptors points to the `i8259A_irq_type` variable, which describes the 8259A PIC. This variable is initialized as follows:

```
struct hw_interrupt_type i8259A_irq_type = {
    "XT-PIC",
    startup_8259A_irq,
    shutdown_8259A_irq,
    do_8259A_IRQ,
    enable_8259A_irq,
    disable_8259A_irq
};
```

The first field in this structure, `"XT-PIC"`, is a name. Following that, `i8259A_irq_type` includes pointers to five different functions used to program the PIC. The first two functions start up and shut down an IRQ line of the chip, respectively. But in the case of the 8259A chip these functions coincide with the last two functions, which enable and disable the line. The `do_8259A_IRQ()` function will be described in the later section "The do_IRQ() Function."

The irqaction descriptor

As described earlier, multiple devices can share a single IRQ. Therefore, the kernel maintains `irqaction` descriptors, each of which refers to a specific hardware device and a specific interrupt. The descriptor includes the following fields.

handler
> Points to the interrupt service routine for an I/O device. This is the key field that allows many devices to share the same IRQ.

flags
> Describes the relationships between IRQ line and I/O device in a set of flags:

> SA_INTERRUPT
>> The handler must execute with interrupts disabled.

> SA_SHIRQ
>> The device permits its IRQ line to be shared with other devices.

> SA_SAMPLE_RANDOM
>> The device may be considered as a source of events occurring randomly; it can thus be used by the kernel random number generator. (Users can access this feature by taking random numbers from the */dev/random* and */dev/urandom* device files.)

> SA_PROBE
>> The kernel is using the IRQ line while performing a hardware device probe.

name
> Names of the I/O device (shown when listing the serviced IRQs by reading the */proc/interrupts* file).

dev_id
> The major and minor numbers that identify the I/O device (see the section "Device Files" in Chapter 13, *Managing I/O Devices*).

next
> Points to the next element of a list of irqaction descriptors. The elements in the list refer to hardware devices that share the same IRQ.

Saving the Registers for the Interrupt Handler

As with other context switches, the need to save registers leaves the kernel developer a somewhat messy coding job because the registers have to be saved and restored using assembly language code, but within those operations the processor is expected to call and return from a C function. In this section we'll describe the assembly language task of handling registers, while in the next we'll show some of the acrobatics required in the C function that is subsequently invoked.

Saving registers is the first task of the interrupt handler. As already mentioned, the interrupt handler for IRQ*n* is named IRQ*n*_interrupt, and its address is included in the interrupt gate stored in the proper IDT entry.

The same BUILD_IRQ macro is duplicated 16 times, once for each IRQ number, in order to yield 16 different interrupt handler entry points. Each BUILD_IRQ expands to the following assembly language fragment:

```
IRQn_interrupt:
    pushl $n-256
    jmp common_interrupt
```

The result is to save on the stack the IRQ number associated with the interrupt minus 256;[*] the same code for all interrupt handlers can then be executed while referring to this number. The common code can be found in the BUILD_COMMON_IRQ macro, which expands to the following assembly language fragment:

```
common_interrupt:
    SAVE_ALL
    call do_IRQ
    jmp ret_from_intr
```

The SAVE_ALL macro, in turn, expands to the following fragment:

```
cld
push %es
push %ds
pushl %eax
pushl %ebp
pushl %edi
pushl %esi
pushl %edx
pushl %ecx
pushl %ebx
movl $__KERNEL_DS,%edx
mov %dx,%ds
mov %dx,%es
```

SAVE_ALL saves all the CPU registers that may be used by the interrupt handler on the stack, except for eflags, cs, eip, ss, and esp, which are already saved automatically by the control unit (see the earlier section "Hardware Handling of Interrupts and Exceptions"). The macro then loads the selector of the kernel data segment into ds and es.

After saving the registers, BUILD_COMMON_IRQ invokes the do_IRQ() function and jumps to the ret_from_intr() address (see the later section "Returning from Interrupts and Exceptions").

The do_IRQ() Function

The do_IRQ() function is invoked to execute all interrupt service routines associated with an interrupt. When it starts, the kernel stack contains from the top down:

* The do_IRQ() return address
* The group of register values pushed on by SAVE_ALL

---

[*] Subtracting 256 from an IRQ number yields a negative number. Positive numbers are reserved to identify system calls (see Chapter 8).

- The encoding of the IRQ number

- The registers saved automatically by the control unit when it recognized the interrupt

Since the C compiler places all the parameters on top of the stack, the `do_IRQ()` function is declared as follows:

```
void do_IRQ(struct pt_regs regs)
```

where the **pt_regs** structure consists of 15 fields:

- The first nine fields correspond to the register values pushed by `SAVE_ALL`.

- The tenth field, referenced through a field called `orig_eax`, encodes the IRQ number.

- The remaining fields correspond to the register values pushed on automatically by the control unit.*

The `do_IRQ()` function can thus read the IRQ passed as a parameter and decode it as follows:

```
irq = regs.orig_eax & 0xff;
```

The function then executes:

```
irq_desc[irq].handler->handle(irq, &regs);
```

The **handler** field points to the **hw_interrupt_type** descriptor that refers to the PIC model servicing the IRQ line (see the earlier section "IRQ Data Structures"). Assuming that the PIC is an 8259A, the **handle** field points to the `do_8259A_IRQ()` function, which is thus executed.

The `do_8259A_IRQ()` function starts by invoking the `mask_and_ack_8259A()` function, which acknowledges the interrupt to the PIC and disables further interrupts with the same IRQ number.

Then the function checks whether the handler is willing to deal with the interrupt and whether it is already handling it; to that end, it reads the values of the IRQ_DISABLED and IRQ_INPROGRESS flags stored in the **status** field of the IRQ main descriptor. If both flags are cleared, the function picks up the pointer to the first **irqaction** descriptor from the **action** field and sets the IRQ_INPROGRESS flag. It then invokes `handle_IRQ_event()`, which executes each interrupt service routine in turn through the following code. As mentioned previously, if the IRQ is shared by several devices, each corresponding interrupt service routine must be invoked because the kernel does not know which device issued the interrupt:

---

* The `ret_from_intr()` return address is missing from the **pt_regs** structure because the C compiler expects a return address on top of the stack and takes this into account when generating the instructions to address parameters.

```
do {
    action->handler(irq, action->dev_id, regs);
    action = action->next;
} while (action);
```

Notice that the kernel cannot break the loop as soon as one ISR has claimed the interrupt because another device on the same IRQ line might need to be serviced.

Finally, the `do_8259A_IRQ()` function cleans things up by clearing the `IRQ_INPROGRESS` flag just mentioned. Moreover, if the `IRQ_DISABLED` flag is not set, the function invokes the low-level `enable_8259A_irq()` function to enable interrupts that come from the IRQ line.

The control now returns to `do_IRQ()`, which checks whether "bottom halves" tasks are waiting to be executed. (As we shall see, a queue of such bottom halves is maintained by the kernel.) If bottom halves are waiting, the function invokes the `do_bottom_half()` function we'll describe shortly. Finally, `do_IRQ()` terminates and control is transferred to the `ret_from_intr` address.

Interrupt Service Routines

As mentioned previously, an interrupt service routine implements a device-specific operation. All of them act on the same parameters:

`irq`
    The IRQ number

`dev_id`
    The device identifier

`regs`
    A pointer to the Kernel Mode stack area containing the registers saved right after the interrupt occurred

The first parameter allows a single ISR to handle several IRQ lines, the second one allows a single ISR to take care of several devices of the same type, and the last one allows the ISR to access the execution context of the interrupted kernel control path. In practice, most ISRs do not use these parameters.

The `SA_INTERRUPT` flag of the main IRQ descriptor determines whether interrupts are enabled or disabled when the `do_IRQ()` function invokes an ISR. An ISR that has been invoked with the interrupts in one state is allowed to put them in the opposite state through an assembly language instruction: `cli` to disable interrupts and `sti` to enable them.

The structure of an ISR depends on the characteristics of the device handled. We'll give a few examples of ISRs in Chapters 5 and 13.

Bottom Half

A *bottom half* is a low-priority function, usually related to interrupt handling, that is waiting for the kernel to find a convenient moment to run it. Bottom halves that are waiting will be executed only when one of the following events occurs:

- The kernel finishes handling a system call.

- The kernel finishes handling an exception.

- The kernel terminates the `do_IRQ()` function—that is, it finishes handling an interrupt.

- The kernel executes the `schedule()` function to select a new process to run on the CPU.

Thus, when an interrupt service routine activates a bottom half, a long time interval can occur before it is executed.* But as we have seen, the existence of bottom halves is very important to fulfill the kernel's responsibility to service interrupts from multiple devices quickly. This book doesn't talk too much about the contents of bottom halves—they depend on the particular tasks needed to service devices—but just about how the kernel maintains and invokes the bottom halves. You will find an example of a specific bottom half in the section "The TIMER_BH Bottom Half Functions" in Chapter 5.

Linux makes use of an array called the `bh_base` table to group all bottom halves together. It is an array of pointers to bottom halves and can include up to 32 entries, one for each type of bottom half. In practice, Linux uses about half of them; the types are listed in Table 4-3. As you can see from the table, some of the bottom halves are associated with hardware devices that are not necessarily installed in the system or that are specific to platforms besides the IBM PC compatible. But `TIMER_BH`, `CONSOLE_BH`, `TQUEUE_BH`, `SERIAL_BH`, `IMMEDIATE_BH`, and `KEYBOARD_BH` see widespread use.

Table 4-3. The Linux Bottom Halves

Bottom Half	Peripheral Device
AURORA_BH	Aurora multiport card (SPARC)
CM206_BH	CD-ROM Philips/LMS cm206 disk
CONSOLE_BH	Virtual console
CYCLADES_BH	Cyclades Cyclom-Y serial multiport
DIGI_BH	DigiBoard PC/Xe
ESP_BH	Hayes ESP serial card
IMMEDIATE_BH	Immediate task queue

---

* However, the execution of bottom halves will not be deferred forever: the CPU does not switch back to User Mode until there are no bottom halves to be executed; see the later section "Returning from Interrupts and Exceptions."

Table 4-3. The Linux Bottom Halves (continued)

Bottom Half	Peripheral Device
ISICOM_BH	MultiTech's ISI cards
JS_BH	Joystick (PC IBM compatible)
KEYBOARD_BH	Keyboard
MACSERIAL_BH	Power Macintosh's serial port
NET_BH	Network interface
RISCOM8_BH	RISCom/8
SCSI_BH	SCSI interface
SERIAL_BH	Serial port
SPECIALIX_BH	Specialix IO8+
TIMER_BH	Timer
TQUEUE_BH	Periodic task queue

Activating and tracking the state of bottom halves

Before invoking a bottom half for the first time, it must be initialized. This is done by invoking the **init_bh(n, routine)** function, which inserts the **routine** address in the *n*th entry of **bh_base**. Conversely, **remove_bh(n)** removes the *n*th bottom half from the table.

Once a bottom half has been initialized, it can be "activated," thus executed any time one of the previously mentioned events occurs. The **mark_bh(n)** function is used by interrupt handlers to activate the *n*th bottom half. To keep track of the state of all these bottom halves, the **bh_active** variable stores 32 flags that specify which bottom halves are currently activated. When a bottom half concludes its execution, the kernel clears the corresponding **bh_active** flag; thus, any activation causes exactly one execution.

The **do_bottom_half()** function is used to start executing all currently active unmasked bottom halves; it enables the maskable interrupts and then invokes **run_bottom_halves()**. This function makes sure that only one bottom half is ever active at a time by executing the following C code fragment:

```
active = bh_mask & bh_active;
bh_active &= ~active;
bh = bh_base;
do {
    if (active & 1)
        (*bh)();
    bh++;
    active >>= 1;
} while (active);
```

The flags in `bh_active` that refer to the group of bottom halves that must be executed are cleared. This ensures that each bottom half activation causes exactly one execution of the corresponding function.

Each bottom half can be individually "masked"; if this is the case, it won't be executed even if it is activated. The `bh_mask` variable stores 32 bits that specify which bottom halves are currently masked. The `disable_bh(n)` and `enable_bh(n)` functions act on the nth flag of `bh_mask`; they are used to mask and unmask a bottom half, respectively.

Here's why masking bottom halves is useful. Assume that a kernel function is modifying some kernel data structure when an exception (for instance, a "Page fault") occurs. After the kernel finishes handling the exception, all active nonmasked bottom halves will be executed. If one of the bottom halves accesses the same kernel data structure as the suspended kernel function, both the bottom half and the kernel function will find the data structure in a nonconsistent state. In order to avoid this race condition, the kernel function must mask all bottom halves that access the data structure.

Unfortunately, the `bh_mask` variable does not always ensure that bottom halves remain correctly masked. For instance, let us suppose that some bottom half B is masked by a kernel control path P1, which is then interrupted by another kernel control path P2. P2 once again masks the bottom half B, performs its own operations, and terminates by unmasking B. Now P1 resumes its execution, but B is (incorrectly) unmasked.

It is thus necessary to use counters rather than a simple binary flag to keep track of masking and to add one more table called `bh_mask_count` whose entries contain the masking level of each bottom half. The `disable_bh(n)` and `enable_bh(n)` functions update `bh_mask_count[n]` before acting on the nth flag of `bh_mask`.

Extending a bottom half

The motivation for introducing bottom halves is to allow a limited number of functions related to interrupt handling to be executed in a deferred manner. This approach has been stretched in two directions:

- To allow a generic kernel function, and not only a function that services an interrupt, to be executed as a bottom half

- To allow several kernel functions, instead of a single one, to be associated with a bottom half

Groups of functions are represented by *task queues*, which are lists of `struct tq_struct` elements having the following structure:

```
struct tq_struct {
    struct tq_struct *next;    /* linked list of active bh's */
    unsigned long sync;        /* must be initialized to zero */
```

```
        void (*routine)(void *);   /* function to call */
        void *data;                /* argument to function */
    };
```

As we shall see in Chapter 13, I/O device drivers make intensive use of task queues to require the execution of some functions when a specific interrupt occurs.

The DECLARE_TASK_QUEUE macro is used to allocate a new task queue, while queue_task() inserts a new function in a task queue. The run_task_queue() function executes all the functions included in a given task queue. It's worth mentioning two particular task queues, each associated with a specific bottom half:

- The tq_immediate task queue, run by the IMMEDIATE_BH bottom half, includes kernel functions to be executed together with the standard bottom halves. The kernel invokes mark_bh() to activate the IMMEDIATE_BH bottom half whenever a function is added to the tq_immediate task queue.

- The tq_timer task queue is run by the TQUEUE_BH bottom half, which is activated at every timer interrupt. As we'll see in Chapter 5, that means it runs about every 10 ms.

Dynamic Handling of IRQ Lines

With the exception of IRQ0, IRQ2, and IRQ13, the remaining 13 IRQs are dynamically handled. There is, therefore, a way in which the same interrupt can be used by several hardware devices even if they do not allow IRQ sharing: the trick consists in serializing the activation of the hardware devices so that just one at a time owns the IRQ line.

Before activating a device that is going to make use of an IRQ line, the corresponding driver invokes request_irq(). This function creates a new irqaction descriptor and initializes it with the parameter values; it then invokes the setup_x86_irq() function to insert the descriptor in the proper IRQ list. The device driver aborts the operation if setup_x86_irq() returns an error code, which means that the IRQ line is already in use by another device that does not allow interrupt sharing. When the device operation is concluded, the driver invokes the free_irq() function to remove the descriptor from the IRQ list and release the memory area.

Let us see how this scheme works on a simple example. Assume a program wants to address the */dev/fd0* device file, that is, the device file that corresponds to the first floppy disk on the system.* The program can do this either by directly accessing */dev/fd0* or by mounting a filesystem on it. Floppy disk controllers are usually assigned IRQ6; given this, the floppy driver will issue the following request:

```
request_irq(6, floppy_interrupt,
        SA_INTERRUPT|SA_SAMPLE_RANDOM, "floppy", NULL);
```

---

* Floppy disks are "old" devices that do not usually allow IRQ sharing.

As can be observed, the `floppy_interrupt()` interrupt service routine must execute with the interrupts disabled (`SA_INTERRUPT` set) and no sharing of the IRQ (`SA_SHIRQ` flag cleared). When the operation on the floppy disk is concluded (either the I/O operation on */dev/fd0* terminates or the filesystem is unmounted), the driver releases IRQ6:

```
free_irq(6, NULL);
```

In order to insert an `irqaction` descriptor in the proper list, the kernel invokes the `setup_x86_irq()` function, passing to it the parameters `irq_nr`, the IRQ number, and `new`, the address of a previously allocated `irqaction` descriptor. This function:

1. Checks whether another device is already using the `irq_nr` IRQ and, if so, whether the `SA_SHIRQ` flags in the `irqaction` descriptors of both devices specify that the IRQ line can be shared. Returns an error code if the IRQ line cannot be used.

2. Adds `*new` (the new `irqaction` descriptor) at the end of the list to which `irq_desc[irq_nr]->action` points.

3. If no other device is sharing the same IRQ, clears the `IRQ_DISABLED` and `IRQ_INPROGRESS` flags in the `flags` field of `*new` and reprograms the PIC to make sure that IRQ signals are enabled.

Here is an example of how `setup_x86_irq()` is used, drawn from system initialization. The kernel initializes the `irq0` descriptor of the interval timer device by executing the following instructions in the `time_init()` function (see Chapter 5):

```
struct irqaction irq0 =
    {timer_interrupt, SA_INTERRUPT, 0, "timer", NULL,};
setup_x86_irq(0, &irq0);
```

First, the `irq0` variable of type `irqaction` is initialized: the `handler` field is set to the address of the `timer_interrupt()` function, the `flags` field is set to `SA_INTERRUPT`, the `name` field is set to "timer", and the last field is set to `NULL` to show that no `dev_id` value is used. Next, the kernel invokes `setup_x86_irq()` to insert `irq0` in the list of `irqaction` descriptors associated with IRQ0.

Similarly, the kernel initializes the `irqaction` descriptors associated with IRQ2 and IRQ13 and inserts them in the proper lists of `irqaction` descriptors by executing the following instructions in the `init_IRQ()` function:

```
struct irqaction irq2 =
    {no_action, 0, 0, "cascade", NULL,};
struct irqaction irq13 =
    {math_error_irq, 0, 0, "fpu", NULL,};
setup_x86_irq(2, &irq2);
setup_x86_irq(13, &irq13);
```

Returning from Interrupts and Exceptions

We will finish the chapter by examining the termination phase of interrupt and exception handlers. Although the main objective is clear, namely, to resume execution of some program, several issues must be considered before doing it:

- The number of kernel control paths being concurrently executed: if there is just one, the CPU must switch back to User Mode.

- Active bottom halves to be executed: if there are some, they must be executed.

- Pending process switch requests: if there is any request, the kernel must perform process scheduling; otherwise, control is returned to the current process.

- Pending signals: if a signal has been sent to the current process, it must be handled.

The kernel assembly language code that accomplishes all these things is not, technically speaking, a function, since control is never returned to the functions that invoke it. It is a piece of code with three different entry points called ret_from_intr, ret_from_sys_call, and ret_from_exception. We will refer to it as three different functions since this makes the description simpler. We shall thus refer quite often to the following three entry points as functions:

ret_from_intr()
> Terminates interrupt handlers

ret_from_sys_call()
> Terminates system calls, that is, kernel control paths engendered by 0x80 exceptions

ret_from_exception()
> Terminates all exceptions except the 0x80 ones

The general flow diagram with the corresponding three entry points is illustrated in Figure 4-5. Besides these three labels, a few other ones have been added to allow you to relate the assembly language code more easily to the flow diagram. Let us now examine in detail how the termination occurs in each case.

The ret_from_intr() Function

When ret_from_intr() is invoked, the do_IRQ() function has already executed all active bottom halves (see the earlier section "The do_IRQ() Function"). The initial part of the ret_from_intr() function is implemented by the following code:

```
ret_from_intr:
  movl %esp, %ebx
  andl $0xffffe000, %ebx
  movl 0x30(%esp), %eax
  movb 0x2c(%esp), %al
  testl $(0x00020000 | 3), %eax
```

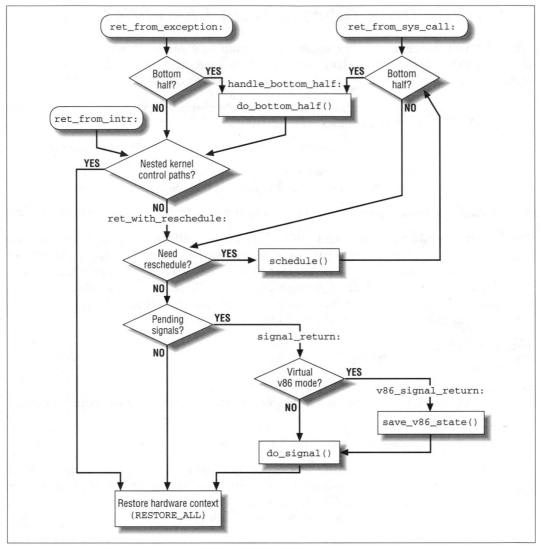

Figure 4-5. Returning from interrupts and exceptions

```
jne ret_with_reschedule
RESTORE_ALL
```

The address of the **current**'s process descriptor is stored in **ebx** (see the section "Identifying a Process" in Chapter 3). Then the values of the **cs** and **eflags** registers, which were pushed on the stack when the interrupt occurred, are used by the function to determine whether the interrupted program was running in Kernel Mode. If so, a nesting of interrupts has occurred and the interrupted kernel control path is restarted by executing the following code, yielded by the **RESTORE_ALL** macro:

```
popl %ebx
popl %ecx
popl %edx
popl %esi
popl %edi
popl %ebp
popl %eax
popl %ds
popl %es
addl $4,%esp
iret
```

This macro loads the registers with the values saved by the SAVE_ALL macro and yields control to the interrupted program by executing the iret instruction.

If, on the other hand, the interrupted program was running in User Mode or if the VM flag of eflags was set,[*] a jump is made to the ret_with_reschedule address:

```
ret_with_reschedule:
  cmpl $0,20(%ebx)
  jne reschedule
  cmpl $0,8(%ebx)
  jne signal_return
  RESTORE_ALL
```

As we said previously, the ebx register points to the current process descriptor; within that descriptor, the need_resched field is at offset 20, which is checked by the first cmpl instruction. Therefore, if the need_resched field is 1, the schedule() function is invoked to perform a process switch.

The offset of the sigpending field inside the process descriptor is 8. If it is null, current resumes execution in User Mode. Otherwise, the code jumps to signal_return to process the pending signals of current:

```
signal_return:
  sti
  testl $(0x00020000),0x30(%esp)
  movl %esp,%eax
  jne v86_signal_return
  xorl %edx,%edx
  call do_signal
  RESTORE_ALL
v86_signal_return:
  call save_v86_state
  movl %eax,%esp
  xorl %edx,%edx
  call do_signal
  RESTORE_ALL
```

---

[*] This flag allows programs to be executed in Virtual-8086 Mode; see the Pentium manuals for further details.

If the interrupted process was in VM86 mode, the `save_v86_state()` function is invoked. The `do_signal()` function (see Chapter 9) is then invoked to handle the pending signals. Finally, `current` can resume execution in User Mode.

The ret_from_sys_call() Function

The `ret_from_sys_call()` function is equivalent to the following assembly language code:

```
ret_from_sys_call:
    movl bh_mask, %eax
    andl bh_active, %eax
    je ret_with_reschedule
handle_bottom_half:
    call do_bottom_half
    jmp ret_from_intr
```

First, the `bh_mask` and `bh_active` variables are checked to determine whether active unmasked bottom halves exist. If no bottom half must be executed, a jump is made to the `ret_with_reschedule` address. Otherwise, the `do_bottom_half()` function is invoked; then control is transferred to `ret_from_intr`.

The ret_from_exception() Function

The `ret_from_exception()` function is equivalent to the following assembly language code:

```
ret_from_exception:
    movl bh_mask,%eax
    andl bh_active,%eax
    jne handle_bottom_half
    jmp ret_from_intr
```

First, the `bh_mask` and `bh_active` global variables are checked to determine whether active unmasked bottom halves exist. If so, they are executed. In any case, a jump is made to the `ret_from_intr` address. Therefore exceptions terminate in the same way as interrupts.

Anticipating Linux 2.4

Linux 2.4 introduces a new mechanism called *software interrupt*. Software interrupts are similar to Linux 2.2's bottom halves, in that they allow you to defer the execution of a kernel function. However, while bottom halves were strictly serialized (because no two bottom halves can be executed at the same time even on different CPUs), software interrupts are not serialized in any way. It is quite possible that two CPUs run two instances of the same software interrupt at the same time. In this case, of course, the software interrupt must be reentrant. Networking, in particular, greatly benefits from software interrupts: it is much more efficient on multiprocessor systems because it uses two software interrupts in place of the old NET_BH bottom half.

Linux 2.4 introduces another mechanism similar to the bottom half called *tasklet*. Tasklets are built on top of software interrupts, but they are serialized with respect to themselves: two CPUs can execute two tasklets at the same time, but these tasklets must be different. Tasklets are much easier to write than generic software interrupts, because they need not be reentrant.

Bottom halves continue to exist in Linux 2.4, but they are now built on top of tasklets. As usual, no two bottom halves can execute at the same time, not even on two different CPUs of a multiprocessor system. Device driver developers are expected to update their old drivers and replace bottom halves with tasklets, because bottom halves degrade significantly the performance of multiprocessor systems.

On the hardware side, Linux 2.4 now supports IO-APIC chips even in uniprocessor systems and is able to handle several external IO-APIC chips in multiprocessor systems. (This feature was required for porting Linux to large enterprise systems.)

CHAPTER FIVE

TIMING MEASUREMENTS

Countless computerized activities are driven by timing measurements, often behind the user's back. For instance, if the screen is automatically switched off after you have stopped using the computer's console, this is due to a timer that allows the kernel to keep track of how much time has elapsed since you pushed a key or moved the mouse. If you receive a warning from the system asking you to remove a set of unused files, this is the outcome of a program that identifies all user files that have not been accessed for a long time. In order to do these things, programs must be able to retrieve from each file a timestamp identifying its last access time, and therefore such a timestamp must be automatically written by the kernel. More significantly, timing drives process switches along with even more basic kernel activities like checking for time-outs.

We can distinguish two main kinds of timing measurement that must be performed by the Linux kernel:

- Keeping the current time and date, so that they can be returned to user programs through the `time()`, `ftime()`, and `gettimeofday()` system calls (see the section "The time(), ftime(), and gettimeofday() System Calls" later in this chapter) and used by the kernel itself as timestamps for files and network packets

- Maintaining timers, that is, mechanisms that are able to notify the kernel (see the later section "The Role of Timers") or a user program (see the later section "The setitimer() and alarm() System Calls") that a certain interval of time has elapsed

Timing measurements are performed by several hardware circuits based on fixed-frequency oscillators and counters. This chapter consists of three different parts. The first section describes the hardware devices that underlie timing; the next three sections describe the kernel data structures and functions introduced to measure time; then a section discusses the system calls related to timing measurements and the corresponding service routines.

Hardware Clocks

The kernel must explicitly interact with three clocks: the Real Time Clock, the Time Stamp Counter, and the Programmable Interval Timer. The first two hardware devices allow the kernel to keep track of the current time of day; the latter device is programmed by the kernel so that it issues interrupts at a fixed, predefined frequency. Such periodic interrupts are crucial for implementing the timers used by the kernel and the user programs.

Real Time Clock

All PCs include a clock called *Real Time Clock* (*RTC*), which is independent of the CPU and all other chips.

The RTC continues to tick even when the PC is switched off, since it is energized by a small battery or accumulator. The CMOS RAM and RTC are integrated in a single chip, the Motorola 146818 or an equivalent.

The RTC is capable of issuing periodic interrupts on IRQ8 at frequencies ranging between 2 Hz and 8192 Hz. It can also be programmed to activate the IRQ8 line when the RTC reaches a specific value, thus working as an alarm clock.

Linux uses the RTC only to derive the time and date; however, it allows processes to program the RTC by acting on the */dev/rtc* device file (see Chapter 13, *Managing I/O Devices*). The kernel accesses the RTC through the 0x70 and 0x71 I/O ports. The system administrator can set up the clock by executing the */sbin/clock* system program that acts directly on these two I/O ports.

Time Stamp Counter

All Intel 80x86 microprocessors include a CLK input pin, which receives the clock signal of an external oscillator.

Starting with the Pentium, many recent Intel 80x86 microprocessors include a 64-bit *Time Stamp Counter* (*TSC*) register that can be read by means of the rdtsc assembly language instruction. This register is a counter that is incremented at each clock signal: if, for instance, the clock ticks at 400 MHz, the Time Stamp Counter is incremented once every 2.5 nanoseconds.

Linux takes advantage of this register to get much more accurate time measurements than the ones delivered by the Programmable Interval Timer. In order to do this, Linux must determine the clock signal frequency while initializing the system: in fact, since this frequency is not declared when compiling the kernel, the same kernel image may run on CPUs whose clocks may tick at any frequency. The task of figuring out the actual frequency is accomplished during the system's boot by the `calibrate_tsc()` function, which returns the number:

$$\left\lceil \frac{2^{32}}{f} \right\rceil , \quad f = \text{CPU frequency in MHz}$$

The value of f is computed by counting the number of clock signals that occur in a relatively long time interval, namely 50.00077 milliseconds. This time constant is produced by setting up one of the channels of the Programmable Interval Timer properly (see the next section). The long execution time of `calibrate_tsc()` does not create problems, since the function is invoked only during system initialization.

Programmable Interval Timer

Besides the Real Time Clock and the Time Stamp Counter, IBM-compatible PCs include a third type of time-measuring device called *Programmable Interval Timer* (*PIT*). The role of a PIT is similar to the alarm clock of a microwave oven: to make the user aware that the cooking time interval has elapsed. Instead of ringing a bell, this device issues a special interrupt called *timer interrupt*, which notifies the kernel that one more time interval has elapsed.[*] Another difference from the alarm clock is that the PIT goes on issuing interrupts forever at some fixed frequency established by the kernel. Each IBM-compatible PC includes at least one PIT, which is usually implemented by a 8254 CMOS chip using the `0x40–0x43` I/O ports.

As we shall see in detail in the next paragraphs, Linux programs the first PC's PIT to issue timer interrupts on the IRQ0 at a (roughly) 100-Hz frequency, that is, once every 10 milliseconds. This time interval is called a *tick*, and its length in microseconds is stored in the `tick` variable. The ticks beat time for all activities in the system; in some sense, they are like the ticks sounded by a metronome while a musician is rehearsing.

Generally speaking, shorter ticks yield better system responsiveness. This is because system responsiveness largely depends on how fast a running process is preempted by a higher-priority process once it becomes runnable (see Chapter 10, *Process Scheduling*); moreover, the kernel usually checks whether the running process should be preempted while handling the timer interrupt. This is a trade-off however: shorter ticks require the CPU to spend a larger fraction of its time in Kernel Mode, that is, a smaller fraction of time in User Mode. As a consequence, user programs run slower. Therefore, only very powerful machines can adopt very short ticks and afford the consequent overhead. Currently, only Compaq's Alpha port of the Linux kernel issues 1024 timer interrupts per second, corresponding to a tick of roughly 1 millisecond.

---

[*] The PIT is also used to drive an audio amplifier connected to the computer's internal speaker.

A few macros in the Linux code yield some constants that determine the frequency of timer interrupts:

- HZ yields the number of timer interrupts per second, that is, the frequency of timer interrupts. This value is set to 100 for IBM PCs and most other hardware platforms.

- CLOCK_TICK_RATE yields the value 1193180, which is the 8254 chip's internal oscillator frequency.

- LATCH yields the ratio between CLOCK_TICK_RATE and HZ. It is used to program the PIT.

The first PIT is initialized by init_IRQ() as follows:

```
outb_p(0x34,0x43);
outb_p(LATCH & 0xff , 0x40);
outb(LATCH >> 8 , 0x40);
```

The outb() C function is equivalent to the outb assembly language instruction: it copies the first operand into the I/O port specified as the second operand. The outb_p() function is similar to outb(), except that it introduces a pause by executing a no-op instruction. The first outb_p() invocation is a command to the PIT to issue interrupts at a new rate. The next two outb_p() and outb() invocations supply the new interrupt rate to the device. The 16-bit LATCH constant is sent to the 8-bit 0x40 I/O port of the device as 2 consecutive bytes. As a result, the PIT will issue timer interrupts at a (roughly) 100-Hz frequency, that is, once every 10 ms.

Now that we understand what the hardware timers do, the following sections describe all the actions performed by the kernel when it receives a timer interrupt—that is, when a tick has elapsed.

The Timer Interrupt Handler

Each occurrence of a timer interrupt triggers the following major activities:

- Updates the time elapsed since system startup.

- Updates the time and date.

- Determines how long the current process has been running on the CPU and preempts it if it has exceeded the time allocated to it. The allocation of time slots (also called *quanta*) is discussed in Chapter 10.

- Updates resource usage statistics.

- Checks whether the interval of time associated with each software timer (see the later section "The Role of Timers") has elapsed; if so, invokes the proper function.

The first activity is considered urgent, so it is performed by the timer interrupt handler itself. The remaining four activities are less urgent; they are performed by the functions invoked by the `TIMER_BH` and `TQUEUE_BH` bottom halves (see the section "Bottom Half" in Chapter 4, *Interrupts and Exceptions*).

The kernel uses two basic timekeeping functions: one to keep the current time up to date and another to count the number of microseconds that have elapsed within the current second. There are two different ways to maintain such values: a more precise method that is available if the chip has a Time Stamp Counter (TSC) and a less precise method used in other cases. So the kernel creates two variables to store the functions it uses, pointing the variables to the functions using the TSC if it exists:

- The current time is calculated by `do_gettimeofday()` if the CPU has the TSC register and by `do_normal_gettime()` otherwise. A pointer to the proper function is stored in the variable `do_get_fast_time`.

- The number of microseconds is calculated by `do_fast_gettimeoffset()` when the TSC register is available and by `do_slow_gettimeoffset()` otherwise. The address of this function is stored in the variable `do_gettimeoffset`.

The `time_init()` function, which runs during kernel startup, sets the variables to point to the right functions and sets up the interrupt gate corresponding to IRQ0.

PIT's Interrupt Service Routine

Once the IRQ0 interrupt gate has been initialized, the `handler` field of IRQ0's `irqaction` descriptor contains the address of the `timer_interrupt()` function. This function starts running with the interrupts disabled, since the `status` field of IRQ0's main descriptor has the `SA_INTERRUPT` flag set. It performs the following steps:

1. If the CPU has a TSC register, it performs the following substeps:

   a. Executes an `rdtsc` Assembly instruction to store the value of the TSC register in the `last_tsc_low` variable

   b. Reads the state of the 8254 chip device internal oscillator and computes the delay between the timer interrupt occurrence and the execution of the interrupt service routine[*]

   c. Stores that delay (in microseconds) in the `delay_at_last_interrupt` variable

2. It invokes `do_timer_interrupt()`.

`do_timer_interrupt()`, which may be considered as the interrupt service routine common to all 80x86 models, executes the following operations:

---

[*] The 8254 oscillator drives a counter that is continuously decremented. When the counter becomes 0, the chip raises an IRQ0. So reading the counter indicates how much time has elapsed since the interrupt occurred.

1. It invokes the do_timer() function, which is fully explained shortly.

2. If an adjtimex() system call has been issued, it invokes the set_rtc_mmss() function once every 660 seconds, that is, every 11 minutes, to adjust the Real Time Clock. This feature helps systems on a network synchronize their clocks (see the later section "The adjtimex() System Call").

The do_timer() function, which runs with the interrupts disabled, must be executed as quickly as possible. For this reason, it simply updates one fundamental value—the time elapsed from system startup—while delegating all remaining activities to two bottom halves. The function refers to three main variables related to timing measurements; the first is the fundamental uptime just mentioned, while the latter two are needed to store lost ticks that take place before the bottom half functions have a chance to run. Thus, the first is absolute (it just keeps incrementing) while the other two are relative to another variable called xtime that stores the approximate current time. (This variable will be described in the later section "Updating the Time and Date").

The three do_timer() variables are:

jiffies
> The number of elapsed ticks since the system was started; it is set to 0 during kernel initialization and incremented by 1 when a timer interrupt occurs, that is, on every tick.*

lost_ticks
> The number of ticks that has occurred since the last update of xtime.

lost_ticks_system
> The number of ticks that has occurred while the process was running in Kernel Mode since the last update of xtime. The user_mode macro examines the CPL field of the cs register saved in the stack to determine if the process was running in Kernel Mode.

The do_timer() function is equivalent to:

```
void do_timer(struct pt_regs * regs)
{
    jiffies++;
    lost_ticks++;
    mark_bh(TIMER_BH);
    if (!user_mode(regs))
        lost_ticks_system++;
    if (tq_timer)
        mark_bh(TQUEUE_BH);
}
```

---

* Since jiffies is stored as a 32-bit unsigned integer, it returns to 0 about 497 days after the systems has been booted.

Note that the `TQUEUE_BH` bottom half is activated only if the `tq_timer` task queue is not empty (see the section "Bottom Half" in Chapter 4).

The TIMER_BH Bottom Half Functions

The `timer_bh()` function associated with the `TIMER_BH` bottom half invokes the `update_times()`, `run_old_timers()`, and `run_timer_list()` auxiliary functions, which are described next.

Updating the Time and Date

The `xtime` variable of type `struct timeval` is where user programs get the current time and date. The kernel also occasionally refers to it, for instance, when updating inode timestamps (see the section "File Descriptor and Inode" in Chapter 1, *Introduction*). In particular, `xtime.tv_sec` stores the number of seconds that have elapsed since midnight of January 1, 1970*, while `xtime.tv_usec` stores the number of microseconds that have elapsed within the last second (its value thus ranges between 0 and 999999).

During system initialization, the `time_init()` function is invoked to set up the time and date: it reads them from the Real Time Clock by invoking the `get_cmos_time()` function, then it initializes `xtime`. Once this has been done, the kernel does not need the RTC anymore: it relies instead on the `TIMER_BH` bottom half, which is activated once every tick.

The `update_times()` function invoked by the `TIMER_BH` bottom half updates `xtime` by disabling interrupts and executing the following statement:

```
if (lost_ticks)
    update_wall_time(lost_ticks);
```

The `update_wall_time()` function invokes the `update_wall_time_one_tick()` function `lost_ticks` consecutive times; each invocation adds 10000 to the `xtime.tv_usec` field.† If `xtime.tv_usec` has become greater than 999999, the `update_wall_time()` function also updates the `tv_sec` field of `xtime`.

Updating Resource Usage Statistics

The value of `lost_ticks` is also used, together with that of `lost_ticks_system`, to update resource usage statistics. These statistics are used by various administration utilities such as `top`. A user who enters the `uptime` command sees the statistics as the

---

* This date is traditionally used by all Unix systems as the earliest moment in counting time.

† In fact, the function is much more complex since it might slightly tune the value 10000. This may be necessary if an `adjtimex()` system call has been issued (see the section "The adjtimex() System Call" later in this chapter).

"load average" relative to the last minute, the last 5 minutes, and the last 15 minutes. A value of 0 means that there are no active processes (besides the *swapper* process 0) to run, while a value of 1 means that the CPU is 100% busy with a single process, and values greater than 1 mean that the CPU is shared among several active processes.

After updating the system clock, `update_times()` reenables the interrupts and performs the following actions:

- Clears `lost_ticks` after storing its value in `ticks`

- Clears `lost_ticks_system` after storing its value in `system`

- Invokes `calc_load(ticks)`

- Invokes `update_process_times(ticks, system)`

The `calc_load()` function counts the number of processes in the `TASK_RUNNING` or `TASK_UNINTERRUPTIBLE` state and uses this number to update the CPU usage statistics.

The `update_process_times()` function updates some kernel statistics stored in the `kstat` variable of type `kernel_stat`; it then invokes `update_one_process()` to update some fields storing statistics that can be exported to user programs through the `times()` system call. In particular, a distinction is made between CPU time spent in User Mode and in Kernel Mode. The function perform the following actions:

- Updates the `per_cpu_utime` field of `current`'s process descriptor, which stores the number of ticks during which the process has been running in User Mode.

- Updates the `per_cpu_stime` field of `current`'s process descriptor, which stores the number of ticks during which the process has been running in Kernel Mode.

- Invokes `do_process_times()`, which checks whether the total CPU time limit has been reached; if so, sends `SIGXCPU` and `SIGKILL` signals to `current`. The section "Process Usage Limits" in Chapter 3, *Processes*, describes how the limit is controlled by the `rlim[RLIMIT_CPU].rlim_cur` field of each process descriptor.

- Invokes the `do_it_virt()` and `do_it_prof()` functions, which are described in the later section "The setitimer() and alarm() System Calls."

Two additional fields called `times.tms_cutime` and `times.tms_cstime` are provided in the process descriptor to count the number of CPU ticks spent by the process children in User Mode and in Kernel Mode, respectively. For reasons of efficiency, these fields are not updated by `do_process_times()` but rather when the parent process queries the state of one of its children (see the section "Destroying Processes" in Chapter 3).

CPU's Time Sharing

Timer interrupts are essential for time sharing the CPU among runnable processes (that is, those in the `TASK_RUNNING` state). As we shall see in Chapter 10, each process is

usually allowed a *quantum* of time of limited duration: if the process is not terminated when its quantum expires, the `schedule()` function selects the new process to
run.

The `counter` field of the process descriptor specifies how many ticks of CPU time are
left to the process. The quantum is always a multiple of a tick, that is, a multiple of
about 10 ms. The value of `counter` is updated at every tick by `update_process_`
`times()` as follows:

```
if (current->pid) {
    current->counter -= ticks;
    if (current->counter < 0) {
        current->counter = 0;
        current->need_resched = 1;
    }
}
```

As stated in the section "Identifying a Process" in Chapter 3, the process having PID 0
(*swapper*) must not be time-shared, because it is the process that runs on the CPU
when no other `TASK_RUNNING` processes exist.

Since `counter` is updated in a deferred manner by a bottom half, the decrement might
be larger than a single tick. Thus, the `ticks` local variable denotes the number of ticks
that occurred since the bottom half was activated. When `counter` becomes smaller
than 0, the `need_resched` field of the process descriptor is set to 1. In that case, the
`schedule()` function will be invoked before resuming User Mode execution, and
other `TASK_RUNNING` processes will have a chance to resume execution on the CPU.

The Role of Timers

A *timer* is a software facility that allows functions to be invoked at some future
moment, after a given time interval has elapsed; a *time-out* denotes a moment at
which the time interval associated with a timer has elapsed.

Timers are widely used both by the kernel and by processes. Most device drivers
make use of timers to detect anomalous conditions: floppy disk drivers, for instance,
use timers to switch off the device motor after the floppy has not been accessed for a
while, and parallel printer drivers use them to detect erroneous printer conditions.

Timers are also used quite often by programmers to force the execution of specific
functions at some future time (see the later section "The setitimer() and alarm() System Calls").

Implementing a timer is relatively easy: each timer contains a field that indicates how
far in the future the timer should expire. This field is initially calculated by adding the
right number of ticks to the current value of `jiffies`. The field does not change.
Every time the kernel checks a timer, it compares the expiration field to the value of
`jiffies` at the current moment, and the timer expires when `jiffies` is greater or

equal to the stored value. This comparison is made via the `time_after`, `time_before`, `time_after_eq`, and `time_before_eq` macros, which take care of possible overflows of `jiffies`.

Linux considers three types of timers called *static timers*, *dynamic timers*, and *interval timers*. The first two types are used by the kernel, while interval timers may be created by processes in User Mode.

One word of caution about Linux timers: since checking for timer functions is always done by bottom halves that may be executed a long time after they have been activated, the kernel cannot ensure that timer functions will start right at their expiration times; it can only ensure that they will be executed either at the proper time or after they are supposed to with a delay of up to a few hundreds of milliseconds. For that reason, timers are not appropriate for real-time applications in which expiration times must be strictly enforced.

Static Timers

The first versions of Linux allowed only 32 different timers;* these static timers, which rely on statically allocated kernel data structure, still continue to be used. Since they were the first to be introduced, Linux code refers to them as *old timers*.

Static timers are stored in the `timer_table` array, which includes 32 entries. Each entry consists of the following `timer_struct` structure:

```
struct timer_struct {
    unsigned long expires;
    void (*fn)(void);
};
```

The `expires` field specifies when the timer expires; the time is expressed as the number of ticks that have elapsed since the system was started up. All timers having an `expires` value smaller than or equal to the value of `jiffies` are considered to be expired or decayed. The `fn` field contains the address of the function to be executed when the timer expires.

Although `timer_table` includes 32 entries, Linux uses only those listed in Table 5-1.

Table 5-1. Static Timers

Static Timer	Time-out Effect
BACKGR_TIMER	Background I/O operation request
BEEP_TIMER	Loudspeaker tone
BLANK_TIMER	Switch off the screen

---

* This value was chosen so that the corresponding active flags could be stored in a single variable.

Table 5-1. Static Timers (continued)

Static Timer	Time-out Effect
COMTROL_TIMER	Comtrol serial card
COPRO_TIMER	i80387 coprocessor
DIGI_TIMER	Digiboard card
FLOPPY_TIMER	Floppy disk
GDTH_TIMER	GDTH SCSI driver
GSCD_TIMER	Goldstar CD-ROM
HD_TIMER	Hard disk (old IDE driver)
MCD_TIMER	Mitsumi CD-ROM
QIC02_TAPE_TIMER	QIC-02 tape driver
RS_TIMER	RS-232 serial port
SWAP_TIMER	*kswapd* kernel thread activation

The `timer_active` variable is used to identify the active static timers: each bit of this 32-bit variable is a flag that specifies whether the corresponding timer is activated.

In order to activate a static timer, the kernel must simply:

- Register the function to be executed in the `fn` field of the timer.

- Compute the expiration time (this is usually done by adding some specified value to the value of `jiffies`) and store it in the `expires` field of the timer.

- Set the proper flag in `timer_active`.

The job of checking for decayed static timers is done by the `run_old_timers()` function, which is invoked by the `TIMER_BH` bottom half:

```
void run_old_timers(void)
{
    struct timer_struct *tp;
    unsigned long mask;
    for (mask = 1, tp = timer_table; mask;
            tp++, mask += mask) {
        if (mask > timer_active)
            break;
        if (!(mask & timer_active))
            continue;
        if (tp->expires > jiffies)
            continue;
        timer_active &= ~mask;
        tp->fn();
        sti();
    }
}
```

Once a decayed active timer has been identified, the corresponding active flag is cleared before executing the function that the **fn** field points to, thus ensuring that the timer won't be invoked again at each future execution of **run_old_timers()**.

Dynamic Timers

Dynamic timers may be dynamically created and destroyed. No limit is placed on the number of currently active dynamic timers.

A dynamic timer is stored in the following **timer_list** structure:

```
struct timer_list {
    struct timer_list *next;
    struct timer_list *prev;
    unsigned long expires;
    unsigned long data;
    void (*function)(unsigned long);
};
```

The **function** field contains the address of the function to be executed when the timer expires. The **data** field specifies a parameter to be passed to this timer function. Thanks to the **data** field, it is possible to define a single general-purpose function that handles the time-outs of several device drivers; the **data** field could store the device ID or other meaningful data that could be used by the function to differentiate the device.

The meaning of the **expires** field is the same as the corresponding field for static timers.

The **next** and **prev** fields implement links for a doubly linked circular list. In fact, each active dynamic timer is inserted in exactly one of 512 doubly linked circular lists, depending on the value of the **expires** field. The algorithm that uses this list is described later in the chapter.

In order to create and activate a dynamic timer, the kernel must:

1. Create a new **struct timer_list** object, say **t**. This can be done in several ways by:

   —Defining a static global variable in the code

   —Defining a local variable inside a function: in this case, the object is stored on the Kernel Mode stack

   —Including the object in a dynamically allocated descriptor

2. Initialize the object by invoking the **init_timer(&t)** function. This simply sets the **next** and **prev** fields to **NULL**.

3. If the dynamic timer is not already inserted in a list, assign a proper value to the expires field. Otherwise, if the dynamic timer is already inserted in a list, update the expires field by invoking the mod_timer() function, which also takes care of moving the object into the proper list (discussed shortly).

4. Load the function field with the address of the function to be activated when the timer decays. If required, load the data field with a parameter value to be passed to the function.

5. If the dynamic timer is not already inserted in a list, insert the t element in the proper list by invoking the add_timer(&t) function.

Once the timer has decayed, the kernel automatically removes the t element from its list. Sometimes, however, a process should explicitly remove a timer from its list using the del_timer() function. Indeed, a sleeping process may be woken up before the time-out is over, and in this case the process may choose to destroy the timer. Invoking del_timer() on a timer already removed from a list does no harm, so calling del_timer() from the timer function is considered a good practice.

We saw previously how the run_old_timers() function was able to identify the active decayed static timers by executing a single for loop on the 32 timer_table components. This approach is no longer applicable to dynamic timers, since scanning a long list of dynamic timers at every tick would be too costly. On the other hand, maintaining a sorted list would not be much more efficient, since the insertion and deletion operations would also be costly.

The solution adopted is based on a clever data structure that partitions the expires values into blocks of ticks and allows dynamic timers to percolate efficiently from lists with larger expires values to lists with smaller ones.

The main data structure is an array called tvecs, whose elements point to five groups of lists identified by the tv1, tv2, tv3, tv4, and tv5 structures (see Figure 5-1).

The tv1 structure is of type struct timer_vec_root, which includes an index field and a vec array of 256 pointers to timer_list elements, that is, to lists of dynamic timers. It contains all dynamic timers that will decay within the next 255 ticks.

The index field specifies the currently scanned list; it is initialized to 0 and incremented by 1 (modulo 256) at every tick. The list referenced by index contains all dynamic timers that have expired during the current tick; the next list contains all dynamic timers that will expire in the next tick; the (index+k)-th list contains all dynamic timers that will expire in exactly k ticks. When index returns to 0, this means that all the timers in tv1 have been scanned: in this case, the list pointed to by tv2.vec[tv2.index] is used to replenish tv1.

The tv2, tv3, and tv4 structures of type struct timer_vec contain all dynamic timers that will decay within the next 2^{14}-1, 2^{20}-1, and 2^{26}-1 ticks, respectively.

The `tv5` structure is identical to the previous ones, except that the last entry of the `vec` array includes dynamic timers with arbitrarily large `expires` fields; it needs never be replenished from another array.

The `timer_vec` structure is very similar to `timer_vec_root`: it contains an `index` field and a `vec` array of 64 pointers to dynamic timer lists. The `index` field specifies the currently scanned list; it is incremented by 1 (modulo 64) every 256^{i-1} ticks, where *i* ranging between 2 and 5 is the `tvi` group number. As in the case of `tv1`, when `index` returns to 0, the list pointed to by `tvj.vec[tvj.index]` is used to replenish `tvi` (*i* ranges between 2 and 4, *j* is equal to *i+1*).

A single entry of `tv2` is sufficient to replenish the whole array `tv1`; similarly, a single entry of `tv3` is sufficient to replenish the whole array `tv2` and so on.

Figure 5-1 shows how these data structures are connected together.

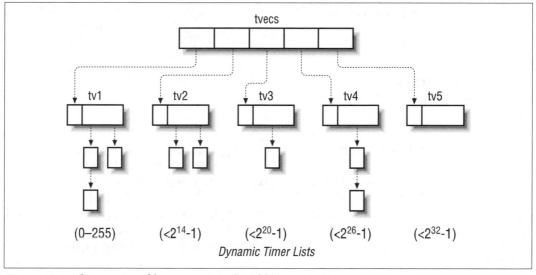

Figure 5-1. The groups of lists associated with dynamic timers

The `timer_bh()` function associated with the **TIMER_BH** bottom half invokes the `run_timer_list()` auxiliary function to check for decayed dynamic timers. The function relies on a variable similar to `jiffies` called `timer_jiffies`. This new variable is needed because a few timer interrupts might occur before the activated **TIMER_BH** bottom half has a chance to run; this happens typically when several interrupts of different types are issued in a short interval of time.

The value of `timer_jiffies` represents the expiration time of the dynamic timer list yet to be checked: if it coincides with the value of `jiffies`, no backlog of bottom half functions has accumulated; if it is smaller than `jiffies`, then bottom half functions that refer to previous ticks have to be dealt with. The variable is set to 0 at system startup and is incremented only by `run_timer_list()`, which is invoked once every tick. Its value can never be greater than `jiffies`.

The `run_timer_list()` function includes the following C fragment (assuming a uniprocessor system):

```
cli();
while ((long)(jiffies - timer_jiffies) >= 0) {
    struct timer_list *timer;
    if (!tv1.index) {
        int n = 1;
        do {
            cascade_timers(tvecs[n]);
        } while (tvecs[n]->index == 1 && ++n < 5));
    }
    while ((timer = tv1.vec[tv1.index])) {
        detach_timer(timer);
        timer->next = timer->prev = NULL;
        sti();
        timer->function(timer->data);
        cli();
    }
    ++timer_jiffies;
    tv1.index = (tv1.index + 1) & 0xff;
}
sti();
```

The outermost `while` loop ends when `timer_jiffies` becomes greater than the value of `jiffies`. Since the values of `jiffies` and `timer_jiffies` usually coincide, the outermost `while` cycle will often be executed only once. In general, the outermost loop will be executed `jiffies - timer_jiffies + 1` consecutive times. Moreover, if a timer interrupt occurs while `run_timer_list()` is being executed, dynamic timers that decay at this tick occurrence will also be considered, since the `jiffies` variable is asynchronously incremented by the IRQ0 interrupt handler (see the earlier section "PIT's Interrupt Service Routine").

During a single execution of the outermost `while` cycle, the dynamic timer functions included in the `tv1.vec[tv1.index]` list are executed. Before executing a dynamic timer function, the loop invokes the `detach_timer()` function to remove the dynamic timer from the list. Once the list is emptied, the values of `tv1.index` is incremented (modulo 256) and the value of `timer_jiffies` is incremented.

When `tv1.index` becomes equal to 0, all the lists of `tv1` have been checked; in this case, it is necessary to refill the `tv1` structure. This is accomplished by the `cascade_timers()` function, which transfers the dynamic timers included in `tv2.vec[tv2.index]` into `tv1.vec`, since they will necessarily decay within the next 256 ticks. If `tv2.index` is equal to 0, it is necessary to refill the `tv2` array of lists with the elements of `tv3.vec[tv3.index]` and so on.

Notice that `run_timer_list()` disables interrupts just before entering the outermost loop; interrupts are enabled right before invoking each dynamic timer function, and again disabled right after its termination. This ensures that the dynamic timer data structures are not corrupted by interleaved kernel control paths.

To sum up, this rather complex algorithm ensures excellent performance. To see why, assume for the sake of simplicity that the `TIMER_BH` bottom half is executed right after the corresponding timer interrupt has occurred. Then in 255 timer interrupt occurrences out of 256, that is in 99.6% of the cases, the `run_timer_list()` function just runs the functions of the decayed timers, if any. In order to replenish `tv1.vec` periodically, it will be sufficient 63 times out of 64 to partition the list pointed to by `tv2.vec[tv2.index]` into the 256 lists pointed to by `tv1.vec`. The `tv2.vec` array, in turn, must be replenished in 0.02% of the cases, that is, once every 163 seconds. Similarly, `tv3` is replenished every 2 hours and 54 minutes, `tv4` every 7 days and 18 hours, while `tv5` doesn't need to be replenished.

An Application of Dynamic Timers

On some occasions, for instance when it is unable to provide a given service, the kernel may decide to suspend the current process for a fixed amount of time. This is usually done by performing a *process time-out*.

Let us assume that the kernel has decided to suspend the current process for two seconds. It does this by executing the following code:

```
timeout = 2 * HZ;
current->state = TASK_INTERRUPTIBLE;
timeout = schedule_timeout(timeout);
```

The kernel implements process time-outs by using dynamic timers. They appear in the `schedule_timeout()` function, which executes the following statements:

```
struct timer_list timer;
expire = timeout + jiffies;
init_timer(&timer);
timer.expires = expire;
timer.data = (unsigned long) current;
timer.function = process_timeout;
add_timer(&timer);
schedule();      /* process suspended until timer expires */
del_timer(&timer);
timeout = expire - jiffies;
return (timeout < 0 ? 0 : timeout);
```

When `schedule()` is invoked, another process is selected for execution; when the former process resumes its execution, the function removes the dynamic timer. In the last statement, the function returns either 0 if the time-out is expired or the number of ticks left to the time-out expiration if the process has been awoken for some other reason.

When the time-out expires, the kernel executes the following function:

```
void process_timeout(unsigned long data)
{
    struct task_struct * p = (struct task_struct *) data;
    wake_up_process(p);
}
```

The `run_timer_list()` function invokes `process_timeout()`, passing as its parameter the process descriptor pointer stored in the `data` field of the `timer` object. As a result, the suspended process is woken up.

System Calls Related to Timing Measurements

Several system calls allow User Mode processes to read and modify the time and date and to create timers. Let us briefly review them and discuss how the kernel handles them.

The time(), ftime(), and gettimeofday() System Calls

Processes in User Mode can get the current time and date by means of several system calls:

`time()`
> Returns the number of elapsed seconds since midnight at the start of January 1, 1970

`ftime()`
> Returns, in a data structure of type `timeb`, the number of elapsed seconds since midnight of January 1, 1970; the number of elapsed milliseconds in the last second; the time zone; and the current status of daylight saving time

`gettimeofday()`
> Returns the same information as `ftime()` in two data structures named `timeval` and `timezone`

The former system calls are superseded by `gettimeofday()`, but they are still included in Linux for backward compatibility. We don't discuss them further.

The `gettimeofday()` system call is implemented by the `sys_gettimeofday()` function. In order to compute the current date and time of the day, this function invokes `do_gettimeofday()`, which executes the following actions:

- Copies the contents of `xtime` into the user-space buffer specified by the system call parameter `tv`:

  ```
  *tv = xtime;
  ```

- Updates the number of microseconds by invoking the function addressed by the `do_gettimeoffset` variable:

```
tv->tv_usec += do_gettimeoffset();
```

  If the CPU has a Time Stamp Counter, the `do_fast_gettimeoffset()` function is executed. It reads the TSC register by using the `rdtsc` Assembly instruction; it then subtracts the value stored in `last_tsc_low` to obtain the number of CPU cycles elapsed since the last timer interrupt was handled. The function converts that number to microseconds and adds in the delay that elapsed before the activation of the timer interrupt handler, which is stored in the `delay_at_last_interrupt` variable mentioned earlier in the section "PIT's Interrupt Service Routine."

  If the CPU does not have a TSC register, `do_gettimeoffset` points to the `do_slow_gettimeoffset()` function. It reads the state of the 8254 chip device internal oscillator and then computes the time length elapsed since the last timer interrupt. Using that value and the contents of `jiffies`, it can derive the number of microseconds elapsed in the last second.

- Further increases the number of microseconds to take into account all timer interrupts whose bottom halves have not yet been executed:

```
if (lost_ticks)
    tv->tv_usec += lost_ticks * (1000000/HZ);
```

- Finally, checks for an overflow in the microseconds field, adjusting both that field and the second field if necessary:

```
while (tv->tv_usec >= 1000000) {
    tv->tv_usec -= 1000000;
    tv->tv_sec++;
}
```

Processes in User Mode with root privilege may modify the current date and time by using either the obsolete `stime()` or the `settimeofday()` system call. The `sys_settimeofday()` function invokes `do_settimeofday()`, which executes operations complementary to those of `do_gettimeofday()`.

Notice that both system calls modify the value of `xtime` while leaving unchanged the RTC registers. Therefore, the new time will be lost when the system shuts down, unless the user executes the `/sbin/clock` program to change the RTC value.

The adjtimex() System Call

Although clock drift ensures that all systems eventually move away from the correct time, changing the time abruptly is both an administrative nuisance and risky behavior. Imagine, for instance, programmers trying to build a large program and depending on filetime stamps to make sure that out-of-date object files are recompiled. A large change in the system's time could confuse the **make** program and lead to an incorrect build. Keeping the clocks tuned is also important when implementing a distributed filesystem on a network of computers: in this case, it is wise to adjust the clocks of the interconnected PCs so that the timestamp values associated with the inodes of the accessed files are coherent. Thus, systems are often configured to run a time synchronization protocol such as Network Time Protocol (NTP) on a regular basis to change the time gradually at each tick. This utility depends on the `adjtimex()` system call in Linux.

This system call is present in several Unix variants, although it should not be used in programs intended to be portable. It receives as its parameter a pointer to a `timex` structure, updates kernel parameters from the values in the `timex` fields, and returns the same structure with current kernel values. Such kernel values are used by `update_wall_time_one_tick()` to slightly adjust the number of microseconds added to `xtime.tv_usec` at each tick.

The setitimer() and alarm() System Calls

Linux allows User Mode processes to activate special timers called *interval timers*.* The timers cause Unix signals (see Chapter 9, *Signals*) to be sent periodically to the process. It is also possible to activate an interval timer so that it sends just one signal after a specified delay. Each interval timer is therefore characterized by:

- The frequency at which the signals must be emitted, or a null value if just one signal has to be generated

- The time remaining until the next signal is to be generated

The warning earlier in the chapter about accuracy applies to these timers. They are guaranteed to execute after the requested time has elapsed, but it is impossible to predict exactly when they will be delivered.

Interval timers are activated by means of the POSIX `setitimer()` system call. The first parameter specifies which of the following policies should be adopted:

ITIMER_REAL
    The actual elapsed time; the process receives **SIGALRM** signals

ITIMER_VIRTUAL
    The time spent by the process in User Mode; the process receives **SIGVTALRM** signals

ITIMER_PROF
    The time spent by the process both in User and in Kernel Mode; the process receives **SIGPROF** signals

---

* These software constructs have nothing in common with the Programmable Interval Timer chips described earlier in this chapter.

In order to implement an interval timer for each of the preceding policies, the process descriptor includes three pairs of fields:

- `it_real_incr` and `it_real_value`
- `it_virt_incr` and `it_virt_value`
- `it_prof_incr` and `it_prof_value`

The first field of each pair stores the interval in ticks between two signals; the other field stores the current value of the timer.

The `ITIMER_REAL` interval timer is implemented by making use of dynamic timers, because the kernel must send signals to the process even when it is not running on the CPU. Therefore, each process descriptor includes a dynamic timer object called `real_timer`. The `setitimer()` system call initializes the `real_timer` fields and then invokes `add_timer()` to insert the dynamic timer in the proper list. When the timer expires, the kernel executes the `it_real_fn()` timer function. In turn, the `it_real_fn()` function sends a `SIGALRM` signal to the process; if `it_real_incr` is not null, it sets the `expires` field again, reactivating the timer.

The `ITIMER_VIRTUAL` and `ITIMER_PROF` interval timers do not require dynamic timers, since they can be updated while the process is running: the `do_it_virt()` and `do_it_prof()` functions are invoked by `update_one_process()`, which runs when the `TIMER_BH` bottom half is executed. Therefore, the two interval timers are usually updated once every tick, and if they are expired, the proper signal is sent to the current process.

The `alarm()` system call sends a `SIGALRM` signal to the calling process when a specified time interval has elapsed. It is very similar to `setitimer()` when invoked with the `ITIMER_REAL` parameter, since it makes use of the `real_timer` dynamic timer included in the process descriptor. Therefore, `alarm()` and `setitimer()` with parameter `ITIMER_REAL` cannot be used at the same time.

Anticipating Linux 2.4

Linux 2.4 introduces no significant change to the time-handling functions of the 2.2 version.

CHAPTER SIX

MEMORY MANAGEMENT

We saw in Chapter 2, *Memory Addressing*, how Linux takes advantage of Intel's segmentation and paging circuits to translate logical addresses into physical ones. In the same chapter, we mentioned that some portion of RAM is permanently assigned to the kernel and used to store both the kernel code and the static kernel data structures.

The remaining part of the RAM is called *dynamic memory*. It is a valuable resource, needed not only by the processes but also by the kernel itself. In fact, the performance of the entire system depends on how efficiently dynamic memory is managed. Therefore, all current multitasking operating systems try to optimize the use of dynamic memory, assigning it only when it is needed and freeing it as soon as possible.

This chapter, which consists of three main sections, describes how the kernel allocates dynamic memory for its own use. The sections "Page Frame Management" and "Memory Area Management" illustrate two different techniques for handling physically contiguous memory areas, while the section "Noncontiguous Memory Area Management" illustrates a third technique that handles noncontiguous memory areas.

Page Frame Management

We saw in the section "Paging in Hardware" in Chapter 2 how the Intel Pentium processor can use two different page frame sizes: 4 KB and 4 MB. Linux adopts the smaller 4 KB page frame size as the standard memory allocation unit. This makes things simpler for two reasons:

- The paging circuitry automatically checks whether the page being addressed is contained in some page frame; furthermore, each page frame is hardware-protected through the flags included in the Page Table entry that points to it. By choosing a 4 KB allocation unit, the kernel can directly determine the memory allocation unit associated with the page where a page fault exception occurs.

- The 4 KB size is a multiple of most disk block sizes, so transfers of data between main memory and disks are more efficient. Yet this smaller size is much more manageable than the 4 MB size.

The kernel must keep track of the current status of each page frame. For instance, it must be able to distinguish the page frames used to contain pages belonging to processes from those that contain kernel code or kernel data structures; similarly, it must be able to determine whether a page frame in dynamic memory is free or not. This sort of state information is kept in an array of descriptors, one for each page frame. The descriptors of type **struct page** have the following format:

```
typedef struct page {
    struct page *next;
    struct page *prev;
    struct inode *inode;
    unsigned long offset;
    struct page *next_hash;
    atomic_t count;
    unsigned long flags;
    struct wait_queue *wait;
    struct page **pprev_hash;
    struct buffer_head * buffers;
} mem_map_t;
```

We shall describe only a few fields (the remaining ones will be discussed in later chapters dealing with filesystems, I/O buffers, memory mapping, and so on):

count

> Set to 0 if the corresponding page frame is free; set to a value greater than 0 if the page frame has been assigned to one or more processes or if it is used for some kernel data structures.

prev, next

> Used to insert the descriptor in a doubly linked circular list. The meaning of these fields depends on the current use of the page frame.

flags

> An array of up to 32 flags (see Table 6-1) describing the status of the page frame. For each **PG_***xyz* flag, a corresponding **Page***Xyz* macro has been defined to read or set its value.

Some of the flags listed in Table 6-1 are explained in later chapters. The **PG_DMA** flag exists because of a limitation on Direct Memory Access (DMA) processors for ISA buses: such DMA processors are able to address only the first 16 MB of RAM, hence page frames are divided into two groups depending on whether they can be addressed by the DMA or not. (The section "Direct Memory Access (DMA)" in Chapter 13, *Managing I/O Devices*, gives further details on DMAs.) In this chapter, the term "DMA" will always refer to DMA for ISA buses.

Table 6-1. Flags Describing the Status of a Page Frame

Flag Name	Meaning
PG_decr_after	See the section "The read_swap_cache_async( ) Function" in, Chapter 16, *Swapping: Methods for Freeing Memory.*
PG_dirty	Not used.
PG_error	An I/O error occurred while transferring the page.
PG_free_after	See the section "Reading from a Regular File" in Chapter 15, *Accessing Regular Files.*
PG_DMA	Usable by ISA DMA (see text).
PG_locked	Page cannot be swapped out.
PG_referenced	Page frame has been accessed through the hash table of the page cache (see the section "The Page Cache" in Chapter 14, *Disk Caches*).
PG_reserved	Page frame reserved to kernel code or unusable.
PG_skip	Used on SPARC/SPARC64 architectures to "skip" some parts of the address space.
PG_Slab	Included in a slab: see the section "Memory Area Management" later in this chapter.
PG_swap_cache	Included in the swap cache; see "The Swap Cache" in Chapter 16
PG_swap_unlock_after	See the section "The read_swap_cache_async( ) Function" in Chapter 16.
PG_uptodate	Set after completing a read operation, unless a disk I/O error happened.

All the page frame descriptors on the system are included in an array called mem_map. Since each descriptor is less than 64 bytes long, mem_map requires about four page frames for each megabyte of RAM. The MAP_NR macro computes the number of the page frame whose address is passed as a parameter, and thus the index of the corresponding descriptor in mem_map:

```
#define MAP_NR(addr)    (_ _pa(addr) >> PAGE_SHIFT)
```

The macro makes use of the __pa macro, which converts a logical address to a physical one.

Dynamic memory, and the values used to refer to it, are illustrated in Figure 6-1. Page frame descriptors are initialized by the `free_area_init()` function, which acts on two parameters: `start_mem` denotes the first linear address of the dynamic memory immediately after the kernel memory, while `end_mem` denotes the last linear address of the dynamic memory plus 1 (see the sections "Reserved Page Frames" and "Kernel Page Tables" in Chapter 2). The `free_area_init()` function also considers the `i386_endbase` variable, which stores the initial address of the reserved page frames. The function allocates a suitably sized memory area to `mem_map`. The function then initializes the area by setting all fields to 0, except for the `flags` fields, in which it sets the `PG_DMA` and `PG_reserved` flags:

```
mem_map = (mem_map_t *) start_mem;
p = mem_map + MAP_NR(end_mem);
start_mem = ((unsigned long) p + sizeof(long) - 1) &
                  ~(sizeof(long)-1);
memset(mem_map, 0, start_mem - (unsigned long) mem_map);
do {
    --p;
    p->count = 0;
    p->flags = (1 << PG_DMA) | (1 << PG_reserved);
} while (p > mem_map);
```

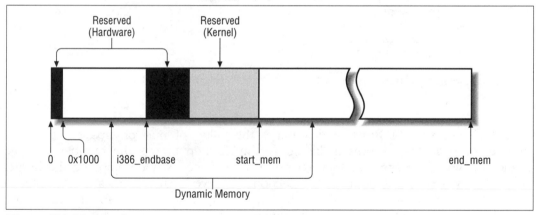

Figure 6-1. Memory layout

Subsequently, the `mem_init()` function clears both the `PG_reserved` flag of the page frames, so they can be used as dynamic memory (see the section "Reserved Page Frames" in Chapter 2), and the `PG_DMA` flags of all page frames having physical addresses greater than or equal to `0x1000000`. This is done by the following fragment of code:

```
start_low_mem = PAGE_SIZE + PAGE_OFFSET;
num_physpages = MAP_NR(end_mem);
while (start_low_mem < i386_endbase) {
    clear_bit(PG_reserved,
```

```
                    &mem_map[MAP_NR(start_low_mem)].flags);
        start_low_mem += PAGE_SIZE;
    }
    while (start_mem < end_mem) {
        clear_bit(PG_reserved,
                    &mem_map[MAP_NR(start_mem)].flags);
        start_mem += PAGE_SIZE;
    }
    for (tmp = PAGE_OFFSET ; tmp < end_mem ; tmp += PAGE_SIZE) {
        if (tmp >= PAGE_OFFSET+0x1000000)
            clear_bit(PG_DMA, &mem_map[MAP_NR(tmp)].flags);
        if (PageReserved(mem_map+MAP_NR(tmp))) {
            if (tmp >= (unsigned long) &_text
                    && tmp < (unsigned long) &_edata)
                if (tmp < (unsigned long) &_etext)
                    codepages++;
                else
                    datapages++;
            else if (tmp >= (unsigned long) &__init_begin
                        && tmp < (unsigned long) &__init_end)
                initpages++;
            else if (tmp >= (unsigned long) &__bss_start
                        && tmp < (unsigned long) start_mem)
                datapages++;
            else
                reservedpages++;
            continue;
        }
        mem_map[MAP_NR(tmp)].count = 1;
        free_page(tmp);
    }
```

First, the `mem_init()` function determines the value of `num_physpages`, the total number of page frames present in the system. It then counts the number of page frames of type `PG_reserved`. Several symbols produced while compiling the kernel (we described some of them in the section "Reserved Page Frames" in Chapter 2) enable the function to count the number of page frames reserved for the hardware, kernel code, and kernel data and the number of page frames used during kernel initialization that can be successively released.

Finally, `mem_init()` sets the `count` field of each page frame descriptor associated with the dynamic memory to 1 and calls the `free_page()` function (see the section "The Buddy System Algorithm" later in this chapter). Since this function increments the value of the variable `nr_free_pages`, that variable will contain the total number of page frames in the dynamic memory at the end of the loop.

Requesting and Releasing Page Frames

After having seen how the kernel allocates and initializes the data structures for page frame handling, we now look at how page frames are allocated and released. Page frames can be requested by making use of four slightly differing functions and macros:

__get_free_pages(gfp_mask, order)
> Function used to request 2^{order} contiguous page frames.

__get_dma_pages(gfp_mask, order)
> Macro used to get page frames suitable for DMA; it expands to:
>
> _ _get_free_pages(gfp_mask | GFP_DMA, order)

__get_free_page(gfp_mask)
> Macro used to get a single page frame; it expands to:
>
> _ _get_free_pages(gfp_mask, 0)

get_free_page(gfp_mask):
> Function that invokes:
>
> _ _get_free_page(gfp_mask)
>
> and then fills the page frame obtained with zeros.

The parameter **gfp_mask** specifies how to look for free page frames. It consists of the following flags:

__GFP_WAIT
> Set if the kernel is allowed to discard the contents of page frames in order to free memory before satisfying the request.

__GFP_IO
> Set if the kernel is allowed to write pages to disk in order to free the corresponding page frames. (Since swapping can block the process in Kernel Mode, this flag must be cleared when handling interrupts or modifying critical kernel data structures.)

__GFP_DMA
> Set if the requested page frames must be suitable for DMA. (The hardware limitation that gives rise to this flag was explained in the earlier section "Page Frame Management.")

__GFP_HIGH, __GFP_MED, __GFP_LOW
> Specify the request priority. __GFP_LOW is usually associated with dynamic memory requests issued by User Mode processes, while the other priorities are associated with kernel requests.

In practice, Linux uses the predefined combinations of flag values shown in Table 6-2; the group name is what you'll encounter in the source code.

Table 6-2. Groups of Flag Values Used to Request Page Frames

Group Name	__GFP_WAIT	__GFP_IO	Priority
GFP_ATOMIC	0	0	__GFP_HIGH
GFP_BUFFER	1	0	__GFP_LOW
GFP_KERNEL	1	1	__GFP_MED
GFP_NFS	1	1	__GFP_HIGH
GFP_USER	1	1	__GFP_LOW

Page frames can be released through any of the following three functions and macros:

`free_pages(addr, order)`
> This function checks the page descriptor of the page frame having physical address `addr`; if the page frame is not reserved (i.e., if the `PG_reserved` flag is equal to 0), it decrements the `count` field of the descriptor. If `count` becomes 0, it assumes that 2^{order} contiguous page frames starting from `addr` are no longer used. In that case, the function invokes `free_pages_ok()` to insert the page frame descriptor of the first free page in the proper list of free page frames (described in the following section).

`__free_page(p)`
> Similar to the previous function, except that it releases the page frame whose descriptor is pointed to by parameter `p`.

`free_page(addr)`
> Macro used to release the page frame having physical address `addr`; it expands

to `free_pages(addr, 0)`.

The Buddy System Algorithm

The kernel must establish a robust and efficient strategy for allocating groups of contiguous page frames. In doing so, it must deal with a well-known memory management problem called *external fragmentation*: frequent requests and releases of groups of contiguous page frames of different sizes may lead to a situation in which several small blocks of free page frames are "scattered" inside blocks of allocated page frames. As a result, it may become impossible to allocate a large block of contiguous page frames, even if there are enough free pages to satisfy the request.

There are essentially two ways to avoid external fragmentation:

• Make use of the paging circuitry to map groups of noncontiguous free page frames into intervals of contiguous linear addresses.

• Develop a suitable technique to keep track of the existing blocks of free contiguous page frames, avoiding as much as possible the need to split up a large free block in order to satisfy a request for a smaller one.

The second approach is the one preferred by the kernel for two good reasons:

- In some cases, contiguous page frames are really necessary, since contiguous linear addresses are not sufficient to satisfy the request. A typical example is a memory request for buffers to be assigned to a DMA processor (see Chapter 13). Since the DMA ignores the paging circuitry and accesses the address bus directly while transferring several disk sectors in a single I/O operation, the buffers requested must be located in contiguous page frames.

- Even if contiguous page frame allocation is not strictly necessary, it offers the big advantage of leaving the kernel paging tables unchanged. What's wrong with modifying the page tables? As we know from Chapter 2, frequent page table modifications lead to higher average memory access times, since they make the CPU flush the contents of the translation lookaside buffers.

The technique adopted by Linux to solve the external fragmentation problem is based on the well-known *buddy system* algorithm. All free page frames are grouped into 10 lists of blocks that contain groups of 1, 2, 4, 8, 16, 32, 64, 128, 256, and 512 contiguous page frames, respectively. The physical address of the first page frame of a block is a multiple of the group size: for example, the initial address of a 16-page-frame block is a multiple of 16×2^{12}.

We'll show how the algorithm works through a simple example.

Assume there is a request for a group of 128 contiguous page frames (i.e., a half-megabyte). The algorithm checks first whether a free block in the 128-page-frame list exists. If there is no such block, the algorithm looks for the next larger block, that is, a free block in the 256-page-frame list. If such a block exists, the kernel allocates 128 of the 256 page frames to satisfy the request and inserts the remaining 128 page frames into the list of free 128-page-frame blocks. If there is no free 256-page block, it then looks for the next larger block, that is, a free 512-page-frame block. If such a block exists, it allocates 128 of the 512 page frames to satisfy the request, inserts the first 256 of the remaining 384 page frames into the list of free 256-page-frame blocks, and inserts the last 128 of the remaining 384 page frames into the list of free 128-page-frame blocks. If the list of 512-page-frame blocks is empty, the algorithm gives up and signals an error condition.

The reverse operation, releasing blocks of page frames, gives rise to the name of this algorithm. The kernel attempts to merge together pairs of free buddy blocks of size b into a single block of size $2b$. Two blocks are considered buddy if:

- Both blocks have the same size, say b.

- They are located in contiguous physical addresses.

- The physical address of the first page frame of the first block is a multiple of $2 \times b \times 2^{12}$.

The algorithm is iterative; if it succeeds in merging released blocks, it doubles *b* and tries again so as to create even bigger blocks.

Data structures

Linux makes use of two different buddy systems: one handles the page frames suitable for ISA DMA, while the other one handles the remaining page frames. Each buddy system relies on the following main data structures:

- The mem_map array introduced previously.

- An array having 10 elements of type free_area_struct, one element for each group size. The variable free_area[0] points to the array used by the buddy system for the page frames that are not suitable for ISA DMA, while free_area[1] points to the array used by the buddy system for page frames suitable for ISA DMA.

- Ten binary arrays named *bitmaps*, one for each group size. Each buddy system has its own set of bitmaps, which it uses to keep track of the blocks it allocates.

Each element of the free_area[0] and free_area[1] arrays is a structure of type free_area_struct, which is defined as follows:

```
struct free_area_struct {
    struct page *next;
    struct page *prev;
    unsigned int *map;
    unsigned long count;
};
```

Notice that the first two fields of this structure match the corresponding fields of a page descriptor; in fact, pointers to free_area_struct structures are sometimes used as pointers to page descriptors.

The *k*th element of either the free_area[0] or the free_area[1] array is associated with a doubly linked circular list of blocks of size 2^k, implemented through the **next** and **prev** fields. Each member of such a list is the descriptor of the first page frame of a block. The **count** field of each free_area_struct structure stores the number of elements in the corresponding list.

The **map** field points to a bitmap whose size depends on the number of existing page frames. Each bit of the bitmap of the *k*th entry of either free_area[0] or free_area[1] describes the status of two buddy blocks of size 2^k page frames. If a bit of the bitmap is equal to 0, either both buddy blocks of the pair are free or both are busy; if it is equal to 1, exactly one of the blocks is busy. When both buddies are free, the kernel treats them as a single free block of size 2^{k+1}.

Let us consider, for sake of illustration, a 128 MB RAM and the bitmaps associated with the non-DMA page frames. The 128 MB can be divided into 32768 single pages, 16384 groups of 2 pages each, or 8192 groups of 4 pages each and so on up to 64 groups of 512 pages each. So the bitmap corresponding to `free_area[0][0]` consists of 16384 bits, one for each pair of the 32768 existing page frames; the bitmap corresponding to `free_area[0][1]` consists of 8192 bits, one for each pair of blocks of two consecutive page frames; the last bitmap corresponding to `free_area[0][9]` consists of 32 bits, one for each pair of blocks of 512 contiguous page frames.

Figure 6-2 illustrates with a simple example the use of the data structures introduced by the buddy system algorithm. The array `mem_map` contains nine free page frames grouped in one block of one (that is, a single page frame) at the top and two blocks of four further down. The double arrows denote doubly linked circular lists implemented by the `next` and `prev` fields. Notice that the bitmaps are not drawn to scale.

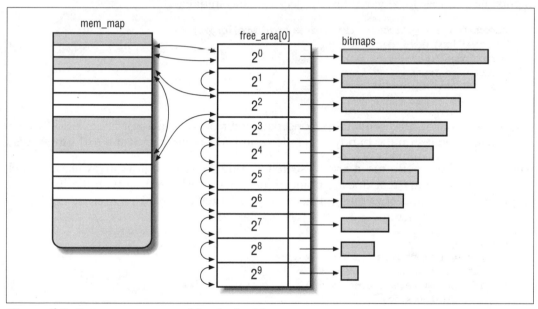

Figure 6-2. Data structures used by the buddy system

Allocating a block

The `__get_free_pages()` function implements the buddy system strategy for allocating page frames. This function checks first whether there are enough free pages, that is, if `nr_free_pages` is greater than `freepages.min`. If not, it may decide to reclaim page frames (see "The try_to_free_pages() Function" in Chapter 16). Otherwise, it goes on with the allocation by executing the code included in the RMQUEUE_TYPE macro:

```
if (!(gfp_mask & _ _GFP_DMA))
    RMQUEUE_TYPE(order, 0);
RMQUEUE_TYPE(order, 1);
```

The **order** parameter denotes the logarithm of the size of the requested block of free pages (0 for a one-page block, 1 for a two-page block, and so forth). The second parameter is the index into **free_area**, which is 0 for non-DMA blocks and 1 for DMA blocks. So the code checks **gfp_mask** to see whether non-DMA blocks are allowed and, if so, tries to get blocks from that list (index 0), because it would be better to save DMA blocks for requests that really need them. If the page frames are successfully allocated, the code in the **RMQUEUE_TYPE** macro executes a return statement, thus terminating the **__get_free_pages()** function. Otherwise, the code in the **RMQUEUE_TYPE** macro is executed again with the second parameter equal to 1, that is, the memory allocation request is satisfied using page frames suitable for DMA.

The code yielded by the **RMQUEUE_TYPE** macro is equivalent to the following fragments. First, a few local variables are declared and initialized:

```
struct free_area_struct * area = &free_area[type][order];
unsigned long new_order = order;
struct page *prev;
struct page *ret;
unsigned long map_nr;
struct page * next;
```

The **type** variable represents the second parameter of the macro: it is equal to 0 when the macro operates on the buddy system for non-DMA page frames and to 1 otherwise.

The macro then performs a cyclic search through each list for an available block (denoted by an entry that doesn't point to the entry itself), starting with the list for the requested **order** and continuing if necessary to larger orders. This cycle is equivalent to the following structure:

```
do {
    prev = (struct page *)area;
    ret = prev->next;
    if ((struct page *) area != ret)
        goto block_found;
    new_order++;
    area++;
} while (new_order < 10);
```

If the **while** loop terminates, no suitable free block has been found, so **__get_free_pages()** returns a NULL value. Otherwise, a suitable free block has been found; in this case, the descriptor of its first page frame is removed from the list, the corresponding bitmap is updated, and the value of **nr_free_pages** is decreased:

```
block_found:
    prev->next = ret->next;
    prev->next->prev = prev;
    map_nr = ret-mem_map;
    change_bit(map_nr>>(1+new_order), area->map);
    nr_free_pages -= 1 << order;
    area->count--;
```

If the block found comes from a list of size **new_order** greater than the requested size **order**, a **while** cycle is executed. The rationale behind these lines of codes is the following: when it becomes necessary to use a block of 2^k page frames to satisfy a request for 2^h page frames ($h < k$), the program allocates the last 2^h page frames and iteratively reassigns the first $2^k - 2^h$ page frames to the **free_area** lists having indexes between h and k.

```
size = 1 << new_order;
while (new_order > order) {
    area--;
    new_order--;
    size >>= 1;
    /* insert *ret as first element in the list
       and update the bitmap */
    next = area->next;
    ret->prev = (struct page *) area;
    ret->next = next;
    next->prev = ret;
    area->next = ret;
    area->count++;
    change_bit(map_nr >> (1+new_order), area->map);
    /* now take care of the second half of
       the free block starting at *ret */
    map_nr += size;
    ret += size;
}
```

Finally, RMQUEUE_TYPE updates the count field of the page descriptor associated with the selected block and executes a **return** instruction:

```
ret->count = 1;
return PAGE_OFFSET + (map_nr << PAGE_SHIFT);
```

As a result, the **__get_free_pages()** function returns the address of the block found.

Freeing a block

The **free_pages_ok()** function implements the buddy system strategy for freeing page frames. It makes use of three input parameters:

map_nr
> The page number of one of the page frames included in the block to be released

order
> The logarithmic size of the block

type
> Equal to 1 if the page frames are suitable for DMA and to 0 if they are not

The function starts by declaring and initializing a few local variables:

```
struct page * next, * prev;
struct free_area_struct *area = &free_area[type][order];
unsigned long index = map_nr >> (1 + order);
unsigned long mask = (~0UL) << order;
unsigned long flags;
```

The `mask` variable contains the two's complement of 2^{order}. It is used to transform `map_nr` into the number of the first page frame of the block to be released and to increment `nr_free_pages`:

```
map_nr &= mask;
nr_free_pages -= mask;
```

The function now starts a cycle executed at most (9 − `order`), once for each possibility for merging a block with its buddy. The function starts with the smallest sized block and moves up to the top size. The condition driving the `while` loop is:

```
(mask + (1 << 9))
```

where the single bit set in `mask` is shifted to the left at each iteration. The body of the loop checks whether the buddy block of the block having number `map_nr` is free:

```
if (!test_and_change_bit(index, area->map))
    break;
```

If the buddy block is not free, the function breaks out of the cycle; if it is free, the function detaches it from the corresponding list of free blocks. The block number of the buddy is derived from `map_nr` by switching a single bit:

```
area->count--;
next = mem_map[map_nr ^ -mask].next;
prev = mem_map[map_nr ^ -mask].prev;
next->prev = prev;
prev->next = next;
```

At the end of each iteration, the function updates the `mask`, `area`, `index`, and `map_nr` variables:

```
mask <<= 1;
area++;
index >>= 1;
map_nr &= mask;
```

The function then continues the next iteration, trying to merge free blocks twice as large as the ones considered in the previous cycle. When the cycle is finished, the free block obtained cannot be further merged with other free blocks. It is then inserted in the proper list:

```
next = area->next;
mem_map[map_nr].prev = (struct page *) area;
```

```
mem_map[map_nr].next = next;
next->prev = &mem_map[map_nr];
area->next = &mem_map[map_nr];
area->count++;
```

Memory Area Management

This section deals with *memory areas*, that is, with sequences of memory cells having contiguous physical addresses and an arbitrary length.

The buddy system algorithm adopts the page frame as the basic memory area. This is fine for dealing with relatively large memory requests, but how are we going to deal with requests for small memory areas, say a few tens or hundred of bytes?

Clearly, it would be quite wasteful to allocate a full page frame to store a few bytes. The correct approach instead consists of introducing new data structures that describe how small memory areas are allocated within the same page frame. In doing so, we introduce a new problem called *internal fragmentation*. It is caused by a mismatch between the size of the memory request and the size of the memory area allocated to satisfy the request.

A classical solution adopted by Linux 2.0 consists of providing memory areas whose sizes are geometrically distributed: in other words, the size depends on a power of 2 rather than on the size of the data to be stored. In this way, no matter what the memory request size is, we can ensure that the internal fragmentation is always smaller than 50%. Following this approach, Linux 2.0 creates 13 geometrically distributed lists of free memory areas whose sizes range from 32 to 131056 bytes. The buddy system is invoked both to obtain additional page frames needed to store new memory areas and conversely to release page frames that no longer contain memory areas. A dynamic list is used to keep track of the free memory areas contained in each page frame.

The Slab Allocator

Running a memory area allocation algorithm on top of the buddy algorithm is not particularly efficient. Linux 2.2 reexamines the memory area allocation from scratch and comes out with some very clever improvements.

The new algorithm is derived from the *slab allocator* schema developed in 1994 for the Sun Microsystem Solaris 2.4 operating system. It is based on the following premises:

* The type of data to be stored may affect how memory areas are allocated; for instance, when allocating a page frame to a User Mode process, the kernel invokes the `get_free_page()` function, which fills the page with zeros.

    The concept of a slab allocator expands upon this idea and views the memory areas as *objects* consisting of both a set of data structures and a couple of functions or methods called the *constructor* and *destructor*: the former initializes the memory area while the latter deinitializes it.

In order to avoid initializing objects repeatedly, the slab allocator does not discard the objects that have been allocated and then released but saves them in memory. When a new object is then requested, it can be taken from memory without having to be reinitialized.

In practice, the memory areas handled by Linux do not need to be initialized or deinitialized. For efficiency reasons, Linux does not rely on objects that need constructor or destructor methods; the main motivation for introducing a slab allocator is to reduce the number of calls to the buddy system allocator. Thus, although the kernel fully supports the constructor and destructor methods, the pointers to these methods are NULL.

- The kernel functions tend to request memory areas of the same type repeatedly. For instance, whenever the kernel creates a new process, it allocates memory areas for some fixed size tables such as the process descriptor, the open file object, and so on (see Chapter 3, *Processes*). When a process terminates, the memory areas used to contain these tables can be reused. Since processes are created and destroyed quite frequently, previous versions of the Linux kernel wasted time allocating and deallocating the page frames containing the same memory areas repeatedly; in Linux 2.2 they are saved in a cache and reused instead.

- Requests for memory areas can be classified according to their frequency. Requests of a particular size that are expected to occur frequently can be handled most efficiently by creating a set of special purpose objects having the right size, thus avoiding internal fragmentation. Meanwhile, sizes that are rarely encountered can be handled through an allocation scheme based on objects in a series of geometrically distributed sizes (such as the power-of-2 sizes used in Linux 2.0), even if this approach leads to internal fragmentation.

- There is another subtle bonus in introducing objects whose sizes are not geometrically distributed: the initial addresses of the data structures are less prone to be concentrated on physical addresses whose values are a power of 2. This, in turn, leads to better performance by the processor hardware cache.

- Hardware cache performance creates an additional reason for limiting calls to the buddy system allocator as much as possible: every call to a buddy system function "dirties" the hardware cache, thus increasing the average memory access time.[*]

The slab allocator groups objects into *caches*. Each cache is a "store" of objects of the same type. For instance, when a file is opened, the memory area needed to store the

---

[*] The impact of a kernel function on the hardware cache is denoted as the function *footprint*; it is defined as the percentage of cache overwritten by the function when it terminates. Clearly, large footprints lead to a slower execution of the code executed right after the kernel function, since the hardware cache is by now filled with useless information.

corresponding "open file" object is taken from a slab allocator cache named *filp* (for "file pointer"). The slab allocator caches used by Linux may be viewed at runtime by reading the */proc/slabinfo* file.

The area of main memory that contains a cache is divided into *slabs*; each slab consists of one or more contiguous page frames that contain both allocated and free objects (see Figure 6-3).

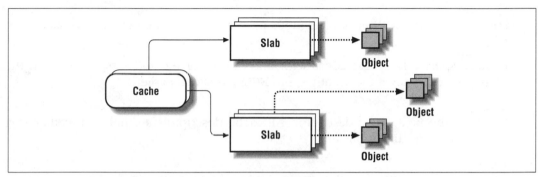

Figure 6-3. The slab allocator components

The slab allocator never releases the page frames of an empty slab on its own. It would not know when free memory is needed, and there is no benefit to releasing objects when there is still plenty of free memory for new objects. Therefore, releases occur only when the kernel is looking for additional free page frames (see the section "Releasing an Object from a Cache" later in this chapter and the section "Freeing Page Frames" in Chapter 16).

Cache Descriptor

Each cache is described by a table of type **struct kmem_cache_s** (which is equivalent to the type **kmem_cache_t**). The most significant fields of this table are:

c_name
Points to the name of the cache.

c_firstp, c_lastp
Point, respectively, to the first and last slab descriptor of the cache. The slab descriptors of a cache are linked together through a doubly linked, circular, partially ordered list: the first elements of the list include slabs with no free objects, then come the slabs that include used objects along with at least one free object, and finally the slabs that include only free objects.

c_freep
Points to the **s_nextp** field of the first slab descriptor that includes at least one free object.

`c_num`

> Number of objects packed into a single slab. (All slabs of the cache have the same size.)

`c_offset`

> Size of the objects included in the cache. (This size may be rounded up if the initial addresses of the objects must be memory aligned.)

`c_gfporder`

> Logarithm of the number of contiguous page frames included in a single slab.

`c_ctor, c_dtor`

> Point, respectively, to the constructor and destructor methods associated with the cache objects. They are currently set to NULL, as stated earlier.

`c_nextp`

> Points to the next cache descriptor. All cache descriptors are linked together in a simple list by means of this field.

`c_flags`

> An array of flags that describes some permanent properties of the cache. There is, for instance, a flag that specifies which of two possible alternatives (see the following section) has been chosen to store the object descriptors in memory.

`c_magic`

> A magic number selected from a predefined set of values. Used to check both the current state of the cache and its consistency.

Slab Descriptor

Each slab of a cache has its own descriptor of type **struct kmem_slab_s** (equivalent to the type `kem_slab_t`).

Slab descriptors can be stored in two possible places, the choice depending normally on the size of the objects in the slab. If the object size is smaller than 512 bytes, the slab descriptor is stored at the end of the slab; otherwise, it is stored outside of the slab. The latter option is preferable for large objects whose sizes are a submultiple of the slab size. In some cases, the kernel may violate this rule by setting the `c_flags` field of the cache descriptor differently.

The most significant fields of a slab descriptor are:

`s_inuse`

> Number of objects in the slab that are currently allocated.

`s_mem`

> Points to the first object (either allocated or free) inside the slab.

s_freep

    Points to the first free object (if any) in the slab.

s_nextp, s_prevp

    Point, respectively, to the next and previous slab descriptor. The **s_nextp** field of the last slab descriptor in the list points to the **c_offset** field of the corresponding cache descriptor.

s_dma

    Flag set if the objects included in the slab can be used by the DMA processor.

s_magic

    Similar to the **c_magic** field of the cache descriptor. It contains a magic number selected from a predefined set of values and is used to check both the current state of the slab and its consistency. The values of this field are different from those of the corresponding **c_magic** field of the cache descriptor. The offset of **s_magic** within the slab descriptor is equal to the offset of **c_magic** with respect to **c_offset** inside the cache descriptor; the checking routine relies on their being the same.

Figure 6-4 illustrates the major relationships between cache and slab descriptors. Full slabs precede partially full slabs that precede empty slabs.

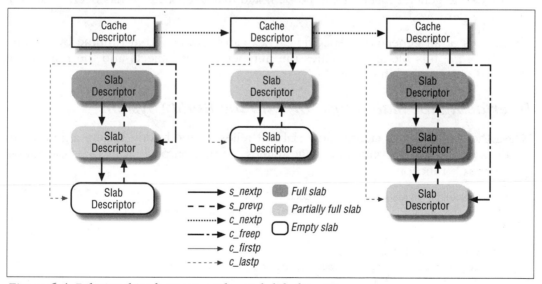

Figure 6-4. Relationships between cache and slab descriptors

General and Specific Caches

Caches are divided into two types: general and specific. General caches are used only by the slab allocator for its own purposes, while specific caches are used by the remaining parts of the kernel.

The general caches are:

- A first cache contains the cache descriptors of the remaining caches used by the kernel. The `cache_cache` variable contains its descriptor.

- A second cache contains the slab descriptors that are not stored inside the slabs. The `cache_slabp` variable points to its descriptor.

- Thirteen additional caches contain geometrically distributed memory areas. The table called `cache_sizes` whose elements are of type `cache_sizes_t` points to the 13 cache descriptors associated with memory areas of size 32, 64, 128, 256, 512, 1024, 2048, 4096, 8192, 16384, 32768, 65536, and 131072 bytes, respectively. The table `cache_sizes` is used to efficiently derive the cache address corresponding to a given size.

The `kmem_cache_init()` and `kmem_cache_sizes_init()` functions are invoked during system initialization to set up the general caches.

Specific caches are created by the `kmem_cache_create()` function. Depending on the parameters, the function first determines the best way to handle the new cache (for instance, whether to include the slab descriptor inside or outside of the slab); it then creates a new cache descriptor for the new cache and inserts the descriptor in the `cache_cache` general cache. It should be noted that once a cache has been created, it cannot be destroyed.

The names of all general and specific caches can be obtained at runtime by reading */proc/slabinfo*; this file also specifies the number of free objects and the number of allocated objects in each cache.

Interfacing the Slab Allocator with the Buddy System

When the slab allocator creates new slabs, it relies on the buddy system algorithm to obtain a group of free contiguous page frames. To that purpose, it invokes the `kmem_getpages()` function:

```
void * kmem_getpages(kmem_cache_t *cachep,
                     unsigned long flags, unsigned int *dma)
{
    void    *addr;
    *dma = flags & SLAB_DMA;
    addr = (void*) __get_free_pages(flags, cachep->c_gfporder);
    if (!*dma && addr) {
        struct page *page = mem_map + MAP_NR(addr);
        *dma = 1<<cachep->c_gfporder;
        while ((*dma)--) {
            if (!PageDMA(page)) {
                *dma = 0;
                break;
            }
```

```
            page++;
        }
    }
    return addr;
}
```

The parameters have the following meaning:

cachep
> Points to the cache descriptor of the cache that needs additional page frames (the number of required page frames is in the cachep->c_gfporder field)

flags
> Specifies how the page frame is requested (see the section "Requesting and Releasing Page Frames" earlier in this chapter)

dma
> Points to a variable that is set to 1 by kmem_getpages() if the allocated page frames are suitable for ISA DMA

In the reverse operation, page frames assigned to a slab allocator can be released (see the section "Releasing a Slab from a Cache" later in this chapter) by invoking the kmem_freepages() function:

```
void kmem_freepages(kmem_cache_t *cachep, void *addr)
{
    unsigned long i = (1<<cachep->c_gfporder);
    struct page *page = &mem_map[MAP_NR(addr)];
    while (i--) {
        PageClearSlab(page);
        page++;
    }
    free_pages((unsigned long)addr, cachep->c_gfporder);
}
```

The function releases the page frames, starting from the one having physical address addr, that had been allocated to the slab of the cache identified by cachep.

Allocating a Slab to a Cache

A newly created cache does not contain any slab and therefore no free objects. New slabs are assigned to a cache only when both of the following are true:

• A request has been issued to allocate a new object.

• The cache does not include any free object.

When this occurs, the slab allocator assigns a new slab to the cache by invoking kmem_cache_grow(). This function calls kmem_getpages() to obtain a group of page frames from the buddy system; it then calls kmem_cache_slabmgmt() to get a new slab descriptor. Next, it calls `kmem_cache_init_objs()`, which applies the constructor method (if defined) to all the objects contained in the new slab. It then calls `kmem_slab_link_end()`, which inserts the slab descriptor at the end of the cache slab list:

```
void kmem_slab_link_end(kmem_cache_t *cachep,
                        kmem_slab_t *slabp)
{
    kmem_slab_t *lastp = cachep->c_lastp;
    slabp->s_nextp = kmem_slab_end(cachep);
    slabp->s_prevp = lastp;
    cachep->c_lastp = slabp;
    lastp->s_nextp = slabp;
}
```

The `kmem_slab_end` macro yields the address of the `c_offset` field of the corresponding cache descriptor (as stated before, the last element of a slab list points to that field).

After inserting the new slab descriptor into the list, `kmem_cache_grow()` loads the `next` and `prev` fields, respectively, of the descriptors of all page frames included in the new slab with the address of the cache descriptor and the address of the slab descriptor. This works correctly because the `next` and `prev` fields are used by functions of the buddy system only when the page frame is free, while page frames handled by the slab allocator functions are not free as far as the buddy system is concerned. Therefore, the buddy system will not be confused by this specialized use of the page frame descriptor.

Releasing a Slab from a Cache

As stated previously, the slab allocator never releases the page frames of an empty slab on its own. In fact, a slab is released only if both the following conditions hold:

- The buddy system is unable to satisfy a new request for a group of page frames.

- The slab is empty, that is, all the objects included in it are free.

When the kernel looks for additional free page frames, it calls `try_to_free_pages()`; this function, in turn, may invoke `kmem_cache_reap()`, which selects a cache that contains at least one empty slab. The `kmem_slab_unlink()` function then removes the slab from the cache list of slabs:

```
void kmem_slab_unlink(kmem_slab_t *slabp)
{
    kmem_slab_t *prevp = slabp->s_prevp;
    kmem_slab_t *nextp = slabp->s_nextp;
    prevp->s_nextp = nextp;
    nextp->s_prevp = prevp;
}
```

Subsequently, the slab—together with the objects in it—is destroyed by invoking `kmem_slab_destroy()`:

```
void kmem_slab_destroy(kmem_cache_t *cachep, kmem_slab_t *slabp)
{
    if (cachep->c_dtor) {
        unsigned long num = cachep->c_num;
        void *objp = slabp->s_mem;
        do {
            (cachep->c_dtor)(objp, cachep, 0);
            objp += cachep->c_offset;
            if (!slabp->s_index)
                objp += sizeof(kmem_bufctl_t);
        } while (--num);
    }
    slabp->s_magic = SLAB_MAGIC_DESTROYED;
    if (slabp->s_index)
        kmem_cache_free(cachep->c_index_cachep, slabp->s_index);
    kmem_freepages(cachep, slabp->s_mem-slabp->s_offset);
    if (SLAB_OFF_SLAB(cachep->c_flags))
        kmem_cache_free(cache_slabp, slabp);
}
```

The function checks whether the cache has a destructor method for its objects (the `c_dtor` field is not NULL), in which case it applies the destructor to all the objects in the slab; the `objp` local variable keeps track of the currently examined object. Next, it calls `kmem_freepages()`, which returns all the contiguous page frames used by the slab to the buddy system. Finally, if the slab descriptor is stored outside of the slab (in this case the `s_index` and `c_index_cachep` fields are not NULL, as explained later in this chapter), the function releases it from the cache of the slab descriptors.

Some modules of Linux (see Appendix B, *Modules*) may create caches. In order to avoid wasting memory space, the kernel must destroy all slabs in all caches created by a module before removing it.[*] The `kmem_cache_shrink()` function destroys all the slabs in a cache by invoking `kmem_slab_destroy()` iteratively. The `c_growing` field of the cache descriptor is used to prevent `kmem_cache_shrink()` from shrinking a cache while another kernel control path attempts to allocate a new slab for it.

Object Descriptor

Each object has a descriptor of type `struct kmem_bufctl_s` (equivalent to the type `kmem_bufctl_t`). Like the slab descriptors themselves, the object descriptors of a slab can be stored in two possible ways, illustrated by Figure 6-5.

---

[*] We stated previously that Linux does not destroy caches. Thus, when linking in a new module, the kernel must check whether the new cache descriptors requested by it were already created in a previous installation of that module or another one.

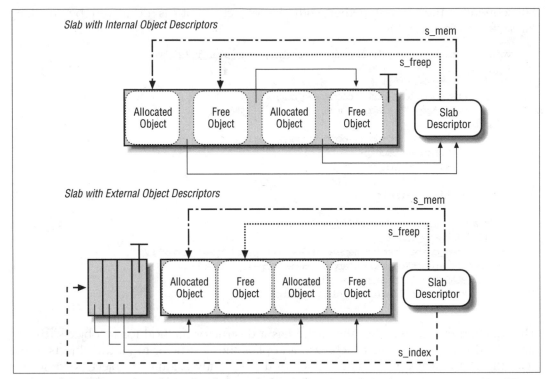

Figure 6-5. Relationships between slab and object descriptors

External object descriptors

Stored outside the slab, in one of the general caches pointed to by **cache_sizes**. In this case, the first object descriptor in the memory area describes the first object in the slab and so on. The size of the memory area, and thus the particular general cache used to store object descriptors, depends on the number of objects stored in the slab (**c_num** field of the cache descriptor). The cache containing the objects themselves is tied to the cache containing their descriptors through two fields. First, the **c_index_cachep** field of the cache containing the slab points to the cache descriptor of the cache containing the object descriptors. Second, the **s_index** field of the slab descriptor points to the memory area containing the object descriptors.

Internal object descriptors

Stored inside the slab, right after the objects they describe. In this case, the **c_index_cachep** field of the cache descriptor and the **s_index** field of the slab descriptor are both NULL.

The slab allocator chooses the first solution when the size of the objects is a multiple of 512, 1024, 2048, or 4096: in this case, storing control structures inside the slab would result in a high level of internal fragmentation. If the size of the objects is smaller than 512 bytes or not a multiple of 512, 1024, 2048, or 4096 the slab allocator stores the object descriptors inside the slab.

Object descriptors are simple structures consisting of a single field:

```
typedef struct kmem_bufctl_s {
    union {
        struct kmem_bufctl_s * buf_nextp;
        kmem_slab_t *          buf_slabp;
        void *                 buf_objp;
    } u;
} kmem_bufctl_t;
#define    buf_nextp    u.buf_nextp
#define    buf_slabp    u.buf_slabp
#define    buf_objp     u.buf_objp
```

This field has the following meaning, depending on the state of the object and the locations of the object descriptors:

buf_nextp
> If the object is free, it points to the next free object in the slab, thus implementing a simple list of free objects inside the slab.

buf_objp
> If the object is allocated and its object descriptor is stored outside of the slab, it points to the object.

buf_slabp
> If the object is allocated and its object descriptor is stored inside the slab, it points to the slab descriptor of the slab in which the object is stored. This holds whether the slab descriptor is stored inside or outside of the slab.

Figure 6-5 illustrates the relationships among slabs, slab descriptors, objects, and object descriptors. Notice that, although the figure suggests that the slab descriptor is stored outside of the slab, it remains unchanged if the descriptor is stored inside it.

Aligning Objects in Memory

The objects managed by the slab allocator can be *aligned* in memory, that is, they can be stored in memory cells whose initial physical addresses are multiples of a given constant, usually a power of 2. This constant is called the *alignment factor*, and its value is stored in the c_align field of the cache descriptor. The c_offset field, which contains the object size, takes into account the number of padding bytes added to obtain the proper alignment. If the value of c_align is 0, no alignment is required for the objects.

The largest alignment factor allowed by the slab allocator is 4096, that is, the page frame size. This means that objects can be aligned by referring either to their physical addresses or to their linear addresses: in both cases, only the 12 least significant bits of the address may be altered by the alignment.

Usually, microcomputers access memory cells more quickly if their physical addresses are aligned with respect to the word size, that is, to the width of the internal memory bus of the computer. Thus, the `kmem_cache_create()` function attempts to align objects according to the word size specified by the `BYTES_PER_WORD` macro. For Intel Pentium processors, the macro yields the value 4 because the word is 32 bits long. However, the function does not align objects if this leads to a consistent waste of memory.

When creating a new cache, it's possible to specify that the objects included in it be aligned in the first-level cache. To achieve this, set the `SLAB_HWCACHE_ALIGN` cache descriptor flag. The `kmem_cache_create()` function handles the request as follows:

- If the object's size is greater than half of a cache line, it is aligned in RAM to a multiple of `L1_CACHE_BYTES`, that is, at the beginning of the line.

- Otherwise, the object size is rounded up to a factor of `L1_CACHE_BYTES`; this ensures that an object will never span across two cache lines.

Clearly, what the slab allocator is doing here is trading memory space for access time: it gets better cache performance by artificially increasing the object size, thus causing additional internal fragmentation.

Slab Coloring

We know from Chapter 2 that the same hardware cache line maps many different blocks of RAM. In this chapter we have also seen that objects of the same size tend to be stored at the same offset within a cache. Objects that have the same offset within different slabs will, with a relatively high probability, end up mapped in the same cache line. The cache hardware might therefore waste memory cycles transferring two objects from the same cache line back and forth to different RAM locations, while other cache lines go underutilized. The slab allocator tries to reduce this unpleasant cache behavior by a policy called *slab coloring*: different arbitrary values called *colors* are assigned to the slabs.

Before examining slab coloring, we have to look at the layout of objects in the cache. Let us consider a cache whose objects are aligned in RAM. Thus, the `c_align` field of the cache descriptor has a positive value, say *aln*. Even taking into account the alignment constraint, there are many possible ways to place objects inside the slab. The choices depend on decisions made for the following variables:

num
> Number of objects that can be stored in a slab (its value is in the `c_num` field of the cache descriptor).

osize
> Object size including the alignment bytes (its value is in the `c_offset` field) plus object descriptor size (if the descriptor is contained inside the slab).

dsize
> Slab descriptor size; its value is equal to 0 if the slab descriptor is stored outside of the slab.

free
> Number of unused bytes (bytes not assigned to any object) inside the slab.

The total length in bytes of a slab can then be expressed as:

$$slab\ length = (num \times osize) + dsize + free$$

free is always smaller than *osize*, since otherwise it would be possible to place additional objects inside the slab. However, *free* could be greater than *aln*.

The slab allocator takes advantage of the *free* unused bytes to color the slab. The term "color" is used simply to subdivide the slabs and allow the memory allocator to spread objects out among different linear addresses. In this way, the kernel obtains the best possible performance from the microprocessor's hardware cache.

Slabs having different colors store the first object of the slab in different memory locations, while satisfying the alignment constraint. The number of available colors is *free/aln*+1. The first color is denoted as 0 and the last one (whose value is in the c_colour field of the cache descriptor) is denoted as *free/aln*.

If a slab is colored with color *col*, the offset of the first object (with respect to the slab initial address) is equal to *col*×*aln* bytes; this value is stored in the s_offset field of the slab descriptor. Figure 6-6 illustrates how the placement of objects inside the slab depends on the slab color. Coloring essentially leads to moving some of the free area of the slab from the end to the beginning.

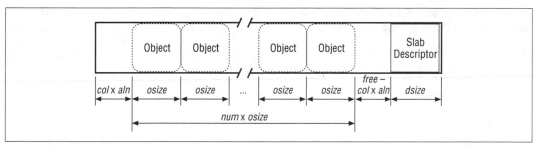

Figure 6-6. Slab with color col and alignment aln

Coloring works only when *free* is large enough. Clearly, if no alignment is required for the objects or if the number of unused bytes inside the slab is smaller than the required alignment (*free* < *aln*), the only possible slab coloring is the one having the color 0, that is, the one that assigns a zero offset to the first object.

The various colors are distributed equally among slabs of a given object type by storing the current color in a field of the cache descriptor called c_colour_next. The `kmem_cache_grow()` function assigns the color specified by `c_colour_next` to a new slab and then decrements the value of this field. After reaching 0, it wraps around again to the maximum available value:

```
if (!(offset = cachep->c_colour_next--))
    cachep->c_colour_next = cachep->c_colour;
offset *= cachep->c_align;
slabp->s_offset = offset;
```

In this way, each slab is created with a different color from the previous one, up to the maximum available colors.

Allocating an Object to a Cache

New objects may be obtained by invoking the `kmem_cache_alloc()` function. The parameter `cachep` points to the cache descriptor from which the new free object must be obtained. `kmem_cache_alloc()` first checks whether the cache descriptor exists; it then retrieves from the `c_freep` field the address of the `s_nextp` field of the first slab that includes at least one free object:

```
slabp = cachep->c_freep;
```

If `slabp` does not point to a slab, it then jumps to `alloc_new_slab` and invokes `kmem_cache_grow()` to add a new slab to the cache:

```
if (slabp->s_magic != SLAB_MAGIC_ALLOC)
    goto alloc_new_slab;
```

The value `SLAB_MAGIC_ALLOC` in the `s_magic` field indicates that the slab contains at least one free object. If the slab is full, `slabp` points to the `cachep->c_offset` field, and thus `slabp->s_magic` coincides with `cachep->c_magic`: in this case, however, this field contains a magic number for the cache different from `SLAB_MAGIC_ALLOC`.

After obtaining a slab with a free object, the function increments the counter containing the number of objects currently allocated in the slab:

```
slabp->s_inuse++;
```

It then loads `bufp` with the address of the first free object inside the slab and, correspondingly, updates the `slabp->s_freep` field of the slab descriptor to point to the next free object:

```
bufp = slabp->s_freep;
slabp->s_freep = bufp->buf_nextp;
```

If `slabp->s_freep` becomes NULL, the slab no longer includes free objects, so the `c_freep` field of the cache descriptor must be updated:

```
if (!slabp->s_freep)
    cachep->c_freep = slabp->s_nextp;
```

Notice that there is no need to change the position of the slab descriptor inside the list since it remains partially ordered. Now the function must derive the address of the free object and update the object descriptor.

If the `slabp->s_index` field is null, the object descriptors are stored right after the objects inside the slab. In this case, the address of the slab descriptor is first stored in the object descriptor's single field to denote the fact that the object is no longer free; then the object address is derived by subtracting from the address of the object descriptor the object size included in the `cachep->c_offset` field:

```
if (!slabp->s_index) {
    bufp->buf_slabp = slabp;
    objp = ((void*)bufp) - cachep->c_offset;
}
```

If the `slabp->s_index` field is not zero, it points to a memory area outside of the slab where the object descriptors are stored. In this case, the function first computes the relative position of the object descriptor in the outside memory area; it then multiplies this number by the object size; finally, it adds the result to the address of the first object in the slab, thus yielding the address of the object to be returned. As in the previous case, the object descriptor single field is updated and points now to the object:

```
if (slabp->s_index) {
    objp = ((bufp-slabp->s_index)*cachep->c_offset) +
               slabp->s_mem;
    bufp->buf_objp = objp;
}
```

The function terminates by returning the address of the new object:

```
return objp;
```

Releasing an Object from a Cache

The `kmem_cache_free()` function releases an object previously obtained by the slab allocator. Its parameters are `cachep`, the address of the cache descriptor, and `objp`, the address of the object to be released. The function starts by checking the parameters, after which it determines the address of the object descriptor and that of the slab containing the object. It uses the `cachep->c_flags` flag, included in the cache descriptor, to determine whether the object descriptor is located inside or outside of the slab.

In the former case, it determines the address of the object descriptor by adding the object's size to its initial address. The address of the slab descriptor is then extracted from the appropriate field in the object descriptor:

```
if (!SLAB_BUFCTL(cachep->c_flags)) {
    bufp = (kmem_bufctl_t *)(objp+cachep->c_offset);
    slabp = bufp->buf_slabp;
}
```

In the latter case, it determines the address of the slab descriptor from the `prev` field of the descriptor of the page frame containing the object (refer to the earlier section "Allocating a Slab to a Cache" for the role of `prev`). The address of the object descriptor is derived by first computing the sequence number of the object inside the slab (object address minus first object address divided by object length). This number is then used to determine the position of the object descriptor starting from the beginning of the outside area pointed to by the `slabp->s_index` field of the slab descriptor. To be on the safe side, the function checks that the object's address passed as a parameter coincides with the address that its object descriptor says it should have:

```
if (SLAB_BUFCTL(cachep->c_flags)) {
    slabp = (kmem_slab_t *)((&mem_map[MAP_NR(objp)])->prev);
    bufp =    &slabp->s_index[(objp - slabp->s_mem) /
                            cachep->c_offset];
    if (objp != bufp->buf_objp)
        goto bad_obj_addr;
}
```

Now the function checks whether the `slabp->s_magic` field of the slab descriptor contains the correct magic number and whether the `slabp->s_inuse` field is greater than 0. If everything is okay, it decrements the value of `slabp->s_inuse` and inserts the object into the slab list of free objects:

```
slabp->s_inuse--;
bufp->buf_nextp = slabp->s_freep;
slabp->s_freep = bufp;
```

If `bufp->buf_nextp` is NULL, the list of free objects includes only one element: the object that is being released. In this case, the slab was previously filled to capacity and it might be necessary to reinsert its slab descriptor in a new position in the list of slab descriptors. (Remember that completely filled slabs appear before slabs with some free objects in the partially ordered list.) This is done by the `kmem_cache_one_free()` function:

```
if (!bufp->buf_nextp)
    kmem_cache_one_free(cachep, slabp);
```

If the slab includes other free objects besides the one being released, it is necessary to check whether *all* objects are free. As in the previous case, this would make it necessary to reinsert the slab descriptor in a new position in the list of slab descriptors. The move is done by the `kmem_cache_full_free()` function:

```
if (bufp->buf_nextp)
    if (!slabp->s_inuse)
        kmem_cache_full_free(cachep, slabp);
```

The `kmem_cache_free()` function terminates here.

General Purpose Objects

As stated in the section "The Buddy System Algorithm," infrequent requests for memory areas are handled through a group of general caches whose objects have geometrically distributed sizes ranging from a minimum of 32 to a maximum of 131072 bytes.

Objects of this type are obtained by invoking the `kmalloc()` function:

```
void * kmalloc(size_t size, int flags)
{
    cache_sizes_t *csizep = cache_sizes;
    for (; csizep->cs_size; csizep++) {
        if (size > csizep->cs_size)
            continue;
        return __kmem_cache_alloc(csizep->cs_cachep, flags);
    }
    printk(KERN_ERR "kmalloc: Size (%lu) too large\n",
                    (unsigned long) size);
    return NULL;
}
```

The function uses the **cache_sizes** table to locate the cache descriptor of the cache containing objects of the right size. It then calls `kmem_cache_alloc()` to allocate the object.[*]

Objects obtained by invoking `kmalloc()` can be released by calling `kfree()`:[†]

```
void kfree(const void *objp)
{
    struct page *page;
    int    nr;
    if (!objp)
        goto null_ptr;
    nr = MAP_NR(objp);
    if (nr >= num_physpages)
        goto bad_ptr;
    page = &mem_map[nr];
    if (PageSlab(page)) {
        kmem_cache_t    *cachep;
        cachep = (kmem_cache_t *)(page->next);
        if (cachep && (cachep->c_flags & SLAB_CFLGS_GENERAL)) {
            __kmem_cache_free(cachep, objp);
            return;
        }
    }
```

---

[*] Actually, for efficiency reasons, the code of `kmem_cache_alloc()` is copied inside the body of `kmalloc()`. The `__kmem_cache alloc()` function, which implements `kmem_cache_alloc()`, is declared `inline`.

[†] A similar function called `kfree_s()` requires an additional parameter, namely, the size of the object to be released. This function was used in previous versions of Linux where the size of the memory area had to be determined before releasing it. It is still used by some modules of the filesystem.

```
    }
bad_ptr:
    printk(KERN_ERR "kfree: Bad obj %p\n", objp);
    *(int *) 0 = 0; /* FORCE A KERNEL DUMP */
null_ptr:
    return;
}
```

The proper cache descriptor is identified by reading the next field of the descriptor of the first page frame containing the memory area. If this field points to a valid descriptor, the memory area is released by invoking kmem_cache_free().[*]

Noncontiguous Memory Area Management

We already know from an earlier discussion that it is preferable to map memory areas into sets of contiguous page frames, thus making better use of the cache and achieving lower average memory access times. Nevertheless, if the requests for memory areas are infrequent, it makes sense to consider an allocation schema based on noncontiguous page frames accessed through contiguous linear addresses. The main advantage of this schema is to avoid external fragmentation, while the disadvantage is that it is necessary to fiddle with the kernel page tables. Clearly, the size of a noncontiguous memory area must be a multiple of 4096. Linux uses noncontiguous memory areas sparingly, for instance, to allocate data structures for active swap areas (see the section "Activating and Deactivating a Swap Area" in Chapter 16), to allocate space for a module (see Appendix B), or to allocate buffers to some I/O drivers.

Linear Addresses of Noncontiguous Memory Areas

To find a free range of linear addresses, we can look in the area starting from PAGE_OFFSET (usually 0xc0000000, the beginning of the fourth gigabyte). We learned in the Chapter 2 section "Process Page Tables" that the kernel reserved this whole upper area of memory to map available RAM for kernel use. But available RAM occupies only a small fraction of the gigabyte, starting at the PAGE_OFFSET address. All the linear addresses above that reserved area are available for mapping noncontiguous memory areas. The linear address that corresponds to the end of physical memory is stored in the high_memory variable.

Figure 6-7 shows how linear addresses are assigned to noncontiguous memory areas. A safety interval of size 8 MB (macro VMALLOC_OFFSET) is inserted between the end of the physical memory and the first memory area; its purpose is to "capture" out-of-bounds memory accesses. For the same reason, additional safety intervals of size 4 KB are inserted to separate noncontiguous memory areas.

---

[*] As for kmalloc(), the code of kmem_cache_free() is copied inside kfree(). __kmem_cache_free(), which implements kmem_cache_free(), is declared inline.

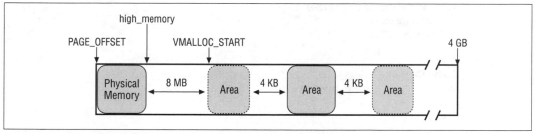

Figure 6-7. The linear address interval starting from PAGE_OFFSET

The `VMALLOC_START` macro defines the starting address of the linear space reserved for noncontiguous memory areas. It is defined as follows:

```
#define VMALLOC_START (((unsigned long) high_memory + \
                        VMALLOC_OFFSET) & ~(VMALLOC_OFFSET-1))
```

Descriptors of Noncontiguous Memory Areas

Each noncontiguous memory area is associated with a descriptor of type `struct vm_struct`:

```
struct vm_struct {
    unsigned long flags;
    void * addr;
    unsigned long size;
    struct vm_struct * next;
};
```

These descriptors are inserted in a simple list by means of the `next` field; the address of the first element of the list is stored in the `vmlist` variable. The `addr` field contains the linear address of the first memory cell of the area; the `size` field contains the size of the area plus 4096 (the size of the previously mentioned interarea safety interval).

The `get_vm_area()` function creates new descriptors of type `struct vm_struct`; its parameter `size` specifies the size of the new memory area:

```
struct vm_struct * get_vm_area(unsigned long size)
{
    unsigned long addr;
    struct vm_struct **p, *tmp, *area;
    area = (struct vm_struct *) kmalloc(sizeof(*area),
                                        GFP_KERNEL);
    if (!area)
        return NULL;
    addr = VMALLOC_START;
    for (p = &vmlist; (tmp = *p) ; p = &tmp->next) {
        if (size + addr < (unsigned long) tmp->addr)
            break;
        addr = tmp->size + (unsigned long) tmp->addr;
```

```
                  if (addr > 0xffffd000-size) {
                      kfree(area);
                      return NULL;
                  }
              }
              area->addr = (void *)addr;
              area->size = size + PAGE_SIZE;
              area->next = *p;
              *p = area;
              return area;
      }
```

The function first calls `kmalloc()` to obtain a memory area for the new descriptor. It then scans the list of descriptors of type `struct vm_struct` looking for an available range of linear addresses that includes at least `size+4096` addresses. If such an interval exists, the function initializes the fields of the descriptor and terminates by returning the initial address of the noncontiguous memory area. Otherwise, when `addr + size` exceeds the 4 GB limit, `get_vm_area()` releases the descriptor and returns NULL.

Allocating a Noncontiguous Memory Area

The `vmalloc()` function allocates a noncontiguous memory area to the kernel. The parameter `size` denotes the size of the requested area. If the function is able to satisfy the request, then it returns the initial linear address of the new area; otherwise, it returns a NULL pointer:

```
      void * vmalloc(unsigned long size)
      {
          void * addr;
          struct vm_struct *area;
          size = (size+PAGE_SIZE-1)&PAGE_MASK;
          if (!size || size > (num_physpages << PAGE_SHIFT))
              return NULL;
          area = get_vm_area(size);
          if (!area)
              return NULL;
          addr = area->addr;
          if (vmalloc_area_pages((unsigned long) addr, size)) {
              vfree(addr);
              return NULL;
          }
          return addr;
      }
```

The function starts by rounding up the value of the `size` parameter to a multiple of 4096 (the page frame size). It also performs a sanity check to make sure the size is greater than 0 and less than or equal to the existing number of page frames. If the size fits available memory, `vmalloc()` invokes `get_vm_area()`, which creates a new descriptor and returns the linear addresses assigned to the memory area. Then `vmalloc()` invokes `vmalloc_area_pages()` to request noncontiguous page frames and terminates by returning the initial linear address of the noncontiguous memory area.

The `vmalloc_area_pages()` function makes use of two parameters: `address`, the initial linear address of the area, and `size`, its size. The linear address of the end of the area is assigned to the `end` local variable:

```
end = address + size;
```

The function then uses the `pgd_offset_k` macro to derive the entry in the Page Global Directory related to the initial linear address of the area:

```
dir = pgd_offset_k(address);
```

The function then executes the following cycle:

```
while (address < end) {
    pmd_t *pmd = pmd_alloc_kernel(dir, address);
    if (!pmd)
        return -ENOMEM;
    if (alloc_area_pmd(pmd, address, end - address))
        return -ENOMEM;
    set_pgdir(address, *dir);
    address = (address + PGDIR_SIZE) & PGDIR_MASK;
    dir++;
}
```

In each cycle, it first invokes `pmd_alloc_kernel()` to create a Page Middle Directory for the new area. It then calls `alloc_area_pmd()` to allocate all the Page Tables associated with the new Page Middle Directory. Next, it invokes `set_pgdir()` to update the entry corresponding to the new Page Middle Directory in all existing Page Global Directories (see the section "Process Page Tables" in Chapter 2). It adds the constant 2^{22}, that is, the size of the range of linear addresses spanned by a single Page Middle Directory, to the current value of `address`, and it increases the pointer `dir` to the Page Global Directory.

The cycle is repeated until all page table entries referring to the noncontiguous memory area have been set up.

The `alloc_area_pmd()` function executes a similar cycle for all the Page Tables that a Page Middle Directory points to:

```
while (address < end) {
    pte_t * pte = pte_alloc_kernel(pmd, address);
    if (!pte)
        return -ENOMEM;
    if (alloc_area_pte(pte, address, end - address))
        return -ENOMEM;
```

```
        address = (address + PMD_SIZE) & PMD_MASK;
        pmd++;
    }
```

The `pte_alloc_kernel()` function (see the section "Page Table Handling" in Chapter 2) allocates a new Page Table and updates the corresponding entry in the Page Middle Directory. Next, `alloc_area_pte()` allocates all the page frames corresponding to the entries in the Page Table. The value of **address** is increased by 2^{22}, that is, the size of the linear address interval spanned by a single Page Table, and the cycle is repeated.

The main cycle of `alloc_area_pte()` is:

```
while (address < end) {
    unsigned long page;
    if (!pte_none(*pte))
        printk("alloc_area_pte: page already exists\n");
    page = _ _get_free_page(GFP_KERNEL);
    if (!page)
        return -ENOMEM;
    set_pte(pte, mk_pte(page, PAGE_KERNEL));
    address += PAGE_SIZE;
    pte++;
}
```

Each page frame is allocated through `_ _get_free_page()`. The physical address of the new page frame is written into the Page Table by the **set_pte** and **mk_pte** macros. The cycle is repeated after adding the constant 4096, that is, the length of a page frame, to **address**.

Releasing a Noncontiguous Memory Area

The `vfree()` function releases noncontiguous memory areas. Its parameter **addr** contains the initial linear address of the area to be released. `vfree()` first scans the list pointed by **vmlist** to find the address of the area descriptor associated with the area to be released:

```
for (p = &vmlist ; (tmp = *p) ; p = &tmp->next) {
    if (tmp->addr == addr) {
        *p = tmp->next;
        vmfree_area_pages((unsigned long)(tmp->addr),
                          tmp->size);
        kfree(tmp);
        return;
    }
}
printk("Trying to vfree() nonexistent vm area (%p)\n", addr);
```

The `size` field of the descriptor specifies the size of the area to be released. The area itself is released by invoking `vmfree_area_pages()`, while the descriptor is released by invoking `kfree()`.

The `vmfree_area_pages()` function takes two parameters: the initial linear address and the size of the area. It executes the following cycle to reverse the actions performed by `vmalloc_area_pages()`:

```
while (address < end) {
    free_area_pmd(dir, address, end - address);
    address = (address + PGDIR_SIZE) & PGDIR_MASK;
    dir++;
}
```

In turn, `free_area_pmd()` reverses the actions of `alloc_area_pmd()` in the cycle:

```
while (address < end) {
    free_area_pte(pmd, address, end - address);
    address = (address + PMD_SIZE) & PMD_MASK;
    pmd++;
}
```

Again, `free_area_pte()` reverses the activity of `alloc_area_pte()` in the cycle:

```
while (address < end) {
    pte_t page = *pte;
    pte_clear(pte);
    address += PAGE_SIZE;
    pte++;
    if (pte_none(page))
        continue;
    if (pte_present(page)) {
        free_page(pte_page(page));
        continue;
    }
    printk("Whee... Swapped out page in kernel page table\n");
}
```

Each page frame assigned to the noncontiguous memory area is released by means of the buddy system `free_page()` function. The corresponding entry in the Page Table is set to 0 by the `pte_clear` macro.

Anticipating Linux 2.4

Linux 2.2 has two buddy systems: the first one handles page frames suitable for ISA DMA, while the second one handles page frames not suitable for ISA DMA. Linux 2.4 adds a third buddy system for the high physical memory, that is, for the page frames not permanently mapped by the kernel. Using a high-memory page frame implies changing an entry in a special kernel Page Table to map the page frame physical addresses in the 4 GB linear address space.

Actually, Linux 2.4 views the three portions of RAM as different "zones." Each zone has its own counters and watermarks to monitor the number of free page frames. When a memory allocation request takes place, the kernel first tries to fetch the page frames from the most suitable zone; if it fails, it may fall back on another zone.

The slab allocator is mostly unchanged. However, Linux 2.4 allows a slab allocator cache that is no longer useful to be destroyed. Recall that in Linux 2.2 a slab allocator cache can be dynamically created but not destroyed. Modules that create their own slab allocator cache when loaded are now expected to destroy it when unloaded.

CHAPTER SEVEN

PROCESS ADDRESS SPACE

As seen in the previous chapter, a kernel function gets dynamic memory in a fairly straightforward manner by invoking one of a variety of functions: `__get_free_pages()` to get pages from the buddy system algorithm, `kmem_cache_alloc()` or `kmalloc()` to use the slab allocator for specialized or general-purpose objects, and `vmalloc()` to get a noncontiguous memory area. If the request can be satisfied, each of these functions returns a linear address identifying the beginning of the allocated dynamic memory area.

These simple approaches work for two reasons:

- The kernel is the highest priority component of the operating system: if some kernel function makes a request for dynamic memory, it must have some valid reason to issue that request, and there is no point in trying to defer it.

- The kernel trusts itself: all kernel functions are assumed error-free, so it does not need to insert any protection against programming errors.

When allocating memory to User Mode processes, the situation is entirely different:

- Process requests for dynamic memory are considered nonurgent. When a process's executable file is loaded, for instance, it is unlikely that the process will address all the pages of code in the near future. Similarly, when a process invokes `malloc()` to get additional dynamic memory, it doesn't mean the process will soon access all the additional memory obtained. So as a general rule, the kernel tries to defer allocating dynamic memory to User Mode processes.

- Since user programs cannot be trusted, the kernel must be prepared to catch all addressing errors caused by processes in User Mode.

As we shall see in this chapter, the kernel succeeds in deferring the allocation of dynamic memory to processes by making use of a new kind of resource. When a User Mode process asks for dynamic memory, it doesn't get additional page frames; instead, it gets the right to use a new range of linear addresses, which become part of its address space. This interval is called a *memory region*.

We start in the section "The Process's Address Space" by discussing how the process views dynamic memory. We then describe the basic components of the process address space in the section "Memory Regions." Next, we examine in detail the role played by the page fault exception handler in deferring the allocation of page frames to processes. We then illustrate how the kernel creates and deletes whole process address spaces. Last, we discuss the APIs and system calls related to address space management.

The Process's Address Space

The *address space* of a process consists of all linear addresses that the process is allowed to use. Each process sees a different set of linear addresses; the address used by one process bears no relation to the address used by another. As we shall see later, the kernel may dynamically modify a process address space by adding or removing intervals of linear addresses.

The kernel represents intervals of linear addresses by means of resources called *memory regions*, which are characterized by an initial linear address, a length, and some access rights. For reasons of efficiency, both the initial address and the length of a memory region must be multiples of 4096, so that the data identified by each memory region entirely fills up the page frames allocated to it. Let us briefly mention typical situations in which a process gets new memory regions:

- When the user types a command at the console, the shell process creates a new process to execute the command. As a result, a fresh address space, thus a set of memory regions, is assigned to the new process (see the section "Creating and Deleting a Process Address Space" later in this chapter and Chapter 19, *Program Execution*).

- A running process may decide to load an entirely different program. In this case, the process ID remains unchanged but the memory regions used before loading the program are released, and a new set of memory regions is assigned to the process (see the section "The exec-like Functions" in Chapter 19).

- A running process may perform a "memory mapping" on a file (or on a portion of it). In such cases, the kernel assigns a new memory region to the process to map the file (see the section "Memory Mapping" in Chapter 15, *Accessing Regular Files*).

- A process may keep adding data on its User Mode stack until all addresses in the memory region that map the stack have been used. In such cases, the kernel may decide to expand the size of that memory region (see the section "Page Fault Exception Handler" later in this chapter).

- A process may create an IPC shared memory region to share data with other cooperating processes. In such cases, the kernel assigns a new memory region to the process to implement this construct (see the section "IPC Shared Memory" in Chapter 18, *Process Communication*).

- A process may expand its dynamic area (the heap) through a function such as `malloc()`. As a result, the kernel may decide to expand the size of the memory region assigned to the heap (see the section "Managing the Heap" later in this chapter).

Table 7-1 illustrates some of the system calls related to the previously mentioned tasks. With the exception of `brk()`, which is discussed at the end of this chapter, the system calls are described in other chapters.

Table 7-1. System Calls Related to Memory Region Creation and Deletion

System Call	Description
`brk()`	Changes the heap size of the process
`execve()`	Loads a new executable file, thus changing the process address space
`exit()`	Terminates the current process and destroys its address space
`fork()`	Creates a new process, and thus a new address space
`mmap()`	Creates a memory mapping for a file, thus enlarging the process address space
`munmap()`	Destroys a memory mapping for a file, thus contracting the process address space
`shmat()`	Creates a shared memory region
`shmdt()`	Destroys a shared memory region

As we shall see in the section "Page Fault Exception Handler," it is essential for the kernel to identify the memory regions currently owned by a process (that is, the address space of a process) since that allows the "Page fault" exception handler to efficiently distinguish between two types of invalid linear addresses that cause it to be invoked:

- Those caused by programming errors.

- Those caused by a missing page; even though the linear address belongs to the process's address space, the page frame corresponding to that address has yet to be allocated.

The latter addresses are not invalid from the process's point of view; the kernel handles the page fault by providing the page frame and letting the process continue.

The Memory Descriptor

All information related to the process address space is included in a table referenced by the mm field of the process descriptor. This table is a structure of type mm_struct as follows:

```
struct mm_struct {
    struct vm_area_struct *mmap, *mmap_avl, *mmap_cache;
    pgd_t * pgd;
    atomic_t count;
    int map_count;
    struct semaphore mmap_sem;
    unsigned long context;
    unsigned long start_code, end_code, start_data, end_data;
    unsigned long start_brk, brk, start_stack;
    unsigned long arg_start, arg_end, env_start, env_end;
    unsigned long rss, total_vm, locked_vm;
    unsigned long def_flags;
    unsigned long cpu_vm_mask;
    unsigned long swap_cnt;
    unsigned long swap_address;
    void * segments;
};
```

For the present discussion, the most important fields are:

pgd *and* segments
> Point, respectively, to the Page Global Directory and Local Descriptor Table of the process.

rss
> Specifies the number of page frames allocated to the process.

total_vm
> Denotes the size of the process address space expressed as a number of pages.

locked_vm
> Counts the number of "locked" pages, that is, pages that cannot be swapped out (see Chapter 16, *Swapping: Methods for Freeing Memory*).

count
> Denotes the number of processes that share the same struct mm_struct descriptor. If count is greater than 1, the processes are lightweight processes sharing the same address space, that is, using the same memory descriptor.

The mm_alloc() function is invoked to get a new memory descriptor. Since these descriptors are stored in a slab allocator cache, mm_alloc() calls kmem_cache_alloc(), initializes the new memory descriptor by duplicating the content of the memory descriptor of current, and sets the count field to 1.

Conversely, the `mmput()` function decrements the `count` field of a memory descriptor. If that field becomes 0, the function releases the Local Descriptor Table, the memory region descriptors (see later in this chapter), the page tables referenced by the memory descriptor, and the memory descriptor itself.

The `mmap`, `mmap_avl`, and `mmap_cache` fields are discussed in the next section.

Memory Regions

Linux implements memory regions by means of descriptors of type `vm_area_struct`:

```
struct vm_area_struct {
    struct mm_struct * vm_mm;
    unsigned long vm_start;
    unsigned long vm_end;
    struct vm_area_struct *vm_next;
    pgprot_t vm_page_prot;
    unsigned short vm_flags;
    short vm_avl_height;
    struct vm_area_struct *vm_avl_left, *vm_avl_right;
    struct vm_area_struct *vm_next_share, **vm_pprev_share;
    struct vm_operations_struct * vm_ops;
    unsigned long vm_offset;
    struct file * vm_file;
    unsigned long vm_pte;
};
```

Each memory region descriptor identifies a linear address interval. The `vm_start` field contains the first linear address of the interval, while the `vm_end` field contains the first linear address outside of the interval; `vm_end - vm_start` thus denotes the length of the memory region. The `vm_mm` field points to the `mm_struct` memory descriptor of the process that owns the region. We shall describe the other fields of `vm_area_struct` later.

Memory regions owned by a process never overlap, and the kernel tries to merge regions when a new one is allocated right next to an existing one. Two adjacent regions can be merged if their access rights match.

As shown in Figure 7-1, when a new range of linear addresses is added to the process address space, the kernel checks whether an already existing memory region can be enlarged (case *a*). If not, a new memory region is created (case *b*). Similarly, if a range of linear addresses is removed from the process address space, the kernel resizes the affected memory regions (case *c*). In some cases, the resizing forces a memory region to be split into two smaller ones (case *d*).[*]

---

[*] Removing a linear address interval may theoretically fail because no free memory is available for a new memory descriptor.

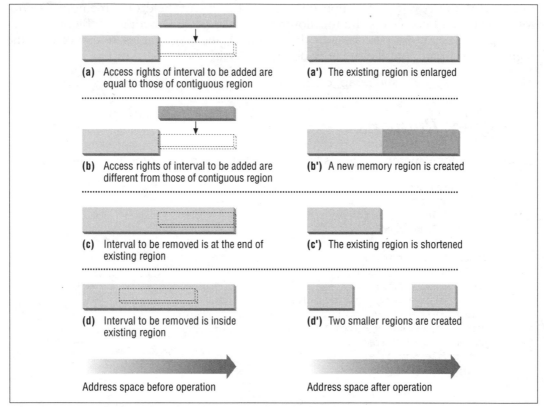

Figure 7-1. Adding or removing a linear address interval

Memory Region Data Structures

All the regions owned by a process are linked together in a simple list. Regions appear in the list in ascending order by memory address; however, each two regions can be separated by an area of unused memory addresses. The vm_next field of each vm_area_struct element points to the next element in the list. The kernel finds the memory regions through the mmap field of the process memory descriptor, which points to the vm_next field of the first memory region descriptor in the list.

The map_count field of the memory descriptor contains the number of regions owned by the process. A process may own up to MAX_MAP_COUNT different memory regions (this value is usually set to 65536).

Figure 7-2 illustrates the relationships among the address space of a process, its memory descriptor, and the list of memory regions.

A frequent operation performed by the kernel is to search the memory region that includes a specific linear address. Since the list is sorted, the search can terminate as soon as a memory region that ends after the specific linear address has been found.

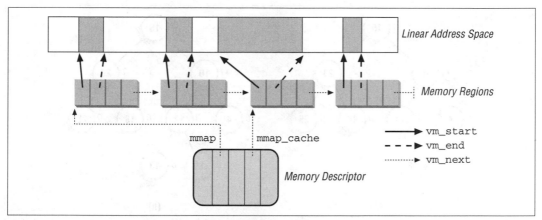

Figure 7-2. Descriptors related to the address space of a process

However, using the list is convenient only if the process has very few memory regions, let's say less than a few tens of them. Searching, inserting elements, and deleting elements in the list involve a number of operations whose times are linearly proportional to the list length.

Although most Linux processes use very few memory regions, there are some large applications like object-oriented databases that one might consider "pathological" in that they have many hundreds or even thousands of regions. In such cases, the memory region list management becomes very inefficient, hence the performance of the memory-related system calls degrades to an intolerable point.

When processes have a large number of memory regions, Linux stores their descriptors in data structures called *AVL trees*, which were invented in 1962 by Adelson-Velskii and Landis.

In an AVL tree, each element (or *node*) usually has two children: a *left child* and a *right child*. The elements in the AVL tree are sorted: for each node *N*, all elements of the subtree rooted at the left child of *N* precede *N*, while, conversely, all elements of the subtree rooted at the right child of *N* follow *N* (see Figure 7-3 (*a*); the key of the node is written inside the node itself).

Every node *N* of an AVL tree has a *balancing factor*, which shows how well balanced the branches under the node are. The balancing factor is the depth of the subtree rooted at *N*'s left child minus the depth of the subtree rooted at *N*'s right child. Every node of a properly balanced AVL tree must have a balancing factor equal to -1, 0, or +1 (see Figure 7-3 (*a*); the balancing factor of the node is written to the left of the node itself).

Searching an element in an AVL tree is very efficient, since it requires operations whose execution time is linearly proportional to the logarithm (of 2) of the tree size. In other words, doubling the number of memory regions adds just one more iteration to the operation.

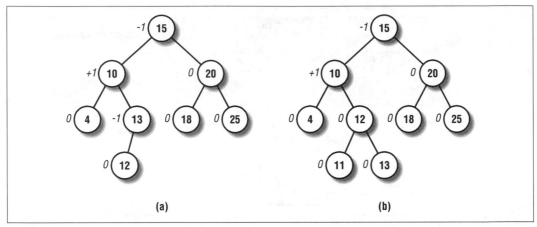

Figure 7-3. Example of AVL trees

Inserting and deleting an element in an AVL tree is also efficient, since the algorithm can quickly traverse the tree in order to locate the position at which the element will be inserted or from which it will be removed. However, such operations could make the AVL tree unbalanced. For instance, let's suppose that an element having value 11 must be inserted in the AVL tree shown in Figure 7-3 (*a*). Its proper position is the left child of node having key 12, but once it is inserted, the balancing factor of the node having key 13 becomes -2. In order to rebalance the AVL tree, the algorithm performs a "rotation" on the subtree rooted at the node having the key 13, thus producing the new AVL tree shown in Figure 7-3 (*b*). This looks complicated, but inserting or deleting an element in an AVL tree requires a small number of operations—a number linearly proportional to the logarithm of the tree size.

Still, AVL trees have their drawbacks. The functions that handle them are a lot more complex than the functions that handle lists. When the number of elements is small, it is far more efficient to put them in a list instead of in an AVL tree.

Therefore, in order to store the memory regions of a process, Linux generally makes use of the linked list referred by the `mmap` field of the memory descriptor; it starts using an AVL tree only when the number of memory regions of the process becomes higher than `AVL_MIN_MAP_COUNT` (usually 32 elements). Thus, the memory descriptor of a process includes another field named `mmap_avl` pointing to the AVL tree. This field has the value 0 until the kernel decides it needs to create the tree. Once an AVL tree has been created to handle memory regions of a process, Linux keeps both the linked list and the AVL tree up-to-date. Both data structures contain pointers to the same memory region descriptors. When inserting or removing a memory region descriptor, the kernel searches the previous and next elements through the AVL tree and uses them to quickly update the list without scanning it.

The addresses of the left and right children of every AVL node are stored in the `vm_avl_left` and `vm_avl_right` fields, respectively, of the `vm_area_struct` descriptor.

This descriptor also includes the `vm_avl_height` field, which stores the height of the subtree rooted at the memory region itself. The tree is sorted on the `vm_end` field value.

The `avl_rebalance()` function receives a path in a memory region's AVL tree as a parameter. It rebalances the tree, if necessary, by properly rotating a subtree branching off from a node of the path. The function is invoked by the `avl_insert()` and `avl_remove()` functions, which insert and remove a memory region descriptor in a tree, respectively. Linux also makes use of the `avl_insert_neighbours()` function to insert an element into the tree and return the addresses of the nearest nodes at the left and the right of the new element.

Memory Region Access Rights

Before moving on, we should clarify the relation between a page and a memory region. As mentioned in Chapter 2, *Memory Addressing*, we use the term "page" to refer both to a set of linear addresses and to the data contained in this group of addresses. In particular, we denote the linear address interval ranging between 0 and 4095 as page 0, the linear address interval ranging between 4096 and 8191 as page 1, and so forth. Each memory region thus consists of a set of pages having consecutive page numbers.

We have already discussed in previous chapters two kinds of flags associated with a page:

- A few flags such as `Read/Write`, `Present`, or `User/Supervisor` stored in each page table entry (see the section "Regular Paging" in Chapter 2).

- A set of flags stored in the `flags` field of each `page` descriptor (see the section "Page Frame Management" in Chapter 6, *Memory Management*).

The first kind of flag is used by the Intel 80x86 hardware to check whether the requested kind of addressing can be performed; the second kind is used by Linux for many different purposes (see Table 6-1).

We now introduce a third kind of flags: those associated with the pages of a memory region. They are stored in the `vm_flags` field of the `vm_area_struct` descriptor (see Table 7-2). Some flags offer the kernel information about all the pages of the memory region, such as what they contain and what rights the process has to access each page. Other flags describe the region itself, such as how it can grow.

Table 7-2. The Memory Region Flags

Flag Name	Description
VM_DENYWRITE	The region maps a file that cannot be opened for writing.
VM_EXEC	Pages can be executed.
VM_EXECUTABLE	Pages contain executable code.

Table 7-2. The Memory Region Flags (continued)

Flag Name	Description
VM_GROWSDOWN	The region can expand toward lower addresses.
VM_GROWSUP	The region can expand toward higher addresses.
VM_IO	The region maps the I/O address space of a device.
VM_LOCKED	Pages are locked and cannot be swapped out.
VM_MAYEXEC	VM_EXEC flag may be set.
VM_MAYREAD	VM_READ flag may be set.
VM_MAYSHARE	VM_SHARE flag may be set.
VM_MAYWRITE	VM_WRITE flag may be set.
VM_READ	Pages can be read.
VM_SHARED	Pages can be shared by several processes.
VM_SHM	Pages are used for IPC's shared memory.
VM_WRITE	Pages can be written.

Page access rights included in a memory region descriptor may be combined arbitrarily: it is possible, for instance, to allow the pages of a region to be executed but not to be read. In order to implement this protection scheme efficiently, the read, write, and execute access rights associated with the pages of a memory region must be duplicated in all the corresponding page table entries, so that checks can be directly performed by the Paging Unit circuitry. In other words, the page access rights dictate what kinds of access should generate a "Page fault" exception. As we shall see shortly, Linux delegates the job of figuring out what caused the page fault to the page fault handler, which implements several page-handling strategies.

The initial values of the page table flags (which must be the same for all pages in the memory region, as we have seen) are stored in the **vm_page_prot** field of the **vm_area_struct** descriptor. When adding a page, the kernel sets the flags in the corresponding page table entry according to the value of the **vm_page_prot** field.

However, translating the memory region's access rights into the page protection bits is not straightforward, for the following reasons:

- In some cases, a page access should generate a "Page fault" exception even when its access type is granted by the page access rights specified in the **vm_flags** field of the corresponding memory region. For instance, the kernel might decide to store two identical, writable private pages (whose VM_SHARE flags are cleared) belonging to two different processes into the same page frame; in this case, an exception should be generated when either one of the processes tries to modify the page (see the section "Copy On Write" later in this chapter).

- Intel 80x86 processors's page tables have just two protection bits, namely the `Read/Write` and `User/Supervisor` flags. Moreover, the `User/Supervisor` flag of any page included in a memory region must always be set, since the page must always be accessible by User Mode processes.

In order to overcome the hardware limitation of the Intel microprocessors, Linux adopts the following rules:

- The read access right always implies the execute access right.

- The write access right always implies the read access right.

Moreover, in order to correctly defer the allocation of page frames through the "Copy On Write" technique (see later in this chapter), the page frame is write-protected whenever the corresponding page must not be shared by several processes. Therefore, the 16 possible combinations of the read, write, execute, and share access rights are scaled down to the following three:

- If the page has both write and share access rights, the `Read/Write` bit is set.

- If the page has the read or execute access right but does not have either the write or the share access right, the `Read/Write` bit is cleared.

- If the page does not have any access rights, the `Present` bit is cleared, so that each access generates a "Page fault" exception. However, in order to distinguish this condition from the real page-not-present case, Linux also sets the `Page size` bit to 1.[*]

The downscaled protection bits corresponding to each combination of access rights are stored in the `protection_map` array.

Memory Region Handling

Having the basic understanding of data structures and state information that control memory handling, we can look at a group of low-level functions that operate on memory region descriptors. They should be considered as auxiliary functions that simplify the implementation of `do_mmap()` and `do_munmap()`. Those two functions, which are described in the sections "Allocating a Linear Address Interval" and "Releasing a Linear Address Interval" later in this chapter, respectively, enlarge and shrink the address space of a process. Working at a higher level than the functions we consider here, they do not receive a memory region descriptor as their parameter, but rather the initial address, the length, and the access rights of a linear address interval.

---

[*] You might consider this use of the `Page size` bit to be a dirty trick, since the bit was meant to indicate the real page size. But Linux can get away with the deception because the Intel chip checks the `Page size` bit in Page Directory entries, but not in Page Table entries.

Finding the closest region to a given address

The find_vma() function acts on two parameters: the address mm of a process memory descriptor and a linear address addr. It locates the first memory region whose vm_end field is greater than addr and returns the address of its descriptor; if no such region exists, it returns a NULL pointer. Notice that the region selected by find_vma() does not necessarily include addr.

Each memory descriptor includes a mmap_cache field that stores the descriptor address of the region that was last referenced by the process. This additional field is introduced to reduce the time spent in looking for the region that contains a given linear address: locality of address references in programs makes it highly likely that if the last linear address checked belonged to a given region, the next one to be checked belongs to the same region.

The function thus starts by checking whether the region identified by mmap_cache includes addr. If so, it returns the region descriptor pointer:

```
vma = mm->mmap_cache;
if (vma && vma->vm_end > addr && vma->vm_start <= addr)
    return vma;
```

Otherwise, the memory regions of the process must be scanned. If the process does not make use of an AVL tree, the function simply scans the linked list:

```
if (!mm->mmap_avl) {
    vma = mm->mmap;
    while (vma && vma->vm_end <= addr)
        vma = vma->vm_next;
    if (vma)
        mm->mmap_cache = vma;
    return vma;
}
```

Otherwise, the function looks up the memory region in the AVL tree:

```
tree = mm->mmap_avl;
vma = NULL;
for (;;) {
    if (tree == NULL)
        break;
    if (tree->vm_end > addr) {
        vma = tree;
        if (tree->vm_start <= addr)
            break;
        tree = tree->vm_avl_left;
    } else
        tree = tree->vm_avl_right;
```

```
    }
    if (vma)
        mm->mmap_cache = vma;
    return vma;
```

The kernel also makes use of the `find_vma_prev()` function, which returns the descriptor addresses of the memory region that precedes the linear address given as parameter and of the memory region that follows it.

Finding a region that overlaps a given address interval

The `find_vma_intersection()` function finds the first memory region that overlaps a given linear address interval; the mm parameter points to the memory descriptor of the process, while the `start_addr` and `end_addr` linear addresses specify the interval:

```
    vma = find_vma(mm, start_addr);
    if (vma && end_addr <= vma->vm_start)
        vma = NULL;
    return vma;
```

The function returns a NULL pointer if no such region exists. To be exact, if `find_vma()` returns a valid address but the memory region found starts after the end of the linear address interval, `vma` is set to NULL.

Finding a free address interval

The `get_unmapped_area()` function searches the process address space to find an available linear address interval. The `len` parameter specifies the interval length, while the `addr` parameter may specify the address from which the search is started. If the search is successful, the function returns the initial address of the new interval; otherwise, it returns 0:

```
    if (len > PAGE_OFFSET)
        return 0;
    if (!addr)
        addr = PAGE_OFFSET / 3;
    addr = (addr + 0xfff) & 0xfffff000;
    for (vmm = find_vma(current->mm, addr); ; vmm = vmm->vm_next) {
        if (addr + len > PAGE_OFFSET)
            return 0;
        if (!vmm || addr + len <= vmm->vm_start)
            return addr;
        addr = vmm->vm_end;
    }
```

The function starts by checking to make sure the interval length is within the limit imposed on User Mode linear addresses, usually 3 GB. If `addr` is NULL, the search's starting point is set to one-third of the User Mode linear address space. To be on the safe side, the function rounds up the value of `addr` to a multiple of 4 KB. Starting from `addr`, it then repeatedly invokes `find_vma()` with increasing values of `addr` to find the required free interval. During this search, the following cases may occur:

- The requested interval is larger than the portion of linear address space yet to be scanned (`addr + len > PAGE_OFFSET`): since there are not enough linear addresses to satisfy the request, return 0.

- The hole following the last scanned region is not large enough (`vmm != NULL && vmm->vm_start < addr + len`): consider the next region.

- If neither one of the preceding conditions holds, a large enough hole has been found: return `addr`.

Inserting a region in the memory descriptor list

`insert_vm_struct()` inserts a `vm_area_struct` structure in the list of memory descriptors and, if necessary, in the AVL tree. It makes use of two parameters: `mm`, which specifies the address of a process memory descriptor, and `vmp`, which specifies the address of the `vm_area_struct` descriptor to be inserted:

```
if (!mm->mmap_avl) {
    pprev = &mm->mmap;
    while (*pprev && (*pprev)->vm_start <= vmp->vm_start)
        pprev = &(*pprev)->vm_next;
} else {
    struct vm_area_struct *prev, *next;
    avl_insert_neighbours(vmp, &mm->mmap_avl, &prev, &next);
    pprev = (prev ? &prev->vm_next : &mm->mmap);
}
vmp->vm_next = *pprev;
*pprev = vmp;
```

If the process makes use of the AVL tree, the `avl_insert_neighbours()` function is invoked to insert the memory region descriptor in the proper position; otherwise, `insert_vm_struct()` scans forward through the linked list using the `pprev` local variable until it finds the descriptor that should precede `vmp`. At the end of the search, `pprev` points to the `vm_next` field of the memory region descriptor that should precede `vmp` in the list, hence `*pprev` yields the address of the memory region descriptor that should follow `vmp`. The descriptor can thus be inserted into the list.

```
mm->map_count++;
if (mm->map_count >= AVL_MIN_MAP_COUNT && !mm->mmap_avl)
    build_mmap_avl(mm);
```

The `map_count` field of the process memory descriptor is then incremented by 1. Moreover, if the process was not using the AVL tree up to now but the number of memory regions becomes greater than or equal to `AVL_MIN_MAP_COUNT`, the `build_mmap_avl()` function is invoked:

```
void build_mmap_avl(struct mm_struct * mm)
{
    struct vm_area_struct * vma;
    mm->mmap_avl = NULL;
    for (vma = mm->mmap; vma; vma = vma->vm_next)
        avl_insert(vma, &mm->mmap_avl);
}
```

From now on, the process will use an AVL tree.

If the region contains a memory mapped file, the function performs additional tasks that are described in Chapter 16.

No explicit function exists for removing a region from the memory descriptor list (see the later section "Releasing a Linear Address Interval").

Merging contiguous regions

The `merge_segments()` function attempts to merge together the memory regions included in a given linear address interval. As illustrated in Figure 7-1, this can be achieved only if the contiguous regions have the same access rights. The parameters of `merge_segments()` are a memory descriptor pointer `mm` and two linear addresses `start_addr` and `end_addr`, which delimit the interval. The function finds the last memory region that ends before `start_addr` and puts the address of its descriptor in the `prev` local variable. Then it iteratively executes the following actions:

- Loads the `mpnt` local variable with `prev->vm_next`, that is, the descriptor address of the first memory region that starts after `start_addr`. If no such region exists, no merging is possible.

- Cycles through the list as long as `prev->vm_start` is smaller than `end_addr`. Checks whether it is possible to merge the memory regions associated with `prev` and `mpnt`. This is possible if:

  — The memory regions are contiguous: `prev->vm_end = mpnt->vm_start`.

  — They have the same flags: `prev->vm_flags = mpnt->vm_flags`.

  — When they map files or are shared among processes, they satisfy additional requirements to be discussed in later chapters.

  If merging is possible, remove the memory region descriptor from the list and, if necessary, from the AVL tree.

- Decrement the `map_count` field of the memory descriptor by 1, and resume the search by setting `prev` so that it points to the merged memory region descriptor.

The function ends by setting the `mmap_cache` field of the memory descriptor to NULL, since the memory region cache could now refer to a memory region that no longer exists.

Allocating a Linear Address Interval

Now let's discuss how new linear address intervals are allocated. In order to do this, the do_mmap() function creates and initializes a new memory region for the current process. However, after a successful allocation, the memory region could be merged with other memory regions defined for the process.

The function makes use of the following parameters:

file *and* off
> File descriptor pointer file and file offset off are used if the new memory region will map a file into memory. This topic will be discussed in Chapter 15. In this section, we'll assume that no memory mapping is required and that file and off are both NULL.

addr
> This linear address specifies where the search for a free interval must start (see the previous description of the get_unmapped_area() function).

len
> The length of the linear address interval.

prot
> This parameter specifies the access rights of the pages included in the memory region. Possible flags are PROT_READ, PROT_WRITE, PROT_EXEC, and PROT_NONE. The first three flags mean the same things as the VM_READ, VM_WRITE, and VM_EXEC flags. PROT_NONE indicates that the process has none of those access rights.

flag
> This parameter specifies the remaining memory region flags:
>
> MAP_GROWSDOWN, MAP_LOCKED, MAP_DENYWRITE, *and* MAP_EXECUTABLE
> > Their meanings are identical to those of the flags listed in Table 7-2.
>
> MAP_SHARED *and* MAP_PRIVATE
> > The former flag specifies that the pages in the memory region can be shared among several processes; the latter flag has the opposite effect. Both flags refer to the VM_SHARED flag in the vm_area_struct descriptor.
>
> MAP_ANONYMOUS
> > No file is associated with the memory region (see Chapter 15).
>
> MAP_FIXED
> > The initial linear address of the interval must be the one specified in the addr parameter.
>
> MAP_NORESERVE
> > The function doesn't have to do a preliminary check of the number of free page frames.

The `do_mmap()` function starts by checking whether the parameter values are correct and whether the request can be satisfied. In particular, it checks for the following conditions that prevent it from satisfying the request:

- The linear address interval includes addresses greater than `PAGE_OFFSET`.

- The process has already mapped too many memory regions: the value of the `map_count` field of its `mm` memory descriptor exceeds the `MAX_MAP_COUNT` value.

- The `file` parameter is equal to NULL and the `flag` parameter specifies that the pages of the new linear address interval must be shared.

- The `flag` parameter specifies that the pages of the new linear address interval must be locked in RAM, and the number of pages locked by the process exceeds the threshold stored in the `rlim[RLIMIT_MEMLOCK].rlim_cur` field of the process descriptor.

If any of the preceding conditions holds, `do_mmap()` terminates by returning a negative value. If the linear address interval has a zero length, the function returns without performing any action.

The next step consists of obtaining a linear address interval; if the `MAP_FIXED` flag is set, a check is made on the proper alignment of the `addr` value; then the `get_unmapped_area()` function is invoked to get it:

```
if (flags & MAP_FIXED) {
    if (addr & 0xfffff000)
        return -EINVAL;
} else {
    addr = get_unmapped_area(addr, len);
    if (!addr)
        return -ENOMEM;
}
```

Now a `vm_area_struct` descriptor must be allocated for the new region. This is done by invoking the `kmem_cache_alloc()` slab allocator function:

```
vma = kmem_cache_alloc(vm_area_cachep, SLAB_KERNEL);
if (!vma)
    return -ENOMEM;
```

The memory region descriptor is then initialized. Notice how the value of the `vm_flags` field is determined both by the `prot` and `flags` parameters (joined together by means of the `vm_flags()` function) and by the `def_flags` field of the memory descriptor. The latter field allows the kernel to define a set of flags that should be set for every memory region in the process.[*]

---

[*] Actually, this field is modified only by the `mlockall()` system call, which can be used to set the `VM_LOCKED` flag, thus locking all future pages of the calling process in RAM.

```
vma->vm_mm = current->mm;
vma->vm_start = addr;
vma->vm_end = addr + len;
vma->vm_flags = vm_flags(prot,flags) | current->mm->def_flags;
vma->vm_flags |= VM_MAYREAD | VM_MAYWRITE | VM_MAYEXEC;
vma->vm_page_prot = protection_map[vma->vm_flags & 0x0f];
```

The do_mmap() function then checks whether any of these error conditions holds:

- The process already includes in its address space a memory region that overlaps the linear address interval ranging from addr to addr+len, and moreover the do_munmap () function fails in releasing the overlapping region.

- The size in pages of the process address space exceeds the threshold stored in the rlim[RLIMIT_AS].rlim_cur field of the process descriptor.

- The MAP_NORESERVE flag was not set in the flags parameter, the new memory region must contain private writable pages, and the number of free page frames is less than the size (in pages) of the linear address interval; this last check is performed by the vm_enough_memory() function.

If any of the preceding conditions holds, do_mmap() releases the vm_area_struct descriptor obtained and terminates by returning the −ENOMEM value.

Once all checks have been performed, do_mmap() increments the size of current's address space stored in the total_vm field of the memory descriptor. It then invokes insert_vm_struct(), which inserts the new region in the list of regions owned by current (and, if necessary, in its AVL tree), and merge_segments(), which checks whether regions can be merged. Since the new region may be destroyed by a merge, the values of vm_flags and vm_start, which may be needed later, are saved in the flags and addr local variables:

```
current->mm->total_vm += len >> PAGE_SHIFT;
flags = vma->vm_flags;
addr = vma->vm_start;
insert_vm_struct(current->mm, vma);
merge_segments(current->mm, vma->vm_start, vma->vm_end);
```

The final step is executed only if the MAP_LOCKED flag is set. First, the number of pages in the memory region is added to the locked_vm field of the memory descriptor. Then the make_pages_present() function is invoked to allocate all the pages of the memory region in succession and lock them in RAM. The core code of make_pages_present() is:

```
vma = find_vma(current->mm, addr);
write = (vma->vm_flags & VM_WRITE) != 0;
while (addr < addr + len) {
```

```
while (addr < addr + len) {
    handle_mm_fault(current, vma, addr, write);
    addr += PAGE_SIZE;
}
```

As we shall see in the section "Handling a Faulty Address Inside the Address Space," `handle_mm_fault()` allocates one page and sets its page table entry according to the `vm_flags` field of the memory region descriptor.

Finally, the `do_mmap()` function terminates by returning the linear address of the new memory region.

Releasing a Linear Address Interval

The `do_munmap()` function deletes a linear address interval from the address space of the current process. The parameters are the starting address `addr` of the interval and its length `len`. The interval to be deleted does not usually correspond to a memory region: it may be included in one memory region, or it may span two or more regions.

The function goes through two main phases. First, it scans the list of memory regions owned by the process and removes all regions that overlap the linear address interval. In the second phase, the function updates the process page tables and reinserts a downsized version of the memory regions that were removed during the first phase.

First phase: scanning the memory regions

A preliminary check is made on the parameter values: if the linear address interval includes addresses greater than `PAGE_OFFSET`, if `addr` is not a multiple of 4096, or if the linear address interval has a zero length, the function returns a negative error code.

Next, the function locates the first memory region that overlaps the linear address interval to be deleted:

```
mpnt = find_vma_prev(current->mm, addr, &prev);
if (!mpnt || mpnt->vm_start >= addr + len)
    return 0;
```

If the linear address interval is located inside a memory region, its deletion will split the region into two smaller ones. In this case, `do_munmap()` checks whether `current` is allowed to obtain an additional memory region:

```
if ((mpnt->vm_start < addr && mpnt->vm_end > addr + len) &&
    current->mm->map_count > MAX_MAP_COUNT)
    return -ENOMEM;
```

The function then attempts to get a new `vm_area_struct` descriptor. There may be no need for it, but the function makes the request anyway so that it can terminate right away if the allocation fails. This cautious approach simplifies the code since it allows an easy error exit:

```
extra = kmem_cache_alloc(vm_area_cachep, SLAB_KERNEL);
if (!extra)
    return -ENOMEM;
```

Now the function builds up a list including all descriptors of the memory regions that overlap the linear address interval. This list is created by setting the **vm_next** field of the memory region descriptor (temporarily) so it points to the previous item in the list; this field thus acts as a backward link. As each region is added to this backward list, a local variable named **free** points to the last inserted element. The regions inserted in the list are also removed from the list of memory regions owned by the process and, if necessary, from the AVL tree:

```
npp = (prev ? &prev->vm_next : &current->mm->mmap);
free = NULL;
for ( ; mpnt && mpnt->vm_start < addr + len; mpnt = *npp) {
    *npp = mpnt->vm_next;
    mpnt->vm_next = free;
    free = mpnt;
    if (current->mm->mmap_avl)
        avl_remove(mpnt, &current->mm->mmap_avl);
}
```

Second phase: updating the page tables

A **while** cycle is used to scan the list of memory regions built in the first phase, starting with the memory region descriptor that **free** points to.

In each iteration, the **mpnt** local variable points to the descriptor of a memory region in the list. The **map_count** field of the **current->mm** memory descriptor is decremented (since the region has been removed in the first phase from the list of regions owned by the process) and a check is made (by means of two question-mark conditional expressions) to determine whether the **mpnt** region must be eliminated or simply downsized:

```
current->mm->map_count--;
st = addr < mpnt->vm_start ? mpnt->vm_start : addr;
end = addr + len;
end = end > mpnt->vm_end ? mpnt->vm_end : end;
size = end - st;
```

The **st** and **end** local variables delimit the linear address interval in the **mpnt** memory region that should be deleted; the **size** local variable specifies the length of the interval.

Next, **do_munmap()** releases the page frames allocated for the pages included in the interval from **st** to **end**:

```
zap_page_range(current->mm, st, size);
flush_tlb_range(current->mm, st, end);
```

The `zap_page_range()` function deallocates the page frames included in the interval from `st` to `end` and updates the corresponding page table entries. The function invokes in nested fashion the `zap_pmd_range()` and `zap_pte_range()` functions for scanning the page tables; the latter function uses the `pte_clear` macro to clear the page table entries and the `free_pte()` function to free the corresponding page frames.

The `flush_tlb_range()` function is then invoked to invalidate the TLB entries corresponding to the interval from `st` to `end`. In the Intel 80x86 architecture that function simply invokes `__flush_tlb()`, thus invalidating all TLB entries.

The last action performed in each iteration of the `do_munmap()` loop is to check whether a downsized version of the `mpnt` memory region must be reinserted in the list of regions of `current`:

```
extra = unmap_fixup(mpnt, st, size, extra);
```

The `unmap_fixup()` function considers four possible cases:

* The memory region has been totally canceled. Return the address stored in the `extra` local variable, thus signaling that the extra memory region descriptor can be released by invoking `kmem_cache_free()`.

* Only the lower part of the memory region has been removed, that is:

  ```
  (mpnt->vm_start < st) && (mpnt->vm_end == end)
  ```

  In this case, update the `vm_end` field of `mnpt`, invoke `insert_vm_struct()` to insert the downsized region in the list of regions belonging to the process, and return the address stored in `extra`.

* Only the upper part of the memory region has been removed, that is:

  ```
  (mpnt->vm_start == st) && (mpnt->vm_end > end)
  ```

  In this case, update the `vm_start` field of `mnpt`, invoke `insert_vm_struct()` to insert the downsized region in the list of regions belonging to the process, and return the address stored in `extra`.

* The linear address interval is in the middle of the memory region, that is:

  ```
  (mpnt->vm_start < st) && (mpnt->vm_end > end)
  ```

  Update the `vm_start` and `vm_end` fields of `mnpt` and `extra` (the previously allocated extra memory region descriptor) so that they refer to the linear address intervals, respectively, from `mpnt->vm_start` to `st` and from `end` to `mpnt->vm_end`. Then invoke `insert_vm_struct()` twice to insert the two regions in the list of regions belonging to the process (and, if necessary, in the AVL tree) and return NULL, thus preserving the extra memory region descriptor previously allocated.

This terminates the description of what must be done in a single iteration of the second-phase loop.

After handling all the memory region descriptors in the list built during the first phase, do_munmap() checks if the additional extra memory descriptor has been used. If extra is NULL, the descriptor has been used; otherwise, do_munmap() invokes kmem_cache_free() to release it. Finally, if the process address space has been modified, do_munmap() sets the mmap_cache field of the memory descriptor to NULL and returns 0.

Page Fault Exception Handler

As stated previously, the Linux "Page fault" exception handler must distinguish exceptions caused by programming errors from those caused by a reference to a page that legitimately belongs to the process address space but simply hasn't been allocated yet.

The memory region descriptors allow the exception handler to perform its job quite efficiently. The do_page_fault() function, which is the "Page fault" interrupt service routine, compares the linear address that caused the page fault against the memory regions of the current process; it can thus determine the proper way to handle the exception according to the scheme illustrated in Figure 7-4.

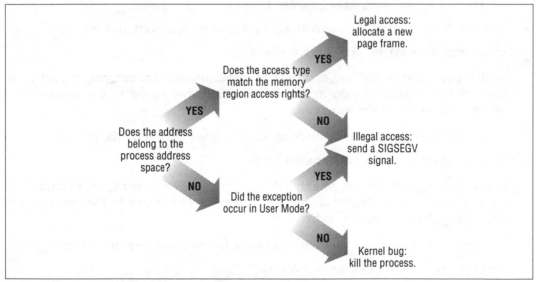

Figure 7-4. Overall scheme for the page fault handler

In practice, things are a lot more complex since the page fault handler must recognize several particular subcases that fit awkwardly into the overall scheme, and it must distinguish several kinds of legal access. A detailed flow diagram of the handler is illustrated in Figure 7-5.

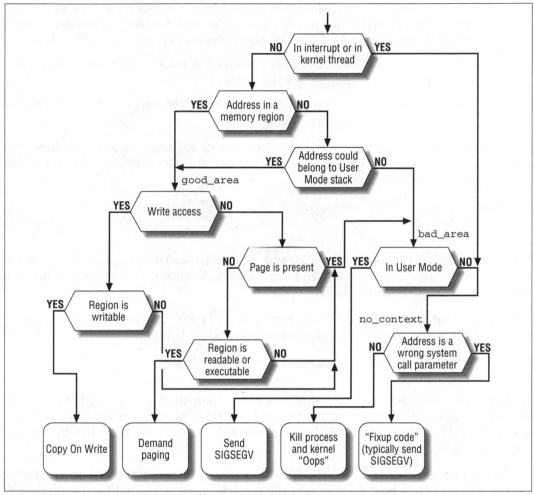

Figure 7-5. The flow diagram of the page fault handler

The identifiers **good_area**, **bad_area**, and **no_context** are labels appearing in **do_page_fault()** that should help you to relate the blocks of the flow diagram to specific lines of code.

The **do_page_fault()** function accepts the following input parameters:

- The **regs** address of a **pt_regs** structure containing the values of the microprocessor registers when the exception occurred.

- A 3-bit **error_code**, which is pushed on the stack by the control unit when the exception occurred (see "Hardware Handling of Interrupts and Exceptions" in Chapter 4, *Interrupts and Exceptions*). The bits have the following meanings.

— If bit 0 is clear, the exception was caused by an access to a page that is not present (the **Present** flag in the Page Table entry is clear); otherwise, if bit 0 is set, the exception was caused by an invalid access right.

— If bit 1 is clear, the exception was caused by a read or execute access; if set, the exception was caused by a write access.

— If bit 2 is clear, the exception occurred while the processor was in Kernel Mode; otherwise, it occurred in User Mode.

The first operation of **do_page_fault()** consists of reading the linear address that caused the page fault. When the exception occurs, the CPU control unit stores that value in the **cr2** control register:

```
asm("movl %%cr2,%0":"=r" (address));
tsk = current;
mm = tsk->mm;
```

The linear address is saved in the **address** local variable. The function also saves the pointers to the process descriptor and the memory descriptor of **current** in the **tsk** and **mm** local variables, respectively.

As shown at the top of Figure 7-5, **do_page_fault()** first checks whether the exception occurred while handling an interrupt or executing a kernel thread:

```
if (in_interrupt() || mm == &init_mm)
    goto no_context;
```

In both cases, **do_page_fault()** does not try to compare the linear address with the memory regions of **current**, since it would not make any sense: interrupt handlers and kernel threads never use linear addresses below **PAGE_OFFSET**, and thus never rely on memory regions.

Let us suppose that the page fault did not occur in an interrupt handler or in a kernel thread. Then the function must inspect the memory regions owned by the process to determine whether the faulty linear address is included in the process address space:

```
vma = find_vma(mm, address);
if (!vma)
    goto bad_area;
if (vma->vm_start <= address)
    goto good_area;
```

Now the function has determined that **address** is not included in any memory region; however, it must perform an additional check, since the faulty **address** may have been caused by a **push** or **pusha** instruction on the User Mode stack of the process.

Let us make a short digression to explain how stacks are mapped into memory regions. Each region that contains a stack expands toward lower addresses; its **VM_GROWSDOWN** flag is set, thus the value of its **vm_end** field remains fixed while the value of its **vm_start** field may be decreased. The region boundaries include, but do not delimit precisely, the current size of the User Mode stack. The reasons for the fuzz factor are:

- The region size is a multiple of 4 KB (it must include complete pages) while the stack size is arbitrary.

- Page frames assigned to a region are never released until the region is deleted; in particular, the value of the **vm_start** field of a region that includes a stack can only decrease; it can never increase. Even if the process executes a series of **pop** instructions, the region size remains unchanged.

It should now be clear how a process that has filled up the last page frame allocated to its stack may cause a "Page fault" exception: the **push** refers to an address outside of the region (and to a nonexistent page frame). Notice that this kind of exception is not caused by a programming error; it must thus be handled separately by the page fault handler.

We now return to the description of **do_page_fault()**, which checks for the case described previously:

```
if (!(vma->vm_flags & VM_GROWSDOWN))
    goto bad_area;
if (error_code & 4        /* User Mode */
    && address + 32 < regs->esp)
    goto bad_area;
if (expand_stack(vma, address))
    goto bad_area;
goto good_area;
```

If the **VM_GROWSDOWN** flag of the region is set and the exception occurred in User Mode, the function checks whether **address** is smaller than the **regs->esp** stack pointer (it should be only a little smaller). Since a few stack-related assembly language instructions (like **pusha**) perform a decrement of the **esp** register only after the memory access, a 32-byte tolerance interval is granted to the process. If the address is high enough (within the tolerance granted), the code invokes the **expand_stack()** function to check whether the process is allowed to extend both its stack and its address space; if everything is OK, it sets the **vm_start** field of **vma** to **address** and returns 0; otherwise, it returns 1.

Note that the preceding code skips the tolerance check whenever the **VM_GROWSDOWN** flag of the region is set and the exception did not occur in User Mode. Those conditions mean that the kernel is addressing the User Mode stack and that the code should always run **expand_stack()**.

Handling a Faulty Address Outside the Address Space

If `address` does not belong to the process address space, `do_page_fault()` proceeds to execute the statements at the label `bad_area`. If the error occurred in User Mode, it sends a `SIGSEGV` signal to `current` (see the section "Sending a Signal" in Chapter 9, *Signals*) and terminates:

```
bad_area:
if (error_code & 4) {    /* User Mode */
    tsk->tss.cr2 = address;
    tsk->tss.error_code = error_code;
    tsk->tss.trap_no = 14;
    force_sig(SIGSEGV, tsk);
    return;
}
```

If, however, the exception occurred in Kernel Mode (bit 2 of `error_code` is clear), there are still two alternatives:

- The exception occurred while using some linear address that has been passed to the kernel as parameter of a system call.

- The exception is due to a real kernel bug.

The function distinguishes these two alternatives as follows:

```
no_context:
if ((fixup = search_exception_table(regs->eip)) != 0) {
    regs->eip = fixup;
    return;
}
```

In the first case, it jumps to some "fixup code," which typically sends a `SIGSEGV` signal to `current` or terminates a system call handler with a proper error code (see the section "Dynamic Address Checking: The Fixup Code" in Chapter 8, *System Calls*).

In the second case, the function prints a complete dump of the CPU registers and the Kernel Mode stack on the console and on a system message buffer, then kills the current process by invoking the `do_exit()` function (see Chapter 19). This is the so-called *"Kernel oops"* error, named after the message displayed. The dumped values can be used by kernel hackers to reconstruct the conditions that triggered the bug, thus find and correct it.

Handling a Faulty Address Inside the Address Space

If `address` belongs to the process address space, `do_page_fault()` proceeds to the statement labeled `good_area`:

```
good_area:
write = 0;
```

```
if (error_code & 2) { /* write access */
    if (!(vma->vm_flags & VM_WRITE))
        goto bad_area;
    write++;
} else                  /* read access */
    if (error_code & 1 ||
        !(vma->vm_flags & (VM_READ | VM_EXEC)))
        goto bad_area;
```

If the exception was caused by a write access, the function checks whether the memory region is writable. If not, it jumps to the **bad_area** code; if so, it sets the **write** local variable to 1.

If the exception was caused by a read or execute access, the function checks whether the page is already present in RAM. In this case, the exception occurred because the process tried to access a privileged page frame (one whose **User/Supervisor** flag is clear) in User Mode, so the function jumps to the **bad_area** code.* If the page is not present, the function also checks whether the memory region is readable or executable.

If the memory region access rights match the access type that caused the exception, the **handle_mm_fault()** function is invoked:

```
if (!handle_mm_fault(tsk, vma, address, write)) {
    tsk->tss.cr2 = address;
    tsk->tss.error_code = error_code;
    tsk->tss.trap_no = 14;
    force_sig(SIGBUS, tsk);
    if (!(error_code & 4)) /* Kernel Mode */
        goto no_context;
}
```

The **handle_mm_fault()** function returns 1 if it succeeded in allocating a new page frame for the process; otherwise, it returns an appropriate error code so that **do_page_fault()** can send a **SIGBUS** signal to the process. It acts on four parameters:

tsk

A pointer to the descriptor of the process that was running on the CPU when the exception occurred

vma

A pointer to the descriptor of the memory region including the linear address that caused the exception

address

The linear address that caused the exception

---

* However, this case should never happen, since the kernel does not assign privileged page frames to the processes.

`write_access`

Set to 1 if `tsk` attempted to write in `address` and to 0 if `tsk` attempted to read or execute it

The function starts by checking whether the Page Middle Directory and the Page Table used to map `address` exist. Even if `address` belongs to the process address space, the corresponding page tables might not have been allocated, so the task of allocating them precedes everything else:

```
pgd = pgd_offset(vma->vm_mm, address);
pmd = pmd_alloc(pgd, address);
if (!pmd)
    return -1;
pte = pte_alloc(pmd, address);
if (!pte)
    return -1;
```

The `pgd` local variable contains the Page Global Directory entry that refers to `address`; `pmd_alloc()` is invoked to allocate, if needed, a new Page Middle Directory.* `pte_alloc()` is then invoked to allocate, if needed, a new Page Table. If both operations are successful, the `pte` local variable points to the Page Table entry that refers to `address`. The `handle_pte_fault()` function is then invoked to inspect the Page Table entry corresponding to `address`:

```
return handle_pte_fault(tsk, vma, address, write_access, pte);
```

The `handle_pte_fault()` function determines how to allocate a new page frame for the process:

- If the accessed page is not present—that is, if it is not already stored in any page frame—the kernel allocates a new page frame and initializes it properly; this technique is called *demand paging.*

- If the accessed page is present but is marked read only—that is, if it is already stored in a page frame—the kernel allocates a new page frame and initializes its contents by copying the old page frame data; this technique is called *Copy On Write.*

Demand Paging

The term *demand paging* denotes a dynamic memory allocation technique that consists of deferring page frame allocation until the last possible moment, that is, until the process attempts to address a page that is not present in RAM, thus causing a "Page fault" exception.

---

* On Intel 80x86 microprocessors, this kind of allocation never occurs since Page Middle Directories are included in the Page Global Directory.

The motivation behind demand paging is that processes do not address all the addresses included in their address space right from the start; in fact, some of these addresses may never be used by the process. Moreover, the program locality principle (see the section "Hardware Cache" in Chapter 2) ensures that, at each stage of program execution, only a small subset of the process pages are really referenced, and therefore the page frames containing the temporarily useless pages can be used by other processes. Demand paging is thus preferable to global allocation (assigning all page frames to the process right from the start and leaving them in memory until program termination) since it increases the average number of free page frames in the system and hence allows better use of the available free memory. From another viewpoint, it allows the system as a whole to get a better throughput with the same amount of RAM.

The price to pay for all these good things is system overhead: each "Page fault" exception induced by demand paging must be handled by the kernel, thus wasting CPU cycles. Fortunately, the locality principle ensures that once a process starts working with a group of pages, it will stick with them without addressing other pages for quite a while: "Page fault" exceptions may thus be considered rare events.

An addressed page may not be present in main memory for the following reasons:

- The page was never accessed by the process. The kernel can recognize this case since the Page Table entry is filled with zeros, that is, the `pte_none` macro returns the value 1.

- The page was already accessed by the process, but its content is temporarily saved on disk. The kernel can recognize this case since the Page Table entry is not filled with zeros (however, the `Present` flag is cleared, since the page is not present in RAM).

The `handle_pte_fault()` function distinguishes the two cases by inspecting the Page Table entry that refers to `address`:

```
entry = *pte;
if (!pte_present(entry)) {
    if (pte_none(entry))
        return do_no_page(tsk, vma, address, write_access,
                          pte);
    return do_swap_page(tsk, vma, address, pte, entry,
                        write_access);
}
```

We'll examine the case in which the page is saved on disk (`do_swap_page()` function) in the section "Page Swap-In" in Chapter 16.

In the other situation, when the page was never accessed, the `do_no_page()` function is invoked. There are two ways to load the missing page, depending on whether the page is mapped to a disk file. The function determines this by checking a field called **nopage** in the **vma** memory region descriptor, which points to the function that loads the missing page from disk into RAM if the page is mapped to a file. Therefore, the possibilities are:

- The **vma->vm_ops->nopage** field is not NULL. In this case, the memory region maps a disk file and the field points to the function that loads the page. This case will be covered in the section "Memory Mapping" in Chapter 15 and in the section "IPC Shared Memory" in Chapter 18.

- Either the **vm_ops** field or the **vma->vm_ops->nopage** field is NULL. In this case, the memory region does not map a file on disk, that is, it is an *anonymous mapping*. Thus, **do_no_page()** invokes the **do_anonymous_page()** function to get a new page frame:

```
if (!vma->vm_ops || !vma->vm_ops->nopage)
    return do_anonymous_page(tsk, vma, page_table,
                    write_access);
```

The **do_anonymous_page()** function handles write and read requests separately:

```
if (write_access) {
    page = __get_free_page(GFP_USER);
    memset((void *)(page), 0, PAGE_SIZE)
    entry = pte_mkwrite(pte_mkdirty(mk_pte(page,
            vma->vm_page_prot)));
    vma->vm_mm->rss++;
    tsk->min_flt++;
    set_pte(pte, entry);
    return 1;
}
```

When handling a write access, the function invokes **__get_free_page()** and fills the new page frame with zeros by using the **memset** macro. The function then increments the **min_flt** field of **tsk** to keep track of the number of *minor page faults* (those that require only a new page frame) caused by the process and the **rss** field of the **vma-> vm_mm** process memory descriptor to keep track of the number of page frames allocated to the process.* The Page Table entry is then set to the physical address of the page frame, which is marked as writable and dirty.

Conversely, when handling a read access, the content of the page is irrelevant because the process is addressing it for the first time. It is safer to give to the process a page filled with zeros rather than an old page filled with information written by some other process. Linux goes one step further in the spirit of demand paging. There is no need to assign a new page frame filled with zeros to the process right away, since we might

---

* Linux records the number of minor page faults for each process. This information, together with several other statistics, may be used to tune the system. The value stored in the **rss** field of memory descriptors is also used by the kernel to select the region from which to steal page frames (see the section "Freeing Page Frames" in Chapter 16).

as well give it an existing page called *zero page*, thus deferring further page frame allocation. The zero page is allocated statically during kernel initialization in the `empty_zero_page` variable (an array of 1024 long integers filled with zeros); it is stored in the sixth page frame, starting from physical address 0x00005000, and it can be referenced by means of the `ZERO_PAGE` macro.

The Page Table entry is thus set with the physical address of the zero page:

```
entry = pte_wrprotect(mk_pte(ZERO_PAGE, vma->vm_page_prot));
set_pte(pte, entry);
return 1;
```

Since the page is marked as nonwritable, if the process attempts to write in it, the Copy On Write mechanism will be activated. Then, and only then, will the process get a page of its own to write in. The mechanism is described in the next section.

Copy On Write

First-generation Unix systems implemented process creation in a rather clumsy way: when a `fork()` system call was issued, the kernel duplicated the whole parent address space in the literal sense of the word and assigned the copy to the child process. This activity was quite time-consuming since it required:

- Allocating page frames for the page tables of the child process

- Allocating page frames for the pages of the child process

- Initializing the page tables of the child process

- Copying the pages of the parent process into the corresponding pages of the child process

This way of creating an address space involved many memory accesses, used up many CPU cycles, and entirely spoiled the cache contents. Last but not least, it was often pointless because many child processes start their execution by loading a new program, thus discarding entirely the inherited address space (see Chapter 19).

Modern Unix kernels, including Linux, follow a more efficient approach called *Copy On Write*, or *COW*. The idea is quite simple: instead of duplicating page frames, they are shared between the parent and the child process. However, as long as they are shared, they cannot be modified. Whenever the parent or the child process attempts to write into a shared page frame, an exception occurs, and at this point the kernel duplicates the page into a new page frame that it marks as writable. The original page frame remains write-protected: when the other process tries to write into it, the kernel checks whether the writing process is the only owner of the page frame; in such a case, it makes the page frame writable for the process.

The `count` field of the page descriptor is used to keep track of the number of processes that are sharing the corresponding page frame. Whenever a process releases a page frame or a Copy On Write is executed on it, its **count** field is decremented; the page frame is freed only when **count** becomes NULL.

Let us now describe how Linux implements COW. When **handle_pte_fault()** determines that the "Page fault" exception was caused by a request to write into a write-protected page present in memory, it executes the following instructions:

```
if (pte_present(pte)) {
    entry = pte_mkyoung(entry);
    set_pte(pte, entry);
    flush_tlb_page(vma, address);
    if (write_access) {
        if (!pte_write(entry))
            return do_wp_page(tsk, vma, address, pte);
        entry = pte_mkdirty(entry);
        set_pte(pte, entry);
        flush_tlb_page(vma, address);
        }
    return 1;
    }
```

First, the **pte_mkyoung()** and **set_pte()** functions are invoked in order to set the **Accessed** bit in the Page Table entry of the page that caused the exception. This setting makes the page "younger" and reduces its chances of being swapped out to disk (see Chapter 16). If the exception was caused by a write-protection violation, **handle_pte_fault()** returns the value yielded by the **do_wp_page()** function; otherwise, some error condition has been detected (for instance, a page inside the User Mode process address space with the **User/Supervisor** flag equal to 0), and the function returns the value 1.

The **do_wp_page()** function starts by loading the **pte** local variable with the Page Table entry referenced by the **page_table** parameter and by getting a new page frame:

```
pte = *page_table;
new_page = _ _get_free_page(GFP_USER);
```

Since the allocation of a page frame can block the process, the function performs the following consistency checks on the Page Table entry once the page frame has been obtained:

- Whether the page has been swapped out while the process waited for a free page frame (**pte** and ***page_table** do not have the same value)

- Whether the page is no longer in RAM (the page's **Present** flag is 0 in its Page Table entry)

- Whether the page can now be written (the page's **Read/Write** flag is 1 in its Page Table entry)

If any of these conditions occurs, do_wp_page() releases the page frame obtained previously and returns the value 1.

Now the function updates the number of minor page faults and stores in the page_map local variable a pointer to the page descriptor of the page that caused the exception:

```
tsk->min_flt++;
page_map = mem_map + MAP_NR(old_page);
```

Next, the function must determine whether the page must really be duplicated. If only one process owns the page, Copy On Write does not apply and the process should be free to write the page. Thus, the page frame is marked as writable so that it will not cause further "Page fault" exceptions when writes are attempted, the previously allocated new page frame is released, and the function terminates with a return value of 1. This check is made by reading the value of the count field of the page descriptor:[*]

```
if (page_map->count == 1) {
    set_pte(page_table, pte_mkdirty(pte_mkwrite(pte)));
    flush_tlb_page(vma, address);
    if (new_page)
        free_page(new_page);
    return 1;
}
```

Conversely, if the page frame is shared among two or more processes, the function copies the content of the old page frame (old_page) into the newly allocated one (new_page):

```
if (old_page == ZERO_PAGE)
    memset((void *) new_page, 0, PAGE_SIZE);
else
    memcpy((void *) new_page, (void *) old_page, PAGE_SIZE);
set_pte(page_table, pte_mkwrite(pte_mkdirty(
        mk_pte(new_page, vma->vm_page_prot))));
flush_tlb_page(vma, address);
__free_page(page_map);
return 1;
```

If the old page is the zero page, the new frame is efficiently filled with zeros by using the memset macro. Otherwise, the page frame content is copied using the memcpy macro. Special handling for the zero page is not strictly required, but it improves the system performance since it preserves the microprocessor hardware cache by making fewer address references.

---

[*] Actually, the check is slightly more complicated, since the count field is also incremented when the page is inserted into the swap cache (see the section "The Swap Cache" in Chapter 16).

The Page Table entry is then updated with the physical address of the new page frame, which is also marked as writable and dirty. Finally, the function invokes __free_page() to decrement the usage counter of the old page frame.

Creating and Deleting a Process Address Space

Out of the six typical cases mentioned in the section "The Process's Address Space" in which a process gets new memory regions, the first one—issuing a fork() system call—requires the creation of a whole new address space for the child process. Conversely, when a process terminates, the kernel destroys its address space. In this section we'll discuss how these two activities are performed by Linux.

Creating a Process Address Space

We have mentioned in the section "The clone(), fork(), and vfork() System Calls" in Chapter 3, *Processes*, that the kernel invokes the copy_mm() function while creating a new process. This function takes care of the process address space creation by setting up all page tables and memory descriptors of the new process.

Each process usually has its own address space, but lightweight processes can be created by calling __clone() with the CLONE_VM flag set. These share the same address space; that is, they are allowed to address the same set of pages.

Following the COW approach described earlier, traditional processes inherit the address space of their parent: pages stay shared as long as they are only read. When one of the processes attempts to write one of them, however, the page is duplicated; after some time, a forked process usually gets its own address space different from that of the parent process. Lightweight processes, on the other hand, use the address space of their parent process: Linux implements them simply by not duplicating address space. Lightweight processes can be created considerably faster than normal processes, and the sharing of pages can also be considered a benefit so long as the parent and children coordinate their accesses carefully.

If the new process has been created by means of the __clone() system call and if the CLONE_VM flag of the flag parameter is set, copy_mm() gives the clone the address space of its parent:

```
if (clone_flags & CLONE_VM) {
    mmget(current->mm);
    copy_segments(nr, tsk, NULL);
    SET_PAGE_DIR(tsk, current->mm->pgd);
    return 0;
}
```

The `copy_segments()` function sets up the LDT for the clone process, because even a lightweight process must have a separate LDT entry in the GDT. The `SET_PAGE_DIR` macro sets the Page Global Directory of the new process and stores the Page Global Directory address in the `mm->pgd` field of the new memory descriptor.

If the `CLONE_VM` flag is not set, `copy_mm()` must create a new address space (even though no memory is allocated within address space until the process requests an address). The function allocates a new memory descriptor and stores its address in the `mm` field of the new process descriptor; it then initializes several fields in the new process descriptor to 0 and, as in the previous case, sets up the LDT descriptor by invoking `copy_segments()`:

```
mm = mm_alloc();
if (!mm)
    return -ENOMEM;
tsk->mm = mm;
copy_segments(nr, tsk, mm);
```

Next, `copy_mm()` invokes `new_page_tables()` to allocate the Page Global Directory. The last entries of this table, which correspond to linear addresses greater than `PAGE_OFFSET`, are copied from the Page Global Directory of the *swapper* process, while the remaining entries are set to 0 (in particular, the `Present` and `Read/Write` flags are cleared). Finally, `new_page_tables()` stores the Page Global Directory address in the `mm->pgd` field of the new memory descriptor. The `dup_mmap()` function is then invoked to duplicate both the memory regions and the Page Tables of the parent process:

```
new_page_tables(tsk);
dup_mmap(mm);
return 0;
```

The `dup_mmap()` function scans the list of regions owned by the parent process, starting from the one pointed by `current->mm->mmap`. It duplicates each `vm_area_struct` memory region descriptor encountered and inserts the copy in the list of regions owned by the child process.

Right after inserting a new memory region descriptor, `dup_mmap()` invokes `copy_page_range()` to create, if necessary, the Page Tables needed to map the group of pages included in the memory region and to initialize the new Page Table entries. In particular, any page frame corresponding to a private, writable page (`VM_SHARE` flag off and `VM_MAYWRITE` flag on) is marked as read only for both the parent and the child, so that it will be handled with the Copy On Write mechanism. Finally, if the number of memory regions is greater than or equal to `AVL_MIN_MAP_COUNT`, the memory region AVL tree of the child process is created by invoking the `build_mmap_avl()` function.

Deleting a Process Address Space

When a process terminates, the kernel invokes the `exit_mm()` function to release the address space owned by that process. Since the process is entering the `TASK_ZOMBIE` state, the function assigns the address space of the *swapper* process to it:

```
flush_tlb_mm(mm);
tsk->mm = &init_mm;
tsk->swappable = 0;
SET_PAGE_DIR(tsk, swapper_pg_dir);
mm_release();
mmput(mm);
```

The function then invokes `mm_release()` and `mmput()` to release the process address space. The first function clears the `fs` and `gs` segmentation registers and restores the LDT of the process to `default_ldt`; the second function decrements the value of the `mm->count` field and releases the LDT, the memory region descriptors, and the page tables referred by `mm`. Finally, the `mm` memory descriptor itself is released.

Managing the Heap

Each Unix process owns a specific memory region called *heap*, which is used to satisfy the process's dynamic memory requests. The `start_brk` and `brk` fields of the memory descriptor delimit the starting and ending address, respectively, of that region.

The following C library functions can be used by the process to request and release dynamic memory:

`malloc(size)`
    Request `size` bytes of dynamic memory; if the allocation succeeds, it returns the linear address of the first memory location.

`calloc(n,size)`
    Request an array consisting of `n` elements of size `size`; if the allocation succeeds, it initializes the array components to 0 and returns the linear address of the first element.

`free(addr)`
    Release the memory region allocated by `malloc()` or `calloc()` having initial address `addr`.

`brk(addr)`
    Modify the size of the heap directly; the `addr` parameter specifies the new value of `current->mm->brk`, and the return value is the new ending address of the memory region (the process must check whether it coincides with the requested `addr` value).

The `brk()` function differs from the other functions listed because it is the only one implemented as a system call: all the other functions are implemented in the C library by making use of `brk()` and `mmap()`.

When a process in User Mode invokes the `brk()` system call, the kernel executes the `sys_brk(addr)` function (see Chapter 8). This function verifies first whether the `addr` parameter falls inside the memory region that contains the process code; if so, it returns immediately:

```
mm = current->mm;
if (addr < mm->end_code)
    return mm->brk;
```

Since the `brk()` system call acts on a memory region, it allocates and deallocates whole pages. Therefore, the function aligns the value of `addr` to a multiple of `PAGE_SIZE`, then compares the result with the value of the `brk` field of the memory descriptor:

```
newbrk = (addr + 0xfff) & 0xfffff000;
oldbrk = (mm->brk + 0xfff) & 0xfffff000;
if (oldbrk == newbrk) {
    mm->brk = addr;
    return mm->brk;
}
```

If the process has asked to shrink the heap, `sys_brk()` invokes the `do_munmap()` function to do the job and then returns:

```
if (addr <= mm->brk) {
    if (!do_munmap(newbrk, oldbrk-newbrk))
        mm->brk = addr;
    return mm->brk;
}
```

If the process has asked to enlarge the heap, `sys_brk()` checks first whether the process is allowed to do so. If the process is trying to allocate memory outside its limit, the function simply returns the original value of `mm->brk` without allocating more memory:

```
rlim = current->rlim[RLIMIT_DATA].rlim_cur;
if (rlim < RLIM_INFINITY && addr - mm->end_code > rlim)
    return mm->brk;
```

The function then checks whether the enlarged heap would overlap some other memory region belonging to the process and, if so, returns without doing anything:

```
if (find_vma_intersection(mm, oldbrk, newbrk+PAGE_SIZE))
    return mm->brk;
```

The last check before proceeding to the expansion consists of verifying whether the available free virtual memory is sufficient to support the enlarged heap (see the earlier section "Allocating a Linear Address Interval"):

```
if (!vm_enough_memory((newbrk-oldbrk) >> PAGE_SHIFT))
    return mm->brk;
```

If everything is OK, the `do_mmap()` function is invoked with the `MAP_FIXED` flag set: if it returns the `oldbrk` value, the allocation was successful and `sys_brk()` returns the value `addr`; otherwise, it returns the old `mm->brk` value:

```
if (do_mmap(NULL, oldbrk, newbrk-oldbrk,
        PROT_READ|PROT_WRITE|PROT_EXEC,
        MAP_FIXED|MAP_PRIVATE, 0) == oldbrk)
    mm->brk = addr;
return mm->brk;
```

Anticipating Linux 2.4

Beside minor optimizations and adjustments, the process address space is handled in the same way by Linux 2.4.

CHAPTER EIGHT

SYSTEM CALLS

Operating systems offer processes running in User Mode a set of interfaces to interact with hardware devices such as the CPU, disks, printers, and so on. Putting an extra layer between the application and the hardware has several advantages. First, it makes programming easier, freeing users from studying low-level programming characteristics of hardware devices. Second, it greatly increases system security, since the kernel can check the correctness of the request at the interface level before attempting to satisfy it. Last but not least, these interfaces make programs more portable since they can be compiled and executed correctly on any kernel that offers the same set of interfaces.

Unix systems implement most interfaces between User Mode processes and hardware devices by means of *system calls* issued to the kernel. This chapter examines in detail how system calls are implemented by the Linux kernel.

POSIX APIs and System Calls

Let us start by stressing the difference between an application programmer interface (API) and a system call. The former is a function definition that specifies how to obtain a given service, while the latter is an explicit request to the kernel made via a software interrupt.

Unix systems include several libraries of functions that provide APIs to programmers. Some of the APIs defined by the *libc* standard C library refer to *wrapper routines*, that is, routines whose only purpose is to issue a system call. Usually, each system call corresponds to a wrapper routine; the wrapper routine defines the API that application programs should refer to.

The converse is not true, by the way—an API does not necessarily correspond to a specific system call. First of all, the API could offer its services directly in User Mode. (For something abstract like math functions, there may be no reason to make system calls.) Second, a single API function could make several system calls. Moreover, several API functions could make the same system call but wrap extra functionality around it. For instance, in Linux the `malloc()`, `calloc()`, and `free()` POSIX APIs are implemented in the *libc* library: the code in that library keeps track of the allocation and deallocation requests and uses the `brk()` system call in order to enlarge or shrink the process heap (see the section "Managing the Heap" in Chapter 7, *Process Address Space*).

The POSIX standard refers to APIs and not to system calls. A system can be certified as POSIX-compliant if it offers the proper set of APIs to the application programs, no matter how the corresponding functions are implemented. As a matter of fact, several non-Unix systems have been certified as POSIX-compliant since they offer all traditional Unix services in User Mode libraries.

From the programmer's point of view, the distinction between an API and a system call is irrelevant: the only things that matter are the function name, the parameter types, and the meaning of the return code. From the kernel designer's point of view, however, the distinction does matter since system calls belong to the kernel, while User Mode libraries don't.

Most wrapper routines return an integer value, whose meaning depends on the corresponding system call. A return value of –1 denotes in most cases, but not always, that the kernel was unable to satisfy the process request. A failure in the system call handler may be caused by invalid parameters, a lack of available resources, hardware problems, and so on. The specific error code is contained in the `errno` variable, which is defined in the *libc* library.

Each error code is associated with a macro, which yields a corresponding positive integer value. The POSIX standard specifies the macro names of several error codes. In Linux on Intel 80x86 systems, those macros are defined in a header file called *include/asm-i386/errno.h*. To allow portability of C programs among Unix systems, the *include/asm-i386/errno.h* header file is included, in turn, in the standard */usr/include/errno.h* C library header file. Other systems have their own specialized subdirectories of header files.

System Call Handler and Service Routines

When a User Mode process invokes a system call, the CPU switches to Kernel Mode and starts the execution of a kernel function. In Linux the system calls must be invoked by executing the `int $0x80` Assembly instruction, which raises the programmed exception having vector 128 (see the section "Interrupt, Trap, and System Gates" and the section "Hardware Handling of Interrupts and Exceptions" in Chapter 4, *Interrupts and Exceptions*).

Since the kernel implements many different system calls, the process must pass a parameter called the *system call number* to identify the required system call; the `eax` register is used for that purpose. As we shall see in the section "Parameter Passing" later in this chapter, additional parameters are usually passed when invoking a system call.

All system calls return an integer value. The conventions for these return values are different from those for wrapper routines. In the kernel, positive or null values denote a successful termination of the system call, while negative values denote an error condition. In the latter case, the value is the negation of the error code that must be returned to the application program. The **errno** variable is not set or used by the kernel.

The system call handler, which has a structure similar to that of the other exception handlers, performs the following operations:

- Saves the contents of most registers in the Kernel Mode stack (this operation is common to all system calls and is coded in assembly language).

- Handles the system call by invoking a corresponding C function called the *system call service routine*.

- Exits from the handler by means of the **ret_from_sys_call()** function (this function is coded in assembly language).

The name of the service routine associated with the *xyz()* system call is usually **sys_xyz()**; there are, however, a few exceptions to this rule.

Figure 8-1 illustrates the relationships among the application program that invokes a system call, the corresponding wrapper routine, the system call handler, and the system call service routine. The arrows denote the execution flow between the functions.

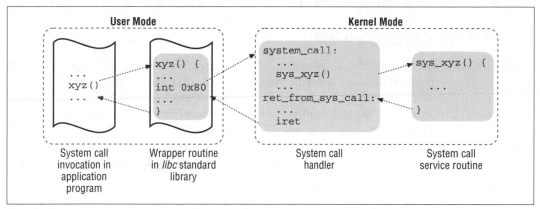

Figure 8-1. Invoking a system call

In order to associate each system call number with its corresponding service routine, the kernel makes use of a *system call dispatch table*; this table is stored in the **sys_call_table** array and has **NR_syscalls** entries (usually 256): the *n*th entry contains the service routine address of the system call having number *n*.

The `NR_syscalls` macro is just a static limit on the maximum number of implement-able system calls: it does not indicate the number of system calls actually implemented. Indeed, any entry of the dispatch table may contain the address of the `sys_ni_syscall()` function, which is the service routine of the "nonimplemented" system calls: it just returns the error code `-ENOSYS`.

Initializing System Calls

The `trap_init()` function, invoked during kernel initialization, sets up the IDT entry corresponding to vector 128 as follows:

```
set_system_gate(0x80, &system_call);
```

The call loads the following values into the gate descriptor fields (see the section "Interrupt, Trap, and System Gates" in Chapter 4):

Segment Selector
> The `__KERNEL_CS` Segment Selector of the kernel code segment.

Offset
> Pointer to the `system_call()` exception handler.

Type
> Set to 15. Indicates that the exception is a Trap and that the corresponding handler does not disable maskable interrupts.

DPL (Descriptor Privilege Level)
> Set to 3; this allows processes in User Mode to invoke the exception handler (see the section "Hardware Handling of Interrupts and Exceptions" in Chapter 4).

The system_call() Function

The `system_call()` function implements the system call handler. It starts by saving the system call number and all the CPU registers that may be used by the exception handler on the stack, except for `eflags`, `cs`, `eip`, `ss`, and `esp`, which have already been saved automatically by the control unit (see the section "Hardware Handling of Interrupts and Exceptions" in Chapter 4). The `SAVE_ALL` macro, which was already discussed in the section "Saving the Registers for the Interrupt Handler" in Chapter 4, also loads the Segment Selector of the kernel data segment in `ds` and `es`:

```
system_call:
  pushl %eax
  SAVE_ALL
  movl %esp, %ebx
  andl $0xffffe000, %ebx
```

The function also stores in `ebx` the address of the `current` process descriptor; this is done by taking the value of the kernel stack pointer and rounding it up to a multiple of 8 KB (see the section "Identifying a Process" in Chapter 3, *Processes*).

A validity check is then performed on the system call number passed by the User Mode process. If it is greater than or equal to NR_syscalls, the system call handler terminates:

```
    cmpl $(NR_syscalls), %eax
    jb nobadsys
    movl $(-ENOSYS), 24(%esp)
    jmp ret_from_sys_call
nobadsys:
```

If the system call number is not valid, the function stores the -ENOSYS value in the stack location where the eax register has been saved (at offset 24 from the current stack top). It then jumps to ret_from_sys_call(). In this way, when the process resumes its execution in User Mode, it will find a negative return code in eax.

Next, the system_call() function checks whether the PF_TRACESYS flag included in the flags field of current is equal to 1, that is, whether the system call invocations of the executed program are being traced by some debugger. If this is the case, system_call() invokes the syscall_trace() function twice, once right before and once right after the execution of the system call service routine. This function stops current and thus allows the debugging process to collect information about it.

Finally, the specific service routine associated with the system call number contained in eax is invoked:

```
    call *sys_call_table(0, %eax, 4)
```

Since each entry in the dispatch table is 4 bytes long, the kernel finds the address of the service routine to be invoked by first multiplying the system call number by 4, adding the initial address of the sys_call_table dispatch table, and extracting a pointer to the service routine from that slot in the table.

When the service routine terminates, system_call() gets its return code from eax and stores it in the stack location where the User Mode value of the eax register has been saved. It then jumps to ret_from_sys call(), which terminates the execution of the system call handler (see the section "The ret_from_sys_call() Function" in Chapter 4):

```
    movl %eax, 24(%esp)
    jmp ret_from_sys_call
```

When the process resumes its execution in User Mode, it will find in eax the return code of the system call.

Parameter Passing

Like ordinary functions, system calls often require some input/output parameters, which may consist of actual values (i.e., numbers) or addresses of functions and variables in the address space of the User Mode process. Since the system_call() function is the unique entry point for all system calls in Linux, each of them has at least one parameter: the system call number passed in the **eax** register. For instance, if an application program invokes the **fork()** wrapper routine, the **eax** register is set to 2 (however, system call numbers are subject to change, so check the actual number in your source code) before executing the **int $0x80** Assembly instruction. Because the register is set by the wrapper routines included in the *libc* library, programmers do not usually care about the system call number.

The **fork()** system call does not require other parameters. However, many system calls do require additional parameters, which must be explicitly passed by the application program. For instance, the **mmap()** system call may require up to six parameters (besides the system call number).

The parameters of ordinary functions are passed by writing their values in the active program stack (either the User Mode stack or the Kernel Mode stack). But system call parameters are usually passed to the system call handler in the CPU registers, then copied onto the Kernel Mode stack, since system call service routines are ordinary C functions.

Why doesn't the kernel copy parameters directly from the User Mode stack to the Kernel Mode stack? First of all, working with two stacks at the same time is complex; moreover, the use of registers makes the structure of the system call handler similar to that of other exception handlers.

However, in order to pass parameters in registers, two conditions must be satisfied:

- The length of each parameter cannot exceed the length of a register, that is 32 bits.*

- The number of parameters must not exceed six (including the system call number passed in **eax**), since the Intel Pentium has a very limited number of registers.

The first condition is always true since, according to the POSIX standard, large parameters that cannot be stored in a 32-bit register must be passed by specifying their addresses. A typical example is the **settimeofday()** system call, which must read two 64-bit structures.

However, system calls that have more than six parameters exist: in such cases, a single register is used to point to a memory area in the process address space that contains the parameter values. Of course, programmers do not have to care about this workaround. As with any C call, parameters are automatically saved on the stack when the wrapper routine is invoked. This routine will find the appropriate way to pass the parameters to the kernel.

The six registers used to store system call parameters are, in increasing order: **eax** (for the system call number), **ebx**, **ecx**, **edx**, **esi**, and **edi**. As seen before, **system_ call()** saves the values of these registers on the Kernel Mode stack by using the

---

* We refer as usual to the 32-bit architecture of the Intel 80x86 processors. The discussion in this section does not apply to Compaq's Alpha 64-bit processors.

SAVE_ALL macro. Therefore, when the system call service routine goes to the stack, it finds the return address to system_call(), followed by the parameter stored in ebx (that is, the first parameter of the system call), the parameter stored in ecx, and so on (see the section "Saving the Registers for the Interrupt Handler" in Chapter 4). This stack configuration is exactly the same as in an ordinary function call, and therefore the service routine can easily refer to its parameters by using the usual C-language constructs.

Let's look at an example. The sys_write() service routine, which handles the write() system call, is declared as:

```
int sys_write (unsigned int fd, const char * buf,
               unsigned int count)
```

The C compiler produces an assembly language function that expects to find the fd, buf, and count parameters on top of the stack, right below the return address, in the locations used to save the contents of the ebx, ecx, and edx registers, respectively.

In a few cases, even if the system call doesn't make use of any parameters, the corresponding service routine needs to know the contents of the CPU registers right before the system call was issued. As an example, the do_fork() function that implements fork() needs to know the value of the registers in order to duplicate them in the child process TSS. In these cases, a single parameter of type pt_regs allows the service routine to access the values saved in the Kernel Mode stack by the SAVE_ALL macro (see the section "The do_IRQ() Function" in Chapter 4):

```
int sys_fork (struct pt_regs regs)
```

The return value of a service routine must be written into the eax register. This is automatically done by the C compiler when a return n; instruction is executed.

Verifying the Parameters

All system call parameters must be carefully checked before the kernel attempts to satisfy a user request. The type of check depends both on the system call and on the specific parameter. Let us go back to the write() system call introduced before: the fd parameter should be a file descriptor that describes a specific file, so sys_write() must check whether fd really is a file descriptor of a file previously opened and whether the process is allowed to write into it (see the section "File-Handling System Calls" in Chapter 1, *Introduction*). If any of these conditions is not true, the handler must return a negative value, in this case the error code −EBADF.

One type of checking, however, is common to all system calls: whenever a parameter specifies an address, the kernel must check whether it is inside the process address space. There are two possible ways to perform this check:

- Verify that the linear address belongs to the process address space and, if so, that the memory region including it has the proper access rights.

- Verify just that the linear address is lower than PAGE_OFFSET (i.e., that it doesn't fall within the range of interval addresses reserved to the kernel).

Previous Linux kernels performed the first type of checking. But it is quite time-consuming since it must be executed for each address parameter included in a system call; furthermore, it is usually pointless because faulty programs are not very common.

Therefore, the Linux 2.2 kernel performs the second type of checking. It is much more efficient because it does not require any scan of the process memory region descriptors. Obviously, it is a very coarse check: verifying that the linear address is smaller than PAGE_OFFSET is a necessary but not sufficient condition for its validity. But there's no risk in confining the kernel to this limited kind of check because other errors will be caught later.

The approach followed in Linux 2.2 is thus to defer the real checking until the last possible moment, that is, until the Paging Unit translates the linear address into a physical one. We shall discuss in the section "Dynamic Address Checking: The Fixup Code" later in this chapter how the "Page fault" exception handler succeeds in detecting those bad addresses issued in Kernel Mode that have been passed as parameters by User Mode processes.

One might wonder at this point why the coarse check is performed at all. This type of checking is actually crucial to preserve both process address spaces and the kernel address space from illegal accesses. We have seen in Chapter 2, *Memory Addressing*, that the RAM is mapped starting from PAGE_OFFSET. This means that kernel routines are able to address all pages present in memory. Thus, if the coarse check were not performed, a User Mode process might pass an address belonging to the kernel address space as a parameter and then be able to read or write any page present in memory without causing a "Page fault" exception!

The check on addresses passed to system calls is performed by the verify_area() function, which acts on two* parameters denoted as addr and size. The function checks the address interval delimited by addr and addr + size - 1, and is essentially equivalent to the following C function:

```
int verify_area(const void * addr, unsigned long size)
{
    unsigned long a = (unsigned long) addr;
    if (a + size < a || a + size > current->addr_limit.seg)
        return -EFAULT;
    return 0;
}
```

---

* A third parameter named type specifies whether the system call should read or write the referred memory locations. It is used only in systems having buggy versions of the Intel 80486 microprocessor, in which writing in Kernel Mode to a write-protected page does not generate a page fault. We don't discuss this case further.

The function verifies first whether `addr + size`, the highest address to be checked, is larger than 2^{32}-1; since unsigned long integers and pointers are represented by the GNU C compiler (`gcc`) as 32-bit numbers, this is equivalent to checking for an overflow condition. The function also checks whether `addr` exceeds the value stored in the `addr_limit.seg` field of `current`. This field usually has the value `PAGE_OFFSET-1` for normal processes and the value `0xffffffff` for kernel threads. The value of the `addr_limit.seg` field can be dynamically changed by the `get_fs` and `set_fs` macros; this allows the kernel to invoke system call service routines directly and pass addresses in the kernel data segment to them.

The `access_ok` macro performs the same check as `verify_area()`. It yields 1 if the specified address interval is valid and 0 otherwise.

Accessing the Process Address Space

System call service routines quite often need to read or write data contained in the process's address space. Linux includes a set of macros that make this access easier. We'll describe two of them, called `get_user()` and `put_user()`. The first can be used to read 1, 2, or 4 consecutive bytes from an address, while the second can be used to write data of those sizes into an address.

Each function accepts two arguments, a value `x` to transfer and a variable `ptr`. The second variable also determines how many bytes to transfer. Thus, in `get_user(x,ptr)`, the size of the variable pointed to by `ptr` causes the function to expand into a `__get_user_1()`, `__get_user_2()`, or `__get_user_4()` assembly language function. Let us consider one of them, for instance, `__get_user_2()`:

```
__get_user_2:
    addl $1, %eax
    jc bad_get_user
    movl %esp, %edx
    andl $0xffffe000, %edx
    cmpl 12(%edx), %eax
    jae bad_get_user
2:  movzwl -1(%eax), %edx
    xorl %eax, %eax
    ret
bad_get_user:
    xorl %edx, %edx
    movl $-EFAULT, %eax
    ret
```

The `eax` register contains the address `ptr` of the first byte to be read. The first six instructions essentially perform the same checks as the `verify_area()` functions: they ensure that the 2 bytes to be read have addresses less than 4 GB as well as less than the `addr_limit.seg` field of the `current` process. (This field is stored at offset 12 in the process descriptor, which appears in the first operand of the `cmpl` instruction.)

If the addresses are valid, the function executes the `movzwl` instruction to store the data to be read in the 2 least significant bytes of `edx` register while setting the high-order bytes of `edx` to 0; then it sets a 0 return code in `eax` and terminates. If the addresses are not valid, the function clears `edx`, sets the −EFAULT value into `eax`, and terminates.

The `put_user(x,ptr)` macro is similar to the one discussed before, except that it writes the value `x` into the process address space starting from address `ptr`. Depending on the size of `x` (1, 2, or 4 bytes), it invokes the `__put_user_1()`, `__put_user_2()`, or `__put_user_4()` function. Let's consider `__put_user_4()` for our example this time. The function performs the usual checks on the `ptr` address stored in the `eax` register, then executes a `movl` instruction to write the 4 bytes stored into the `edx` register. The function returns the value 0 in the `eax` register if it succeeds, and −EFAULT otherwise.

Several other functions and macros are available to access the process address space in Kernel Mode; they are listed in Table 8-1. Notice that many of them also have a variant prefixed by two underscores (_ _). The ones without initial underscores take extra time to check the validity of the linear address interval requested, while the ones with the underscores bypass that check. Whenever the kernel must repeatedly access the same memory area in the process address space, it is more efficient to check the address once at the start, then access the process area without making any further checks.

Table 8-1. Functions and Macros that Access the Process Address Space

Function	Action
get_user _ _get_user	Reads an integer value from user space (1, 2, or 4 bytes)
put_user _ _put_user	Writes an integer value to user space (1, 2, or 4 bytes)
get_user_ret _ _get_user_ret	Like get_user, but returns a specified value on error
put_user_ret _ _put_user_ret	Like put_user, but returns a specified value on error
copy_from_user _ _copy_from_user	Copies a block of arbitrary size from user space
copy_to_user _ _copy_to_user	Copies a block of arbitrary size to user space
copy_from_user_ret	Like copy_from_user, but returns a specified value on error
copy_to_user_ret	Like copy_to_user, but returns a specified value on error
strncpy_from_user _ _strncpy_from_user	Copies a null-terminated string from user space

Table 8-1. Functions and Macros that Access the Process Address Space (continued)

Function	Action
strlen_user strnlen_user	Returns the length of a null-terminated string in user space
clear_user __clear_user	Fills a memory area in user space with zeros

Dynamic Address Checking: The Fixup Code

As seen previously, the `verify_area()` function and the `access_ok` macro make only a coarse check on the validity of linear addresses passed as parameters of a system call. Since they do not ensure that these addresses are included in the process address space, a process could cause a "Page fault" exception by passing a wrong address.

Before describing how the kernel detects this type of error, let us specify the three cases in which "Page fault" exceptions may occur in Kernel Mode:

- The kernel attempts to address a page belonging to the process address space, but either the corresponding page frame does not exist, or the kernel is trying to write a read-only page.

- Some kernel function includes a programming bug that causes the exception to be raised when that program is executed; alternatively, the exception might be caused by a transient hardware error.

- The case introduced in this chapter: a system call service routine attempts to read or write into a memory area whose address has been passed as a system call parameter, but that address does not belong to the process address space.

These cases must be distinguished by the page fault handler, since the actions to be taken are quite different. In the first case, the handler must allocate and initialize a new page frame (see the section "Demand Paging" and the section "Copy On Write" in Chapter 7); in the second case, the handler must perform a kernel oops (see the section "Handling a Faulty Address Outside the Address Space" in Chapter 7); in the third case, the handler must terminate the system call by returning a proper error code.

The page fault handler can easily recognize the first case by determining whether the faulty linear address is included in one of the memory regions owned by the process. Let us now explain how the handler distinguishes the remaining two cases.

The exception tables

The key to determining the source of a page fault lies in the narrow range of calls that the kernel uses to access the process address space. Only the small group of functions and macros described in the previous section are ever used to access that address space; thus, if the exception is caused by an invalid parameter, the instruction that caused it *must* be included in one of the functions or be generated by expanding one of the macros. If you add up the code in all these functions and macros, they consist of a fairly small set of addresses.

Therefore, it would not take much effort to put the address of any kernel instruction that accesses the process address space into a structure called the *exception table*. If we succeed in doing this, the rest is easy. When a "Page fault" exception occurs in Kernel Mode, the `do_page_fault()` handler examines the exception table: if it includes the address of the instruction that triggered the exception, the error is caused by a bad system call parameter; otherwise, it is caused by some more serious bug.

Linux defines several exception tables. The main exception table is automatically generated by the C compiler when building the kernel program image. It is stored in the `__ex_table` section of the kernel code segment, and its starting and ending addresses are identified by two symbols produced by the C compiler: `__start___ex_table` and `__stop___ex_table`.

Moreover, each dynamically loaded module of the kernel (see Appendix B, *Modules*) includes its own local exception table. This table is automatically generated by the C compiler when building the module image, and it is loaded in memory when the module is inserted in the running kernel.

Each entry of an exception table is an `exception_table_entry` structure having two fields:

`insn`
> The linear address of an instruction that accesses the process address space

`fixup`
> The address of the assembly language code to be invoked when a "Page fault" exception triggered by the instruction located at `insn` occurs

The fixup code consists of a few assembly language instructions that solve the problem triggered by the exception. As we shall see later in this section, the fix usually consists of inserting a sequence of instructions that forces the service routine to return an error code to the User Mode process. Such instructions are usually defined in the same macro or function that accesses the process address space; sometimes, they are placed by the C compiler in a separate section of the kernel code segment called `.fixup`.

The `search_exception_table()` function is used to search for a specified address in all exception tables: if the address is included in a table, the function returns the corresponding `fixup` address; otherwise, it returns 0. Thus the page fault handler `do_page_fault()` executes the following statements:

```
if ((fixup = search_exception_table(regs->eip)) != 0) {
    regs->eip = fixup;
    return;
}
```

The `regs->eip` field contains the value of the `eip` register saved on the Kernel Mode stack when the exception occurred. If the value in the register (the instruction pointer) is in an exception table, `do_page_fault()` replaces the saved value with the address returned by `search_exception_table()`. Then the page fault handler terminates and the interrupted program resumes with execution of the fixup code.

Generating the exception tables and the fixup code

The GNU Assembler `.section` directive allows programmers to specify which section of the executable file contains the code that follows. As we shall see in Chapter 19, *Program Execution*, an executable file includes a code segment, which in turn may be subdivided into sections. Thus, the following assembly language instructions add an entry into an exception table; the `"a"` attribute specifies that the section must be loaded in memory together with the rest of the kernel image:

```
.section __ex_table, "a"
    .long faulty_instruction_address, fixup_code_address
.previous
```

The `.previous` directive forces the assembler to insert the code that follows into the section that was active when the last `.section` directive was encountered.

Let us consider again the `__get_user_1()`, `__get_user_2()`, and `__get_user_4()` functions mentioned before:

```
__get_user_1:
    [...]
1:  movzbl (%eax), %edx
    [...]
__get_user_2:
    [...]
2:  movzwl -1(%eax), %edx
    [...]
__get_user_4:
    [...]
3:  movl -3(%eax), %edx
    [...]
bad_get_user:
    xorl %edx, %edx
    movl $-EFAULT, %eax
    ret
.section __ex_table,"a"
    .long 1b, bad_get_user
    .long 2b, bad_get_user
    .long 3b, bad_get_user
.previous
```

The instructions that access the process address space are those labeled as 1, 2, and 3. The fixup code is common to the three functions and is labeled as `bad_get_user`. Each exception table entry consists simply of two labels. The first one is a numeric label with a **b** suffix to indicate that the label is a "backward" one: in other words, it appears in a previous line of the program. The fixup code at **bad_get_user** returns an **EFAULT** error code to the process that issued the system call.

Let us consider a second example, the **strlen_user(string)** macro. This returns the length of a null-terminated string in the process address space or the value 0 on error. The macro essentially yields the following assembly language instructions:

```
        movl $0, %eax
        movl $0x7fffffff, %ecx
        movl %ecx, %edx
        movl string, %edi
   0:   repne; scasb
        subl %ecx, %edx
        movl %edx, %eax
   1:
   .section .fixup,"ax"
   2:   movl $0, %eax
        jmp 1b
   .previous
   .section __ex_table,"a"
        .long 0b, 2b
   .previous
```

The **ecx** and **edx** registers are initialized with the **0x7fffffff** value, which represents the maximum allowed length for the string. The **repne; scasb** assembly language instructions iteratively scan the string pointed to by the **edi** register, looking for the value 0 (the end of string \0 character) in **eax**. Since the **ecx** register is decremented at each iteration, the **eax** register will ultimately store the total number of bytes scanned in the string; that is, the length of the string.

The fixup code of the macro is inserted into the **.fixup** section. The **"ax"** attributes specify that the section must be loaded in memory and that it contains executable code. If a page fault exception is generated by the instructions at label 0, the fixup code is executed: it simply loads the value 0 in **eax**, thus forcing the macro to return a 0 error code instead of the string length, then jumps to the 1 label, which corresponds to the instruction following the macro.

Wrapper Routines

Although system calls are mainly used by User Mode processes, they can also be invoked by kernel threads, which cannot make use of library functions. In order to simplify the declarations of the corresponding wrapper routines, Linux defines a set of six macros called **_syscall0** through **_syscall5**.

The numbers 0 through 5 in the name of each macro correspond to the number of parameters used by the system call (excluding the system call number). The macros may also be used to simplify the declarations of the wrapper routines in the *libc* standard library; however, they cannot be used to define wrapper routines for system calls having more than five parameters (excluding the system call number) or for system calls that yield nonstandard return values.

Each macro requires exactly $2+2\times n$ parameters, with n being the number of parameters of the system call. The first two parameters specify the return type and the name of the system call; each additional pair of parameters specifies the type and the name of the corresponding system call parameter. Thus, for instance, the wrapper routine of the **fork()** system call may be generated by:

```
_syscall0(int,fork)
```

while the wrapper routine of the **write()** system call may be generated by:

```
_syscall3(int,write,int,fd,const char *,buf,unsigned int,count)
```

In the latter case, the macro yields the following code:

```
int write(int fd,const char * buf,unsigned int count)
{
    long _ _res;
    asm("int $0x80"
        : "=a" (_ _res)
        : "0" (_ _NR_write), "b" ((long)fd),
          "c" ((long)buf), "d" ((long)count));
    if ((unsigned long)_ _res >= (unsigned long)-125) {
        errno = -_ _res;
        _ _res = -1;
    }
    return (int) _ _res;
}
```

The **_ _NR_write** macro is derived from the second parameter of **_syscall3**; it expands into the system call number of **write()**. When compiling the preceding function, the following assembly language code is produced:

```
write:
        pushl %ebx              ; push ebx into stack
        movl 8(%esp), %ebx      ; put first parameter in ebx
        movl 12(%esp), %ecx     ; put second parameter in ecx
        movl 16(%esp), %edx     ; put third parameter in edx
        movl $4, %eax           ; put _ _NR_write in eax
        int $0x80               ; invoke system call
        cmpl $-126, %eax        ; check return code
        jbe .L1                 ; if no error, jump
        negl %eax               ; complement the value of eax
        movl %eax, errno        ; put result in errno
        movl $-1, %eax          ; set eax to -1
.L1:    popl %ebx               ; pop ebx from stack
        ret                     ; return to calling program
```

Notice how the parameters of the `write()` function are loaded into the CPU registers before the `int $0x80` instruction is executed. The value returned in `eax` must be interpreted as an error code if it lies between -1 and -125 (the kernel assumes that the largest error code defined in *include/asm-i386/errno.h* is 125). If this is the case, the wrapper routine will store the value of `-eax` in `errno` and return the value -1; otherwise, it will return the value of `eax`.

Anticipating Linux 2.4

Beside adding a few new system calls, Linux 2.4 does not introduce any change to the system call mechanism of Linux 2.2.

CHAPTER NINE

SIGNALS

Signals were introduced by the first Unix systems to simplify interprocess communication. The kernel also uses them to notify processes of system events. In contrast to interrupts and exceptions, most signals are visible to User Mode processes.

Signals have been around for 30 years with only minor changes. Due to their relative simplicity and efficiency, they continue to be widely used, although as we shall see in Chapter 18, *Process Communication*, other higher-level tools have been introduced for the same purpose.

The first sections of this chapter examine in detail how signals are handled by the Linux kernel, then we discuss the system calls that allow processes to exchange signals.

The Role of Signals

A *signal* is a very short message that may be sent to a process or to a group of processes. The only information given to the process is usually the number identifying the signal; there is no room in standard signals for arguments, a message, or other accompanying information.

A set of macros whose names start with the prefix SIG is used to identify signals; we have already made a few references to them in previous chapters. For instance, the SIGCHLD macro has been mentioned in the section "The clone( ), fork( ), and vfork( ) System Calls" in Chapter 3, *Processes*. This macro, which expands into the value 17 in Linux, yields the identifier of the signal that is sent to a parent process when some child stops or terminates. The SIGSEGV macro, which expands into the value 11, has been mentioned in the section "Page Fault Exception Handler" in Chapter 7, *Process Address Space*: it yields the identifier of the signal that is sent to a process when it makes an invalid memory reference.

Signals serve two main purposes:

- To make a process aware that a specific event has occurred
- To force a process to execute a signal handler function included in its code

Of course, the two purposes are not mutually exclusive, since often a process must react to some event by executing a specific routine.

Table 9-1 lists the first 31 signals handled by Linux 2.2 for the Intel 80x86 architecture (some signal numbers such as SIGCHLD or SIGSTOP are architecture-dependent; furthermore, some signals are defined only for specific architectures). Besides the signals described in this table, the POSIX standard has introduced a new class of signals called "real-time." They will be discussed separately in the section "Real-Time Signals" later in this chapter.

Table 9-1. The First 31 Signals in Linux/i386

#	Signal Name	Default Action	Comment	POSIX
1	SIGHUP	Abort	Hangup of controlling terminal or process	Yes
2	SIGINT	Abort	Interrupt from keyboard	Yes
3	SIGQUIT	Dump	Quit from keyboard	Yes
4	SIGILL	Dump	Illegal instruction	Yes
5	SIGTRAP	Dump	Breakpoint for debugging	No
6	SIGABRT	Dump	Abnormal termination	Yes
6	SIGIOT	Dump	Equivalent to SIGABRT	No
7	SIGBUS	Abort	Bus error	No
8	SIGFPE	Dump	Floating point exception	Yes
9	SIGKILL	Abort	Forced process termination	Yes
10	SIGUSR1	Abort	Available to processes	Yes
11	SIGSEGV	Dump	Invalid memory reference	Yes
12	SIGUSR2	Abort	Available to processes	Yes
13	SIGPIPE	Abort	Write to pipe with no readers	Yes
14	SIGALRM	Abort	Real timer clock	Yes
15	SIGTERM	Abort	Process termination	Yes
16	SIGSTKFLT	Abort	Coprocessor stack error	No
17	SIGCHLD	Ignore	Child process stopped or terminated	Yes
18	SIGCONT	Continue	Resume execution, if stopped	Yes
19	SIGSTOP	Stop	Stop process execution	Yes
20	SIGTSTP	Stop	Stop process issued from tty	Yes
21	SIGTTIN	Stop	Background process requires input	Yes
22	SIGTTOU	Stop	Background process requires output	Yes

Table 9-1. The First 31 Signals in Linux/i386 (continued)

#	Signal Name	Default Action	Comment	POSIX
23	SIGURG	Ignore	Urgent condition on socket	No
24	SIGXCPU	Abort	CPU time limit exceeded	No
25	SIGXFSZ	Abort	File size limit exceeded	No
26	SIGVTALRM	Abort	Virtual timer clock	No
27	SIGPROF	Abort	Profile timer clock	No
28	SIGWINCH	Ignore	Window resizing	No
29	SIGIO	Abort	I/O now possible	No
29	SIGPOLL	Abort	Equivalent to SIGIO	No
30	SIGPWR	Abort	Power supply failure	No
31	SIGUNUSED	Abort	Not used	No

A number of system calls allow programmers to send signals and determine how their processes exploit the signals they receive. Table 9-2 describes these calls succinctly; their behavior is described in detail later in the later section "System Calls Related to Signal Handling."

Table 9-2. System Calls Related to Signals

System Call	Description
kill()	Send a signal to a process.
sigaction()	Change the action associated with a signal.
signal()	Similar to sigaction().
sigpending()	Check whether there are pending signals.
sigprocmask()	Modify the set of blocked signals.
sigsuspend()	Wait for a signal.
rt_sigaction()	Change the action associated with a real-time signal.
rt_sigpending()	Check whether there are pending real-time signals.
rt_sigprocmask()	Modify the set of blocked real-time signals.
rt_sigqueueinfo()	Send a real-time signal to a process.
rt_sigsuspend()	Wait for a real-time signal.
rt_sigtimedwait()	Similar to rt_sigsuspend().

An important characteristic of signals is that they may be sent at any time to processes whose state is usually unpredictable. Signals sent to a nonrunning process must be saved by the kernel until that process resumes execution. Blocking signals (described later) require signals to be queued, which exacerbates the problem of signals being raised before they can be delivered.

Therefore, the kernel distinguishes two different phases related to signal transmission:

Signal sending
> The kernel updates the descriptor of the destination process to represent that a new signal has been sent.

Signal receiving
> The kernel forces the destination process to react to the signal by changing its execution state or by starting the execution of a specified signal handler or both.

Each signal sent can be received no more than once. Signals are consumable resources: once they have been received, all process descriptor information that refers to their previous existence is canceled.

Signals that have been sent but not yet received are called *pending signals*. At any time, only one pending signal of a given type may exist for a process; additional pending signals of the same type to the same process are not queued but simply discarded. In general, a signal may remain pending for an unpredictable amount of time. Indeed, the following factors must be taken into consideration:

- Signals are usually received only by the currently running process (that is, by the current process).

- Signals of a given type may be selectively *blocked* by a process (see the section "Modifying the Set of Blocked Signals"): in this case, the process will not receive the signal until it removes the block.

- When a process executes a signal-handler function, it usually "masks" the corresponding signal, that is, it automatically blocks the signal until the handler terminates. A signal handler therefore cannot be interrupted by another occurrence of the handled signal, and therefore the function doesn't need to be reentrant. A *masked* signal is always blocked, but the converse does not hold.

Although the notion of signals is intuitive, the kernel implementation is rather complex. The kernel must:

- Remember which signals are blocked by each process.

- When switching from Kernel Mode to User Mode, check whether a signal for any process has arrived. This happens at almost every timer interrupt, that is, roughly every 10 ms.

- Determine whether the signal can be ignored. This happens when all of the following conditions are fulfilled:

— The destination process is not traced by another process (the `PF_TRACED` flag in the process descriptor `flags` field is equal to 0).[*]

— The signal is not blocked by the destination process.

— The signal is being ignored by the destination process (either because the process has explicitly ignored it or because the process did not change the default action of the signal and that action is "ignore").

- Handle the signal, which may require switching the process to a handler function at any point during its execution and restoring the original execution context after the function returns.

Moreover, Linux must take into account the different semantics for signals adopted by BSD and System V; furthermore, it must comply with the rather cumbersome POSIX requirements.

Actions Performed upon Receiving a Signal

There are three ways in which a process can respond to a signal:

- *Explicitly ignore* the signal.

- *Execute the default action* associated with the signal (see Table 9-1). This action, which is predefined by the kernel, depends on the signal type and may be any one of the following:

Abort
  The process is destroyed (killed).

Dump
  The process is destroyed (killed) and a `core` file containing its execution context is created, if possible; this file may be used for debug purposes.

Ignore
  The signal is ignored.

Stop
  The process is stopped, that is, put in a `TASK_STOPPED` state (see the section "Process State" in Chapter 3).

Continue
  If the process is stopped (`TASK_STOPPED`), it is put into the `TASK_RUNNING` state.

- *Catch* the signal by invoking a corresponding signal-handler function.

---

[*] If a process receives a signal while it is being traced, the kernel stops the process and notifies the tracing process by sending a `SIGCHLD` signal to it. The tracing process may, in turn, resume execution of the traced process by means of a `SIGCONT` signal.

Notice that blocking a signal is different from ignoring it: a signal is never received while it is blocked; an ignored signal is always received, and there is simply no further action.

The SIGKILL and SIGSTOP signals cannot be explicitly ignored or caught, and thus their default actions must always be executed. Therefore, SIGKILL and SIGSTOP allow a user with appropriate privileges to destroy and to stop, respectively, any process[*] regardless of the defenses taken by the program it is executing.

Data Structures Associated with Signals

The basic data structure used to store the signals sent to a process is a sigset_t array of bits, one for each signal type:

```
typedef struct {
    unsigned long sig[2];
} sigset_t;
```

Since each unsigned long number consists of 32 bits, the maximum number of signals that may be declared in Linux is 64 (the _NSIG macro denotes this value). No signal has the number 0, so the other 31 bits in the first element of sigset_t are the standard ones listed in Table 9-1. Signal 1 is mapped to bit 1, signal 2 to bit 1, and so on. The bits in the second element are the real-time signals. The following fields are included in the process descriptor to keep track of the signals sent to the process:

signal
    A sigset_t variable that denotes the signals sent to the process

blocked
    A sigset_t variable that denotes the blocked signals

sigpending
    A flag set if one or more nonblocked signals are pending

gsig
    A pointer to a signal_struct data structure that describes how each signal must be handled

The signal_struct structure, in turn, is defined as follows:

```
struct signal_struct {
    atomic_t           count;
    struct k_sigaction action[64];
    spinlock_t         siglock;
};
```

---

[*] Actually, there are two exceptions: all signals sent to process 0 (*swapper*) are discarded, while those sent to process 1 (*init*) are always discarded unless they are caught. Therefore, process 0 never dies, while process 1 dies only when the *init* program terminates.

As mentioned in the section "The clone( ), fork( ), and vfork( ) System Calls" in Chapter 3, this structure may be shared by several processes by invoking the `clone( )` system call with the `CLONE_SIGHAND` flag set.* The `count` field specifies the number of processes that share the `signal_struct` structure, while the `siglock` field is used to ensure exclusive access to its fields (see Chapter 11, *Kernel Synchronization*). The `action` field is an array of 64 `k_sigaction` structures that specify how each signal must be handled.

Some architectures assign properties to a signal that are visible only to the kernel. Thus, the properties of a signal are stored in a `k_sigaction` structure, which contains both the properties hidden from the User Mode process and the more familiar `sigaction` structure that holds all the properties a User Mode process can see. Actually, on the Intel platform all signal properties are visible to User Mode processes. So the `k_sigaction` structure simply reduces to a single `sa` structure of type `sigaction`, which includes the following fields:

`sa_handler`
> This field specifies the type of action to be performed; its value can be a pointer to the signal handler, `SIG_DFL` (that is, the value 0) to specify that the default action must be executed or `SIG_IGN` (that is, the value 1) to specify that the signal must be explicitly ignored.

`sa_flags`
> This set of flags specifies how the signal must be handled; some of them are listed in Table 9-3.

`sa_mask`
> This `sigset_t` variable specifies the signals to be masked when running the signal handler.

Table 9-3. Flags Specifying How to Handle a Signal

Flag Name	Description
SA_NOCLDSTOP	Do not send SIGCHLD to the parent when the process is stopped.
SA_NODEFER, SA_NOMASK	Do not mask the signal while executing the signal handler.
SA_RESETHAND, SA_ONESHOT	Reset to default action after executing the signal handler.
SA_ONSTACK	Use an alternate stack for the signal handler (see the later section "Catching the Signal").
SA_RESTART	Interrupted system calls are automatically restarted (see the later section "Reexecution of System Calls").
SA_SIGINFO	Provide additional information to the signal handler (see the later section "Changing a Signal Action").

---

* If this is not done, about 1300 bytes are added to the process data structures just to take care of signal handling.

Operations on Signal Data Structures

Several functions and macros are used by the kernel to handle signals. In the following description, set is a pointer to a sigset_t variable, nsig is the number of a signal, and mask is an unsigned long bit mask.

sigaddset(set,nsig) *and* sigdelset(set,nsig)

Sets the bit of the sigset_t variable corresponding to signal nsig to 1 or 0, respectively. In practice, sigaddset() reduces to:

```
set->sig[(nsig - 1) / 32] |= 1UL << ((nsig - 1) % 32);
```

and sigdelset() to:

```
set->sig[(nsig - 1) / 32] &= ~(1UL << ((nsig - 1) % 32));
```

sigaddsetmask(set,mask) *and* sigdelsetmask(set,mask)

Sets all the bits of the sigset_t variable whose corresponding bits of mask are on to 1 or 0, respectively. The corresponding functions reduce to:

```
set->sig[0] |= mask;
```

and to:

```
set->sig[0] &= ~mask;
```

sigismember(set,nsig)

Returns the value of the bit of the sigset_t variable corresponding to the signal nsig. In practice, this function reduces to:

```
1 & (set->sig[(nsig - 1) / 32] >> ((nsig - 1) % 32))
```

sigmask(nsig)

Yields the bit index of the signal nsig. In other words, if the kernel needs to set, clear, or test a bit in an element of sigset_t that corresponds to a particular signal, it can derive the proper bit through this macro.

signal_pending(p)

Returns the value 1 (true) if the process identified by the *p process descriptor has nonblocked pending signals and the value 0 (false) if it doesn't. The function is implemented as a simple check on the sigpending field of the process descriptor.

recalc_sigpending(t)

Checks whether the process identified by the process descriptor at *t has nonblocked pending signals, by looking at the sig and blocked fields of the process, then sets the sigpending field properly as follows:

```
ready = t->signal.sig[1] &~ t->blocked.sig[1];
ready |= t->signal.sig[0] &~ t->blocked.sig[0];
t->sigpending = (ready != 0);
```

sigandsets(d,s1,s2), sigorsets(d,s1,s2), *and* signandsets(d,s1,s2)

Performs a logical AND, a logical OR, and a logical NAND, respectively, between the sigset_t variables to which s1 and s2 point; the result is stored in the sigset_t variable to which d points.

dequeue_signal(mask, info)

Checks whether the current process has nonblocked pending signals. If so, returns the lowest-numbered pending signal and updates the data structures to indicate it is no longer pending. This task involves clearing the corresponding bit in current->signal, updating the value of current->sigpending, and storing the signal number of the dequeued signal into the *info table. In the mask parameter each bit that is set represents a blocked signal:

```
sig = 0;
if (((x = current->signal.sig[0]) & ~mask->sig[0]) != 0)
    sig = 1 + ffz(~x);
else if (((x = current->signal.sig[1]) &
            ~mask->sig[1]) != 0)
    sig = 33 + ffz(~x);
if (sig) {
    sigdelset(&current->signal, sig);
    recalc_sigpending(current);
}
return sig;
```

The collection of currently pending signals is ANDed with the blocked signals (the complement of mask). If anything is left, it represents a signal that should be delivered to the process. The ffz() function returns the index of the first 0 bit in its parameter; this value is used to compute the lowest-number signal to be delivered.

flush_signals(t)

Deletes all signals sent to the process identified by the process descriptor at *t. This is done by clearing both the t->sigpending and the t->signal fields and by emptying the real-time queue of signals (see the later section "Real-Time Signals").

Sending a Signal

When a signal is sent to a process, either from the kernel or from another process, the kernel delivers it by invoking the send_sig_info(), send_sig(), force_sig(), or force_sig_info() functions. These accomplish the first phase of signal handling described earlier in the section "The Role of Signals": updating the process descriptor as needed. They do not directly perform the second phase of receiving the signal but, depending on the type of signal and the state of the process, may wake up the process and force it to receive the signal.

The *send_sig_info()* and *send_sig()* Functions

The `send_sig_info()` function acts on three parameters:

sig
> The signal number.

info
> Either the address of a `siginfo_t` table associated with real-time signals or one of two special values: 0 means that the signal has been sent by a User Mode process, while 1 means that it has been sent by the kernel. The `siginfo_t` data structure has information that must be passed to the process receiving the real-time signal, such as the PID of the sender process and the UID of its owner.

t
> A pointer to the descriptor of the destination process.

The `send_sig_info()` function starts by checking whether the parameters are correct:

```
if (sig < 0 || sig > 64)
    return -EINVAL;
```

The function checks then if the signal is being sent by a User Mode process. This occurs when `info` is equal to 0 or when the `si_code` field of the `siginfo_t` table is negative or zero (the positive values of this field are reserved to identify the kernel function that sent the signal):

```
if ((!info || ((unsigned long)info != 1 && (info->si_code <=0)))
    && ((sig != SIGCONT) || (current->session != t->session))
    && (current->euid ^ t->suid) && (current->euid ^ t->uid)
    && (current->uid ^ t->suid) && (current->uid ^ t->uid)
    && !capable(CAP_KILL))
        return -EPERM;
```

If the signal is sent by a User Mode process, the function determines whether the operation is allowed. The signal is delivered only if the owner of the sending process has the proper capability (see Chapter 19, *Program Execution*), the signal is SIGCONT, the destination process is in the same login session of the sending process, or both processes belong to the same user.

If the `sig` parameter has the value 0, the function returns immediately without sending any signal: since 0 is not a valid signal number, it is used to allow the sending process to check whether it has the required privileges to send a signal to the destination process. The function returns also if the destination process is in the TASK_ZOMBIE state, indicated by checking whether its `siginfo_t` table has been released:

```
if (!sig || !t->sig)
    return 0;
```

Some types of signals might nullify other pending signals for the destination process. Therefore, the function checks whether one of the following cases occurs:

- `sig` is a `SIGKILL` or `SIGCONT` signal. If the destination process is stopped, it is put in the `TASK_RUNNING` state so that it will be able to execute the `do_exit()` function; moreover, if the destination process has `SIGSTOP`, `SIGTSTP`, `SIGTTOU`, or `SIGTTIN` pending signals, they are removed:

```
if (t->state == TASK_STOPPED)
    wake_up_process(t);
t->exit_code = 0;
sigdelsetmask(&t->signal, (sigmask(SIGSTOP) |
        sigmask(SIGTSTP) | sigmask(SIGTTOU) |
        sigmask(SIGTTIN)));
recalc_sigpending(t);
```

- `sig` is a `SIGSTOP`, `SIGTSTP`, `SIGTTIN`, or `SIGTTOU` signal. If the destination process has a pending `SIGCONT` signal, it is destroyed:

```
sigdelset(&t->signal, SIGCONT);
recalc_sigpending(t);
```

Next, `send_sig_info()` checks whether the new signal can be handled immediately. In this case, the function also takes care of the receiving phase of the signal:

```
if (ignored_signal(sig, t)) {
  out:
    if (t->state == TASK_INTERRUPTIBLE && signal_pending(t))
        wake_up_process(t);
    return 0;
}
```

The `ignored_signal()` function returns the value 1 when all three conditions for ignoring a signal mentioned in the section "The Role of Signals" are satisfied. However, in order to fulfill a POSIX requirement, the `SIGCHLD` signal is handled specially. POSIX distinguishes between explicitly setting the "ignore" action for the `SIGCHLD` signal and leaving the default in place (even if the default is to ignore the signal). In order to let the kernel clean up a terminated child process and prevent it from becoming a zombie (see the section "Process Removal" in Chapter 3) the parent must explicitly set the action to "ignore" the signal. So `ignored_signal()` handles as follows: if the signal is explicitly ignored, `ignored_signal()` returns 0, but if the default action was "ignore" and the process didn't change that default, `ignored_signal()` returns 1.

If `ignored_signal()` returns 1, the `siginfo_t` table of the destination process must not be updated; however, if the process is in the `TASK_INTERRUPTIBLE` state and if it has other nonblocked pending signals, `send_sig_info()` invokes the `wake_up_process()` function to wake it up.

If `ignored_signal()` returns 0, the phase of signal receiving has to be deferred, therefore `send_sig_info()` may have to modify the data structures of the destination process to let it know later that a new signal has been sent to it. Since standard signals are not queued, `send_sig_info()` must check whether another instance of the same signal is already pending, then leave its mark on the proper data structures of the process descriptor:

```
if (sigismember(&t->signal, sig))
    goto out;
sigaddset(&t->signal, sig);
if (!sigismember(&t->blocked, sig))
    t->sigpending = 1;
goto out;
```

The `sigaddset()` function is invoked to set the proper bit in `t->signal`. The `t->sigpending` flag is also set, unless the destination process has blocked the `sig` signal. The function terminates in the usual way by waking up, if necessary, the destination process. In the section "Receiving a Signal," we'll discuss the actions performed by the process.

The `send_sig()` function is similar to `send_sig_info()`. However, the `info` parameter is replaced by a `priv` flag, which is true if the signal is sent by the kernel and false if it is sent by a process. The `send_sig()` function is implemented as a special case of `send_sig_info()`:

```
return send_sig_info(sig, (void*)(priv != 0), t);
```

The force_sig_info() and force_sig() Functions

The `force_sig_info()` function is used by the kernel to send signals that cannot be explicitly ignored or blocked by the destination processes. The function's parameters are the same as those of `send_sig_info()`. The `force_sig_info()` function acts on the `signal_struct` data structure that is referenced by the `sig` field included in the descriptor `t` of the destination process:

```
if (t->sig->action[sig-1].sa.sa_handler == SIG_IGN)
    t->sig->action[sig-1].sa.sa_handler = SIG_DFL;
sigdelset(&t->blocked, sig);
return send_sig_info(sig, info, t);
```

`force_sig()` is similar to `force_sig_info()`. Its use is limited to signals sent by the kernel; it can be implemented as a special case of the `force_sig_info()` function:

```
force_sig_info(sig, (void*)1L, t);
```

Receiving a Signal

We assume that the kernel has noticed the arrival of a signal and has invoked one of the functions in the previous section to prepare the process descriptor of the process that is supposed to receive the signal. But in case that process was not running on the

CPU at that moment, the kernel deferred the task of waking the process, if necessary, and making it receive the signal. We now turn to the activities that the kernel performs to ensure that pending signals of a process are handled.

As mentioned in the section "The ret_from_intr() Function" in Chapter 4, *Interrupts and Exceptions*, the kernel checks whether there are nonblocked pending signals before allowing a process to resume its execution in User Mode. This check is performed in `ret_from_intr()` every time an interrupt or an exception has been handled by the kernel routines.

In order to handle the nonblocked pending signals, the kernel invokes the `do_signal()` function, which receives two parameters:

`regs`
> The address of the stack area where the User Mode register contents of the current process have been saved

`oldset`
> The address of a variable where the function is supposed to save the bit mask array of blocked signals (actually, this parameter is NULL when invoked from `ret_from_intr()`)

The function starts by checking whether the interrupt occurred while the process was running in User Mode; if not, it simply returns:

```
if ((regs->xcs & 3) != 3)
    return 1;
```

However, as we'll see in the section "Reexecution of System Calls," this does not mean that a system call cannot be interrupted by a signal.

If the `oldset` parameter is NULL, the function initializes it with the address of the `current->blocked` field:

```
if (!oldset)
    oldset = &current->blocked;
```

The heart of the `do_signal()` function consists of a loop that repeatedly invokes `dequeue_signal()` until no more nonblocked pending signals are left. The return code of `dequeue_signal()` is stored in the `signr` local variable: if its value is 0, it means that all pending signals have been handled and `do_signal()` can finish. As long as a nonzero value is returned, a pending signal is waiting to be handled and `dequeue_signal()` is invoked again after `do_signal()` handles the current signal.

If the `current` receiver process is being monitored by some other process, the `do_signal()` function invokes `notify_parent()` and `schedule()` to make the monitoring process aware of the signal handling.

Then `do_signal()` loads the `ka` local variable with the address of the `k_sigaction` data structure of the signal to be handled:

```
ka = &current->sig->action[signr-1];
```

Depending on the contents, three kinds of actions may be performed: ignoring the signal, executing a default action, or executing a signal handler.

Ignoring the Signal

When a received signal is explicitly ignored, the `do_signal()` function normally just continues with a new execution of the loop and therefore considers another pending signal. One exception exists, as described earlier:

```
if (ka->sa.sa_handler == SIG_IGN) {
    if (signr == SIGCHLD)
        while (sys_wait4(-1, NULL, WNOHANG, NULL) > 0)
            /* nothing */;
    continue;
}
```

If the signal received is `SIGCHLD`, the `sys_wait4()` service routine of the `wait4()` system call is invoked to force the process to read information about its children, thus cleaning up memory left over by the terminated child processes (see the section "Destroying Processes" in Chapter 3).

Executing the Default Action for the Signal

If `ka->sa.sa_handler` is equal to `SIG_DFL`, `do_signal()` must perform the default action of the signal. The only exception comes when the receiving process is *init,* in which case the signal is discarded as described in the earlier section "Actions Performed upon Receiving a Signal":

```
if (current->pid == 1)
    continue;
```

For other processes, since the default action depends on the type of signal, the function executes a `switch` statement based on the value of `signr`.

The signals whose default action is "ignore" are easily handled:

```
case SIGCONT: case SIGCHLD: case SIGWINCH:
    continue;
```

The signals whose default action is "stop" may stop the current process. In order to do this, `do_signal()` sets the state of `current` to `TASK_STOPPED` and then invokes the `schedule()` function (see the section "The schedule() function" in Chapter 10, *Process Scheduling*). The `do_signal()` function also sends a `SIGCHLD` signal to the parent process of `current`, unless the parent has set the `SA_NOCLDSTOP` flag of `SIGCHLD`:

```
case SIGTSTP: case SIGTTIN: case SIGTTOU:
    if (is_orphaned_pgrp(current->pgrp))
        continue;
case SIGSTOP:
    current->state = TASK_STOPPED;
    current->exit_code = signr;
    if (!(SA_NOCLDSTOP &
        current->p_pptr->sig->action[SIGCHLD-1].sa.sa_flags))
        notify_parent(current, SIGCHLD);
    schedule();
    continue;
```

The difference between `SIGSTOP` and the other signals is subtle: `SIGSTOP` always stops the process, while the other signals stop the process only if it is not in an "orphaned process group"; the POSIX standard specifies that a process group is *not* orphaned as long as there is a process in the group that has a parent in a different process group but in the same session.

The signals whose default action is "dump" may create a **core** file in the process working directory; this file lists the complete contents of the process's address space and CPU registers. After the `do_signal()` creates the core file, it kills the process. The default action of the remaining 18 signals is "abort," which consists of just killing the process:

```
exit_code = sig_nr;
case SIGQUIT: case SIGILL: case SIGTRAP:
case SIGABRT: case SIGFPE: case SIGSEGV:
    if (current->binfmt
        && current->binfmt->core_dump
        && current->binfmt->core_dump(signr, regs))
        exit_code |= 0x80;
default:
    sigaddset(&current->signal, signr);
    current->flags |= PF_SIGNALED;
    do_exit(exit_code);
```

The `do_exit()` function receives as its input parameter the signal number ORed with a flag set when a core dump has been performed. That value is used to determine the exit code of the process. The function terminates the current process, and hence never returns (see Chapter 19).

Catching the Signal

If the signal has a specific handler, the `do_signal()` function must enforce its execution. It does this by invoking `handle_signal()`:

```
handle_signal(signr, ka, &info, oldset, regs);
return 1;
```

Notice how `do_signal()` returns after having handled a single signal: other pending signals won't be considered until the next invocation of `do_signal()`. This approach ensures that real-time signals will be dealt in the proper order (see the later section "Real-Time Signals").

Executing a signal handler is a rather complex task because of the need to juggle stacks carefully while switching between User Mode and Kernel Mode. We'll explain exactly what is entailed here.

Signal handlers are functions defined by User Mode processes and included in the User Mode code segment. The `handle_signal()` function runs in Kernel Mode while signal handlers run in User Mode; this means that the current process must first execute the signal handler in User Mode before being allowed to resume its "normal" execution. Moreover, when the kernel attempts to resume the normal execution of the process, the Kernel Mode stack no longer contains the hardware context of the interrupted program because the Kernel Mode stack is emptied at every transition from User Mode to Kernel Mode.

An additional complication is that signal handlers may invoke system calls: in this case, after having executed the service routine, control must be returned to the signal handler instead of to the code of the interrupted program.

The solution adopted in Linux consists of copying the hardware context saved in the Kernel Mode stack onto the User Mode stack of the current process. The User Mode stack is also modified in such a way that, when the signal handler terminates, the `sigreturn()` system call is automatically invoked to copy the hardware context back on the Kernel Mode stack and restore the original content of the User Mode stack.

Figure 9-1 illustrates the flow of execution of the functions involved in catching a signal. A nonblocked signal is sent to a process. When an interrupt or exception occurs, the process switches into Kernel Mode. Right before returning to User Mode, the kernel executes the `do_signal()` function, which in turn handles the signal (by invoking `handle_signal()`) and sets up the User Mode stack (by invoking `setup_frame()`). When the process switches again to User Mode, it starts executing the signal handler because the handler's starting address was forced into the program counter. When that function terminates, the return code placed on the User Mode stack by the `setup_frame()` function is executed. This code invokes the `sigreturn()` system call, whose service routine copies the hardware context of the normal program in the Kernel Mode stack and restores the User Mode stack back to its original state (by invoking `restore_sigcontext()`). When the system call terminates, the normal program can thus resume its execution.

Let us now examine in detail how this scheme is carried out.

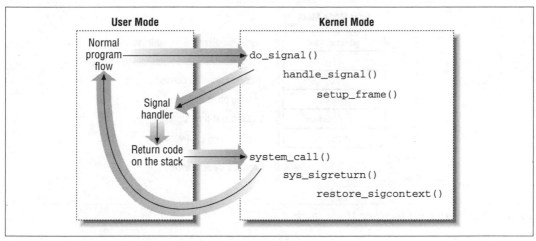

Figure 9-1. Catching a signal

Setting up the frame

In order to properly set the User Mode stack of the process, the `handle_signal()` function invokes either `setup_frame()` (for signals without `siginfo_t` table) or `setup_rt_frame()`.

The `setup_frame()` function receives four parameters, which have the following meanings:

sig
> Signal number

ka
> Address of the `k_sigaction` table associated with the signal

oldset
> Address of a bit mask array of blocked signals

regs
> Address in the Kernel Mode stack area where the User Mode register contents have been saved

The function pushes onto the User Mode stack a data structure called a *frame*, which contains the information needed to handle the signal and to ensure the correct return to the `sys_sigreturn()` function. A frame is a `sigframe` table that includes the following fields (see Figure 9-2):

pretcode
> Return address of the signal handler function; it points to the `retcode` field (later in this list) in the same table.

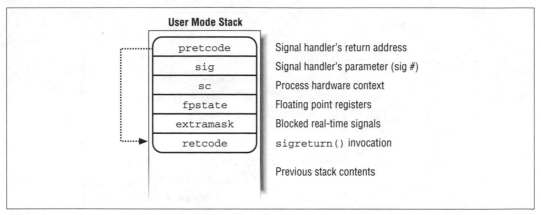

Figure 9-2. Frame on the User Mode stack

`sig`

> The signal number; this is the parameter required by the signal handler.

`sc`

> Structure of type `sigcontext` containing the hardware context of the User Mode process right before switching to Kernel Mode (this information is copied from the Kernel Mode stack of `current`). It also contains a bit array that specifies the blocked standard signals of the process.

`fpstate`

> Structure of type `_fpstate` that may be used to store the floating point registers of the User Mode process (see the section "Saving the Floating Point Registers" in Chapter 3).

`extramask`

> Bit array that specifies the blocked real-time signals.

`retcode`

> Eight-byte code issuing a `sigreturn()` system call; this code is executed when returning from the signal handler.

The `setup_frame()` function starts by invoking `get_sigframe()` to compute the first memory location of the frame. That memory location is usually* in the User Mode stack, thus the function returns the value:

```
(regs->esp - sizeof(struct sigframe)) & 0xfffffff8
```

---

* Linux allows processes to specify an alternate stack for their signal handlers by invoking the `sigaltstack()` system call; this feature is also requested by the X/Open standard. When an alternate stack is present, the `get_sigframe()` function returns an address inside that stack. We don't discuss this feature further, since it is conceptually similar to standard signal handling.

Since stacks grow toward lower addresses, the initial address of the frame is obtained by subtracting its size from the address of the current stack top and aligning the result to a multiple of 8.

The returned address is then verified by means of the **access_ok** macro; if it is valid, the function repeatedly invokes **__put_user()** to fill all the fields of the frame. Once this is done, it modifies the **regs** area of the Kernel Mode stack, thus ensuring that control will be transferred to the signal handler when **current** resumes its execution in User Mode:

```
regs->esp = (unsigned long) frame;
regs->eip = (unsigned long) ka->sa.sa_handler;
```

The **setup_frame()** function terminates by resetting the segmentation registers saved on the Kernel Mode stack to their default value. Now the information needed by the signal handler is on the top of the User Mode stack.

The **setup_rt_frame()** function is very similar to **setup_frame()**, but it puts on the User Mode stack an *extended frame* (stored in the **rt_sigframe** data structure) that also includes the content of the **siginfo_t** table associated with the signal.

Evaluating the signal flags

After setting up the User Mode stack, the **handle_signal()** function checks the values of the flags associated with the signal.

If the received signal has the **SA_ONESHOT** flag set, it must be reset to its default action so that further occurrences of the same signal will not trigger the execution of the signal handler:

```
if (ka->sa.sa_flags & SA_ONESHOT)
    ka->sa.sa_handler = SIG_DFL;
```

Moreover, if the signal does not have the **SA_NODEFER** flag set, the signals in the **sa_mask** field of the **sigaction** table must be blocked during the execution of the signal handler:

```
if (!(ka->sa.sa_flags & SA_NODEFER)) {
    sigorsets(&current->blocked,
              &current->blocked,
              &ka->sa.sa_mask);
    sigaddset(&current->blocked,sig);
    recalc_sigpending(current);
}
```

The function returns then to **do_signal()**, which also returns immediately.

Starting the signal handler

When do_signal() returns, the current process resumes its execution in User Mode. Because of the preparation by setup_frame() described earlier, the eip register points to the first instruction of the signal handler, while esp points to the first memory location of the frame that has been pushed on top of the User Mode stack. As a result, the signal handler is executed.

Terminating the signal handler

When the signal handler terminates, the return address on top of the stack points to the code in the retcode field of the frame. For signals without siginfo_t table, the code is equivalent to the following Assembly instructions:

```
popl %eax
movl $__NR_sigreturn, %eax
int $0x80
```

Therefore, the signal number (that is, the sig field of the frame) is discarded from the stack, and the sigreturn() system call is then invoked.

The sys_sigreturn() function receives as its parameter the pt_regs data structure regs, which contains the hardware context of the User Mode process (see the section "Parameter Passing" in Chapter 8, *System Calls*). It can thus derive the frame address inside the User Mode stack:

```
frame = (struct sigframe *)(regs.esp - 8);
```

The function reads from the sc field of the frame the bit array of signals that were blocked before invoking the signal handler and writes it in the blocked field of current. As a result, all signals that have been masked for the execution of the signal handler are unblocked. The recalc_sigpending() function is then invoked.

The sys_sigreturn() function must at this point copy the process hardware context from the sc field of the frame to the Kernel Mode stack; it then removes the frame from the User Mode stack by invoking the restore_sigcontext() function.

For signals having a siginfo_t table, the mechanism is very similar. The return code in the retcode field of the extended frame invokes the rt_sigreturn() system call; the corresponding sys_rt_sigreturn() service routine copies the process hardware context from the extended frame to the Kernel Mode stack and restores the original User Mode stack content by removing the extended frame from it.

Reexecution of System Calls

In some cases, the request associated with a system call cannot be immediately satisfied by the kernel; when this happens the process that issued the system call is put in a TASK_INTERRUPTIBLE or TASK_UNINTERRUPTIBLE state.

If the process is put in a `TASK_INTERRUPTIBLE` state and some other process sends a signal to it, the kernel puts it in the `TASK_RUNNING` state without completing the system call (see the section "Returning from Interrupts and Exceptions" in Chapter 4). When this happens, the system call service routine does not complete its job but returns an `EINTR`, `ERESTARTNOHAND`, `ERESTARTSYS`, or `ERESTARTNOINTR` error code. The process receives the signal while switching back to User Mode.

In practice, the only error code a User Mode process can get in this situation is `EINTR`, which means that the system call has not been completed. (The application programmer may check this code and decide whether to reissue the system call.) The remaining error codes are used internally by the kernel to specify whether the system call may be reexecuted automatically after the signal handler termination.

Table 9-4 lists the error codes related to unfinished system calls and their impact for each of the three possible signal actions. The meaning of the terms appearing in the entries is the following:

Terminate
> The system call will not be automatically reexecuted; the process will resume its execution in User Mode at the instruction following the `int $0x80` one and the `eax` register will contain the `-EINTR` value.

Reexecute
> The kernel forces the User Mode process to reload the `eax` register with the system call number and to reexecute the `int $0x80` instruction; the process is not aware of the reexecution and the error code is not passed to it.

Depends
> The system call is reexecuted only if the `SA_RESTART` flag of the received signal is set; otherwise, the system call terminates with a `-EINTR` error code.

Table 9-4. Reexecution of System Calls

Signal Action	Error Codes and Their Impact on System Call Execution			
	EINTR	**ERESTARTSYS**	**ERESTARTNOHAND**	**ERESTARTNOINTR**
Default	Terminate	Reexecute	Reexecute	Reexecute
Ignore	Terminate	Reexecute	Reexecute	Reexecute
Catch	Terminate	Depends	Terminate	Reexecute

When receiving a signal, the kernel must be sure that the process really issued a system call before attempting to reexecute it. This is where the `orig_eax` field of the `regs` hardware context plays a critical role. Let us recall how this field is initialized when the interrupt or exception handler starts:

Interrupt
> The field contains the IRQ number associated with the interrupt minus 256 (see the section "Saving the Registers for the Interrupt Handler" in Chapter 4).

0x80 *exception*

The field contains the system call number (see the section "The system_call() Function" in Chapter 8).

Other exceptions

The field contains the value -1 (see the section "Saving the Registers for the Exception Handler" in Chapter 4).

Therefore, a nonnegative value in the `orig_eax` field means that the signal has woken up a `TASK_INTERRUPTIBLE` process that was sleeping in a system call. The service routine recognizes that the system call was interrupted, and thus returns one of the previously mentioned error codes.

If the signal is explicitly ignored or if its default action has been executed, `do_signal()` analyzes the error code of the system call to decide whether the unfinished system call must be automatically reexecuted, as specified in Table 9-4. If the call must be restarted, the function modifies the `regs` hardware context so that, when the process is back in User Mode, `eip` points to the `int $0x80` instruction and `eax` contains the system call number:

```
if (regs->orig_eax >= 0) {
    if (regs->eax == -ERESTARTNOHAND ||
        regs->eax == -ERESTARTSYS ||
        regs->eax == -ERESTARTNOINTR) {
        regs->eax = regs->orig_eax;
        regs->eip -= 2;
    }
}
```

The `regs->eax` field has been filled with the return code of a system call service routine (see the section "The system_call() Function" in Chapter 8).

If the signal has been caught, `handle_signal()` analyzes the error code and, possibly, the `SA_RESTART` flag of the `sigaction` table to decide whether the unfinished system call must be reexecuted:

```
if (regs->orig_eax >= 0) {
    switch (regs->eax) {
        case -ERESTARTNOHAND:
            regs->eax = -EINTR;
            break;
        case -ERESTARTSYS:
            if (!(ka->sa.sa_flags & SA_RESTART)) {
                regs->eax = -EINTR;
                break;
            }
            /* fallthrough */
        case -ERESTARTNOINTR:
```

```
            regs->eax = regs->orig_eax;
            regs->eip -= 2;
        }
    }
```

If the system call must be restarted, `handle_signal()` proceeds exactly as `do_signal()`; otherwise, it returns an `-EINTR` error code to the User Mode process.

Real-Time Signals

The POSIX standard introduced a new class of signals denoted as *real-time signals*; the corresponding signal numbers range from 32 to 63. The main difference with respect to standard signals is that real-time signals of the same kind may be queued. This ensures that multiple signals sent will be received. Although the Linux kernel does not make use of real-time signals, it fully supports the POSIX standard by means of several specific system calls (see the later section "System Calls for Real-Time Signals").

The queue of real-time signals is implemented as a list of `signal_queue` elements:

```
struct signal_queue {
    struct signal_queue *next;
    siginfo_t info;
};
```

The `info` table of type `siginfo_t` was explained in the section "The send_sig_info() and send_sig() Functions"; the `next` field points to the next element in the list.

Each process descriptor has two specific fields; `sigqueue` points to the first element of the queue of received real-time signals, while `sigqueue_tail` points to the `next` field of the last element of the queue.

When sending a signal, the `send_sig_info()` function checks whether its number is greater than 31; if so, it inserts the signal in the queue of real-time signals for the destination process.

Similarly, when receiving a signal, `dequeue_signal()` checks whether the signal number of the pending signal is greater than 31; if so, it extracts from the queue the element corresponding to the received signal. If the queue does not contain other signals of the same type, the function also clears the corresponding bit in `current->signal`.

System Calls Related to Signal Handling

As stated in the introduction of this chapter, programs running in User Mode are allowed to send and receive signals. This means that a set of system calls must be defined to allow these kinds of operations. Unfortunately, due to historical reasons, several noncompatible system calls exist that serve essentially the same purpose. In order to ensure full compatibility with older Unix versions, Linux supports both older system calls and newer ones introduced in the POSIX standard. We shall describe some of the most significant POSIX system calls.

The kill( ) System Call

The `kill(pid,sig)` system call is commonly used to send signals; its corresponding service routine is the `sys_kill()` function. The integer `pid` parameter has several meanings, depending on its numerical value:

pid > 0
> The `sig` signal is sent to the process whose PID is equal to `pid`.

pid = 0
> The `sig` signal is sent to all processes in the same group of the calling process.

pid = -1
> The signal is sent to all processes, except *swapper* (PID 0), *init* (PID 1), and `current`.

pid < -1
> The signal is sent to all processes in the process group *-pid*.

The `sys_kill()` function invokes `kill_something_info()`. This in turn invokes either `send_sig_info()`, to send the signal to a single process, or `kill_pg_info()`, to scan all processes and invoke `send_sig_info()` for each process in the destination group.

System V and BSD Unix variants also have a `killpg()` system call, which is able to explicitly send a signal to a group of processes. In Linux the function is implemented as a library function that makes use of the `kill()` system call.

Changing a Signal Action

The `sigaction(sig,act,oact)` system call allows users to specify an action for a signal; of course, if no signal action is defined, the kernel executes the default action associated with the received signal.

The corresponding `sys_sigaction()` service routine acts on two parameters: the `sig` signal number and the `act` table of type `sigaction` that specifies the new action. A third `oact` optional output parameter may be used to get the previous action associated with the signal.

The function checks first whether the `act` address is valid. Then it fills the `sa_handler`, `sa_flags`, and `sa_mask` fields of a `new_ka` local variable of type `k_sigaction` with the corresponding fields of `*act`:

```
__get_user(new_ka.sa.sa_handler, &act->sa_handler);
__get_user(new_ka.sa.sa_flags, &act->sa_flags);
__get_user(mask, &act->sa_mask);
new_ka.sa.sa_mask.sig[0] = mask;
new_ka.sa.sa_mask.sig[1] = 0
```

The function invokes `do_sigaction()` to copy the new `new_ka` table into the entry at the `sig-1` position of `current->sig->action`:

```
k = &current->sig->action[sig-1];
if (act) {
    *k = *act;
    sigdelsetmask(&k->sa.sa_mask, sigmask(SIGKILL)
                                  | sigmask(SIGSTOP));
    if (k->sa.sa_handler == SIG_IGN
        || (k->sa.sa_handler == SIG_DFL
        && (sig == SIGCONT ||
            sig == SIGCHLD ||
            sig == SIGWINCH))) {
        sigdelset(&current->signal, sig);
        recalc_sigpending(current);
    }
}
```

The POSIX standard requires that setting a signal action either to `SIG_IGN`, or to `SIG_DFL` when the default action is "ignore," will cause any pending signal of the same type to be discarded. Moreover, notice that, no matter what the requested masked signals are for the signal handler, `SIGKILL` and `SIGSTOP` are never masked.

If the `oact` parameter is not NULL, the contents of the previous `sigaction` table are copied to the process address space at the address specified by that parameter:

```
if (oact) {
    __put_user(old_ka.sa.sa_handler, &oact->sa_handler);
    __put_user(old_ka.sa.sa_flags, &oact->sa_flags);
    __put_user(old_ka.sa.sa_mask.sig[0], &oact->sa_mask);
}
```

Older System V Unix variants offered the `signal()` system call, which is still widely used by programmers. Recent C libraries implement `signal()` by means of `sigaction()`. However, Linux still supports old C libraries and offers the `sys_signal()` service routine:

```
new_sa.sa.sa_handler = handler;
new_sa.sa.sa_flags = SA_ONESHOT | SA_NOMASK;
ret = do_sigaction(sig, &new_sa, &old_sa);
return ret ? ret : (unsigned long)old_sa.sa.sa_handler;
```

Examining the Pending Blocked Signals

The `sigpending()` system call allows a process to examine the set of pending blocked signals, that is, those that have been raised while blocked. This system call fetches only the standard signals.

The corresponding `sys_sigpending()` service routine acts on a single parameter, `set`, namely, the address of a user variable where the array of bits must be copied:

```
pending = current->blocked.sig[0] & current->signal.sig[0];
if (copy_to_user(set, &pending, sizeof(*set)))
    return -EFAULT;
return 0;
```

Modifying the Set of Blocked Signals

The `sigprocmask()` system call allows processes to modify the set of blocked signals; like `sigpending()`, this system call applies only to the standard signals.

The corresponding `sys_sigprocmask()` service routine acts on three parameters:

`oset`

Pointer in the process address space to a bit array where the previous bit mask must be stored

`set`

Pointer in the process address space to the bit array containing the new bit mask

`how`

Flag that may have one of the following values:

`SIG_BLOCK`

The `*set` bit mask array specifies the signals that must be added to the bit mask array of blocked signals.

`SIG_UNBLOCK`

The `*set` bit mask array specifies the signals that must be removed from the bit mask array of blocked signals.

`SIG_SETMASK`

The `*set` bit mask array specifies the new bit mask array of blocked signals.

The function invokes `copy_from_user()` to copy the value pointed to by the `set` parameter into the `new_set` local variable and copies the bit mask array of standard blocked signals of `current` into the `old_set` local variable. It then acts as the `how` flag specifies on these two variables:

```
if (copy_from_user(&new_set, set, sizeof(*set)))
    return -EFAULT;
new_set &= ~(sigmask(SIGKILL)|sigmask(SIGSTOP));
```

```
    old_set = current->blocked.sig[0];
    if (how == SIG_BLOCK)
        sigaddsetmask(&current->blocked, new_set);
    else if (how == SIG_UNBLOCK)
        sigdelsetmask(&current->blocked, new_set);
    else if (how == SIG_SETMASK)
        current->blocked.sig[0] = new_set;
    else
        return -EINVAL;
    recalc_sigpending(current);
    if (oset) {
        if (copy_to_user(oset, &old_set, sizeof(*oset)))
            return -EFAULT;
    }
    return 0;
```

Suspending the Process

The sigsuspend() system call puts the process in the TASK_INTERRUPTIBLE state, after having blocked the standard signals specified by a bit mask array to which the mask parameter points. The process will wake up only when a nonignored, non-blocked signal is sent to it.

The corresponding sys_sigsuspend() service routine executes these statements:

```
    mask &= ~(sigmask(SIGKILL) | sigmask(SIGSTOP));
    saveset = current->blocked;
    current->blocked.sig[0] = mask;
    current->blocked.sig[1] = 0;
    recalc_sigpending(current);
    regs->eax = -EINTR;
    while (1) {
        current->state = TASK_INTERRUPTIBLE;
        schedule();
        if (do_signal(regs, &saveset))
            return -EINTR;
    }
```

The schedule() function selects another process to run. When the process that issued the sigsuspend() system call is executed again, sys_sigsuspend() invokes the do_signal() function in order to receive the signal that has woken up the process. If that function returns the value 1, the signal is not ignored, therefore the system call terminates by returning the error code −EINTR.

The sigsuspend() system call may appear redundant, since the combined execution of sigprocmask() and sleep() apparently yields the same result. But this is not true: because of interleaving of process executions, one must be conscious that invoking a system call to perform action A followed by another system call to perform action B is not equivalent to invoking a single system call that performs action A and then action B.

In the particular case, `sigprocmask()` might unblock a signal that will be received before invoking `sleep()`. If this happens, the process might remain in a `TASK_INTERRUPTIBLE` state forever, waiting for the signal that was already received. On the other hand, the `sigsuspend()` system call does not allow signals to be sent after unblocking and before the `schedule()` invocation because other processes cannot grab the CPU during that time interval.

System Calls for Real-Time Signals

Since the system calls previously examined apply only to standard signals, additional system calls must be introduced to allow User Mode processes to handle real-time signals.

Several system calls for real-time signals (`rt_sigaction()`, `rt_sigpending()`, `rt_sigprocmask()`, and `rt_sigsuspend()` are similar to those described earlier and won't be further discussed.

Two other system calls have been introduced to deal with queues of real-time signals:

`rt_sigqueueinfo()`
> Sends a real-time signal so that it is added to the real-time signal queue of the destination process

`rt_sigtimedwait()`
> Similar to `rt_sigsuspend()`, but the process remains suspended only for a fixed time interval

We do not discuss these system calls because they are quite similar to those used for standard signals.

Anticipating Linux 2.4

Signals are pretty much the same in Linux 2.2 and Linux 2.4.

CHAPTER TEN

PROCESS SCHEDULING

Like any time-sharing system, Linux achieves the magical effect of an apparent simultaneous execution of multiple processes by switching from one process to another in a very short time frame. Process switch itself was discussed in Chapter 3, *Processes*; this chapter deals with *scheduling*, which is concerned with when to switch and which process to choose.

The chapter consists of three parts. The section "Scheduling Policy" introduces the choices made by Linux to schedule processes in the abstract. The section "The Scheduling Algorithm" discusses the data structures used to implement scheduling and the corresponding algorithm. Finally, the section "System Calls Related to Scheduling" describes the system calls that affect process scheduling.

Scheduling Policy

The scheduling algorithm of traditional Unix operating systems must fulfill several conflicting objectives: fast process response time, good throughput for background jobs, avoidance of process starvation, reconciliation of the needs of low- and high-priority processes, and so on. The set of rules used to determine when and how selecting a new process to run is called *scheduling policy*.

Linux scheduling is based on the *time-sharing* technique already introduced in the section "CPU's Time Sharing" in Chapter 5, *Timing Measurements*: several processes are allowed to run "concurrently," which means that the CPU time is roughly divided into "slices," one for each runnable process.* Of course, a single processor can run only one process at any given instant. If a currently running process is not terminated when its

---

* Recall that stopped and suspended processes cannot be selected by the scheduling algorithm to run on the CPU.

277

time slice or *quantum* expires, a process switch may take place. Time-sharing relies on timer interrupts and is thus transparent to processes. No additional code needs to be inserted in the programs in order to ensure CPU time-sharing.

The scheduling policy is also based on ranking processes according to their priority. Complicated algorithms are sometimes used to derive the current priority of a process, but the end result is the same: each process is associated with a value that denotes how appropriate it is to be assigned to the CPU.

In Linux, process priority is dynamic. The scheduler keeps track of what processes are doing and adjusts their priorities periodically; in this way, processes that have been denied the use of the CPU for a long time interval are boosted by dynamically increasing their priority. Correspondingly, processes running for a long time are penalized by decreasing their priority.

When speaking about scheduling, processes are traditionally classified as "I/O-bound" or "CPU-bound." The former make heavy use of I/O devices and spend much time waiting for I/O operations to complete; the latter are number-crunching applications that require a lot of CPU time.

An alternative classification distinguishes three classes of processes:

Interactive processes
> These interact constantly with their users, and therefore spend a lot of time waiting for keypresses and mouse operations. When input is received, the process must be woken up quickly, or the user will find the system to be unresponsive. Typically, the average delay must fall between 50 and 150 ms. The variance of such delay must also be bounded, or the user will find the system to be erratic. Typical interactive programs are command shells, text editors, and graphical applications.

Batch processes
> These do not need user interaction, and hence they often run in the background. Since such processes do not need to be very responsive, they are often penalized by the scheduler. Typical batch programs are programming language compilers, database search engines, and scientific computations.

Real-time processes
> These have very strong scheduling requirements. Such processes should never be blocked by lower-priority processes, they should have a short response time and, most important, such response time should have a minimum variance. Typical real-time programs are video and sound applications, robot controllers, and programs that collect data from physical sensors.

The two classifications we just offered are somewhat independent. For instance, a batch process can be either I/O-bound (e.g., a database server) or CPU-bound (e.g., an image-rendering program). While in Linux real-time programs are explicitly recognized as such by the scheduling algorithm, there is no way to distinguish between interactive and batch programs. In order to offer a good response time to interactive applications, Linux (like all Unix kernels) implicitly favors I/O-bound processes over CPU-bound ones.

Programmers may change the scheduling parameters by means of the system calls illustrated in Table 10-1. More details will be given in the section "System Calls Related to Scheduling."

Table 10-1. System Calls Related to Scheduling

System Call	Description
nice()	Change the priority of a conventional process.
getpriority()	Get the maximum priority of a group of conventional processes.
setpriority()	Set the priority of a group of conventional processes.
sched_getscheduler()	Get the scheduling policy of a process.
sched_setscheduler()	Set the scheduling policy and priority of a process.
sched_getparam()	Get the scheduling priority of a process.
sched_setparam()	Set the priority of a process.
sched_yield()	Relinquish the processor voluntarily without blocking.
sched_get_priority_min()	Get the minimum priority value for a policy.
sched_get_priority_max()	Get the maximum priority value for a policy.
sched_rr_get_interval()	Get the time quantum value for the Round Robin policy.

Most system calls shown in the table apply to real-time processes, thus allowing users to develop real-time applications. However, Linux does not support the most demanding real-time applications because its kernel is nonpreemptive (see the later section "Performance of the Scheduling Algorithm").

Process Preemption

As mentioned in the first chapter, Linux processes are *preemptive*. If a process enters the TASK_RUNNING state, the kernel checks whether its dynamic priority is greater than the priority of the currently running process. If it is, the execution of current is interrupted and the scheduler is invoked to select another process to run (usually the process that just became runnable). Of course, a process may also be preempted when its time quantum expires. As mentioned in the section "CPU's Time Sharing" in Chapter 5, when this occurs, the need_resched field of the current process is set, so the scheduler is invoked when the timer interrupt handler terminates.

For instance, let us consider a scenario in which only two programs—a text editor and a compiler—are being executed. The text editor is an interactive program, therefore it has a higher dynamic priority than the compiler. Nevertheless, it is often suspended, since the user alternates between pauses for think time and data entry; moreover, the average delay between two keypresses is relatively long. However, as soon as the user presses a key, an interrupt is raised, and the kernel wakes up the text editor process. The kernel also determines that the dynamic priority of the editor is higher than the priority of current, the currently running process (that is, the compiler), and hence it sets the need_resched field of this process, thus forcing the scheduler to be activated when the kernel finishes handling the interrupt. The scheduler selects the editor and performs a task switch; as a result, the execution of the editor is resumed very quickly and the character typed by the user is echoed to the screen. When the character has been processed, the text editor process suspends itself waiting for another keypress, and the compiler process can resume its execution.

Be aware that a preempted process is not suspended, since it remains in the TASK_RUNNING state; it simply no longer uses the CPU.

Some real-time operating systems feature preemptive kernels, which means that a process running in Kernel Mode can be interrupted after any instruction, just as it can in User Mode. The Linux kernel is not preemptive, which means that a process can be preempted only while running in User Mode; nonpreemptive kernel design is much simpler, since most synchronization problems involving the kernel data structures are easily avoided (see the section "Nonpreemptability of Processes in Kernel Mode" in Chapter 11, *Kernel Synchronization*).

How Long Must a Quantum Last?

The quantum duration is critical for system performances: it should be neither too long nor too short.

If the quantum duration is too short, the system overhead caused by task switches becomes excessively high. For instance, suppose that a task switch requires 10 milliseconds; if the quantum is also set to 10 milliseconds, then at least 50% of the CPU cycles will be dedicated to task switch.[*]

If the quantum duration is too long, processes no longer appear to be executed concurrently. For instance, let's suppose that the quantum is set to five seconds; each runnable process makes progress for about five seconds, but then it stops for a very long time (typically, five seconds times the number of runnable processes).

It is often believed that a long quantum duration degrades the response time of interactive applications. This is usually false. As described in the section "Process Preemption" earlier in this chapter, interactive processes have a relatively high priority, therefore they quickly preempt the batch processes, no matter how long the quantum duration is.

In some cases, a quantum duration that is too long degrades the responsiveness of the system. For instance, suppose that two users concurrently enter two commands at the

---

[*] Actually, things could be much worse than this; for example, if the time required for task switch is counted in the process quantum, all CPU time will be devoted to task switch and no process can progress toward its termination. Anyway, you got the point.

respective shell prompts; one command is CPU-bound, while the other is an interactive application. Both shells fork a new process and delegate the execution of the user's command to it; moreover, suppose that such new processes have the same priority initially (Linux does not know in advance if an executed program is batch or interactive). Now, if the scheduler selects the CPU-bound process to run, the other process could wait for a whole time quantum before starting its execution. Therefore, if such duration is long, the system could appear to be unresponsive to the user that launched it.

The choice of quantum duration is always a compromise. The rule of thumb adopted by Linux is: choose a duration as long as possible, while keeping good system response time.

The Scheduling Algorithm

The Linux scheduling algorithm works by dividing the CPU time into *epochs*. In a single epoch, every process has a specified time quantum whose duration is computed when the epoch begins. In general, different processes have different time quantum durations. The time quantum value is the maximum CPU time portion assigned to the process in that epoch. When a process has exhausted its time quantum, it is preempted and replaced by another runnable process. Of course, a process can be selected several times from the scheduler in the same epoch, as long as its quantum has not been exhausted—for instance, if it suspends itself to wait for I/O, it preserves some of its time quantum and can be selected again during the same epoch. The epoch ends when all runnable processes have exhausted their quantum; in this case, the scheduler algorithm recomputes the time-quantum durations of all processes and a new epoch begins.

Each process has a *base time quantum*: it is the time-quantum value assigned by the scheduler to the process if it has exhausted its quantum in the previous epoch. The users can change the base time quantum of their processes by using the `nice()` and `setpriority()` system calls (see the section "System Calls Related to Scheduling" later in this chapter). A new process always inherits the base time quantum of its parent.

The `INIT_TASK` macro sets the value of the base time quantum of process 0 (*swapper*) to `DEF_PRIORITY`; that macro is defined as follows:

```
#define DEF_PRIORITY (20*HZ/100)
```

Since `HZ`, which denotes the frequency of timer interrupts, is set to 100 for IBM PCs (see the section "Programmable Interval Timer" in Chapter 5), the value of `DEF_PRIORITY` is 20 ticks, that is, about 210 ms.

Users rarely change the base time quantum of their processes, so `DEF_PRIORITY` also denotes the base time quantum of most processes in the system.

In order to select a process to run, the Linux scheduler must consider the priority of each process. Actually, there are two kinds of priority:

Static priority
> This kind is assigned by the users to real-time processes and ranges from 1 to 99. It is never changed by the scheduler.

Dynamic priority
> This kind applies only to conventional processes; it is essentially the sum of the base time quantum (which is therefore also called the *base priority* of the process) and of the number of ticks of CPU time left to the process before its quantum expires in the current epoch.

Of course, the static priority of a real-time process is always higher than the dynamic priority of a conventional one: the scheduler will start running conventional processes only when there is no real-time process in a `TASK_RUNNING` state.

Data Structures Used by the Scheduler

We recall from the section "Process Descriptor" in Chapter 3 that the process list links together all process descriptors, while the runqueue list links together the process descriptors of all runnable processes—that is, of those in a `TASK_RUNNING` state. In both cases, the `init_task` process descriptor plays the role of list header.

Each process descriptor includes several fields related to scheduling:

`need_resched`
> A flag checked by `ret_from_intr()` to decide whether to invoke the `schedule()` function (see the section "The ret_from_intr() Function" in Chapter 4, *Interrupts and Exceptions*).

`policy`
> The scheduling class. The values permitted are:
>
> `SCHED_FIFO`
>> A First-In, First-Out real-time process. When the scheduler assigns the CPU to the process, it leaves the process descriptor in its current position in the runqueue list. If no other higher-priority real-time process is runnable, the process will continue to use the CPU as long as it wishes, even if other real-time processes having the same priority are runnable.
>
> `SCHED_RR`
>> A Round Robin real-time process. When the scheduler assigns the CPU to the process, it puts the process descriptor at the end of the runqueue list. This policy ensures a fair assignment of CPU time to all `SCHED_RR` real-time processes that have the same priority.

SCHED_OTHER
> A conventional, time-shared process.

The `policy` field also encodes a SCHED_YIELD binary flag. This flag is set when the process invokes the `sched_yield()` system call (a way of voluntarily relinquishing the processor without the need to start an I/O operation or go to sleep; see the section "System Calls Related to Real-Time Processes"). The scheduler puts the process descriptor at the bottom of the runqueue list (see the later section "System Calls Related to Scheduling").

rt_priority
> The static priority of a real-time process. Conventional processes do not make use of this field.

priority
> The base time quantum (or base priority) of the process.

counter
> The number of ticks of CPU time left to the process before its quantum expires; when a new epoch begins, this field contains the time-quantum duration of the process. Recall that the `update_process_times()` function decrements the `counter` field of the current process by 1 at every tick.

When a new process is created, `do_fork()` sets the `counter` field of both `current` (the parent) and `p` (the child) processes in the following way:

```
current->counter >>= 1;
p->counter = current->counter;
```

In other words, the number of ticks left to the parent is split in two halves, one for the parent and one for the child. This is done to prevent users from getting an unlimited amount of CPU time by using the following method: the parent process creates a child process that runs the same code and then kills itself; by properly adjusting the creation rate, the child process would always get a fresh quantum before the quantum of its parent expires. This programming trick does not work since the kernel does not reward forks. Similarly, a user cannot hog an unfair share of the processor by starting lots of background processes in a shell or by opening a lot of windows on a graphical desktop. More generally speaking, a process cannot hog resources (unless it has privileges to give itself a real-time policy) by forking multiple descendents.

Notice that the `priority` and `counter` fields play different roles for the various kinds of processes. For conventional processes, they are used both to implement time-sharing and to compute the process dynamic priority. For SCHED_RR real-time processes, they are used only to implement time-sharing. Finally, for SCHED_FIFO real-time processes, they are not used at all, because the scheduling algorithm regards the quantum duration as unlimited.

The schedule() Function

schedule() implements the scheduler. Its objective is to find a process in the run-queue list and then assign the CPU to it. It is invoked, directly or in a lazy way, by several kernel routines.

Direct invocation

The scheduler is invoked directly when the current process must be blocked right away because the resource it needs is not available. In this case, the kernel routine that wants to block it proceeds as follows:

1. Inserts current in the proper wait queue

2. Changes the state of current either to TASK_INTERRUPTIBLE or to TASK_UNINTERRUPTIBLE

3. Invokes schedule()

4. Checks if the resource is available; if not, goes to step 2

5. Once the resource is available, removes current from the wait queue

As can be seen, the kernel routine checks repeatedly whether the resource needed by the process is available; if not, it yields the CPU to some other process by invoking schedule(). Later, when the scheduler once again grants the CPU to the process, the availability of the resource is again checked.

You may have noticed that these steps are similar to those performed by the sleep_on() and interruptible_sleep_on() functions described in the section "Wait Queues" in Chapter 3. However, the functions we discuss here immediately remove the process from the wait queue as soon as it is woken up.

The scheduler is also directly invoked by many device drivers that execute long iterative tasks. At each iteration cycle, the driver checks the value of the need_resched field and, if necessary, invokes schedule() to voluntarily relinquish the CPU.

Lazy invocation

The scheduler can also be invoked in a lazy way by setting the need_resched field of current to 1. Since a check on the value of this field is always made before resuming the execution of a User Mode process (see the section "Returning from Interrupts and Exceptions" in Chapter 4), schedule() will definitely be invoked at some close future time.

Lazy invocation of the scheduler is performed in the following cases:

- When **current** has used up its quantum of CPU time; this is done by the **update_process_times()** function.

- When a process is woken up and its priority is higher than that of the current process; this task is performed by the **reschedule_idle()** function, which is invoked by the **wake_up_process()** function (see the section "Identifying a Process" in Chapter 3):

```
if (goodness(current, p) > goodness(current, current))
    current->need_resched = 1;
```

(The **goodness()** function will be described later in the section "How Good Is a Runnable Process?")

- When a **sched_setscheduler()** or **sched_yield()** system call is issued (see the section "System Calls Related to Scheduling" later in this chapter).

Actions performed by schedule()

Before actually scheduling a process, the **schedule()** function starts by running the functions left by other kernel control paths in various queues. The function invokes **run_task_queue()** on the **tq_scheduler** task queue. Linux puts a function in that task queue when it must defer its execution until the next **schedule()** invocation:

```
run_task_queue(&tq_scheduler);
```

The function then executes all active unmasked bottom halves. These are usually present to perform tasks requested by device drivers (see the section "Bottom Half" in Chapter 4):

```
if (bh_active & bh_mask)
    do_bottom_half();
```

Now comes the actual scheduling, and therefore a potential process switch.

The value of **current** is saved in the **prev** local variable and the **need_resched** field of **prev** is set to 0. The key outcome of the function is to set another local variable called **next** so that it points to the descriptor of the process selected to replace **prev**.

First, a check is made to determine whether **prev** is a Round Robin real-time process (**policy** field set to SCHED_RR) that has exhausted its quantum. If so, **schedule()** assigns a new quantum to **prev** and puts it at the bottom of the runqueue list:

```
if (!prev->counter && prev->policy == SCHED_RR) {
    prev->counter = prev->priority;
    move_last_runqueue(prev);
}
```

Now **schedule()** examines the state of **prev**. If it has nonblocked pending signals and its state is TASK_INTERRUPTIBLE, the function wakes up the process as follows.

This action is not the same as assigning the processor to **prev**; it just gives **prev** a chance to be selected for execution:

```
if (prev->state == TASK_INTERRUPTIBLE &&
    signal_pending(prev))
    prev->state = TASK_RUNNING;
```

If **prev** is not in the **TASK_RUNNING** state, **schedule()** was directly invoked by the process itself because it had to wait on some external resource; therefore, **prev** must be removed from the runqueue list:

```
if (prev->state != TASK_RUNNING)
    del_from_runqueue(prev);
```

Next, **schedule()** must select the process to be executed in the next time quantum. To that end, the function scans the runqueue list. It starts from the process referenced by the **next_run** field of **init_task**, which is the descriptor of process 0 (*swapper*). The objective is to store in **next** the process descriptor pointer of the highest priority process. In order to do this, **next** is initialized to the first runnable process to be checked, and **c** is initialized to its "goodness" (see the later section "How Good Is a Runnable Process?"):

```
if (prev->state == TASK_RUNNING) {
    next = prev;
    if (prev->policy & SCHED_YIELD) {
        prev->policy &= ~SCHED_YIELD;
        c = 0;
    } else
        c = goodness(prev, prev);
} else {
    c = -1000;
    next = &init_task;
}
```

If the **SCHED_YIELD** flag of **prev->policy** is set, **prev** has voluntarily relinquished the CPU by issuing a **sched_yield()** system call. In this case, the function assigns a zero goodness to it.

Now **schedule()** repeatedly invokes the **goodness()** function on the runnable processes to determine the best candidate:

```
p = init_task.next_run;
while (p != &init_task) {
    weight = goodness(prev, p);
    if (weight > c) {
        c = weight;
        next = p;
    }
    p = p->next_run;
}
```

The **while** loop selects the first process in the runqueue having maximum weight. If the previous process is runnable, it is preferred with respect to other runnable processes having the same weight.

Notice that if the runqueue list is empty (no runnable process exists except for *swapper*), the cycle is not entered and **next** points to **init_task**. Moreover, if all processes in the runqueue list have a priority lesser than or equal to the priority of **prev**, no process switch will take place and the old process will continue to be executed.

A further check must be made at the exit of the loop to determine whether **c** is 0. This occurs only when all the processes in the runqueue list have exhausted their quantum, that is, all of them have a zero **counter** field. When this happens, a new epoch begins, therefore **schedule()** assigns to all existing processes (not only to the **TASK_RUNNING** ones) a fresh quantum, whose duration is the sum of the **priority** value plus half the **counter** value:

```
if (!c) {
    for_each_task(p)
        p->counter = (p->counter >> 1) + p->priority;
}
```

In this way, suspended or stopped processes have their dynamic priorities periodically increased. As stated earlier, the rationale for increasing the **counter** value of suspended or stopped processes is to give preference to I/O-bound processes. However, even after an infinite number of increases, the value of **counter** can never become larger than twice[*] the **priority** value.

Now comes the concluding part of **schedule()**: if a process other than **prev** has been selected, a process switch must take place. Before performing it, however, the **context_swtch** field of **kstat** is increased by 1 to update the statistics maintained by the kernel:

```
if (prev != next) {
    kstat.context_swtch++;
    switch_to(prev,next);
}
return;
```

Notice that the **return** statement that exits from **schedule()** will not be performed right away by the **next** process but at a later time by the **prev** one when the scheduler selects it again for execution.

---

[*] Assume both **priority** and **counter** equal to P; then the geometric series $P \times (1 + \frac{1}{2} + \frac{1}{4} + \frac{1}{8} + \ldots)$ converges to $2 \times P$.

How Good Is a Runnable Process?

The heart of the scheduling algorithm includes identifying the best candidate among all processes in the runqueue list. This is what the **goodness()** function does. It receives as input parameters **prev** (the descriptor pointer of the previously running process) and **p** (the descriptor pointer of the process to evaluate). The integer value **c** returned by **goodness()** measures the "goodness" of **p** and has the following meanings:

c = -1000

p must never be selected; this value is returned when the runqueue list contains only init_task.

c = 0

p has exhausted its quantum. Unless p is the first process in the runqueue list and all runnable processes have also exhausted their quantum, it will not be selected for execution.

0 < c < 1000

p is a conventional process that has not exhausted its quantum; a higher value of c denotes a higher level of goodness.

c >= 1000

p is a real-time process; a higher value of c denotes a higher level of goodness.

The **goodness()** function is equivalent to:

```
if (p->policy != SCHED_OTHER)
        return 1000 + p->rt_priority;
if (p->counter == 0)
        return 0;
if (p->mm == prev->mm)
        return p->counter + p->priority + 1;
return p->counter + p->priority;
```

If the process is real-time, its goodness is set to at least 1000. If it is a conventional process that has exhausted its quantum, its goodness is set to 0; otherwise, it is set to **p->counter + p->priority**.

A small bonus is given to **p** if it shares the address space with **prev** (i.e., if their process descriptors' **mm** fields point to the same memory descriptor). The rationale for this bonus is that if p runs right after **prev**, it will use the same page tables, hence the same memory; some of the valuable data may still be in the hardware cache.

The Linux/SMP Scheduler

The Linux scheduler must be slightly modified in order to support the symmetric multiprocessor (SMP) architecture. Actually, each processor runs the **schedule()** function on its own, but processors must exchange information in order to boost system performance.

When the scheduler computes the goodness of a runnable process, it should consider whether that process was previously running on the same CPU or on another one. A process that was running on the same CPU is always preferred, since the hardware cache of the CPU could still include useful data. This rule helps in reducing the number of cache misses.

Let us suppose, however, that CPU 1 is running a process when a second, higher-priority process that was last running on CPU 2 becomes runnable. Now the kernel is faced with an interesting dilemma: should it immediately execute the higher-priority process on CPU 1, or should it defer that process's execution until CPU 2 becomes available? In the former case, hardware caches contents are discarded; in the latter case, parallelism of the SMP architecture may not be fully exploited when CPU 2 is running the idle process (*swapper*).

In order to achieve good system performance, Linux/SMP adopts an empirical rule to solve the dilemma. The adopted choice is always a compromise, and the trade-off mainly depends on the size of the hardware caches integrated into each CPU: the larger the CPU cache is, the more convenient it is to keep a process bound on that CPU.

Linux/SMP scheduler data structures

An `aligned_data` table includes one data structure for each processor, which is used mainly to obtain the descriptors of current processes quickly. Each element is filled by every invocation of the `schedule()` function and has the following structure:

```
struct schedule_data {
    struct task_struct * curr;
    unsigned long last_schedule;
};
```

The `curr` field points to the descriptor of the process running on the corresponding CPU, while `last_schedule` specifies when `schedule()` selected `curr` as the running process.

Several SMP-related fields are included in the process descriptor. In particular, the `avg_slice` field keeps track of the average quantum duration of the process, and the `processor` field stores the logical identifier of the last CPU that executed it.

The `cacheflush_time` variable contains a rough estimate of the minimal number of CPU cycles it takes to entirely overwrite the hardware cache content. It is initialized by the `smp_tune_scheduling()` function to:

$$\left\lfloor \frac{cache\ size\ in\ KB}{5000} \times cpu\ frequency\ in\ kHz \right\rfloor$$

Intel Pentium processors have a hardware cache of 8 KB, so their `cacheflush_time` is initialized to a few hundred CPU cycles, that is, a few microseconds. Recent Intel processors have larger hardware caches, and therefore the minimal cache flush time could range from 50 to 100 microseconds.

As we shall see later, if `cacheflush_time` is greater than the average time slice of some currently running process, no process preemption is performed because it is convenient in this case to bind processes to the processors that last executed them.

The schedule() function

When the `schedule()` function is executed on an SMP system, it carries out the following operations:

1. Performs the initial part of `schedule()` as usual.

2. Stores the logical identifier of the executing processor in the `this_cpu` local variable; such value is read from the `processor` field of `prev` (that is, of the process to be replaced).

3. Initializes the `sched_data` local variable so that it points to the `schedule_data` structure of the `this_cpu` CPU.

4. Invokes `goodness()` repeatedly to select the new process to be executed; this function also examines the `processor` field of the processes and gives a consistent bonus (`PROC_CHANGE_PENALTY`, usually 15) to the process that was last executed on the `this_cpu` CPU.

5. If needed, recomputes process dynamic priorities as usual.

6. Sets `sched_data->curr` to `next`.

7. Sets `next->has_cpu` to 1 and `next->processor` to `this_cpu`.

8. Stores the current Time Stamp Counter value in the `t` local variable.

9. Stores the last time slice duration of `prev` in the `this_slice` local variable; this value is the difference between `t` and `sched_data->last_schedule`.

10. Sets `sched_data->last_schedule` to `t`.

11. Sets the `avg_slice` field of `prev` to (`prev->avg_slice+this_slice`)/2; in other words, updates the average.

12. Performs the context switch.

13. When the kernel returns here, the original previous process has been selected again by the scheduler; the `prev` local variable now refers to the process that has just been replaced. If `prev` is still runnable and it is not the idle task of this CPU, invokes the `reschedule_idle()` function on it (see the next section).

14. Sets the `has_cpu` field of `prev` to 0.

The reschedule_idle() function

The `reschedule_idle()` function is invoked when a process `p` becomes runnable (see the earlier section "The schedule() Function"). On an SMP system, the function determines whether the process should preempt the current process of some CPU. It performs the following operations:

1. If `p` is a real-time process, always attempts to perform preemption: go to step 3.

2. Returns immediately (does not attempt to preempt) if there is a CPU whose current process satisfies both of the following conditions:[*]

   — `cacheflush_time` is greater than the average time slice of the current process. If this is true, the process is not dirtying the cache significantly.

   — Both `p` and the current process need the global kernel lock (see the section "Global and Local Kernel Locks" in Chapter 11) in order to access some critical kernel data structure. This check is performed because replacing a process holding the lock with another one that needs it is not fruitful.

3. If the `p->processor` CPU (the one on which `p` was last running) is idle, selects it.

4. Otherwise, computes the difference:

   $$\text{goodness(tsk, p)} - \text{goodness(tsk, tsk)}$$

   for each task `tsk` running on some CPU and selects the CPU for which the difference is greatest, provided it is a positive value.

5. If CPU has been selected, sets the `need_resched` field of the corresponding running process and sends a "reschedule" message to that processor (see the section "Interprocessor Interrupts" in Chapter 11).

Performance of the Scheduling Algorithm

The scheduling algorithm of Linux is both self-contained and relatively easy to follow. For that reason, many kernel hackers love to try to make improvements. However, the scheduler is a rather mysterious component of the kernel. While you can change its performance significantly by modifying just a few key parameters, there is usually no theoretical support to justify the results obtained. Furthermore, you can't be sure that the positive (or negative) results obtained will continue to hold when the mix of requests submitted by the users (real-time, interactive, I/O-bound, background, etc.) varies significantly. Actually, for almost every proposed scheduling strategy, it is possible to derive an artificial mix of requests that yields poor system performances.

---

[*] These conditions look like voodoo magic; perhaps, they are empirical rules that make the SMP scheduler work better.

Let us try to outline some pitfalls of the Linux scheduler. As it will turn out, some of these limitations become significant on large systems with many users. On a single workstation that is running a few tens of processes at a time, the Linux scheduler is quite efficient. Since Linux was born on an Intel 80386 and continues to be most popular in the PC world, we consider the current Linux scheduler quite appropriate.

The algorithm does not scale well

If the number of existing processes is very large, it is inefficient to recompute all dynamic priorities at once.

In old traditional Unix kernels, the dynamic priorities were recomputed every second, thus the problem was even worse. Linux tries instead to minimize the overhead of the scheduler. Priorities are recomputed only when all runnable processes have exhausted their time quantum. Therefore, when the number of processes is large, the recomputation phase is more expensive but is executed less frequently.

This simple approach has the disadvantage that when the number of runnable processes is very large, I/O-bound processes are seldom boosted, and therefore interactive applications have a longer response time.

The predefined quantum is too large for high system loads

The system responsiveness experienced by users depends heavily on the *system load*, which is the average number of processes that are runnable, and hence waiting for CPU time.*

As mentioned before, system responsiveness depends also on the average time-quantum duration of the runnable processes. In Linux, the predefined time quantum appears to be too large for high-end machines having a very high expected system load.

I/O-bound process boosting strategy is not optimal

The preference for I/O-bound processes is a good strategy to ensure a short response time for interactive programs, but it is not perfect. Indeed, some batch programs with almost no user interaction are I/O-bound. For instance, consider a database search engine that must typically read lots of data from the hard disk or a network application that must collect data from a remote host on a slow link. Even if these kinds of processes do not need a short response time, they are boosted by the scheduling algorithm.

On the other hand, interactive programs that are also CPU-bound may appear unresponsive to the users, since the increment of dynamic priority due to I/O blocking operations may not compensate for the decrement due to CPU usage.

---

* The uptime program returns the system load for the past 1, 5, and 15 minutes. The same information can be obtained by reading the /proc/loadavg file.

Support for real-time applications is weak

As stated in the first chapter, nonpreemptive kernels are not well suited for real-time applications, since processes may spend several milliseconds in Kernel Mode while handling an interrupt or exception. During this time, a real-time process that becomes runnable cannot be resumed. This is unacceptable for real-time applications, which require predictable and low response times.*

Future versions of Linux will likely address this problem, either by implementing SVR4's "fixed preemption points" or by making the kernel fully preemptive.

However, kernel preemption is just one of several necessary conditions for implementing an effective real-time scheduler. Several other issues must be considered. For instance, real-time processes often must use resources also needed by conventional processes. A real-time process may thus end up waiting until a lower-priority process releases some resource. This phenomenon is called *priority inversion*. Moreover, a real-time process could require a kernel service that is granted on behalf of another lower-priority process (for example, a kernel thread). This phenomenon is called *hidden scheduling*. An effective real-time scheduler should address and resolve such problems.

System Calls Related to Scheduling

Several system calls have been introduced to allow processes to change their priorities and scheduling policies. As a general rule, users are always allowed to lower the priorities of their processes. However, if they want to modify the priorities of processes belonging to some other user or if they want to increase the priorities of their own processes, they must have superuser privileges.

The nice() System Call

The `nice()`† system call allows processes to change their base priority. The integer value contained in the `increment` parameter is used to modify the `priority` field of the process descriptor. The `nice` Unix command, which allows users to run programs with modified scheduling priority, is based on this system call.

The `sys_nice()` service routine handles the `nice()` system call. Although the `increment` parameter may have any value, absolute values larger than 40 are trimmed down to 40. Traditionally, negative values correspond to requests for priority incre-

---

* The Linux kernel has been modified in several ways so it can handle a few hard real-time jobs if they remain short. Basically, hardware interrupts are trapped and kernel execution is monitored by a kind of "superkernel." These changes do not make Linux a true real-time system, though.

† Since this system call is usually invoked to lower the priority of a process, users who invoke it for their processes are "nice" toward other users.

ments and require superuser privileges, while positive ones correspond to requests for priority decrements.

The function starts by copying the value of `increment` into the `newprio` local variable. In the case of a negative increment, the function invokes the `capable()` function to verify whether the process has a `CAP_SYS_NICE` capability. We shall discuss that function, together with the notion of capability, in Chapter 19, *Program Execution*. If the user turns out to have the capability required to change priorities, `sys_nice()` changes the sign of `newprio` and it sets the `increase` local flag:

```
increase = 0
newprio = increment;
if (increment < 0) {
    if (!capable(CAP_SYS_NICE))
        return -EPERM;
    newprio = -increment;
    increase = 1;
}
```

If `newprio` has a value larger than 40, the function trims it down to 40. At this point, the `newprio` local variable may have any value included from 0 to 40, inclusive. The value is then converted according to the priority scale used by the scheduling algorithm. Since the highest base priority allowed is $2 \times$ DEF_PRIORITY, the new value is:

$$\lfloor (\text{newprio} \times 2 \times \text{DEF\_PRIORITY})/40 + 0.5 \rfloor$$

The resulting value is copied into `increment` with the proper sign:

```
if (newprio > 40)
    newprio = 40;
newprio = (newprio * DEF_PRIORITY + 10) / 20;
increment = newprio;
if (increase)
    increment = -increment;
```

Since `newprio` is an integer variable, the expression in the code is equivalent to the formula shown earlier.

The function then sets the final value of `priority` by subtracting the value of `increment` from it. However, the final base priority of the process cannot be smaller than 1 or larger than $2 \times$ DEF_PRIORITY:

```
if (current->priority - increment < 1)
    current->priority = 1;
else if (current->priority > DEF_PRIORITY*2)
    current->priority = DEF_PRIORITY*2;
else
    current->priority -= increment;
return 0;
```

A `niced` process changes over time like any other process, getting extra priority if necessary or dropping back in deference to other processes.

The getpriority() and setpriority() System Calls

The `nice()` system call affects only the process that invokes it. Two other system calls, denoted as `getpriority()` and `setpriority()`, act on the base priorities of all processes in a given group. `getpriority()` returns 20 plus the highest base priority among all processes in a given group; `setpriority()` sets the base priority of all processes in a given group to a given value.

The kernel implements these system calls by means of the `sys_getpriority()` and `sys_setpriority()` service routines. Both of them act essentially on the same group of parameters:

`which`
> Identifies the group of processes; it can assume one of the following values:
>
> `PRIO_PROCESS`
>> Select the processes according to their process ID (`pid` field of the process descriptor).
>
> `PRIO_PGRP`
>> Select the processes according to their group ID (`pgrp` field of the process descriptor).
>
> `PRIO_USER`
>> Select the processes according to their user ID (`uid` field of the process descriptor).

`who`
> Value of the `pid`, `pgrp`, or `uid` field (depending on the value of `which`) to be used for selecting the processes. If `who` is 0, its value is set to that of the corresponding field of the `current` process.

`niceval`
> The new base priority value (needed only by `sys_setpriority()`). It should range between -20 (highest priority) and +20 (minimum priority).

As stated before, only processes with a `CAP_SYS_NICE` capability are allowed to increase their own base priority or to modify that of other processes.

As we have seen in Chapter 8, system calls return a negative value only if some error occurred. For that reason, `getpriority()` does not return a normal nice value ranging between -20 and 20, but rather a nonnegative value ranging between 0 and 40.

System Calls Related to Real-Time Processes

We now introduce a group of system calls that allow processes to change their scheduling discipline and, in particular, to become real-time processes. As usual, a process must have a CAP_SYS_NICE capability in order to modify the values of the rt_priority and policy process descriptor fields of any process, including itself.

The sched_getscheduler( ) and sched_setscheduler( ) system calls

The sched_getscheduler() system call queries the scheduling policy currently applied to the process identified by the pid parameter. If pid equals 0, the policy of the calling process will be retrieved. On success, the system call returns the policy for the process: SCHED_FIFO, SCHED_RR, or SCHED_OTHER. The corresponding sys_sched_getscheduler() service routine invokes find_task_by_pid(), which locates the process descriptor corresponding to the given pid and returns the value of its policy field.

The sched_setscheduler() system call sets both the scheduling policy and the associated parameters for the process identified by the parameter pid. If pid is equal to 0, the scheduler parameters of the calling process will be set.

The corresponding sys_sched_setscheduler() function checks whether the scheduling policy specified by the policy parameter and the new static priority specified by the param->sched_priority parameter are valid. It also checks whether the process has CAP_SYS_NICE capability or whether its owner has superuser rights. If everything is OK, it executes the following statements:

```
p->policy = policy;
p->rt_priority = param->sched_priority;
if (p->next_run)
    move_first_runqueue(p);
current->need_resched = 1;
```

The sched_getparam( ) and sched_setparam( ) system calls

The sched_getparam() system call retrieves the scheduling parameters for the process identified by pid. If pid is 0, the parameters of the current process are retrieved. The corresponding sys_sched_getparam() service routine, as one would expect, finds the process descriptor pointer associated with pid, stores its rt_priority field in a local variable of type sched_param, and invokes copy_to_user() to copy it into the process address space at the address specified by the param parameter.

The sched_setparam() system call is similar to sched_setscheduler(): it differs from the latter by not letting the caller set the policy field's value.* The corresponding

---

* This anomaly is caused by a specific requirement of the POSIX standard.

`sys_sched_setparam()` service routine is almost identical to `sys_sched_setscheduler()`, but the policy of the affected process is never changed.

The sched_yield() system call

The `sched_yield()` system call allows a process to relinquish the CPU voluntarily without being suspended; the process remains in a `TASK_RUNNING` state, but the scheduler puts it at the end of the runqueue list. In this way, other processes having the same dynamic priority will have a chance to run. The call is used mainly by `SCHED_FIFO` processes.

The corresponding `sys_sched_yield()` service routine executes these statements:

```
if (current->policy == SCHED_OTHER)
    current->policy |= SCHED_YIELD;
current->need_resched = 1;
move_last_runqueue(current);
```

Notice that the `SCHED_YIELD` field is set in the `policy` field of the process descriptor only if the process is a conventional `SCHED_OTHER` process. As a result, the next invocation of `schedule()` will view this process as one that has exhausted its time quantum (see how `schedule()` handles the `SCHED_YIELD` field).

The sched_get_priority_min() and sched_get_priority_max() system calls

The `sched_get_priority_min()` and `sched_get_priority_max()` system calls return, respectively, the minimum and the maximum real-time static priority value that can be used with the scheduling policy identified by the `policy` parameter.

The `sys_sched_get_priority_min()` service routine returns 1 if `current` is a real-time process, 0 otherwise.

The `sys_sched_get_priority_max()` service routine returns 99 (the highest priority) if `current` is a real-time process, 0 otherwise.

The sched_rr_get_interval() system call

The `sched_rr_get_interval()` system call should get the round robin time quantum for the named real-time process.

The corresponding `sys_sched_rr_get_interval()` service routine does not operate as expected, since it always returns a 150-millisecond value in the `timespec` structure pointed to by `tp`. This system call remains effectively unimplemented in Linux.

Anticipating Linux 2.4

Linux 2.4 introduces a subtle optimization concerning TLB flushing for kernel threads and zombie processes. As a result, the active Page Global Directory is set by the `schedule()` function rather than by the `switch_to` macro.

The Linux 2.4 scheduling algorithm for SMP machines has been improved and simplified. Whenever a new process becomes runnable, the kernel checks whether the preferred CPU of the process, that is, the CPU on which it was last running, is idle; in this case, the kernel assigns the process to that CPU. Otherwise, the kernel assigns the process to another idle CPU, if any. If all CPUs are busy, the kernel checks whether the process has enough priority to preempt the process running on the preferred CPU. If not, the kernel tries to preempt some other CPU only if the new runnable process is real-time or if it has short average time slices compared to the hardware cache rewriting time. (Roughly, preemption occurs if the new runnable process is interactive and the preferred CPU will not reschedule shortly.)

CHAPTER ELEVEN

KERNEL SYNCHRONIZATION

You could think of the kernel as a server that answers requests; these requests can come either from a process running on a CPU or an external device issuing an interrupt request. We make this analogy to underscore that parts of the kernel are not run serially but in an interleaved way. Thus, they can give rise to race conditions, which must be controlled through proper synchronization techniques. A general introduction to these topics can be found in the section "An Overview of Unix Kernels" in Chapter 1, *Introduction*.

We start this chapter by reviewing when, and to what extent, kernel requests are executed in an interleaved fashion. We then introduce four basic synchronization techniques implemented by the kernel and illustrate how they are applied by means of examples.

The next two sections deal with the extension of the Linux kernel to multiprocessor architectures. The first describes some hardware features of the Symmetric Multiprocessor (SMP) architecture, while the second discusses additional mutual exclusion techniques adopted by the SMP version of the Linux kernel.

Kernel Control Paths

As we said, kernel functions are executed following a request that may be issued in two possible ways:

- A process executing in User Mode causes an exception, for instance by executing an int 0x80 assembly language instruction.

- An external device sends a signal to a Programmable Interrupt Controller by using an IRQ line, and the corresponding interrupt is enabled.

The sequence of instructions executed in Kernel Mode to handle a kernel request is denoted as *kernel control path*: when a User Mode process issues a system call request, for instance, the first instructions of the corresponding kernel control path are those included in the initial part of the `system_call()` function, while the last instructions are those included in the `ret_from_sys_call()` function.

In the section "Nested Execution of Exception and Interrupt Handlers" in Chapter 4, *Interrupts and Exceptions*, a kernel control path was defined as a sequence of instructions executed by the kernel to handle a system call, an exception, or an interrupt. Kernel control paths play a role similar to that of processes, except that they are much more rudimentary: first, no descriptor of any kind is attached to them; second, they are not scheduled through a single function, but rather by inserting sequences of instructions that stop or resume the paths into the kernel code.

In the simplest cases, the CPU executes a kernel control path sequentially from the first instruction to the last. When one of the following events occurs, however, the CPU interleaves kernel control paths:

- A context switch occurs. As we have seen in Chapter 10, *Process Scheduling*, a context switch can occur only when the `schedule()` function is invoked.

- An interrupt occurs while the CPU is running a kernel control path with interrupts enabled. In this case, the first kernel control path is left unfinished and the CPU starts processing another kernel control path to handle the interrupt.

It is important to interleave kernel control paths in order to implement multiprocessing. In addition, as already noticed in the section, "Nested Execution of Exception and Interrupt Handlers" in Chapter 4, interleaving improves the throughput of programmable interrupt controllers and device controllers.

While interleaving kernel control paths, special care must be applied to data structures that contain several related member variables, for instance, a buffer and an integer indicating its length. All statements affecting such a data structure must be put into a single critical section, otherwise, it is in danger of being corrupted.

Synchronization Techniques

Chapter 1 introduced the concepts of race condition and critical region for processes. The same definitions apply to kernel control paths. In this chapter, a race condition can occur when the outcome of some computation depends on how two or more interleaved kernel control paths are nested. A critical region is any section of code that should be completely executed by each kernel control path that begins it, before another kernel control path can enter it.

We now examine how kernel control paths can be interleaved while avoiding race conditions among shared data. We'll distinguish four broad types of synchronization techniques:

- Nonpreemptability of processes in Kernel Mode
- Atomic operations
- Interrupt disabling
- Locking

Nonpreemptability of Processes in Kernel Mode

As already pointed out, the Linux kernel is not preemptive, that is, a running process cannot be preempted (replaced by a higher-priority process) while it remains in Kernel Mode. In particular, the following assertions always hold in Linux:

- No process running in Kernel Mode may be replaced by another process, except when the former voluntarily relinquishes control of the CPU.*

- Interrupt or exception handling can interrupt a process running in Kernel Mode; however, when the interrupt handler terminates, the kernel control path of the process is resumed.

- A kernel control path performing interrupt or exception handling can be interrupted only by another control path performing interrupt or exception handling.

Thanks to the above assertions, kernel control paths dealing with nonblocking system calls are atomic with respect to other control paths started by system calls. This simplifies the implementation of many kernel functions: any kernel data structures that are not updated by interrupt or exception handlers can be safely accessed. However, if a process in Kernel Mode voluntarily relinquishes the CPU, it must ensure that all data structures are left in a consistent state. Moreover, when it resumes its execution, it must recheck the value of all previously accessed data structures that could be changed. The change could be caused by a different kernel control path, possibly running the same code on behalf of a separate process.

Atomic Operations

The easiest way to prevent race conditions is by ensuring that an operation is atomic at the chip level: the operation must be executed in a single instruction. These very small atomic operations can be found at the base of other, more flexible mechanisms to create critical sections.

Thus, an *atomic operation* is something that can be performed by executing a single assembly language instruction in an "atomic" way, that is, without being interrupted in the middle.

---

* Of course, all context switches are performed in Kernel Mode. However, a context switch may occur only when the current process is going to return in User Mode.

Let's review Intel 80x86 instructions according to that classification:

- Assembly language instructions that make zero or one memory access are atomic.

- *Read/modify/write* assembly language instructions such as `inc` or `dec` that read data from memory, update it, and write the updated value back to memory are atomic if no other processor has taken the memory bus after the read and before the write. Memory bus stealing, naturally, never happens in a uniprocessor system, because all memory accesses are made by the same processor.

- Read/modify/write assembly language instructions whose opcode is prefixed by the `lock` byte (`0xf0`) are atomic even on a multiprocessor system. When the control unit detects the prefix, it "locks" the memory bus until the instruction is finished. Therefore, other processors cannot access the memory location while the locked instruction is being executed.

- Assembly language instructions whose opcode is prefixed by a `rep` byte (`0xf2`, `0xf3`), which forces the control unit to repeat the same instruction several times, are not atomic: the control unit checks for pending interrupts before executing a new iteration.

When you write C code, you cannot guarantee that the compiler will use a single, atomic instruction for an operation like `a=a+1` or even for `a++`. Thus, the Linux kernel provides special functions (see Table 11-1) that it implements as single, atomic assembly language instructions; on multiprocessor systems each such instruction is prefixed by a `lock` byte.

Table 11-1. Atomic Operations in C

Function	Description
`atomic_read(v)`	Return `*v`
`atomic_set(v,i)`	Set `*v` to `i`.
`atomic_add(i,v)`	Add `i` to `*v`.
`atomic_sub(i,v)`	Subtract `i` from `*v`.
`atomic_inc(v)`	Add 1 to `*v`.
`atomic_dec(v)`	Subtract 1 from `*v`.
`atomic_dec_and_test(v)`	Subtract 1 from `*v` and return 1 if the result is null, 0 otherwise.
`atomic_inc_and_test_greater_zero(v)`	Add 1 to `*v` and return 1 if the result is positive, 0 otherwise.
`atomic_clear_mask(mask,addr)`	Clear all bits of `addr` specified by `mask`.
`atomic_set_mask(mask,addr)`	Set all bits of `addr` specified by `mask`.

Interrupt Disabling

For any section of code too large to be defined as an atomic operation, more complicated means of providing critical sections are needed. To ensure that no window is left open for a race condition to slip in, even a window one instruction long, these critical sections always have an atomic operation at their base.

Interrupt disabling is one of the key mechanisms used to ensure that a sequence of kernel statements is operated as a critical section. It allows a kernel control path to continue executing even when hardware devices issue IRQ signals, thus providing an effective way to protect data structures that are also accessed by interrupt handlers.

However, interrupt disabling alone does not always prevent kernel control path interleaving. Indeed, a kernel control path could raise a "Page fault" exception, which in turn could suspend the current process (and thus the corresponding kernel control path). Or again, a kernel control path could directly invoke the schedule() function. This happens during most I/O disk operations because they are potentially blocking, that is, they may force the process to sleep until the I/O operation completes. Therefore, the kernel must never execute a blocking operation when interrupts are disabled, since the system could freeze.

Interrupts can be disabled by means of the `cli` assembly language instruction, which is yielded by the `__cli()` and `cli()` macros. Interrupts can be enabled by means of the `sti` assembly language instruction, which is yielded by the `__sti()` and `sti()` macros. On a uniprocessor system `cli()` is equivalent to `__cli()` and `sti()` is equivalent to `__sti()`; however, as we shall see later in this chapter, these macros are quite different on a multiprocessor system.

When the kernel enters a critical section, it clears the `IF` flag of the `eflags` register in order to disable interrupts. But at the end of the critical section, the kernel can't simply set the flag again. Interrupts can execute in nested fashion, so the kernel does not know what the `IF` flag was before the current control path executed. Each control path must therefore save the old setting of the flag and restore that setting at the end.

In order to save the `eflags` content, the kernel uses the `__save_flags` macro; on a uniprocessor system it is identical to the `save_flags` macro. In order to restore the `eflags` content, the kernel uses the `__restore_flags` and (on a uniprocessor system) `restore_flags` macros. Typically, these macros are used in the following way:

```
__save_flags(old);
__cli();
[...]
__restore_flags(old);
```

The `__save_flags` macro copies the content of the `eflags` register into the `old` local variable; the `IF` flag is then cleared by `__cli()`. At the end of the critical region, the `__restore_flags` macro restores the original content of `eflags`; therefore, interrupts are enabled only if they were enabled before this control path issued the `__cli()` macro.

Linux offers several additional synchronization macros that are important on a multiprocessor system (see the section "Spin Locks" later in this chapter) but are somewhat redundant on a uniprocessor system (see Table 11-2). Notice that some functions do not perform any visible operation. They just act as "barriers" for the `gcc` compiler, since they prevent the compiler from optimizing the code by moving around assembly language instructions. The `lck` parameter is always ignored.

Table 11-2. Interrupt Disabling/Enabling Macros on a Uniprocessor System

Macro	Description
`spin_lock_init(lck)`	No operation
`spin_lock(lck)`	No operation
`spin_unlock(lck)`	No operation
`spin_unlock_wait(lck)`	No operation
`spin_trylock(lck)`	Return always 1
`spin_lock_irq(lck)`	`__cli()`
`spin_unlock_irq(lck)`	`__sti()`
`spin_lock_irqsave(lck, flags)`	`__save_flags(flags); __cli()`
`spin_unlock_irqrestore(lck, flags)`	`__restore_flags(flags)`
`read_lock_irq(lck)`	`__cli()`
`read_unlock_irq(lck)`	`__sti()`
`read_lock_irqsave(lck, flags)`	`__save_flags(flags); __cli()`
`read_unlock_irqrestore(lck, flags)`	`__restore_flags(flags)`
`write_lock_irq(lck)`	`__cli()`
`write_unlock_irq(lck)`	`__sti()`
`write_lock_irqsave(lck, flags)`	`__save_flags(flags); __cli()`
`write_unlock_irqrestore(lck, flags)`	`__restore_flags(flags)`

Let us recall a few examples of how these macros are used in functions introduced in previous chapters:

- The `add_wait_queue()` and `remove_wait_queue()` functions protect the wait queue list with the `write_lock_irqsave()` and `write_unlock_irqrestore()` functions.

- The `setup_x86_irq()` adds a new interrupt handler for a specific IRQ; the `spin_lock_irqsave()` and `spin_unlock_irqrestore()` functions are used to protect the corresponding list of handlers.

- The `run_timer_list()` function protects the dynamic timer data structures with the `spin_lock_irq()` and `spin_unlock_irq()` functions.

- The `handle_signal()` function protects the `blocked` field of `current` with the `spin_lock_irq()` and `spin_unlock_irq()` functions.

Because of its simplicity, interrupt disabling is widely used by kernel functions for implementing critical regions. Clearly, the critical regions obtained by interrupt disabling must be short, because any kind of communication between the I/O device controllers and the CPU is blocked when the kernel enters one. Longer critical regions should be implemented by means of locking.

Locking Through Kernel Semaphores

A widely used synchronization technique is *locking*: when a kernel control path must access a shared data structure or enter a critical region, it must acquire a "lock" for it. A resource protected by a locking mechanism is quite similar to a resource confined in a room whose door is locked when someone is inside. If a kernel control path wishes to access the resource, it tries to "open the door" by acquiring the lock. It will succeed only if the resource is free. Then, as long as it wants to use the resource, the door remains locked. When the kernel control path releases the lock, the door is unlocked and another kernel control path may enter the room.

Linux offers two kinds of locking: *kernel semaphores*, which are widely used both on uniprocessor systems and multiprocessor ones, and *spin locks*, which are used only on multiprocessors systems. We'll discuss just kernel semaphores here; the other solution will be discussed in the section "Spin Locks" later in this chapter. When a kernel control path tries to acquire a busy resource protected by a kernel semaphore, the corresponding process is suspended. It will become runnable again when the resource is released.

Kernel semaphores are objects of type `struct semaphore` and have these fields:

count
: Stores an integer value. If it is greater than 0, the resource is free, that is, it is currently available. Conversely, if `count` is less than or equal to 0, the semaphore is busy, that is, the protected resource is currently unavailable. In the latter case, the absolute value of `count` denotes the number of kernel control paths waiting for the resource. Zero means that a kernel control path is using the resource but no other kernel control path is waiting for it.

wait
: Stores the address of a wait queue list that includes all sleeping processes that are currently waiting for the resource. Of course, if `count` is greater than or equal to 0, the wait queue is empty.

`waking`

Ensures that, when the resource is freed and the sleeping processes is woken up, only one of them succeeds in acquiring the resource. We'll see this field in operation soon.

The `count` field is decremented when a process tries to acquire the lock and incremented when a process releases it. The `MUTEX` and `MUTEX_LOCKED` macros may be used to initialize a semaphore for exclusive access: they set the `count` field, respectively, to 1 (free resource with exclusive access) and 0 (busy resource with exclusive access currently granted to the process that initializes the semaphore). Note that a semaphore could also be initialized with an arbitrary positive value n for `count`: in this case, at most n processes will be allowed to concurrently access the resource.

When a process wishes to acquire a kernel semaphore lock, it invokes the `down()` function. The implementation of `down()` is quite involved, but it is essentially equivalent to the following:

```
void down(struct semaphore * sem)
{
    /* BEGIN CRITICAL SECTION */
    --sem->count;
    if (sem->count < 0) {
    /* END CRITICAL SECTION */
        struct wait_queue wait = { current, NULL };
        current->state = TASK_UNINTERRUPTIBLE;
        add_wait_queue(&sem->wait, &wait);
        for (;;) {
            unsigned long flags;
            spin_lock_irqsave(&semaphore_wake_lock, flags);
            if (sem->waking > 0) {
                sem->waking--;
                break;
            }
            spin_unlock_irqrestore(&semaphore_wake_lock, flags);
            schedule();
            current->state = TASK_UNINTERRUPTIBLE;
        }
        spin_unlock_irqrestore(&semaphore_wake_lock, flags);
        current->state = TASK_RUNNING;
        remove_wait_queue(&sem->wait, &wait);
    }
}
```

The function decrements the `count` field of the `*sem` semaphore, then checks whether its value is negative. The decrement and the test must be atomically executed, otherwise another kernel control path could concurrently access the field value, with disastrous results (see the section "Synchronization and Critical Regions" in Chapter 1). Therefore, these two operations are implemented by means of the following assembly language instructions:

```
movl sem, %ecx
lock /* only for multiprocessor systems */
decl (%ecx)
js 2f
```

On a multiprocessor system, the `decl` instruction is prefixed by a `lock` prefix to ensure the atomicity of the decrement operation (see the previous section "Atomic Operations").

If `count` is greater than or equal to 0, the current process acquires the resource and the execution continues normally. Otherwise, `count` is negative and the current process must be suspended. It is inserted into the wait queue list of the semaphore and put to sleep by directly invoking the `schedule()` function.

The process is woken up when the resource is freed. Nonetheless, it cannot assume that the resource is now available, since several processes in the semaphore wait queue could be waiting for it. In order to select a winning process, the `waking` field is used: when the releasing process is going to wake up the processes in the wait queue, it increments `waking`; each awakened process then enters a critical region of the `down()` function and tests whether `waking` is positive. If an awakened process finds the field to be positive, it decrements `waking` and acquires the resource; otherwise it goes back to sleep. The critical region is protected by the `semaphore_wake_lock` global spin lock and by interrupt disabling.

Notice that an interrupt handler or a bottom half must not invoke `down()`, since this function suspends the process when the semaphore is busy.[*] For that reason, Linux provides the `down_trylock()` function, which may be safely used by one of the previously mentioned asynchronous functions. It is identical to `down()` except when the resource is busy: in this case, the function returns immediately instead of putting the process to sleep.

A slightly different function called `down_interruptible()` is also defined. It is widely used by device drivers since it allows processes that receive a signal while being blocked on a semaphore to give up the "down" operation. If the sleeping process is awakened by a signal before getting the needed resource, the function increments the `count` field of the semaphore and returns the value `-EINTR`. On the other hand, if `down_interruptible()` runs to normal completion and gets the resource, it returns 0. The device driver may thus abort the I/O operation when the return value is `-EINTR`.

When a process releases a kernel semaphore lock, it invokes the `up()` function, which is essentially equivalent to the following:

```
void up(struct semaphore * sem)
{
```

---

[*] Exception handlers can block on a semaphore. Linux takes special care to avoid the particular kind of race condition in which two nested kernel control paths compete for the same semaphore; naturally, one of them waits forever because the other cannot run and free the semaphore.

```
        /* BEGIN CRITICAL SECTION */
        ++sem->count;
        if (sem->count <= 0) {
        /* END CRITICAL SECTION */
            unsigned long flags;
            spin_lock_irqsave(&semaphore_wake_lock, flags);
            if (atomic_read(&sem->count) <= 0)
                sem->waking++;
            spin_unlock_irqrestore(&semaphore_wake_lock, flags);
            wake_up(&sem->wait);
        }
    }
```

The function increments the **count** field of the ***sem** semaphore, then checks whether its value is negative or null. The increment and the test must be atomically executed, so these two operations are implemented by means of the following assembly language instructions:

```
    movl sem, %ecx
    lock
    incl (%ecx)
    jle 2f
```

If the new value of **count** is positive, no process is waiting for the resource, and thus the function terminates. Otherwise, it must wake up the processes in the semaphore wait queue. In order to do this, it increments the **waking** field, which is protected by the **semaphore_wake_lock** spin lock and by interrupt disabling, then invokes **wake_up()** on the semaphore wait queue.

The increment of the **waking** field is included in a critical region because there can be several processes that concurrently access the same protected resource; therefore, a process could start executing **up()** while the waiting processes have already been woken up and one of them is already accessing the **waking** field. This also explains why **up()** checks whether **count** is nonpositive right before incrementing **waking**: another process could have executed the **up()** function after the first **count** check and before entering the critical region.

We now examine how semaphores are used in Linux. Since the kernel is nonpreemptive, only a few semaphores are needed. Indeed, on a uniprocessor system race conditions usually occur either when a process is blocked during an I/O disk operation or when an interrupt handler accesses a global kernel data structure. Other kinds of race conditions may occur in multiprocessor systems, but in such cases Linux tends to make use of spin locks (see the section "Spin Locks" later in this chapter).

The following sections discuss a few typical examples of semaphore use.

Slab cache list semaphore

The list of slab cache descriptors (see the section "Cache Descriptor" in Chapter 6, *Memory Management*) is protected by the `cache_chain_sem` semaphore, which grants an exclusive right to access and modify the list.

A race condition is possible when `kmem_cache_create()` adds a new element in the list, while `kmem_cache_shrink()` and `kmem_cache_reap()` sequentially scan the list. However, these functions are never invoked while handling an interrupt, and they can never block while accessing the list. Since the kernel is nonpreemptive, this semaphore plays an active role only in multiprocessor systems.

Memory descriptor semaphore

Each memory descriptor of type `mm_struct` includes its own semaphore in the `mmap_sem` field (see the section "The Memory Descriptor" in Chapter 7, *Process Address Space*). The semaphore protects the descriptor against race conditions that could arise because a memory descriptor can be shared among several lightweight processes.

For instance, let us suppose that the kernel must create or extend a memory region for some process; in order to do this, it invokes the `do_mmap()` function, which allocates a new `vm_area_struct` data structure. In doing so, the current process could be suspended if no free memory is available, and another process sharing the same memory descriptor could run. Without the semaphore, any operation of the second process that requires access to the memory descriptor (for instance, a page fault due to a Copy On Write) could lead to severe data corruption.

Inode semaphore

This example refers to filesystem handling, which this book has not examined yet. Therefore, we shall limit ourselves to giving the general picture without going into too many details. As we shall see in Chapter 12, *The Virtual Filesystem*, Linux stores the information on a disk file in a memory object called an *inode*. The corresponding data structure includes its own semaphore in the `i_sem` field.

A huge number of race conditions can occur during filesystem handling. Indeed, each file on disk is a resource held in common for all users, since all processes may (potentially) access the file content, change its name or location, destroy or duplicate it, and so on.

For example, let us suppose that a process is listing the files contained in some directory. Each disk operation is potentially blocking, and therefore even in uniprocessor systems other processes could access the same directory and modify its content while the first process is in the middle of the listing operation. Or again, two different processes could modify the same directory at the same time. All these race conditions are avoided by protecting the directory file with the inode semaphore.

Avoiding Deadlocks on Semaphores

Whenever a program uses two or more semaphores, the potential for deadlock is present because two different paths could end up waiting for each other to release a semaphore. A typical deadlock condition occurs when a kernel control path gets the lock for semaphore A and is waiting for semaphore B, while another kernel control path holds the lock for semaphore B and is waiting for semaphore A. Linux has few problems with deadlocks on semaphore requests, since each kernel control path usually needs to acquire just one semaphore at a time.

However, in a couple of cases the kernel must get two semaphore locks. This occurs in the service routines of the `rmdir()` and the `rename()` system calls (notice that in both cases two inodes are involved in the operation). In order to avoid such deadlocks, semaphore requests are performed in the order given by addresses: the semaphore request whose `semaphore` data structure is located at the lowest address is issued first.

The SMP Architecture

Symmetrical multiprocessing (*SMP*) denotes a multiprocessor architecture in which no CPU is selected as the Master CPU, but rather all of them cooperate on an equal basis, hence the name "symmetrical." As usual, we shall focus on Intel SMP architectures.

How many independent CPUs are most profitably included in a multiprocessor system is a hot issue. The troubles are mainly due to the impressive progress reached in the area of cache systems. Many of the benefits introduced by hardware caches are lost by wasting bus cycles in synchronizing the local hardware caches located on the CPU chips. The higher the number of CPUs, the worse the problem becomes.

From the kernel design point of view, however, we can completely ignore this issue: an SMP kernel remains the same no matter how many CPUs are involved. The big jump in complexity occurs when moving from one CPU (a uniprocessor system) to two.

Before proceeding in describing the changes that had to be made to Linux in order to make it a true SMP kernel, we shall briefly review the hardware features of the Pentium dual-processing systems. These features lie in the following areas of computer architecture:

- Shared memory
- Hardware cache synchronization
- Atomic operations
- Distributed interrupt handling
- Interrupt signals for CPU synchronization

Some hardware issues are completely resolved within the hardware, so we don't have to say much about them.

Common Memory

All the CPUs share the same memory; that is, they are connected to a common bus. This means that RAM chips may be accessed concurrently by independent CPUs. Since read or write operations on a RAM chip must be performed serially, a hardware circuit called a *memory arbiter* is inserted between the bus and every RAM chip. Its role is to grant access to a CPU if the chip is free and to delay it if the chip is busy. Even uniprocessor systems make use of memory arbiters, since they include a specialized processor called DMA that operates concurrently with the CPU (see the section "Direct Memory Access (DMA)," in Chapter 13, *Managing I/O Devices*).

In the case of multiprocessor systems, the structure of the arbiter is more complex since it has more input ports. The dual Pentium, for instance, maintains a two-port arbiter at each chip entrance and requires that the two CPUs exchange synchronization messages before attempting to use the bus. From the programming point of view, the arbiter is hidden since it is managed by hardware circuits.

Hardware Support to Cache Synchronization

The section "Hardware Cache" in Chapter 2, *Memory Addressing*, explained that the contents of the hardware cache and the RAM maintain their consistency at the hardware level. The same approach holds in the case of a dual processor. As shown in Figure 11-1, each CPU has its own local hardware cache. But now updating becomes more time-consuming: whenever a CPU modifies its hardware cache it must check whether the same data is contained in the other hardware cache and, if so, notify the other CPU to update it with the proper value. This activity is often called *cache snooping*. Luckily, all this is done at the hardware level and is of no concern to the kernel.

SMP Atomic Operations

Atomic operations for uniprocessor systems have already been introduced in the section "Atomic Operations." Since standard read-modify-write instructions actually access the memory bus twice, they are not atomic on a multiprocessor system.

Let us give a simple example of what might happen if an SMP kernel used standard instructions. Consider the semaphore implementation described in the section "Locking Through Kernel Semaphores" earlier in this chapter and assume that the `down()` function decrements and tests the `count` field of the semaphore with a simple `decl` assembly language instruction. What happens if two processes running on two different CPUs simultaneously execute the `decl` instruction on the same semaphore? Well, `decl` is a read-modify-write instruction that accesses the same memory location twice: once to read the old value and again to write the new value.

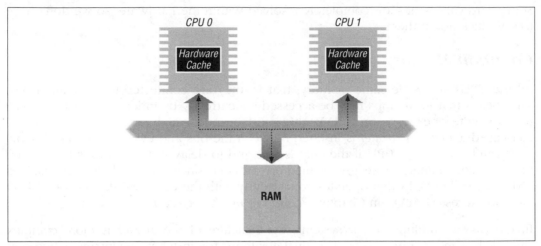

Figure 11-1. The caches in a dual processor

At first, both CPUs are trying to read the same memory location, but the memory arbiter steps in to grant access to one of them and delay the other. However, when the first read operation is complete the delayed CPU reads exactly the same (old) value from the memory location. Both CPUs then try to write the same (new) value on the memory location; again, the bus memory access is serialized by the memory arbiter, but eventually both write operations will succeed and the memory location will contain the old value decremented by 1. But of course, the global result is completely incorrect. For instance, if count was previously set to 1, both kernel control paths will simultaneously gain mutual exclusive access to the protected resource.

Since the early days of the Intel 80286, lock instruction prefixes have been introduced to solve that kind of problem. From the programmer's point of view, lock is just a special byte that is prefixed to an assembly language instruction. When the control unit detects a lock byte, it locks the memory bus so that no other processor can access the memory location specified by the destination operand of the following assembly language instruction. The bus lock is released only when the instruction has been executed. Therefore, read-modify-write instructions prefixed by lock are atomic even in a multiprocessor environment.

The Pentium allows a lock prefix on 18 different instructions. Moreover, some kind of instructions like xchg do not require the lock prefix because the bus lock is implicitly enforced by the CPU's control unit.

Distributed Interrupt Handling

Being able to deliver interrupts to any CPU in the system is crucial for fully exploiting the parallelism of the SMP architecture. For that reason, Intel has introduced a new component designated as the *I/O APIC* (*I/O Advanced Programmable Interrupt Controller*), which replaces the old 8259A Programmable Interrupt Controller.

Figure 11-2 illustrates in a schematic way the structure of a multi-APIC system. Each CPU chip has its own integrated *Local APIC*. An *Interrupt Controller Communication* (*ICC*) bus connects a frontend I/O APIC to the Local APICs. The IRQ lines coming from the devices are connected to the I/O APIC, which therefore acts as a router with respect to the Local APICs.

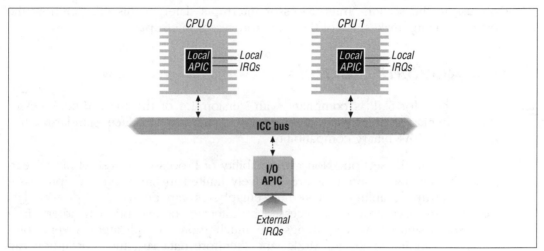

Figure 11-2. APIC system

Each Local APIC has 32-bit registers, an internal clock, a timer device, 240 different interrupt vectors, and two additional IRQ lines reserved for local interrupts, which are typically used to reset the system.

The I/O APIC consists of a set of IRQ lines, a 24-entry *Interrupt Redirection Table*, programmable registers, and a message unit for sending and receiving APIC messages over the ICC bus. Unlike IRQ pins of the 8259A, interrupt priority is not related to pin number: each entry in the Redirection Table can be individually programmed to indicate the interrupt vector and priority, the destination processor, and how the processor is selected. The information in the Redirection Table is used to translate any external IRQ signal into a message to one or more Local APIC units via the ICC bus.

Interrupt requests can be distributed among the available CPUs in two ways:

Fixed mode
> The IRQ signal is delivered to the Local APICs listed in the corresponding Redirection Table entry.

Lowest-priority mode
> The IRQ signal is delivered to the Local APIC of the processor which is executing the process with the lowest priority. Any Local APIC has a programmable *task priority register*, which contains the priority of the currently running process. It must be modified by the kernel at each task switch.

Another important feature of the APIC allows CPUs to generate *interprocessor inter-rupts*. When a CPU wishes to send an interrupt to another CPU, it stores the interrupt vector and the identifier of the target's Local APIC in the Interrupt Command Register of its own Local APIC. A message is then sent via the ICC bus to the target's Local APIC, which therefore issues a corresponding interrupt to its own CPU.

We'll discuss in the section "Interprocessor Interrupts" later in this chapter how the SMP version of Linux makes use of these interprocessor interrupts.

The Linux/SMP Kernel

Linux 2.2 support for SMP is compliant with Version 1.4 of the Intel MultiProcessor Specification, which establishes a multiprocessor platform interface standard while maintaining full PC/AT binary compatibility.

As we have seen in the section "Nonpreemptability of Processes in Kernel Mode" earlier in this chapter, race conditions are relatively limited in Linux on a uniprocessor system, so interrupt disabling and kernel semaphores can be used to protect data structures that are asynchronously accessed by interrupt or exception handlers. In a multiprocessor system, however, things are much more complicated: several processes may be running in Kernel Mode, and therefore data structure corruption can occur even if no running process is preempted. The usual way to synchronize access to SMP kernel data structures is by means of semaphores and spin locks (see the later section "Spin Locks").

Before discussing in detail how Linux 2.2 serializes the accesses to kernel data structures in multiprocessor systems, let us make a brief digression to how this goal was achieved when Linux first introduced SMP support. In order to facilitate the transition from a uniprocessor kernel to a multiprocessor one, the old 2.0 version of Linux/SMP adopted this drastic rule:

> *At any given instant, at most one processor is allowed to access the kernel data structures and to handle the interrupts.*

This rule dictates that each processor wishing to access the kernel data structures must get a global lock. As long as it holds the lock, it has exclusive access to all kernel data structures. Of course, since the processor will also handle any incoming interrupts, the data structures that are asynchronously accessed by interrupt and exception handlers must still be protected with interrupt disabling and kernel semaphores.

Although very simple, this approach has a serious drawback: processes spend a significant fraction of their computing time in Kernel Mode, therefore this rule may force I/O-bound processes to be sequentially executed. The situation was far from satisfactory, hence the rule was not strictly enforced in the next stable version of Linux/SMP (2.2). Instead, many locks were added, each of which grants exclusive access to single kernel data structure or a single critical region. Therefore, several processes are allowed to concurrently run in Kernel Mode as long as each of them accesses different data structures protected by locks. However, a global kernel lock is still present (see the section "Global and Local Kernel Locks" later in this chapter), since not all kernel data structures have been protected with specific locks.

Figure 11-3 illustrates the more flexible Linux 2.2 system. Five kernel control paths—P0, P1, P2, P3, and P4—are trying to access two critical regions—C1 and C2. Kernel control path P0 is inside C1, while P2 and P4 are waiting to enter it. At the same time, P1 is inside C2, while P3 is waiting to enter it. Notice that P0 and P1 could run concurrently. The lock for critical region C3 is open since no kernel control path needs to enter it.

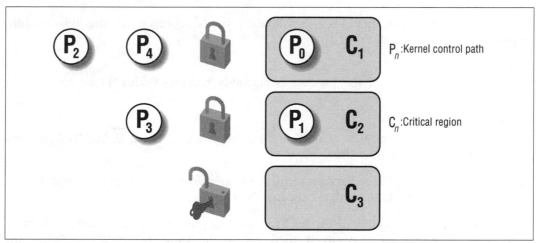

Figure 11-3. Protecting critical regions with several locks

Main SMP Data Structures

In order to handle several CPUs, the kernel must be able to represent the activity that takes place on each of them. In this section we'll consider some significant kernel data structures that have been added to allow multiprocessing.

The most important information is what process is currently running on each CPU, but this information actually does not require a new CPU-specific data structure. Instead, each CPU retrieves the current process through the same **current** macro defined for uniprocessor systems: since it extracts the process descriptor address from the **esp** stack pointer register, it yields a value that is CPU-dependent.

A first group of new CPU-specific variables refers to the SMP architecture. Linux/SMP has a hard-wired limit on the number of CPUs, which is defined by the NR_CPUS macro (usually 32).

During the initialization phase, Linux running on the booting CPU probes whether other CPUs exist (some CPU slots of an SMP board may be empty). As a result, both a counter and a bitmap are initialized: `max_cpus` stores the number of existing CPUs while `cpu_present_map` specifies which slots contain a CPU.

An existing CPU is not necessarily activated, that is, initialized and recognized by the kernel. Another pair of variables, a counter called `smp_num_cpus` and a bitmap called `cpu_online_map`, keeps track of the activated CPUs. If some CPU cannot be properly initialized, the kernel clears the corresponding bit in `cpu_online_map`.

Each active CPU is identified in Linux by a sequential logical number called *CPU ID*, which does not necessarily coincide with the CPU slot number. The `cpu_number_map` and `__cpu_logical_map` arrays allow conversion between CPU IDs and CPU slot numbers.

The process descriptor includes the following fields representing the relationships between the process and a processor:

`has_cpu`
> Flag denoting whether the process is currently running (value 1) or not running (value 0)

`processor`
> Logical number of the CPU that is running the process, or `NO_PROC_ID` if the process is not running

The `smp_processor_id()` macro returns the value of `current->processor`, that is, the logical number of the CPU that executes the process.

When a new process is created by `fork()`, the `has_cpu` and `processor` fields of its descriptor are initialized respectively to 0 and to the value `NO_PROC_ID`. When the `schedule()` function selects a new process to run, it sets its `has_cpu` field to 1 and its `processor` field to the logical number of the CPU that is doing the task switch. The corresponding fields of the process being replaced are set to 0 and to `NO_PROC_ID`, respectively.

During system initialization `smp_num_cpus` different *swapper* processes are created. Each of them has a PID equal to 0 and is bound to a specific CPU. As usual, a *swapper* process is executed only when the corresponding CPU is idle.

Spin Locks

Spin locks are a locking mechanism designed to work in a multiprocessing environment. They are similar to the kernel semaphores described earlier, except that when a process finds the lock closed by another process, it "spins" around repeatedly, executing a tight instruction loop.

Of course, spin locks would be useless in a uniprocessor environment, since the waiting process would keep running, and therefore the process that is holding the lock would not have any chance to release it. In a multiprocessing environment, however, spin locks are much more convenient, since their overhead is very small. In other words, a context switch takes a significant amount of time, so it is more efficient for each process to keep its own CPU and simply spin while waiting for a resource.

Each spin lock is represented by a `spinlock_t` structure consisting of a single `lock` field; the values 0 and 1 correspond, respectively, to the "unlocked" and the "locked" state. The `SPIN_LOCK_UNLOCKED` macro initializes a spin lock to 0.

The functions that operate on spin locks are based on atomic read/modify/write operations; this ensures that the spin lock will be properly updated by a process running on a CPU even if other processes running on different CPUs attempt to modify the spin lock at the same time.*

The `spin_lock` macro is used to acquire a spin lock. It takes the address `slp` of the spin lock as its parameter and yields essentially the following code:

```
1: lock; btsl $0, slp
   jnc  3f
2: testb $1,slp
   jne 2b
   jmp 1b
3:
```

The `btsl` atomic instruction copies into the carry flag the value of bit 0 in `*slp`, then sets the bit. A test is then performed on the carry flag: if it is null, it means that the spin lock was unlocked and hence normal execution continues at label 3 (the `f` suffix denotes the fact that the label is a "forward" one: it appear in a later line of the program). Otherwise, the tight loop at label 2 (the `b` suffix denotes a "backward" label) is executed until the spin lock assumes the value 0. Then execution restarts from label 1, since it would be unsafe to proceed without checking whether another processor has grabbed the lock.†

The `spin_unlock` macro releases a previously acquired spin lock; it essentially yields the following code:

```
lock; btrl $0, slp
```

The `btrl` atomic assembly language instruction clears the bit 0 of the spin lock `*slp`.

Several other macros have been introduced to handle spin locks; their definitions on a multiprocessor system are described in Table 11-3 (see Table 11-2 for their definitions on a uniprocessor system).

---

* Spin locks, ironically enough, are global and therefore must themselves be protected against concurrent access.

† The actual implementation of `spin_lock` is slightly more complicated. The code at label 2, which is executed only if the spin lock is busy, is included in an auxiliary section so that in the most frequent case (free spin lock) the hardware cache is not filled with code that won't be executed. In our discussion we omit these optimization details.

Table 11-3. Spin Lock Macros on a Multiprocessor System

Macro	Description
spin_lock_init(slp)	Set slp->lock to 0
spin_trylock (slp)	Set slp->lock to 1, return 1 if got the lock, 0 otherwise
spin_unlock_wait(slp)	Cycle until slp->lock becomes 0
spin_lock_irq(slp)	__cli(); spin_lock(slp)
spin_unlock_irq(slp)	spin_unlock(slp); __sti()
spin_lock_irqsave(slp,flags)	__save_flags(flags); __cli(); spin_lock(slp)
spin_unlock_irqrestore(slp,flags)	spin_unlock(slp); __restore_flags(flags)

Notice that **spin_lock** and **spin_unlock** can protect only kernel data structures that are never accessed by interrupt handlers. With the added complication of interrupt handlers, the kernel must use spin lock macros that also disable and reenable interrupts on the local CPU. Otherwise, deadlocks could occur if an interrupt handler tries to get a busy spin lock.*

Read/Write Spin Locks

Read/write spin locks have been introduced to increase the amount of concurrency inside the kernel. They allow several kernel control paths to simultaneously read the same data structure, as long as no kernel control path modifies it. If a kernel control path wishes to write to the structure, it must acquire the write version of the read/write lock, which grants exclusive access to the resource. Of course, allowing concurrent reads on data structures improves system performance.

Figure 11-4 illustrates two critical regions, C1 and C2, protected by read/write locks. Kernel control paths R0 and R1 are reading the data structures in C1 at the same time, while W0 is waiting to acquire the lock for writing. Kernel control path W1 is writing the data structures in C2, while both R2 and W2 are waiting to acquire the lock for reading and writing, respectively.

Each read/write spin lock is a **rwlock_t** structure; its **lock** field is a 32-bit counter that represents the number of kernel control paths currently reading the protected data structure. The highest-order bit of the **lock** field is the write lock: it is set when a kernel control path is modifying the data structure.† The **RW_LOCK_UNLOCKED** macro initializes the **lock** field of a read/write spin lock to 0. The **read_lock** macro, applied to the address **rwlp** of a read/write spin lock, essentially yields the following code:

---

* Interrupts need to be disabled only on the local CPU: no deadlock occurs if an interrupt handler tries to get a spin lock that is assigned to a kernel control path on another CPU.

† It would also be set if there are more than 2,147,483,647 readers: of course, such a huge limit is never reached.

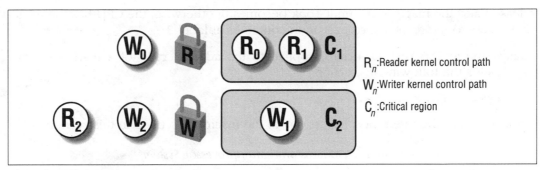

Figure 11-4. Read/write spin locks

```
1: lock; incl rwlp
   jns 3f
   lock; decl rwlp
2: cmpl $0, rwlp
   js 2b
   jmp 1b
3:
```

After increasing by 1 the value of **rwlp->lock**, the function checks whether the field has a negative value—that is, if it is already locked for writing. If not, execution continues at label 3. Otherwise, the macro restores the previous value and spins around until the highest-order bit becomes 0; then it starts back from the beginning.

The **read_unlock** function, applied to the address **rwlp** of a read/write spin lock, yields the following assembly language instruction:

```
lock; decl rwlp
```

The **write_lock** function applied to the address **rwlp** of a read/write spin lock yields the following instructions:

```
1: lock; btsl $31, rwlp
   jc 2f
   testl $0x7fffffff, rwlp
   je 3f
   lock; btrl $31, rwlp
2: cmp $0, rwlp
   jne 2b
   jmp 1b
3:
```

The highest-order bit of **rwlp->lock** is set. If its old value was 1, the write lock is already busy, and therefore the execution continues at label 2. Here the macro executes a tight loop waiting for the **lock** field to become 0 (meaning that the write lock was released). If the old value of the highest-order bit was 0 (meaning there is no write lock), the macro checks whether there are readers. If so, the write lock is released and the macro waits until `lock` becomes 0; otherwise, the CPU has the exclusive access to the resource, so execution continues at label 3.

Finally, the `write_unlock` macro, applied to the address `rwlp` of a read/write spin lock, yields the following instruction:

```
lock; btrl $31, rwlp
```

Table 11-4 lists the interrupt-safe versions of the macros described in this section.

Table 11-4. Read/Write Spin Lock Macros on a Multiprocessor System

Function	Description
`read_lock_irq(rwlp)`	`__cli(); read_lock(rwlp)`
`read_unlock_irq(rwlp)`	`read_unlock(rwlp); __sti()`
`write_lock_irq(rwlp)`	`__cli(); write_lock(rwlp)`
`write_unlock_irq(rwlp)`	`write_unlock(rwlp); __sti()`
`read_lock_irqsave(rwlp,flags)`	`__save_flags(flags); __cli(); read_lock(rwlp)`
`read_unlock_irqrestore(rwlp,flag)`	`read_unlock(rwlp); __restore_flags(flags)`
`write_lock_irqsave(rwlp,flags)`	`__save_flags(flags); __cli(); write_lock(rwlp)`
`write_unlock_irqrestore(rwlp,flags)`	`write_unlock(rwlp); __restore_flags(flags)`

Linux/SMP Interrupt Handling

We stated previously that, on Linux/SMP, interrupts are broadcast by the I/O APIC to all Local APICs; that is, to all CPUs. This means that all CPUs having the `IF` flags set will receive the same interrupt. However, only one CPU must handle the interrupt, although all of them must acknowledge to their Local APICs they received it.

In order to do this, each IRQ main descriptor (see the section "IRQ Data Structures" in Chapter 4) includes an `IRQ_INPROGRESS` flag. If it is set, the corresponding interrupt handler is already running on some CPU. Therefore, when each CPU acknowledges to its Local APIC that the interrupt was accepted, it checks whether the flag is already set. If it is, the CPU does not handle the interrupt and exits back to what it was running; otherwise, the CPU sets the flag and starts executing the interrupt handler.

Of course, accesses to the IRQ main descriptor must be mutually exclusive; therefore, each CPU always acquires the `irq_controller_lock` spin lock before checking the value of `IRQ_INPROGRESS`. The same lock also prevents several CPUs from fiddling with the interrupt controller simultaneously; this precaution is necessary for old SMP machines that have just one external interrupt controller shared by all CPUs.

The `IRQ_INPROGRESS` flag ensures that each specific interrupt handler is atomic with respect to itself among all CPUs. However, several CPUs may concurrently handle different interrupts. The `global_irq_count` variable contains the number of interrupt handlers that are being handled at each given instant on all CPUs. This value could be greater than the number of CPUs, since any interrupt handler can be interrupted by another interrupt handler of a different kind. Similarly, the `local_irq_count` array stores the number of interrupt handlers being handled on each CPU.

As we have already seen, the kernel must often disable interrupts in order to prevent corruption of a kernel data structure that may be accessed by interrupt handlers. Of course, local CPU interrupt disabling provided by the `__cli()` macro is not enough, since it does not prevent some other CPU from accessing the kernel data structure. The usual solution consists of acquiring a spin lock with an IRQ-safe macro (like `spin_lock_irqsave`).

In a few cases, however, interrupts should be disabled on all CPUs. In order to achieve such a result, the kernel does not clear the **IF** flags on all CPUs; instead it uses the `global_irq_lock` spin lock to delay the execution of the interrupt handlers. The `global_irq_holder` variable contains the logical identifier of the CPU that is holding the lock. The `get_irqlock()` function acquires the spin lock and waits for the termination of all interrupt handlers running on the other CPUs. Moreover, if the caller is not a bottom half itself, the function waits for the termination of all bottom halves running on the other CPUs. No further interrupt handler on other CPUs will start running until the lock is released by invoking `release_irqlock()`.

Global interrupt disabling is performed by the `cli()` macro, which just invokes the `__global_cli()` function:

```
__save_flags(flags);
if (!(flags & (1 << 9))) /* testing IF flag */
    return;
cpu = smp_processor_id();
__cli();
if (!local_irq_count[cpu])
    return;
get_irqlock(cpu);
```

Notice that global interrupt disabling is not performed when the CPU is running with local interrupts already disabled or when the CPU is running an interrupt handler itself.*

---

* Deadlock conditions can easily occur if such constraints are removed. For instance, suppose that `cli()` could "promote" a local interrupt disabling to a global one. Consider a kernel control path that is executing a critical region protected by some spin lock and with local interrupt disabled. The critical region can legally include a `cli()` macro, since it could invoke a function that is also accessed with local interrupts enabled. The `get_irqlock()` function starts waiting for interrupt handlers to complete on the other CPUs. However, an interrupt handler in another kernel control path could be stuck on the spin lock that protects the critical region, waiting for the first kernel control path to release it: deadlock!

Global interrupt enabling is performed by the `sti()` macro, which just invokes the `__global_sti()` function:

```
cpu = smp_processor_id();
if (!local_irq_count[cpu])
    release_irqlock(cpu);
__sti();
```

Linux also provides SMP versions of the `__save_flags` and `__restore_flags` macros, which are called `save_flags` and `restore_flags`: they save and reload, respectively, information controlling the interrupt handling for the executing CPU. As illustrated in Figure 11-5, `save_flags` yields an integer value that depends on three conditions; `restore_flags` performs actions based on the value yielded by `save_flags`.

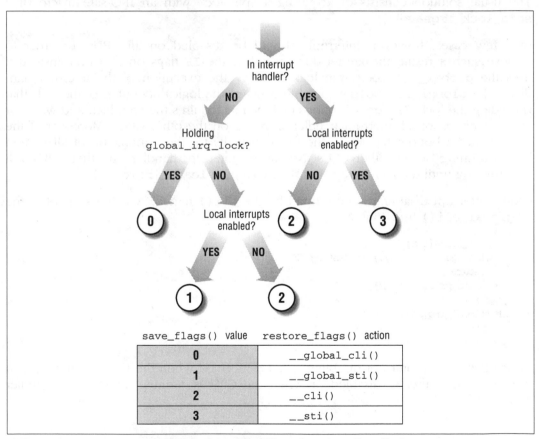

save_flags() value	restore_flags() action
0	__global_cli()
1	__global_sti()
2	__cli()
3	__sti()

Figure 11-5. Actions performed by save_flags() and restore_flags()

Finally, the `synchronize_irq()` function is called when a kernel control path wishes to synchronize itself with all interrupt handlers:

```
if (atomic_read(&global_irq_count)) {
```

```
    cli();
    sti();
}
```

By invoking `cli()`, the function acquires the `global_irq_lock` spin lock and then waits until all executing interrupt handlers terminate; once this is done, it reenables interrupts. The `synchronize_irq()` function is usually called by device drivers when they want to make sure that all activities carried on by interrupt handlers are over.

Linux/SMP Bottom Half Handling

Bottom halves are handled much like interrupt handlers, but no bottom half can ever run concurrently with other bottom halves. Moreover, disabling interrupts also disables the running of bottom halves. The `global_bh_count` variable is a flag that specifies whether a bottom half is currently active on some CPU. The `synchronize_bh()` function is called when a kernel control path must wait for the termination of a currently executing bottom half.

The `global_bh_lock` variable is used to disable the execution of bottom halves on all CPUs; in other words, it ensures that some critical region is atomic with respect to all bottom halves on all CPUs.

The `start_bh_atomic()` function, which locks out bottom halves, consists of:

```
atomic_inc(&global_bh_lock);
synchronize_bh();
```

The complementary `end_bh_atomic()` function is used to reenable the bottom halves by executing:

```
atomic_dec(&global_bh_lock);
```

Therefore, the `do_bottom_half()` function starts bottom halves only if:

- No other bottom half is currently running on any CPU (`global_bh_count` is null).

- The bottom halves are not disabled (`global_bh_lock` is null).

- No interrupt handler is running on any CPU (`global_irq_count` is null).

- Interrupts are globally enabled (`global_irq_lock` is free).

Serial execution of bottom halves is inherited from previous versions of Linux. Allowing bottom halves to be executed concurrently would require a full revision of all device drivers that use them.

Global and Local Kernel Locks

As we have already mentioned, in the Version 2.2 of Linux/SMP a *global kernel lock* named `kernel_flag` is still widely used. In Version 2.0, this spin lock was relatively crude, ensuring simply that only one processor at a time could run in Kernel Mode. The 2.2 kernel is considerably more flexible and no longer relies on a single spin lock; however, it is still used to protect a very large number of kernel data structures, namely:

- All data structures related to the Virtual Filesystem and to file handling (see Chapter 12)

- Most kernel data structures related to networking

- All kernel data structures for interprocess communication (IPC); see Chapter 18, *Process Communication*

- Several less important kernel data structures

The global kernel lock still exists because introducing new locks is not trivial: both deadlocks and race conditions must be carefully avoided.

All system call service routines related to files, including the ones related to file memory mapping, must acquire the global kernel lock before starting their operations and must release it when they terminate. Therefore, a very large number of system calls cannot concurrently execute on Linux/SMP.

Every process descriptor includes a `lock_depth` field, which allows the same process to acquire the global kernel lock several times. Therefore, two consecutive requests for it will not hang the processor (as for normal spin locks). If the process does not want the lock, the field has the value -1. If the process wants it, the field value plus 1 specifies how many times the lock has been requested. The `lock_depth` field is crucial for interrupt handlers, exception handlers, and bottom halves. Without it, any asynchronous function that tries to get the global kernel lock could generate a deadlock if the current process already owns the lock.

The `lock_kernel()` and `unlock_kernel()` functions are used to get and release the global kernel lock. The former function is equivalent to:

```
if (++current->lock_depth == 0)
    spin_lock(&kernel_flag);
```

while the latter is equivalent to:

```
if (--current->lock_depth < 0)
    spin_unlock(&kernel_flag);
```

Notice that the `if` statements of the `lock_kernel()` and `unlock_kernel()` functions need not be executed atomically because `lock_depth` is not a global variable: each CPU addresses a field of its own current process descriptor. Local interrupts inside the `if` statements do not induce race conditions either: even if the new kernel control path invokes `lock_kernel()`, it must release the global kernel lock before terminating.

Although the global kernel lock still protects a large number of kernel data structures, work is in progress to reduce that number by introducing many additional smaller locks. Table 11-5 lists some kernel data structures that are already protected by specific (read/write) spin locks.

Table 11-5. Various Kernel Spin Locks

Spin Lock	Protected Resource
console_lock	Console
dma_spin_lock	DMA's data structures
inode_lock	Inode's data structures
io_request_lock	Block IO subsystem
kbd_controller_lock	Keyboard
page_alloc_lock	Buddy system's data structures
runqueue_lock	Runqueue list
semaphore_wake_lock	Semaphores's waking fields
tasklist_lock (rw)	Process list
taskslot_lock	List of free entries in task
timerlist_lock	Dynamic timer lists
tqueue_lock	Task queues' lists
uidhash_lock	UID hash table
waitqueue_lock (rw)	Wait queues' lists
xtime_lock (rw)	xtime and lost_ticks

As already explained, finer granularity in the lock mechanism enhances system performance, since less serialization is enforced among the processors. For instance, a kernel control path that accesses the runqueue list is allowed to concurrently run with another kernel control path that is servicing a file-related system call. Similarly, using a read/write lock, two kernel control paths may concurrently access the process list as long as neither of them wants to modify it.

Interprocessor Interrupts

Interprocessor interrupts (in short, IPIs) are part of the SMP architecture and are actively used by Linux in order to exchange messages among CPUs. Linux/SMP provides the following functions to handle them:

send_IPI_all()
 Sends an IPI to all CPUs (including the sender)

send_IPI_allbutself()
 Sends an IPI to all CPUs except the sender

`send_IPI_self()`
Sends an IPI to the sender CPU

`send_IPI_single()`
Sends an IPI to a single, specified CPU

Depending on the I/O APIC configuration, the kernel may sometimes need to invoke the `send_IPI_self()` function. The other functions are used to implement interprocessor messages.

Linux/SMP recognizes five kinds of messages, which are interpreted by the receiving CPU as different interrupt vectors:

RESCHEDULE_VECTOR *(0x30)*
Sent to a single CPU in order to force the execution of the `schedule()` function on it. The corresponding Interrupt Service Routine (ISR) is named `smp_reschedule_interrupt()`. This message is used by `reschedule_idle()` and by `send_sig_info()` to preempt the running process on a CPU.

INVALIDATE_TLB_VECTOR *(0x31)*
Sent to all CPUs but the sender, forcing them to invalidate their translation lookaside buffers. The corresponding ISR, named `smp_invalidate_interrupt()`, invokes the `__flush_tlb()` function.* This message is used whenever the kernel modifies a page table of some process.

STOP_CPU_VECTOR *(0x40)*
Sent to all CPUs but the sender, forcing the receiving CPUs to halt. The corresponding Interrupt Service Routine is named `smp_stop_cpu_interrupt()`. This message is used only when the kernel detects an unrecoverable internal error.

LOCAL_TIMER_VECTOR *(0x41)*
A timer interrupt automatically sent to all CPUs by the I/O APIC. The corresponding Interrupt Service Routine is named `smp_apic_timer_interrupt()`.

CALL_FUNCTION_VECTOR *(0x50)*
Sent to all CPUs but the sender, forcing those CPUs to run a function passed by the sender. The corresponding ISR is named `smp_call_function_interrupt()`. A typical use of this message is to force CPUs to synchronize and to reload the state of the Memory Type Range Registers (MTRRs). Starting with the Pentium Pro model, Intel microprocessors include these additional registers to easily customize cache operations. Linux uses these registers to disable the hardware cache for the addresses mapping the frame buffer of a PCI/AGP graphic card while maintaining the "write combining" mode of operation: the paging unit combines write transfers into larger chunks before copying them into the frame buffer.

---

* A subtle concurrency problem occurs when trying to flush the translation lookaside buffers of all processors while some of them run with the interrupts disabled. Therefore, while spinning in tight loops, the kernel control paths keep checking whether some CPU has sent an "invalidate TLB" message.

Anticipating Linux 2.4

Linux 2.4 changes a bit the way semaphores are implemented. Essentially, they are now more efficient because, when a semaphore is released, usually only one sleeping process is awoken.

As already mentioned, Linux 2.4 enhances support for high-end SMP architectures. It is now possible to make use of multiple external I/O APIC chips, and all the code that handles interprocessor interrupts (IPIs) has been rewritten.

However, the most important change is that Linux 2.4 is much more multithreaded than Linux 2.2. In other words, it makes use of many new spin locks and reduces the role of the global kernel lock, particularly in the networking code. Linux 2.4 is therefore much more efficient on SMP architectures and performs much better as a high-end server.

CHAPTER TWELVE

THE VIRTUAL FILESYSTEM

One of Linux's keys to success is its ability to coexist comfortably with other systems. You can transparently mount disks or partitions that host file formats used by Windows, other Unix systems, or even systems with tiny market shares like the Amiga. Linux manages to support multiple disk types in the same way other Unix variants do, through a concept called the Virtual Filesystem.

The idea behind the Virtual Filesystem is that the internal objects representing files and filesystems in kernel memory embody a wide range of information; there is a field or function to support any operation provided by any real filesystem supported by Linux. For each read, write, or other function called, the kernel substitutes the actual function that supports a native Linux filesystem, the NT filesystem, or whatever other filesystem the file is on.

This chapter discusses the aims, the structure, and the implementation of Linux's Virtual Filesystem. It focuses on three of the five standard Unix file types, namely, regular files, directories, and symbolic links. Device files will be covered in Chapter 13, *Managing I/O Devices*, while pipes will be discussed in Chapter 18, *Process Communication*. To show how a real filesystem works, Chapter 17, *The Ext2 Filesystem*, covers the Second Extended Filesystem that appears on nearly all Linux systems.

The Role of the VFS

The *Virtual Filesystem* (also known as Virtual Filesystem Switch or VFS) is a kernel software layer that handles all system calls related to a standard Unix filesystem. Its main strength is providing a common interface to several kinds of filesystems.

For instance, let us assume that a user issues the shell command:

```
$ cp /floppy/TEST /tmp/test
```

where */floppy* is the mount point of an MS-DOS diskette and */tmp* is a normal Ext2 (Second Extended Filesystem) directory. As shown in Figure 12-1 (a), the VFS is an abstraction layer between the application program and the filesystem implementations. Therefore, the *cp* program is not required to know the filesystem types of */floppy/ TEST* and */tmp/test*. Instead, *cp* interacts with the VFS by means of generic system calls well known to anyone who has done Unix programming (see also the section "File-Handling System Calls" in Chapter 1, *Introduction*); the code executed by *cp* is shown in Figure 12-1 (b).

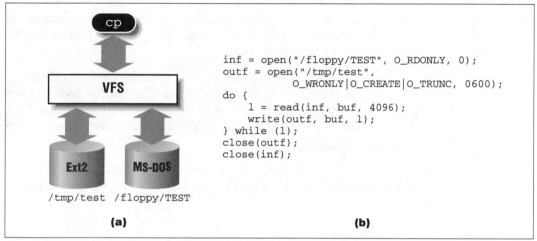

```
inf = open("/floppy/TEST", O_RDONLY, 0);
outf = open("/tmp/test",
            O_WRONLY|O_CREATE|O_TRUNC, 0600);
do {
    l = read(inf, buf, 4096);
    write(outf, buf, l);
} while (l);
close(outf);
close(inf);
```

/tmp/test /floppy/TEST

(a)   (b)

Figure 12-1. VFS role in a simple file copy operation

Filesystems supported by the VFS may be grouped into three main classes:

Disk-based filesystems

Manage the memory space available in a local disk partition. The official Linux disk-based filesystem is Ext2. Other well-known disk-based filesystems supported by the VFS are:

— Filesystems for Unix variants like System V and BSD

— Microsoft filesystems like MS-DOS, VFAT (Windows 98), and NTFS (Windows NT)

— ISO9660 CD-ROM filesystem (formerly High Sierra Filesystem)

— Other proprietary filesystems like HPFS (IBM's OS/2), HFS (Apple's Macintosh), FFS (Amiga's Fast Filesystem), and ADFS (Acorn's machines)

Network filesystems

Allow easy access to files included in filesystems belonging to other networked computers. Some well-known network filesystems supported by the VFS are NFS, Coda, AFS (Andrew's filesystem), SMB (Microsoft's Windows and IBM's OS/2 LAN Manager), and NCP (Novell's NetWare Core Protocol).

Special filesystems (also called virtual filesystems)

Do not manage disk space. Linux's `/proc` filesystem provides a simple interface that allows users to access the contents of some kernel data structures. The `/dev/pts` filesystem is used for pseudo-terminal support as described in the Open Group's Unix98 standard.

In this book we describe only the Ext2 filesystem, which is the topic of Chapter 17; the other filesystems will not be covered for lack of space.

As mentioned in the section "An Overview of the Unix Filesystem" in Chapter 1, Unix directories build a tree whose root is the / directory. The root directory is contained in the *root filesystem*, which in Linux is usually of type Ext2. All other filesystems can be "mounted" on subdirectories of the root filesystem.*

A disk-based filesystem is usually stored in a hardware block device like a hard disk, a floppy, or a CD-ROM. A useful feature of Linux's VFS allows it to handle *virtual block devices* like */dev/loop0*, which may be used to mount filesystems stored in regular files. As a possible application, a user may protect his own private filesystem by storing an encrypted version of it in a regular file.

The first Virtual Filesystem was included in Sun Microsystems's SunOS in 1986. Since then, most Unix filesystems include a VFS. Linux's VFS, however, supports the widest range of filesystems.

The Common File Model

The key idea behind the VFS consists of introducing a *common file model* capable of representing all supported filesystems. This model strictly mirrors the file model provided by the traditional Unix filesystem. This is not surprising, since Linux wants to run its native filesystem with minimum overhead. However, each specific filesystem implementation must translate its physical organization into the VFS's common file model.

For instance, in the common file model each directory is regarded as a normal file, which contains a list of files and other directories. However, several non-Unix disk-based filesystems make use of a File Allocation Table (FAT), which stores the position of each file in the directory tree: in these filesystems, directories are not files. In order to stick to the VFS's common file model, the Linux implementations of such FAT-based filesystems must be able to construct on the fly, when needed, the files corresponding to the directories. Such files exist only as objects in kernel memory.

---

* When a filesystem is mounted on some directory, the contents of the directory in the parent filesystem are no longer accessible, since any pathname including the mount point will refer to the mounted filesystem. However, the original directory's content will show up again when the filesystem is unmounted. This somewhat surprising feature of Unix filesystems is used by system administrators to hide files; they simply mount a filesystem on the directory containing the files to be hidden.

More essentially, the Linux kernel cannot hardcode a particular function to handle an operation such as `read()` or `ioctl()`. Instead, it must use a pointer for each operation; the pointer is made to point to the proper function for the particular filesystem being accessed.

Let's illustrate this concept by showing how the `read()` shown in Figure 12-1 would be translated by the kernel into a call specific to the MS-DOS filesystem. The application's call to `read()` makes the kernel invoke `sys_read()`, just like any other system call. The file is represented by a `file` data structure in kernel memory, as we shall see later in the chapter. This data structure contains a field called `f_op` that contains pointers to functions specific to MS-DOS files, including a function that reads a file. `sys_read()` finds the pointer to this function and invokes it. Thus, the application's `read()` is turned into the rather indirect call:

```
file->f_op->read(...);
```

Similarly, the `write()` operation triggers the execution of a proper Ext2 write function associated with the output file. In short, the kernel is responsible for assigning the right set of pointers to the `file` variable associated with each open file, then for invoking the call specific to each filesystem that the `f_op` field points to.

One can think of the common file model as object-oriented, where an *object* is a software construct that defines both a data structure and the methods that operate on it. For reasons of efficiency, Linux is not coded in an object-oriented language like C++. Objects are thus implemented as data structures with some fields pointing to functions that correspond to the object's methods.

The common file model consists of the following object types:

The superblock object
> Stores information concerning a mounted filesystem. For disk-based filesystems, this object usually corresponds to a *filesystem control block* stored on disk.

The inode object
> Stores general information about a specific file. For disk-based filesystems, this object usually corresponds to a *file control block* stored on disk. Each inode object is associated with an *inode number*, which uniquely identifies the file within the filesystem.

The file object
> Stores information about the interaction between an open file and a process. This information exists only in kernel memory during the period each process accesses a file.

The dentry object
> Stores information about the linking of a directory entry with the corresponding file. Each disk-based filesystem stores this information in its own particular way on disk.

Figure 12-2 illustrates with a simple example how processes interact with files. Three different processes have opened the same file, two of them using the same hard link. In this case, each of the three processes makes use of its own file object, while only two dentry objects are required, one for each hard link. Both dentry objects refer to the same inode object, which identifies the superblock object and, together with the latter, the common disk file.

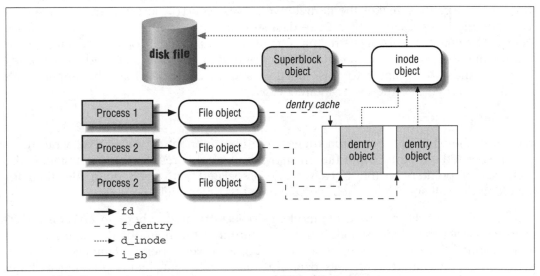

Figure 12-2. Interaction between processes and VFS objects

Besides providing a common interface to all filesystem implementations, the VFS has another important role related to system performance. The most recently used dentry objects are contained in a disk cache named the *dentry cache*, which speeds up the translation from a file pathname to the inode of the last pathname component.

Generally speaking, a *disk cache* is a software mechanism that allows the kernel to keep in RAM some information that is normally stored on a disk, so that further accesses to that data can be quickly satisfied without a slow access to the disk itself.[*] Beside the dentry cache, Linux uses other disk caches, like the buffer cache and the page cache, which will be described in forthcoming chapters.

---

[*] Notice how a disk cache differs from a hardware cache or a memory cache, neither of which has anything to do with disks or other devices. A hardware cache is a fast static RAM that speeds up requests directed to the slower dynamic RAM (see the section "Hardware Cache" in Chapter 2, *Memory Addressing*). A memory cache is a software mechanism introduced to bypass the Kernel Memory Allocator (see the section "The Slab Allocator" in Chapter 6, *Memory Management*).

System Calls Handled by the VFS

Table 12-1 illustrates the VFS system calls that refer to filesystems, regular files, directories, and symbolic links. A few other system calls handled by the VFS, such as `ioperm()`, `ioctl()`, `pipe()`, and `mknod()`, refer to device files and pipes and hence will be discussed in later chapters. A last group of system calls handled by the VFS, such as `socket()`, `connect()`, `bind()`, and `protocols()`, refer to sockets and are used to implement networking; they will not be covered in this book. Some of the kernel service routines that correspond to the system calls listed in Table 12-1 are discussed either in this chapter or in Chapter 17.

Table 12-1. Some System Calls Handled by the VFS

System Call Name	Description
`mount()` `umount()`	Mount/Unmount filesystems
`sysfs()`	Get filesystem information
`statfs()` `fstatfs()` `ustat()`	Get filesystem statistics
`chroot()`	Change root directory
`chdir()` `fchdir()` `getcwd()`	Manipulate current directory
`mkdir()` `rmdir()`	Create and destroy directories
`getdents()` `readdir()` `link()` `unlink()` `rename()`	Manipulate directory entries
`readlink()` `symlink()`	Manipulate soft links
`chown()` `fchown()` `lchown()`	Modify file owner
`chmod()` `fchmod()` `utime()`	Modify file attributes
`stat()` `fstat()` `lstat()` `access()`	Read file status
`open()` `close()` `creat()` `umask()`	Open and close files
`dup()` `dup2()` `fcntl()`	Manipulate file descriptors
`select()` `poll()`	Asynchronous I/O notification
`truncate()` `ftruncate()`	Change file size
`lseek()` `_llseek()`	Change file pointer
`read()` `write()` `readv()` `writev()` `sendfile()`	File I/O operations
`pread()` `pwrite()`	Seek file and access it
`mmap()` `munmap()`	File memory mapping
`fdatasync()` `fsync()` `sync()` `msync()`	Synchronize file data
`flock()`	Manipulate file lock

We said earlier that the VFS is a layer between application programs and specific filesystems. However, in some cases a file operation can be performed by the VFS itself, without invoking a lower-level procedure. For instance, when a process closes an open file, the file on disk doesn't usually need to be touched, and hence the VFS simply releases the corresponding file object. Similarly, when the `lseek()` system call modifies a file pointer, which is an attribute related to the interaction between an opened file and a process, the VFS needs to modify only the corresponding file object without accessing the file on disk and therefore does not have to invoke a specific filesystem procedure. In some sense, the VFS could be considered as a "generic" filesystem that relies, when necessary, on specific ones.

VFS Data Structures

Each VFS object is stored in a suitable data structure, which includes both the object attributes and a pointer to a table of object methods. The kernel may dynamically modify the methods of the object, and hence it may install specialized behavior for the object. The following sections explain the VFS objects and their interrelationships in detail.

Superblock Objects

A superblock object consists of a `super_block` structure whose fields are described in Table 12-2.

Table 12-2. The Fields of the Superblock Object

Type	Field	Description
struct list_head	s_list	Pointers for superblock list
kdev_t	s_dev	Device identifier
unsigned long	s_blocksize	Block size in bytes
unsigned char	s_blocksize_bits	Block size in number of bits
unsigned char	s_lock	Lock flag
unsigned char	s_rd_only	Read-only flag
unsigned char	s_dirt	Modified (dirty) flag
struct file_system_type *	s_type	Filesystem type
struct super_operations *	s_op	Superblock methods
struct dquot_operations *	dq_op	Disk quota methods
unsigned long	s_flags	Mount flags
unsigned long	s_magic	Filesystem magic number
unsigned long	s_time	Time of last superblock change
struct dentry *	s_root	Dentry object of mount directory
struct wait_queue *	s_wait	Mount wait queue
struct inode *	s_ibasket	Future development
short int	s_ibasket_count	Future development

Table 12-2. The Fields of the Superblock Object (continued)

Type	Field	Description
short int	s_ibasket_max	Future development
struct list_head	s_dirty	List of modified inodes
union	u	Specific filesystem information

All superblock objects (one per mounted filesystem) are linked together in a circular doubly linked list. The addresses of the first and last elements of the list are stored in the **next** and **prev** fields, respectively, of the **s_list** field in the **super_blocks** variable. This field has the data type **struct list_head**, which is also found in the **s_dirty** field of the superblock and in a number of other places in the kernel; it consists simply of pointers to the next and previous elements of a list. Thus, the **s_list** field of a superblock object includes the pointers to the two adjacent superblock objects in the list. Figure 12-3 illustrates how the **list_head** elements, **next** and **prev**, are embedded in the superblock object.

The last u union field includes superblock information that belongs to a specific filesystem; for instance, as we shall see later in Chapter 17, if the superblock object refers to an Ext2 filesystem, the field stores an **ext2_sb_info** structure, which includes the disk allocation bit masks and other data of no concern to the VFS common file model.

In general, data in the u field is duplicated in memory for reasons of efficiency. Any disk-based filesystem needs to access and update its allocation bitmaps in order to allocate or release disk blocks. The VFS allows these filesystems to act directly on the u union field of the superblock in memory, without accessing the disk.

This approach leads to a new problem, however: the VFS superblock might end up no longer synchronized with the corresponding superblock on disk. It is thus necessary to introduce an **s_dirt** flag, which specifies whether the superblock is dirty, that is, whether the data on the disk must be updated. The lack of synchronization leads to the familiar problem of a corrupted filesystem when a site's power goes down without giving the user the chance to shut down a system cleanly. As we shall see in the section "Writing Dirty Buffers to Disk" in Chapter 14, *Disk Caches*, Linux minimizes this problem by periodically copying all dirty superblocks to disk.

The methods associated with a superblock are called *superblock operations*. They are described by the **super_operations** structure whose address is included in the **s_op** field.

Each specific filesystem can define its own superblock operations. When the VFS needs to invoke one of them, say **read_inode()**, it executes:

```
sb->s_op->read_inode(inode);
```

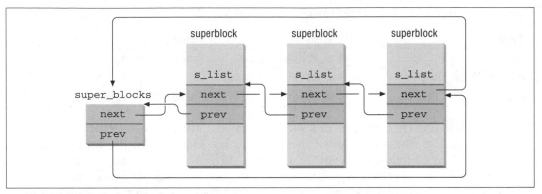

Figure 12-3. The superblock list

where **sb** stores the address of the superblock object involved. The **read_inode** field of the **super_operations** table contains the address of the suitable function, which is thus directly invoked.

Let us briefly describe the superblock operations, which implement higher-level operations like deleting files or mounting disks. They are listed in the order they appear in the **super_operations** table:

read_inode(inode)
> Fills the fields of the inode object whose address is passed as the parameter from the data on disk; the **i_ino** field of the inode object identifies the specific filesystem inode on disk to be read.

write_inode(inode)
> Updates a filesystem inode with the contents of the inode object passed as the parameter; the **i_ino** field of the inode object identifies the filesystem inode on disk that is concerned.

put_inode(inode)
> Releases the inode object whose address is passed as the parameter. As usual, releasing an object does not necessarily mean freeing memory since other processes may still use that object.

delete_inode(inode)
> Deletes the data blocks containing the file, the disk inode, and the VFS inode.

notify_change(dentry, iattr)
> Changes some attributes of the inode according to the **iattr** parameter. If the **notify_change** field is **NULL**, the VFS falls back on the **write_inode()** method.

put_super(super)
> Releases the superblock object whose address is passed as the parameter (because the corresponding filesystem is unmounted).

`write_super(super)`
>   Updates a filesystem superblock with the contents of the object indicated.

`statfs(super, buf, bufsize)`
>   Returns statistics on a filesystem by filling the **buf** buffer.

`remount_fs(super, flags, data)`
>   Remounts the filesystem with new options (invoked when a mount option must be changed).

`clear_inode(inode)`
>   Like **put_inode**, but also releases all pages that contain data concerning the file that corresponds to the indicated inode.

`umount_begin(super)`
>   Interrupts a mount operation, because the corresponding unmount operation has been started (used only by network filesystems).

The preceding methods are available to all possible filesystem types. However, only a subset of them applies to each specific filesystem; the fields corresponding to unimplemented methods are set to NULL. Notice that no **read_super** method to read a superblock is defined: how could the kernel invoke a method of an object yet to be read from disk? We'll find the **read_super** method in another object describing the filesystem type (see the later section "Filesystem Mounting").

Inode Objects

All information needed by the filesystem to handle a file is included in a data structure called an inode. A filename is a casually assigned label that can be changed, but the inode is unique to the file and remains the same as long as the file exists. An inode object in memory consists of an **inode** structure whose fields are described in Table 12-3.

Table 12-3. The Fields of the Inode Object

Type	Field	Description
`struct list_head`	`i_hash`	Pointers for the hash list
`struct list_head`	`i_list`	Pointers for the inode list
`struct list_head`	`i_dentry`	Pointers for the dentry list
`unsigned long`	`i_ino`	inode number
`unsigned int`	`i_count`	Usage counter
`kdev_t`	`i_dev`	Device identifier
`umode_t`	`i_mode`	File type and access rights
`nlink_t`	`i_nlink`	Number of hard links
`uid_t`	`i_uid`	Owner identifier

Table 12-3. The Fields of the Inode Object (continued)

Type	Field	Description
gid_t	i_gid	Group identifier
kdev_t	i_rdev	Real device identifier
off_t	i_size	File length in bytes
time_t	i_atime	Time of last file access
time_t	i_mtime	Time of last file write
time_t	i_ctime	Time of last inode change
unsigned long	i_blksize	Block size in bytes
unsigned long	i_blocks	Number of blocks of the file
unsigned long	i_version	Version number, automatically incremented after each use
unsigned long	i_nrpages	Number of pages containing file data
struct semaphore	i_sem	inode semaphore
struct semaphore	i_atomic_write	inode semaphore for atomic write
struct inode_operations *	i_op	inode operations
struct super_block *	i_sb	Pointer to superblock object
struct wait_queue *	i_wait	inode wait queue
struct file_lock *	i_flock	Pointer to file lock list
struct vm_area_struct *	i_mmap	Pointer to memory regions used to map the file
struct page *	i_pages	Pointer to page descriptor
struct dquot **	i_dquot	inode disk quotas
unsigned long	i_state	inode state flag
unsigned int	i_flags	Filesystem mount flag
unsigned char	i_pipe	True if file is a pipe
unsigned char	i_sock	True if file is a socket
int	i_writecount	Usage counter for writing process
unsigned int	i_attr_flags	File creation flags
__u32	i_generation	Reserved for future development
union	u	Specific filesystem information

The final u union field is used to include inode information that belongs to a specific filesystem. For instance, as we shall see in Chapter 17, if the inode object refers to an Ext2 file, the field stores an **ext2_inode_info** structure.

Each inode object duplicates some of the data included in the disk inode, for instance, the number of blocks allocated to the file. When the value of the **i_state** field is equal to I_DIRTY, the inode is dirty, that is, the corresponding disk inode must be updated. Other values of the `i_state` field are `I_LOCK` (which means that the inode object is locked) and `I_FREEING` (which means that the inode object is being freed).

Each inode object always appears in one of the following circular doubly linked lists:

- The list of unused inodes. The first and last elements of this list are referenced by the `next` and `prev` fields, respectively, of the `inode_unused` variable. This list acts as a memory cache.

- The list of in-use inodes. The first and last elements are referenced by the `inode_in_use` variable.

- The list of dirty inodes. The first and last elements are referenced by the `s_dirty` field of the corresponding superblock object.

Each of the lists just mentioned links together the `i_list` fields of the proper inode objects.

Inode objects belonging to the "in use" or "dirty" lists are also included in a hash table named `inode_hashtable`. The hash table speeds up the search of the inode object when the kernel knows both the inode number and the address of the superblock object corresponding to the filesystem that includes the file.* Since hashing may induce collisions, the inode object includes an `i_hash` field that contains a backward and a forward pointer to other inodes that hash to the same position; this field creates a doubly linked list of those inodes.

The methods associated with an inode object are also called *inode operations*. They are described by an `inode_operations` structure, whose address is included in the `i_op` field. The structure also includes a pointer to the file operation methods (see the next section, "File Objects"). Here are the inode operations, in the order they appear in the `inode_operations` table:

`create(dir, dentry, mode)`
Creates a new disk inode for a regular file associated with a dentry object in some directory.

`lookup(dir, dentry)`
Searches a directory for an inode corresponding to the filename included in a dentry object.

`link(old_dentry, dir, new_dentry)`
Creates a new hard link that refers to the file specified by `old_dentry` in the directory `dir`; the new hard link has the name specified by `new_dentry`.

---

* Actually, a Unix process may open a file and then unlink it: the `i_nlink` field of the inode could become 0, yet the process is still able to act on the file. In this particular case, the inode is removed from the hash table, even if it still belongs to the in-use or dirty list.

`unlink(dir, dentry)`

Removes the hard link of the file specified by a dentry object from a directory.

`symlink(dir, dentry, symname)`

Creates a new inode for a symbolic link associated with a dentry object in some directory.

`mkdir(dir, dentry, mode)`

Creates a new inode for a directory associated with a dentry object in some directory.

`rmdir(dir, dentry)`

Removes from a directory the subdirectory whose name is included in a dentry object.

`mknod(dir, dentry, mode, rdev)`

Creates a new disk inode for a special file associated with a dentry object in some directory. The `mode` and `rdev` parameters specify, respectively, the file type and the device's major number.

`rename(old_dir, old_dentry, new_dir, new_dentry)`

Moves the file identified by `old_entry` from the `old_dir` directory to the `new_dir` one. The new filename is included in the dentry object that `new_dentry` points to.

`readlink(dentry, buffer, buflen)`

Copies into a memory area specified by `buffer` the file pathname corresponding to the symbolic link specified by the dentry.

`follow_link(inode, dir)`

Translates a symbolic link specified by an inode object; if the symbolic link is a relative pathname, the lookup operation starts from the specified directory.

`readpage(file, pg)`

Reads a page of data from an open file. As we shall see in Chapter 15, *Accessing Regular Files*, regular files are read by this method.

`writepage(file, pg)`

Writes a page of data into an open file. Most filesystems do not make use of this method when writing regular files.

`bmap(inode, block)`

Returns the logical block number corresponding to the file block number of the file associated with an inode.

`truncate(inode)`

Modifies the size of the file associated with an inode. Before invoking this method, it is necessary to set the `i_size` field of the inode object to the required new size.

`permission(inode, mask)`

Checks whether the specified access mode is allowed for the file associated with `inode`.

smap(inode, sector)
　　Similar to **bmap()**, but determines the disk sector number; used by FAT-based filesystems.

updatepage(inode, pg, buf, offset, count, sync)
　　Updates, if needed, a page of data of a file associated with an inode (usually invoked by network filesystems, which may have to wait a long time before updating remote files).

revalidate(dentry)
　　Updates the cached attributes of a file specified by a dentry object (usually invoked by the network filesystem).

The methods just listed are available to all possible inodes and filesystem types. However, only a subset of them applies to any specific inode and filesystem; the fields corresponding to unimplemented methods are set to **NULL**.

File Objects

A file object describes how a process interacts with a file it has opened. The object is created when the file is opened and consists of a **file** structure, whose fields are described in Table 12-4. Notice that file objects have no corresponding image on disk, and hence no "dirty" field is included in the **file** structure to specify that the file object has been modified.

The main information stored in a file object is the *file pointer*, that is, the current position in the file from which the next operation will take place. Since several processes may access the same file concurrently, the file pointer cannot be kept in the inode object.

Table 12-4. The Fields of the File Object

Type	Field	Description
struct file *	f_next	Pointer to next file object
struct file **	f_pprev	Pointer to previous file object
struct dentry *	f_dentry	Pointer to associated dentry object
struct file_operations *	f_op	Pointer to file operation table
mode_t	f_mode	Process access mode
loff_t	f_pos	Current file offset (file pointer)
unsigned int	f_count	File object's usage counter
unsigned int	f_flags	Flags specified when opening the file
unsigned long	f_reada	Read-ahead flag
unsigned long	f_ramax	Maximum number of pages to be read-ahead
unsigned long	f_raend	File pointer after last read-ahead

Table 12-4. The Fields of the File Object (continued)

Type	Field	Description
unsigned long	f_ralen	Number of read-ahead bytes
unsigned long	f_rawin	Number of read-ahead pages
struct fown_struct	f_owner	Data for asynchronous I/O via signals
unsigned int	f_uid	User's UID
unsigned int	f_gid	User's GID
int	f_error	Error code for network write operation
unsigned long	f_version	Version number, automatically incremented after each use
void *	private_data	Needed for tty driver

Each file object is always included in one of the following circular doubly linked lists:

- The list of "unused" file objects. This list acts both as a memory cache for the file objects and as a reserve for the superuser; it allows the superuser to open a file even if the dynamic memory in the system is exhausted. Since the objects are unused, their **f_count** fields are null. The address of the first element in the list is stored in the **free_filps** variable. The kernel makes sure that the list always contains at least **NR_RESERVED_FILES** objects, usually 10.

- The list of "in use" file objects. Each element in the list is used by at least one process, and hence its **f_count** field is not null. The address of the first element in the list is stored in the **inuse_filps** variable.

Regardless of which list a file object is in at the moment, its **f_next** field points to the next element in the list, while the **f_pprev** field points to the **f_next** field of the previous element.

The size of the list of "unused" file objects is stored in the **nr_free_files** variable. The **get_empty_filp()** function is invoked when the VFS must allocate a new file object. The function checks whether the "unused" list has more than **NR_RESERVED_FILES** items, in which case one can be used for the newly opened file. Otherwise, it falls back to normal memory allocation.

As we explained in the section "The Common File Model," each filesystem includes its own set of *file operations* that perform such activities as reading and writing a file. When the kernel loads an inode into memory from disk, it stores a pointer to these file operations in a **file_operations** structure whose address is contained in the **default_file_ops** field of the **inode_operations** structure of the inode object. When a process opens the file, the VFS initializes the **f_op** field of the new file object with the address stored in the inode so that further calls to file operations can use these functions. If necessary, the VFS may later modify the set of file operations by storing a new value in **f_op**.

The following list describes the file operations in the order in which they appear in the `file_operations` table:

`llseek(file, offset, whence)`
Updates the file pointer.

`read(file, buf, count, offset)`
Reads `count` bytes from a file starting at position `*offset`; the value `*offset` (which usually corresponds to the file pointer) is then incremented.

`write(file, buf, count, offset)`
Writes `count` bytes into a file starting at position `*offset`; the value `*offset` (which usually corresponds to the file pointer) is then incremented.

`readdir(dir, dirent, filldir)`
Returns the next directory entry of a directory in `dirent`; the `filldir` parameter contains the address of an auxiliary function that extracts the fields in a directory entry.

`poll(file, poll_table)`
Checks whether there is activity on a file and goes to sleep until something happens on it.

`ioctl(inode, file, cmd, arg)`
Sends a command to an underlying hardware device. This method applies only to device files.

`mmap(file, vma)`
Performs a memory mapping of the file into a process address space (see the section "Memory Mapping" in Chapter 15, *Accessing Regular Files*).

`open(inode, file)`
Opens a file by creating a new file object and linking it to the corresponding inode object (see the section "The open( ) System Call" later in this chapter).

`flush(file)`
Called when a reference to an open file is closed, that is, the `f_count` field of the file object is decremented. The actual purpose of this method is filesystem-dependent.

`release(inode, file)`
Releases the file object. Called when the last reference to an open file is closed, that is, the `f_count` field of the file object becomes 0.

`fsync(file, dentry)`
Writes all cached data of the file to disk.

`fasync(file, on)`
Enables or disables asynchronous I/O notification by means of signals.

`check_media_change(dev)`
> Checks whether there has been a change of media since the last operation on the device file (applicable to block devices that support removable media, such as floppies and CD-ROMs).

`revalidate(dev)`
> Restores the consistency of a device (used by network filesystems after a media change has been recognized on a remote device).

`lock(file, cmd, file_lock)`
> Applies a lock to the file (see the section "File Locking" later in this chapter).

The methods just described are available to all possible file types. However, only a subset of them applies to a specific file type; the fields corresponding to unimplemented methods are set to NULL.

Special Handling for Directory File Objects

Directories must be handled with care because several processes can change their contents concurrently. Explicit locking, which is frequently performed on regular files (see the section "File Locking" later in this chapter), is not well suited for directories because it prevents other processes from accessing the whole subtree of files rooted at the locked directory. Therefore, the **f_version** field of the file object is used together with the **i_version** field of the inode object to ensure that accesses to each directory file maintain consistency.

We'll explain the use of these fields by describing the most common operation in which they are needed, the **readdir()** system call. Each invocation of this call is supposed to return a directory entry and update the directory's file pointer so that the next invocation of the same system call will return the next directory entry. But the directory could be modified by another process that concurrently accesses it. Without some kind of consistency check, the **readdir()** system call could return the wrong directory entry. Long intervals—potentially hours—could elapse between a process's calls to **readdir()**, and the process may choose to stop calling it at any time, so we don't want to lock the directory. What we want is a way to make **readdir()** adapt to changes.

The problem is solved by introducing the **global_event** variable, which plays the role of version stamp. Whenever the inode object of a directory file is modified, the **global_event** is increased by 1, and the new version stamp is stored in the **i_version** field of the object. Whenever a file object is created or its file pointer is modified, **global_event** is increased by 1, and the new version stamp is stored in the **f_version** field of the object. When servicing the **readdir()** system call, the VFS checks whether the version stamps contained in the **i_version** and **f_version** fields coincide. If not, the directory may have been modified by some other process after the previous execution of **readdir()**.

When the `readdir()` call detects this consistency problem, it recomputes the directory's file pointer by reading again the whole directory contents. The system call returns the directory entry immediately following the entry that was returned by the process's last `readdir()`. `f_version` is then set to `i_version` to indicate that `readdir()` is now synchronized with the actual state of the directory.

Dentry Objects

We mentioned in the section "The Common File Model" that each directory is considered by the VFS as a normal file that contains a list of files and other directories. We shall discuss in Chapter 17 how directories are implemented on a specific filesystem. Once a directory entry has been read into memory, however, it is transformed by the VFS into a dentry object based on the `dentry` structure, whose fields are described in Table 12-5. A dentry object is created by the kernel for every component of a pathname that a process looks up; the dentry object associates the component to its corresponding inode. For example, when looking up the */tmp/test* pathname, the kernel creates a dentry object for the / root directory, a second dentry object for the *tmp* entry of the root directory, and a third dentry object for the *test* entry of the */tmp* directory.

Notice that dentry objects have no corresponding image on disk, and hence no field is included in the `dentry` structure to specify that the object has been modified. Dentry objects are stored in a slab allocator cache called `dentry_cache`; dentry objects are thus created and destroyed by invoking `kmem_cache_alloc()` and `kmem_cache_free()`.

Table 12-5. The Fields of the Dentry Object

Type	Field	Description
int	d_count	Dentry object usage counter
unsigned int	d_flags	Dentry flags
struct inode *	d_inode	Inode associated with filename
struct dentry *	d_parent	Dentry object of parent directory
struct dentry *	d_mounts	For a mount point, the dentry of the root of the mounted filesystem
struct dentry *	d_covers	For the root of a filesystem, the dentry of the mount point
struct list_head	d_hash	Pointers for list in hash table entry
struct list_head	d_lru	Pointers for unused list
struct list_head	d_child	Pointers for the list of dentry objects included in parent directory
struct list_head	d_subdirs	For directories, list of dentry objects of subdirectories
struct list_head	d_alias	List of associated inodes (alias)
struct qstr	d_name	Filename

Table 12-5. The Fields of the Dentry Object (continued)

Type	Field	Description
unsigned long	d_time	Used by **d_revalidate** method
structdentry_operations*	d_op	Dentry methods
struct super_block *	d_sb	Superblock object of the file
unsigned long	d_reftime	Time when dentry was discarded
void *	d_fsdata	Filesystem-dependent data
unsigned char	d_iname[16]	Space for short filename

Each dentry object may be in one of four states:

Free

The dentry object contains no valid information and is not used by the VFS. The corresponding memory area is handled by the slab allocator.

Unused

The dentry object is not currently used by the kernel. The **d_count** usage counter of the object is null, but the **d_inode** field still points to the associated inode. The dentry object contains valid information, but its contents may be discarded if necessary to reclaim memory.

In use

The dentry object is currently used by the kernel. The **d_count** usage counter is positive and the **d_inode** field points to the associated inode object. The dentry object contains valid information and cannot be discarded.

Negative

The inode associated with the dentry no longer exists, because the corresponding disk inode has been deleted. The **d_inode** field of the dentry object is set to NULL, but the object still remains in the dentry cache so that further lookup operations to the same file pathname can be quickly resolved. The term "negative" is misleading since no negative value is involved.

The Dentry Cache

Since reading a directory entry from disk and constructing the corresponding dentry object requires considerable time, it makes sense to keep in memory dentry objects that you've finished with but might need later. For instance, people often edit a file and then compile it or edit, then print or copy, then edit. In any case like these, the same file needs to be repeatedly accessed.

In order to maximize efficiency in handling dentries, Linux uses a dentry cache, which consists of two kinds of data structures:

- A set of dentry objects in the in-use, unused, or negative state.

- A hash table to derive the dentry object associated with a given filename and a given directory quickly. As usual, if the required object is not included in the dentry cache, the hashing function returns a null value.

The dentry cache also acts as a controller for an *inode cache*. The inodes in kernel memory that are associated with unused dentries are not discarded, since the dentry cache is still using them and therefore their i_count fields are not null. Thus, the inode objects are kept in RAM and can be quickly referenced by means of the corresponding dentries.

All the "unused" dentries are included in a doubly linked "Least Recently Used" list sorted by time of insertion. In other words, the dentry object that was last released is put in front of the list, so the least recently used dentry objects are always near the end of the list. When the dentry cache has to shrink, the kernel removes elements from the tail of this list so that the most recently used objects are preserved. The addresses of the first and last elements of the LRU list are stored in the next and prev fields of the dentry_unused variable. The d_lru field of the dentry object contains pointers to the adjacent dentries in the list.

Each "in use" dentry object is inserted into a doubly linked list specified by the i_dentry field of the corresponding inode object (since each inode could be associated with several hard links, a list is required). The d_alias field of the dentry object stores the addresses of the adjacent elements in the list. Both fields are of type struct list_head.

An "in use" dentry object may become "negative" when the last hard link to the corresponding file is deleted. In this case, the dentry object is moved into the LRU list of unused dentries. Each time the kernel shrinks the dentry cache, negative dentries move toward the tail of the LRU list so that they are gradually freed (see the section "Reclaiming Pages from the Dentry and Inode Caches" in Chapter 16, *Swapping: Methods for Freeing Memory*).

The hash table is implemented by means of a dentry_hashtable array. Each element is a pointer to a list of dentries that hash to the same hash table value. The array's size depends on the amount of RAM installed in the system. The d_hash field of the dentry object contains pointers to the adjacent elements in the list associated with a single hash value. The hash function produces its value from both the address of the dentry object of the directory and the filename.

The methods associated with a dentry object are called *dentry operations*; they are described by the dentry_operations structure, whose address is stored in the d_op field. Although some filesystems define their own dentry methods, the fields are usually NULL, and the VFS replaces them with default functions. Here are the methods, in the order they appear in the dentry_operations table.

d_revalidate(dentry)

Determines whether the dentry object is still valid before using it for translating a file pathname. The default VFS function does nothing, although network filesystems may specify their own functions.

d_hash(dentry, hash)

Creates a hash value; a filesystem-specific hash function for the dentry hash table. The **dentry** parameter identifies the directory containing the component. The **hash** parameter points to a structure containing both the pathname component to be looked up and the value produced by the hash function.

d_compare(dir, name1, name2)

Compares two filenames; **name1** should belong to the directory referenced by **dir**. The default VFS function is a normal string match. However, each filesystem can implement this method in its own way. For instance, MS-DOS does not distinguish capital from lowercase letters.

d_delete(dentry)

Called when the last reference to a dentry object is deleted (**d_count** becomes 0). The default VFS function does nothing.

d_release(dentry)

Called when a dentry object is going to be freed (released to the slab allocator). The default VFS function does nothing.

d_iput(dentry, ino)

Called when a dentry object becomes "negative," that is, it loses its inode. The default VFS function invokes **iput()** to release the inode object.

Files Associated with a Process

We mentioned in the section "An Overview of the Unix Filesystem" in Chapter 1 that each process has its own current working directory and its own root directory. This information is stored in an **fs_struct** kernel table, whose address is contained in the **fs** field of the process descriptor.

```
struct fs_struct {
    atomic_t count;
    int umask;
    struct dentry * root, * pwd;
};
```

The **count** field specifies the number of processes sharing the same **fs_struct** table (see the section "The clone(), fork(), and vfork() System Calls" in Chapter 3, *Processes*). The **umask** field is used by the **umask()** system call to set initial file permissions on newly created files.

A second table, whose address is contained in the **files** field of the process descriptor, specifies which files are currently opened by the process. It is a **files_struct** structure whose fields are illustrated in Table 12-6. A process cannot have more than NR_OPEN (usually, 1024) file descriptors. It is possible to define a smaller, dynamic bound on the maximum number of allowed open files by changing the rlim[RLIMIT_NOFILE] structure in the process descriptor.

Table 12-6. The Fields of the files_struct Structure

Type	Field	Description
int	count	Number of processes sharing this table
int	max_fds	Current maximum number of file objects
int	max_fdset	Current maximum number of file descriptors
int	next_fd	Maximum file descriptors ever allocated plus 1
struct file **	fd	Pointer to array of file object pointers
fd_set *	close_on_exec	Pointer to file descriptors to be closed on exec()
fd_set *	open_fds	Pointer to open file descriptors
fd_set	close_on_exec_init	Initial set of file descriptors to be closed on exec()
fd_set	open_fds_init	Initial set of file descriptors
struct file *	fd_array[32]	Initial array of file object pointers

The fd field points to an array of pointers to file objects. The size of the array is stored in the max_fds field. Usually, fd points to the fd_array field of the files_struct structure, which includes 32 file object pointers. If the process opens more than 32 files, the kernel allocates a new, larger array of file pointers and stores its address in the fd fields; it also updates the max_fds field.

For every file with an entry in the fd array, the array index is the *file descriptor*. Usually, the first element (index 0) of the array is associated with the standard input of the process, the second with the standard output, and the third with the standard error (see Figure 12-4). Unix processes use the file descriptor as the main file identifier. Notice that, thanks to the dup(), dup2(), and fcntl() system calls, two file descriptors may refer to the same opened file, that is, two elements of the array could point to the same file object. Users see this all the time when they use shell constructs like 2>&1 to redirect the standard error to the standard output.

The open_fds field contains the address of the open_fds_init field, which is a bitmap that identifies the file descriptors of currently opened files. The max_fdset field stores the number of bits in the bitmap. Since the fd_set data structure includes 1024 bits, there is usually no need to expand the size of the bitmap. However, the kernel may dynamically expand the size of the bitmap if this turns out to be necessary, much as in the case of the array of file objects.

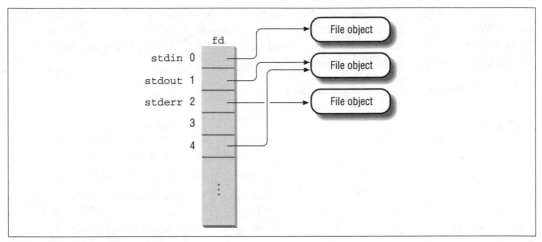

Figure 12-4. The fd array

The kernel provides an `fget()` function to be invoked when it starts using a file object. This function receives as its parameter a file descriptor `fd`. It returns the address in `current->files->fd[fd]`, that is, the address of the corresponding file object, or `NULL` if no file corresponds to `fd`. In the first case, `fget()` increments by 1 the file object usage counter `f_count`.

The kernel also provides an `fput()` function to be invoked when a kernel control path finishes using a file object. This function receives as its parameter the address of a file object and decrements its usage counter `f_count`. Moreover, if this field becomes null, the function invokes the `release` method of the file operations (if defined), releases the associated dentry object, decrements the `i_writeaccess` field in the inode object (if the file was opened for writing), and finally moves the file object from the "in use" list to the "unused" one.

Filesystem Mounting

Now we'll focus on how the VFS keeps track of the filesystems it is supposed to support. Two basic operations must be performed before making use of a filesystem: registration and mounting.

Registration is done either when the system boots or when the module implementing the filesystem is being loaded. Once a filesystem has been registered, its specific functions are available to the kernel, so that kind of filesystem can be mounted on the system's directory tree.

Each filesystem has its own *root directory*. The filesystem whose root directory is the root of the system's directory tree is called *root filesystem*. Other filesystems can be mounted on the system's directory tree: the directories on which they are inserted are called *mount points*.

Filesystem Registration

Often, the user configures Linux to recognize all the filesystems needed when compiling the kernel for her system. But the code for a filesystem actually may either be included in the kernel image or dynamically loaded as a module (see Appendix B). The VFS must keep track of all filesystems whose code is currently included in the kernel. It does this by performing *filesystem registrations*.

Each registered filesystem is represented as a `file_system_type` object whose fields are illustrated in Table 12-7. All filesystem-type objects are inserted into a simply linked list. The `file_systems` variable points to the first item.

Table 12-7. The Fields of the file_system_type Object

Type	Field	Description
`const char *`	`name`	Filesystem name
`int`	`fs_flag`	Mount flags
`struct super_block *(*)()`	`read_super`	Method for reading superblock
`struct file_system_type *`	`next`	Pointer to next list element

During system initialization, the `filesystem_setup()` function is invoked to register the filesystems specified at compile time. For each filesystem type, the `register_filesystem()` function is invoked with a parameter pointing to the proper `file_system_type` object, which is thus inserted into the filesystem-type list.

The `register_filesystem()` is also invoked when a module implementing a filesystem is loaded. In this case, the filesystem may also be unregistered (by invoking the `unregister_filesystem()` function) when the module is unloaded.

The `get_fs_type()` function, which receives a filesystem name as its parameter, scans the list of registered filesystems and returns a pointer to the corresponding `file_system_type` object if it is present.

Mounting the Root Filesystem

Mounting the root filesystem is a crucial part of system initialization. While the system boots, it finds the major number of the disk containing the root filesystem in the `ROOT_DEV` variable. The root filesystem can be specified as a device file in the */dev* directory either when compiling the kernel or by passing a suitable option to the initial bootstrap loader. Similarly, the mount flags of the root filesystem are stored in the `root_mountflags` variable. The user specifies these flags either by using the */sbin/rdev* external program on a compiled kernel image or by passing suitable options to the initial bootstrap loader (see Appendix A, *System Startup*).

During system initialization, right after the `filesystem_setup()` invocation, the `mount_root()` function is executed. It performs the following operations (assuming that the filesystem to be mounted is a disk-based one):[*]

1. Initializes a dummy, local file object `filp`. The `f_mode` field is set according to the mount flags of the root, while all other fields are set to 0.

2. Creates a dummy inode object and initializes it by setting its `i_rdev` field to `ROOT_DEV`.

3. Invokes the `blkdev_open()` function, passing the dummy inode and the file object. As we shall see later in Chapter 13, the function checks whether the disk exists and is properly working.

4. Releases the dummy inode object, which was needed just to verify the disk.

5. Scans the filesystem-type list. For each `file_system_type` object, invokes `read_super()` to attempt to read the corresponding superblock. This function checks that the device is not already mounted and attempts to fill a superblock object by using the method to which the `read_super` field of the `file_system_type` object points. Since each filesystem-specific method uses unique magic numbers, all `read_super()` invocations will fail except the one that attempts to fill the superblock by using the method of the filesystem really used on the root device. The `read_super()` method also creates an inode object and a dentry object for the root directory; the dentry object maps / to the inode object.

6. Sets the `root` and `pwd` fields of the `fs_struct` table of `current` (the *init* process) to the dentry object of the root directory.

7. Invokes `add_vfsmnt()` to insert a first element into the list of mounted filesystems (see next section).

Mounting a Generic Filesystem

Once the root filesystem has been initialized, additional filesystems may be mounted. Each of them must have its own mount point, which is just an already existing directory in the system's directory tree.

All mounted filesystems are included in a list, whose first element is referenced by the `vfsmntlist` variable. Each element is a structure of type `vfsmount`, whose fields are shown in Table 12-8.

---

[*] Diskless workstations can mount the root directory over a network-based filesystem such as NFS, but we don't describe how this is done.

Table 12-8. The Fields of the vfsmount Data Structure

Type	Field	Description
kdev_t	mnt_dev	Device number
char *	mnt_devname	Device name
char *	mnt_dirname	Mount point
unsigned int	mnt_flags	Device flags
struct super_block *	mnt_sb	Superblock pointer
struct quota_mount_options	mnt_dquot	Disk quota mount options
struct vfsmount *	mnt_next	Pointer to next list element

Three low-level functions are used to handle the list and are invoked by the service routines of the `mount()` and `umount()` system calls. The `add_vfsmnt()` and `remove_vfsmnt()` functions add and remove, respectively, an element in the list. The `lookup_vfsmnt()` function searches a specific mounted filesystem and returns the address of the corresponding `vfsmount` data structure.

The `mount()` system call is used to mount a filesystem; its `sys_mount()` service routine acts on the following parameters:

- The pathname of a device file containing the filesystem or `NULL` if it is not required (for instance, when the filesystem to be mounted is network-based)

- The pathname of the directory on which the filesystem will be mounted (the mount point)

- The filesystem type, which must be the name of a registered filesystem

- The mount flags (permitted values are listed in Table 12-9)

- A pointer to a filesystem-dependent data structure (which may be `NULL`)

Table 12-9. Filesystem Mounting Options

Macro	Value	Description
MS_MANDLOCK	0x040	Mandatory locking allowed.
MS_NOATIME	0x400	Do not update file access time.
MS_NODEV	0x004	Forbid access to device files.
MS_NODIRATIME	0x800	Do not update directory access time.
MS_NOEXEC	0x008	Disallow program execution.
MS_NOSUID	0x002	Forbid *setuid* and *setgid* flags.
MS_RDONLY	0x001	Files can only be read.
MS_REMOUNT	0x020	Remount the filesystem.
MS_SYNCHRONOUS	0x010	Write operations are immediate.

Table 12-9. Filesystem Mounting Options (continued)

Macro	Value	Description
S_APPEND	0x100	Allow append-only file.
S_IMMUTABLE	0x200	Allow immutable file.
S_QUOTA	0x080	Initialize disk quota.

The sys_mount() function performs the following operations:

1. Checks whether the process has the required capability to mount a filesystem.

2. If the MS_REMOUNT option has been specified, invokes do_remount() to modify the mount flags and terminate.

3. Otherwise, gets a pointer to the proper file_system_type object by invoking get_fs_type().

4. If the filesystem to be mounted refers to a hardware device like */dev/hda1*, checks whether the device exists and is operational. This is done as follows:

   a. Invokes namei() to get the dentry object of the corresponding device file (see the section "Pathname Lookup" later in this chapter).

   b. Checks whether the inode associated with the device file refers to a valid block device (see the section "Device Files" in Chapter 13).

   c. Initializes a dummy file object that refers to the device file, then opens the device file by using the open method of the file operations. If this operation succeeds, the device is operational.

5. If the filesystem to be mounted does not refer to a hardware device, gets a fictitious block device with major number 0 by invoking get_unnamed_dev().

6. Invokes do_mount(), passing the parameters dev (device number), dev_name (device filename), dir_name (mount point), type (filesystem type), flags (mount flags), and data (pointer to optional data area). This function mounts the required filesystem by performing the following operations:

   a. Invokes namei() to locate the dir_d dentry object corresponding to dir_name; if it does not exist, creates it (see Figure 12-5 (a)).

   b. Acquires the mount_sem semaphore, which is used to serialize the mounting and unmounting operations.

   c. Checks to make sure that dir_d->d_inode is the inode of a directory and that the directory is not the root of a filesystem that is already mounted (dir_d->d_covers must be equal to dir_d).

   d. Invokes read_super() to get the superblock object sb of the new filesystem. (If the object does not exist, it is created and filled with information read from the **dev** device.) The **s_root** field of the superblock object points to the dentry object of the root directory of the filesystem to be mounted (see Figure 12-5 (b)).

e. The previous operation could have suspended the current process; therefore, checks that no other process is using the superblock and that no process has already succeeded in mounting the same filesystem.

f. Invokes **add_vfsmnt()** in order to insert a new element in the list of mounted filesystems.

g. Sets the **d_mounts** field of **dir_d** to the **s_root** field of the superblock, that is, to the root directory of the mounted filesystem.

h. Sets the **d_covers** field of the dentry object of the root directory of the mounted filesystem to **dir_d** (see Figure 12-5 (c)).

i. Releases the **mount_sem** semaphore.

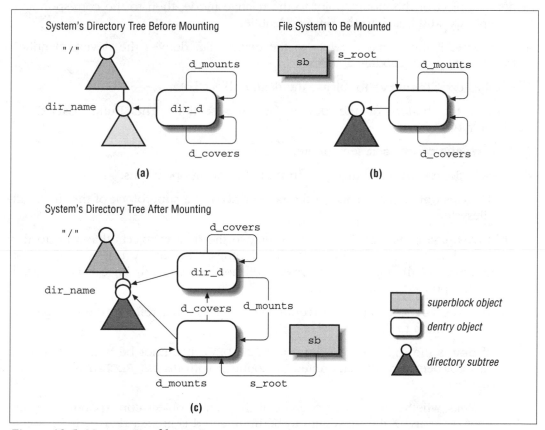

Figure 12-5. Mounting a filesystem

Now, the `dir_d` dentry object of the mount point is linked through the `d_mounts` field to the root directory dentry object of the mounted filesystem; this latter object is linked to the `dir_d` dentry object through the `d_covers` field.

Unmounting a Filesystem

The `umount()` system call is used to unmount a filesystem. The corresponding `sys_umount()` service routine acts on two parameters: a filename (either a mount directory or a block device file) and a set of flags. It performs the following actions:

1. Checks whether the process has the required capability to unmount the filesystem.

2. Invokes `namei()` on the filename to derive the `dentry` pointer to the associated dentry object.

3. If the filename refers to the mount point, derives the device identifier from `dentry->d_inode->i_sb->s_dev`. In other words, the function goes from the dentry object of the mount point to the relative inode, then to the corresponding superblock, and finally to the device identifier.

4. Otherwise, if the filename refers to the device file, derives the device identifier from `dentry->d_inode->i_rdev`.

5. Invokes `dput(dentry)` to release the dentry object.

6. Flushes the buffers of the device (see the section "The Buffer Cache" in Chapter 14).

7. Acquires the `mount_sem` semaphore.

8. Invokes `do_umount()`, which performs the following operations:

    a. Invokes `get_super()` to get the pointer `sb` of the superblock of the mounted filesystem.

    b. Invokes `shrink_dcache_sb()` to remove the dentry objects that refer to the `dev` device without disturbing other dentries. The dentry object of the root directory of the mounted filesystem will not be removed, since it is still used by the process doing the unmount.

    c. Invokes `fsync_dev()` to force all "dirty" buffers that refer to the `dev` device to be written to disk.

    d. If `dev` is the root device (`dev == ROOT_DEV`), it cannot be unmounted. If it has not been already remounted, remounts it with the `MS_RDONLY` flag set and returns.

    e. Checks whether the usage counter of the dentry object corresponding to the root directory of the filesystem to be unmounted is greater than 1. If so, some process is accessing a file in the filesystem, so returns an error code.

f. Decrements the usage counter of `sb->s_root->d_covers` (the dentry object of the mount point directory).

g. Sets `sb->s_root->d_covers->d_mounts` to `sb->s_root->d_covers`. This removes the link from the inode of the mount point to the inode of the root directory of the filesystem.

h. Releases the dentry object to which `sb->s_root` (the root directory of the previously mounted filesystem) points and sets `sb->s_root` to NULL.

i. If the superblock has been modified and the `write_super` superblock's method is defined, executes it.

j. If defined, invokes the `put_super()` method of the superblock.

k. Sets `sb->s_dev` to 0.

l. Invokes `remove_vfsmnt()` to remove the proper element from the list of mounted filesystems.

9. Invokes `fsync_dev()` to force a write to disk for all remaining "dirty" buffers that refer to the `dev` device (presumably, the buffers containing the superblock information), then invokes the `release()` method of the device file operations.

10. Releases the `mount_sem` semaphore.

Pathname Lookup

We illustrate in this section how the VFS derives an inode from the corresponding file pathname. When a process must identify a file, it passes its file pathname to some VFS system call, such as `open()`, `mkdir()`, `rename()`, `stat()`, and so on.

The standard procedure for performing this task consists of analyzing the pathname and breaking it into a sequence of filenames. All filenames except the last must identify directories.

If the first character of the pathname is /, the pathname is absolute, and the search starts from the directory identified by `current->fs->root` (the process root directory). Otherwise, the pathname is relative, and the search starts from the directory identified by `current->fs->pwd` (the process current directory).

Having in hand the inode of the initial directory, the code examines the entry matching the first name to derive the corresponding inode. Then the directory file having that inode is read from disk and the entry matching the second name is examined to derive the corresponding inode. This procedure is repeated for each name included in the path.

The dentry cache considerably speeds up the procedure, since it keeps the most recently used dentry objects in memory. As we have seen before, each such object associates a filename in a specific directory to its corresponding inode. In many cases, therefore, the analysis of the pathname can avoid reading the intermediate directories from the disk.

However, things are not as simple as they look, since the following Unix and VFS filesystem features must be taken into consideration:

- The access rights of each directory must be checked to verify whether the process is allowed to read the directory's content.

- A filename can be a symbolic link that corresponds to an arbitrary pathname: in that case, the analysis must be extended to all components of that pathname.

- Symbolic links may induce circular references: the kernel must take this possibility into account and break endless loops when they occur.

- A filename can be the mount point of a mounted filesystem: this situation must be detected, and the lookup operation must continue into the new filesystem.

The `namei()` and `lnamei()` functions derive an inode from a pathname. The difference between them is that `namei()` follows a symbolic link if it appears as the last component in a pathname without trailing slashes, while `lnamei()` does not. Both functions delegate the heavy work by invoking the `lookup_dentry()` function, which acts on three parameters: `name` points to a file pathname, `base` points to the dentry object of the directory from which to start searching, and `lookup_flags` is a bit array that includes the following flags:

LOOKUP_FOLLOW
> If the last component of the pathname is a symbolic link, interpret (follow) it. This flag is set when `lookup_dentry()` is invoked by `namei()` and cleared when it is invoked by `lnamei()`.

LOOKUP_DIRECTORY
> The last component of the pathname must be a directory.

LOOKUP_SLASHOK
> A trailing / in the pathname is allowed even if the last filename does not exist.

LOOKUP_CONTINUE
> There are still filenames to be examined in the pathname. This flag is used internally by `lookup_dentry()`.

The `lookup_dentry()` function is recursive, since it may end up invoking itself. Therefore, `name` could represent the still unresolved trailing portion of a complete pathname. In this case, `base` points to the dentry object of the last resolved pathname component. `lookup_dentry()` executes the following actions:

1. Examines both the first character of name and the value of base to identify the directory from which the search should start. Three cases can occur.

   — The first character of name is /: the pathname is an absolute pathname, thus base is set to current->fs->root.

   — The first character of name is different from "/" and base is NULL: the pathname is a relative pathname and base is set to current->fs->pwd.

   — The first character of name is different from "/" and base is not NULL: the pathname is a relative pathname and base is left unchanged. (This case should occur only when lookup_dentry() is recursively invoked.)

2. Gets the inode of the initial directory from base->d_inode.

3. Clears the LOOKUP_Follow flag in lookup_flags.

4. Iteratively repeats the following procedure on each filename included in the path. If an error condition is encountered, exits from the cycle and returns a NULL dentry pointer, else returns the dentry pointer corresponding to the file pathname. At the start of each iteration, name points to the next filename to be examined and base points to the dentry object of the current directory.

   a. Checks whether the process is allowed to access the base directory (if defined, uses the permission method of inode).

   b. Computes a hash value from the first component name in name to be used in searching for the corresponding entry in the dentry cache. Moreover, if the base directory is in a filesystem that has its own d_hash() dentry hashing method, invokes base->d_op->d_hash() to compute the hash value based on the directory, the component name, and the previous hash value.

   c. Updates name so that it points to the first character of the next component name (if any), skipping any "/" separator.

   d. Sets the flag local variable to the value previously set in lookup_flags. Additionally, if the currently resolved component was followed by a trailing /, sets the LOOKUP_DIRECTORY flag (requiring a check on whether the component is a directory) and the LOOKUP_FOLLOW flag (interprets the component even if it is a symbolic link). Moreover, if there is a non-null component after the component currently resolved, sets the LOOKUP_CONTINUE flag.

   e. Invokes reserved_lookup() to perform the following actions:

      1. If the first component name is a single period (.), sets the dentry local variable to base.

      2. If the first component name is a double period (..) and base is equal to current->fs->root, sets the dentry local variable to base (because the process is already in its root directory).

3. If the first component name is a double period (..) and `base` is not equal to `current->fs->root`, sets the `dentry` local variable to `base->d_covers->d_parent`. Usually, `d_covers` points to `base` itself and `dentry` is set to the directory that includes `base`; however, if the `base` directory is the root of a mounted filesystem, the `d_covers` field points to the inode of the mount point and `dentry` is set to the directory that includes the mount point.

   If the first component name is neither (.) nor (..) invokes `cached_lookup()`, passing as parameters `base` and the hash number previously derived. If the dentry hash table includes the required object, returns its address in `dentry`.

   If the required dentry object is not in the dentry cache, invokes `real_lookup()` to read the directory from disk and creates a new dentry object. This function, which acts on the `base` and `name` parameters, performs the following steps:

4. Gets the `i_sem` semaphore of the directory inode.

5. Checks again whether the dentry object is in the cashe, since the required dentry object could have been inserted in the cache while the process was waiting for the directory semaphore.

6. We assume that the previous attempt failed. Invokes `d_alloc()` to allocate a new dentry object.

7. Invokes the `lookup` method of the inode associated with the `base` directory to find the directory entry containing the required `name` and fills the new dentry object. This method is filesystem-dependent. We'll describe its Ext2 implementation in Chapter 17.

8. Releases the `i_sem` semaphore of the directory inode.

9. Returns the address of the new object in `dentry` or an error code if the entry was not found.

f. Invokes `follow_mount()` to check whether the `d_mounts` field of `dentry` has the same value as `dentry`. If not, `dentry` is the mount point of a filesystem. In this case, the old `dentry` object is replaced by the one having the address in `dentry->d_mounts`.

g. Invokes `do_follow_link()` to check whether `name` is a symbolic link. This function receives as its parameters `base`, `dentry`, and `flags` and executes the following steps:

   1. If the `LOOKUP_FOLLOW` flag is not set, returns immediately. Since the flag is not set by `lnamei()`, this ensures that `lnamei()` does not follow a symbolic link if it appears as the last component in a pathname without trailing slashes.

2. Checks whether `dentry->d_inode` contains the `follow_link` method. If not, the inode is not a symbolic link, so the function returns the `dentry` input parameter.

3. Invokes the `follow_link` inode method. This filesystem-dependent function reads the pathname associated with the symbolic link from the disk and recursively invokes `lookup_dentry()` to resolve it. The function then returns a pointer to the dentry object referred by the symbolic link (we shall describe in Chapter 17 how symbolic links are handled by Ext2).

   Since `lookup_dentry()` invokes `do_follow_link()`, which may in turn invoke the `follow_link` inode method, which invokes, in turn, `lookup_dentry()`, recursive cycles of function calls may be created. The `link_count` field of `current` is used to avoid endless recursive calls due to circular references inside the symbolic links. This field is incremented before each recursive execution of `follow_link()` and decremented right after. If it reaches the value 5, `do_follow_link()` terminates with an error code. Therefore, while there is no limit on the number of symbolic links in a pathname, the level of nesting of symbolic links can be at most five.

h. If everything went smoothly, `base` now points to the dentry object associated to the currently resolved component, so sets `inode` to `base->d_inode`.

i. If the `LOOKUP_DIRECTORY` flag of `flag` is not set, the currently resolved component is the last one in the file pathname, so returns the address in `base`. Note that `base` could point to a negative dentry object; that is, there might be no associated inode. This is fine for the lookup operation, since the last component must not be followed.

j. Otherwise, if `LOOKUP_DIRECTORY` is set, there is a slash after the currently resolved component. There are two cases to consider:

   - `inode` points to a valid inode object. In this case, checks that it is a directory by seeing whether the `lookup` method of the inode operations is defined; if not, returns an error code. Then either starts a new cycle iteration if the `LOOKUP_CONTINUE` flag in `flags` is set (meaning that the currently resolved component is not the last one) or returns the address in `base` (meaning that the component is the last one, even if it is followed by a trailing slash).

   - `inode` is `NULL` (meaning that `base` points to a negative dentry object). Returns `base` only if `LOOKUP_CONTINUE` is cleared and `LOOKUP_SLASHOK` is set; otherwise, returns an error code. Since a negative dentry object represents a file that was removed, it must not appear in the middle of a pathname lookup (which happens when `LOOKUP_CONTINUE` is set). Moreover, a negative dentry object must not appear as the last component in the pathname when a trailing slash is present, unless explicitly allowed by setting `LOOKUP_SLASHOK`.

Implementations of VFS System Calls

For the sake of brevity, we cannot discuss the implementation of all VFS system calls listed in Table 12-1. However, it could be useful to sketch out the implementation of a few system calls, just to show how VFS's data structures interact.

Let us reconsider the example proposed at the beginning of this chapter: a user issues a shell command that copies an MS-DOS file */floppy/TEST* in an Ext2 file */tmp/test*. The command shell invokes an external program like *cp*, which we assume executes the following code fragment:

```
inf = open("/floppy/TEST", O_RDONLY, 0);
outf = open("/tmp/test", O_WRONLY | O_CREAT | O_TRUNC, 0600);
do {
    l = read(inf, buf, 4096);
    write(outf, buf, l);
} while (l);
close(outf);
close(inf);
```

Actually, the code of the real *cp* program is more complicated, since it must also check for possible error codes returned by each system call. In our example, we just focus our attention on the "normal" behavior of a copy operation.

The open( ) System Call

The `open()` system call is serviced by the `sys_open()` function, which receives as parameters the pathname `filename` of the file to be opened, some access mode flags `flags`, and a permission bit mask `mode` if the file must be created. If the system call succeeds, it returns a file descriptor, that is, the index in the `current->files->fd` array of pointers to file objects; otherwise, it returns -1.

In our example, `open()` is invoked twice: the first time to open */floppy/TEST* for reading (`O_RDONLY` flag) and the second time to open */tmp/test* for writing (`O_WRONLY` flag). If */tmp/test* does not already exist, it will be created (`O_CREAT` flag) with exclusive read and write access for the owner (octal `0600` number in the third parameter).

Conversely, if the file already exists, it will be rewritten from scratch (`O_TRUNC` flag). Table 12-10 lists all flags of the `open()` system call.

Table 12-10. The Flags of the open( ) System Call

Flag Name	Description
FASYNC	Asynchronous I/O notification via signals
O_APPEND	Write always at end of the file
O_CREAT	Create the file if it does not exist
O_DIRECTORY	Fail if file is not a directory

Table 12-10. The Flags of the open() System Call (continued)

Flag Name	Description
O_EXCL	With O_CREAT, fail if the file already exists
O_LARGEFILE	Large file (size greater than 2 GB)
O_NDELAY	Same as O_NONBLOCK
O_NOCTTY	Never consider the file as a controlling terminal
O_NOFOLLOW	Do not follow a trailing symbolic link in pathname
O_NONBLOCK	No system calls will block on the file
O_RDONLY	Open for reading
O_RDWR	Open for both reading and writing
O_SYNC	Synchronous write (block until physical write terminates)
O_TRUNC	Truncate the file
O_WRONLY	Open for writing

Let us describe the operation of the **sys_open()** function. It performs the following:

1. Invokes **getname()** to read the file pathname from the process address space.

2. Invokes **get_unused_fd()** to find an empty slot in **current->files->fd**. The corresponding index (the new file descriptor) is stored in the **fd** local variable.

3. Invokes the **filp_open()** function, passing as parameters the pathname, the access mode flags, and the permission bit mask. This function, in turn, executes the following steps:

   a. Invokes **get_empty_filp()** to get a new file object.

   b. Sets the **f_flags** and **f_mode** fields of the file object according to the values of the **flags** and **modes** parameters.

   c. Invokes **open_namei()**, which executes the following operations:

      1. Invokes **lookup_dentry()** to interpret the file pathname and gets the dentry object associated with the requested file.

      2. Performs a series of checks to verify whether the process is permitted to open the file as specified by the values of the **flags** parameter. If so, returns the address of the dentry object; otherwise, returns an error code.

   d. If the access is for writing, checks the value of the **i_writecount** field of the inode object. A negative value means that the file has been memory-mapped, specifying that write accesses must be denied (see the section "Memory Mapping" in Chapter 15). In this case, returns an error code. Any other value specifies the number of processes that are actually writing into the file. In the latter case, increments the counter.

e. Initializes the fields of the file object; in particular, sets the `f_op` field to the contents of the `i_op->default_file_ops` field of the inode object. This sets up all the right functions for future file operations.

f. If the `open` method of the (default) file operations is defined, invokes it.

g. Clears the O_CREAT, O_EXCL, O_NOCTTY, and O_TRUNC flags in `f_flags`.

h. Returns the address of the file object.

4. Sets `current->files->fd[fd]` to the address of the file object.

5. Returns `fd`.

The read() and write() System Calls

Let's return to the code in our *cp* example. The `open()` system calls return two file descriptors, which are stored in the `inf` and `outf` variables. Then the program starts a loop: at each iteration, a portion of the */floppy/TEST* file is copied into a local buffer (`read()` system call), and then the data in the local buffer is written into the */tmp/test* file (`write()` system call).

The `read()` and `write()` system calls are quite similar. Both require three parameters: a file descriptor `fd`, the address `buf` of a memory area (the buffer containing the data to be transferred), and a number `count` that specifies how many bytes should be transferred. Of course, `read()` will transfer the data from the file into the buffer, while `write()` will do the opposite. Both system calls return the number of bytes that were successfully transferred or -1 to signal an error condition.[*]

The read or write operation always takes place at the file offset specified by the current file pointer (field `f_pos` of the file object). Both system calls update the file pointer by adding the number of transferred bytes to it.

In short, both `sys_read()` (the `read()`'s service routine) and `sys_write()` (the `write()`'s service routine) perform almost the same steps:

1. Invokes `fget()` to derive from `fd` the address `file` of the corresponding file object and increments the usage counter `file->f_count`.

2. Checks whether the flags in `file->f_mode` allow the requested access (read or write operation).

---

[*] A return value less than `count` does not mean that an error occurred. The kernel is always allowed to terminate the system call even if not all requested bytes were transferred, and the user application must accordingly check the return value and reissue, if necessary, the system call. Typically, a small value is returned when reading from a pipe or a terminal device, when reading past the end of the file, or when the system call is interrupted by a signal. The End-Of-File condition (EOF) can easily be recognized by a null return value from `read()`. This condition will not be confused with an abnormal termination due to a signal, because if `read()` is interrupted by a signal before any data was read, an error occurs.

3. Invokes `locks_verify_area()` to check whether there are mandatory locks for the file portion to be accessed (see the section "File Locking" later in this chapter).

4. If executing a write operation, acquires the `i_sem` semaphore included in the inode object. This semaphore forbids a process to write into the file while another process is flushing to disk buffers relative to the same file (see the section "Writing Dirty Buffers to Disk" in Chapter 14). It also forbids two processes to write into the same file at the same time. Notice that, unless the `O_APPEND` flag is set, POSIX does not require serialized file accesses: if a programmer wants exclusive access to a file, he must use a file lock (see next section). Thus, it is possible that a process is reading from a file while another process is writing to it.

5. Invokes either `file->f_op->read` or `file->f_op->write` to transfer the data. Both functions return the number of bytes that were actually transferred. As a side effect, the file pointer is properly updated.

6. Invokes `fput()` to decrement the usage counter `file->f_count`.

7. Returns the number of bytes actually transferred.

The close() System Call

The loop in our example code terminates when the `read()` system call returns the value 0, that is, when all bytes of */floppy/TEST* have been copied into */tmp/test*. The program can then close the open files, since the copy operation has been completed.

The `close()` system call receives as its parameter `fd` the file descriptor of the file to be closed. The `sys_close()` service routine performs the following operations:

1. Gets the file object address stored in `current->files->fd[fd]`; if it is `NULL`, returns an error code.

2. Sets `current->files->fd[fd]` to `NULL`. Releases the file descriptor `fd` by clearing the corresponding bits in the `open_fds` and `close_on_exec` fields of `current->files` (see Chapter 19, *Program Execution*, for the Close on Execution flag).

3. Invokes `filp_close()`, which performs the following operations:

   a. Invokes the `flush` method of the file operations, if defined

   b. Releases any mandatory lock on the file

   c. Invokes `fput()` to release the file object

4. Returns the error code of the `flush` method (usually 0).

File Locking

When a file can be accessed by more than one process, a synchronization problem occurs: what happens if two processes try to write in the same file location? Or again, what happens if a process reads from a file location while another process is writing into it?

In traditional Unix systems, concurrent accesses to the same file location produce unpredictable results. However, the systems provide a mechanism that allows the processes to *lock* a file region so that concurrent accesses may be easily avoided.

The POSIX standard requires a file-locking mechanism based on the `fcntl()` system call. It is possible to lock an arbitrary region of a file (even a single byte) or to lock the whole file (including data appended in the future). Since a process can choose to lock just a part of a file, it can also hold multiple locks on different parts of the file.

This kind of lock does not keep out another process that is ignorant of locking. Like a critical region in code, the lock is considered "advisory" because it doesn't work unless other processes cooperate in checking the existence of a lock before accessing the file. Therefore, POSIX's locks are known as *advisory locks*.

Traditional BSD variants implement advisory locking through the `flock()` system call. This call does not allow a process to lock a file region, just the whole file.

Traditional System V variants provide the `lockf()` system call, which is just an interface to `fcntl()`. More importantly, System V Release 3 introduced *mandatory locking*: the kernel checks that every invocation of the `open()`, `read()`, and `write()` system calls does not violate a mandatory lock on the file being accessed. Therefore, mandatory locks are enforced even between noncooperative processes.* A file is marked as a candidate for mandatory locking by setting its set-group bit (SGID) and clearing the group-execute permission bit. Since the set-group bit makes no sense when the group-execute bit is off, the kernel interprets that combination as a hint to use mandatory locks instead of advisory ones.

Whether processes use advisory or mandatory locks, they can make use of both shared *read locks* and exclusive *write locks*. Any number of processes may have read locks on some file region, but only one process can have a write lock on it at the same time. Moreover, it is not possible to get a write lock when another process owns a read lock for the same file region and vice versa (see Table 12-11).

---

* Oddly enough, a process may still unlink (delete) a file even if some other process owns a mandatory lock on it! This perplexing situation is possible because, when a process deletes a file hard link, it does not modify its contents but only the contents of its parent directory.

Table 12-11. Whether a Lock Is Granted

Current Locks	Requested Lock	
	Read	Write
No lock	Yes	Yes
Read locks	Yes	No
Write lock	No	No

Linux File Locking

Linux supports all fashions of file locking: advisory and mandatory locks and the `fcntl()`, `flock()`, and the `lockf()` system calls. However, the `lockf()` system call is just a library wrapper routine, and therefore will not be discussed here.

Mandatory locks can be enabled and disabled on a per-filesystem basis using the `MS_MANDLOCK` flag of the `mount()` system call. The default is to switch off mandatory locking: in this case, both `flock()` and `fcntl()` create advisory locks. When the flag is set, `flock()` still produces advisory locks, while `fcntl()` produces mandatory locks if the file has the set-group bit on and the group-execute bit off; it produces advisory locks otherwise.

Beside the checks in the `read()` and `write()` system calls, the kernel takes into consideration the existence of mandatory locks when servicing all system calls that could modify the contents of a file. For instance, an `open()` system call with the `O_TRUNC` flag set fails if any mandatory lock exists for the file.

A lock produced by `fcntl()` is of type `FL_POSIX`, while a lock produced by `flock()` is of type `FL_LOCK`. These two types of locks may safely coexist, but neither one has any effect on the other. Therefore, a file locked through `fcntl()` does not appear locked to `flock()` and vice versa.

An `FL_POSIX` lock is always associated with a process *and* with an inode; the lock is automatically released either when the process dies or when a file descriptor is closed (even if the process opened the same file twice or duplicated a file descriptor). Moreover, `FL_POSIX` locks are never inherited by the child across a `fork()`.

An `FL_LOCK` lock is always associated with a file object. When a lock is requested, the kernel replaces any other lock that refers to the same file object. This happens only when a process wants to change an already owned read lock into a write one or vice versa. Moreover, when a file object is being freed by the `fput()` function, all `FL_LOCK` locks that refer to the file object are destroyed. However, there could be other `FL_LOCK` read locks set by other processes for the same file (inode), and they still remain active.

File-Locking Data Structures

The `file_lock` data structure represents file locks; its fields are shown in Table 12-12. All `file_lock` data structures are included in a doubly linked list. The address of the first element is stored in `file_lock_table`, while the fields `fl_nextlink` and `fl_prevlink` store the addresses of the adjacent elements in the list.

Table 12-12. The Fields of the file_lock Data Structure

Type	Field	Description
struct file_lock *	fl_next	Next element in inode list
struct file_lock *	fl_nextlink	Next element in global list
struct file_lock *	fl_prevlink	Previous element in global list
struct file_lock *	fl_nextblock	Next element in process list
struct file_lock *	fl_prevblock	Previous element in process list
struct files_struct *	fl_owner	Owner's `files_struct`
unsigned int	fl_pid	PID of the process owner
struct wait_queue *	fl_wait	Wait queue of blocked processes
struct file *	fl_file	Pointer to file object
unsigned char	fl_flags	Lock flags
unsigned char	fl_type	Lock type
off_t	fl_start	Starting offset of locked region
off_t	fl_end	Ending offset of locked region
void (*)(struct file_lock *)	fl_notify	Callback function when lock is unblocked
union	u	Filesystem-specific information

All `lock_file` structures that refer to the same file on disk are collected in a simply linked list, whose first element is pointed to by the `i_flock` field of the inode object. The `fl_next` field of the `lock_file` structure specifies the next element in the list.

When a process tries to get an advisory or mandatory lock, it may be suspended until the previously allocated lock on the same file region is released. All processes sleeping on some lock are inserted into a wait queue, whose address is stored in the `fl_wait` field of the `file_lock` structure. Moreover, all processes sleeping on any file locks are inserted into a global circular list implemented by means of the `fl_nextblock` and `fl_prevblock` fields.

The following sections examine the differences between the two lock types.

FL_LOCK Locks

The flock() system call acts on two parameters: the fd file descriptor of the file to be acted upon and a cmd parameter that specifies the lock operation. A cmd parameter of LOCK_SH requires a shared lock for reading, LOCK_EX requires an exclusive lock for writing, and LOCK_UN releases the lock. If the LOCK_NB value is ORed to the LOCK_SH or LOCK_EX operation, the system call does not block; in other words, if the lock cannot be immediately obtained, the system call returns an error code. Note that it is not possible to specify a region inside the file: the lock always applies to the whole file.

When the sys_flock() service routine is invoked, it performs the following steps:

1. Checks whether fd is a valid file descriptor; if not, returns an error code. Gets the address of the corresponding file object.

2. Invokes flock_make_lock() to initialize a file_lock structure by setting the fl_flags field to FL_LOCK; sets the fl_type field to F_RDLCK, F_WRLCK, or F_UNLCK, depending on the value of cmd, and sets the fl_file field to the address of the file object.

3. If the lock must be acquired, checks that the process has both read and write permission on the open file; if not, returns an error code.

4. Invokes flock_lock_file(), passing as parameters the file object pointer filp, a pointer caller to the initialized file_lock structure, and a flag wait. This last parameter is set if the system call should block and cleared otherwise. This function performs, in turn, the following actions:

   a. Searches the list that filp->f_dentry->d_inode->i_flock points to. If an FL_LOCK lock for the same file object is found and an F_UNLCK operation is required, removes the file_lock element from the inode list and the global list, wakes up all processes sleeping in the lock's wait queue, frees the file_lock structure, and returns.

   b. Otherwise, searches the inode list again to verify that no existing FL_LOCK lock conflicts with the requested one. There must be no FL_LOCK write lock in the inode list; and moreover there must be no FL_LOCK lock at all if the processing is requesting a write lock. However, a process may want to change the type of a lock it already owns; this is done by issuing a second flock() system call. Therefore, the kernel always allows the process to change locks that refer to the same file object. If a conflicting lock is found and the LOCK_NB flag was specified, returns an error code, otherwise inserts the current process in the circular list of blocked processes and invokes interruptible_sleep_on() to suspend it.

   c. Otherwise, if no incompatibility exists, inserts the file_lock structure into the global lock list and the inode list, then returns 0 (success).

FL_POSIX Locks

When used to lock files, the fcntl() system call acts on three parameters: the fd file descriptor of the file to be acted upon, a cmd parameter that specifies the lock operation, and an fl pointer to a flock structure.

Locks of type FL_POSIX are able to protect an arbitrary file region, even a single byte. The region is specified by three fields of the flock structure. l_start is the initial offset of the region and is relative to the beginning of the file (if field l_whence is set to SEEK_SET), to the current file pointer (if l_whence is set to SEEK_CUR), or to the end of the file (if l_whence is set to SEEK_END). The l_len field specifies the length of the file region (or 0, which means that the region extends beyond the end of the file).

The sys_fcntl() service routine behaves differently depending on the value of the flag set in the cmd parameter:

F_GETLK

Determines whether the lock described by the flock structure conflicts with some FL_POSIX lock already obtained by another process. In that case, the flock structure is overwritten with the information about the existing lock.

F_SETLK

Sets the lock described by the flock structure. If the lock cannot be acquired, the system call returns an error code.

F_SETLKW

Sets the lock described by the flock structure. If the lock cannot be acquired, the system call blocks; that is, the calling process is put to sleep.

When sys_fcntl() acquires a lock, it performs the following:

1. Reads the flock structure from user space.

2. Gets the file object corresponding to fd.

3. Checks whether the lock should be a mandatory one. In that case, returns an error code if the file has a shared memory mapping (see the section "Memory Mapping" in Chapter 15).

4. Invokes the posix_make_lock() function to initialize a new file_lock structure.

5. Returns an error code if the file does not allow the access mode specified by the type of the requested lock.

6. Invokes the lock method of the file operations, if defined.

7. Invokes the posix_lock_file() function, which executes the following actions:

   a. Invokes posix_locks_conflict() for each FL_POSIX lock in the inode's lock list. The function checks whether the lock conflicts with the requested one. Essentially, there must be no FL_POSIX write lock for the same region in the inode list, and there may be no FL_POSIX lock at all for the same region if the process is requesting a write lock. However, locks owned by the same process never conflict; this allows a process to change the characteristics of a lock it already owns.

b. If a conflicting lock is found and fcntl() was invoked with the F_SETLK flag, returns an error code. Otherwise, the current process should be suspended. In this case, invokes posix_locks_deadlock() to check that no deadlock condition is being created among processes waiting for FL_POSIX locks, then inserts the current process in the circular list of blocked processes and invokes interruptible_sleep_on() to suspend it.

c. As soon as the inode's lock list includes no conflicting lock, checks all the FL_POSIX locks of the current process that overlap the file region that the current process wants to lock and combines and splits adjacent areas as required. For example, if the process requested a write lock for a file region that falls inside a read-locked wider region, the previous read lock is split into two parts covering the nonoverlapping areas, while the central region is protected by the new write lock. In case of overlaps, newer locks always replace older ones.

d. Inserts the new file_lock structure in the global lock list and in the inode list.

8. Returns the value 0 (success).

Anticipating Linux 2.4

The Linux 2.4 VFS handles eight new filesystems, among them the udf for handling DVD devices. The maximum file size has been considerably increased (at least from the VFS point of view) by expanding the i_size field of the inode from 32 to 64 bits.

CHAPTER THIRTEEN

MANAGING I/O DEVICES

The Virtual File System in the last chapter depends on lower-level functions to carry out each read, write, or other operation in a manner suited to each device. The previous chapter included a brief discussion of how operations are handled by different filesystems. In this chapter, we'll look at how the kernel invokes the operations on actual devices.

In the section "I/O Architecture" we give a brief survey of the Intel 80x86 I/O architecture. In "Associating Files with I/O Devices" we show how the VFS associates a "device file" with each different hardware device so that application programs can use all kinds of devices in the same way. Most of the chapter focuses on the two types of drivers, character and block.

The aim of this chapter is to illustrate the overall organization of device drivers in Linux. Readers interested in developing device drivers on their own may want to refer to Alessandro Rubini's *Linux Device Drivers* book from O'Reilly.

I/O Architecture

In order to make a computer work properly, data paths must be provided that let information flow between CPU(s), RAM, and the score of I/O devices that can be connected nowadays to a personal computer. These data paths, which are denoted collectively as the *bus*, act as the primary communication channel inside the computer.

Several types of buses, such as the ISA, EISA, PCI, and MCA, are currently in use. In this section we'll discuss the functional characteristics common to all PC architectures, without giving details about a specific bus type.

In fact, what is commonly denoted as bus consists of three specialized buses:

Data bus
> A group of lines that transfers data in parallel. The Pentium has a 64-bit-wide data bus.

Address bus
> A group of lines that transmits an address in parallel. The Pentium has a 32-bit-wide address bus.

Control bus
> A group of lines that transmits control information to the connected circuits. The Pentium makes use of control lines to specify, for instance, whether the bus is used to allow data transfers between a processor and the RAM or alternatively between a processor and an I/O device. Control lines also determine whether a read or a write transfer must be performed.

When the bus connects the CPU to an I/O device, it is called an *I/O bus*. In this case, Intel 80x86 microprocessors use 16 out of the 32 address lines to address I/O devices and 8, 16, or 32 out of the 64 data lines to transfer data. The I/O bus, in turn, is connected to each I/O device by means of a hierarchy of hardware components including up to three elements: I/O ports, interfaces, and device controllers. Figure 13-1 shows the components of the I/O architecture.

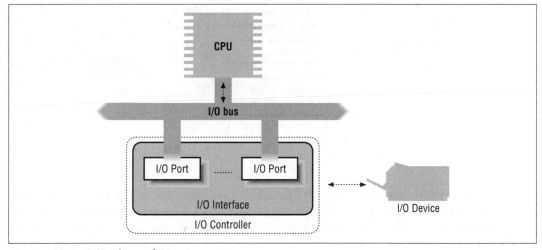

Figure 13-1. PC's I/O architecture

I/O Ports

Each device connected to the I/O bus has its own set of I/O addresses, which are usually called *I/O ports*. In the IBM PC architecture, the I/O address space provides up to 65,536 8-bit I/O ports. Two consecutive 8-bit ports may be regarded as a single 16-bit port, which must start on an even address. Similarly, two consecutive 16-bit ports may be regarded as a single 32-bit port, which must start on an address that is a multiple of 4. Four special assembly language instructions called in, ins, out, and outs allow the CPU to read from and write into an I/O port. While executing one of these instructions, the CPU makes use of the address bus to select the required I/O port and of the data bus to transfer data between a CPU register and the port.

I/O ports may also be mapped into addresses of the physical address space: the processor is then able to communicate with an I/O device by issuing assembly language instructions that operate directly on memory (for instance, mov, and, or, and so on). Modern hardware devices tend to prefer mapped I/O, since it is faster and can be combined with DMA.

An important objective for system designers is to offer a unified approach to I/O programming without sacrificing performance. Toward that end, the I/O ports of each device are structured into a set of specialized registers as shown in Figure 13-2. The CPU writes into the *control register* the commands to be sent to the device and reads from the *status register* a value that represents the internal state of the device. The CPU also fetches data from the device by reading bytes from the *input register* and pushes data to the device by writing bytes into the *output register*.

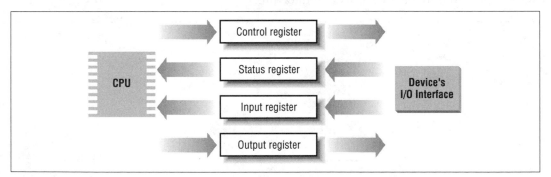

Figure 13-2. Specialized I/O ports

In order to lower costs, the same I/O port is often used for different purposes. For instance, some bits describe the device state, while others specify the command to be issued to the device. Similarly, the same I/O port may be used as an input register or an output register.

I/O Interfaces

An *I/O interface* is a hardware circuit inserted between a group of I/O ports and the corresponding device controller. It acts as an interpreter that translates the values in the I/O ports into commands and data for the device. In the opposite direction, it detects changes in the device state and correspondingly updates the I/O port that plays the role of status register. This circuit can also be connected through an IRQ line to a Programmable Interrupt Controller, so that it issues interrupt requests on behalf of the device.

There are two types of interfaces:

Custom I/O interfaces
> Devoted to one specific hardware device. In some cases, the device controller is located in the same *card** that contains the I/O interface. The devices attached to a custom I/O interface can be either *internal devices* (devices located inside the PC's cabinet) or *external devices* (devices located outside the PC's cabinet).

General-purpose I/O interfaces
> Used to connect several different hardware devices. Devices attached to a general-purpose I/O interface are always external devices.

Custom I/O interfaces

Just to give an idea of how much variety is encompassed by custom I/O interfaces, thus by the devices currently installed in a PC, we'll list some of the most commonly found:

Keyboard interface
> Connected to a keyboard controller that includes a dedicated microprocessor. This microprocessor decodes the combination of pressed keys, generates an interrupt, and puts the corresponding scan code in an input register.

Graphic interface
> Packed together with the corresponding controller in a graphic card that has its own *frame buffer*, as well as a specialized processor and some code stored in a Read-Only Memory chip (ROM). The frame buffer is an on-board memory containing the graphics description of the current screen contents.

Disk interface
> Connected by a cable to the disk controller, which is usually integrated with the disk. For instance, the IDE interface is connected by a 40-wire flat conductor cable to an intelligent disk controller that can be found on the disk itself.

---

* Each card must be inserted in one of the available free bus slots of the PC. If the card can be connected to an external device through an external cable, the card sports a suitable connector in the rear panel of the PC.

Bus mouse interface

> The corresponding controller is included in the mouse, which is connected via a cable to the interface.

Network interface

> Packed together with the corresponding controller in a network card used to receive or transmit network packets. Although there are several widely adopted network standards, Ethernet is the most common.

General-purpose I/O interfaces

Modern PCs include several general-purpose I/O interfaces, which are used to connect a wide range of external devices. The most common interfaces are:

Parallel port

> Traditionally used to connect printers, it can also be used to connect removable disks, scanners, backup units, other computers, and so on. The data is transferred 1 byte (8 bits) at the time.

Serial port

> Like the parallel port, but the data is transferred 1 bit at a time. It includes a Universal Asynchronous Receiver and Transmitter (UART) chip to string out the bytes to be sent into a sequence of bits and to reassemble the received bits into bytes. Since it is intrinsically slower than the parallel port, this interface is mainly used to connect external devices that do not operate at a high speed, like modems, mouses, and printers.

Universal serial bus (USB)

> A recent general-purpose I/O interface that is quickly gaining in popularity. It operates at a high speed, and it may be used for the external devices traditionally connected to the parallel port and the serial port.

PCMCIA interface

> Included mostly on portable computers. The external device, which has the shape of a credit card, can be inserted into and removed from a slot without rebooting the system. The most common PCMCIA devices are hard disks, modems, network cards, and RAM expansions.

SCSI (Small Computer System Interface) interface

> A circuit that connects the main PC bus to a secondary bus called the *SCSI bus*. The SCSI-2 bus allows up to eight PCs and external devices—hard disks, scanners, CD-ROM writers, and so on—to be connected together. Wide SCSI-2 and the recent SCSI-3 interfaces allow you to connect 16 devices or more if additional interfaces are present. The *SCSI standard* is the communication protocol used to connect devices via the SCSI bus.

Device Controllers

A complex device may require a *device controller* to drive it. Essentially, the controller plays two important roles:

- It interprets the high-level commands received from the I/O interface and forces the device to execute specific actions by sending proper sequences of electrical signals to it.

- It converts and properly interprets the electrical signals received from the device and modifies (through the I/O interface) the value of the status register.

A typical device controller is the *disk controller*, which receives high-level commands such as a "write this block of data" from the microprocessor (through the I/O interface) and converts them into low-level disk operations such as "position the disk head on the right track" and "write the data inside the track." Modern disk controllers are very sophisticated, since they can keep the disk data in fast memory caches and can reorder the CPU high-level requests optimized for the actual disk geometry.

Simpler devices do not have a device controller; the Programmable Interrupt Controller (see the section "Interrupts and Exceptions" in Chapter 4, *Interrupts and Exceptions*) and the Programmable Interval Timer (see the section "Programmable Interval Timer" in Chapter 5, *Timing Measurements*) are examples of such devices.

Direct Memory Access (DMA)

All PCs include an auxiliary processor called the *Direct Memory Access Controller*, or *DMAC*, which can be instructed to transfer data between the RAM and an I/O device. Once activated by the CPU, the DMAC is able to carry on the data transfer on its own; when the data transfer has been completed, the DMAC issues an interrupt request. The conflicts occurring when both CPU and DMAC need to access the same memory location at the same time are resolved by a hardware circuit called a *memory arbiter* (see also the section "Common Memory" in Chapter 11, *Kernel Synchronization*).

The DMAC is mostly used by disk drivers and other slow devices that transfer a large number of bytes at once. Because setup time for the DMAC is relatively high, it is more efficient to directly use the CPU for the data transfer when the number of bytes is small.

The first DMACs for the old ISA buses were complex and hard to program. More recent DMACs for the PCI and SCSI buses rely on dedicated hardware circuits in the buses and make life easier for device driver developers.

Until now we have distinguished three kinds of memory addresses: logical and linear addresses, which are used internally by the CPU, and physical addresses, which are the memory addresses used by the CPU to physically drive the data bus. However, there is a fourth kind of memory address, the so-called *bus address*: it corresponds to the memory addresses used by all hardware devices except the CPU to drive the data bus. In the PC architecture, bus addresses coincide with physical addresses; however, in other architectures, like Sun's SPARC and Compaq's Alpha, these two kinds of addresses differ.

Why should the kernel be concerned at all about bus addresses? Well, in a DMA operation the data transfer takes place without CPU intervention: the data bus is directly driven by the I/O device and the DMAC. Therefore, when the kernel sets up a DMA operation, it must write the bus address of the memory buffer involved in the proper I/O ports of the DMAC or I/O device.

Associating Files with I/O Devices

As mentioned in Chapter 1, *Introduction*, Unix-like operating systems are based on the notion of a *file*, which is just an information container structured as a sequence of bytes. According to this approach, I/O devices are treated as files; thus, the same system calls used to interact with regular files on disk can be used to directly interact with I/O devices. As an example, the same `write()` system call may be used to write data into a regular file, or to send it to a printer by writing to the */dev/lp0* device file. Let's now examine in more detail how this schema is carried out.

Device Files

Device files are used to represent most of the I/O devices supported by Linux. Besides its name, each device file has three main attributes:

Type
Either *block* or *character* (we'll discuss the difference shortly).

Major number
A number ranging from 1 to 255 that identifies the device type. Usually, all device files having the same major number and the same type share the same set of file operations, since they are handled by the same device driver.

Minor number
A number that identifies a specific device among a group of devices that share the same major number.

The `mknod()` system call is used to create device files. It receives the name of the device file, its type, and the major and minor numbers as parameters. The last two parameters are merged in a 16-bit `dev_t` number: the eight most significant bits identify the major number, while the remaining ones identify the minor number. The `MAJOR` and `MINOR` macros extract the two values from the 16-bit number, while the `MKDEV` macro merges a major and minor number into a 16-bit number. Actually, `dev_t` is the data type specifically used by application programs; the kernel uses the `kdev_t` data type. In Linux 2.2 both types reduce to an unsigned short integer, but `kdev_t` will become a complete device file descriptor in some future Linux version.

Device files are usually included in the */dev* directory. Table 13-1 illustrates the attributes of some device files.[*] Notice how the same major number may be used to identify both a character and a block device.

Table 13-1. Examples of Device Files

Name	Type	Major	Minor	Description
/dev/fd0	block	2	0	Floppy disk
/dev/hda	block	3	0	First IDE disk
/dev/hda2	block	3	2	Second primary partition of first IDE disk
/dev/hdb	block	3	64	Second IDE disk
/dev/hdb3	block	3	67	Third primary partition of second IDE disk
/dev/ttyp0	char	3	0	Terminal
/dev/console	char	5	1	Console
/dev/lp1	char	6	1	Parallel printer
/dev/ttyS0	char	4	64	First serial port
/dev/rtc	char	10	135	Real time clock
/dev/null	char	1	3	Null device (black hole)

Usually, a device file is associated with a hardware device, like a hard disk (for instance, */dev/hda*), or with some physical or logical portion of a hardware device, like a disk partition (for instance, */dev/hda2*). In some cases, however, a device file is not associated to any real hardware device, but represents a fictitious logical device. For instance, */dev/null* is a device file corresponding to a "black hole": all data written into it are simply discarded, and the file appears always empty.

As far as the kernel is concerned, the name of the device file is irrelevant. If you created a device file named */tmp/disk* of type "block" with major number 3 and minor number 0, it would be equivalent to the */dev/hda* device file shown in the table. On the other hand, device filenames may be significant for some application programs. As an example, a communication program might assume that the first serial port is associated with the */dev/ttyS0* device file. But usually most application programs can be configured to interact with arbitrarily named device files.

---

[*] The official registry of allocated device numbers and */dev* directory nodes is stored in the *Documentation/devices. txt* file. The major numbers of the devices supported may also be found in the *include/linux/major.h* file.

Block versus character devices

Block devices have the following characteristics:

- They are able to transfer a fixed-size block of data in a single I/O operation.

- Blocks stored in the device can be addressed randomly: the time needed to transfer a data block can be assumed independent of the block address inside the device and of the current device state.

Typical examples of block devices are hard disks, floppy disks, and CD-ROMs. *RAM disks*, which are obtained by configuring portions of the RAM as fast hard disks and can make temporary storage very efficient for application programs, are also treated as block devices.

Character devices have the following characteristics:

- They are able to transfer arbitrary-sized data in a single I/O operation. Actually, some character devices—such as printers—transfer 1 byte at a time, while others, such as tape units, transfer variable-length blocks of data.

- They usually address characters sequentially.

Network cards

Some I/O devices have no corresponding device file. The most significant example is network cards. Essentially, a network card places outgoing data on a line going to remote computer systems and receives packets from those systems into kernel memory. Although this book does not cover networking, it is worth spending a few moments on the kernel and programming interfaces to these cards.

Starting with BSD, all Unix systems assign a different symbolic name to each network card included in the computer; for instance, the first Ethernet card gets the `eth0` name. However, the name does not correspond to any device file and has no corresponding inode.

Instead of using the filesystem, the system administrator has to set up a relationship between the device name and a network address. Therefore, data communication between application programs and the network interface is not based on the standard file-related system calls; it is based instead on the `socket()`, `bind()`, `listen()`, `accept()`, and `connect()` system calls, which act on network addresses. This group of system calls, introduced first by Unix BSD, has become the standard programming model for network devices.

VFS Handling of Device Files

Device files live in the system directory tree but are intrinsically different from regular files and directories. When a process accesses a regular file, it is accessing some data blocks in some disk partition through a filesystem, but when a process accesses a device file, it is just driving a hardware device. For instance, a process might access a device file to read the room temperature from a digital thermometer connected to the computer. It is the VFS's responsibility to hide the differences between device files and regular files from application programs.

In order to do this, the VFS changes the default file operations of an opened device file; as result, any system call on the device file will be translated to an invocation of a device-related function instead of the corresponding function of the hosting filesystem. The device-related function acts on the hardware device to perform the operation requested by the process.*

The set of device-related functions that control an I/O device is called a *device driver*. Since each device has a unique I/O controller, and thus unique commands and unique state information, most I/O device types have their own drivers.

Device file class descriptors

Each class of device files having the same major number and the same type is described by a `device_struct` data structure, which includes two fields: the name (`name`) of the device class and a pointer (`fops`) to the file operation table. All `device_struct` descriptors for character device files are included in the `chrdevs` table. It includes 255 elements, one for each possible major number. (No device file can have major number 255, since that value is reserved for future extensions.) Similarly, all 255 descriptors for block device files are included in the `blkdevs` table. The first entry of both tables is always empty, since no device file can have major number 0.

The `chrdevs` and `blkdevs` tables are initially empty. The `register_chrdev()` and `register_blkdev()` functions are used to insert a new entry into one of the tables, while `unregister_chrdev()` and `unregister_blkdev()` are used to remove an entry.

As an example, the descriptor for the parallel printer driver class is inserted in the `chrdevs` table as follows:

```
register_chrdev(6, "lp", &lp_fops);
```

The first parameter denotes the major number, the second denotes the device class name, and the last is a pointer to the table of file operations.

If a device driver is statically included in the kernel, the corresponding device file class is registered during system initialization. However, if a device driver is dynamically loaded as a module (see Appendix B, *Modules*), the corresponding device file class is registered when the module is loaded and unregistered when the module is unloaded.

---

* Notice that, thanks to the name-resolving mechanism explained in the section "Pathname Lookup" in Chapter 12, *The Virtual Filesystem*, symbolic links to device files work just like device files.

Opening a device file

We discussed in the section "The open() System Call" in Chapter 12 how files are opened. Let us suppose that a process opens a device file. The VFS initializes, if necessary, the file object, the dentry object, and the inode object that refer to the device file. In particular, if the inode object does not already exist, the VFS invokes the read_ inode method of the proper superblock object to retrieve the file information from disk. In doing so, the method records the device major and minor numbers in the i_ rdev field of the inode object and the device file type in the i_mode field (S_IFCHR for character device files or S_IFBLK for block device files). Moreover, it installs a pointer to the appropriate inode operations as follows:

```
if ((inode->i_mode & 00170000) == S_IFCHR)
    inode->i_op = &chrdev_inode_operations;
else if ((inode->i_mode & 00170000) == S_IFBLK)
    inode->i_op = &blkdev_inode_operations;
```

All fields of the chrdev_inode_operations and blkdev_inode_operations tables are null except for the default_file_ops fields, which point to the def_chr_fops table and to the def_blk_fops table, respectively. All the methods of def_chr_fops and def_blk_fops in turn are null except for the open methods, which point to the chrdev_open() function and to the blkdev_open() function, respectively.

The filp_open() function fills the new file object and in particular initializes the f_ op field with the contents of i_op->default_file_ops field of the inode object. As a consequence, the file operation table will be def_chr_fops or def_blk_fops. Then filp_open() invokes the open method, thus executing either chrdev_open() or blkdev_open(). These functions essentially perform three operations:

1. Derive the major number of the device driver from the i_rdev field of the inode object:

   ```
   major = MAJOR(inode->i_rdev);
   ```

2. Install the proper file operations for the device file:

   ```
   filp->f_op = chrdevs[major].fops;
   ```

   (The example, of course, is for character device files; blkdev_open() uses the blkdevs table instead.)

3. Invoke, if defined, the open method of the file operations table:

   ```
   if (filp->f_op != NULL && filp->f_op->open != NULL)
       return filp->f_op->open(inode, filp);
   ```

Notice that the final invocation of the open() method does not cause recursion, since now the field contains the address of a device-dependent function whose job is to set up the device. Typically, that function performs the following operations:

1. If the device driver is included in a kernel module, increments its usage counter, so that it cannot be unloaded until the device file is closed. (Appendix B describes how users can load and unload modules.)

2. If the device driver handles several devices of the same kind, selects the proper one by making use of the minor number and further specializes, if needed, the table of file operations.

3. Checks whether the device really exists and is currently working.

4. If necessary, sends an initialization command sequence to the hardware device.

5. Initializes the data structures of the device driver.

Device Drivers

We have seen that the VFS uses a canonical set of common functions (*open, read, lseek,* and so on) to control a device. The actual implementation of all these functions is delegated to the device driver. Since each device has a unique I/O controller, and thus unique commands and unique state information, most I/O devices have their own drivers.

We shall not attempt to describe any of the hundreds of existing device drivers but concentrate rather on how the kernel supports them. In doing so, we shall describe several I/O architecture features that must be taken into consideration by device driver programmers.

Level of Kernel Support

The kernel can support access to hardware devices in three possible ways:

No support at all
> The application program interacts directly with the device's I/O ports by issuing suitable in and out assembly language instructions.

Minimal support
> The kernel does not recognize the hardware device but only its I/O interface. User programs are able to treat the interface as a sequential device capable of reading and/or writing sequences of characters.

Extended support
> The kernel recognizes the hardware device and handles the I/O interface itself. In fact, there might not even be a device file for the device.

The most common example of the first approach, which does not rely on any kernel device driver, is how the X Window System handles the graphic display. The approach is quite efficient, although it restrains the X server from making use of the hardware interrupts issued by the I/O device. This approach also requires some additional effort in order to allow the X server to access the required I/O ports. As mentioned in the section "Task State Segment" in Chapter 3, *Processes*, the `iopl()` and `ioperm()` system calls grant a process the privilege to access I/O ports. They can be invoked only by programs having root privileges. But such programs can be made available to users by setting the `fsuid` field of the executable file to 0, the UID of the superuser (see the section "Process Credentials and Capabilities" in Chapter 19, *Program Execution*).

The minimal support approach is used to handle external hardware devices connected to a general-purpose I/O interface. The kernel takes care of the I/O interface by offering a device file (and thus a device driver); the application program handles the external hardware device by reading and writing the device file.

Minimal support is preferable to extended support because it keeps the kernel size small. However, among the general-purpose I/O interfaces commonly found on a PC, only the serial port is handled with this approach. Thus, a serial mouse is directly controlled by an application program, like the X server, and a serial modem always requires a communication program like Minicom, Seyon, or a PPP (Point-to-Point Protocol) daemon.

Minimal support has a limited range of applications because it cannot be used when the external device must interact heavily with internal kernel data structures. As an example, consider a removable hard disk that is connected to a general-purpose I/O interface. An application program cannot interact with all kernel data structures and functions needed to recognize the disk and to mount its filesystem, so extended support is mandatory in this case.

In general, any hardware device directly connected to the I/O bus, such as the internal hard disk, is handled according to the extended support approach: the kernel must provide a device driver for each such device. External devices attached to the parallel port, the Universal Serial Bus (USB), the PCMCIA port found in many laptops, or the SCSI interface—in short, any general-purpose I/O interface except the serial port—also require extended support.

It is worth noting that the standard file-related system calls like `open()`, `read()`, and `write()` do not always give the application full control of the underlying hardware device. In fact, the lowest-common-denominator approach of the VFS does not include room for special commands that some devices need or let an application check whether the device is in some specific internal state.

The POSIX `ioctl()` system call has been introduced to satisfy such needs. Besides the file descriptor of the device file and a second 32-bit parameter specifying the request, the system call can accept an arbitrary number of additional parameters. For example, specific `ioctl()` requests exist to get the CD-ROM sound volume or to eject the CD-ROM media. Application programs may simulate the user interface of a CD player using these kinds of `ioctl()` requests.

Monitoring I/O Operations

The duration of an I/O operation is often unpredictable. It can depend on mechanical considerations (the current position of a disk head with respect to the block to be transferred), on truly random events (when a data packet will arrive on the network card), or on human factors (when a user will press a key on the keyboard or when she will notice that a paper jam occurred in the printer). In any case, the device driver that started an I/O operation must rely on a monitoring technique that signals either the termination of the I/O operation or a time-out.

In the case of a terminated operation, the device driver reads the status register of the I/O interface to determine if the I/O operation was carried out successfully. In the case of a time-out, the driver knows that something went wrong, since the maximum time interval allowed to complete the operation elapsed and nothing happened.

The two techniques available to monitor the end of an I/O operation are called the *polling mode* and the *interrupt mode*.

Polling mode

According to this technique, the CPU checks (polls) the device's status register repeatedly until its value signals that the I/O operation has been completed. We have already encountered a technique based on polling in the section "Spin Locks" in Chapter 11: when a processor tries to acquire a busy spin lock, it repeatedly polls the variable until its value becomes 0. However, polling applied to I/O operations is usually more elaborate, since the delays involved may be huge and the driver must remember to check for possible time-outs, too. In order to avoid wasting precious machine cycles, device drivers voluntarily relinquish the CPU after each polling operation so that other runnable processes can continue their execution:

```
for (;;) {
    if (read_status(device) & DEVICE_END_OPERATION)
        break;
    schedule();
    if (--count == 0)
        break;
}
```

The count variable, which was initialized before entering the loop, is decremented at each iteration, and thus can be used to implement a rough time-out mechanism. Alternatively, a more precise time-out mechanism could be implemented by reading the value of the tick counter jiffies at each iteration (see the section "PIT's Interrupt Service Routine" in Chapter 5) and comparing it with the old value read before starting the wait loop.

Interrupt mode

Interrupt mode can be used only if the I/O controller is capable of signaling, via an IRQ line, the end of an I/O operation. The device driver starts the I/O operation and invokes `interruptible_sleep_on()` or `sleep_on()`, passing as the parameter a pointer to the I/O device wait queue.

When the interrupt occurs, the interrupt handler invokes `wake_up()` to wake up all processes sleeping in the device wait queue. The awakened device driver can thus check the result of the I/O operation.

Time-out control is implemented through static or dynamic timers (see Chapter 5); the timer must be set to the right time before starting the I/O operation and removed when the operation terminates.

Accessing I/O Ports

The `in`, `out`, `ins`, and `outs` assembly language instructions access I/O ports. The following auxiliary functions are included in the kernel to simplify such accesses:

`inb()`, `inw()`, `inl()`
> Read 1, 2, or 4 consecutive bytes, respectively, from an I/O port. The suffix "b," "w," or "l" refers, respectively, to a byte (8 bits), a word (16 bits), and a long (32 bits).

`inb_p()`, `inw_p()`, `inl_p()`
> Read 1, 2, or 4 consecutive bytes, respectively, from an I/O port and then execute a "dummy" instruction to introduce a pause.

`outb()`, `outw()`, `outl()`
> Write 1, 2, or 4 consecutive bytes respectively to an I/O port.

`outb_p()`, `outw_p()`, `outl_p()`
> Write 1, 2, and 4 consecutive bytes, respectively, to an I/O port and then execute a "dummy" instruction to introduce a pause.

`insb()`, `insw()`, `insl()`
> Read sequences of consecutive bytes, in groups of 1, 2, or 4, respectively, from an I/O port. The length of the sequence is specified as a parameter of the functions.

`outsb()`, `outsw()`, `outsl()`
> Write sequences of consecutive bytes, in groups of 1, 2, or 4, respectively, to an I/O port.

While accessing I/O ports is simple, detecting which I/O ports have been assigned to I/O devices may not be, in particular for systems based on an ISA bus. Often a device driver must blindly write into some I/O port in order to probe the hardware device; if, however, this I/O port is already used by some other hardware device, a system crash could occur. In order to prevent such situations, the kernel keeps track of I/O ports assigned to each hardware device by means of the `iotable` table. Any device driver may thus use the following three functions:

`request_region()`
> Assigns a given interval of I/O ports to an I/O device

`check_region()`
> Checks whether a given interval of I/O ports is free or whether some of them have already been assigned to some I/O device

`release_region()`
> Releases a given interval of I/O ports previously assigned to an I/O device

The I/O addresses currently assigned to I/O devices can be obtained from the */proc/ ioports* file.

Requesting an IRQ

We have seen in the section "Dynamic Handling of IRQ Lines" in Chapter 4 that the assignment of IRQs to devices is usually made dynamically, right before using them, since several devices may share the same IRQ line. To make sure the IRQ is obtained when needed but not requested in a redundant manner when it is already in use, device drivers usually adopt the following schema:

- A usage counter keeps track of the number of processes that are currently accessing the device file. The counter is incremented in the **open** method of the device file and decremented in the **release** method.*

- The **open** method checks the value of the usage counter before the increment. If the counter is null, the device driver must allocate the IRQ and enable interrupts on the hardware device. Therefore, it invokes `request_irq()` and configures the I/O controller properly.

- The **release** method checks the value of the usage counter after the decrement. If the counter is null, no more processes are using the hardware device. If so, the method invokes `free_irq()`, thus releasing the IRQ line, and disables interrupts on the I/O controller.

Putting DMA to Work

As mentioned in the section "Direct Memory Access (DMA)," several I/O drivers make use of the Direct Memory Access Controller (DMAC) to speed up operations. The DMAC interacts with the device's I/O controller to perform a data transfer; as we shall see later, the kernel includes an easy-to-use set of routines to program the DMAC. The I/O controller signals to the CPU, via an IRQ, when the data transfer has finished.

---

* More precisely, the usage counter keeps track of the number of file objects referring to the device file, since clone processes could share the same file object.

When a device driver sets up a DMA operation for some I/O device, it must specify the memory buffer involved by using bus addresses. The kernel provides the `virt_to_bus` and `bus_to_virt` macros, respectively, to translate a linear address into a bus address and vice versa.

As with IRQ lines, the DMAC is a resource that must be assigned dynamically to the drivers that need it. The way the driver starts and ends DMA operations depends on the type of bus.

DMA for ISA bus

Each ISA DMAC can control a limited number of *channels*. Each channel includes an independent set of internal registers, so that the DMAC can control several data transfers at the same time.

Device drivers normally reserve and release the ISA DMAC in the following manner. As usual, the device driver relies on a usage counter to detect when a device file is no longer accessed by any process. The driver performs the following:

*   In the `open()` method of the device file, increment the device's usage counter. If the previous value was 0, the driver performs the following operations:

    a. Invokes `request_irq()` to allocate the IRQ line used by the ISA DMAC

    b. Invokes `request_dma()` to allocate a DMA channel

    c. Notifies the hardware device that it should use DMA and issue interrupts

    d. Allocates, if necessary, a storage area for the DMA buffer

*   When the DMA operation must be started, performs the following operations in the proper methods of the device file (typically, `read` and `write`):

    a. Invokes `set_dma_mode()` to set the channel to read or write mode.

    b. Invokes `set_dma_addr()` to set the bus address of the DMA buffer. (Only the 24 least-significant bits of the address are sent to the DMAC, so the buffer must be included in the first 16 MB of RAM.)

    c. Invokes `set_dma_count()` to set the number of bytes to be transferred.

    d. Invokes `enable_dma()` to enable the DMA channel.

    e. Puts the current process in the device's wait queue and suspends it. When the DMAC terminates the transfer operation, the device's I/O controller issues an interrupt and the corresponding interrupt handler wakes up the sleeping process.

    f. Once awakened, invokes `disable_dma()` to disable the DMA channel.

    g. Invokes `get_dma_residue()` to check whether all bytes have been transferred.

- In the `release` method of the device file, decrements the device's usage counter. If it becomes 0, execute the following operations:

  a. Disables the DMA and the corresponding interrupt on the hardware device

  b. Invokes `free_dma()` to release the DMA channel

  c. Invokes `free_irq()` to release the IRQ line used for DMA

DMA for PCI bus

Making use of DMA for a PCI bus is much simpler, since the DMAC is somewhat integrated into the I/O interface. As usual, in the open method, the device driver must allocate the IRQ line used for signaling the termination of the DMA operation. However, there is no need to allocate a DMA channel, since each hardware device directly controls the electrical signals of the PCI bus. To start a DMA operation, the device driver simply writes in some I/O port of the hardware device the bus address of the DMA buffer, the transfer direction, and the size of the data; the driver then suspends the current process. The `release` method releases the IRQ line when the file object is closed by the last process.

Device Controller's Local Memory

Several hardware devices include their own memory, which is often called *I/O shared memory*. For instance, all recent graphic cards include a few megabytes of RAM called a *frame buffer*, which is used to store the screen image to be displayed on the monitor.

Mapping addresses

Depending on the device and on the bus type, I/O shared memory in the PC's architecture may be mapped within three different physical address ranges:

For most devices connected to the ISA bus
The I/O shared memory is usually mapped into the physical addresses ranging from `0xa0000` to `0xfffff`; this gives rise to the "hole" between 640 KB and 1 MB mentioned in the section "Reserved Page Frames" of Chapter 2, *Memory Addressing*.

For some old devices using the VESA Local Bus (VLB)
This is a specialized bus mainly used by graphic cards: the I/O shared memory is mapped into the physical addresses ranging from `0xe00000` to `0xffffff`, that is between 14 MB and 16 MB. These devices, which further complicate the initialization of the paging tables, are going out of production.

For devices connected to the PCI bus
The I/O shared memory is mapped into very large physical addresses, well above the end of RAM's physical addresses. This kind of device is much simpler to handle.

Accessing the I/O shared memory

How 'does the kernel access an I/O shared memory location? Let's start with the PC's architecture, which is relatively simple to handle and then extend the discussion to other architectures.

Remember that kernel programs act on linear addresses, so the I/O shared memory locations must be expressed as addresses greater than PAGE_OFFSET. In the following discussion, we assume that PAGE_OFFSET is equal to 0xc0000000, that is, that the kernel linear addresses are in the fourth gigabyte.

Kernel drivers must translate I/O physical addresses of I/O shared memory locations into linear addresses in kernel space. In the PC architecture, this can be achieved simply by ORing the 32-bit physical address with the 0xc0000000 constant. For instance, suppose the kernel needs to store in t1 the value in the I/O location at physical address 0x000b0fe4 and in t2 the value in the I/O location at physical address 0xfc000000. One might think that the following statements could do the job:

```
t1 = *((unsigned char *)(0xc00b0fe4));
t2 = *((unsigned char *)(0xfc000000));
```

During the initialization phase, the kernel has mapped the available RAM's physical addresses into the initial portion of the fourth gigabyte of the linear address space. Therefore, the Paging Unit maps the 0xc00b0fe4 linear address appearing in the first statement back to the original I/O physical address 0x000b0fe4, which falls inside the "ISA hole" between 640 KB and 1 MB (see the section "Paging in Linux" in Chapter 2). This works fine.

There is a problem, however, for the second statement because the I/O physical address is greater than the last physical address of the system RAM. Therefore, the 0xfc000000 linear address does not necessarily correspond to the 0xfc000000 physical address. In such cases, the kernel page tables must be modified in order to include a linear address that maps the I/O physical address: this can be done by invoking the ioremap() function. This function, which is similar to vmalloc(), invokes get_vm_area() to create a new vm_struct descriptor (see the section "Descriptors of Noncontiguous Memory Areas" in Chapter 6, *Memory Management*) for a linear address interval having the size of the required I/O shared memory area. The ioremap() function then updates properly the corresponding page table entries of all processes.

The correct form for the second statement might therefore look like:

```
io_mem = ioremap(0xfb000000, 0x200000);
t2 = *((unsigned char *)(io_mem + 0x100000));
```

The first statement creates a new 2 MB linear address interval, starting from 0xfb000000; the second one reads the memory location having the 0xfc000000 address. To remove the mapping later, the device driver must use the iounmap() function.

Now let's consider architectures other than the PC. In this case, adding to an I/O physical address the 0xc0000000 constant to obtain the corresponding linear address does not always work. In order to improve kernel portability, Linux therefore includes the following macros to access the I/O shared memory:

readb, readw, readl
> Reads 1, 2, or 4 bytes, respectively, from an I/O shared memory location

writeb, writew, writel
> Writes 1, 2, or 4 bytes, respectively, into an I/O shared memory location

memcpy_fromio, memcpy_toio
> Copies a block of data from an I/O shared memory location to dynamic memory and vice versa

memset_io
> Fills an I/O shared memory area with a fixed value

The recommended way to access the 0xfc000000 I/O location is thus:

```
io_mem = ioremap(0xfb000000, 0x200000);
t2 = readb(io_mem + 0x100000);
```

Thanks to these macros, all dependences on platform-specific ways of accessing the I/O shared memory can be hidden.

Character Device Handling

Handling a character device is relatively easy, since no data buffering is needed and no disk caches are involved. Of course, character devices differ in their requirements: some of them must implement a sophisticated communication protocol to drive the hardware device, while others just have to read a few values from a couple of I/O ports of the hardware devices. For instance, the device driver of a multiport serial card device (a hardware device offering many serial ports) is much more complicated than the device driver of a bus mouse.

Let's briefly sketch out the functioning of a very simple character device driver, namely the driver of the Logitech bus mouse. It is associated with the */dev/logibm* character device file, which has major number 10 and minor number 0.

Suppose that a process opens the */dev/logibm* file; as explained in the section "VFS Handling of Device Files" earlier in this chapter, the VFS ends up invoking the **open** method of the device file operations common to all character devices having major number 10. This device class covers a series of heterogeneous devices, and hence the method, a function called **misc_open()**, installs yet a more specialized set of file operations according to the device's minor number. As the final result, the field **f_op** of the file object points to the **bus_mouse_fops** table, and the **open_mouse()** function is invoked. This function performs the following operations:

1. Checks whether the bus mouse is connected.

2. Requests the IRQ line used by the bus mouse, that is IRQ5, and registers the **mouse_interrupt()** Interrupt Service Routine.

3. Initializes a small **mouse** data structure of type **mouse_status**, which stores the information about the status of the bus mouse. This status information includes which buttons are pressed, along with the horizontal and vertical displacements of the mouse pointer after the last read of the device file.

4. Writes the value 0 in the **0x23e** control register to enable bus mouse interrupts (the Logitech bus mouse uses I/O ports from **0x23c** to **0x23f**).

The **mouse** data structure is filled asynchronously: every time the user changes the mouse position or presses a mouse button, the mouse controller generates an interrupt, and hence the **mouse_interrupt()** function is activated. It performs the following operations:

1. Asks the bus mouse device about its state by writing suitable commands in the **0x23e** control register and reading the corresponding values from the **0x23c** input register.

2. Updates the **mouse** data structure.

3. Writes the value 0 in the **0x23e** control register to reenable bus mouse interrupts (they are automatically disabled by the bus mouse device each time one of them occurs).

The process must read the */dev/logibm* file to get the mouse status. Each **read()** system call ends up invoking the **read_mouse()** function associated with the **read** method of the file operations. It performs the following operations:

1. Checks that the process requested at least 3 bytes and returns **-EINVAL** otherwise.

2. Checks whether the mouse status has changed after the last read operation of */dev/ logibm*; if not, return **-EAGAIN**.

3. Invokes **disable_irq()** to disable interrupt handling of IRQ5, and reads the values stored in the **mouse** data structure; then reenables interrupt handling of IRQ5 by invoking **enable_irq()**.

4. Writes into the User Mode buffer 3 bytes representing the mouse status (buttons status, horizontal and vertical displacements) after the last read operation.

5. If the process requested more than 3 bytes, fills the User Mode buffer with zeros.

6. Returns the number of written bytes.

Block Device Handling

Typical block devices like hard disks have very high average access times. Each operation requires several milliseconds to complete, mainly because the hard disk controller must move the heads on the disk surface to reach the exact position where the data is recorded. However, when the heads are correctly placed, data transfer can be sustained at rates of tens of megabytes per second.

In order to achieve acceptable performance, hard disks and similar devices transfer several adjacent bytes at once. In the following discussion, we'll say that groups of bytes are *adjacent* when they are recorded on the disk surface in such a manner that a single seek operation can access them.

The organization of Linux block device handlers is quite involved. We won't be able to discuss in detail all the functions that have been included in the kernel to support the handlers. But we'll outline the general software architecture and introduce the main data structures. Kernel support for block device handlers includes the following features:

- Offers a uniform interface through the VFS

- Implements efficient read-ahead of disk data

- Provides disk caching for the data

The kernel basically distinguishes two kinds of I/O data transfer:

Buffer I/O operations
> Here the transferred data is kept in buffers, the kernel's generic memory containers for disk-based data. Each buffer is associated with a specific block identified by a device number and a block number. Linux misleadingly calls these operations "synchronous I/O operations." The term "synchronous" is not well-suited in this context because a buffer I/O operation is really asynchronous: in other words, the kernel control path that starts the operation may continue its execution without waiting for the operation to end. The term is probably inherited from very old versions of Linux.

Page I/O operations
> Here the transferred data is kept in page frames; each page frame contains data belonging to a regular file. Since this data is not necessarily stored in adjacent disk blocks, it is identified by the file's inode and by an offset within the file. Again, Linux inappropriately calls these operations "asynchronous I/O operations."

Buffer I/O operations are most often used either when a process directly reads a block device file or when the kernel reads particular types of blocks in a filesystem (for example, a block containing inodes or a superblock). In Linux 2.2 buffer operations are also used to write disk-based regular files. Page I/O operations are used mainly for reading regular files, file memory mapping, and swapping. Both kinds of I/O data transfer rely on the same driver to access a block device, but the kernel uses different algorithms and buffering techniques with them.

Sectors, Blocks, and Buffers

Each data transfer operation for a block device acts on a group of adjacent bytes called a *sector*. In most disk devices, the size of a sector is 512 bytes, although a few devices have recently appeared that make use of larger sectors (1024 and 2048 bytes). Notice that the sector should be considered the basic unit of data transfer: it is never possible to transfer less than a sector, although most disk devices are capable of transferring several adjacent sectors at once.

The kernel stores the sector size of each hardware block device in a table named `hardsect_size`. Each element in the table is indexed by the major number and the minor number of the corresponding block device file. Thus, `hardsect_size[3][2]` represents the sector size of */dev/hda2*, the second primary partition of the first IDE disk (see Table 13-1). If `hardsect_size[M]` is NULL, all block devices sharing the major number *M* have a standard sector size of 512 bytes.

Block device drivers transfer a large number of adjacent bytes called a *block* in a single operation. A block should not be confused with a sector: the sector is the basic unit of data transfer for the hardware device, while the block is simply a group of adjacent bytes involved in an I/O operation requested by a device driver.

In Linux, the block size must be a power of 2 and cannot be larger than a page frame. Moreover, it must be a multiple of the sector size, since each block must include an integral number of sectors. Therefore, on PC architecture, the permitted block sizes are 512, 1024, 2048, and 4096 bytes. The same block device driver may operate with several block sizes, since it has to handle a set of device files sharing the same major number, while each block device file has its own predefined block size. For instance, a block device driver could handle a hard disk with two partitions containing an Ext2 filesystem and a swap area (see Chapter 16, *Swapping: Methods for Freeing Memory*, and Chapter 17, *The Ext2 Filesystem*). In this case, the device driver makes use of two different block sizes: 1024 bytes for the Ext2 partition* and 4096 bytes for the swap partition.

The kernel stores the block size in a table named `blksize_size`; each element in the table is indexed by the major number and the minor number of the corresponding block device file. If `blksize_size[M]` is NULL, all block devices sharing the major number *M* have a standard block size of 1024 bytes.

Each block requires its own *buffer*, which is a RAM memory area used by the kernel to store the block's content. When a device driver reads a block from disk, it fills the corresponding buffer with the values obtained from the hardware device; similarly,

---

* 1024 is the standard Ext2 block size, although other block sizes are allowed.

when a device driver writes a block on disk, it updates the corresponding group of adjacent bytes on the hardware device with the actual values of the associated buffer. The size of a buffer always matches the size of the corresponding block.

An Overview of Buffer I/O Operations

Figure 13-3 illustrates the architecture of a generic block device driver and the main components that interact with it when servicing a buffer I/O operation.

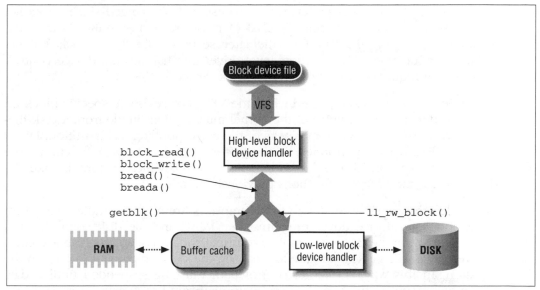

Figure 13-3. Block device handler architecture for buffer I/O operations

A block device driver is usually split in two parts: a high-level driver, which interfaces with the VFS layer, and a low-level driver, which handles the hardware device.

Suppose a process issues a `read()` or `write()` system call on a device file. The VFS executes the **read** or **write** method of the corresponding file object, and thus invokes a procedure within the high-level block device handler. This procedure performs all actions related to the read or write request that are specific to the hardware device. The kernel offers two general functions called `block_read()` and `block_write()` that take care of almost everything (see the section "The block_read() and block_write() Functions" later in this chapter). Therefore, in most cases, the high-level hardware device drivers must do nothing, and the **read** and **write** methods of the device file point, respectively, to `block_read()` and `block_write()`.

However, some block device handlers require their own customized high-level device drivers. A significant example is the device driver of the floppy disk: it must check that the disk in the drive has not been changed by the user since the last disk access; if a new disk has been inserted, the device driver must invalidate all buffers already filled with data of the old disk media.

Even when a high-level device driver includes its own `read` and `write` methods, they usually end up invoking `block_read()` and `block_write()`. These functions translate the access request involving an I/O device file into a request for some blocks from the corresponding hardware device. As we'll see in the section "The Buffer Cache" in Chapter 14, *Disk Caches*, the blocks required may already be in main memory, so both `block_read()` and `block_write()` invoke the `getblk()` function to check the cache first in case a block was prefetched or has stayed unchanged since an earlier access. If the block is not in the cache, `getblk()` must proceed to request it from the disk by invoking `ll_rw_block()` (see the later section "The ll_rw_block() Function"). This latter function activates a low-level driver that handles the device controller to perform the requested operation on the block device.

Buffer I/O operations are also triggered when the VFS accesses some specific block on a block device directly. For instance, if the kernel must read an inode from a disk filesystem, it must transfer the data from blocks of the corresponding disk partition. Direct access to specific blocks is performed by the `bread()` and `breada()` functions (see the later section "The bread() and breada() Functions"), which in turn invoke the `getblk()` and `ll_rw_block()` functions previously mentioned.

Since block devices are slow, buffer I/O data transfers are always handled asynchronously: the low-level device driver programs the DMAC and the disk controller and then terminates. When the transfer completes, an interrupt is issued, and the low-level device driver is activated a second time to clean up the data structures involved in the I/O operation. In this way, no kernel control path must be suspended until a data transfer completes (unless the kernel control path explicitly has to wait for some block of data).

The Role of Read-Ahead

Many disk accesses are sequential. As we shall see in Chapter 17, files are stored on disk in large groups of adjacent sectors, so that they can be retrieved quickly with few moves of the disk heads. When a program reads or copies a file, it usually accesses it sequentially, from the first byte to the last one. Therefore, many adjacent sectors on disk are likely to be fetched in several I/O operations.

Read-ahead is a technique that consists of reading several adjacent blocks of a block device in advance, before they are actually requested. In most cases, read-ahead significantly enhances disk performance, since it lets the disk controller handle fewer commands that refer to larger groups of adjacent sectors. Moreover, system responsiveness improves. A process that is sequentially reading a block device can get the requested data faster because the driver performs fewer disk accesses.

However, read-ahead is of no use for random accesses to block devices; in that case, it is actually detrimental since it tends to waste space in the disk caches with useless information. Therefore, the kernel stops read-ahead when it determines that the most recently issued I/O access is not sequential to the previous one. The `f_reada` field of the file object is a flag that is set when read-ahead is enabled for the corresponding file (or block device file) and cleared otherwise.

The kernel stores in a table named `read_ahead` the number of bytes (the number of standard 512-byte sectors, to be precise) to be read in advance when a device file is being read sequentially. A "zero" value specifies a default number of 8 512-byte sectors, that is, 4 KB. All block device files having the same major number share the same predefined number of 512-byte sectors to be read in advance; therefore, each element in `read_ahead` is indexed by the major device number.

The block_read() and block_write() Functions

The `block_read()` and `block_write()` functions are invoked by a high-level device driver whenever a process issues a read or write operation on a device file. For example, the *superformat* program formats a diskette by writing blocks into the */dev/fd0* device file. The `write` method of the corresponding file object invokes the `block_write()` function.

The `block_read()` and `block_write()` functions receive the following parameters:

`filp`
: Address of a file object associated with the device file.

`buf`
: Address of a memory area in User Mode address space. `block_read()` writes the data fetched from the block device into this memory area; conversely, `block_write()` reads the data to be written on the block device from the memory area.

`count`
: Number of bytes to be transferred.

`ppos`
: Address of a variable containing an offset in the device file; usually, this parameter points to `filp->f_pos`, that is, to the file pointer of the device file.

The `block_read()` function performs the following operations:

1. Derives the major number and the minor number of the block device from `filp->f_dentry->d_inode->i_rdev`.

2. Derives the block size of the device file from `blksize_size`.

3. Computes from `*ppos` and the block size the sequential number of the first block to be read on the device. Also computes the offset of the first byte to be read inside that block.

4. Derives the size of the block hardware device. This value is stored in a table named `blk_size`. As with similar data structures introduced earlier in the chapter, each element is indexed by the major number and the minor number of the corresponding device file and represents the size of the block device in units of 1024 bytes. If necessary, modifies `count` in order to prevent any read operation from going beyond the end of the device.

5. Computes the number of blocks to be read from the devices from a combination of `count`, the block size, and the offset inside the first block. If `filp->f_reada` is set, also takes into consideration the number of blocks to be read in advance, which is specified in the `read_ahead` table.

6. For any block to be read, performs the following operations:

    a. Searches for the block in the buffer cache by using the `getblk()` function (see the section "The Buffer Cache" in Chapter 14). If it is not found, a new buffer is allocated and inserted into the cache.

    b. If the buffer does not contain valid data (for instance, because it has been allocated just now), starts a read operation by using the `ll_rw_block()` function (see the later section "The ll_rw_block( ) Function"), and suspends the current process until the data has been transferred in the buffer.

    c. If the block has been requested by the process, that is, if it is not read in advance, copies the buffer content into the user memory area pointed to by `buf`.

    Actually, the algorithm is more elaborate than what we've just explained, since it is optimized to make maximum use of the buffer cache. The function operates by requesting large groups of blocks from the low-level driver at once; it does not wait until all of them have been transferred before searching for the next group of blocks in the buffer cache. However, the final result is the same: after this step, all buffers of the blocks involved contain valid data, and the bytes requested by the user process are copied into the user memory area.

7. Adds to `*ppos` the number of bytes copied into the user memory area.

8. Sets the `filp->f_reada` flag, so that the read-ahead mechanism will be used next time (unless the process modifies the file pointer, in which case the flag is cleared).

9. Returns the number of bytes copied in the user memory area.

The `block_write()` function is similar to `block_read()`, so we won't describe it in detail. However, some important differences should be underlined:

• Before starting the write operation, the `block_write()` function must check whether the block hardware device is read-only and, in this case, returns an error code. This happens, for example, when attempting to write on a block device file associated with a CD-ROM disk. The `ro_bits` table includes a bit for each block hardware device: a bit is set if the corresponding device cannot be written and cleared if it can be written.

- The `block_write()` function must check the offset of the first byte to be written inside the first block. If the offset is not null and the buffer cache does not already contain valid data for the first block, the function must read the block from disk before rewriting it. In fact, since the block device driver operates on whole blocks, the portions of the first block that precedes the bytes being written must be preserved by the write operation. Similarly, the function must also read from disk the last block to be written before rewriting it, unless the last byte to be written falls in the last position of the last block.

- The `block_write()` function does not necessarily invoke `ll_rw_block()` to force a write to disk. Usually, it just marks the buffers of the blocks to be written as "dirty," thus deferring the actual updating of the corresponding sectors on disk (see the section "Writing Dirty Buffers to Disk" in Chapter 14). However, the function does invoke `ll_rw_block()` if the call opening the block device file has specified the `O_SYNC` flag. In this case, the calling process wants to wait (sleep) until the data has been physically written in the hardware device, so that the disk always reflects what the process thinks it does.

The bread() and breada() Functions

The `bread()` function checks whether a specific block is already included in the buffer cache; if not, the function reads the block from a block device. `bread()` is widely used by filesystems to read from disk bitmaps, inodes, and other block-based data structures. (Recall that `block_read()` is used instead of `bread()` when a process wants to read a block device file.) The function receives as parameters the device identifier, the block number, and the block size, and performs the following operations:

1. Invokes the `getblk()` function to search for the block in the buffer cache; if the block is not included in the cache, `getblk()` allocates a new buffer for it.

2. If the buffer already contains up-to-date data, terminates.

3. Invokes `ll_rw_block()` to start the read operation.

4. Waits until the data transfer completes. This is done by invoking a function named `wait_on_buffer()`, which inserts the `current` process in the `b_wait` wait queue and suspends the process until the buffer is unlocked.

`breada()` is very similar to `bread()`, but it also reads in advance some extra blocks in addition to the one required. Notice that there is no function that directly writes some block to disk. Write operations are never critical for system performance, thus are always deferred (see the section "Writing Dirty Buffers to Disk" in Chapter 14).

Buffer Heads

The *buffer head* is a descriptor of type **buffer_head** associated with each buffer. It contains all the information needed by the kernel to know how to handle the buffer; thus, before operating on each buffer the kernel checks its buffer head.

The buffer head fields are listed in Table 13-2. The **b_data** field of each buffer head stores the starting address of the corresponding buffer. Since a page frame may store several buffers, the **b_this_page** field points to the buffer head of the next buffer in the page. This field facilitates the storage and retrieval of entire page frames. The **b_blocknr** field stores the *logical block number*, that is, the index of the block inside the disk partition.

Table 13-2. The Fields of a Buffer Head

Type	Field	Description
unsigned long	b_blocknr	Logical block number
unsigned long	b_size	Block size
kdev_t	b_dev	Virtual device identifier
kdev_t	b_rdev	Real device identifier
unsigned long	b_rsector	Number of initial sector in real device
unsigned long	b_state	Buffer status flags
unsigned int	b_count	Block usage counter
char *	b_data	Pointer to buffer
unsigned long	b_flushtime	Flushing time for buffer
struct wait_queue *	b_wait	Buffer wait queue
struct buffer_head *	b_next	Next item in collision hash list
struct buffer_head **	b_pprev	Previous item in collision hash list
struct buffer_head *	b_this_page	Per-page buffer list
struct buffer_head *	b_next_free	Next item in list
struct buffer_head *	b_prev_free	Previous item in list
unsigned int	b_list	LRU list including the buffer
struct buffer_head *	b_reqnext	Request's buffer list
void (*)()	b_end_io	I/O completion method
void (*)	b_dev_id	Specialized device driver data

The **b_state** field stores the following flags:

BH_Uptodate
> Set if the buffer contains valid data. The value of this flag is returned by the **buffer_uptodate()** function.

BH_Dirty
>   Set if the buffer is dirty, that is, if it contains data that must be written to the block device. The value of this flag is returned by the `buffer_dirty()` function.

BH_Lock
>   Set if the buffer is locked, which happens if the buffer is involved in a disk transfer. The value of this flag is returned by the `buffer_locked()` function.

BH_Req
>   Set if the corresponding block has been requested (see next section) and has valid (up-to-date) data. The value of this flag is returned by the `buffer_req()` function.

BH_Protected
>   Set if the buffer is protected (protected buffers never get freed). The value of this flag is returned by the `buffer_protected()` function. This flag is used only to implement RAM disks on top of the buffer cache.

The `b_dev` field identifies the virtual device containing the block stored in the buffer, while the `b_rdev` field identifies the real device. This distinction, which is meaningless for simple hard disks, has been introduced to model RAID (Redundant Array of Independent Disks) storage units consisting of several disks operating in parallel. For reasons of safety and efficiency, files stored in a RAID array are scattered across several disks that the applications think of as a single logical disk. Besides the `b_blocknr` field representing the logical block number, it is thus necessary to specify the specific disk unit in the `b_rdev` field, and the corresponding sector number in the `b_rsector` field.

Block Device Requests

Although block device drivers are able to transfer a single block at a time, the kernel does not perform an individual I/O operation for each block to be accessed on disk: this would lead to poor disk performances, since locating the physical position of a block on the disk surface is quite time-consuming. Instead, the kernel tries, whenever possible, to cluster several blocks and handle them as a whole, thus reducing the average number of head movements.

When a process, the VFS layer, or any other kernel component wishes to read or write a disk block, it actually creates a *block device request*. That request essentially describes the requested block and the kind of operation to be performed on it (read or write). However, the kernel does not satisfy a request as soon as it is created: the I/O operation is just scheduled and will be performed at a later time. This artificial delay is paradoxically the crucial mechanism for boosting the performance of block devices. When a new block data transfer is requested, the kernel checks whether it can be satisfied by slightly enlarging a previous request that is still waiting, that is, whether the new request can be satisfied without further seek operations. Since disks tend to be accessed sequentially, this simple mechanism is very effective.

Deferring requests complicates block device handling. For instance, suppose that a process opens a regular file and, consequently, a filesystem driver wants to read the corresponding inode from disk. The high-level block device driver puts the request on a queue and the process is suspended until the block storing the inode is transferred. However, the high-level block device driver cannot be blocked, because any other process trying to access the same disk would be blocked as well.

In order to keep the block device driver from being suspended, each I/O operation is being processed asynchronously, as already mentioned in the section "An Overview of Buffer I/O Operations." Thus, no kernel control path is forced to wait until a data transfer completes. In particular, block device drivers are interrupt-driven (see the section "Monitoring I/O Operations" earlier in this chapter), so that the high-level driver can terminate its execution as soon as it has issued the block request. The low-level driver, which is activated at a later time, invokes a so-called *strategy routine*, which takes the request from a queue and satisfies it by issuing suitable commands to the disk controller. When the I/O operation terminates, the disk controller raises an interrupt and the corresponding handler invokes the strategy routine again, if necessary, to process another request in the queue.

Each block device driver maintains its own *request queues*; there should be one request queue for each physical block device, so that the requests can be ordered in such a way as to increase disk performance. The strategy routine can thus sequentially scan the queue and service all requests with the minimum number of head movements.

Each block device request is represented by a *request descriptor*, which is stored in the `request` data structure illustrated in Table 13-3. The direction of the data transfer is stored in the `cmd` field: it is either READ (from block device to RAM) or WRITE (from RAM to block device). The `rq_status` field is used to specify the status of the request: for most block devices, it is simply set either to RQ_INACTIVE (request descriptor not in use) or to RQ_ACTIVE (valid request, to be serviced or already being serviced by the low-level device driver).

Table 13-3. The Fields of a Request Descriptor

Type	Field	Description
int	rq_status	Request status
kdev_t	rq_dev	Device identifier
int	cmd	Requested operation
int	errors	Success or failure code
unsigned long	sector	First sector number
unsigned long	nr_sector	Number of sectors of request
unsigned long	current_nr_sector	Number of sectors of current block
char *	buffer	Memory area for I/O transfer

Table 13-3. The Fields of a Request Descriptor (continued)

Type	Field	Description
struct semaphore *	sem	Request semaphore
struct buffer_head *	bh	First buffer descriptor
struct buffer_head *	bhtail	Last buffer descriptor
struct request *	next	Request queue link

The request may encompass many adjacent blocks on the same device. The `rq_dev` field identifies the block device, while the `sector` field specifies the number of the first sector corresponding to the first block in the request. Both `nr_sector` and `current_nr_sector` specify the number of sectors to be transferred. As we'll later see in the section "Low-Level Request Handling," the `sector`, `nr_sector`, and `current_nr_sector` fields could be dynamically updated while the request is being serviced.

All buffer heads of the blocks in the request are collected in a simply linked list. The `b_reqnext` field of each buffer head points to the next element in the list, while the `bh` and `bhtail` fields of the request descriptor point, respectively, to the first element and the last element in the list.

The `buffer` field of the request descriptor points to the memory area used for the actual data transfer. If the request involves a single block, `buffer` is just a copy of the `b_data` field of the buffer head. However, if the request encompasses several blocks whose buffers are not consecutive in memory, the buffers are linked through the `b_reqnext` fields of their buffer heads as shown in Figure 13-4. On a read, the low-level device driver could choose to allocate a large memory area referred by `buffer`, read all sectors of the request at once, and then copy the data into the various buffers. Similarly, for a write, the low-level device driver could copy the data from many nonconsecutive buffers into a single memory area referred by `buffer` and then perform the whole data transfer at once.

Figure 13-4 illustrates a request descriptor encompassing three blocks. The buffers of two of them are consecutive in RAM, while the third buffer is by itself. The corresponding buffer heads identify the logical blocks on the block device; the blocks must necessarily be adjacent. Each logical block includes two sectors. The `sector` field of the request descriptor points to the first sector of the first block on disk, and the `b_reqnext` field of each buffer head points to the next buffer head.

The kernel statically allocates a fixed number of request descriptors to handle all the requests for block devices: there are `NR_REQUEST` descriptors (usually 128) stored in the `all_requests` array. Since the efficiency of read operations have a larger impact on system performance than does the efficiency of write operations (because the data to be read is probably needed for some computation to progress), the last third of request descriptors in `all_requests` is reserved for read operations.

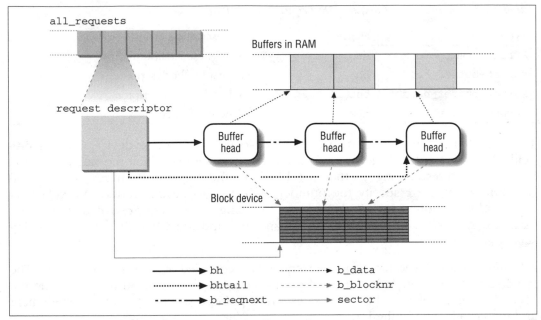

Figure 13-4. A request descriptor and its buffers and sectors

The fixed number of request descriptors may become, under very heavy loads and high disk activity, a bottleneck. A dearth of free descriptors may force processes to wait until an ongoing data transfer terminates. Thus, a `wait_for_request` wait queue is used to queue processes waiting for a free `request` element. The `get_request_wait()` tries to get a free request descriptor and puts the current process to sleep in the wait queue if none is found; the `get_request()` function is similar but simply returns `NULL` if no free request descriptor is available.

Request Queues and Block Device Driver Descriptors

A request queue is a simply linked list whose elements are request descriptors. The **next** field in each request descriptor points to the next item in the queue and is null for the last element. The list is usually ordered first according to the device identifier and next according to the number of the initial sector.

As mentioned earlier, device drivers usually have one request queue for each disk they serve. However, some device drivers have just one request queue that includes the requests for all physical devices handled by the driver. This approach simplifies the design of the driver but degrades overall performances, since no simple ordering strategy can be imposed on the queue.

The address of the request being serviced, together with a few other pieces of relevant information, are stored in a descriptor associated with each block device driver. The descriptor is a data structure of type `blk_dev_struct`, whose fields are listed in

Table 13-4. The descriptors for all the block devices are stored in the `blk_dev` table, which is indexed by the major number of the block device.

Table 13-4. The Fields of a Block Device Driver Descriptor

Type	Field	Description
`void *(*)(void)`	`request_fn`	Strategy routine
`void *`	`data`	Driver's private data common queue
`struct request`	`plug`	Dummy plug request
`struct request *`	`current_request`	Current request in single common queue
`struct request **(*)(kdev_t)`	`queue`	Method for getting a request from one of the queues
`struct tq_struct`	`plug_tq`	Plug task queue element

If the block device driver has a unique request queue for all physical block devices, the `queue` field is null and the `current_request` field points to the descriptor of the request being serviced in the queue. If the queue is empty, `current_request` is null.

Conversely, if the block device driver maintains several queues, the `queue` field points to a custom driver method that receives the identifier of the block device file, selects one of the queues according to the device number, then returns the address of the descriptor of the request being serviced, if any. In this case, the `current_request` field points to the descriptor of the request being serviced, if any. (There can be at most one request at a time, since the same device driver does not allow requests to be processed concurrently even if they refer to different disks.)

The `request_fn()` field contains the address of the driver's strategy routine, the crucial function in the low-level block device driver that actually interacts with the physical block device (usually the disk controller) in order to start the data transfer specified by a request in the queue.

The ll_rw_block() Function

The `ll_rw_block()` function creates a block device request; as we have seen earlier in this chapter, it is invoked from several places in the kernel and device drivers. It receives the following parameters:

- The type of operation, `rw`, whose value can be READ, WRITE, READA, or WRITEA. The last two operation types differ from the former in that the function does not block when no request descriptor is available.

- The number, `nr`, of blocks to be transferred.

- A `bh` array of `nr` pointers to buffer heads describing the blocks (all of them must have the same block size and must refer to the same block device).

The buffer heads have been previously initialized, so each specifies the block number, the block size, and the virtual device identifier (see the earlier section "Buffer Heads"). All blocks must belong to the same virtual device.

The function enters a loop considering all non-null elements of the bh array. For each buffer head, it performs the following actions:

1. Checks that the block size b_size matches the block size of the virtual device b_dev.

2. Sets the real device identifier (usually just sets b_rdev to be b_dev).

3. Sets the sector number b_rsector according to the block number and the block size.

4. If the operation is WRITE or WRITEA, checks that the block device is not read-only.

5. Sets the BH_Req flag of the buffer head to show other kernel control paths that the block has been requested.

6. Invokes the make_request() function, passing to it the real device's major number, the type of I/O operation, and the address of the buffer head.

The make_request() function, in turn, performs the following operations:

1. Sets the BH_Lock flag of the buffer head.

2. Checks that b_rsector does not exceed the number of sectors of the block device.

3. If the block must be read, checks that it is not already valid (that is, the BH_Uptodate flag must be off). If the block must be written, checks that it is actually dirty (that is, the BH_Dirty flag must be on). If either one of these conditions does not hold, returns without requesting the data transfer, because it is really useless.

4. Disables local interrupts and gets the io_request_lock spin lock (see the section "Spin Locks" in Chapter 11).

5. Invokes the queue method, if defined, or reads the current_request field in the block device descriptor to get the address of the real device's request queue.

6. Performs one of the following substeps:

   a. If the request queue is empty, inserts a new request descriptor in it and schedules activation of the strategy routine at a later time.

   b. If the request queue is not empty, inserts a new request descriptor in it, trying to cluster it with other requests already queued. As we'll see shortly, there is no need to schedule the activation of the strategy routine.

Let's look closer at the last two substeps.

Scheduling the activation of the strategy routine

As we saw earlier, it's expedient to delay activation of the strategy routine in order to increase the chances of clustering requests for adjacent blocks. The delay is accomplished through a technique known as device plugging and unplugging.

If the real device's request queue is empty and the device is not already plugged, `make_request()` does a *device plugging*: it sets the `current_request` field of the block device driver descriptor to the address of a dummy request descriptor, namely, the `plug` field of the same block device driver descriptor. The function then allocates a new request descriptor and initializes it with the information read from the buffer head. Next, `make_request()` inserts the new request descriptor into the proper real device's request queue. If there is just one queue, the request is inserted into the queue right after the dummy element consisting of the `plug` field in the block device descriptor. Finally, `make_request()` inserts the `plug_tq` task queue descriptor (statically included in the block device driver descriptor) in the `tq_disk` task queue (see the section "Bottom Half" in Chapter 4) to cause the device's strategy routine to be activated later. Actually, the task queue element refers to the `unplug_device()` function, which executes the device's strategy routine.

The kernel checks periodically whether the `tq_disk` task queue contains any `plug_tq` task queue elements. This occurs in a kernel thread such as *kswapd* and *bdflush* or when the kernel must wait for some resource related to block device drivers, such as buffers or request descriptors. During the `tq_disk` check, the kernel removes any element in the queue and executes the corresponding `unplug_device()` function. This activity is referred to as *unplugging* the device.

Extending the request queue

If the request queue is not empty, the low-level block device driver keeps handling requests until the queue has been emptied (see the next section), so `make_request()` does not have to schedule the activation of the strategy routine.

In this case, `make_request()` just modifies the request queue by adding a new element or by merging the new request with existing elements; the second case is known as *block clustering*.

Block clustering is implemented only for blocks belonging to certain block devices, namely the EIDE and SCSI hard disks, the floppy disk, and a few others. Moreover, a block can be included in a request only if all the following conditions are satisfied:

- The block to be inserted belongs to the same block device as the other blocks in the request and is adjacent to them: it either immediately precedes the first block in the request or immediately follows the last block in the request.

- The blocks in the request have the same I/O operation type (READ or WRITE) as the block to be inserted.

- The extended request does not exceed the allowed maximum number of sectors. This value is stored in the `max_sectors` table, which is indexed by the major number and the minor number of the block device. The default value is 244 sectors.

- The request is not currently being handled by the low-level device driver.

The `make_request()` function scans all the requests in the queue. If one of them satisfies all the conditions just mentioned, the buffer head is inserted in the request's list, and the fields of the `request` data structure are updated. If the block was appended to the end of a request, the function also tries to merge this request with the next element of the queue. Nothing else has to be done, and hence `make_request()` releases the `io_request_lock` spin lock and terminates.

Conversely, if no existing request can include the block, `make_request()` allocates a new request descriptor* and initializes it properly with the information read from the buffer head.

Finally, `make_request()` invokes the `add_request()` function, which inserts the new request in the proper position in the request queue, according to its initial sector number. The `io_request_lock` spin lock is then released and the execution terminates.

Low-Level Request Handling

We have now reached the lowest level of Linux's block device–handling architecture: this level is implemented by the strategy routine, which interacts with the physical block device in order to satisfy the requests collected in the queue.

As mentioned earlier, the strategy routine is usually started after inserting a new request in an empty request queue. Once activated, the low-level block device driver should handle all requests in the queue and terminate when the queue is empty.

A naive implementation of the strategy routine could be the following: for each element in the queue, interact with the block device controller to service the request and wait until the data transfer completes, then remove the serviced request from the queue and proceed with the next one.

Such an implementation is not very efficient. Even assuming that data can be transferred using DMA, the strategy routine must suspend itself while waiting for I/O completion, and hence an unrelated user process would be heavily penalized. (The strategy routine does not necessarily execute on behalf of the process that has requested the I/O operation but at some random later time, since it is activated by means of the `tq_disk` task queue.)

Therefore, many low-level block device drivers adopt the following schema:

---

* If there is no free request descriptor, the current process is suspended until a request descriptor is freed.

- The strategy routine handles the current request in the queue and sets up the block device controller so that it raises an interrupt when the data transfer completes. Then the strategy routine terminates.

- When the block device controller raises the interrupt, the interrupt handler activates a bottom half. The bottom half handler removes the request from the queue and reexecutes the strategy routine to service the next request in the queue.

Basically, low-level block device drivers can be further classified into the following:

- Drivers that service each block in a request separately

- Drivers that service several blocks in a request together

Drivers of the second type are much more complicated to design and implement than drivers of the first type. Indeed, although the sectors are adjacent on the physical block devices, the buffers in RAM are not necessarily consecutive. Therefore, any such driver may have to allocate a temporary area for the DMA data transfer, then perform a memory-to-memory copy of the data between the temporary area and each buffer in the request's list.

Since clustered requests refer to adjacent blocks on disk, they improve the performance of both types of drivers because the requests may be serviced by issuing fewer seek commands. Transferring several blocks from disk at once is not as effective in boosting disk performance.

The kernel doesn't offer any support for the second type of drivers: they must handle the request queues and the buffer head lists on their own. The choice to leave the job up to the driver is not capricious or lazy. Each physical block device is inherently different from all others (for example, a floppy driver groups blocks in disk tracks and transfers a whole track in a single I/O operation), so making general assumptions on how to service each clustered request would make very little sense.

However, the kernel offers a limited degree of support for the low-level block device drivers in the first class. So we'll spend a little more time on such drivers.

A typical strategy routine should perform the following actions:

1. Get the current request from a request queue. If all request queues are empty, terminate the routine.

2. Check that the current request has consistent information. In particular, compare the major number of the block device with the value stored in the `rq_rdev` field of the request descriptor. Moreover, check that the first buffer head in the list is locked (that is, the `BH_Lock` flag has been set by `make_request()`).

3. Program the block device controller for the data transfer of the first block. The data transfer direction can be found in the `cmd` field of the request descriptor and the address of the buffer in the `buffer` field, while the initial sector number and

the number of sectors to be transferred are stored in the `sector` and `current_nr_sectors` fields, respectively.* Also, set up the block device controller so that an interrupt is raised when the DMA data transfer completes.

4. If the routine is handling a block device file for which `ll_rw_block()` accomplishes block clustering, increment the `sector` field and decrement the `nr_sectors` field of the request descriptor to keep track of the blocks to be transferred.

The interrupt handler associated with the termination of the DMA data transfer for the block device should invoke (either directly or via a bottom half) the `end_request()` function. It receives as its parameter the value 1 if the data transfer succeeded and the value 0 if an error occurred. `end_request()` performs the following operations:

1. If an error occurred (parameter value is 0), updates the `sector` and `nr_sectors` fields so as to skip the remaining sectors of the block. In step 3a, the buffer content will also be marked as not up-to-date.

2. Removes the buffer head of the transferred block from the request's list.

3. Invokes the `b_end_io` method of the buffer head. When the `getblk()` function allocates the buffer head, it loads this field with the address of the `end_buffer_io_sync()` function, which performs two operations:

   a. Sets the `BH_Uptodate` flag of the buffer head to 1 or 0, according to the success or failure of the data transfer

   b. Clears the `BH_Lock` flag of the buffer head and wakes up all processes sleeping in the wait queue to which the `b_wait` field of the buffer head points

4. If there is another buffer head on the request's list, performs the following actions:

   a. Sets the `current_nr_sectors` field of the request descriptor to the number of sectors of the new block

   b. Sets the `buffer` field with the address of the new buffer (from the `b_data` field of the new buffer head)

5. Otherwise, if the request's list is empty, all blocks have been processed. Therefore, performs the following operations:

   a. Sets the current request pointer to the next element in the request queue

   b. Sets the `rq_status` field of the processed request to `RQ_INACTIVE`

   c. Wakes up all processes sleeping in the `wait_for_request` wait queue

After invoking `end_request()`, the low-level block device driver checks the value of the `current_request` field in the block device driver descriptor; if it is not `NULL`, the request queue is not empty, and the strategy routine is executed again. Notice that

---

* Recall that `current_nr_sectors` contains the number of sectors in the first block of the request, while `nr_sectors` contains the total number of sectors in the request.

`end_request()` actually performs two nested iterations: the outer one on the elements of the request queue and the inner one on the elements in the buffer head list of each request. The strategy routine is thus invoked once for each block in the request queue.

Page I/O Operations

Block devices transfer information one block at a time, while process address spaces (or to be more precise, memory regions allocated for the process) are defined as sets of pages. This mismatch can be hidden to some extent by using page I/O operations (see the section "Block Device Handling"). They may be activated in the following cases:

- A process issues a `read()` or `write()` system call on a regular file (see the section "Reading and Writing a Regular File" in Chapter 15, *Accessing Regular Files*).

- A process reads a location of a page that maps a file in memory (see the section "Memory Mapping" in Chapter 15).

- The kernel flushes some dirty pages related to a file memory mapping to disk (see the section "Flushing Dirty Memory Mapping Pages to Disk" in Chapter 15).

- When swapping in or swapping out, the kernel loads from disk or saves to disk the contents of whole page frames (see Chapter 16).

We'll use the rest of this chapter to describe how these operations are carried out.

Starting Page I/O Operations

A page I/O operation is activated by invoking the `brw_page()` function, which receives the following parameters:

`rw`
   Type of I/O operation (`READ` or `WRITE`)

`page`
   Address of a page descriptor

`dev`
   Block device number

`b`
   Array of logical block numbers

`size`
   Block size

`bmap`
   Flag specifying whether the block numbers in `b` were computed by using the `bmap` method of the inode operations (see the section "Inode Objects" in Chapter 12)

The page descriptor refers to the page involved in the page I/O operation. It must already be locked (PG_locked flag on) before invoking brw_page() so that no other kernel control path can access it. The page is considered as split into 4096/size buffers; the *i*th buffer in the page is associated with the block b[i] of device dev.

The function performs the following operations:

1. Invokes create_buffers() to allocate temporary buffer heads for all buffers included in the page (such buffer heads are called asynchronous; they will be discussed in the section "Buffer Head Data Structures" in Chapter 14). The function returns the address of the first buffer head, while the b_this_page field of each buffer head points to the buffer head of the next buffer in the page.

2. For each buffer head in the page, performs the following substeps:

   a. Initializes the buffer head fields; since it is an asynchronous buffer head, sets the b_end_io method to end_buffer_io_async().

   b. If the bmap parameter flag is not null, checks whether the buffer head refers to a block having number 0. This is because the bmap method of the inode operations uses block number 0 to represent a file hole (see Chapter 17). In this case, fills the buffer with zeros, sets the BH_Uptodate flag of the buffer head, and continues with the next asynchronous buffer head.

   c. Invokes find_buffer() to check whether the block associated with the buffer head is already present in memory (see the section "The Buffer Cache" in Chapter 14). If so, performs the following substeps:

      1. Increments the usage counter of the buffer head found in the cache.

      2. If the I/O operation is READ and if the buffer in the cache is not up-to-date, invokes ll_rw_block() to issue a READ request; then invokes wait_on_buffer() to wait for the I/O to complete. Notice that ll_rw_block() acts on the buffer head included in the buffer cache, and thus triggers a buffer I/O operation.

      3. If the I/O operation is READ, copies the data from the buffer in the cache into the page buffer.

      4. If the I/O operation is WRITE, copies the data from the page buffer into the buffer in the cache, and invokes mark_buffer_dirty() to set the BH_Dirty flag of the buffer head in the cache.

      5. Sets the BH_Uptodate field of the asynchronous buffer head, decrements the usage counter of the buffer head in the cache, and continues with the next asynchronous buffer head.

d. The block required is not in the cache. Therefore, if the I/O operation is a READ, clears the BH_Uptodate flag of the asynchronous buffer head; if it is a WRITE, sets the BH_Dirty flag.

e. Inserts the pointer to the asynchronous buffer head into a local array, and continues with the next asynchronous buffer head.

Now all asynchronous buffer heads have been considered.

3. If the local array of asynchronous buffer head pointers is empty, all requested blocks were included in the buffer cache, thus the page I/O operation is not necessary. In this case, performs the following substeps:

a. Clears the PG_locked flag of the page descriptor, thus unlocking the page frame.

b. Sets the PG_uptodate flag of the page descriptor.

c. Wakes up any process sleeping on the wait wait queue of the page descriptor.

d. Invokes free_async_buffers() to release the asynchronous buffer heads.

e. Invokes the after_unlock_page() function (see Chapter 16). This function releases the page frame if the PG_free_after flag of the page descriptor is set.

f. Returns the value 0.

4. If we have reached this point, the local array of asynchronous buffer head pointers is not empty, thus a page I/O operation is really necessary. Invokes ll_rw_block() to issue an rw request for all buffer heads included in the local array and immediately returns the value 0.

Terminating Page I/O Operations

The ll_rw_block() function activates the device driver of the block device being accessed (see the section "The ll_rw_block() Function"). As described in the earlier section "Low-Level Request Handling," the device driver performs the actual data transfer, and then invokes the b_end_io method of all asynchronous buffer heads that have been transferred. The b_end_io field points to the end_buffer_io_async() function, which performs the following operations:

1. Invokes the mark_buffer_uptodate() function, which in turn performs the following substeps:

a. Sets the BH_Uptodate flag of the asynchronous buffer head according to the result of the I/O operation.

b. If the BH_Uptodate flag is set, checks whether all other asynchronous buffer heads in the page are up-to-date; if so, sets the PG_uptodate flag of the page descriptor.

2. Clears the BH_Lock flag of the asynchronous buffer head.

3. If the `BH_Uptodate` flag is off, sets the `PG_error` flag of the page descriptor because an error occurred while transferring the block.

4. Decrements the usage counter of the asynchronous buffer head (it becomes 0).

5. Checks whether all asynchronous buffer heads that refer to the page have null usage counters. If so, all data transfers for the buffers in the page have been completed, thus performs the following substeps:

   a. Invokes the `free_async_buffers()` function to release all asynchronous buffer heads.

   b. Clears the `PG_locked` bit of the page descriptor, thus unlocking the page frame.

   c. Wakes up all processes sleeping in the `wait` wait queue of the page descriptor.

   d. Invokes the `after_unlock_page()` function (see Chapter 16). This function releases the page frame if the `PG_free_after` flag of the page descriptor is set.

Anticipating Linux 2.4

Linux 2.4 heavily changes how I/O device drivers are handled. The main improvement consists of a new Resource Management Subsystem used to allocate IRQ lines, DMA channels, I/O ports, and so on. Thanks to this new subsystem, Linux now fully supports hot-pluggable Plug-And-Play hardware devices, USB buses, and PCMCIA cards.

Linux 2.4 reorganizes the block device driver layer and adds support for the *Logical Volume Manager*. The Logical Volume Manager allows filesystems to span several disk partitions and to be resized dynamically. This new feature brings Linux closer to enterprise-class operating systems.

The new kernel introduces a class of character devices called *raw I/O devices*. These devices allow applications like DBMS to directly access disks without making use of the kernel caches.

Another significant addition is kernel support for Intelligent Input/Output (I2O) hardware. The goal of this new standard, derived from the PCI architecture, is to write OS-independent device drivers for several kind of devices like disks, SCSI devices, and network cards.

Finally, Linux 2.4 includes the *devfs* virtual filesystem, which replaces the old static */dev* directory of device files. Virtual files appear only when the corresponding device driver is present in the kernel. The device filenames have also been changed. As an example, all disc devices are placed under the */dev/discs* directory: */dev/hda* might become */dev/discs/disc0*, */dev/hdb* might become */dev/discs/disc1*, and so on. Users can still refer to the old name scheme by properly configuring a device management daemon.

CHAPTER FOURTEEN

DISK CACHES

This chapter deals with disk caches. It shows how Linux makes use of sophisticated techniques to improve system performances by reducing disk accesses as much as possible.

As mentioned in the section "The Common File Model" in Chapter 12, *The Virtual Filesystem*, a disk cache is a software mechanism that allows the system to keep in RAM some data normally stored on a disk, so that further accesses to that data can be satisfied quickly without accessing the disk.

Besides the dentry cache, which is used by the VFS to speed up the translation of a file pathname to the corresponding inode, two main disk caches—the buffer cache and the page cache—are used by Linux. Most of this chapter describes the buffer cache, and a short section near the end covers the page cache.

We learned in the section "Sectors, Blocks, and Buffers" in Chapter 13, *Managing I/O Devices*, that a buffer is a memory area containing the data of a disk block. Each block refers to physically adjacent bytes on the disk surface; the block size depends on the type of the filesystem it comes from. As suggested by its name, the *buffer cache* is a disk cache that stores buffers.

Conversely, the *page cache* is a disk cache storing page frames that contain data belonging to regular files. It is inherently different from the buffer cache, since page frames in the page cache do not necessarily correspond to physically adjacent disk blocks.

Buffer I/O operations (see the section "Block Device Handling" in Chapter 13) make use of the buffer cache only. Page I/O operations use the page cache and optionally the buffer cache as well. As we'll see in the following sections, both caches are implemented by making use of proper data structures storing pointers to buffer heads and page descriptors.

Table 14-1 shows how some widely used I/O operations make use of the buffer and page caches.

Table 14-1. Use of the Buffer Cache and Page Cache

I/O Operation	Cache	System Call	Kernel Function
Read a block device file[a]	Buffer	`read()`	`block_read()`
Write a block device file[a]	Buffer	`write()`	`block_write()`
Read an Ext2 directory[b]	Buffer	`getdents()`	`ext2_bread()`
Read an Ext2 regular file[b]	Page	`read()`	`generic_file_read()`
Write an Ext2 regular file[b]	Page, buffer	`write()`	`ext2_file_write()`
Access to memory-mapped file[c]	Page	None	`file_map_nopage()`
Access to swapped-out page[d]	Page	None	`do_swap_page()`

[a] See the section "The block_read() and block_write() Functions" in Chapter 13.
[b] See Chapter 17, *The Ext2 Filesystem*.
[c] See the section "Memory Mapping" in Chapter 15, *Accessing Regular Files*.
[d] See Chapter 16, *Swapping: Methods for Freeing Memory*.

For each type of I/O activity, the table also shows the system call required to start it (if any) and the main corresponding kernel function that handles it.

You'll notice in the table that accesses to memory-mapped files and swapped-out pages do not require system calls; they are transparent to the programmer. Once a file memory mapping has been set up and once swapping has been activated, the application program can access the mapped file or the swapped-out page as if it were present in memory. It is the kernel's responsibility to delay the process until the required page has been located on disk and brought into RAM.

The Buffer Cache

The whole idea behind the buffer cache is to relieve processes from having to wait for relatively slow disks to retrieve or store data. Thus, it would be counterproductive to write a lot of data at once; instead, data should be written piecemeal at regular intervals so that I/O operations have a minimal impact on the speed of the user processes and on response time experienced by human users.

The kernel maintains a lot of information about each buffer to help it pace the writes, including a "dirty" bit to indicate the buffer has been changed in memory and needs to be written and a timestamp to indicate how long the buffer should be kept in memory before being flushed to disk. Information on buffers is kept in buffer heads (introduced in the previous chapter), so these data structures require maintenance along with the buffers of user data themselves.

The size of the buffer cache may vary. Page frames are allocated on demand when a new buffer is required and one is not available. When free memory becomes scarce, as we shall see in Chapter 16, buffers are released and the corresponding page frames are recycled.

The buffer cache consists of two kinds of data structures:

- A set of buffer heads describing the buffers in the cache (see the section "Buffer Heads" in Chapter 13)

- A hash table to help the kernel quickly derive the buffer head that describes the buffer associated with a given pair of device and block numbers

Buffer Head Data Structures

As mentioned in the section "Buffer Heads" in Chapter 13, each buffer head is stored in a data structure of type `buffer_head`. These data structures have their own slab allocator cache called `bh_cachep`, which should not be confused with the buffer cache itself. The slab allocator cache is a memory cache (see the section "Identifying a Process" in Chapter 3, *Processes*) for the buffer head objects, meaning that it has no interaction with disks and is simply a way of managing memory efficiently.

In contrast, the buffer cache is a disk cache for the data in the buffers. The number of allocated buffer heads, that is, the number of objects obtained from the slab allocator, is stored in the `nr_buffer_heads` variable.

Each buffer used by a block device driver must have a corresponding buffer head that describes the buffer's current status. The converse is not true: a buffer head may be unused, which means it is not bound to any buffer. The kernel keeps a certain number of unused buffer heads to avoid the overhead of constantly allocating and deallocating memory.

In general, a buffer head may be in any one of the following states:

Unused buffer head
　　The object is available; the values of its fields are meaningless.

Buffer head for a free buffer
　　Its `b_data` field points to a free buffer, and its `b_dev` field has the value `B_FREE` (`0xffff`). Notice that the buffer is available, not the buffer head itself.

Buffer head for a cached buffer
　　Its `b_data` field points to a buffer stored in the buffer cache.

Asynchronous buffer head
　　Its `b_data` field points to a temporary buffer used to implement a page I/O operation (see the section "Page I/O Operations" in Chapter 13).

Strictly speaking, the buffer cache data structures include only pointers to buffer heads for a cached buffer. For sake of completeness, we shall examine the data structures and the methods used by the kernel to handle all kinds of buffer heads, not just those in the buffer cache.

The list of unused buffer heads

All unused buffer heads are collected in a simply linked list, whose first element is addressed by the `unused_list` variable. Each buffer head stores the address of the next list element in the `b_next_free` field. The current number of elements in the list is stored in the `nr_unused_buffer_heads` variable.

The list of unused buffer heads acts as a primary memory cache for the buffer head objects, while the `bh_cachep` slab allocator cache is a secondary memory cache. When a buffer head is no longer needed, it is inserted into the list of unused buffer heads. Buffer heads are released to the slab allocator (a preliminary step to letting the kernel free the memory associated with them altogether) only when the number of list elements exceeds `MAX_UNUSED_BUFFERS` (usually 36 elements). In other words, a buffer head in this list is considered as an allocated object by the slab allocator and as an unused data structure by the buffer cache.

A subset of `NR_RESERVED` (usually 16) elements in the list is reserved for page I/O operations. This is done to prevent nasty deadlocks caused by the lack of free buffer heads. As we shall see in Chapter 16, if free memory is scarce, the kernel can try to free a page frame by swapping out some page to disk. In order to do this, it requires at least one additional buffer head to perform the page I/O file operation. If the swapping algorithm fails to get a buffer head, it simply keeps waiting and lets writes to files proceed in order to free up buffers, since at least `NR_RESERVED` buffer heads are going to be released as soon as the ongoing file operations terminate.

The `get_unused_buffer_head()` function is invoked to get a new buffer head. It essentially performs the following operations:

1. Invokes the `recover_reusable_buffer_heads()` function (more on this later).

2. If the list of unused buffer heads has more than `NR_RESERVED` elements, removes one of them from the list and returns its address.

3. Otherwise, invokes `kmem_cache_alloc()` to allocate a new buffer head; if the operation succeeds, returns its address.

4. No free memory is available. If the buffer head has been requested for a buffer I/O operation, returns `NULL` (failure).

5. If this point is reached, the buffer head has been requested for a page I/O operation. If the list of unused buffer heads is not empty, removes one element and returns its address.

The `put_unused_buffer_head()` function performs the reverse operation, releasing a buffer head. It inserts the object in the list of unused buffer heads if that list has fewer than `MAX_UNUSED_BUFFERS` elements; otherwise, it releases the object to the slab allocator.

Lists of buffer heads for free buffers

Since Linux uses several block sizes (see the section "Sectors, Blocks, and Buffers" in Chapter 13), it uses several circular lists, one for each buffer size, to collect the buffer heads of free buffers. Such lists act as a memory cache. Thanks to them, a free buffer of a given size can be obtained quickly when needed, without relying on the time-consuming Buddy system procedures.

Seven lists of buffer heads for free buffers are defined; the corresponding buffer sizes are 512, 1024, 2048, 4096, 8192, 16384, and 32768 bytes. The size of a block, how-ever, cannot exceed the size of a page frame; only the first four lists are thus actually used on PC architecture.

The `free_list` array points to all seven lists; for each list, there is one element in the array to hold the address of the list's first element. The `BUFSIZE_INDEX` macro accepts a block size as input and derives from it the corresponding index in the array. For instance, buffer size 512 maps to `free_list[0]`, buffer size 1024 to `free_list[1]`, and so on. The lists are doubly linked by means of the `b_next_free` and `b_prev_free` fields of each buffer head.

Lists of buffer heads for cached buffers

When a buffer belongs to the buffer cache, the flags of the corresponding buffer head describe its current status (see the section "Buffer Heads" in Chapter 13). For instance, when a block not present in the cache must be read from disk, a new buffer is allo-cated and the `BH_Uptodate` flag of the buffer head is cleared because the buffer's contents are meaningless. While filling the buffer by reading from disk, the `BH_Lock` flag is set to protect the buffer from being reclaimed. If the read operation terminates successfully, the `BH_Uptodate` flag is set and the `BH_Lock` flag is cleared. If the block must be written to disk, the buffer content is modified and the `BH_Dirty` flag is set; the flag will be cleared only after the buffer is successfully written to disk.

Any buffer head associated with a used buffer is contained in a doubly linked list, implemented by means of the `b_next_free` and `b_prev_free` fields. There are three different lists, identified by an index defined as a macro (`BUF_CLEAN`, `BUF_DIRTY`, and `BUF_LOCKED`). We'll define these lists in a moment.

The three lists are introduced to speed up the functions that flush dirty buffers to disk (see the section "Writing Dirty Buffers to Disk" later in this chapter). For reasons of efficiency, a buffer head is not moved right away from one list to another when it changes status; this makes the following description a bit murky.

BUF_CLEAN

This list collects buffer heads of nondirty buffers (BH_Dirty flag is off). Notice that buffers in this list are not necessarily up-to-date, that is, they don't necessarily contain valid data. If the buffer is not up-to-date, it could even be locked (BH_Lock is on) and selected to be read from the physical device while being on this list. The buffer heads in this list are guaranteed only to be not dirty—in other words, the corresponding buffers are ignored by the functions that flush dirty buffers to disk.

BUF_DIRTY

This list mainly collects buffer heads of dirty buffers that have not been selected to be written into the physical device, that is, dirty buffers that have not yet been included in a block request for a block device driver (BH_Dirty is on and BH_Lock is off). However, this list could also include nondirty buffers, since in a few cases the BH_Dirty flag of a dirty buffer is cleared without flushing it to disk and without removing the buffer head from the list (for instance, whenever a floppy disk is removed from its drive without unmounting—an event that most probably leads to data loss, of course).

BUF_LOCKED

This list mainly collects buffer heads of dirty buffers that have been selected to be written to the block device (BH_Lock is on; BH_Dirty is clear because the add_request() function resets it before including the buffer head in a block request). However, when a write operation for some locked buffer has been completed, the low-level block device handler clears the BH_Lock flag without removing the buffer head from the list (see the section "Low-Level Request Handling" in Chapter 13). The buffer heads in this list are guaranteed only to be not dirty, or dirty but selected to be written.

For any buffer head associated with a used buffer, the b_list field of the buffer head stores the index of the list containing the buffer. The lru_list array* stores the address of the first element in each list, while the nr_buffers_type array stores the number of elements in each list.

The mark_buffer_dirty() and mark_buffer_clean() functions set and clear, respectively, the BH_Dirty flag of a buffer head. They also invoke the refile_buffer() function, which moves the buffer head into the proper list according to the value of the BH_Dirty and BH_Lock flags.

The hash table of cached buffer heads

The addresses of the buffer heads belonging to the buffer cache are inserted into a large hash table. Given a device identifier and a block number, the kernel can use the hash table to quickly derive the address of the corresponding buffer head, if one

---

* The name of the array derives from the abbreviation for Least Recently Used: in earlier versions of Linux, these lists were ordered according to the time when each buffer was last accessed.

exists. The hash table noticeably improves kernel performance because checks on buffer heads are frequent. Before starting a buffer I/O operation, the kernel must check whether the required block is already in the buffer cache; in this situation, the hash table lets the kernel avoid a lengthy sequential scan of the lists of cached buffers.

The hash table is stored in the `hash_table` array, which is allocated during system initialization and whose size depends on the amount of RAM installed on the system. As an example, for systems having 64 MB of RAM, `hash_table` is stored in 64 page frames and includes 65,536 buffer head pointers. As usual, entries causing a collision are chained in doubly linked lists implemented by means of the `b_next` and `b_pprev` fields of each buffer head. The total number of buffer heads in the hash table is stored in the `nr_hashed_buffer` variable.

The `find_buffer()` function receives as parameters the device number and the block number of a buffer head to be searched, hashes the values of the parameters and looks into the hash table to find the first element in the collision list, then checks the `b_dev` and `b_blocknr` fields of each element in the list and returns the address of the requested buffer head. If the buffer head is not in the cache, the function returns NULL.

The `insert_into_queues()` and `remove_from_queues()` functions insert an element into the hash table and remove it from the hash table, respectively. Both functions also take care of the buffer head's other data structures. For instance, when `insert_into_queues()` is invoked on a buffer head that should be cached, the function inserts it into both the proper `lru_list` and the hash table.

Lists of asynchronous buffer heads

Asynchronous buffer heads are used by page I/O file operations (see the section "Page I/O Operations" in Chapter 13). Even if a page I/O operation transfers a whole page, the actual data transfer is done one block at a time by the proper block device handler. In other words, the operation views the page frame containing the page as a group of buffers. The number of buffers in the group depends on the block size used: a 4 KB page frame may include, for instance, a group of four 1 KB buffers if the block size is 1024 or a single 4 KB buffer if the block size is 4096. During the page I/O operation, any buffer in the page must have its corresponding asynchronous buffer head. These buffer heads, however, are discarded as soon as the I/O operation completes, since from now on the page can be regarded as a whole and referenced by means of its page descriptor.

Since each page can consist of many buffers, the goal at this point is to try to find whether all buffers used by a page have been transferred.

As discussed in the section "Low-Level Request Handling" in Chapter 13, when a block transfer terminates, the interrupt handler invokes `end_request()`. This function takes care of removing the block request from the request queue and invokes the `b_end_io` method of all buffer heads included in the request. When a buffer is involved in a page I/O operation (instead of a buffer I/O operation), the `end_request()` field points to the `end_buffer_io_async()` function, which decrements the usage counter of the buffer head and checks whether all buffer heads in the page have a null usage counter. If they turn out to be unused, the function invokes `free_async_buffers()` to release the asynchronous buffer heads. Notice that the usage counter of an asynchronous buffer head is used as a flag specifying whether the buffer data has been transferred.

The `free_async_buffers()` function cannot, however, insert the asynchronous buffer heads into the unused list right away, since a customized block device driver's `end_request()` function might need to access them later. Therefore, `free_async_buffers()` inserts these buffer heads in a special list denoted as the *reuse list*, which is implemented by means of the `b_next_free` field. The `reuse_list` variable points to the first element of the list. Elements in the reuse list are moved into the unused list by `recover_reusable_buffer_heads()` just before getting a buffer head from the unused list. But this never happens before `end_request()` terminates, so there is no danger of a race condition involving accesses to the reuse list.

The getblk() Function

The `getblk()` function is the main service routine for the buffer cache. When the kernel needs to read or write the contents of some block of a physical device, it must check whether the buffer head for the required buffer is already included in the buffer cache. If the buffer is not there, the kernel must create a new entry in the cache. In order to do this, the kernel invokes `getblk()`, specifying as parameters the device identifier, the block number, and the block size. This function returns the address of the buffer head associated with the buffer.

Remember that having a buffer head in the cache does not imply that the data in the buffer is valid. (For instance, the buffer has yet to be read from disk.) Any function that reads blocks, such as `block_read()`, must check whether the buffer obtained from `getblk()` is up-to-date; if not, it must read the block first from disk before using the buffer.

The `getblk()` function performs the following operations:

1. Invokes `find_buffer()`, which makes use of the hash table to check whether the required buffer head is already in the cache.

2. If the buffer head has been found, increments its usage counter (`b_count` field) and returns its address. The next section explains the purpose of this field.

3. If the buffer head is not in the cache, a new buffer and a new buffer head must be allocated. Derives from the block size an index in the `free_list` array and checks whether the corresponding free list is empty.

4. If the free list is not empty, performs the following operations:

   a. Removes the first buffer head from the list

   b. Initializes the buffer head with the device identifier, the block number, and the block size; stores in the b_end_io field a pointer to the end_buffer_io_ sync() function;* and sets the b_count usage counter to 1

   c. Invokes insert_into_queues() to insert the buffer head into the hash table and the lru_list[BUF_CLEAN] list

   d. Returns the address of the buffer head

5. If the free list is empty, invokes the refill_freelist() function to replenish it (see the later section "Buffer Allocation").

6. Invokes find_buffer() to check once more whether some other process has put the buffer in the cache while the kernel control path was waiting for the completion of the previous step. If so, goes to step 2; otherwise, goes to step 3.

Buffer Usage Counter

The b_count field of the buffer head is a usage counter for the corresponding buffer. The counter is incremented right before any operation on the buffer and decremented right after. It acts mainly as a safety lock, since the kernel never destroys a buffer (or its contents) as long as it has a non-null usage counter. Instead, the cached buffers are examined either periodically or when the free memory becomes scarce, and only those buffers having null counters may be destroyed (see Chapter 16). In other words, a buffer with a null usage counter may belong to the buffer cache, but it cannot be determined for how long the buffer will stay in the cache.

When a kernel control path wishes to access a buffer, it should increment the usage counter first. This task is performed by the getblk() function, which is usually invoked to locate the buffer, so that the increment need not be done explicitly by higher-level functions. When a kernel control path stops accessing a buffer, it may invoke either brelse() or bforget() to decrement the corresponding usage counter.

The brelse() function receives as its parameter the address of a buffer head. It checks whether the buffer is dirty and, if so, writes the time when the buffer should be flushed in the b_flushtime field of the buffer head (see the later section "Writing Dirty Buffers to Disk"). The function also invokes refile_buffer() to move the buffer head to the proper list, if necessary. Finally, the PG_referenced flag of the page frame containing the buffer is set (see Chapter 16), and the b_count field is decremented.

---

* The buffer cache is reserved for buffer I/O operations, which require the b_end_io method to point to the end_ buffer_io_sync() function; asynchronous buffer heads are left out of the buffer cache.

The `bforget()` function is similar to `brelse()`, except that if the usage counter becomes 0 and the buffer is not locked (`BH_Lock` flag cleared), the buffer head is removed from the buffer cache and inserted into the proper list of free buffers. In other words, the data included in the buffer, as well the association between the buffer and a specific block of a physical device, is lost.

Buffer Allocation

For reasons of efficiency, buffers are not allocated as single memory objects. Instead, buffers are stored in dedicated pages called *buffer pages*. All the buffers within a single buffer page must be the same size. Depending on the block size, a buffer page can include eight, four, two, or just one buffer on the PC architecture. The buffer head's `b_this_page` field links all buffers included in a single buffer page together in a circular list.

If the page descriptor refers to a buffer page, its `buffers` field points to the buffer head of the first buffer included in the page; otherwise, this field is set to `NULL`. Figure 14-1 shows a page containing four buffers and the corresponding buffer heads.

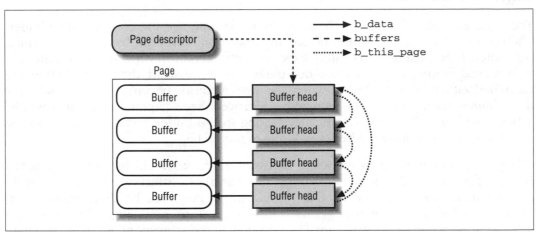

Figure 14-1. A page including four buffers and their buffer heads

The number of buffer pages must never become too small, or buffer I/O operations would be delayed for lack of buffers. The minimum percentage of buffer pages among all page frames is stored in the `min_percent` field of the `buffer_mem` table,* which is accessible either from the */proc/sys/vm/buffermem* file or by using the `sysctl()` system call.

---

* The table also includes two other fields, `borrow_percent` and `max_percent`, which are not used in Linux 2.2.

When the `getblk()` function needs a free buffer, it tries to get an element of the list pointing to free buffers of the right size. If that list is empty, the kernel must allocate additional page frames and then create new buffers of the required block size. This task is performed by the `refill_freelist()` function, which receives as a parameter the block size of the buffers to be allocated. Actually, the function just invokes `grow_buffers()`, which basically tries to allocate new buffers and returns the value 1 if it succeeded, 0 otherwise. If `grow_buffers()` failed to obtain new buffers because available memory is scarce, `refill_freelist()` wakes up the *bdflush* kernel thread (see the next section). It then relinquishes the CPU by setting the `SCHED_YIELD` flag of `current` and by invoking `schedule()`, thus allowing *bdflush* to run. The `getblk()` function invokes `refill_freelist()` repeatedly until it succeeds.

The `grow_buffers()` function receives as a parameter the size of the buffers to be allocated and performs the following operations:

1. Invokes `__get_free_page()` with priority `GFP_BUFFER` to get a new page frame from the Buddy system. The `GFP_BUFFER` priority indicates that the current process could be suspended while executing this function.

2. If no page frame is available, returns 0.

3. If a page frame is available, invokes the `create_buffers()` function, which in turn performs the following operations:

   a. Tries to allocate the buffer heads for all buffers in the page by repeatedly invoking `get_unused_buffer_head()`.

   b. If all the buffer heads needed have been obtained, initializes them properly; in particular, sets the `b_dev` field to `B_FREE`, the `b_size` field to the buffer size, and the `b_data` field to the starting address of the buffer in the page; then links together the buffer heads by means of the `b_this_page` field. Finally, returns the address of the buffer head of the first buffer in the page.

   c. If not all buffer heads have been obtained, releases all buffer heads already obtained by repeatedly invoking `put_unused_buffer_head()`.

   d. If the buffer has been requested for a buffer I/O operation, returns `NULL` (failure). This will cause `grow_buffers()` to return 0.

   e. If we reach this point, `get_unused_buffer_head()` failed and the buffer has been requested for a page I/O operation. In this case, the unused list is empty and all `NR_RESERVED` asynchronous buffer heads in the list are being used for other page I/O operations. Executes the function in the `tq_disk` task queue (see the section "The ll_rw_block() Function" in Chapter 13) and sleeps on the `buffer_wait` wait queue until some asynchronous buffer head becomes free.

   f. Goes to step a and tries again to allocate all buffer heads for a page.

4. If `create_buffers()` returned `NULL`, releases the page frame and returns 0.

5. Otherwise, all the buffer heads needed are now available. Inserts the buffer heads corresponding to the new buffers in the proper free list.

6. Adds the number of newly created buffers to `nr_buffers`, which always stores the total number of existing buffers.

7. Sets the `buffers` field of the page descriptor to the address of the first buffer head in the page.

8. Updates the `buffermem` variable, which stores the total number of bytes in the buffer pages.

9. Returns the value 1 (success).

Writing Dirty Buffers to Disk

Unix systems allow the deferred writing of dirty buffers into block devices, since that strategy noticeably improves system performance. Several write operations on a buffer could be satisfied by just one slow physical update of the corresponding disk block. Moreover, write operations are less critical than read operations since a process is usually not suspended because of delaying writings, while it is most often suspended because of delayed readings. Thanks to deferred writing, any physical block device will service, on the average, many more read requests than write ones.

A dirty buffer might stay in main memory until the last possible moment, that is, until system shutdown. However, pushing the delayed-write strategy to its limits has two major drawbacks:

- If a hardware or power supply failure occurs, the contents of RAM can no longer be retrieved, so a lot of file updates made since the time the system was booted are lost.

- The size of the buffer cache, and hence of the RAM required to contain it, would have to be huge—at least as big as the size of the accessed block devices.

Therefore, dirty buffers are *flushed* (written) to disk under the following conditions:

- The buffer cache gets too full and more buffers are needed, or the number of dirty buffers becomes too large: when one of these conditions occurs, the *bdflush* kernel thread is activated.

- Too much time has elapsed since a buffer has stayed dirty: the *kupdate* kernel thread regularly flushes old buffers.

- A process requests all the buffers of block devices or of particular files to be flushed: it does this by invoking the `sync()`, `fsync()`, or `fdatasync()` system call.

The bdflush kernel thread

The *bdflush* kernel thread (also called *kflushd*) is created during system initialization. It executes the `bdflush()` function, which selects some dirty buffers and forces an update of the corresponding blocks on the physical block devices.

Some system parameters control the behavior of *bdflush*; they are stored in the `b_un` field of the `bdf_prm` table and are accessible either by means of the */proc/sys/vm/ bdflush* file or by invoking the `bdflush()` system call. Each parameter has a default standard value, although it may vary within a minimum and a maximum value stored in the `bdflush_min` and `bdflush_max` tables, respectively. The parameters are listed in Table 14-2; remember that 1 tick corresponds to about 10 milliseconds.[*]

Table 14-2. Buffer Cache Tuning Parameters

Parameter	Default	Min	Max	Description
age_buffer	3000	100	60,000	Time-out in ticks of a normal dirty buffer for being written to disk
age_super	500	100	60,000	Time-out in ticks of a superblock dirty buffer for being written to disk
interval	500	0	6000	Delay in ticks between *kupdate* activations
ndirty	500	10	5000	Maximum number of dirty buffers written to disk during an activation of *bdflush*
nfract	40	0	100	Threshold percentage of dirty buffers for waking up *bdflush*

In order to implement deferred writing effectively, it would be counterproductive to write a lot of data at once; that would degrade system response time more than simply writing each buffer as soon as it's dirty. Therefore, not all dirty buffers are written to disk at each activation of *bdflush*. The maximum number of dirty buffers to be flushed in each activation is stored in the `ndirty` parameter of `bdf_prm`.

The kernel thread is woken up in a few specific cases:

- When a buffer head is inserted into the `BUF_DIRTY` list and the number of elements in the list becomes larger than:

$$\text{nr\_buffers} \times \text{bdf\_prm.b\_un.nfract} / 100$$

  that is, the percentage of dirty buffers exceeds the threshold represented by the `nfract` system parameter.

- When the `grow_buffers()` function, invoked by `refill_freelist()`, fails to replenish a list of free buffers as described earlier in the section "Buffer Allocation."

---

[*] The `bdf_prm` table also includes several other unused fields.

- When the kernel tries to get some free pages by releasing some buffers in the buffer cache (see Chapter 16).

- When a user presses some specific combinations of keys on the console (usually ALT+SysRq+U and ALT+SysRq+S). These key combinations, which are enabled only if the Linux kernel has been compiled with the Magic SysRq Key option, allow Linux hackers to have some explicit control over kernel behavior.

In order to wake up *bdflush*, the kernel invokes the wakeup_bdflush() function. It receives as its parameter a wait flag that indicates whether the calling kernel control path wishes to wait until some buffers have been successfully flushed to disk. The function performs the following actions:

1. Invokes wake_up() to wake up the process suspended in the bdflush_wait task queue. There is just one process in this wait queue, namely *bdflush* itself.

2. If the wait parameter indicates that the calling process wishes to wait, invokes sleep_on() to insert the current process in a specific wait queue named bdflush_done.

At each activation of the *bdflush* kernel thread, the bdflush() function performs the following operations:

1. Initializes the ndirty local variable to 0; this variable denotes the number of dirty buffers written to disk during a single activation of bdflush().

2. Scans the BUF_DIRTY and BUF_LOCKED lists of buffer heads. If a dirty, unlocked buffer is found, increments ndirty and invokes ll_rw_block() to issue a WRITE request for the buffer. Moreover, if a buffer head in the wrong list is found, invokes refile_buffer() on it (see the section "Buffer Head Data Structures" earlier in this chapter).

3. If ndirty is smaller than bdf_prm.b_un.ndirty and there are other buffer heads to be checked, reruns step 2.

4. Invokes run_task_queue() to execute the functions in the tq_disk task queue, thus starting the effective low-level block device drivers.

5. Invokes wake_up() to wake up all processes suspended in the bdflush_done wait queue.

6. If some buffers have been flushed in this iteration and the percentage of dirty buffers is greater than bdf_prm.b_un.nfract, goes to step 1 and starts a new iteration: the buffer cache still contains too many dirty buffers.

7. Otherwise, suspends the *bdflush* kernel thread, as follows: invokes flush_signals() to flush all pending signals of *bdflush* and invokes interruptible_sleep_on() to insert *bdflush* in the bdflush_wait wait queue. When the kernel thread is awakened, it will resume its execution from step 1.

The kupdate kernel thread

Since the *bdflush* kernel thread is usually activated only when there are too many dirty buffers or when more buffers are needed and available memory is scarce, some dirty buffers might stay in RAM for an arbitrarily long time before being flushed to disk. The *kupdate* kernel thread is thus introduced to flush the older dirty buffers.*

The kernel distinguishes the buffers used by disk superblocks from other buffers. A superblock includes very critical information, and its corruption could lead to severe problems: in fact, the whole partition could become unreadable. As shown in Table 14-2, there are two time-out parameters: `age_buffer` is the time for normal buffers to age before *kupdate* writes them to disk (usually 30 seconds), while `age_super` is the corresponding time for superblocks (usually 5 seconds).

The `interval` field of the `bdf_prm` table stores the delay in ticks between two activations of the *kupdate* kernel thread (usually five seconds). If this field is null, the kernel thread is normally stopped, and it is activated only when it receives a `SIGCONT` signal.

When the kernel modifies the contents of some buffer, it sets the `b_flushtime` field of the corresponding buffer head to the time (in jiffies) when it should later be flushed to disk. The *kupdate* kernel thread selects only the dirty buffers whose `b_flushtime` field is smaller than the current value of `jiffies`.

The *kupdate* kernel thread consists of the `kupdate()` function, which executes the following endless loop:

```
for (;;) {
    if (bdf_prm.b_un.interval) {
        tsk->state = TASK_INTERRUPTIBLE;
        schedule_timeout(bdf_prm.b_un.interval);
    } else {
        tsk->state = TASK_STOPPED;
        schedule(); /* wait for SIGCONT */
    }
    sync_old_buffers();
}
```

If `bdf_prm.b_un.interval` is not null, the thread suspends itself for the specified amount of ticks (see the section "An Application of Dynamic Timers" in Chapter 5, *Timing Measurements*); otherwise, the thread stops itself until a `SIGCONT` signal is received (see the section "The Role of Signals" in Chapter 9, *Signals*).

The core of the `kupdate()` function consists of the `sync_old_buffers()` function. The operations to be performed are very simple for standard filesystems used with

---

* In an earlier version of Linux 2.2, the same task was achieved by means of the `bdflush()` system call, which was invoked every five seconds by a User Mode system process launched at system startup and which executed the */sbin/update* program. In more recent kernel versions, the `bdflush()` system call is used only to allow users to modify the system parameters in the `bdf_prm` table.

Unix; all the function has to do is write dirty buffers to disk. However, some nonnative filesystems introduce complexities because they store their superblock or inode information in complicated ways. `sync_old_buffers()` executes the following steps:

1. Invokes `sync_supers ()`, which accesses the `super_blocks` array to scan the superblocks of all currently mounted filesystems (see the section "Filesystem Mounting" in Chapter 12). It then invokes, for each superblock, the corresponding `write_super` superblock operation, if one is defined (see the section "Super-block Objects" in Chapter 12). The `write_super` method is not defined for any Unix filesystem.

2. Invokes `sync_inodes()`, which takes care of inodes used by filesystems that do not store all the inode data in a single disk block (an example is the MS-DOS filesystem). The function scans the superblocks of all currently mounted filesystems and, for each superblock, the list of dirty inodes to which the `s_dirty` field of the superblock object points. The function invokes the `write_inode` superblock operation on each element of the list, if that method is defined. The `write_inode` method is not defined for any Unix filesystem.

3. Scans the `BUF_DIRTY` and `BUF_LOCKED` lists and writes to disk all old dirty buffers, that is, those whose `b_flushtime` buffer head fields have a value smaller than or equal to `jiffies`. The code used to perform this step is almost identical to the code used by `bdflush()`, but `sync_old_buffers()` does not flush young buffers to disk, and it doesn't limit the number of buffers checked on each activation.

4. Executes the functions in the `tq_disk` task queue, thus starting up (unplugging) any low-level block device drivers needed to write blocks to disk.

The sync(), fsync(), and fdatasync() system calls

Three different system calls are available to user applications to flush dirty buffers to disk:

`sync()`
   Usually issued before a shutdown, since it flushes all dirty buffers to disk

`fsync()`
   Allows a process to flush all blocks belonging to a specific open file to disk

`fdatasync()`
   Very similar to `fsync()` but doesn't flush the inode block of the file

The core of the `sync()` system call is the `fsync_dev()` function, which performs the following actions:

1. Invokes sync_buffers(), which scans the BUF_DIRTY and BUF_LOCKED lists and issues a WRITE request, via ll_rw_block(), for all dirty, unlocked buffers the lists contain

2. Invokes sync_supers() to write the dirty superblocks to disk, if necessary, by using the write_super methods (see earlier in this section)

3. Invokes sync_inodes() to write the dirty inodes to disk, if necessary, by using the write_inode methods (see earlier in this section)

4. Invokes sync_buffers() once again, since sync_supers() and sync_inodes() might have marked additional buffers as dirty

The fsync() system call forces the kernel to write to disk all dirty buffers belonging to the file specified by the fd file descriptor parameter (including the buffer containing its inode, if necessary). The system service routine derives the address of the file object and then invokes its fsync method. This method is filesystem-dependent, since it must know how files are stored on disk in order to be able to identify the dirty buffers associated with a given file. Once the correspondence between file and buffers has been established, the rest of the job can be delegated to ll_rw_block(). The fsync method suspends the calling process until all dirty buffers of the file have been written to disk. In order to do this, it scans both the BUF_DIRTY and BUF_LOCKED lists and invokes wait_on_buffer() for each locked buffer found.

The fdatasync() system call is very similar to fsync(), but it is supposed to write to disk only the buffers that contain the file's data, not those that contain inode information. Since Linux 2.2 does not have a specific file method for fdatasync(), this system call uses the fsync method and is thus identical to fsync().

The Page Cache

The page cache, which is thankfully much simpler than the buffer cache, is a disk cache for the data accessed by page I/O operations. As we shall see in Chapter 15, all access to regular files made by read(), write(), and mmap() system calls is done through the page cache. Of course, the unit of information kept in the cache is a whole page, since page I/O operations transfer whole pages of data. A page does not necessarily contain physically adjacent disk blocks, and it cannot thus be identified by a device number and a block number. Instead, a page in the page cache is identified by a file's inode and by the offset within the file.

There are three main activities related to the page cache: adding a page when accessing a file portion not already in the cache, removing a page when the cache gets too big, and finding the page including a given file offset.

Page Cache Data Structures

The page cache makes use of two main data structures:

A page hash table
> Lets the kernel quickly derive the page descriptor address for the page associated with a specified inode and file offset

An inode queue
> A list of page descriptors corresponding to pages of data of a particular file (distinguished by a unique inode)

Manipulation of the page cache involves adding and removing entries from these data structures, as well as updating the fields in all inode objects referencing cached files.

The page hash table

When a process reads a large file, the page cache may become filled with pages related to that file. In such cases, scanning the proper inode queue to find the page that maps the required file portion could become a time-consuming operation.

For that reason, Linux makes use of a hash table of page descriptor pointers named `page_hash_table`. Its size depends on the amount of available RAM; as an example, for systems having 64 MB of RAM, `page_hash_table` is stored in 16 page frames and includes 16,384 page descriptor pointers.

The `page_hash()` function derives from the address of an inode object and from an offset value the address of the corresponding element in the hash table. As usual, chaining is introduced to handle entries that cause a collision: the `next_hash` and `pprev_hash` fields of the page descriptors are used to implement doubly circular lists of entries having the same hash value. The `page_cache_size` variable specifies the number of page descriptors included in the collision lists of the page hash table (and therefore in the page cache).

The `add_page_to_hash_queue()` and `remove_page_from_hash_queue()` functions are used to add an element into the hash table and remove an element from it, respectively.

The inode queue

A queue of pages is associated with each inode object in kernel memory. The `i_pages` field of each inode object stores the address of the first page descriptor in its inode queue, while the `i_nrpages` field stores the length of the list.

The `add_page_to_inode_queue()` and `remove_page_from_inode_queue()` functions are used to insert a page descriptor into an inode queue and to remove it, respectively.

Page descriptor fields related to the page cache

When a page frame is included in the page cache, some fields of the corresponding page descriptor have special meanings:

`inode`
> Contains the address of the inode object of the file to which the data included in the page belongs; if the page does not belong to the page cache, this field is `NULL`.*

`offset`
> Specifies the relative address of the data inside the file.

`next`
> Points to the next element in the inode queue.

`prev`
> Points to the previous element in the inode queue.

`next_hash`
> Points to the next colliding page descriptor in the page hash list.

`pprev_hash`
> Points to the previous colliding page descriptor in the page hash list.

In addition, when a page frame is inserted into the page cache, the usage counter (`count` field) of the corresponding page descriptor is incremented. If the `count` field is exactly 1, the page frame belongs to the cache but is not being accessed by any process: it can thus be removed from the page cache whenever free memory becomes scarce, as described in Chapter 16.

Page Cache Handling Functions

The high-level functions using the page cache involve finding, adding, and removing a page.

The `find_page()` function receives as parameters the address of an inode object and an offset value. It invokes `page_hash()` to derive the address of the first element in the collision list, then scans the list until the requested page is found. If the page is present, the function increments the `count` field of the page descriptor, sets the `PG_referenced` flag, and returns its address; otherwise, it returns `NULL`.

The `add_to_page_cache()` function inserts a new page descriptor in the page cache. This is achieved by performing the following operations:

1. Increments the `count` field of the page descriptor

---

* As we shall see in Chapter 16, the `inode` field points to a fictitious inode object when the page includes data of a swap partition; actually, the page belongs to a subset of the page cache named "swap cache." In this chapter, we don't care about this special case.

2. Clears the `PG_uptodate`, `PG_error`, and `PG_referenced` flags of the page frame to indicate that the page is present in the cache but not yet filled with data

3. Sets the `offset` field of the page descriptor with the offset of the data within the file

4. Invokes `add_page_to_hash_queue()` to insert the page descriptor in the hash table

5. Invokes `add_page_to_inode_queue()` to insert the page descriptor in the inode queue and to set the `inode` field of the page descriptor

The `remove_inode_page()` function removes a page descriptor from the page cache. This is achieved by invoking `remove_page_from_hash_queue()`, `remove_page_from_inode_queue()`, and `__free_page()` in succession. The latter function decrements the `count` field of the page descriptor, and releases the page frame to the Buddy system if the counter becomes 0.

Tuning the Page Cache

The page cache tends to quickly grow in size, because any access to previously unaccessed portions of files forces the kernel to allocate a new page frame for the accessed data and to insert that page frame in the cache. As we shall see in Chapter 16, when free memory becomes scarce, the kernel prunes the page cache by releasing the oldest unused pages.

However, the page cache size should never fall under some predefined limit, otherwise system performance will quickly degrade. The lower size limit of the page cache can be tuned by means of the `min_percent` parameter stored in the `page_cache` table,* which specifies the minimum percentage of pages among all page frames that should belong to the page cache. The default value is 2%. The parameter's value can be read or modified either by invoking the `sysctl()` system call or by accessing the */proc/sys/vm/pagecache* file.

Anticipating Linux 2.4

Much work has been done on the page cache. First of all, the page cache makes use preferably of page frames in high memory. Moreover, Linux 2.4 introduces a new kind of object that represents a *file address space*: the object refers to a given block of an inode (or of a block device) and includes pointers to both the memory region descriptors mapping the file and the pages containing the file data. The inode object now includes a pointer to the new address space object, and the page cache is indexed by combining the base address of the address space object with the offset inside the file.

---

* The `page_cache` table also includes the `borrow_percent` and `max_percent` parameters, which are no longer used.

The address space object includes methods to read and write a full page of data. These methods take care of inode object management (like updating the file access time), page cache handling, and temporary buffer allocation. This approach leads to a better coupling between the page cache and the buffer cache. Most filesystems can thus use the `generic_file_write()` function (as you'll see in Chapter 15, Linux 2.2 uses this function only for networking filesystems). The synchronization problem between the buffer cache and the page cache has thus been removed: since both read and write operations for regular files make use of the same page cache, it is no longer necessary to synchronize data present in the two caches.

Notice that both the buffer cache and the page cache continue to be used with different purposes. The first acts on disk blocks, the second on pages that have a file image on disk.

CHAPTER FIFTEEN

ACCESSING REGULAR FILES

Accessing a regular file is a complex activity that involves the VFS abstraction (Chapter 12, *The Virtual Filesystem*), the handling of block devices (Chapter 13, *Managing I/O Devices*), and the use of disk caches (Chapter 14, *Disk Caches*). This chapter shows how the kernel builds on all those facilities to accomplish file reads and writes. The topics covered in this chapter apply to regular files stored either in disk-based filesystems or to network filesystems such as NFS or Samba.

The stage we are working at in this chapter starts after the proper read or write method of a particular file has been called (as described in Chapter 12). We show here how each read ends with the desired data delivered to a User Mode process and how each write ends with data marked ready for transfer to disk. The rest of the transfer is handled by the facilities in Chapter 13 and Chapter 14.

In particular, in the section "Reading and Writing a Regular File" we describe how regular files are accessed by means of the **read()** and **write()** system calls. When a process reads from a regular file, data is first moved from the disk itself to a set of buffers in the kernel's address space. This set of buffers is included in a set of pages in the page cache (see the section "Page I/O Operations" in Chapter 13). Next, the pages are copied into the process's user address space. This chapter deals only with the move from the kernel to the user address space. A write is basically the opposite, although some stages are different from reads in important ways.

We also discuss in the section "Memory Mapping" how the kernel allows a process to directly map a regular file into its address space, because that activity also has to deal with pages in kernel memory.

Reading and Writing a Regular File

The Chapter 13 section "The block_read() and block_write() Functions" described how the **read()** and **write()** system calls are implemented. The corresponding service routines end up invoking the file object's `read` and `write` methods, which may be file-system-dependent. For disk-based filesystems, these methods locate the physical blocks containing the data being accessed and activate the block device driver to start the data transfer. However, reading and writing are performed differently in Linux.

Reading a regular file is page-based: the kernel always transfers whole pages of data at once. If a process issues a `read()` system call in order to get a few bytes, and that data is not already in RAM, the kernel allocates a new page frame, fills the page with the suitable portion of the regular file, adds the page to the page cache, and finally copies the requested bytes into the process address space. For most filesystems, reading a page of data from a regular file is just a matter of finding what blocks on disk contain the requested data. Once this is done, the kernel can use one or more page I/O operations to fill the pages.

Write operations for disk-based filesystems are much more complicated to handle, since the file size could change, and therefore the kernel might allocate or release some physical blocks on the disk. Of course, how this is precisely done depends on the filesystem type.

As a matter of fact, the `read` method of most filesystems is implemented by a common function named `generic_file_read()`. However, all disk-based filesystems have a customized `write` method. Since the Second Extended Filesystem is the most efficient and powerful one currently available for Linux and since it is thus the standard filesystem on most Linux systems, we discuss how it implements methods like `write` in Chapter 17, *The Ext2 Filesystem*. The `generic_file_write()` function is used only by NFS and Samba: since they are network filesystems, the kernel does not care about how the data is physically recorded on the remote disks.

Reading from a Regular File

Let's discuss the `generic_file_read()` function, which implements the `read` method for regular files of most filesystems. The function acts on the following parameters:

`file`
Address of the file object

`buf`
Linear address of the User Mode memory area where the characters read from the file must be stored

`count`
Number of characters to be read

`ppos`
Pointer to a variable storing the file offset from which reading must start

The function verifies that the parameters are correct by invoking access_ok() (see the section "Verifying the Parameters" in Chapter 8, *System Calls*), then invokes do_generic_file_read(), which performs the following steps:

1. Determines from *ppos whether the file offset from which reading must start is inside or outside the file's read-ahead window (see the next section).

2. Starts a cycle to read all the pages that include the requested count characters and initializes the pos local variable with the value *ppos. During a single iteration, the function reads a page of data by performing the following substeps:

    a. If pos exceeds the file size, exits from the cycle and goes to step 3.

    b. Invokes find_page() to check whether the page is already in the page cache.

    c. If the page is not in the page cache, allocates a new page frame, adds it to the page cache, and invokes the readpage method of the inode object to fill it. Although its implementation depends on the filesystem, most disk filesystems rely on a common generic_readpage() function, which performs the following operations:

        1. Sets the PG_locked flag of the page so that no other kernel control path can access the page contents.

        2. Increments the usage counter of the page descriptor. This is a fail-safe mechanism ensuring that, if the process that reads the page is killed while sleeping, the page frame won't be released to the Buddy system.

        3. Sets the PG_free_after flag, thus ensuring that the usage counter of the page descriptor is decremented when the page I/O operation terminates (see the section "Page I/O Operations" in Chapter 13). This flag is necessary because device drivers may invoke the brw_page() function without first incrementing the usage counter. Currently no device driver does this, though.

        4. Computes the number of blocks needed to fill the page and derives from the file offset relative to the page the file block number of the first block in the page.

        5. Invokes the bmap method of the inode operation table on each file block number to get the corresponding logical block number.

        6. Invokes brw_page() to transfer the blocks in the page (see the section "Starting Page I/O Operations" in Chapter 13).

    d. Invokes the generic_file_readahead() function (see the next section).

    e. If the page is locked, invokes wait_on_page() to wait for I/O to complete.

    f. Copies the page (or a portion of it) into the process address space, updates `pos` to point to the next position in the file for a read to take place, and goes to step 2a to continue with the next requested page.

3. Assigns to the `*ppos` the current value of `pos`, thus storing the next position where a read is to occur for a future invocation of this function.

4. Sets the `f_reada` field of the file descriptor to 1 (see the next section).

5. Invoke `update_atime()` to store the current time in the `i_atime` field of the file's inode and to mark the inode as dirty.

Read-Ahead for Regular Files

In the section "The Role of Read-Ahead" in Chapter 13, we discussed how sequential disk accesses benefit from reading several adjacent blocks of a block device in advance, before they are actually requested. The same considerations apply to sequential read operations of regular files. However, read-ahead of regular files requires a more sophisticated algorithm than read-ahead of physical blocks for several reasons:

- Since data is read page by page, the read-ahead algorithm does not have to consider the offsets inside the page, but only the positions of the accessed pages inside the file. A sequence of accesses to pages of the same file is considered sequential if the related pages are close to each other. We'll define the word "close" more precisely in a moment.

- Read-ahead must be restarted from scratch when the current access is not sequential with respect to the previous one (random access).

- Read-ahead should be slowed down or even stopped when a process keeps accessing the same pages over and over again (only a small portion of the file is being used).

- If necessary, the read-ahead algorithm must activate the low-level I/O device driver to make sure that the new pages will be read.

We'll try now to sketch out how Linux implements read-ahead. However, we won't be able to cover the algorithm in detail because the motivations behind it appear somewhat empirical.

The read-ahead algorithm identifies a set of pages corresponding to a contiguous portion of the file as the *read-ahead window*. If the next read operation issued by a process falls inside this set of pages, the kernel considers the file access as "sequential" to the previous one. The read-ahead window consists of pages requested by the process or read in advance by the kernel and included in the page cache. The read-ahead window always includes the pages requested in the last read-ahead operation; they are called the *read-ahead group*. Not all the pages in the read-ahead window or group are necessarily up-to-date. They are invalid (that is, their `PG_uptodate` flags are cleared) if their transfer from disk has not yet been completed.

The file object includes the following fields related to read-ahead:

f_raend
> Position of the first byte after the read-ahead group and the read-ahead window

f_rawin
> Length in bytes of the current read-ahead window

f_ralen
> Length in bytes of the current read-ahead group

f_ramax
> Maximum number of characters for the next read-ahead operation

f_reada
> Flag specifying whether the file has been accessed sequentially (used only when accessing a block device file; see the section "The block_read( ) and block_write( ) Functions" in Chapter 13)

Figure 15-1 illustrates how some of the fields are used to delimit the read-ahead window and the read-ahead group. The `generic_file_readahead()` function implements the read-ahead algorithm; its overall scheme is shown later in Figure 15-3.

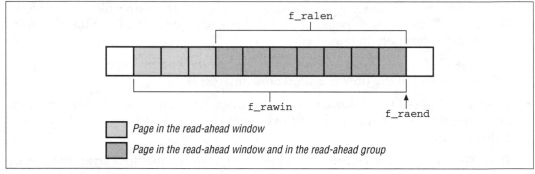

Figure 15-1. Read-ahead window and read-ahead group

Read-ahead operations

The kernel performs a *read-ahead operation* by invoking a function named `try_to_read_ahead()` several times, once for each page to be read ahead.

The number of bytes to be read in advance is stored into the **f_ramax** field of the file object. This number is initially set to **MIN_READAHEAD** (usually three pages); it cannot become larger than **MAX_READAHEAD** (usually 31 pages).

The `try_to_read_ahead()` function checks whether the page considered is already included in the page cache; if not, the page is transferred by invoking the **readpage** method of the corresponding inode object. The function then doubles the value of the **f_ramax** field, so that the next read-ahead operation will be much more aggressive (accesses appear to be really sequential). As mentioned, the field is never allowed to exceed MAX_READAHEAD.

Next, the `generic_file_readahead()` function updates the file's read-ahead window and the read-ahead group. As we shall see later, the function may set up either a short read-ahead window or a long one: the former consists of only the most recent read-ahead group while the latter includes the two most recent read-ahead groups (see Figure 15-2).

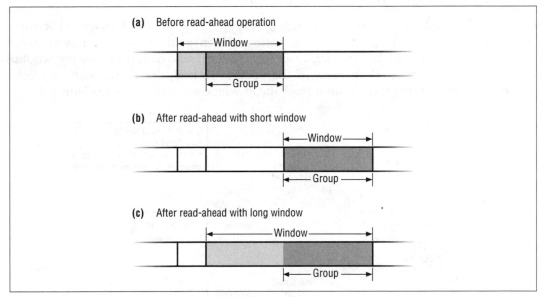

Figure 15-2. Read-ahead group and window

Finally, the `generic_file_readahead()` function may activate the low-level block device driver by executing the `tq_disk` task queue (see Figure 15-3).

A special case occurs for the first read-ahead operation, where the previous read-ahead window and the previous read-ahead group are null (all relative fields are set to 0). The number of bytes to be read in advance in the first read-ahead operation is equal to MIN_READAHEAD or the number of bytes requested by the process in its `read()` system call, whichever value is larger.

Nonsequential access (outside the read-ahead window)

When a process issues a read request through the `read()` system call, the kernel checks whether the first page of the requested data is included in the current read-ahead window of the corresponding file object.

Suppose the first page is not included in the read-ahead window, perhaps because the file has never been accessed by the process or because the process issued an `lseek()` system call to reposition the current file pointer. The kernel considers every page requested by the process in turn; for each such page, it invokes the `generic_file_readahead()` function, which decides whether a read-ahead operation has to be performed.

Basically, two cases may occur (see Figure 15-3). Either the page is locked, meaning that the actual data transfer for the page has not been completed, or the page is unlocked and therefore up-to-date. (For the sake of simplicity, we will not consider I/O errors occurring while transferring the pages in this chapter.)

If the page is unlocked, the read-ahead operation does not take place. This rule ensures that no read-ahead operation is performed on a file whose data is entirely contained in the page cache. In such cases, any further read-ahead processing would be a waste of CPU time. Conversely, if the page is locked, the kernel starts a read-ahead operation and prepares a short read-ahead window for the next read-ahead.

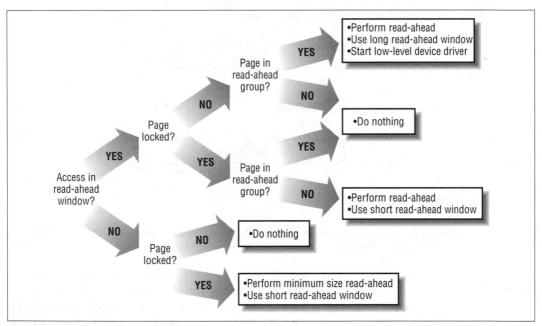

Figure 15-3. Read-ahead scheme

Sequential access (inside the read-ahead window)

Suppose now that the first page accessed by the process through a `read()` system call falls inside the read-ahead window of the previous read-ahead operation. The kernel considers all pages requested by the process in turn; for each of them, it invokes the `generic_file_readahead()` function. Four cases may occur, depending on whether the page is locked and whether it is included in the read-ahead group (see Figure 15-3):

- If the page is not locked but is included in the read-ahead group, the process has progressed to the point where it is accessing a page transferred from disk by the last read-ahead operation, so the process is dangerously close to the end of the pages read in advance. In this case, another read-ahead is performed and a long read-ahead window is used; moreover, the functions in the tq_disk task queue are executed to be sure that the low-level block device driver will be activated.

- If the page is neither locked nor included in the read-ahead group, the process is accessing a page transferred from disk in the next-to-last read-ahead operation. In this case, no reading in advance is done since the process is lagging with respect to read-ahead. This is the best scenario and shows that the kernel has an ample number of read-ahead pages being read sequentially by the process, just as we would hope.

- If the page is both locked and included in the read-ahead group, the process is accessing a page requested in the last read-ahead operation but probably not yet transferred from disk. In this case, it would be pointless to start an additional read-ahead.

- Finally, if the page is locked but not included in the read-ahead group, the process is accessing a page requested in the next-to-last read-ahead operation. In this case, the kernel performs another read-ahead because the page is likely to be written on disk and an additional read-ahead will cause no harm.

Writing to a Regular File

Recall that the write() system call involves moving data from the User Mode address space of the calling process into the kernel data structures, and then to disk. The write method of the file object permits each filesystem type to define a specialized write operation. In Linux 2.2, the write method of each disk-based filesystem is a procedure that basically identifies the disk blocks involved in the write operation, copies the data from the User Mode address space into the corresponding buffers, and then marks those buffers as dirty. The procedure depends on the type of filesystem; we present one example in the section "Reading and Writing an Ext2 Regular File" in Chapter 17.

Disk-based filesystems do not directly use the page cache for writing to a regular file. This is a heritage from older versions of Linux, in which the only disk cache was the buffer cache. However, network-based filesystems always use the page cache for writing to a regular file.

The approach used in Linux 2.2, bypassing the page cache, leads to a synchronization problem. When writing takes place, the valid data is in the buffer cache but not in the page cache; more precisely, when the write method changes any portion of a file, any page in the page cache that corresponds to that portion no longer includes meaningful data. As an example of the problem, one process might think it's reading correct data but fail to see the changes written by another process.

In order to solve this problem, all `write` methods of disk-based filesystems invoke the `update_vm_cache()` function to update the page cache used by reads. This function acts on the following parameters:

`inode`
> Pointer to inode object of the file to which the writes took place

`pos`
> Offset within the file where the writes took place

`buf`
> Address from where the characters to be written into the file must be fetched

`count`
> Number of characters to be written

The function updates page by page the portion of the page cache related to the file being written by performing the following operations:

1. Computes from `pos` the offset relative to a page of the first character to be written

2. Invokes `find_page()` to search in the page cache for the page frame including the character at file offset `pos`

3. If the page is found, performs the following substeps:

    a. Invokes `wait_on_page()` to wait until the page becomes unlocked (in case it is involved in an I/O data transfer).

    b. Fills the page with data from the process address space, starting from the page offset `pos` previously computed. This is the data that has already been written into the buffer cache by the filesystem's customized `write` method.

    c. Invokes `free_page()` to decrement the page's usage counter (it was incremented by the `find_page()` function).

4. If some data in the User Mode address space remains to be copied, updates `pos`, sets the page offset to 0, and goes to step 2

Now we'll briefly describe the write operation for a regular file through the page cache. Recall that this operation is used only by network filesystems. In this case, the `write` method of the file object is implemented by the `generic_file_write()` function, which acts on the following parameters:

`file`
> File object pointer

`buf`
> Address where the characters to be written into the file must be fetched

count
> Number of characters to be written

ppos
> Address of a variable storing the file offset from which writing must start

The function performs the following operations:

1. If the O_APPEND flag of `file->flags` is on, sets `*ppos` to the end of the file so that all new data is appended to it.

2. Starts a cycle to update all the pages involved in the write operation. During each iteration, performs the following substeps:

    a. Tries to find the page in the page cache. If it isn't there, allocates a free page and adds it to the page cache.

    b. Invokes `wait_on_page()` and then sets the PG_locked flag of the page descriptor, thus obtaining exclusive access to the page content.

    c. Invokes `copy_from_user()` to fill the page with data coming from the process address space.

    d. Invokes the inode operation's **updatepage** method. This method is specific to the particular network filesystem being used and is not described in this book. It should ensure that the remote file is properly updated with the newly written data.

    e. Unlocks the page, invokes `wake_up()` to wake up the processes suspended on the page wait queue, and invokes `free_page()` to decrement the page's usage counter (incremented by `find_page()`).

3. Updates the value of `*ppos` to point right after the last character written.

Memory Mapping

As already mentioned in the section "Memory Regions" in Chapter 7, *Process Address Space*, a memory region can be associated with a file (or with some portion of it) of a disk-based filesystem. This means that an access to a byte within a page of the memory region is translated by the kernel into an operation on the corresponding byte of the regular file. This technique is called *memory mapping*.

Two kinds of memory mapping exist:

Shared
> Any write operation on the pages of the memory region changes the file on disk; moreover, if a process writes into a page of a shared memory mapping, the changes are visible to all other processes that map the same file.

Private

> Meant to be used when the process creates the mapping just to read the file, not to write it. For this purpose, private mapping is more efficient than shared mapping. But any write operation on a privately mapped page will cause it not to map the page in the file any longer. Thus, a write does not change the file on disk, nor is the change visible to any other processes that access the same file.

A process can create a new memory mapping by issuing an `mmap()` system call (see the section "Creating a Memory Mapping" later in this chapter). Programmers must specify either the `MAP_SHARED` flag or the `MAP_PRIVATE` flag as a parameter of the system call; as you can probably guess, in the former case the mapping is shared while in the latter it is private. Once the mapping has been created, the process can read the data stored in the file by simply reading from the memory locations of the new memory region. If the memory mapping is shared, the process can also modify the corresponding file by simply writing into the same memory locations. In order to destroy or shrink a memory mapping, the process may use the `munmap()` system call (see the later section "Destroying a Memory Mapping").

As a general rule, if a memory mapping is shared, the corresponding memory region has the `VM_SHARED` flag set; if it is private, the `VM_SHARED` flag is cleared. As we'll see later, an exception to this rule exists for read-only shared memory mappings.

Memory Mapping Data Structures

A memory mapping is represented by a combination of the following data structures:

- The inode object associated with the mapped file
- A file object for each different mapping performed on that file by different processes
- A `vm_area_struct` descriptor for each different mapping on the file
- A page descriptor for each page frame assigned to a memory region that maps the file

Figure 15-4 illustrates how the data structures are linked together. In the upper left corner we show the inode. The `i_mmap` field of each inode object points to the first element of a doubly linked list that includes all memory regions that currently map the file; if `i_mmap` is `NULL`, the file is not mapped by any memory region. The list contains `vm_area_struct` descriptors representing memory regions and is implemented by means of the `vm_next_share` and `vm_pprev_share` fields.

The `vm_file` field of each memory region descriptor contains the address of a file object for the mapped file; if that field is null, the memory region is not used in a memory mapping. The file object contains fields that allow the kernel to identify both the process that owns the memory mapping and the file being mapped.

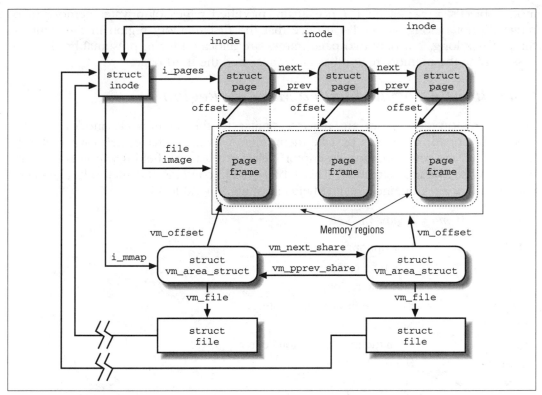

Figure 15-4. Data structures related to memory mapping

The position of the first mapped location is stored into the **vm_offset** field of the memory region descriptor. The length of the mapped file portion is simply the length of the memory region, thus can be computed from the **vm_start** and **vm_end** fields.

Pages of shared memory mappings are always included in the page cache; pages of private memory mappings are included in the page cache as long as they are unmodified. When a process tries to modify a page of a private memory mapping, the kernel duplicates the page frame and replaces the original page frame with the duplicate in the process Page Table; this is one of the applications of the Copy On Write mechanism that we discussed in Chapter 7. The original page frame still remains in the page cache, although it no longer belongs to the memory mapping since it is replaced by the duplicate. In turn, the duplicate is not inserted into the page cache since it no longer contains valid data representing the file on disk.

Figure 15-4 also shows the page descriptors of the pages included in the page cache that refer to the memory-mapped file. As described in the section "Page Cache Data Structures" in Chapter 14, these descriptors are inserted into a doubly linked list implemented through the **next** and **prev** fields. The address of the first list element is in the inode object's `i_pages` field. Once again, modified pages of private memory mappings do not belong to this list. Notice that the first memory region in the figure is three pages long, but only two page frames are allocated for it; presumably, the process owning the memory region has never accessed the third page.

Operations Associated with a Memory Region

Memory region descriptors are objects, similar to the superblock, inode, and file objects described in Chapter 12. Like them, memory regions have their own methods. In fact, each `vm_area_struct` descriptor includes a `vm_ops` field that points to a `vm_operations_struct` structure. This table, which contains the methods associated with a memory region, includes the fields illustrated in Table 15-1.

Table 15-1. Memory Region Methods

Method	Description
open	Open the region.
close	Close the region.
unmap	Unmap a linear address interval.
protect	Not used.
sync	Flush the memory region content.
advise	Not used.
nopage	Demand paging.
wppage	Not used.
swapout	Swap out a page belonging to the region.
swapin	Swap in a page belonging to the region.

The memory region operations allow different filesystems to implement their own memory mapping functions. In practice, most filesystems rely on two standard tables of memory region operations: `file_shared_mmap`, which is used for shared memory mappings, and `file_private_mmap`, which is used for private memory mappings. Table 15-2 shows the names of the relevant methods.

As usual, when a method has a `NULL` value, the kernel invokes either a default function or no function at all. If the `nopage` method has a `NULL` value, the memory region is anonymous; that is, it does not map any file on disk. This use is discussed in the section "Demand Paging" in Chapter 7.

Table 15-2. Methods Used by file_shared_mmap and by file_private_mmap

Method	file_shared_mmap	file_private_mmap
open	NULL	NULL
close	NULL	NULL

Table 15-2. Methods Used by file_shared_mmap and by file_private_mmap (continued)

Method	file_shared_mmap	file_private_mmap
unmap	filemap_unmap	NULL
protect	NULL	NULL
sync	filemap_sync	NULL
advise	NULL	NULL
nopage	filemap_nopage	filemap_nopage
wppage	NULL	NULL
swapout	filemap_swapout	NULL
swapin	NULL	NULL

Creating a Memory Mapping

To create a new memory mapping, a process issues an mmap() system call, passing the following parameters to it:

- A file descriptor identifying the file to be mapped.

- An offset inside the file specifying the first character of the file portion to be mapped.

- The length of the file portion to be mapped.

- A set of flags. The process must explicitly set either the **MAP_SHARED** flag or the **MAP_PRIVATE** flag to specify the kind of memory mapping requested.*

- A set of permissions specifying one or more types of access to the memory region: read access (**PROT_READ**), write access (**PROT_WRITE**), or execution access (**PROT_EXEC**).

- An optional linear address, which is taken by the kernel as a hint of where the new memory region should start. If the **MAP_FIXED** flag is specified and the kernel cannot allocate the new memory region starting from the specified linear address, the system call fails.

The mmap() system call returns the linear address of the first location in the new memory region. The service routine is implemented by the old_mmap() function, which essentially invokes the do_mmap() function already described in the section "Allocating a Linear Address Interval" in Chapter 7. We now complete that description by detailing the steps performed only when creating a memory region that maps a file.

---

* The process could also set the MAP_ANONYMOUS flag to specify that the new memory region is anonymous, that is, not associated with any file (see the section "Demand Paging" in Chapter 7); however, this flag is a Linux extension and it is not defined by the POSIX standard.

1. Checks whether the mmap file operation for the file to be mapped is defined; if not, returns an error code. A NULL value for mmap in the file operation table indicates that the corresponding file cannot be mapped (for instance, because it is a directory).

2. In addition to the usual consistency checks, compares the kind of memory mapping requested and the flags specified when the file was opened. The flags passed as a parameter of the system call specify the kind of mapping required, while the value of the f_mode field of the file object specifies how the file was opened. Depending on these two sources of information, performs the following checks:

    a. If a shared writable memory mapping is required, checks that the file was opened for writing and that it was not opened in append mode (O_APPEND flag of the open() system call)

    b. If a shared memory mapping is required, checks that there is no mandatory lock on the file (see the section "File Locking" in Chapter 12)

    c. For any kind of memory mapping, checks that the file was opened for reading

    If any of these conditions is not fulfilled, returns an error code.

3. When initializing the value of the vm_flags field of the new memory region descriptor, sets the VM_READ, VM_WRITE, VM_EXEC, VM_SHARED, VM_MAYREAD, VM_MAYWRITE, VM_MAYEXEC, and VM_MAYSHARE flags according to the access rights of the file and the kind of requested memory mapping (see the section "Memory Region Access Rights" in Chapter 7). As an optimization, the VM_SHARED flag is cleared for nonwritable shared memory mapping. This can be done because the process is not allowed to write into the pages of the memory region, thus the mapping is treated the same as a private mapping; however, the kernel actually allows other processes that share the file to access the pages in this memory region.

4. Invokes the mmap method for the file being mapped, passing as parameters the address of the file object and the address of the memory region descriptor. For most filesystems, this method is implemented by the generic_file_mmap() function, which performs the following operations:

    a. Initializes the vm_ops field of the memory region descriptor. If VM_SHARED is on, sets the field to file_shared_mmap, otherwise sets the field to file_private_mmap (see Table 15-2). In a sense, this step does something similar to the way opening a file initializes the methods of a file object.

    b. Checks from the inode's i_mode field whether the file to be mapped is a regular one. For other types of files, such as a directory or socket, returns an error code.

    c. Checks from the inode's i_op field whether the readpage() inode operation is defined. If not, returns an error code.

d. Invokes `update_atime()` to store the current time in the `i_atime` field of the file's inode and to mark the inode as dirty.

5. Initializes the `vm_file` field of the memory region descriptor with the address of the file object and increments the file's usage counter.

6. Recall from the section "Allocating a Linear Address Interval" in Chapter 7 that `do_mmap()` invokes `insert_vm_struct()`. During the execution of this function, inserts the memory region descriptor into the list to which the inode's `i_mmap` field points.

Destroying a Memory Mapping

When a process is ready to destroy a memory mapping, it invokes the `munmap()` system call, passing the following parameters to it:

- The address of the first location in the linear address interval to be removed

- The length of the linear address interval to be removed

Notice that the `munmap()` system call can be used to either remove or reduce the size of any kind of memory region. Indeed, the `sys_munmap()` service routine of the system call essentially invokes the `do_munmap()` function already described in the section "Releasing a Linear Address Interval" in Chapter 7. However, if the memory region maps a file, the following additional steps are performed for each memory region included in the range of linear addresses to be released:

1. Checks whether the memory region has an `unmap` method; if so, invokes it. Usually, private memory mappings do not have such a method since the file must not be updated. Shared memory mappings make use of the `filemap_unmap()` function, which invokes, in turn, `filemap_sync()` (see the later section "Flushing Dirty Memory Mapping Pages to Disk").

2. Invokes `remove_shared_vm_struct()` to remove the memory region descriptor from the inode list pointed to by the `i_mmap` field.

Demand Paging for Memory Mapping

For reasons of efficiency, page frames are not assigned to a memory mapping right after it has been created but at the last possible moment—that is, when the process attempts to address one of its pages, thus causing a "Page fault" exception.

We have seen in the section "Page Fault Exception Handler" in Chapter 7 how the kernel verifies whether the faulty address is included in some memory region of the process; in the affirmative case, the kernel checks the page table entry corresponding to the faulty address and invokes the `do_no_page()` function if the entry is null (see the section "Demand Paging" in Chapter 7).

The `do_no_page()` function performs all the operations that are common to all types of demand paging, such as allocating a page frame and updating the page tables. It also checks whether the `nopage` method of the memory region involved is defined. In the Chapter 7 section "Demand Paging," we described the case in which the method is undefined (anonymous memory region); now we complete the description by discussing the actions performed by the function when the method is defined:

1. Invokes the `nopage` method, which returns the address of a page frame that contains the requested page.

2. Increments the `rss` field of the process memory descriptor to indicate that a new page frame has been assigned to the process.

3. Sets up the Page Table entry corresponding to the faulty address with the address of the page frame returned by the `nopage` method and the page access rights included in the memory region `vm_page_prot` field. Further actions depend on the type of access:

   — If the process is trying to write into the page, forces the `Read/Write` and `Dirty` bits of the Page Table entry to 1. In this case, either the page frame is exclusively assigned to the process, or the page is shared: in both cases, writing to it should be allowed. (This avoids a second useless "Page fault" exception caused by the Copy On Write mechanism.)

   — If the process is trying to read from the page, the memory region `VM_SHARED` flag is not set, and the page's usage counter is greater than 1, forces the `Read/Write` bit of the Page Table entry to 0. This is because the page's usage counter indicates that other processes are sharing the page; since the page doesn't belong to a shared memory region, it must be handled through the Copy On Write mechanism.

The core of the demand paging algorithm consists of the memory region's `nopage` method. Generally speaking, it must return the address of a page frame that contains the page accessed by the process. Its implementation depends on the kind of memory region in which the page is included.

When handling memory regions that map files on disk, the `nopage` method must first search for the requested page in the page cache. If the page is not found, the method must read it from disk. Most filesystems implement the `nopage` method by means of the `filemap_nopage()` function, which acts on three parameters:

`area`
    Descriptor address of the memory region including the required page.

`address`
    Linear address of the required page.

no_share

Flag specifying whether the page frame returned by the function must not be shared among many processes. The `do_no_page()` function sets this flag only if the process is trying to write into the page and the VM_SHARED flag is off.

The `filemap_nopage()` function executes the following steps:

1. Gets the file object address from `area->vm_file` field. Derives the inode object address from the `d_inode` field of the `dentry` object to which the `f_dentry` field of the file object points.

2. Uses the `vm_start` and `vm_offset` fields of `area` to determine the offset within the file of the data corresponding to the page starting from `address`.

3. Checks whether the file offset exceeds the file size. If this occurs and the VM_SHARED flag is on, returns 0, thus causing a SIGBUS signal to be sent to the process. (Private memory mappings behave differently: a new page frame filled with zeros is assigned to the process.)

4. Invokes `find_page()` to look in the page cache for the page identified by the inode object and the file offset. If the page isn't there, invokes `try_to_read_ahead()` to allocate a new page frame, to add it to the page cache, and to fill its contents with data read from disk. Actually, the kernel tries to read ahead the next `page_cluster` pages as well (see Chapter 16, *Swapping: Methods for Freeing Memory*).

5. Invokes `wait_on_page()` to wait until the required page becomes unlocked (that is, until any current I/O data transfer for the page terminates).

6. If the no_share flag is 0, the page frame can be shared: returns its address.

7. The no_share flag is 1, so the process tried to write into a page of a private memory mapping (or, more precisely, of a memory region whose VM_SHARED flag is off). Therefore, allocates a new page frame by performing the following operations:

   a. Invokes the `__get_free_page()` function

   b. Copies the page included in the page cache in the new page frame

   c. Decrements the usage counter of the page in the page cache in order to undo the increment done by `find_page()`

   d. Returns the address of the new page frame

Flushing Dirty Memory Mapping Pages to Disk

The `msync()` system call can be used by a process to flush to disk dirty pages belonging to a shared memory mapping. It receives as parameters the starting address of an interval of linear addresses, the length of the interval, and a set of flags that have the following meanings.

MS_SYNC

Asks the system call to suspend the process until the I/O operation completes. In this way the calling process can assume that when the system call terminates, all pages of its memory mapping have been flushed to disk.

MS_ASYNC

Asks the system call to return immediately without suspending the calling process.

MS_INVALIDATE

Asks the system call to remove all pages included in the memory mapping from the process address space.

The `sys_msync()` service routine invokes `msync_interval()` on each memory region included in the interval of linear addresses (see the section "Allocating a Linear Address Interval" in Chapter 7). In turn, the latter function performs the following operations:

1. If the `vm_file` field of the memory region descriptor is `NULL`, returns 0 (the memory region doesn't map a file).

2. Invokes the `sync` method of the memory region operations. In most filesystems, this method is implemented by the `filemap_sync()` function (described shortly).

3. If the `MS_SYNC` flag is on, invokes the `file_fsync()` function to flush to disk all related file information: the file's inode, the filesystem's superblock, and (by means of `sync_buffers()`) all the dirty buffers of the file.

The `filemap_sync()` function copies data included in the memory region to disk. It starts by scanning the Page Table entries corresponding to the linear address intervals included in the memory region. For each page frame found, it performs the following steps:

1. Invokes `flush_tlb_page()` to flush the translation lookaside buffers.

2. If the `MS_INVALIDATE` flag is off, increments the usage counter of the page descriptor.

3. If the `MS_INVALIDATE` flag is on, sets the corresponding Page Table entry to 0, thus specifying that the page is no longer present.

4. Invokes the `filemap_write_page()` function, which in turn performs the following substeps:

   a. Increments the usage counter of the file object associated with the file. This is a fail-safe mechanism, so that the file object is not freed if the process terminates while the I/O data transfer is still going on.

   b. Invokes `do_write_page()`, which essentially executes the `write` method of the file operations, thus simulating a `write()` system call on the file. In this case, of course, the data to be written is not taken from a User Mode buffer but from the page being flushed.

   c. Invokes `fput()` to decrement the usage counter of the file object, thus compensating for the increment made in step 4a.

5. Invokes `free_page()` to decrease the usage counter of the page descriptor; this compensates for the increment performed at step 2 if the `MS_INVALIDATE` flag is off. Otherwise, if the flag is on, the global effect of `filemap_sync()` is to release the page frame (giving it back to the Buddy system if the counter becomes 0).

Anticipating Linux 2.4

The approach followed remains basically the same. However, if a memory region is recognized as "sequential read," read-ahead is performed while reading pages from disk. Moreover, as already mentioned at the end of Chapter 13, writing to a regular file is much simpler in Linux 2.4 because it can be easily done through page I/O operations.

CHAPTER SIXTEEN

SWAPPING: METHODS FOR FREEING MEMORY

The disk caches examined in previous chapters used RAM as an extension of the disk; the goal was to improve system response time and the solution was to reduce the number of disk accesses. In this chapter we introduce an opposite approach called *swapping*: here the kernel uses some space on disk as an extension of RAM. Swapping is transparent to the programmer: once the swapping areas have been properly installed and activated, the processes may run under the assumption that they have all the physical memory available that they can address, never knowing that some of their pages are stored away and retrieved again as needed.

Disk caches enhance system performance at the expense of free RAM, while swapping extends the amount of addressable memory at the expense of access speed. Thus, disk caches are "good" and desirable, while swapping should be regarded as some sort of last resort to be used whenever the amount of free RAM becomes too scarce.

We'll start in "What Is Swapping?" by defining swapping. Then we'll describe in the section "Swap Area" the main data structures introduced by Linux to implement it. We discuss the swap cache and the low-level functions that transfer pages between RAM and swap areas and vice versa. The two crucial sections are: "Page Swap-Out," where we describe the procedure used to select a page to be swapped out to disk, and "Page Swap-In," where we explain how a page stored in a swap area is read back into RAM when the need occurs.

This chapter effectively concludes our discussion of memory management. Just one topic remains to be covered, namely page frame reclaiming; this is done in the last section, which is related only in part to swapping. With so many disk caches around, including the swap cache, all the available RAM could eventually end up in these caches and no more free RAM would be left. We shall see how the kernel prevents this by monitoring the amount of free RAM and by freeing pages from the caches or from the process address spaces, as the need occurs.

What Is Swapping?

Swapping serves two main purposes:

- To expand the address space that is effectively usable by a process

- To expand the amount of dynamic RAM (what is left of the RAM once the kernel code and static data structures have been initialized) to load processes

Let's give a few examples of how swapping benefits the user. The simplest is when a program's data structures take up more space than the size of the available RAM. A swap area will allow this program to be loaded without any problem, thus to run correctly. A more subtle example involves users who issue several commands trying to simultaneously run large applications that require a lot of memory. If no swap area is active, the system might reject requests to launch a new application. In contrast, a swap area allows the kernel to launch it, since some memory can be freed at the expense of some of the already existing processes without killing them.

These two examples illustrate the benefits, but also the drawbacks, of swapping. Simulation of RAM is not like RAM in terms of performance. Every access by a process to a page that is currently swapped-out increases the process execution time by several orders of magnitude. In short, if performance is of great importance, swapping should be used only as a last resort; adding RAM chips still remains the best solution to cope with increasing computing needs. It is fair to say, however, that, in some cases, swapping may be beneficial to the system as a whole. Long-running processes typically access only half of the page frames obtained. Even when some RAM is available, swapping unused pages out and using the RAM for disk cache can improve overall system performance.

Swapping has been around for many years. The first Unix system kernels monitored the amount of free memory constantly. When it became less than a fixed threshold, they performed some swapping-out. This activity consisted of copying the entire address space of a process to disk. Conversely, when the scheduling algorithm selected a swapped-out process, the whole process was swapped in from disk.

This approach has been abandoned by modern Unix kernels, including Linux, mainly because context switches are quite expensive when they involve swapping in swapped-out processes. To compensate for the burden of such swapping activity, the scheduling algorithm must be very sophisticated: it must favor in-RAM processes without completely shutting out the swapped-out ones.

In Linux, swapping is currently performed at the page level rather than at the process address space level. This finer level of granularity has been reached thanks to the inclusion of a hardware paging unit in the CPU. We recall from the section "Regular Paging" in Chapter 2, *Memory Addressing*, that each Page Table entry includes a Present flag: the kernel can take advantage of this flag to signal to the hardware that a page belonging to a process address space has been swapped out. Besides that flag,

Linux also takes advantage of the remaining bits of the Page Table entry to store the location of the swapped-out page on disk. When a "Page fault" exception occurs, the corresponding exception handler can detect that the page is not present in RAM and invoke the function that swaps the missing page in from the disk.

Much of the algorithm's complexity is thus related to swapping-out. In particular, four main issues must be considered:

- Which kind of page to swap out
- How to distribute pages in the swap areas
- How to select the page to be swapped out
- When to perform page swap-out

Let us give a short preview of how Linux handles these four issues before describing the main data structures and functions related to swapping.

Which Kind of Page to Swap Out

Swapping applies only to the following kinds of pages:

- Pages belonging to an anonymous memory region (for instance, a User Mode stack) of a process
- Modified pages belonging to a private memory mapping of a process
- Pages belonging to an IPC shared memory region (see the section "IPC Shared Memory" in Chapter 18, *Process Communication*)

The remaining kinds of pages are either used by the kernel or used to map files on disk. In the first case, they are ignored by swapping because this simplifies the kernel design; in the second case, the best swap areas for the pages are the files themselves.

How to Distribute Pages in the Swap Areas

Each swap area is organized into *slots*, where each slot contains exactly one page. When swapping out, the kernel tries to store pages in contiguous slots so as to minimize disk seek time when accessing the swap area; this is an important element of an efficient swapping algorithm.

If more than one swap area is used, things become more complicated. Faster swap areas—that is, swap areas stored in faster disks—get a higher priority. When looking for a free slot, the search starts in the swap area having the highest priority. If there are several of them, swap areas of the same priority are cyclically selected in order to avoid overloading one of them. If no free slot is found in the swap areas having the highest priority, the search continues in the swap areas having a priority next to the highest one, and so on.

How to Select the Page to Be Swapped Out

With the exception of pages belonging to IPC shared memory, which will be discussed in Chapter 18, the general rule for swapping out is to steal pages from the process having the largest number of pages in RAM. However, a choice must be made among the pages of the process chosen for swap-out: it would be nice to be able to rank them according to some criterion. Several Least Recently Used (LRU) replacement algorithms have been proposed and used in some kernels. The main idea is to associate with each page in RAM a counter storing the age of the page, that is, the interval of time elapsed since the last access to the page. The oldest page of the process can then be swapped out.

Some computer platforms provide sophisticated support for LRU algorithms; for instance, the CPUs of some mainframes automatically update the value of a counter included in each Page Table entry to specify the age of the corresponding page. But Intel 80x86 processors do not offer such a hardware feature, so Linux cannot use a true LRU algorithm. However, when selecting a candidate for swap-out, Linux takes advantage of the `Accessed` flag included in each Page Table entry, which is automatically set by the hardware when the page is accessed. As we'll see later, this flag is set and cleared in a rather simplistic way to keep pages from being swapped in and out too much.

When to Perform Page Swap-out

Swapping out is useful when the kernel is dangerously low on memory. In fact, the kernel keeps a small reserve of free page frames that can be used only by the most critical functions. This turns out to be essential to avoid system crashes, which might occur when a kernel routine invoked to free resources is unable to obtain the memory area it needs to complete its task. In order to protect this reserve of free page frames, Linux performs a swap-out on the following occasions:

- By a kernel thread denoted as *kswapd* activated once every second whenever the number of free page frames falls below a predefined threshold

- When a memory request to the Buddy system (see the section "The Buddy System Algorithm" in Chapter 6, *Memory Management*) cannot be satisfied because the number of free page frames would fall below a predefined threshold

Several functions are concerned with swapping. Figure 16-1 illustrates the most important ones. They will be discussed in the following sections.

Swap Area

The pages swapped out from memory are stored in a *swap area*, which may be implemented either as a disk partition of its own or as a file included in a larger partition. Several different swap areas may be defined, up to a maximum number specified by the `MAX_SWAPFILES` macro (usually set to 8).

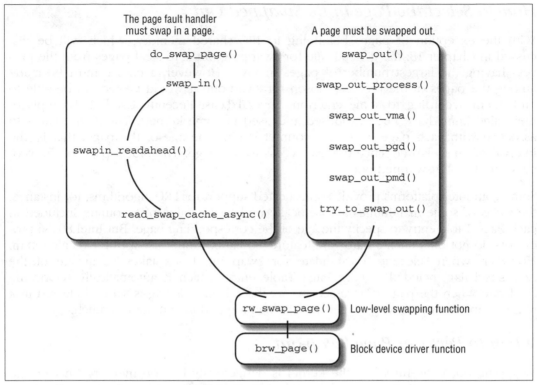

Figure 16-1. Main functions related to swapping

Having multiple swap areas allows a system administrator to spread a lot of swap space among several disks so that the hardware can act on them concurrently; it also lets swap space be increased at runtime without rebooting the system.

Each swap area consists of a sequence of *page slots*, that is, of 4096-byte blocks used to contain a swapped-out page. The first page slot of a swap area is used to persistently store some information about the swap area; its format is described by the `swap_header` union composed of two structures, `info` and `magic`. The `magic` structure provides a string that marks part of the disk unambiguously as a swap area; it consists of just one field, `magic.magic`, containing a 10-character "magic" string. The `magic` structure essentially allows the kernel to unambiguously identify a file or a partition as a swap area; the text of the string depends on the swapping algorithm version. The field is always located at the end of the first page slot.

The `info` structure includes the following fields:

info.bootbits
Not used by the swapping algorithm; this field corresponds to the first 1024 bytes of the swap area, which may store partition data, disk labels, and so on.

`info.version`
> Swapping algorithm version.

`info.last_page`
> Last page slot that is effectively usable.

`info.nr_badpages`
> Number of defective page slots.

`info.padding[125]`
> Padding bytes.

`info.badpages[1]`
> Up to 640 numbers specifying the location of defective page slots.

Usually, the system administrator creates a swap partition when creating the other partitions on the Linux system, then uses the */sbin/mkswap* command to set up the disk area as a new swap area. That command initializes the fields just described within the first page slot. Since the disk may include some bad blocks, the program also examines all other page slots in order to locate the defective ones. But executing the */sbin/mkswap* command leaves the swap area in an inactive state. Each swap area can be activated in a script file at system boot or dynamically after the system is running. An initialized swap area is considered *active* when it effectively represents an extension of the system RAM (see the section "Activating and Deactivating a Swap Area" later in this chapter).

Swap Area Descriptor

Each active swap area has its own `swap_info_struct` descriptor in memory, whose fields are illustrated in Table 16-1.

Table 16-1. Fields of a Swap Area Descriptor

Type	Field	Description
unsigned int	flags	Swap area flags
kdev_t	swap_device	Device number of the swap device
struct dentry *	swap_file	Dentry of the file or device file
unsigned short *	swap_map	Pointer to array of counters, one for each swap area page slot
unsigned char *	swap_lockmap	Pointer to array of bit locks, one for each swap area page slot
unsigned int	lowest_bit	First page slot to be scanned when searching for a free one
unsigned int	highest_bit	Last page slot to be scanned when searching for a free one
unsigned int	cluster_next	Next page slot to be scanned when searching for a free one

Table 16-1. Fields of a Swap Area Descriptor (continued)

Type	Field	Description
unsigned int	cluster_nr	Number of free page slot allocations before restarting from beginning
int	prio	Swap area priority
int	pages	Number of usable page slots
unsigned long	max	Size of swap area in pages
int	next	Pointer to next swap area descriptor

The `flags` field includes two overlapping subfields:

SWP_USED

 1 if the swap area is active; 0 if it is nonactive.

SWP_WRITEOK

 This 2-bit field is set to 3 if it is possible to write into the swap area and 0 otherwise; since the least-significant bit of this field coincides with the bit used to implement SWP_USED, a swap area can be written only if it is active. The kernel is not allowed to write in a swap area when it is being activated or deactivated.

The `swap_map` field points to an array of counters, one for each swap area page slot. If the counter is equal to 0, the page slot is free; if it is positive, the page slot is filled with a swapped-out page (the exact meaning of positive values will be discussed in the section "The Swap Cache"). If the counter has the value SWP_MAP_MAX (equal to 32,767), the page stored in the page slot is "permanent" and cannot be removed from the corresponding slot. If the counter has the value SWP_MAP_BAD (equal to 32,768), the page slot is considered defective, thus unusable.

The `swap_lockmap` field points to an array of bits, one for each swap area page slot. If a bit is set, the page stored in the page slot is currently being swapped in or swapped out. This bit is thus used as a lock to ensure exclusive access to the page slot during an I/O data transfer.

The `prio` field is a signed integer that denotes the "goodness" of the swap area. Swap areas implemented on faster disks should have a higher priority, so that they will be used first. Only when they are filled does the swapping algorithm consider lower-priority swap areas. Swap areas having the same priority are cyclically selected in order to distribute swapped-out pages among them. As we shall see in the section "Activating and Deactivating a Swap Area," the priority is assigned when the swap area is activated.

The `swap_info` array includes MAX_SWAPFILES swap area descriptors. Of course, not all of them are necessarily used, only those having the SWP_USED flag set. Figure 16-2 illustrates the `swap_info` array, one swap area, and the corresponding array of counters.

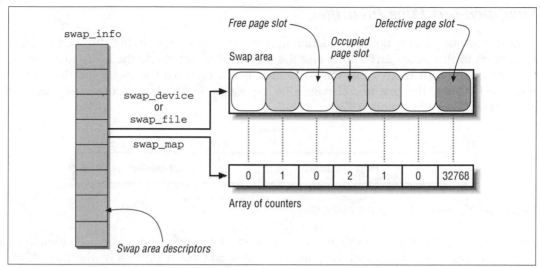

Figure 16-2. Swap area data structures

The **nr_swapfiles** variable stores the index of the last array element that contains, or that has contained, an effectively used swap area descriptor. Despite its name, the variable *does not* contain the number of active swap areas.

Descriptors of active swap areas are also inserted into a list sorted by the swap area priority. The list is implemented through the **next** field of the swap area descriptor, which stores the index of the next descriptor in the **swap_info** array. This use of the field as an index is different from most fields we've seen with the name **next**, which are usually pointers.

The **swap_list** variable, of type **swap_list_t**, includes the following fields:

head

Index in the **swap_info** array of the first list element.

next

Index in the **swap_info** array of the descriptor of the next swap area to be selected for swapping out pages. This field is used to implement a round-robin algorithm among maximum-priority swap areas with free slots.

The **max** field stores the size of the swap area in pages, while the **pages** field stores the number of usable page slots. These numbers differ because **pages** does not take into consideration the first page slot and the defective page slots.

Finally, the **nr_swap_pages** variable contains the total number of free, nondefective page slots in all active swap areas.

Swapped-out Page Identifier

A swapped-out page is uniquely identified quite simply by specifying the index of the swap area in the `swap_info` array and the page slot index inside the swap area. Since the first page (with index 0) of the swap area is reserved for the `swap_header` union discussed earlier, the first useful page slot has index 1. The format of a *swapped-out page identifier* is illustrated in Figure 16-3.

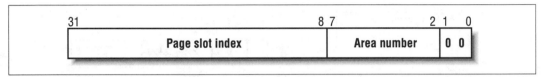

Figure 16-3. Swapped-out page identifier

The `SWP_ENTRY(type,offset)` macro constructs a swapped-out page identifier from the swap area index `type` and the page slot index `offset`. Conversely, the `SWP_TYPE` and `SWP_OFFSET` macros extract from a swapped-out page identifier the swap area index and the page slot index, respectively.

When a page is swapped out, its identifier is inserted as the page's entry into the Page Table so the page can be found again when needed. Notice that the least-significant bit of such an identifier, which corresponds to the `Present` flag, is always cleared to denote the fact that the page is not currently in RAM. However, at least 1 of the 30 most-significant bits has to be set because no page is ever stored in slot 0. It is thus possible to identify, from the value of a Page Table entry, three different cases:

- Null entry: the page does not belong to the process address space.

- First 30 most-significant bits not all equal to 0, last 2 bits equal to 0: the page is currently swapped out.

- Least-significant bit equal to 1: the page is contained in RAM.

Since a page may belong to the address spaces of several processes (see the later section "The Swap Cache"), it may be swapped out from the address space of one process and still remain in main memory; therefore, it is possible to swap out the same page several times. A page is physically swapped out and stored just once, of course, but each subsequent attempt to swap it out increments the `swap_map` counter.

The `swap_duplicate()` function is invoked while trying to swap out an already swapped-out page. It just verifies that the swapped-out page identifier passed as its parameter is valid and increments the corresponding `swap_map` counter. More precisely, it performs the following actions:

1. Uses the `SWP_TYPE` and `SWP_OFFSET` macros to extract from the parameter the partition number `type` and the page slot index `offset`.

2. Checks whether one of the following error conditions occurs:

    a. `type` is greater than `nr_swapfiles`.

    b. The `SWP_USED` flag in `swap_info[type].flags` is cleared, indicating that the swap area is not active.

    c. `offset` is greater than `swap_info[type].max`.

    d. `swap_info[type].swap_map[offset]` is null, indicating that the page slot is free.

    If any of these cases occurs, return 0 (invalid identifier).

3. If the previous tests were passed, the swapped-out page identifier locates a valid page. Therefore, increments `swap_info[type].swap_map[offset]`; however, if the counter is equal to `SWAP_MAP_MAX` or to `SWAP_MAP_BAD`, leaves it unchanged.

4. Returns 1 (valid identifier).

Activating and Deactivating a Swap Area

Once a swap area is initialized, the superuser (or, more precisely, any user having the `CAP_SYS_ADMIN` capability, as described in the section "Process Credentials and Capabilities" in Chapter 19, *Program Execution*) may use the */bin/swapon* and */bin/swapoff* programs to, respectively, activate and deactivate the swap area. These programs make use of the `swapon()` and `swapoff()` system calls; we'll briefly sketch out the corresponding service routines.

The `sys_swapon()` service routine receives as parameters:

`specialfile`
> This parameter contains the pathname of the device file (partition) or plain file used to implement the swap area.

`swap_flags`
> If the `SWAP_FLAG_PREFER` bit is on, the 15 least-significant bits specify the priority of the swap area.

The function checks the fields of the `swap_header` union that was put in the first slot when the swap area was created. The main steps performed by the function are:

1. Checks that the current process has the `CAP_SYS_ADMIN` capability.

2. Searches for the first descriptor in `swap_info` having the `SWP_USED` flag cleared, meaning that the corresponding swap area is inactive. If there is none, returns an error code, because there are already `MAX_SWAPFILES` active swap areas.

3. A descriptor for the swap area has been found; sets its SWP_USED flag. Moreover, if the descriptor's index is greater than nr_swapfiles, updates that variable.

4. Sets the prio field of the descriptor. If the swap_flags parameter does not specify a priority, initializes the field with the lowest priority among all active swap areas minus 1 (thus assuming that the last activated swap area is on the slowest block device). If no other swap areas are already active, assigns the value -1.

5. Initializes the swap_file field of the descriptor to the address of the dentry object associated with specialfile, as returned by the namei() function (see the section "Pathname Lookup" in Chapter 12, *The Virtual Filesystem*).

6. If the specialfile parameter identifies a block device file, stores the device number into the swap_device field of the descriptor, sets the block size in the proper entry of the blksize_size array to PAGE_SIZE, and invokes blkdev_open(). The latter function sets up the f_ops field of a new file object associated with the device file and initializes the hardware device (see the section "VFS Handling of Device Files" in Chapter 13, *Managing I/O Devices*). Moreover, checks that the swap area was not already activated by looking at the swap_device field of the other descriptors in swap_info. If it has been activated, returns an error code.

7. If, on the other hand, the specialfile parameter identifies a regular file, checks that the swap area was already activated by looking at the swap_file->d_inode field of the other descriptors in swap_info. If it was activated, returns an error code.

8. Allocates a page frame and invokes rw_swap_page_nocache() (see the section "Transferring Swap Pages" later in this chapter) to read the first page of the swap area, which stores the swap_header union.

9. Checks that the magic string in the last 10 characters of the first page is equal to SWAP-SPACE or to SWAPSPACE2 (there are two slightly different versions of the swapping algorithm). If not, the specialfile parameter does not specify an already initialized swap area, so returns an error code.

10. Initializes the lowest_bit, highest_bit, and max fields of the swap area descriptor according to the size of the swap area stored in the info.last_page field of the swap_header union.

11. Invokes vmalloc() to create the array of counters associated with the new swap area and store its address in the swap_map field of the swap descriptor. Initializes the elements of the array to 0 or to SWAP_MAP_BAD, according to the list of defective page slots stored in the info.bad_pages field of the swap_header union.

12. Invokes vmalloc() again to create the array of locks and store its address in the swap_lockmap field of the swap descriptor; initializes all bits to 0.

13. Computes the number of useful page slots by accessing the info.last_page and info.nr_badpages fields in the first page slot.

14. Sets the `flags` field of the swap descriptor to `SWP_WRITEOK`, sets the `pages` field to the number of useful page slots, and updates the `nr_swap_pages` variable.

15. Inserts the new swap area descriptor in the list to which the `swap_list` variable points.

16. Releases the page frame containing the data of the first page of the swap area and returns 0 (success).

The `sys_swapoff()` service routine deactivates a swap area identified by the parameter `specialfile`. It is much more complex and time-consuming than `sys_swapon()`, since the partition to be deactivated might still contain pages belonging to several processes. The function is thus forced to scan the swap area and to swap in all existing pages. Since each swap-in requires a new page frame, it might fail if there are no free page frames left. In this case, the function returns an error code. All this is achieved by performing the following steps:

1. Invokes `namei()` on `specialfile` to get a pointer to the dentry object associated with the swap area.

2. Scans the list to which `swap_list` points and locates the descriptor whose `swap_file` field points to the dentry object associated with `specialfile`. If no such descriptor exists, an invalid parameter was passed to the function; if the descriptor exists but the most significant bit of its `SWP_WRITEOK` field is cleared while its SWP_USED flag is set.

3. Removes the descriptor from the list and sets its `flags` field to SWP_USED so the kernel doesn't store more pages in the swap area before this function deactivates it.

4. Invokes the `try_to_unuse()` function to successively force all pages left in the swap area into RAM and to correspondingly update the page tables of the processes that make use of these pages. For each page slot, the function performs the following substeps:

   a. If the counter associated with the page slot is equal to 0 (no page is stored there) or to SWP_MAP_BAD, does nothing (continues with the next page slot).

   b. Otherwise, invokes the `read_swap_cache()` function (see the section "Transferring Swap Pages" later in this chapter) to allocate, if necessary, a new page frame and fill it with the data stored in the page slot.

   c. Invokes `unuse_process()` on each process in the process list. This time-consuming function scans all Page Table entries of the process and replaces any occurrence of the swapped-out page identifier with the physical address of the page frame. To reflect this move, the function also decrements the page slot counter in the `swap_map` array and increments the usage counter of the page frame.

      d. Invokes `shm_unuse()` to check whether the swapped-out page is used for an IPC shared memory resource and to properly handle that case (see the section "IPC Shared Memory" in Chapter 18).

      e. Removes, if necessary, the page frame from the swap cache (see the section "The Swap Cache" later in this chapter).

5. If `try_to_unuse()` fails in allocating all requested page frames, the swap area cannot be deactivated. Reinserts the swap area descriptor in the `swap_list` list, sets its `flags` field to `SWP_WRITEOK` again, and returns an error code.

6. Otherwise, all used page slots have been successfully transferred to RAM. Finishes by releasing the dentry object and the inode object associated with the swap area, releasing the memory areas used to store the `swap_map` and `swap_lockmap` arrays, updating the `nr_swap_pages` variable, and finally returning 0 (success).

Finding a Free Page Slot

As we shall see later, when freeing memory, the kernel swaps out many pages in a short period of time. It is thus important to try to store these pages in contiguous slots so as to minimize disk seek time when accessing the swap area.

A first approach to an algorithm that searches for a free slot could choose one of two simplistic, rather extreme strategies:

- Always start from the beginning of the swap area. This approach may increase the average seek time during swap-out operations, because free page slots may be scattered far away from one another.

- Always start from the last allocated page slot. This approach increases the average seek time during swap-in operations if the swap area is mostly free (as is usually the case): the few occupied page slots may be scattered far away from one another.

Linux adopts a hybrid approach. It always starts from the last allocated page slot unless one of these conditions occurs:

- The end of the swap area is reached

- `SWAPFILE_CLUSTER` (usually 256) free page slots have been allocated after the last restart from the beginning of the swap area

The `cluster_nr` field in the `swap_info_struct` descriptor stores the number of free page slots allocated. This field is reset to 0 when the function restarts allocation from the beginning of the swap area. The `cluster_next` field stores the index of the first page slot to be examined in the next allocation.[*]

---

[*] As you may have noticed, the names of Linux data structures are not always appropriate. In this case, the kernel does not really "cluster" page slots of a swap area.

In order to speed up the search for free page slots, the kernel keeps the `lowest_bit` and `highest_bit` fields of each swap area descriptor up-to-date. These fields specify the first and the last page slots that could be free; in other words, any page slot below `lowest_bit` and above `highest_bit` is known to be occupied.

The `scan_swap_map()` is used to find a free page slot. It acts on a single parameter, which points to a swap area descriptor and returns the index of a free page slot. It returns 0 if the swap area does not contain any free slots. The function performs the following steps:

1. If the `cluster_nr` field of the swap area descriptor is positive, scans the `swap_map` array of counters starting from the element at index `cluster_next` and looks for a null entry. If a null entry is found, decrements the `cluster_nr` field and goes to step 3.

2. If this point is reached, either the `cluster_nr` field is null or the search starting from `cluster_next` didn't find a null entry in the `swap_map` array. It is time to try the second stage of the hybrid search. Reinitializes `cluster_nr` to `SWAPFILE_CLUSTER` and restarts scanning of the array from the `lowest_bit` index. If no null entry is found, returns 0 (the swap area is full).

3. A null entry has been found. Puts the value 1 in the entry, decrements `nr_swap_pages`, updates if necessary the `lowest_bit` and `highest_bit` fields, and sets the `cluster_next` field to the index of the page slot just allocated.

4. Returns the index of the allocated page slot.

Allocating and Releasing a Page Slot

The `get_swap_page()` function returns the index of a newly allocated page slot or 0 if all swap areas are filled. The function takes into consideration the different priorities of the active swap areas.

Two passes are necessary. The first pass is partial and applies only to areas having the same priority; the function searches such areas in a round-robin fashion for a free slot. If no free page slot is found, a second pass is made starting from the beginning of the swap area list; in this second pass all swap areas are examined. More precisely, the function performs the following steps:

1. If `nr_swap_pages` is null, returns 0.

2. Starts by considering the swap area pointed to by `swap_list.next` (recall that the swap area list is sorted by decreasing priorities).

3. If the swap area is active and not being deactivated, invokes `scan_swap_map()` to allocate a free page slot. If `scan_swap_map()` returns a page slot index, the function's job is essentially done, but it must prepare for its next invocation. Thus, it

updates `swap_list.next` to point to the next swap area in the swap area list, if the latter has the same priority (thus continuing the round-robin use of these swap areas). If the next swap area does not have the same priority as the current one, the function sets `swap_list.next` to the first swap area in the list (so that the next search will start with the swap areas having the highest priority). The function finishes by returning the identifier corresponding to the page slot just allocated.

4. Either the swap area is not writable, or it does not have free page slots. If the next swap area in the swap area list has the same priority as the current one, makes it the current one and goes to step 3.

5. At this point, the next swap area in the swap area list has a lower priority than the previous one. The next step depends on which of the two passes the function is performing.

    a. If this is the first (partial) pass, considers the first swap area in the list and goes to step 3, thus starting the second pass.

    b. Otherwise, checks if there is a next element in the list; if so, considers it and goes to step 3.

6. At this point the list has been completely scanned by the second pass, and no free page slot has been found: returns 0.

The `swap_free()` function is invoked when swapping in a page to decrement the corresponding `swap_map` counter (see Table 16-1). When the counter reaches 0, the page slot becomes free since its identifier is no longer included in any Page Table entry. The function acts on a single `entry` parameter that specifies a swapped-out page identifier and performs the following steps:

1. Uses the `SWP_TYPE` and `SWP_OFFSET` macros to derive from `entry` the swap area index and the page slot index.

2. Checks whether the swap area is active; returns right away if it is not.

3. If the priority of the swap area is greater than that of the swap area to which `swap_list.next` points, sets `swap_list.next` to `swap_list.head`, so that the next search for a free page slot starts from the highest priority swap area. In this way, the page slot being released will be reallocated before any other page slot is allocated from lower-priority swap areas.

4. If the `swap_map` counter corresponding to the page slot being freed is smaller than `SWAP_MAP_MAX`, decrements it. Recall that entries having the `SWAP_MAP_MAX` value are considered persistent (undeletable).

5. If the `swap_map` counter becomes 0, increments the value of `nr_swap_pages` and updates, if necessary, the `lowest_bit` and `highest_bit` fields of the swap area descriptor.

The Swap Cache

In Linux, a page frame may be shared among several processes in the following cases:

- The page frame is associated with a shared* memory mapping (see the section "Memory Mapping" in Chapter 15, *Accessing Regular Files*).

- The page frame is handled by means of Copy On Write, perhaps because a new process has been forked (see the section "Copy On Write" in Chapter 7, *Process Address Space*).

- The page frame is allocated to an IPC shared memory resource (see the section "IPC Shared Memory" in Chapter 18).

As we shall see later in this chapter, page frames used for shared memory mappings are never swapped out. Instead, they are handled by another kernel function that writes their data to the proper files and discards them. However, the other two kinds of shared page frames must be carefully handled by the swapping algorithm.

Because the kernel handles each process separately, a page shared by two processes, A and B, may have been swapped out from the address space of A while it is still in B's address space. To handle this peculiar situation, Linux makes use of a swap cache, which collects all shared page frames that have been copied to swap areas. The swap cache does not exist as a data structure on its own, but the pages in the regular page cache are considered to be in the swap cache if certain fields are set.

The reader might ask at this point why the algorithm does not just swap a shared page out from all the process's address spaces at the same time, thus avoiding the need for a swap cache. The answer is that there is no quick way to derive from the page frame the list of processes that own it. Scanning all page table entries of all processes looking for an entry with a given physical address would be too costly.

So shared page swapping works like this. Consider a page P shared among two processes, A and B. Suppose that the swapping algorithm scans the page frames of process A and selects P for swapping out: it allocates a new page slot and copies the data stored in P into the new page slot. It then puts the swapped-out page identifier in the corresponding page table entry of process A. Finally, it invokes `__free_page()` to release the page frame. However, the page's usage counter does not become 0 since P is still owned by B. Thus, the swapping algorithm succeeds in transferring the page into the swap area, but it fails to reclaim the corresponding page frame.

Suppose now that the swapping algorithm scans the page frames of process B at a later time and selects P for swapping out. The kernel must recognize that P has already been transferred into a swap area so that the page won't be swapped out a

---

* Page frames for private memory mappings are handled through the Copy On Write mechanism, and thus fall under the next case.

second time. Moreover, it must be able to derive the swapped-out page identifier so that it can increase the page slot usage counter.

Figure 16-4 illustrates schematically the actions performed by the kernel on a shared page that is swapped out from multiple processes at different times. The numbers inside the swap area and inside P represent the page slot usage counter and the page usage counter, respectively. Notice that any usage count includes every process that is using the page or page slot, plus the swap cache if the page is included in it. Four stages are shown:

1. In (a) P is present in the Page Tables of both A and B.

2. In (b) P has been swapped out from A's address space.

3. In (c) P has been swapped out from both the address spaces of A and B but is still included in the swap cache.

4. Finally, in (d) P has been released to the Buddy system.

The swap cache is implemented by the page cache data structures and procedures described in the section "The Page Cache" in Chapter 14, *Disk Caches*. Recall that the page cache includes pages associated with regular files and that a hash table allows the algorithm to quickly derive the address of a page descriptor from the address of an inode object and an offset inside the file. Pages in the swap cache are stored as any other page in the page cache, with the following special treatment:

- The `inode` field of the page descriptor stores the address of a fictitious inode object contained in the `swapper_inode` variable.

- The `offset` field stores the swapped-out page identifier associated with the page.

- The `PG_swap_cache` flag in the `flags` field is set.

Moreover, when the page is put in the swap cache, both the `count` field of the page descriptor and the page slot usage counters are incremented, since the swap cache makes use of both the page frame and the page slot.

The kernel makes use of several functions to handle the swap cache; they are based mainly on those discussed in the section "The Page Cache" in Chapter 14. We'll show later how these relatively low-level functions are invoked by higher-level functions to swap pages in and out as needed.

The functions that handle the swap cache are:

`in_swap_cache()`
> Checks the `PG_swap_cache` flag of a page to determine whether it belongs to the swap cache; if so, it returns the swapped-out page identifier stored in the `offset` field.

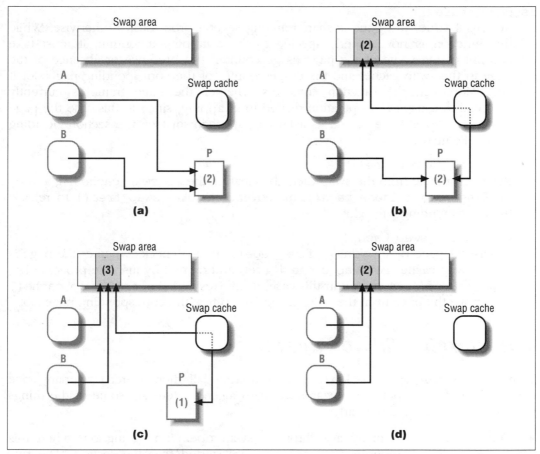

Figure 16-4. The role of the swap cache

`lookup_swap_cache()`

Acts on a swapped-out page identifier passed as its parameter and returns the page address or 0 if the page is not present in the cache. It invokes `find_page()`, passing as parameters the address of the fictitious `swapper_inode` inode object and the swapped-out page identifier to find the required page. If the page is present in the swap cache, `lookup_swap_cache()` checks whether it is locked; if so, the function invokes `wait_on_page()` to suspend the current process until the page becomes unlocked.

`add_to_swap_cache()`

Inserts a page into the swap cache. The inode and offset fields of the page descriptor are set to the address of the fictitious `swapper_inode` inode object and to the swapped-out page identifier, respectively. Then the function invokes the `add_page_to_hash_queue()` and `add_page_to_inode_queue()` functions. The page usage counter is also incremented.

`is_page_shared()`

Returns 1 (true) if a page is shared among several processes, 0 otherwise. While this function is not properly specific to the swapping algorithm, it must take account of the value of the page usage counter, the presence or absence of the page in the swap cache, and the usage counter of the corresponding page slot if any. Moreover, the function considers whether the page frame is currently involved in a page I/O operation related to swapping, since in this case the page usage counter is incremented as a fail-safe mechanism (see the section "Reading from a Regular File" in Chapter 15).

`delete_from_swap_cache()`

Removes a page from the swap cache by clearing the `PG_swap_cache` flag and by invoking `remove_inode_page()`; moreover, it invokes `swap_free()` to release the corresponding page slot.

`free_page_and_swap_cache()`

Releases a page by invoking `__free_page()`. It also checks whether the page is in the swap cache (`PG_swap_cache` flag set) and owned by just one process (`is_page_shared()` returns 0); in this case, it invokes `delete_from_swap_cache()` to remove the page from the swap cache and to free the corresponding page slot.

Transferring Swap Pages

Transferring swap pages wouldn't be so complicated if there weren't so many race conditions and other potential hazards to guard against. Here are some of the things that have to be checked regularly:

- There may be too many asynchronous swap operations going on; when this occurs, only synchronous I/O operations are started (see the section "The rw_swap_page() Function" later in this chapter).

- The process that owns a page may terminate while the page is being swapped in or out.

- Another process may be in the middle of swapping in a page that the current one is trying to swap out or vice versa.

We'll follow a bottom-up approach in the following sections. First we describe the synchronization mechanisms that avoid data corruption caused by simultaneous I/O operations on the same page frame or on the same page slot. Then we illustrate a few functions used to perform the data transfer of a swapped page.

Locking the Page Frame and the Page Slot

Like any other disk access type, I/O data transfers for swap pages are blocking operations. Therefore, the kernel must take care to avoid simultaneous transfers involving the same page frame, the same page slot, or both.

Race conditions can be avoided on the page frame through the mechanisms discussed in Chapter 13. Specifically, before starting an I/O operation on the page frame, the kernel invokes the `wait_on_page()` function to wait until the `PG_locked` flag is off. When the function returns, the page frame lock has been acquired, and therefore no other kernel control path can access the page frame's contents during the I/O operation.

But the state of the page slot must also be tracked. The `PG_locked` flag of the page descriptor is used once again to ensure exclusive access to the page slot involved in the I/O data transfer. Before starting an I/O operation on a swap page, the kernel usually checks that the page frame involved is included in the swap cache; if not, it adds the page frame into the swap cache. Let's suppose some process tries to swap in some page while the same page is currently being transferred. Before doing any work related to the swap-in, the kernel looks in the swap cache for a page frame associated with the given swapped-out page identifier. Since the page frame is found, the kernel knows that it must not allocate a new page frame, but must simply use the cached page frame. Moreover, since the `PG_locked` flag is set, the kernel suspends the kernel control path until the bit becomes 0, so that both the page frame's contents and the page slot in the swap area are preserved until the I/O operation terminates.

In a few specific cases, the `PG_locked` flag and the swap cache are not sufficient to avoid race conditions. Let us suppose, for instance, that the kernel begins a swap-out operation on some page; therefore, it increments the page usage counter, it allocates a page slot, and then it starts the I/O data transfer. Suppose further that during this operation, the process that owns the page dies. The kernel reclaims the process's memory; that is, it releases all page frames and all page slots used by the process. Since the page usage counter was incremented before starting the I/O operation, the page frame involved in the swap I/O operation is not released to the Buddy system; however, the page slot usage counter in the swap area descriptor could become 0, thus it could be used for swapping out another page before the previous I/O operation completes. If this happens, a kernel control path could start a write operation in the page slot while another kernel control path is performing another write operation on the same page slot, that is, on the same physical disk portion. This would lead to unpredictable (and unpleasant) results.

In order to avoid this kind of problem, the kernel uses an array of bits, whose address is stored into the `swap_lockmap` field of the swap area descriptor. Each bit in the array is a lock for a page slot in the swap area. The bit is set before activating an I/O data transfer on the page slot and is cleared when the operation terminates. The `scan_swap_map()` function described in the earlier section "Finding a Free Page Slot" does not consider a page slot as "free" if its lock bit is on, even if its usage counter in the `swap_map` array is null. The `lock_queue` wait queue is used to suspend a process until a bit in the `swap_lockmap` array is cleared.

The rw_swap_page() Function

As illustrated in Figure 16-1, the `rw_swap_page()` function is used to swap in or swap out a page. It receives the following parameters:

buffer
> The initial address of the page frame containing the page to be swapped in or swapped out.

entry
> A swapped-out page identifier. This parameter is somewhat redundant since the same information can be derived from the descriptor of the `buffer` page frame.

rw
> A flag specifying the direction of data transfer: `READ` for swapping in, `WRITE` for swapping out.

wait
> A flag specifying whether the kernel control path must block until the I/O operation completes.

The swap-in operation triggered by a page fault is usually synchronous (`wait` equal to 1), since the process should be suspended until the requested page has been transferred from disk. Conversely, swap-out operations are usually asynchronous (`wait` equal to 0), since there is no need to suspend the current process until they are completed. However, the kernel defines a limit on the number of asynchronous swap operations concurrently being carried on, in order to avoid flooding the block device driver's request queue. The limit is stored in the `swap_cluster` field of the `pager_daemon` variable (see the section "The kswapd Kernel Thread" later in this chapter). If the limit is reached, `rw_swap_page()` ignores the value of the `wait` parameter and proceeds as if it were equal to 1.

In order to swap the page, the function performs the following operations:

1. Computes the address of the page descriptor corresponding to the page frame.

2. Gets the swap area index and the page slot index from `entry`.

3. Tests and sets the lock bit in the `swap_lockmap` array corresponding to the page slot. If the bit was already set, the page is in the middle of being swapped in or out, so we want to wait for that operation to complete. Therefore, executes the functions in the `tq_disk` task queue, thus unplugging any block device driver that is waiting, and sleeps on the `lock_queue` wait queue until the ongoing swap operation terminates.

4. Sets the `PG_swap_unlock_after` flag of the page in order to ensure that the flag in `swap_lockmap` will be cleared at the end of the swap operation that the function will start in step 10. (The effect of the flag is discussed later in this section.)

5. If the data transfer is for a swap-in operation (`rw` set to `READ`), clears the `PG_uptodate` flag of the page frame. The flag will be set again only if the swap-in operation terminates successfully.

6. Increments the page usage counter, so that the page frame is not released to the Buddy system even if the owning process dies (the fail-safe mechanism discussed in the previous section). Also sets the `PG_free_after` flag, thus ensuring that the usage counter of the page descriptor is decremented when the page I/O operation terminates (see the section "Page I/O Operations" in Chapter 13). This flag represents a belt-and-suspenders kind of caution because it might be possible to invoke the `brw_page()` function without first incrementing the usage counter. Actually, the kernel never does this.

7. If the swap area is a disk partition, locates the block associated with the page slot (swap partitions have 4096-byte blocks). Otherwise, if the swap area is a regular file, invokes the `bmap` method of the corresponding inode object (or equivalently the `smap` method for sector-based filesystems like MS-DOS) to derive the logical numbers of the blocks associated with the page slot.

8. If `nr_async_pages` is greater than `pager_daemon.swap_cluster`, forces the `wait` parameter to 1 (too many asynchronous swap operations are being carried on).

9. If `wait` is null, increments `nr_async_pages`. Sets the `PG_decr_after` flag of the page in order to ensure that the variable will be decremented again when the swap operation to be started on the next step terminates. (Like `PG_swap_unlock_after`, the `PG_decr_after` flag will be discussed shortly.)

10. Invokes the `brw_page()` function to start the actual I/O operation. As described in the section "Starting Page I/O Operations" in Chapter 13, this function returns before the data transfer is completed.

11. If `wait` is null, returns without waiting for the completion of the data transfer.

12. Otherwise (`wait` equal to 1), invokes `wait_on_page()` to suspend the current process until the page frame becomes unlocked, that is, until the I/O data transfer terminates.

Notice that the `rw_swap_page()` function relies on the `brw_page()` function to perform the data transfer. As described in the section "Terminating Page I/O Operations" in Chapter 13, whenever the block device driver terminates the data transfer of a block in the page slot, the `b_end_io` method taken from the corresponding asynchronous buffer head is invoked. This method is implemented by the `end_buffer_io_async()` function, which in turn invokes `after_unlock_page()` if all blocks in the page have been transferred. The latter function performs the following operations:

1. If the `PG_decr_after` flag of the page is on, clears it and decrements the `nr_async_pages` variable. As we've seen, this variable helps to put an upper limit on the number of current asynchronous page swaps.

2. If the `PG_swap_unlock_after` flag of the page is on, clears it and invokes `swap_after_unlock_page()`. This function clears the lock bit in the `swap_lockmap` array associated with the page slot and wakes up the processes sleeping in the `lock_queue` wait queue. Thus, processes waiting for the end of the I/O operation on the page slot can start again.

3. If the `PG_free_after` flag of the page is on, clears it and invokes `__free_page()` to release the page frame, thus compensating for the increment of the page usage counter performed by `rw_swap_page()` as a fail-safe mechanism.

The read_swap_cache_async() Function

As shown in Figure 16-1, the `read_swap_cache_async()` function is invoked to swap in a page either from the swap cache or from disk. The function receives the following parameters:

`entry`
> A swapped-out page identifier

`wait`
> A flag specifying whether the kernel is allowed to suspend the current process until the swap's I/O operation completes

Despite the function's name, the `wait` parameter determines whether the I/O swap operation must be synchronous or asynchronous. The `read_swap_cache` macro is often used to invoke `read_swap_cache_async()` passing the value 1 to the `wait` parameter.

The function performs the following operations:

1. Invokes `swap_duplicate()` on `entry` to check whether the page slot is valid and to increment the page slot usage counter. (The increment is a fail-safe mechanism applied to the page slot during the swap cache lookup, to avoid problems in case the process that caused the page fault dies before terminating the swap-in.)

2. Invokes `lookup_swap_cache()` to search for the page in the swap cache. If the page is found, invokes `swap_free()` on `entry` to decrement the page slot usage counter and ends by returning the page's address.

3. The page is not included in the swap cache. Invokes `__get_free_page()` to allocate a new page frame. Then invokes `lookup_swap_cache()` again, because the process may have been suspended while waiting for the new page frame, and some other kernel control path could have created the page in the interim. As in the previous step, if the requested page is found, decreases the page slot usage counter, releases the page frame just allocated, and returns the address of the requested page.

4. Invokes `add_to_swap_cache()` to initialize the `inode` and `offset` fields of the descriptor of the new page frame and to insert it into the swap cache.

5. Sets the `PG_locked` flag of the page frame. Since the page frame is new, no other kernel control path could access it, therefore no check on the previous flag value is necessary.

6. Invokes `rw_swap_page()` to read the page's contents from the swap area, passing to that function the `READ` parameter, the swapped-out page identifier, the page frame address, and the `wait` parameter. As a result, the required page is copied in the page frame.

7. Returns the page's address.

The rw_swap_page_nocache() Function

In a few cases, the kernel wants to read a page from a swap area without putting it in the swap cache. This happens, for instance, when servicing the `swapon()` system call: the kernel reads the first page of a swap area, which contains the `swap_header` union, then immediately discards the page frame. Swapped-out pages of IPC shared memory regions are also never included in the swap cache (see the section "IPC Shared Memory" in Chapter 18).

The `rw_swap_page_nocache()` function receives as parameters the type of I/O operation (`READ` or `WRITE`), a swapped-out page identifier, and the address of a page frame. It performs the following operations:

1. Invokes `wait_on_page()` and then sets the `PG_locked` flag of the page frame.

2. Initializes the `inode` field of the page descriptor with the address of the `swapper_inode` inode object, sets the `offset` field to the swapped-out page identifier, and sets the `PG_swap_cache` flag. Notice, however, that the function does not insert the page frame in the swap cache data structures: the `PG_swap_cache` flag and the `inode` and `offset` fields of the page descriptor are initialized just to satisfy the consistency checks of the `rw_swap_page()` function.

3. Increments the page usage counter (fail-safe mechanism).

4. Invokes `rw_swap_page()` to start the I/O swap operation.

5. Decrements the page usage counter, clears the `PG_swap_cache` flag, and sets the `inode` field of the page descriptor to 0.

Page Swap-Out

The later section "Freeing Page Frames" explains when pages are swapped out. As we indicated at the beginning of the chapter, swapping out pages is a last resort and appears as part of a general strategy to free memory that uses other tactics as well. In this section, we show how the kernel performs swap-out. This is achieved by the `swap_out()` function, which acts on the following parameters.

priority

> An integer value ranging from 0 to 6 that specifies how much time the kernel should spend trying to locate a page to be swapped; lower values correspond to longer search times. We shall describe how this parameter is set in the section "The do_try_to_free_pages() Function" later in this chapter.

gfp_mask

> If the function has been invoked as a consequence of a memory allocation request, this parameter is a copy of the **gfp_mask** parameter passed to the allocator function (see the section "Requesting and Releasing Page Frames" in Chapter 6. The parameter tells the kernel how to treat the page, notably how urgent the request is and whether the kernel control path can be suspended.

The **swap_out()** function scans existing processes and tries to swap out the pages referenced in each process's page tables. It terminates as soon as one of the following conditions occurs:

- The function succeeds in swapping out a page.

- The function performs some blocking operation. It doesn't bother resuming activity because the process being examined could have been destroyed while the current process was sleeping, and thus no further page scanning would be needed.

- The function failed to swap out a page after scanning a predefined number of processes. This is because the kernel does not want to spend too much time in swap-out activities. Specifically, each invocation of **swap_out()** considers at most **nr_tasks/(priority+1)** processes.

How can the kernel select the processes to be penalized? In each invocation, the **swap_out()** function scans the process list and finds the process having the largest value for the **swap_cnt** field of the process descriptor. If all processes have null **swap_cnt** fields, the function scans the process list again and sets each **swap_cnt** field to the number of page frames assigned to the corresponding process (the number can be found in the **mm->rss** field of the process descriptor). In this way, processes with many page frames are generally more penalized (in the long run) than processes owning fewer page frames.

After having selected a process, **swap_out()** invokes the **swap_out_process()** function, passing it the process descriptor pointer and the **gfp_mask** parameter (see Figure 16-1). If the latter function returns the value 1, **swap_out()** terminates its execution, since either a page frame has been swapped out or the current process has been suspended. Otherwise, **swap_out()** tries to select another process, until it reaches the maximum number of processes to be examined.

The **swap_out_process()** scans all the memory regions of a process and invokes the **swap_out_vma()** function on each one. The address of the first memory region scanned by **swap_out_process()** is stored in the **swap_address** field of the process descriptor: since this field identifies the memory region last scanned in the previous invocation of the function, all memory regions of the process are penalized equally. (This appears to be the best strategy since the kernel has no information on how often each memory region is accessed.) swap_out_process() continues to invoke swap_out_vma() until that function returns the value 1 or the end of the memory region list is reached. In the latter case, the swap_cnt field in the process descriptor is set to 0, so that the process will not be considered again by swap_out() before it examines all the other processes in the system that remain to be considered.

The swap_out_vma() function checks that the memory region is not locked, that is, that its VM_LOCKED flag is equal to 0. It then starts a sequence in which it considers all entries in the process's Page Global Directory that refer to linear addresses in the memory region. For each such entry, the function invokes the swap_out_pgd() function, which in turn considers all entries in a Page Middle Directory corresponding to address intervals in the memory region. For each such entry, swap_out_pgd() invokes the swap_out_pmd() function, which considers all entries in a Page Table referencing pages in the memory region. For each such page, swap_out_pmd() invokes the try_to_swap_out() function, which finally determines whether the page can be swapped out. If try_to_swap_out() returns the value 1 (meaning the page frame was freed or the current process is suspended), the chain of nested invocations of the swap_out_vma(), swap_out_pgd(), swap_out_pmd(), and try_to_swap_out() functions terminates.

The try_to_swap_out() Function

The try_to_swap_out() function attempts to free a given page frame, either discarding or swapping out its contents. The parameters of the function are:

tsk
   Process descriptor pointer

vma
   Memory region descriptor pointer

address
   Initial linear address of the page

page_table
   Address of the Page Table entry of tsk that maps address

gfp_mask
   The gfp_mask parameter of the swap_out() function, which is passed along the chain of function invocations described at the end of the previous section

The function returns the value 1 either if it has succeeded in swapping out the page or if it has executed a blocking I/O operation. In this second case, continuing to swap out would be risky since the function might act on a process that no longer actually exists. The function returns 0 if it decided not to swap.

`try_to_swap_out()` must recognize many different situations demanding different responses, but the responses all share many of the same basic operations. In particular, the function performs the following steps:

1. Considers the Page Table entry at address `page_table`. If the `Present` bit is null, no page frame is allocated, so there is nothing to swap and the function returns 0.

2. If the `Accessed` flag of the Page Table entry is set, the page frame is young. In this case, clears the `Accessed` flag, sets the `PG_referenced` flag of the page descriptor, invokes `flush_tlb_page()` to invalidate the TLB entry associated with the page, and returns 0. Only pages whose `Accessed` flag is null can be swapped out. Since this bit is automatically set by the CPU's paging unit at every page access, the page can be swapped out only if it was not accessed after the previous invocation of `try_to_swap_out()` on it. As mentioned previously, the `Accessed` flag offers a limited degree of hardware support that allows Linux to make use of a primitive LRU replacement algorithm.

3. If the `PG_reserved` or `PG_locked` flag of the page descriptor is set, returns 0 (the page cannot be swapped out).

4. If the `PG_DMA` flag is equal to 0 and the `gfp_mask` parameter specifies that the freed page frame should be used for an ISA DMA buffer, returns 0.

5. If the page belongs to the swap cache, it is shared with some other process and it has already been stored in a swap area. In this case, the page must be marked as swapped out but no memory transfer is performed. Does the following:

   a. Gets the swapped-out page's identifier from the `offset` field of the page descriptor

   b. Invokes `swap_duplicate()` to increment the page slot usage counter

   c. Writes the swapped-out page identifier into the Page Table entry

   d. Decrements the `mm->rss` counter of the process

   e. Invokes `flush_tlb_page()` to invalidate the TLB entry associated with the page

   f. Invokes `__free_page()` to decrement the page usage counter

   g. Returns 0 (no page has been swapped out)

6. If the `Dirty` bit of the Page Table entry is null, the page is "clean"; there is no need to write it back to disk, since the kernel is always able to restore its contents with the demand paging mechanism. Therefore, performs the following substeps to remove the page from the process's address space:

   a. Sets the Page Table entry to 0

   b. Decrements the `mm->rss` counter of the process

    c. Invokes `flush_tlb_page()` to invalidate the TLB entry associated with the page

    d. Invoke `__free_page()` to decrement the page usage counter

    e. Returns 0 (no page has been swapped out)

7. The page is dirty and it can be swapped out; however, checks whether the kernel is allowed to perform I/O operations (that is, if the `__GFP_IO` flag in the `gfp_mask` parameter is set); if not, returns 0. The `__GFP_IO` flag is cleared when the kernel control path cannot be suspended (for instance, because it is executing an interrupt handler).

8. Checks whether the `vma` memory region that contains the page has its own `swapout` method. If so, performs the following substeps:

    a. Sets the Page Table entry to 0

    b. Decrements the `mm->rss` counter of the process

    c. Invokes `flush_tlb_page()` to invalidate the TLB entry associated with the page

    d. Invokes the `swapout` method; if this function returns an error code, sends a `SIGBUS` signal to the process `tsk`

    e. Invokes `__free_page()` to decrement the page usage counter

    f. Returns 1 (the `swapout` method invoked in step 8d could block, so the `swap_out()` function must terminate)

9. The `swapout` method of the memory region is not defined, thus the page must be explicitly swapped out. (This is the most frequent case.) Performs the following substeps:

    a. Invokes `get_swap_page()` to allocate a new page slot.

    b. Decrements the `mm->rss` field of the process and increments its `nswap` field (a counter of swapped-out pages).

    c. Writes the swapped-out page identifier into the Page Table entry.

    d. Invokes `flush_tlb_page()` to invalidate the TLB entry associated with the page.

    e. Invokes `swap_duplicate()` to increase the page slot usage counter; it will now have the value 2, one increment for the process and the other for the swap cache.

    f. Invokes `add_to_swap_cache()` to add the page into the swap cache.

    g. Preparatory to the swapping operation to be started in the next step, sets the `PG_locked` flag. (We don't have to test the flag, because we did so already in step 3. No other kernel path could have set the flag since then, because the function didn't perform any blocking operation.)

h. Invokes `rw_swap_page()` to start an asynchronous swapping operation to write the page into the swap area.

i. Invokes `__free_page()` to decrement the page usage counter.

j. Returns 1 (a page was swapped out).

Swapping Out Pages from Shared Memory Mappings

As we saw in the section "Memory Mapping" in Chapter 15, pages in a shared memory mapping correspond to portions of regular files on disk. For that reason, the kernel does not store them in swap areas but rather updates the corresponding files.

Shared memory mapping regions define their own `swapout` method; as shown in Table 15-2 in Chapter 15, this method is implemented by the `filemap_swapout()` function, which just invokes the `filemap_write_page()` function to force the page to be written on disk.

In this case, however, the `filemap_write_page()` function does not explicitly invoke the `do_write_page()` function as described in the section "Flushing Dirty Memory Mapping Pages to Disk" in Chapter 15. The reason is that running the function could induce the following nasty race condition: suppose the kernel gets a critical filesystem lock and then starts swapping out some pages as a consequence of a memory allocation request. The `do_write_page()` function might try to acquire the same lock, thus inducing a deadlock.

In order to avoid this problem, the only part of the kernel allowed to swap out pages belonging to shared memory mappings is a kernel thread named *kpiod*, which services all I/O requests in a special input queue. Since *kpiod* is a separate kernel thread from the process executing `filemap_write_page()`, no deadlock may occur. Even if *kpiod* is suspended while trying to get the filesystem lock, the process executing `filemap_write_page()` can proceed and eventually release that lock.

The *kpiod* kernel thread is woken up whenever a new request is added to its input queue; each request refers to a page of a shared memory region to be written to disk. Since the kernel may attempt to swap out several pages at once (see the section "Freeing Page Frames" later in this chapter), several requests may accumulate in the *kpiod* input queue. The kernel thread continues to process requests until the queue becomes empty.

Each element in the queue is a descriptor of type `pio_request`, which includes the fields illustrated in Table 16-2. The `pio_first` and `pio_last` variables point to the first and last elements in the queue, respectively. The `pio_request` descriptors are handled by the `pio_request_cache` slab allocator cache.

Table 16-2. Fields of a pio_request Descriptor

Type	Field	Description
struct pio_request *	next	Next element in queue
struct file *	file	File object pointer
unsigned long	offset	File offset
unsigned long	page	Page initial address

When invoked by filemap_swapout(), the filemap_write_page() function invokes make_pio_request() to add a request to the *kpiod* input queue, instead of the usual do_write_page() that does its own data transfer. The make_pio_request() function performs the following operations:

1. Increments the usage counter of the page to be written.

2. Allocates a new pio_request descriptor. If no memory is available, tries to prune some disk caches without doing any actual I/O operation. The function does this by invoking try_to_free_pages() with the __GFP_IO flag cleared in its parameter (see the section "The try_to_free_pages() Function" later in this chapter). make_pio_request() then tries again to allocate the request pio_request descriptor.

3. Initializes the fields of the pio_request descriptor.

4. Inserts the pio_request descriptor in the request queue.

5. Wakes up the processes (actually, the *kpiod* kernel thread) in the pio_wait wait queue.

Thus, the make_pio_request() function does not trigger any I/O operation; instead, it wakes up the *kpiod* kernel thread. The thread executes the kpiod() function, which considers all requests in the input queue and invokes the do_write_page() function on each of them to write the corresponding page to disk. The page counter is then decremented and the pio_request descriptor is released to the slab allocator. When all requests in the queue have been processed, kpiod() inserts itself in the pio_wait wait queue and puts itself to sleep.

kpiod() must guard against another potential error. In general, when a kernel thread requests some free page frames and free memory is low, it starts reclaiming pages. In order to do this, it may need to request a few additional page frames. However, during this new request the thread should never try to reclaim pages, or infinite recursion might occur. For this reason, a PF_MEMALLOC flag is defined in each process. It essentially forbids recursive invocations of try_to_free_pages(), so the kernel always sets the flag before invoking that function and clears it when the function returns. In particular, the value of this flag is checked by __get_free_pages(); if it is set, the try_to_free_pages() function is never invoked. The *kpiod* kernel thread always runs with PF_MEMALLOC set.

Page Swap-In

Swap-in must take place when a process attempts to address a page within its address space that has been swapped out to disk. The "Page fault" exception handler triggers a swap-in operation when the following conditions occur (see the section "Handling a Faulty Address Inside the Address Space," Chapter 7):

- The page including the address that caused the exception is a valid one, that is, it belongs to a memory region of the current process.

- The page is not present in memory, that is, the **Present** flag in the Page Table entry is cleared.

- The Page Table entry associated with the page is not null, which means it contains a swapped-out page identifier.

As described in the section "Demand Paging" in Chapter 7, the handle_pte_fault() function, invoked by the do_page_fault() exception handler, checks whether the Page Table entry is non-null. If so, it invokes do_swap_page(), which acts on the following parameters:

tsk
: Process descriptor address of the process that caused the "Page fault" exception

address
: Linear address that caused the exception

vma
: Memory region descriptor address of the region that includes **address**

page_table
: Address of the Page Table entry that maps **address**

entry
: Identifier of the swapped-out page

write_access
: Flag denoting whether the attempted access was a read or a write

Linux allows each memory region to include a customized function for performing swap-in. A region that needs such a customized function stores a pointer to it in the **swapin** field of its descriptor. Until recently, IPC shared memory regions had a special **swapin** method. But from Linux 2.2 on, no memory regions have a customized method. If such a method were provided, do_swap_page() would perform the following operations:

1. Invoke the **swapin** method. It returns a Page Table entry value, which contains the address of the page frame to be assigned to the process.

2. Write the value returned from the `swapin` method into the Page Table entry that `page_table` points to.

3. If the page frame usage counter is greater than 1 and the memory region not is shared, clear the `Read/Write` flag of the Page Table entry.

4. Increment the `mm->rss` and the `tsk->maj_flt` fields of the process.

5. Release the `kernel_flag` global kernel lock, which had been obtained when entering the exception handler.

6. Return the value 1.

Conversely, when the `swapin` method is not defined, `do_swap_page()` invokes the general `swap_in()` function. It acts on the same parameters as `do_swap_page()` and performs the following steps:

1. Invokes `lookup_swap_cache()` to check whether the swap cache already contains the page specified by `entry`. If so, goes to step 4.

2. Invokes the `swapin_readahead()` function to read from the swap area a group of 2^n pages, including the requested one. The value n is stored into the `page_cluster` variable, which is usually set to 4, but it could be lower if the system has less than 32 MB of memory. Each page is read by invoking the `read_swap_cache_async()` function, specifying a null `wait` parameter (asynchronous swap operation).

3. Invokes `read_swap_cache()` on `entry`, just in case the `swapin_readahead()` function failed to read the requested page (for instance, because too many asynchronous swap operations were already being carried out by the system). Recall that `read_swap_cache()` activates a synchronous swap operation. As a consequence, the current process will be suspended until the page has been read from disk.

4. Checks whether the entry to which `page_table` points differs from `entry`. If so, another kernel control path has already swapped in the requested page. Therefore, invokes `free_page_and_swap_cache()` to release the page obtained previously and returns.

5. Invokes `swap_free()` to decrement the usage counter of the page slot corresponding to `entry`.

6. Increments the `mm->rss` and `min_flt` fields of the process.

7. If the page is shared by several processes or the process is attempting only a read on it, the page stays in the swap cache. However, the Page Table of the process must be updated so the process can find the page. Therefore, writes the physical address of the requested page and the protection bits found in the `vm_page_prot` field of the memory region into the Page Table entry to which `page_table` points.

8. Otherwise, if the page is not shared and the process attempted to write it, there is no reason to keep it in the swap cache, since it is private to the process. Therefore, invokes `delete_from_swap_cache()` and writes the same information described by the previous step into the Page Table entry. However, sets the `Read/Write` and `Dirty` bits to 1.

Freeing Page Frames

Page frames can be freed in several possible ways:

*   By reclaiming an unused page frame within a cache. Depending on the type of cache, the following functions are used:

    `shrink_mmap()`
    Used for the page cache, swap cache, and buffer cache

    `shrink_dcache_memory()`
    Used for the dentry cache

    `kmem_cache_reap()`
    Used for the slab cache (see the section "Releasing a Slab from a Cache" in Chapter 6)

*   By swapping out a page belonging to an anonymous memory region of a process or a modified page belonging to a private memory mapping.

*   By swapping out a page belonging to an IPC shared memory region.

As we shall see shortly, the choice among these possibilities is done in a rather empirical way, with very little support from theory. The situation is somewhat similar to evaluating the factors that determine the dynamic priority of a process. The main objective is to get a tuning of the parameters that achieve good system performance, without asking too many questions about why it works.

Monitoring the Free Memory

Besides the `nr_free_pages` variable, which expresses the current number of free page frames, the kernel relies on two values, a kind of low and high watermark. These values are stored in a structure called `freepages` (it also has a `low` field that is no longer used in Linux 2.2):

`min`
    Minimum number of page frames reserved to the kernel to perform crucial operations (e.g., for swapping pages to disk). (`free_area_init()` initializes this field to 2n, where n denotes the size of primary memory expressed in megabytes. The resulting value must lie in the range 10 to 256.

`high`

>   The threshold of `nr_free_pages` that indicates to the kernel that enough free
>   memory is available. In this case, no swapping is done; `free_area_init()` ini-
>   tializes this threshold value to $3 \times$ `freepages.min`.

The contents of `min` and `high` fields can be modified by writing into the file */proc/sys/
vm/freepages*.

Reclaiming Pages from the Page, Swap, and Buffer Caches

In order to reclaim page frames from the disk caches, the kernel makes use of the
`shrink_mmap()` function. It returns 1 if it succeeds in freeing a page frame belonging
to the page cache, the swap cache, or the buffer cache; otherwise, it returns 0. The
function acts on two parameters:

`priority`

>   Fraction of total number of page frames to be checked before the function gives
>   up and terminates with a return value of 0. The parameter's value ranges from 0
>   (very urgent: shrink everything) to 6 (nonurgent: try to shrink a bit).

`gfp_mask`

>   Flags specifying the kind of page frame to be freed.

The function scans the `mem_map` array and looks for a page that can be freed. To fit
the bill, the page must belong to one of the above caches, must be unlocked, must
not be used by any process, and must have the `PG_DMA` flag set if the page frame is
requested for ISA DMA. Moreover, it must have not been recently accessed.

A problem of fairness exists, similar to the one encountered by `swap_out_process()`
when choosing the first memory region of a process to be checked. When `shrink_`
`mmap()` is invoked, it should not always start scanning the `mem_map` array from the
beginning, or pages with lower physical addresses would have much less chance of
being in a disk cache than pages with higher physical addresses. The `clock`* static
local variable plays the same role as the `swap_address` field of a process descriptor: it
points to the next page frame to be checked in the `mem_map` array.

The function scans the page descriptors of `mem_map` by performing the following
steps:

1. Initializes the local variable `count` to the number $n/2^p$ of unlocked, nonshared
    page frames that should be checked during this activation of the function. Here, n
    is the number of page frames in the system as found in the `num_physpages` vari-
    able, and p is equal to `priority`.

---

* The name of this local variable derives from the idea of the hand of a clock moving circularly. The function has
  nothing to do with system timers, of course.

2. If `count` is greater than 0, increments `clock` and performs the following substeps on the page descriptor in `mem_map[clock]`:

   a. If the page is locked, if its `PG_DMA` flag is cleared while the `gfp_mask` parameter specifies an ISA DMA page, or if its usage counter is not equal to 1, skips the page and restarts step 2 on the next page.

   b. The page is unlocked and nonshared, so decrements `count`.

   c. If the `PG_swap_cache` flag is set, the page belongs to the swap cache. It can be reclaimed if either of the following conditions holds:

      • Its `PG_referenced` flag is off, which means that the page has not been accessed since the last invocation of `shrink_mmap()`. (This flag acts like the `Accessed` flag shown earlier as a simple way to hold back swapping.)

      • The page slot usage counter is 1 (no process is referencing it).

      If the page can be reclaimed, invokes `delete_from_swap_cache()`, clears the `PG_referenced` flag, and returns 1 (a page frame has been freed).

   d. If the `PG_referenced` flag of the page is set, the page has been recently accessed, thus it cannot be reclaimed: clears the flag and restarts step 2 on the next page.

   e. If the page belongs to the buffer cache (that is, the `buffers` field of the page descriptor is not null) and the buffer cache size is greater than the threshold specified by the `buffer_mem.min_percent` system parameter, invokes `try_to_free_buffers()` to check if all buffers in the page are unused. In particular, this function performs the following operations:

      1. Considers all buffers in the page to determine whether they can be released. They must all be free (that is, their usage counters must be null), unlocked, not dirty, and not protected. If one of them fails these tests, very little can be done. Invokes `wakeup_bdflush()` (see the section "Writing Dirty Buffers to Disk" in Chapter 14) and returns 0 to signal that the page has not been freed.

      2. All buffers are unused. Invokes `remove_from_queues()` and `put_unused_buffer_head()` repeatedly to release the corresponding buffer heads.

      3. Decrements `nr_buffers` by the number of buffers in the page and decrements `buffermem` by 4 KB.

      4. Wakes up the processes suspended for lack of buffer heads and sleeping in the `buffer_wait` wait queue (see the section "Buffer Allocation" in Chapter 14).

      5. Invokes `__free_page()` to release the page frame to the Buddy system, and returns 1 to signal that the page has been freed.

If `try_to_free_buffers()` returns the value 0, the page cannot be freed: goes to step 2. Otherwise, returns the value 1.

f. If the page belongs to the page cache (that is, the `inode` field of the page descriptor is not null) and the page cache size is greater than the threshold specified by the `page_cache.min_percent` system parameter, invokes `remove_inode_page()` (see the section "Page Cache Handling Functions" in Chapter 14) to remove the page from the page cache and releases the page frame to the Buddy system, then returns the value 1.

3. If this point is reached, no page frame has been freed: returns the value 0.

Reclaiming Pages from the Dentry and Inode Caches

Dentry objects themselves aren't big, but freeing one of them has a cascading effect that can ultimately free a lot of memory by releasing several data structures. The `shrink_dcache_memory()` function is invoked to remove dentry objects from the dentry cache. Clearly, only dentry objects not referenced by any process (defined as unused dentries in the section "Dentry Objects" in Chapter 12) can be removed.

Since the dentry cache objects are allocated through the slab allocator, the `shrink_dcache_memory()` function may force some slabs to become free, thus some page frames may be consequently reclaimed by `kmem_cache_reap()` (see the section "Releasing a Slab from a Cache" in Chapter 6). Moreover, the dentry cache acts as a controller of the inode cache. Therefore, when a dentry object is released, the buffer storing the corresponding inode becomes unused, and the `shrink_mmap()` function may release the corresponding buffer page.

The `shrink_dcache_memory()` function receives the same parameters as the `shrink_mmap()` function. It checks whether the kernel is allowed to perform I/O operations (if the `__GFP_IO` flag is set in the `gfp_mask` parameter) and, if so, invokes `prune_dcache()`.

Two parameters are passed to the latter function: the number of dentry objects `d_nr` to be released and the number of inode objects `i_nr` to be released (because removing a dentry may induce an inode to be released as well). `prune_dcache()` stops shrinking the dentry cache as soon as one of the two targets has been reached. The value of the first parameter `d_nr` depends on `priority`. If it is 0, `shrink_dcache_memory()` passes the value 0 to `prune_dcache()`, which means that all unused dentry objects will be removed. Otherwise, `d_nr` is computed to be `n/priority`, where n is the total number of unused dentry objects. The `shrink_dcache_memory()` function passes -1 as a second parameter to `prune_dcache()`, which means that no limit is enforced on the number of released inodes.

The `prune_dcache()` function scans the list of unused dentries and invokes `prune_one_dentry()` on each object to be released. The latter function, in turn, performs the following operations.

1. Removes the dentry object from the dentry hash table and from the list of dentry objects in its parent's directory.

2. Invokes `dentry_iput()`, which releases the dentry's inode using the `d_iput` dentry method, if defined, or the `iput()` function.

3. Invokes `dput()` on the parent dentry of `dentry`. As a result, its usage counter is decremented.

4. Returns the dentry object to the slab allocator (see the section "Releasing an Object from a Cache" in Chapter 6).

The try_to_free_pages() Function

The `try_to_free_pages()` function is invoked:

- By the `__get_free_pages()` function (see the section "Requesting and Releasing Page Frames" in Chapter 6) when the number of free page frames falls below the threshold specified in `freepages.min` and the `PF_MEMALLOC` flag of the current process is cleared

- By the `make_pio_request()` function (see the section "Swapping Out Pages from Shared Memory Mappings" earlier in this chapter) when it fails to allocate a new `pio_request` descriptor

The function receives as its parameter a set of flags `gfp_mask`, whose meaning is exactly the same as the corresponding parameter of the `__get_free_pages()` function. In particular, the `__GFP_IO` flag is set if the kernel is allowed to activate I/O data transfers, while the `__GFP_WAIT` flag is set if the kernel is allowed to discard the contents of page frames in order to free memory.

The function performs only two operations:

- Wakes up the *kswapd* kernel thread (see the section "The kswapd Kernel Thread" later in this chapter)

- If the `__GFP_WAIT` flag in `gfp_mask` is set, invokes `do_try_to_free_pages()`, passing to it the `gfp_mask` parameter

The do_try_to_free_pages() Function

The `do_try_to_free_pages()` function is invoked by `try_to_free_pages()` and by the *kswapd* kernel thread. It receives the usual `gfp_mask` parameter and tries to free at least `SWAP_CLUSTER_MAX` page frames (usually 32). A few auxiliary functions are invoked to do the job. Some of them return after releasing a single page frame, so they must be invoked repeatedly.

The algorithm implemented by `do_try_to_free_pages()` is quite reasonable, since the page frames are released according to their usage. For instance, the algorithm favors the preservation of page frames used by the dentry cache over the preservation of unused page frames in the slab allocator caches. Moreover, do_try_to_free_pages() tries to free memory by invoking the functions that do the reclaiming with decreasing priority values. In general, a lower value for priority means that more iterations will be performed by the functions before quitting. do_try_to_free_pages() gives up when all functions have been invoked with a 0 priority.

In particular, the function executes the following actions:

1. Acquires the global kernel lock by invoking lock_kernel().

2. Invokes kmem_cache_reap(gfp_mask) to reclaim page frames from the slab allocator caches.

3. Sets a priority local variable to 6 (the lowest priority).

4. Tries to free pages over a series of more and more thorough searches, driven by increasing the priority on each iteration. To be specific, while priority is greater than or equal to 0 and the number of released page frames is lower than SWAP_CLUSTER_MAX, performs the following substeps:

   a. Invokes shrink_mmap(priority, gfp_mask) repeatedly until it fails in releasing a page frame belonging to the page cache, to the swap cache, or to the buffer cache or until the number of released page frames reaches SWAP_CLUSTER_MAX

   b. If the kernel is allowed to write pages to disk (if the __GFP_IO flag in gfp_mask is set), invokes shm_swap(priority, gfp_mask) repeatedly until it fails in releasing a page frame belonging to an IPC shared memory region or until the number of released page frames reaches SWAP_CLUSTER_MAX

   c. Invokes swap_out(priority, gfp_mask) repeatedly until it fails in releasing to the Buddy system a page frame belonging to some process or until the number of released page frames reaches SWAP_CLUSTER_MAX

   d. Invokes shrink_dcache_memory(priority, gfp_mask) to release free elements in the dentry cache

   e. Decrements priority and goes to the start of the loop

5. Invokes unlock_kernel().

6. Returns 1 if at least SWAP_CLUSTER_MAX page frames have been released, 0 otherwise.

The kswapd Kernel Thread

The *kswapd* kernel thread is another kernel mechanism that activates the reclamation of memory. Why is it necessary? Is it not sufficient to invoke try_to_free_pages() when free memory becomes scarce and another memory allocation request is issued?

Unfortunately, this is not the case. Some memory allocation requests are performed by interrupt and exception handlers, which cannot block the current process waiting for some page frame to be freed; moreover, some memory allocation requests are done by kernel control paths that have already acquired exclusive access to critical resources and that, therefore, cannot activate I/O data transfers. In the infrequent case in which all memory allocation requests are done by such sorts of kernel control paths, the kernel would be unable to free memory forever.

In order to avoid this situation, the *kswapd* kernel thread is activated once every 10 seconds. The thread executes the `kswapd()` function, which at each activation performs the following operations:

1. If `nr_free_pages` is greater than the `freepages.high` threshold, no memory reclaiming is necessary: goes to step 5.

2. Invokes `do_try_to_free_pages()` with `gfp_mask` set to `__GFP_IO`. In order to avoid recursive invocations of the function, the kernel thread executes with the `PF_MEMALLOC` flag set (see the section "Swapping Out Pages from Shared Memory Mappings" earlier in this chapter). If the function does not succeed in freeing `SWAP_CLUSTER_MAX` page frames, goes to step 5.

3. If the `need_resched` field of `current` is equal to 0, goes to step 1 (no higher priority process is runnable, so continues to reclaim memory).

4. The `need_resched` field is equal to 1: yields the CPU to some other process by invoking `schedule()`. The *kswapd* kernel thread remains runnable. When the thread resumes execution, goes to step 1.

5. Sets the `state` of `current` to `TASK_INTERRUPTIBLE`.

6. Invokes `schedule_timeout()`, passing as its parameter the value `10*HZ`, thus forcing the process to suspend itself and resume execution 10 seconds later. Then goes to step 1.

Anticipating Linux 2.4

Swapping must now take into consideration the existence of RAM zones; much of the swapping code has thus been rewritten in a simpler and cleaner way, mainly thanks to the new page cache implementation. The swap cache is still implemented on top of the page cache, but the `swapper_inode` fictitious inode object has been replaced by a *file address space* object. The *kpiod* kernel thread has been removed, because it is now safe to directly swap out pages of shared memory mappings. Moreover, the arrays of locks associated with each swap area are no longer used.

The most interesting change concerns the policy used to select the process from which stealing pages when reclaiming memory: it is the one that performed fewer page faults (recall that in Linux 2.2 it is the one that owns the largest number of page frames).

CHAPTER SEVENTEEN

THE EXT2 FILESYSTEM

In this chapter, we finish our extensive discussion of I/O and filesystems by taking a look at the details the kernel has to take care of when interacting with a particular filesystem. Since the Second Extended Filesystem (Ext2) is native to Linux and is used on virtually every Linux system, it made a natural choice for this discussion. Furthermore, Ext2 illustrates a lot of good practices in its support for modern filesystem features with fast performance. To be sure, other filesystems will embody new and interesting requirements, because they are designed for other operating systems, but we cannot examine the oddities of various filesystems and platforms in this book.

After introducing Ext2 in the section "General Characteristics," we describe the data structures needed, just as in other chapters. Since we are looking at a particular way to store data on a disk, we have to consider two versions of data structures: the section "Disk Data Structures" shows the data structures stored by Ext2 on the disk, while "Memory Data Structures" shows how they are duplicated in memory.

Then we get to the operations performed on the filesystem. In the section "Creating the Filesystem," we discuss how Ext2 is created in a disk partition. The next sections describe the kernel activities performed whenever the disk is used. Most of these are relatively low-level activities dealing with the allocation of disk space to inodes and data blocks. Then we'll discuss how Ext2 regular files are read and written.

General Characteristics

Each Unix-like operating system makes use of its own filesystem. Although all such filesystems comply with the POSIX interface, each of them is implemented in a different way.

The first versions of Linux were based on the Minix filesystem. As Linux matured, the *Extended Filesystem (Ext FS)* was introduced; it included several significant extensions but offered unsatisfactory performance. The *Second Extended Filesystem (Ext2)* was introduced in 1994: besides including several new features, it is quite efficient and robust and has become the most widely used Linux filesystem.

The following features contribute to the efficiency of Ext2:

- When creating an Ext2 filesystem, the system administrator may choose the optimal block size (from 1024 to 4096 bytes), depending on the expected average file length. For instance, a 1024 block size is preferable when the average file length is smaller than a few thousand bytes because this leads to less internal fragmentation—that is, less of a mismatch between the file length and the portion of the disk that stores it (see also the section "Memory Area Management" in Chapter 6, *Memory Management*, where internal fragmentation was discussed for dynamic memory). On the other hand, larger block sizes are usually preferable for files greater than a few thousand bytes because this leads to fewer disk transfers, thus reducing system overhead.

- When creating an Ext2 filesystem, the system administrator may choose how many inodes to allow for a partition of a given size, depending on the expected number of files to be stored on it. This maximizes the effectively usable disk space.

- The filesystem partitions disk blocks into groups. Each group includes data blocks and inodes stored in adjacent tracks. Thanks to this structure, files stored in a single block group can be accessed with a lower average disk seek time.

- The filesystem *preallocates* disk data blocks to regular files before they are actually used. Thus, when the file increases in size, several blocks are already reserved at physically adjacent positions, reducing file fragmentation.

- Fast symbolic links are supported. If the pathname of the symbolic link (see the section "Hard and Soft Links" in Chapter 1, *Introduction*) has 60 bytes or less, it is stored in the inode and can thus be translated without reading a data block.

Moreover, the Second Extended File System includes other features that make it both robust and flexible:

- A careful implementation of the file-updating strategy that minimizes the impact of system crashes. For instance, when creating a new hard link for a file, the counter of hard links in the disk inode is incremented first, and the new name is added into the proper directory next. In this way, if a hardware failure occurs after the inode update but before the directory can be changed, the directory is consistent, even if the inode's hard link counter is wrong. Deleting the file does not lead to catastrophic results, although the file's data blocks cannot be automatically reclaimed. If the reverse were done (changing the directory before updating the inode), the same hardware failure would produce a dangerous inconsistency: deleting the original hard link would remove its data blocks from disk, yet the new directory entry would refer to an inode that no longer exists. If that inode number is used later for another file, writing into the stale directory entry will corrupt the new file.

- Support for automatic consistency checks on the filesystem status at boot time. The checks are performed by the */sbin/e2fsck* external program, which may be activated not only after a system crash, but also after a predefined number of filesystem mountings (a counter is incremented after each mount operation) or after a predefined amount of time has elapsed since the most recent check.

- Support for immutable files (they cannot be modified) and for append-only files (data can be added only to the end of them). Even the superuser is not allowed to override these kinds of protection.

- Compatibility with both the Unix System V Release 4 and the BSD semantics of the Group ID for a new file. In SVR4 the new file assumes the Group ID of the process that creates it; in BSD the new file inherits the Group ID of the directory containing it. Ext2 includes a mount option that specifies which semantic is used.

Several additional features are being considered for the next major version of the Ext2 filesystem. Some of them have already been coded and are available as external patches. Others are just planned, but in some cases fields have already been introduced in the Ext2 inode for them. The most significant features are:

Block fragmentation
System administrators usually choose large block sizes for accessing recent disks. As a result, small files stored in large blocks waste a lot of disk space. This problem can be solved by allowing several files to be stored in different fragments of the same block.

Access Control Lists
Instead of classifying the users of a file under three classes—owner, group, and others—an access control list (ACL) is associated with each file to specify the access rights for any specific users or combinations of users.

Handling of compressed and encrypted files
These new options, which must be specified when creating a file, will allow users to store compressed and/or encrypted versions of their files on disk.

Logical deletion
An *undelete* option will allow users to easily recover, if needed, the contents of a previously removed file.

Disk Data Structures

The first block in any Ext2 partition is never managed by the Ext2 filesystem, since it is reserved for the partition boot sector (see Appendix A, *System Startup*). The rest of the Ext2 partition is split into *block groups*, each of which has the layout shown in Figure 17-1. As you will notice from the figure, some data structures must fit in exactly one block while others may require more than one block. All the block groups in the

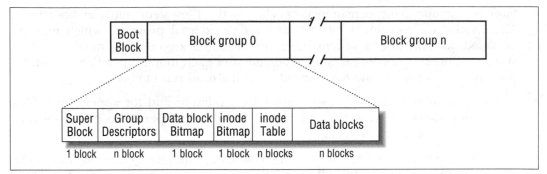

Figure 17-1. Layouts of an Ext2 partition and of an Ext2 block group

filesystem have the same size and are stored sequentially, so the kernel can derive the location of a block group in a disk simply from its integer index.

Block groups reduce file fragmentation, since the kernel tries to keep the data blocks belonging to a file in the same block group if possible. Each block in a block group contains one of the following pieces of information:

- A copy of the filesystem's superblock

- A copy of the group of block group descriptors

- A data block bitmap

- A group of inodes

- An inode bitmap

- A chunk of data belonging to a file; that is, a data block

If a block does not contain any meaningful information, it is said to be free.

As can be seen from Figure 17-1, both the superblock and the group descriptors are duplicated in each block group. Only the superblock and the group descriptors included in block group 0 are used by the kernel, while the remaining superblocks and group descriptors are left unchanged; in fact, the kernel doesn't even look at them. When the */sbin/e2fsck* program executes a consistency check on the filesystem status, it refers to the superblock and the group descriptors stored in block group 0, then copies them into all other block groups. If data corruption occurs and the main superblock or the main group descriptors in block group 0 becomes invalid, the system administrator can instruct */sbin/e2fsck* to refer to the old copies of the superblock and the group descriptors stored in a block groups other than the first. Usually, the redundant copies store enough information to allow */sbin/e2fsck* to bring the Ext2 partition back to a consistent state.

How many block groups are there? Well, that depends both on the partition size and on the block size. The main constraint is that the block bitmap, which is used to identify the blocks that are used and free inside a group, must be stored in a single block.

Therefore, in each block group there can be at most $8 \times b$ blocks, where b is the block size in bytes. Thus, the total number of block groups is roughly $s/(8 \times b)$, where s is the partition size in blocks.

As an example, let's consider an 8 GB Ext2 partition with a 4 KB block size. In this case, each 4 KB block bitmap describes 32 K data blocks, that is, 128 MB. Therefore, at most 64 block groups are needed. Clearly, the smaller the block size, the larger the number of block groups.

Superblock

An Ext2 disk superblock is stored in an `ext2_super_block` structure, whose fields are listed in Table 17-1. The `__u8`, `__u16`, and `__u32` data types denote unsigned numbers of length 8, 16, and 32 bits respectively, while the `__s8`, `__s16`, `__s32` data types denote signed numbers of length 8, 16, and 32 bits.

Table 17-1. The Fields of the Ext2 Superblock

Type	Field	Description
__u32	s_inodes_count	Total number of inodes
__u32	s_blocks_count	Filesystem size in blocks
__u32	s_r_blocks_count	Number of reserved blocks
__u32	s_free_blocks_count	Free blocks counter
__u32	s_free_inodes_count	Free inodes counter
__u32	s_first_data_block	Number of first useful block (always 1)
__u32	s_log_block_size	Block size
__s32	s_log_frag_size	Fragment size
__u32	s_blocks_per_group	Number of blocks per group
__u32	s_frags_per_group	Number of fragments per group
__u32	s_inodes_per_group	Number of inodes per group
__u32	s_mtime	Time of last mount operation
__u32	s_wtime	Time of last write operation
__u16	s_mnt_count	Mount operations counter
__u16	s_max_mnt_count	Number of mount operations before check
__u16	s_magic	Magic signature
__u16	s_state	Status flag
__u16	s_errors	Behavior when detecting errors
__u16	s_minor_rev_level	Minor revision level
__u32	s_lastcheck	Time of last check
__u32	s_checkinterval	Time between checks

Table 17-1. The Fields of the Ext2 Superblock (continued)

Type	Field	Description
__u32	s_creator_os	OS where filesystem was created
__u32	s_rev_level	Revision level
__u16	s_def_resuid	Default UID for reserved blocks
__u16	s_def_resgid	Default GID for reserved blocks
__u32	s_first_ino	Number of first nonreserved inode
__u16	s_inode_size	Size of on-disk inode structure
__u16	s_block_group_nr	Block group number of this superblock
__u32	s_feature_compat	Compatible features bitmap
__u32	s_feature_incompat	Incompatible features bitmap
__u32	s_feature_ro_compat	Read-only-compatible features bitmap
__u8 [16]	s_uuid	128-bit filesystem identifier
char [16]	s_volume_name	Volume name
char [64]	s_last_mounted	Pathname of last mount point
__u32	s_algorithm_usage_bitmap	Used for compression
__u8	s_prealloc_blocks	Number of blocks to preallocate
__u8	s_prealloc_dir_blocks	Number of blocks to preallocate for directories
__u8 [818]	s_padding	Nulls to pad out 1024 bytes

The s_inodes_count field stores the number of inodes, while the s_blocks_count field stores the number of blocks in the Ext2 filesystem.

The s_log_block_size field expresses the block size as a power of 2, using 1024 bytes as the unit. Thus, 0 denotes 1024-byte blocks, 1 denotes 2048-byte blocks, and so on. The s_log_frag_size field is currently equal to s_log_block_size, since block fragmentation is not yet implemented.

The s_blocks_per_group, s_frags_per_group, and s_inodes_per_group fields store the number of blocks, fragments, and inodes in each block group, respectively.

Some disk blocks are reserved to the superuser (or to some other user or group of users selected by the s_def_resuid and s_def_resgid fields). These blocks allow the system administrator to continue to use the filesystem even when no more free blocks are available for normal users.

The s_mnt_count, s_max_mnt_count, s_lastcheck, and s_checkinterval fields set up the Ext2 filesystem to be checked automatically at boot time. These fields cause

/sbin/e2fsck to run after a predefined number of mount operations has been performed, or when a predefined amount of time has elapsed since the last consistency
check. (Both kinds of checks can be used together.) The consistency check is also
enforced at boot time if the filesystem has not been cleanly unmounted (for instance,
after a system crash) or when the kernel discovers some errors in it. The `s_state`
field stores the value 0 if the filesystem is mounted or was not cleanly unmounted, 1 if
it was cleanly unmounted, and 2 if it contains errors.

Group Descriptor and Bitmap

Each block group has its own group descriptor, an `ext2_group_desc` structure whose
fields are illustrated in Table 17-2.

Table 17-2. The Fields of the Ext2 Group Descriptor

Type	Field	Description
__u32	bg_block_bitmap	Block number of block bitmap
__u32	bg_inode_bitmap	Block number of inode bitmap
__u32	bg_inode_table	Block number of first inode table block
__u16	bg_free_blocks_count	Number of free blocks in the group
__u16	bg_free_inodes_count	Number of free inodes in the group
__u16	bg_used_dirs_count	Number of directories in the group
__u16	bg_pad	Alignment to word
__u32 [3]	bg_reserved	Nulls to pad out 24 bytes

The `bg_free_blocks_count`, `bg_free_inodes_count`, and `bg_used_dirs_count`
fields are used when allocating new inodes and data blocks. These fields determine
the most suitable block in which to allocate each data structure. The bitmaps are
sequences of bits, where the value 0 specifies that the corresponding inode or data
block is free and the value 1 specifies that it is used. Since each bitmap must be stored
inside a single block and since the block size can be 1024, 2048, or 4096 bytes, a single bitmap describes the state of 8192, 16,384, or 32,768 blocks.

Inode Table

The inode table consists of a series of consecutive blocks, each of which contains a
predefined number of inodes. The block number of the first block of the inode table is
stored in the `bg_inode_table` field of the group descriptor.

All inodes have the same size, 128 bytes. A 1024-byte block contains 8 inodes, while a
4096-byte block contains 32 inodes. To figure out how many blocks are occupied by
the inode table, divide the total number of inodes in a group (stored in the `s_inodes_`
`per_group` field of the superblock) by the number of inodes per block.

Each Ext2 inode is an `ext2_inode` structure whose fields are illustrated in Table 17-3.

Table 17-3. The Fields of an Ext2 Disk Inode

Type	Field	Description
__u16	i_mode	File type and access rights
__u16	i_uid	Owner identifier
__u32	i_size	File length in bytes
__u32	i_atime	Time of last file access
__u32	i_ctime	Time that inode last changed
__u32	i_mtime	Time that file contents last changed
__u32	i_dtime	Time of file deletion
__u16	i_gid	Group identifier
__u16	i_links_count	Hard links counter
__u32	i_blocks	Number of data blocks of the file
__u32	i_flags	File flags
union	osd1	Specific operating system information
__u32 [EXT2_N_BLOCKS]	i_block	Pointers to data blocks
__u32	i_version	File version (for NFS)
__u32	i_file_acl	File access control list
__u32	i_dir_acl	Directory access control list
__u32	i_faddr	Fragment address
union	osd2	Specific operating system information

Many fields related to POSIX specifications are similar to the corresponding fields of the VFS's inode object and have already been discussed in the section "Inode Objects" in Chapter 12, *The Virtual Filesystem*. The remaining ones refer to the Ext2-specific implementation and deal mostly with block allocation.

In particular, the `i_size` field stores the effective length of the file in bytes, while the `i_blocks` field stores the number of data blocks (in units of 512 bytes) that have been allocated to the file.

The values of `i_size` and `i_blocks` are not necessarily related. Since a file is always stored in an integer number of blocks, a nonempty file receives at least one data block (since fragmentation is not yet implemented) and `i_size` may be smaller than 512×`i_blocks`. On the other hand, as we shall see in the section "File Holes" later in this chapter, a file may contain holes. In that case, `i_size` may be greater than 512×`i_blocks`.

The `i_block` field is an array of `EXT2_N_BLOCKS` (usually 15) pointers to blocks used to identify the data blocks allocated to the file (see the section "Data Blocks Addressing" later in this chapter).

The 32 bits reserved for the i_size field limit the file size to 4 GB. Actually, the highest-order bit of the i_size field is not used, thus the maximum file size is limited to 2 GB. However, the Ext2 filesystem includes a "dirty trick" that allows larger files on 64-bit architectures like Compaq's Alpha. Essentially, the i_dir_acl field of the inode, which is not used for regular files, represents a 32-bit extension of the i_size field. Therefore, the file size is stored in the inode as a 64-bit integer. The 64-bit version of the Ext2 filesystem is somewhat compatible with the 32-bit version because an Ext2 filesystem created on a 64-bit architecture may be mounted on a 32-bit architecture, and vice versa. However, on a 32-bit architecture a large file cannot be accessed.

Recall that the VFS model requires each file to have a different inode number. In Ext2, there is no need to store the inode number of a file on disk because its value can be derived from the block group number and the relative position inside the inode table. As an example, suppose that each block group contains 4096 inodes and that we want to know the address on disk of inode 13021. In this case, the inode belongs to the third block group and its disk address is stored in the 733rd entry of the corresponding inode table. As you can see, the inode number is just a key used by the Ext2 routines to retrieve quickly the proper inode descriptor on disk.

How Various File Types Use Disk Blocks

The different types of files recognized by Ext2 (regular files, pipes, etc.) use data blocks in different ways. Some files store no data and therefore need no data blocks at all. This section discusses the storage requirements for each type.

Regular file

Regular files are the most common case and receive almost all the attention in this chapter. But a regular file needs data blocks only when it starts to have data. When first created, a regular file is empty and needs no data blocks; it can also be emptied by the truncate() system call. Both situations are common; for instance, when you issue a shell command that includes the string *>filename*, the shell creates an empty file or truncates an existing one.

Directory

Ext2 implements directories as a special kind of file whose data blocks store filenames together with the corresponding inode numbers. In particular, such data blocks contain structures of type ext2_dir_entry_2. The fields of that structure are shown in Table 17-4. The structure has a variable length, since the last name field is a variable length array of up to EXT2_NAME_LEN characters (usually 255). Moreover, for reasons of efficiency, the length of a directory entry is always a multiple of 4, and therefore null characters (\0) are added for padding at the end of the filename if necessary. The name_len field stores the actual file name length (see Figure 17-2).

Table 17-4. The Fields of an Ext2 Directory Entry

Type	Field	Description
__u32	inode	Inode number
__u16	rec_len	Directory entry length
__u8	name_len	File name length
__u8	file_type	File type
char [EXT2_NAME_LEN]	name	File name

The `file_type` field stores a value that specifies the file type (see Table 17-5). The `rec_len` field may be interpreted as a pointer to the next valid directory entry: it is the offset to be added to the starting address of the directory entry to get the starting address of the next valid directory entry. In order to delete a directory entry, it is sufficient to set its `inode` field to 0 and to suitably increment the value of the `rec_len` field of the previous valid entry. Read the `rec_len` field of Figure 17-2 carefully; you'll see that the *oldfile* entry has been deleted because the `rec_len` field of *usr* is set to 12+16 (the lengths of the *usr* and *oldfile* entries).

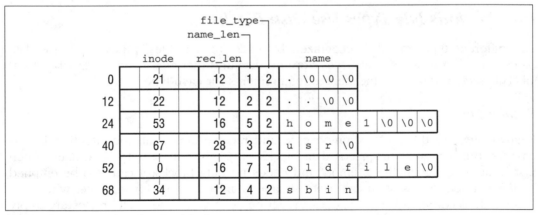

Figure 17-2. An example of EXT2 directory

Symbolic link

As stated before, if the pathname of the symbolic link has up to 60 characters, it is stored in the `i_block` field of the inode, which consists of an array of 15 4-byte integers; no data block is thus required. If the pathname is longer than 60 characters, however, a single data block is required.

Device file, pipe, and socket

No data blocks are required for these kinds of file. All the necessary information is stored in the inode.

Table 17-5. Ext2 File Types

file_type	Description
0	Unknown
1	Regular file
2	Directory
3	Character device
4	Block device
5	Named pipe
6	Socket
7	Symbolic link

Memory Data Structures

For the sake of efficiency, most information stored in the disk data structures of an Ext2 partition are copied into RAM when the filesystem is mounted, thus allowing the kernel to avoid many subsequent disk read operations. To get an idea of how often some data structures change, consider some fundamental operations:

- When a new file is created, the values of the **s_free_inodes_count** field in the Ext2 superblock and of the **bg_free_inodes_count** field in the proper group descriptor must be decremented.

- If the kernel appends some data to an existing file, so that the number of data blocks allocated for it increases, the values of the **s_free_blocks_count** field in the Ext2 superblock and of the **bg_free_blocks_count** field in the group descriptor must be modified.

- Even just rewriting a portion of an existing file involves an update of the **s_wtime** field of the Ext2 superblock.

Since all Ext2 disk data structures are stored in blocks of the Ext2 partition, the kernel uses the buffer cache to keep them up-to-date (see the section "Writing Dirty Buffers to Disk" in Chapter 14, *Disk Caches*).

Table 17-6 specifies, for each type of data related to Ext2 filesystems and files, the data structure used on the disk to represent its data, the data structure used by the kernel in memory, and a rule of thumb used to determine how much caching is used. Data that is updated very frequently is always cached; that is, the data is permanently stored in memory and included in the buffer cache until the corresponding Ext2 partition is unmounted. The kernel gets this result by keeping the buffer's usage counter greater than 0 at all times.

The never-cached data is not kept in the buffer cache since it does not represent meaningful information.

Table 17-6. VFS Images of Ext2 Data Structures

Type	Disk Data Structure	Memory Data Structure	Caching Mode
Superblock	ext2_super_block	ext2_sb_info	Always cached
Group descriptor	ext2_group_desc	ext2_group_desc	Always cached
Block bitmap	Bit array in block	Bit array in buffer	Fixed limit
Inode bitmap	Bit array in block	Bit array in buffer	Fixed limit
Inode	ext2_inode	ext2_inode_info	Dynamic
Data block	Unspecified	Buffer	Dynamic
Free inode	ext2_inode	None	Never
Free block	Unspecified	None	Never

In between these extremes lie two other modes: fixed limit and dynamic. In the fixed limit mode, a specific number of data structures can be kept in the buffer cache; older ones are flushed to disk when the number is exceeded. In the dynamic mode, the data is kept in the buffer cache as long as the associated object (an inode or block) is in use; when the file is closed or the block is deleted, the shrink_mmap() function may remove the associated data from the cache and write it back to disk.

The ext2_sb_info and ext2_inode_info Structures

When an Ext2 filesystem is mounted, the u field of the VFS superblock, which contains filesystem-specific data, is loaded with a structure of type ext2_sb_info so that the kernel can find out things related to the filesystem as a whole. This structure includes the following information:

- Most of the disk superblock fields

- The block bitmap cache, tracked by the **s_block_bitmap** and **s_block_bitmap_number** arrays (see next section)

- The inode bitmap cache, tracked by the **s_inode_bitmap** and **s_inode_bitmap_number** arrays (see next section)

- An **s_sbh** pointer to the buffer head of the buffer containing the disk superblock

- An **s_es** pointer to the buffer containing the disk superblock

- The number of group descriptors, **s_desc_per_block**, that can be packed in a block

- An **s_group_desc** pointer to an array of buffer heads of buffers containing the group descriptors (usually, a single entry is sufficient)

- Other data related to mount state, mount options, and so on

Similarly, when an inode object pertaining to an Ext2 file is initialized, the u field is loaded with a structure of type ext2_inode_info, which includes this information:

- Most of the fields found in the disk's inode structure that are not kept in the generic VFS inode object (see Table 12-3 in Chapter 12)

- The fragment size and the fragment number (not yet used)

- The i_block_group block group index at which the inode belongs (see the section "Disk Data Structures" earlier in this chapter)

- The i_alloc_block and i_alloc_count fields, which are used for data block preallocation (see the section "Allocating a Data Block" later in this chapter)

- The i_osync field, which is a flag specifying whether the disk inode should be synchronously updated (see the section "Reading and Writing an Ext2 Regular File" later in this chapter)

Bitmap Caches

When the kernel mounts an Ext2 filesystem, it allocates a buffer for the Ext2 disk superblock and reads its contents from disk. The buffer is released only when the Ext2 filesystem is unmounted. When the kernel must modify a field in the Ext2 superblock, it simply writes the new value in the proper position of the corresponding buffer and then marks the buffer as dirty.

Unfortunately, this approach cannot be adopted for all Ext2 disk data structures. The tenfold increase in disk capacity reached in recent years has induced a tenfold increase in the size of inode and data block bitmaps, so we have reached the point at which it is no longer convenient to keep all the bitmaps in RAM at the same time.

For instance, consider a 4 GB disk with a 1 KB block size. Since each bitmap fills all the bits of a single block, each of them describes the status of 8192 blocks, that is, of 8 MB of disk storage. The number of block groups is 4096 MB/8 MB=512. Since each block group requires both an inode bitmap and a data block bitmap, 1 MB of RAM would be required to store all 1024 bitmaps in memory!

The solution adopted to limit the memory requirements of the Ext2 descriptors is to use, for any mounted Ext2 filesystem, two caches of size EXT2_MAX_GROUP_LOADED (usually 8). One cache stores the most recently accessed inode bitmaps, while the other cache stores the most recently accessed block bitmaps. Buffers containing bitmaps included in a cache have a usage counter greater than 0, therefore they are never freed by shrink_mmap() (see the section "Reclaiming Pages from the Page, Swap, and Buffer Caches" in Chapter 16, *Swapping: Methods for Freeing Memory*). Conversely, buffers containing bitmaps not included in a bitmap cache have a null usage counter, and thus they can be freed if free memory becomes scarce.

Each cache is implemented by means of two arrays of EXT2_MAX_GROUP_LOADED elements. One array contains the indexes of the block groups whose bitmaps are currently in the cache, while the other array contains pointers to the buffer heads that refer to those bitmaps.

The ext2_sb_info structure stores the arrays pertaining to the inode bitmap cache: indexes of block groups are found in the s_inode_bitmap field and pointers to buffer heads in the s_inode_bitmap_number field. The corresponding arrays for the block bitmap cache are stored in the s_block_bitmap and s_block_bitmap_number fields.

The load_inode_bitmap() function loads the inode bitmap of a specified block group and returns the cache position in which the bitmap can be found.

If the bitmap is not already in the bitmap cache, load_inode_bitmap() invokes read_inode_bitmap(). The latter function gets the number of the block containing the bitmap from the bg_inode_bitmap field of the group descriptor, then invokes bread() to allocate a new buffer and read the block from disk if it is not already included in the buffer cache.

If the number of block groups in the Ext2 partition is less than or equal to EXT2_MAX_GROUP_LOADED, the index of the cache array position in which the bitmap is inserted always matches the block group index passed as the parameter to the load_inode_bitmap() function.

Otherwise, if there are more block groups than cache positions, a bitmap is removed from cache, if necessary, by using a Least Recently Used (LRU) policy, and the requested bitmap is inserted in the first cache position. Figure 17-3 illustrates the three possible cases in which the bitmap in block group 5 is referenced: where the requested bitmap is already in cache, where the bitmap is not in cache but there is a free position, and where the bitmap is not in cache and there is no free position.

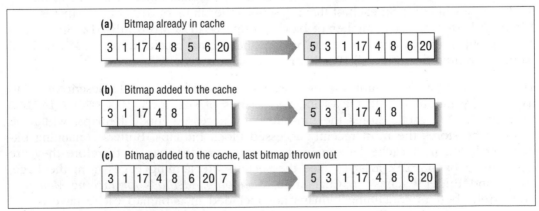

Figure 17-3. Adding a bitmap to the cache

The `load_block_bitmap()` and `read_block_bitmap()` functions are very similar to `load_inode_bitmap()` and `read_inode_bitmap()`, but they refer to the block bitmap cache of an Ext2 partition.

Figure 17-4 illustrates the memory data structures of a mounted Ext2 filesystem. In our example, there are three block groups whose descriptors are stored in three blocks on disk; therefore, the `s_group_desc` field of the `ext2_sb_info` points to an array of three buffer heads. We have shown just one inode bitmap having index 2 and one block bitmap having index 4, although the kernel may keep in the bitmap caches 2×EXT2_MAX_GROUP_LOADED bitmaps, and even more may be stored in the buffer cache.

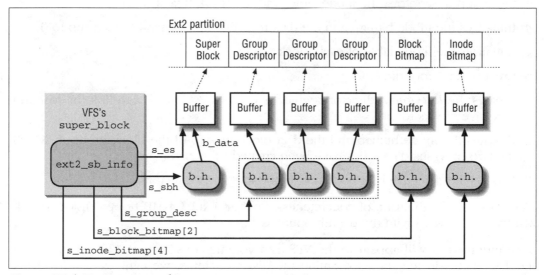

Figure 17-4. Ext2 memory data structures

Creating the Filesystem

Formatting a disk partition or a floppy is not the same thing as creating a filesystem on it. Formatting allows the disk driver to read and write blocks on the disk, while creating a filesystem means setting up the structures described in detail earlier in this chapter.

Modern hard disks come preformatted from the factory and need not be reformatted; floppy disks may be formatted by using the */usr/bin/superformat* utility program.

Ext2 filesystems are created by the */sbin/mke2fs* utility program; it assumes the following default options, which may be modified by the user with flags on the command line:

- Block size: 1024 bytes

- Fragment size: block size

- Number of allocated inodes: one for each group of 4096 bytes

- Percentage of reserved blocks: 5%

The program performs the following actions:

1. Initializes the superblock and the group descriptors

2. Optionally, checks whether the partition contains defective blocks: if so, creates a list of defective blocks

3. For each block group, reserves all the disk blocks needed to store the superblock, the group descriptors, the inode table, and the two bitmaps

4. Initializes the inode bitmap and the data map bitmap of each block group to 0

5. Initializes the inode table of each block group

6. Creates the / root directory

7. Creates the *lost+found* directory, which is used by */sbin/e2fsck* to link the lost and defective blocks found

8. Updates the inode bitmap and the data block bitmap of the block group in which the two previous directories have been created

9. Groups the defective blocks (if any) in the *lost+found* directory

Let's consider, for the sake of concreteness, how an Ext2 1.4 MB floppy disk is initialized by */sbin/mke2fs* with the default options.

Once mounted, it will appear to the VFS as a volume consisting of 1390 blocks, each one 1024 bytes in length. To examine the disk's contents, we can execute the Unix command:

```
$ dd if=/dev/fd0 bs=1k count=1440 | od -tx1 -Ax > /tmp/dump_hex
```

to get in the */tmp* directory a file containing the hexadecimal dump of the floppy disk contents.[*]

By looking at that file, we can see that, due to the limited capacity of the disk, a single group descriptor is sufficient. We also notice that the number of reserved blocks is set to 72 (5% of 1440) and that, according to the default option, the inode table must include 1 inode for each 4096 bytes, that is, 360 inodes stored in 45 blocks.

Table 17-7 summarizes how the Ext2 filesystem is created on a floppy disk when the default options are selected.

---

[*] Some information on an Ext2 filesystem could also be obtained by using the */sbin/dumpe2fs* and */sbin/debugfs* utility programs.

Table 17-7. Ext2 Block Allocation for a Floppy Disk

Block	Content
0	Boot block
1	Superblock
2	Block containing a single block group descriptor
3	Data block bitmap
4	Inode bitmap
5–49	Inode table: inodes up to 10: reserved; inode 11: *lost+found*; inodes 12–360: free
50	Root directory (includes ., .., and *lost+found*)
51	*lost+found* directory (includes . and ..)
52–62	Reserved blocks preallocated for *lost+found* directory
63–1439	Free blocks

Ext2 Methods

Many of the VFS methods described in Chapter 12 have a corresponding Ext2 implementation. Since it would take a whole book to describe all of them, we'll limit ourselves to briefly reviewing the methods implemented in Ext2. Once the disk and the memory data structures are clearly understood, the reader should be able to follow the code of the Ext2 functions that implement them.

Ext2 Superblock Operations

All VFS superblock operations have a specific implementation in Ext2, with the exception of the `clear_inode` and `umount_begin` VFS methods. The addresses of the superblock methods are stored into the `ext2_sops` array of pointers.

Ext2 Inode Operations

Many of the VFS inode operations have a specific implementation in Ext2, which depends on the type of the file to which the inode refers. Table 17-8 illustrates the inode operations implemented for inodes that refer to regular and directory files; their addresses are stored in the `ext2_file_inode_operations` and in the `ext2_dir_inode_operations` tables, respectively. Recall that the VFS uses its own generic functions when the corresponding Ext2 method is undefined (`NULL` pointer).

Table 17-8. Ext2 Inode Operations for Regular and Directory Files

VFS Inode Operation	Ext2 File Inode Method	Ext2 Directory Inode Method
`lookup`	`NULL`	`ext2_lookup()`
`link`	`NULL`	`ext2_link()`
`unlink`	`NULL`	`ext2_unlink()`

Table 17-8. Ext2 Inode Operations for Regular and Directory Files (continued)

VFS Inode Operation	Ext2 File Inode Method	Ext2 Directory Inode Method
symlink	NULL	ext2_symlink()
mkdir	NULL	ext2_mkdir()
rmdir	NULL	ext2_rmdir()
create	NULL	ext2_create()
mknod	NULL	ext2_mknod()
rename	NULL	ext2_rename()
readlink	NULL	NULL
follow_link	NULL	NULL
readpage	generic_readpage()	NULL
writepage	NULL	NULL
bmap	ext2_bmap()	NULL
truncate	ext2_truncate()	NULL
permission	ext2_permission()	ext2_permission()
smap	NULL	NULL
updatepage	NULL	NULL
revalidate	NULL	NULL

If the inode refers to a symbolic link, all inode methods are NULL except for readlink and follow_link, which are implemented by ext2_readlink() and ext2_follow_link(), respectively. The addresses of those methods are stored in the ext2_symlink_inode_operations table.

If the inode refers to a character device file, to a block device file, or to a named pipe (see "FIFOs" in Chapter 18, *Process Communication*), the inode operations do not depend on the filesystem. They are specified in the chrdev_inode_operations, blkdev_inode_operations, and fifo_inode_operations tables, respectively.

Ext2 File Operations

The file operations specific to the Ext2 filesystem are listed in Table 17-9. As you can see, the read and mmap VFS methods are implemented by generic functions that are common to many filesystems. The addresses of these methods are stored in the ext2_file_operations table.

Table 17-9. Ext2 File Operations

VFS File Operation	Ext2 Method
lseek	ext2_file_lseek()
read	generic_file_read()

Table 17-9. Ext2 File Operations (continued)

VFS File Operation	Ext2 Method
write	ext2_file_write()
readdir	NULL
poll	NULL
ioctl	ext2_ioctl()
mmap	generic_file_mmap()
open	ext2_open_file()
flush	NULL
release	ext2_release_file()
fsync	ext2_sync_file()
fasync	NULL
check_media_change	NULL
revalidate	NULL
lock	NULL

Managing Disk Space

The storage of a file on disk differs from the view the programmer has of the file in two ways: blocks can be scattered around the disk (although the filesystem tries hard to keep blocks sequential to improve access time), and files may appear to a programmer to be bigger than they really are because a program can introduce holes into them (through the lseek() system call).

In this section we explain how the Ext2 filesystem manages the disk space, that is, how it allocates and deallocates inodes and data blocks. Two main problems must be addressed:

- Space management must make every effort to avoid *file fragmentation*, that is, the physical storage of a file in several, small pieces located in nonadjacent disk blocks. File fragmentation increases the average time of sequential read operations on the files, since the disk heads must be frequently repositioned during the read operation.* This problem is similar to the external fragmentation of RAM discussed in the section "The Buddy System Algorithm" in Chapter 6.

- Space management must be time-efficient; that is, the kernel should be able to quickly derive from a file offset the corresponding logical block number in the Ext2 partition. In doing so, the kernel should limit as much as possible the number of

---

* Please note that fragmenting a file across block groups (A Bad Thing) is quite different from the not-yet-implemented fragmentation of blocks in order to store many files in one block (A Good Thing).

accesses to addressing tables stored on disk, since each such intermediate access considerably increases the average file access time.

Creating Inodes

The `ext2_new_inode()` function creates an Ext2 disk inode, returning the address of the corresponding inode object (or **NULL** in case of failure). It acts on two parameters: the address `dir` of the inode object that refers to the directory into which the new inode must be inserted and a `mode` that indicates the type of inode being created. The latter argument also includes an **MS_SYNCHRONOUS** flag that requires the current process to be suspended until the inode is allocated. The function performs the following actions:

1. Invokes `get_empty_inode()` to allocate a new inode object and initializes its `i_sb` field to the superblock address stored in `dir->i_sb`.

2. Invokes `lock_super()` to get exclusive access to the superblock object. The function tests and sets the value of the `s_lock` field and, if necessary, suspends the current process until the flag becomes 0.

3. If the new inode is a directory, tries to place it so that directories are evenly scattered through partially filled block groups. In particular, allocates the new directory in the block group that has the maximum number of free blocks among all block groups having a number of free inodes greater than the average. (The average is the total number of free inodes divided by the number of block groups).

4. If the new inode is not a directory, allocates it in a block group having a free inode. Selects the group by starting from the one containing the parent directory and moving farther and farther away from it, to be precise:

    a. Performs a quick logarithmic search starting from the block group that includes the parent directory `dir`. The algorithm searches $\log(n)$ block groups, where n is the total number of block groups. The algorithm jumps further and further ahead until it finds an available block group, as follows: if we call the number of the starting block group i, the algorithm considers block groups $i \ mod \ (n)$, $i+1 \ mod \ (n)$, $i+1+2 \ mod \ (n)$, $i+1+2+4 \ mod \ (n)$, . . .

    b. If the logarithmic search failed in finding a block group with a free inode, performs an exhaustive linear search starting from the first block group.

5. Invokes `load_inode_bitmap()` to get the inode bitmap of the selected block group and searches for the first null bit into it, thus obtaining the number of the first free disk inode.

6. Allocates the disk inode: sets the corresponding bit in the inode bitmap and marks the buffer containing the bitmap as dirty. Moreover, if the filesystem has been mounted specifying the **MS_SYNCHRONOUS** flag, invokes `ll_rw_block()` and waits until the write operation terminates (see the section "Mounting a Generic Filesystem" in Chapter 12).

7. Decrements the `bg_free_inodes_count` field of the block group descriptor. If the new inode is a directory, increments `bg_used_dirs_count`. Marks the buffer containing the group descriptor as dirty.

8. Decrements the `s_free_inodes_count` field of the disk superblock and marks the buffer containing it as dirty. Sets the `s_dirt` field of the VFS's superblock object to 1.

9. Initializes the fields of the inode object. In particular, sets the inode number `i_ino` and copies the value of `xtime.tv_sec` into `i_atime`, `i_mtime`, and `i_ctime`. Also loads the `i_block_group` field in the `ext2_inode_info` structure with the block group index. Refer to Table 17-3 for the meaning of these fields.

10. Inserts the new inode object into `inode_hashtable`.

11. Invokes `mark_inode_dirty()` to move the inode object into the superblock's dirty inode list (see the section "Inode Objects" in Chapter 12).

12. Invokes `unlock_super()` to release the superblock object.

13. Returns the address of the new inode object.

Deleting Inodes

The `ext2_free_inode()` function deletes a disk inode, which is identified by an inode object whose address is passed as the parameter. The kernel should invoke the function after a series of cleanup operations involving internal data structures and the data in the file itself: it should come after the inode object has been removed from the inode hash table, after the last hard link referring to that inode has been deleted from the proper directory, and after the file is truncated to 0 length in order to reclaim all its data blocks (see the section "Releasing a Data Block" later in this chapter). It performs the following actions:

1. Invokes `lock_super()` to get exclusive access to the superblock object.

2. Computes from the inode number and the number of inodes in each block group the index of the block group containing the disk inode.

3. Invokes `load_inode_bitmap()` to get the inode bitmap.

4. Invokes `clear_inode()` to perform the following operations:

    a. Release all pages in the page cache associated with the inode, suspending the current process if some of them are locked. (The pages could be locked because the kernel could be in the process of reading or writing them, and there is no way to stop the block device driver.)

    b. Invoke the `clear_inode` method of the superblock object, if defined; but the Ext2 filesystem does not define it.

5. Increments the `bg_free_inodes_count` field of the group descriptor. If the deleted inode is a directory, decrements the `bg_used_dirs_count` field. Marks the buffer containing the group descriptor as dirty.

6. Increments the `s_free_inodes_count` field of the disk superblock and marks the buffer that contains it as dirty. Also sets the `s_dirt` field of the superblock object to 1.

7. Clears the bit corresponding to the disk inode in the inode bitmap and marks the buffer containing the bitmap as dirty. Moreover, if the filesystem has been mounted with the `MS_SYNCHRONIZE` flag, invokes `ll_rw_block()` and waits until the write operation on the bitmap's buffer terminates.

8. Invokes `unlock_super()` to unlock the superblock object.

Data Blocks Addressing

Each nonempty regular file consists of a group of data blocks. Such blocks may be referred to either by their relative position inside the file (their *file block number*) or by their position inside the disk partition (their logical block number, explained in the section "Buffer Heads" in Chapter 13, *Managing I/O Devices*).

Deriving the logical block number of the corresponding data block from an offset f inside a file is a two-step process:

- Derive from the offset f the file block number, that is, the index of the block containing the character at offset f.

- Translate the file block number to the corresponding logical block number.

Since Unix files do not include any control character, it is quite easy to derive the file block number containing the fth character of a file: simply take the quotient of f and the filesystem's block size and round down to the nearest integer.

For instance, let's assume a block size of 4 KB. If f is smaller than 4096, the character is contained in the first data block of the file, which has file block number 0. If f is equal to or greater than 4096 and less than 8192, the character is contained in the data block having file block number 1 and so on.

This is fine as far as file block numbers are concerned. However, translating a file block number into the corresponding logical block number is not nearly as straightforward, since the data blocks of an Ext2 file are not necessarily adjacent on disk.

The Ext2 filesystem must thus provide a method to store on disk the connection between each file block number and the corresponding logical block number. This mapping, which goes back to early versions of Unix from AT&T, is implemented partly inside the inode. It also involves some specialized data blocks, which may be considered an inode extension used to handle large files.

The `i_block` field in the disk inode is an array of `EXT2_N_BLOCKS` components containing logical block numbers. In the following discussion, we assume that `EXT2_N_BLOCKS` has the default value, namely 15. The array represents the initial part of a larger data structure, which is illustrated in Figure 17-5. As can be noticed from the figure, the 15 components of the array are of four different types:

- The first 12 components yield the logical block numbers corresponding to the first 12 blocks of the file, that is, to the blocks having file block numbers from 0 to 11.

- The component at index 12 contains the logical block number of a block that represents a second-order array of logical block numbers. They correspond to the file block numbers ranging from 12 to $b/4+11$ where b is the filesystem's block size (each logical block number is stored in 4 bytes, so we divide by 4 in the formula). Therefore, the kernel must look in this component for a pointer to a block, then look in that block for another pointer to the ultimate block that contains the file contents.

- The component at index 13 contains the logical block number of a block containing a second-order array of logical block numbers; in turn, the entries of this second-order array point to third-order arrays, which store the logical block numbers corresponding to the file block numbers ranging from $b/4+12$ to $(b/4)^2+(b/4)+11$.

- Finally, the component at index 14 makes use of triple indirection: the fourth-order arrays store the logical block numbers corresponding to the file block numbers ranging from $(b/4)^2+(b/4)+12$ to $(b/4)^3+(b/4)^2+(b/4)+11$ upward.

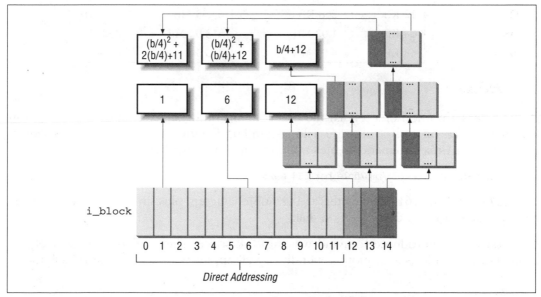

Figure 17-5. Data structures used to address the file's data blocks

In Figure 17-5, the number inside a block represents the corresponding file block number. The arrows, which represent logical block numbers stored in array components, show how the kernel finds its way to reach the block that contains the actual contents of the file.

Notice how this mechanism favors small files. If the file does not require more than 12 data blocks, any data can be retrieved in two disk accesses: one to read a component in the i_block array of the disk inode and the other one to read the requested data block. For larger files, however, three or even four consecutive disk accesses may be needed in order to access the required block. In practice, this is a worst-case estimate, since inode, buffer, and page caches contribute significantly to reduce the number of real disk accesses.

Notice also how the block size of the filesystem affects the addressing mechanism, since a larger block size allows the Ext2 to store more logical block numbers inside a single block. Table 17-10 shows the upper limit placed on a file's size for each block size and each addressing mode. For instance, if the block size is 1024 bytes and the file contains up to 268 kilobytes of data, the first 12 KB of a file can be accessed through direct mapping, and the remaining 13 through 268 KB can be addressed through simple indirection. With 4096-byte blocks, double indirection is sufficient to address a file of 2 GB (the maximum allowed by the Ext2 filesystem on 32-bit architecture).

Table 17-10. File Size Upper Limits for Data Block Addressing

Block Size	Direct	1-Indirect	2-Indirect	3-Indirect
1024	12 KB	268 KB	63.55 MB	2 GB
2048	24 KB	1.02 MB	513.02 MB	2 GB
4096	48 KB	4.04 MB	2 GB	—

File Holes

A *file hole* is a portion of a regular file that contains null characters and is not stored in any data block on disk. Holes are a long-standing feature of Unix files. For instance, the following Unix command creates a file in which the first bytes are a hole:

```
$ echo -n "X" | dd of=/tmp/hole bs=1024 seek=6
```

Now, */tmp/hole* has 6145 characters (6144 null characters plus an X character), yet the file occupies just one data block on disk.

File holes were introduced to avoid wasting disk space. They are used extensively by database applications and, more generally, by all applications that perform hashing on files.

The Ext2 implementation of file holes is based on dynamic data block allocation: a block is actually assigned to a file only when the process needs to write data into it. The i_size field of each inode defines the size of the file as seen by the program, including the hole, while the `i_blocks` field stores the number of data blocks effectively assigned to the file (in units of 512 bytes).

In our earlier example of the `dd` command, suppose the */tmp/hole* file was created on an Ext2 partition having blocks of size 4096. The `i_size` field of the corresponding disk inode stores the number 6145, while the `i_blocks` field stores the number 8 (because each 4096-byte block includes eight 512-byte blocks). The second element of the `i_block` array (corresponding to the block having file block number 1) stores the logical block number of the allocated block, while all other elements in the array are null (see Figure 17-6).

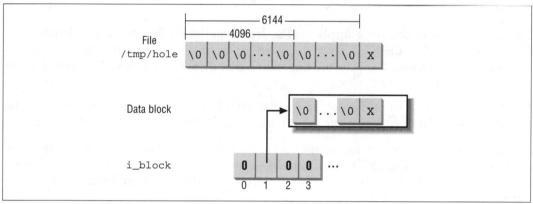

Figure 17-6. A file with an initial hole

Allocating a Data Block

When the kernel has to allocate a new block to hold data for an Ext2 regular file, it invokes the `ext2_getblk()` function. In turn, this function handles the data structures already described in the section "Data Blocks Addressing" and invokes when necessary the `ext2_alloc_block()` function to actually search for a free block in the Ext2 partition.

In order to reduce file fragmentation, the Ext2 filesystem tries to get a new block for a file near the last block already allocated for the file. Failing that, the filesystem searches for a new block in the block group that includes the file's inode. As a last resort, the free block is taken from one of the other block groups.

The Ext2 filesystem uses preallocation of data blocks. The file does not get just the requested block, but rather a group of up to eight adjacent blocks. The `i_prealloc_count` field in the `ext2_inode_info` structure stores the number of data blocks preallocated to some file that are still unused, and the `i_prealloc_block` field stores the logical block number of the next preallocated block to be used. Any preallocated blocks that remain unused are freed when the file is closed, when it is truncated, or when a write operation is not sequential with respect to the write operation that triggered the block preallocation.

The `ext2_alloc_block()` function receives as parameters a pointer to an inode object and a *goal*. The goal is a logical block number that represents the preferred position of the new block. The `ext2_getblk()` function sets the goal parameter according to the following heuristic:

1. If the block being allocated and the previously allocated one have consecutive file block numbers, the goal is the logical block number of the previous block plus 1; it makes sense that consecutive blocks as seen by a program should be adjacent on disk.

2. If the first rule does not apply and at least one block has been previously allocated to the file, the goal is one of these block's logical block number. More precisely, it is the logical block number of the already allocated block that precedes in the file the block to be allocated.

3. If the preceding rules do not apply, the goal is the logical block number of the first block (not necessarily free) in the block group that contains the file's inode.

The `ext2_alloc_block()` function checks whether the goal refers to one of the preallocated blocks of the file. If so, it allocates the corresponding block and return its logical block number; otherwise, the function discards all remaining preallocated blocks and invokes `ext2_new_block()`.

This latter function searches for a free block inside the Ext2 partition with the following strategy:

1. If the preferred block passed to `ext2_alloc_block()` (the goal) is free, allocates it.

2. If the goal is busy, checks whether one of the next 64 blocks after the preferred block is free.

3. If no free block has been found in the near vicinity of the preferred block, considers all block groups, starting from the one including the goal. For each block group:

   a. Looks for a group of at least eight adjacent free blocks.

   b. If no such group is found, looks for a single free block.

The search ends as soon as a free block is found. Before terminating, the `ext2_new_block()` function also tries to preallocate up to eight free blocks adjacent to the free block found and sets the `i_prealloc_block` and `i_prealloc_count` fields of the disk inode to the proper block location and number of blocks.

Releasing a Data Block

When a process deletes a file or truncates it to 0 length, all its data blocks must be reclaimed. This is done by ext2_truncate(), which receives the address of the file's inode object as its parameter. The function essentially scans the disk inode's i_block array to locate all data blocks, partitioning them into physically adjacent groups. Each such group is then released by invoking ext2_free_blocks().

The ext2_free_blocks() function releases a group of one or more adjacent data blocks. Besides its use by ext2_truncate(), the function is invoked mainly when discarding the preallocated blocks of a file (see the earlier section "Allocating a Data Block"). Its parameters are:

inode
> Address of the inode object that describes the file

block
> Logical block number of the first block to be released

count
> Number of adjacent blocks to be released

The function invokes lock_super() to get exclusive access to the filesystem's super-block, then performs the following actions for each block to be released:

1. Gets the block bitmap of the block group including the block to be released

2. Clears the bit in the block bitmap corresponding to the block to be released and marks the buffer containing the bitmap as dirty

3. Increments the bg_free_blocks_count field in the block group descriptor and marks the corresponding buffer as dirty

4. Increments the s_free_blocks_count field of the disk superblock, marks the corresponding buffer as dirty, and sets the s_dirt flag of the superblock object

5. If the filesystem has been mounted with the MS_SYNCHRONOUS flag set, invokes ll_rw_block() and waits until the write operation on the bitmap's buffer terminates

Finally, the function invokes unlock_super() to release the superblock.

Reading and Writing an Ext2 Regular File

In Chapter 12 we described how the Virtual File System recognizes the type of file being accessed by a read() or write() system call and invokes the corresponding method of the proper file operation table. We now have all the needed tools to understand how a regular file is actually read or written in the Ext2 filesystem.

There's nothing more to say about read operations, however, because they have already been completely discussed. As shown in Table 17-9, the Ext2's `read` method is implemented by the `generic_file_read()` function, which is described in the section "Reading from a Regular File" in Chapter 15, *Accessing Regular Files*.

Let's concentrate then on Ext2's `write` method, which is implemented by the `ext2_file_write()` function. It acts on four parameters:

`fd`
> File descriptor of the file being written

`buf`
> Address of a memory area containing the data to be written

`count`
> Number of bytes to be written

`ppos`
> Pointer to a variable storing the file offset where data must be written

The function performs the following actions:

1. Removes any superuser privilege from the file (to guard against tampering with *set-uid* programs, described in Chapter 19, *Program Execution*).

2. If the file has been opened with the `O_APPEND` flag set, sets the file offset where data must be written to the end of the file.

3. If the file has been opened in synchronous mode (`O_SYNC` flag set), sets `i_osync` field in the `ext2_inode_info` structure of the disk inode to 1. This flag is tested when a data block is allocated for the file, so that the kernel can synchronously update the inode on disk as soon as it is modified.

4. As done before, computes from the file offset and the filesystem block size the file block number of the first byte to be written and the relative offset within the block (see the earlier section "Data Blocks Addressing").

5. For each block to be written, performs the following substeps:

    a. Invokes `ext2_getblk()` to get the data block on the disk, allocating it when necessary.

    b. If the block has to be partially rewritten and the buffer is not up-to-date, invokes `ll_rw_block()` and waits until the read operation terminates.

    c. Copies the bytes to be written into the block from the process address space to the buffer and marks the buffer as dirty.

 d. Invokes `update_vm_cache()` to synchronize the contents of the page cache with that of the buffer cache.

 e. If the file has been opened in synchronous mode, inserts the buffer in a local array. If the array becomes filled (it includes 32 elements), invokes `ll_rw_block()` to start the write operations and waits until they terminate.

6. If the file has been opened in synchronous mode, clears the `i_osync` flag of the disk inode; also invokes `ll_rw_block()` to start the write operation for any buffer still remaining in the local array and waits until I/O data transfers terminate.

7. Updates the `i_size` field of the inode object.

8. Sets the `i_ctime` and `i_mtime` fields of the inode object to `xtime.tv_sec` and marks the inode as dirty.

9. Updates the variable `*ppos` storing the file offset where the data has been written (it is usually the file pointer).

10. Returns the number of bytes written into the file.

Anticipating Linux 2.4

Using the `generic_file_write()` function to write in a regular Ext2 file has several beneficial effects. One of them is that the 2 GB limit on the file size is gone and very large files can be accessed even on 32-bit architectures. However, none of the features mentioned at the end of the section "General Characteristics" has been included in Linux 2.4. They will likely come out with the new Ext3 filesystem currently being tested.

CHAPTER EIGHTEEN

PROCESS COMMUNICATION

This chapter explains how User Mode processes can synchronize themselves and exchange data. We have already covered a lot of synchronization topics in Chapter 11, *Kernel Synchronization*, but the actors there were kernel control paths, not User Mode programs. We are now ready, after having discussed I/O management and filesystems at length, to extend the discussion of synchronization to User Mode processes. These processes must rely on the kernel to synchronize themselves and to exchange data.

As we saw in the section "Linux File Locking" in Chapter 12, *The Virtual Filesystem*, a crude form of synchronization among User Mode processes can be achieved by creating a (possibly empty) file and by making use of suitable VFS system calls to lock and unlock it. Similarly, data sharing among processes can be obtained by storing data in temporary files protected by locks. This approach is costly since it requires accesses to the disk filesystem. For that reason, all Unix kernels include a set of system calls that supports process communication without interacting with the filesystem; furthermore, several wrapper functions have been developed and inserted in suitable libraries to expedite how processes issue their synchronization requests to the kernel.

As usual, application programmers have a variety of needs that call for different communication mechanisms. Here are the basic mechanisms that Unix systems, and Linux in particular, offer to allow interprocess communication:

Pipes and FIFOs (named pipes)
> Best suited to implement producer/consumer interactions among processes. Some processes fill the pipe with data while others extract data from the pipe.

Semaphores
> Represents, as the name implies, the User Mode version of the kernel semaphores discussed in the section "Locking Through Kernel Semaphores" in Chapter 11.

Messages

Allow processes to exchange messages (short blocks of data) in an asynchronous way. They can be thought of as signals carrying additional information.

Shared memory regions

Best suited to implement interaction schemes in which processes must share large amounts of data in an efficient way.

This book does not cover another common communication mechanism, sockets. As stated in previous chapters, sockets were introduced initially to allow data communication between application programs and the network interface (see the section "Device Files" in Chapter 13, *Managing I/O Devices*). They can also be used as a communication tool for processes located on the same host computer; the X Window System graphic interface, for instance, uses a socket to allow client programs to exchange data with the X server. We don't include them because they would require a long discussion of networking, which is beyond the scope of the book.

Pipes

Pipes are an interprocess communication mechanism that is provided in all flavors of Unix. A *pipe* is a one-way flow of data between processes: all data written by a process to the pipe is routed by the kernel to another process, which can thus read it.

In Unix command shells, pipes can be created by means of the | operator. For instance, the following statement instructs the shell to create two processes connected by a pipe:

```
$ ls | more
```

The standard output of the first process, which executes the *ls* program, is redirected to the pipe; the second process, which executes the *more* program, reads its input from the pipe.

Note that the same results can also be obtained by issuing two commands such as the following:

```
$ ls > temp
$ more < temp
```

The first command redirects the output of *ls* into a regular file; then the second command forces *more* to read its input from the same file. Of course, using pipes instead of temporary files is usually more convenient since:

- The shell statement is much shorter and simpler.

- There is no need to create temporary regular files, which must be deleted later.

Using a Pipe

Pipes may be considered open files that have no corresponding image in the mounted filesystems. A new pipe can be created by means of the `pipe()` system call, which returns a pair of file descriptors. The process can read from the pipe by using the `read()` system call with the first file descriptor; likewise, it can write into the pipe by using the `write()` system call with the second file descriptor.

POSIX defines only half-duplex pipes, so even though the `pipe()` system call returns two file descriptors, each process must close one before using the other. If a two-way flow of data is required, the processes must use two different pipes by invoking `pipe()` twice.

Several Unix systems, such as System V Release 4, implement full-duplex pipes and allow both descriptors to be written into and read from. Linux adopts another approach: each pipe's file descriptors are still one-way, but it is not necessary to close one of them before using the other.

Let us resume the previous example: when the command shell interprets the `ls|more` statement, it essentially performs the following actions:

1. Invokes the `pipe()` system call; let us assume that `pipe()` returns the file descriptors 3 (the pipe's *read channel*) and 4 (the *write channel*).

2. Invokes the `fork()` system call twice.

3. Invokes the `close()` system call twice to release file descriptors 3 and 4.

The first child process, which must execute the *ls* program, performs the following operations:

1. Invokes `dup2(4,1)` to copy file descriptor 4 to file descriptor 1. From now on, file descriptor 1 refers to the pipe's write channel.

2. Invokes the `close()` system call twice to release file descriptors 3 and 4.

3. Invokes the `execve()` system call to execute the */bin/ls* program (see the section "The exec-like Functions" in Chapter 19, *Program Execution*). By default, such a program writes its output to the file having file descriptor 1 (the standard output), that is, it writes into the pipe.

The second child process must execute the *more* program; therefore, it performs the following operations:

1. Invokes `dup2(3,0)` to copy file descriptor 3 to file descriptor 0. From now on, file descriptor 0 refers to the pipe's read channel.

2. Invokes the `close()` system call twice to release file descriptors 3 and 4.

3. Invokes the `execve()` system call to execute */bin/more*. By default, that program reads its input from the file having file descriptor 0 (the standard input); that is, it reads from the pipe.

In this simple example, the pipe is used by exactly two processes. Because of its implementation, though, a pipe can be used by an arbitrary number of processes.* Clearly, if two or more processes read or write the same pipe, they must explicitly synchronize their accesses by using file locking (see the section "Linux File Locking" in Chapter 12) or IPC semaphores (see the section "IPC Semaphores" later in this chapter).

Many Unix systems provide, besides the `pipe()` system call, two wrapper functions named `popen()` and `pclose()` that handle all the dirty work usually done when using pipes. Once a pipe has been created by means of the `popen()` function, it can be used with the high-level I/O functions included in the C library (`fprintf()`, `fscanf()`, and so on).

In Linux, `popen()` and `pclose()` are included in the C library. The `popen()` function receives two parameters: the `filename` pathname of an executable file and a `type` string specifying the direction of the data transfer. It returns the pointer to a `FILE` data structure. The `popen()` function essentially performs the following operations:

1. Creates a new pipe by making use of the `pipe()` system call

2. Forks a new process, which in turn executes the following operations:

   a. If `type` is `r`, duplicates the file descriptor associated with the pipe's write channel as file descriptor 1 (standard output); otherwise, if `type` is `w`, duplicates the file descriptor associated with the pipe's read channel as file descriptor 0 (standard input)

   b. Closes the file descriptors returned by `pipe()`

   c. Invokes the `execve()` system call to execute the program specified by `filename`

3. If `type` is `r`, closes the file descriptor associated with the pipe's write channel; otherwise, if `type` is `w`, closes the file descriptor associated with the pipe's read channel

4. Returns the address of the `FILE` file pointer that refers to whichever file descriptor for the pipe is still open

After the `popen()` invocation, parent and child can exchange information through the pipe: the parent can read (if `type` is `r`) or write (if `type` is `w`) some data by using the `FILE` pointer returned by the function. The data is written to the standard output or read from the standard input, respectively, by the program executed by the child process.

---

* Since most shells offer pipes that connect only two processes, applications requiring pipes used by more than two processes must be coded in a programming language such as C.

The pclose() function, which receives the file pointer returned by popen() as its parameter, simply invokes the wait4() system call and waits for the termination of the process created by popen().

Pipe Data Structures

We now have to start thinking again on the system call level. Once a pipe has been created, a process uses the read() and write() VFS system calls to access it. Therefore, for each pipe, the kernel creates an inode object plus two file objects, one for reading and the other for writing. When a process wants to read from or write to the pipe, it must use the proper file descriptor.

When the inode object refers to a pipe, its u field consists of a pipe_inode_info structure shown in Table 18-1.

Table 18-1. The pipe_inode_info Structure

Type	Field	Description
char *	base	Address of kernel buffer
unsigned int	start	Read position in kernel buffer
unsigned int	lock	Locking flag for exclusive access
struct wait_queue *	wait	Pipe/FIFO wait queue
unsigned int	readers	Flag for (or number of) reading processes
unsigned int	writers	Flag for (or number of) writing processes
unsigned int	rd_openers	Used while opening a FIFO for reading
unsigned int	wr_openers	Used while opening a FIFO for writing

Besides one inode and two file objects, each pipe has its own *pipe buffer*, that is, a single page frame containing the data written into the pipe and yet to be read. The address of this page frame is stored in the base field of the pipe_inode_info structure. The i_size field of the inode object stores the number of bytes written into the pipe buffer that are yet to be read; in the following, we call that number the current *pipe size*.

The pipe buffer is accessed both by reading processes and by writing ones, so the kernel must keep track of two current positions in the buffer:

- The offset of the next byte to be read, which is stored in the start field of the pipe_inode_info structure

- The offset of the next byte to be written, which is derived from start and the pipe size

To avoid race conditions on the pipe's data structures, the kernel forbids concurrent accesses to the pipe buffer. In order to achieve this, it makes use of the lock field in the pipe_inode_info data structure. Unfortunately, the lock field is not sufficient. As we shall see, POSIX dictates that some pipe operations are atomic. Moreover, the POSIX standard allows the writing process to be suspended when the pipe is full, so that readers can empty the buffer (see the section "Writing into a Pipe" later in this chapter). These requirements are satisfied by using an additional i_atomic_write semaphore that can be found in the inode object: this semaphore keeps a process from starting a write operation while another writer has been suspended because the buffer is full.

Creating and Destroying a Pipe

A pipe is implemented as a set of VFS objects, which have no corresponding disk image. As we shall see from the following discussion, a pipe remains in the system as long as some process owns a file descriptor referring to it.

The pipe() system call is serviced by the sys_pipe() function, which in turn invokes the do_pipe() function. In order to create a new pipe, do_pipe() performs the following operations:

1. Allocates a file object and a file descriptor for the read channel of the pipe, sets the flag field of the file object to O_RDONLY, and initializes the f_op field with the address of the read_pipe_fops table.

2. Allocates a file object and a file descriptor for the write channel of the pipe, sets the flag field of the file object to O_WRONLY, and initializes the f_op field with the address of the write_pipe_fops table.

3. Invokes the get_pipe_inode() function, which allocates and initializes an inode object for the pipe. This function also allocates a page frame for the pipe buffer and stores its address in the base field of the pipe_inode_info structure.

4. Allocates a dentry object and uses it to link together the two file objects and the inode object (see the section "The Common File Model" in Chapter 12).

5. Returns the two file descriptors to the User Mode process.

The process that issues a pipe() system call is initially the only process that can access the new pipe, both for reading and for writing. To represent that the pipe has actually both a reader and a writer, the readers and writers fields of the pipe_inode_info data structure are initialized to 1. In general, each of these two fields is set to 1 if and only if the corresponding pipe's file object is still opened by some process; the field is set to 0 if the corresponding file object has been released, since it is no longer accessed by any process.

Forking a new process does not increase the value of the **readers** and **writers** fields, so they never rise above 1;* however, it does increase the value of the usage counters of all file objects still used by the parent process (see the section "The clone(), fork(), and vfork() System Calls" in Chapter 3, *Processes*). Thus, the objects will not be released even when the parent dies, and the pipe will stay open for use by the children.

Whenever a process invokes the **close()** system call on a file descriptor associated with a pipe, the kernel executes the **fput()** function on the corresponding file object, which decrements the usage counter. If the counter becomes 0, the function invokes the **release** method of the file operations (see the sections "The close() System Call" and "Files Associated with a Process" in Chapter 12).

Both the **pipe_read_release()** and the **pipe_write_release()** functions are used to implement the **release** method of the pipe's file objects. They set to 0 the **readers** and the **writers** fields, respectively, of the **pipe_inode_info** structure. Each function then invokes the **pipe_release()** function. This function wakes up any processes sleeping in the pipe's wait queue so that they can recognize the change in the pipe state. Moreover, the function checks whether both the **readers** and **writers** fields are equal to 0; in this case, it releases the page frame containing the pipe buffer.

Reading from a Pipe

A process wishing to get data from a pipe issues a **read()** system call, specifying as its file descriptor the descriptor associated with the pipe's read channel. As described in the section "The read() and write() System Calls" in Chapter 12, the kernel ends up invoking the **read** method found in the file operation table associated with the proper file object. In the case of a pipe, the entry for the read method in the **read_pipe_fops** table points to the **pipe_read()** function.

The **pipe_read()** function is quite involved, since the POSIX standard specifies several requirements for the pipe's read operations. Table 18-2 illustrates the expected behavior of a **read()** system call that requests n bytes from a pipe having a pipe size (number of bytes in the pipe buffer yet to be read) equal to p. Notice that the read operation can be nonblocking: in this case, it completes as soon as all available bytes (even none) have been copied into the user address space.† Notice also that the value 0 is returned by the **read()** system call only if the pipe is empty and no process is currently using the file object associated with the pipe's write channel.

---

* As we'll see, the **readers** and **writers** fields act as counters instead of flags when associated with FIFOs.

† Nonblocking operations are usually requested by specifying the O_NONBLOCK flag in the open() system call. This method does not work for pipes, since they cannot be opened; a process can, however, require a nonblocking operation on a pipe by issuing a fcntl() system call on the corresponding file descriptor.

Table 18-2. Reading n Bytes from a Pipe

Pipe Size p	At Least One Writing Process		No Writing Process
	Blocking Read	Nonblocking Read	
$p=0$	Wait for some data, copy it, and return its size.	Return -EAGAIN.	Return 0.
$0<p<n$	Copy p bytes and return p: 0 bytes are left in the pipe buffer.		
$p\geq n$	Copy n bytes and return n: p-n bytes are left in the pipe buffer.		

The function performs the following operations:

1. Determines if the pipe size, which is stored into the inode's **i_size** field, is 0. In this case, determines if the function must return or if the process must be blocked while waiting until another process writes some data in the pipe (see Table 18-2). The type of I/O operation (blocking or nonblocking) is specified by the O_ NONBLOCK flag in the **f_flags** field of the file object. If necessary, invokes the **interruptible_sleep_on()** function to suspend the current process after having inserted it in the wait queue to which the **wait** field of the **pipe_inode_info** data structure points.

2. Checks the **lock** field of the **pipe_inode_info** data structure. If it is not null, another process is currently accessing the pipe; in this case, either suspends the current process or immediately terminates the system call, depending on the type of read operation (blocking or nonblocking).

3. Increments the **lock** field.

4. Copies the requested number of bytes (or the number of available bytes, if the buffer size is too small) from the pipe's buffer to the user address space.

5. Decrements the **lock** field.

6. Invokes **wake_up_interruptible()** to wake up all processes sleeping on the pipe's wait queue.

7. Returns the number of bytes copied into the user address space.

Writing into a Pipe

A process wishing to put data into a pipe issues a **write()** system call, specifying as its file descriptor the descriptor associated with the pipe's write channel. The kernel satisfies this request by invoking the **write** method of the proper file object; the corresponding entry in the **write_pipe_fops** table points to the **pipe_write()** function.

Table 18-3 illustrates the behavior, specified by the POSIX standard, of a **write()** system call that requested to write n bytes into a pipe having u unused bytes in its buffer. In particular, the standard requires that write operations involving a small number of bytes must be automatically executed. More precisely, if two or more processes are concurrently writing into a pipe, any write operation involving fewer than 4096 bytes (the pipe buffer size) must finish without being interleaved with write operations of other processes to the same pipe. However, write operations involving more than 4096 bytes may be nonatomic and may also force the calling process to sleep.

Table 18-3. Writing n Bytes to a Pipe

Available Buffer Space u	At Least One Reading Process		No Reading Process
	Blocking Write	Nonblocking Write	
$u < n \leq 4096$	Wait until $n-u$ bytes are freed, copy n bytes, and return n.	Return -EAGAIN.	Send SIGPIPE signal and return -EPIPE.
$n > 4096$	Copy n bytes (waiting when necessary) and return n.	If $u > 0$, copy u bytes and return u, else return -EAGAIN.	
$u \geq n$	Copy n bytes and return n.		

Moreover, any write operation to a pipe must fail if the pipe does not have a reading process (that is, if the **readers** field of the pipe's inode object has the value 0). In that case, the kernel sends a SIGPIPE signal to the writing process and terminates the **write()** system call with the -EPIPE error code, which usually leads to the familiar "Broken pipe" message.

The **pipe_write()** function performs the following operations:

1. Checks whether the pipe has at least one reading process. If not, sends a SIGPIPE signal to the **current** process and return an -EPIPE value.

2. Releases the **i_sem** semaphore of the pipe's inode, which was acquired by the **sys_write()** function (see the section "The read() and write() System Calls" in Chapter 12), and acquires the **i_atomic_write** semaphore of the same inode.[*]

3. Checks whether the number of bytes to be written is within the pipe's buffer size:

    a. If so, the write operation must be atomic. Therefore, checks whether the buffer has enough free space to store all bytes to be written.

    b. If the number of bytes is greater than the buffer size, the operation can start as long as there is any free space at all. Therefore, checks for at least 1 free byte.

4. If the buffer does not have enough free space and the write operation is blocking, inserts the current process into the pipe's wait queue and suspends it until some data is read from the pipe. Notice that the **i_atomic_write** semaphore is not

---

[*] The i_sem semaphore prevents multiple processes from starting write operations on a file, and thus on the pipe. For some reason unknown to the authors, Linux prefers to make use of a specialized pipe semaphore.

released, so no other process can start a write operation on the buffer. If the write operation is nonblocking, returns the **-EAGAIN** error code.

5. Checks the **lock** field of the **pipe_inode_info** data structure. If it is not null, another process is currently reading the pipe, so either suspends the current process or immediately terminates the write depending on whether the write operation is blocking or nonblocking.

6. Increments the **lock** field.

7. Copies the requested number of bytes (or the number of free bytes if the pipe size is too small) from the user address space to the pipe's buffer.

8. If there are bytes yet to be written, goes to step 4.

9. After all requested data is written, decrements the **lock** field.

10. Invokes **wake_up_interruptible()** to wake up all processes sleeping on the pipe's wait queue.

11. Releases the **i_atomic_write** semaphore and acquires the **i_sem** semaphore (so that **sys_write()** can safely release the latter).

12. Returns the number of bytes written into the pipe's buffer.

FIFOs

Although pipes are a simple, flexible, and efficient communication mechanism, they have one main drawback, namely, that there is no way to open an already existing pipe. This makes it impossible for two arbitrary processes to share the same pipe, unless the pipe was created by a common ancestor process.

This drawback is substantial for many application programs. Consider, for instance, a database engine server, which continuously polls client processes wishing to issue some queries and which sends back to them the results of the database lookups. Each interaction between the server and a given client might be handled by a pipe. However, client processes are usually created on demand by a command shell when a user explicitly queries the database; server and client processes thus cannot easily share a pipe.

In order to address such limitations, Unix systems introduce a special file type called a *named pipe* or *FIFO* (which stands for "first in, first out": the first byte written into the special file is also the first byte that will be read).*

FIFO files are similar to device files: they have a disk inode, but they do not make use of data blocks. Thanks to the disk inode, a FIFO can be accessed by any process,

---

* Starting with System V Release 3, FIFOs are implemented as full-duplex (bidirectional) objects.

since the FIFO filename is included in the system's directory tree. In addition to having a filename, FIFOs are similar to unnamed pipes in that they also include a kernel buffer to temporarily store the data exchanged by two or more processes. Since they make use of kernel buffers, FIFOs are much more efficient than temporary files.

Going back to the database example, the communication between server and clients may be easily established by using FIFOs instead of pipes. The server creates, at startup, a FIFO used by client programs to make their requests. Each client program creates, before establishing the connection, another FIFO to which the server program can write the answer to the query and includes the FIFO's name in the initial request to the server.

Creating and Opening a FIFO

A process creates a FIFO by issuing a `mknod()`* system call (see the section "Device Files" in Chapter 13), passing to it as parameters the pathname of the new FIFO and the value `S_IFIFO` (`0x1000`) logically ORed with the permission bit mask of the new file. POSIX introduces a system call named `mkfifo()` specifically to create a FIFO. This call is implemented in Linux, as in System V Release 4, as a C library function that invokes `mknod()`.

Once created, a FIFO can be accessed through the usual `open()`, `read()`, `write()`, and `close()` system calls, yet the VFS handles it in a special way because the FIFO inode and file operations are customized and do not depend on the filesystems in which the FIFO is stored.

The POSIX standard specifies the behavior of the `open()` system call on named pipes; the behavior depends essentially on the requested access type, on the kind of I/O operation (blocking or nonblocking), and on the presence of other processes accessing the FIFO.

A process may open a FIFO for reading, for writing, or for reading and writing. The file operations associated with the corresponding file object are set to special methods for these three cases.

When a process opens a FIFO, the VFS performs the same operations as it does for device files (see the section "VFS Handling of Device Files" in Chapter 13). The inode object associated with the opened FIFO is initialized by a filesystem-dependent `read_inode` superblock method. This method always checks whether the inode on disk represents a FIFO:

```
if ((inode->i_mode & 00170000) == S_IFIFO)
    init_fifo(inode);
```

---

* In fact, `mknod()` can be used to create nearly any kind of file: block and character device files, FIFOs, and even regular files (it cannot create directories or sockets, though).

The `init_fifo()` function sets the `i_op` field of the inode object to the address of the `fifo_inode_operations` table. The function also initializes to 0 all fields of the `pipe_inode_info` data structure stored inside the inode object (see Table 18-1).

The `filp_open()` function (invoked by `sys_open()`, see the section "The open() System Call" in Chapter 12) then fills the remaining fields of the inode object and initializes the `f_op` field of the new file object with the contents of `i_op->default_file_ops` field of the inode object. As a consequence, the file operation table is set to `def_fifo_fops`. Then `filp_open()` invokes the `open` method from that table of operations, which is implemented in this specific case by the `fifo_open()` function.

The `fifo_open()` function examines the values of the **readers** and **writers** fields in the `pipe_inode_info` data structure. When referring to FIFOs, such fields store the number of reading and writing processes, respectively. If necessary, the function suspends the current process until a reader or a writer process accesses the FIFO: Table 18-4 illustrates the possible behaviors of `fifo_open()`. Moreover, the function further determines specialized behavior for the set of file operations to be used by setting the `f_op` field of the file object to the address of some predefined tables shown in Table 18-5. Finally, the function checks whether the **base** field of the **pipe_inode_info** data structure is **NULL**; in this case, it gets a free page frame for the FIFO's kernel buffer and stores its address in **base**.

Table 18-4. Behavior of the fifo_open() Function

Access Type	Blocking	Nonblocking
Read only, with writers	Successfully return	Successfully return
Read only, no writer	Wait for a writer	Successfully return
Write only, with readers	Successfully return	Successfully return
Write only, no reader	Wait for a reader	Return `-ENXIO`
Read/write	Successfully return	Successfully return

The FIFO's four specialized file operation tables differ mainly in the implementation of the **read** and **write** methods. If the access type allows read operations, the **read** method is implemented by the `pipe_read()` function. Otherwise, it is implemented by `bad_pipe_r()`, which just returns an error code. Similarly, if the access type allows write operations, the **write** method is implemented by the `pipe_write()` function; otherwise, it is implemented by `bad_pipe_w()`, which also returns an error code.

According to the POSIX standard, a process may open a FIFO successfully for reading in a nonblocking mode, even if the FIFO has no writers: in this case, the `pipe_read()` function cannot be used right away to implement the **read** method since it returns an `-EAGAIN` error code when it discovers that the pipe is empty and that there are no writers. The solution adopted consists of implementing the **read** method with an intermediate `connect_read()` function; if there are no writers, this function returns 0; otherwise, it sets the `f_op` field of the file object to `read_fifo_fops` and then invokes `pipe_read()`.

Table 18-5. FIFO's File Operations

Access Type	File Operations	read Method	write Method
Read only, with writers	`read_fifo_fops`	`pipe_read()`	`bad_pipe_w()`
Read only, no writer	`connecting_fifo_fops`	`connect_read()`	`bad_pipe_w()`
Write only	`write_fifo_fops`	`bad_pipe_r()`	`pipe_write()`
Read/write	`rdwr_fifo_fops`	`pipe_read()`	`pipe_write()`

Reading from and Writing into a FIFO

The `read()` and `write()` system calls that refer to a FIFO, as well as to any other file type, are handled by the VFS through the `read()` and `write()` file object methods. If the operation is allowed, the corresponding entries in the file operation table point to the `pipe_read()` and `pipe_write()` functions (see the earlier sections "Reading from a Pipe" and "Writing into a Pipe").

The VFS thus handles reading and writing for FIFOs the same as for unnamed pipes. In contrast to unnamed pipes, however, the same file descriptor may be used both for reading and for writing a FIFO.

System V IPC

IPC is an abbreviation that stands for Interprocess Communication. It denotes a set of system calls that allows a User Mode process to:

- Synchronize itself with other processes by means of semaphores

- Send messages to other processes or receive messages from them

- Share a memory area with other processes

IPC was introduced in a development Unix variant called "Columbus Unix" and later adopted by AT&T's System III. It is now commonly found in most Unix systems, including Linux.

IPC data structures are created dynamically when a process requests an *IPC resource* (a semaphore, a message queue, or a shared memory segment). Each IPC resource is persistent: unless explicitly released by a process, it is kept in memory. An IPC resource may be used by any process, including those that do not share the ancestor that created the resource.

Since a process may require several IPC resources of the same type, each new resource is identified by a 32-bit *IPC key*, which is similar to the file pathname in the system's directory tree. Each IPC resource also has a 32-bit *IPC identifier*, which is somewhat similar to the file descriptor associated with an open file. IPC identifiers are assigned to IPC resources by the kernel and are unique within the system, while IPC keys can be freely chosen by programmers.

When two or more processes wish to communicate through an IPC resource, they all refer to the IPC identifier of the resource.

Using an IPC Resource

IPC resources are created by invoking the `semget()`, `msgget()`, or `shmget()` functions, depending on whether the new resource is a semaphore, a message queue, or a shared memory segment.

The main objective of each of these three functions is to derive from the IPC key (passed as the first parameter) the corresponding IPC identifier, which will then be used by the process for accessing the resource. If there is no IPC resource already associated with the IPC key, a new resource is created. If everything goes right, the function returns a positive IPC identifier; otherwise, it returns one of the error codes illustrated in Table 18-6.

Table 18-6. Error Codes Returned While Requiring an IPC Identifier

Error Code	Description
EACCESS	Process does not have proper access rights.
EEXIST	Process tried to create an IPC resource with the same key as one that already exists.
EIDRM	The resource is marked so as to be deleted.
ENOENT	No IPC resource with the requested key exists and the process did not ask to create it.
ENOMEM	No more storage is left for an additional IPC resource.
ENOSPC	Maximum limit on the number of IPC resources has been exceeded.

Assume that two independent processes want to share a common IPC resource. This can be achieved in two possible ways:

- The processes agree on some fixed, predefined IPC key. This is the simplest case, and it works quite well for any complex application implemented by many processes. However, there's a chance that the same IPC key is adopted by another unrelated program. In this case, the IPC functions might be successfully invoked and yet return the IPC identifier of the wrong resource.[*]

---

[*] The `ftok()` function attempts to create a new key from a file pathname and an 8-bit project identifier passed as parameters. It does not guarantee, however, a unique key number, since there is a small chance that it will return the same IPC key to two different applications using different pathnames and project identifiers.

- One process issues a `semget()`, `msgget()`, or `shmget()` function by specifying `IPC_PRIVATE` as its IPC key. A new IPC resource is thus allocated, and the process can either communicate its IPC identifier to the other process in the application[*] or fork the other process itself. This method ensures that the IPC resource cannot be accidentally used by other applications.

The last parameter of the `semget()`, `msgget()`, and `shmget()` functions can include two flags. `IPC_CREAT` specifies that the IPC resource must be created, if it does not already exist; `IPC_EXCL` specifies that the function must fail if the resource already exists and the `IPC_CREAT` flag is set.

Even if the process uses the `IPC_CREAT` and `IPC_EXCL` flags, there is no way to ensure exclusive access to an IPC resource, since other processes may always refer to the resource by using its IPC identifier.

In order to minimize the risk of incorrectly referencing the wrong resource, the kernel does not recycle IPC identifiers as soon as they become free. Instead, the IPC identifier assigned to a resource is almost always larger than the identifier assigned to the previously allocated resource of the same type. (The only exception occurs when the 32-bit IPC identifier overflows.) Each IPC identifier is computed by combining a *slot usage sequence number* relative to the resource type, an arbitrary *slot index* for the allocated resource, and the value chosen in the kernel for the maximum number of allocatable resources. If we choose s to represent the slot usage sequence number, M to represent the maximum number of resources, and i to represent the slot index, where $0 \leq i < M$, each IPC resource's ID is computed as follows:

$$\text{IPC identifier} = s \times M + i$$

The slot usage sequence number s is initialized to 0 and is incremented by 1 at every resource deallocation. In two consecutive resource allocations, the slot index i can only increase; it can decrease only when a resource has been deallocated, but then the increased slot usage sequence number ensures that the new IPC identifier for the next allocated resource is larger than the previous one.

Each IPC resource is associated with an `ipc_perm` data structure, whose fields are shown in Table 18-7. The `uid`, `gid`, `cuid`, and `cgid` fields store the user and group identifiers of the resource's creator and the user and group identifiers of the current resource's owner, respectively. The `mode` bit mask includes six flags, which store the read and write access permissions for the resource's owner, the resource's group, and all other users. IPC access permissions are similar to file access permissions described in the section "Access Rights and File Mode" in Chapter 1, *Introduction*, except that there is no Execute permission flag.

---

[*] This implies, of course, the existence of another communication channel between the processes not based on IPC.

Table 18-7. The Fields in the ipc_perm Structure

Type	Field	Description
int	key	IPC key
unsigned short	uid	Owner user ID
unsigned short	gid	Owner group ID
unsigned short	cuid	Creator user ID
unsigned short	cgid	Creator group ID
unsigned short	mode	Permission bit mask
unsigned short	seq	Slot usage sequence number

The `ipc_perm` data structure also includes a `key` field, which contains the IPC key of the corresponding resource, and a `seq` field, which stores the slot usage sequence number *s* used to compute the IPC identifier of the resource.

The `semctl()`, `msgctl()`, and `shmctl()` functions may be used to handle IPC resources. The `IPC_SET` subcommand allows a process to change the owner's user and group identifiers and the permission bit mask in the `ipc_perm` data structure. The `IPC_STAT` and `IPC_INFO` subcommands retrieve some information concerning a resource. Finally, the `IPC_RMID` subcommand releases an IPC resource. Depending on the type of IPC resource, other specialized subcommands are also available.*

Once an IPC resource has been created, a process may act on the resource by means of a few specialized functions. A process may acquire or release an IPC semaphore by issuing the `semop()` function. When a process wants to send or receive an IPC message, it uses the `msgsnd()` and `msgrcv()` functions, respectively. Finally, a process attaches and detaches a shared memory segment in its address space by means of the `shmat()` and `shmdt()` functions, respectively.

The ipc() System Call

All IPC functions must be implemented through suitable Linux system calls. Actually, in the Intel 80x86 architecture, there is just one IPC system call named `ipc()`. When a process invokes an IPC function, let's say `msgget()`, it really invokes a wrapper function in the C library, which in turn invokes the `ipc()` system call by passing to it all the parameters of `msgget()` plus a proper subcommand code, in this case `MSGGET`. The `sys_ipc()` service routine examines the subcommand code and invokes the kernel function that implements the requested service.

The `ipc()` "multiplexer" system call is a legacy from older Linux versions, which included the IPC code in a dynamic module (see Appendix B). It did not make much

---

* Another IPC design flaw is that a User Mode process cannot atomically create and initialize an IPC resource, since these two operations are performed by two different IPC functions.

sense to reserve several system call entries in the `system_call` table for a kernel component that could be missing, so the kernel designers adopted the multiplexer approach.

Nowadays, System V IPC can no longer be compiled as a dynamic module, and there is no justification for using a single IPC system call. As a matter of fact, Linux provides one system call for each IPC function on Compaq's Alpha architecture.

IPC Semaphores

IPC semaphores are quite similar to the kernel semaphores introduced in Chapter 11: they are counters used to provide controlled access to shared data structures for multiple processes. The semaphore value is positive if the protected resource is available, and negative or 0 if the protected resource is currently not available. A process that wants to access the resource decrements by 1 the semaphore value. It is allowed to use the resource only if the old value was positive; otherwise, the process waits until the semaphore becomes positive. When a process relinquishes a protected resource, it increments its semaphore value by 1; in doing so, any other process waiting for the semaphore is woken up. Actually, IPC semaphores are more complicated to handle than kernel semaphores for two main reasons:

- Each IPC semaphore is a set of one or more semaphore values, not just a single value as for kernel semaphores. This means that the same IPC resource can protect several independent shared data structures. The number of semaphore values in each IPC semaphore must be specified as a parameter of the `semget()` function when the resource is being allocated, but it cannot be greater than SEMMSL (usually 32). From now on, we'll refer to the counters inside an IPC semaphore as *primitive semaphores*.

- The IPC specification creates a fail-safe mechanism for situations in which a process dies without being able to undo the operations that it previously issued on a semaphore. When a process chooses to use this mechanism, the resulting operations are called *undoable* semaphore operations. When the process dies, all of its IPC semaphores can revert to the values they would have had if the process had never started its operations. This can help prevent deadlocks of other processes using the same semaphores.

First, we'll briefly sketch the typical steps performed by a process wishing to access one or more resources protected by an IPC semaphore. The process:

1. Invokes the `semget()` wrapper function to get the IPC semaphore identifier, specifying as the parameter the IPC key of the IPC semaphore that protects the shared resources. If the process wants to create a new IPC semaphore, it also specifies the `IPC_CREATE` or `IPC_PRIVATE` flag and the number of primitive semaphores required (see the section "Using an IPC Resource" earlier in this chapter).

2. Invokes the `semop()` wrapper function to test and decrement all primitive semaphore values involved. If all the tests succeed, the decrements are performed, the

function terminates, and the process is allowed to access the protected resources. If some semaphores are in use, the process is usually suspended until some other process releases the resources. The function receives as parameters the IPC semaphore identifier, an array of numbers specifying the operations to be atomically performed on the primitive semaphores, and the number of such operations. Optionally, the process may specify the SEM_UNDO flag, which instructs the kernel to reverse the operations should the process exit without releasing the primitive semaphores.

3. When relinquishing the protected resources, invokes the semop() function again to atomically increment all primitive semaphores involved.

4. Optionally, invokes the semctl() wrapper function, specifying in its parameter the IPC_RMID flag to remove the IPC semaphore from the system.

Now we can discuss how the kernel implements IPC semaphores. The data structures involved are shown in Figure 18-1. A statically allocated **semary** array includes SEMMNI values (usually 128). Each element in the array can assume one of the following values:

- IPC_UNUSED (-1): no IPC resource refers to this slot.

- IPC_NOID (-2): the IPC resource is being allocated or destroyed.

- The address of a dynamically allocated memory area containing the IPC semaphore resource.

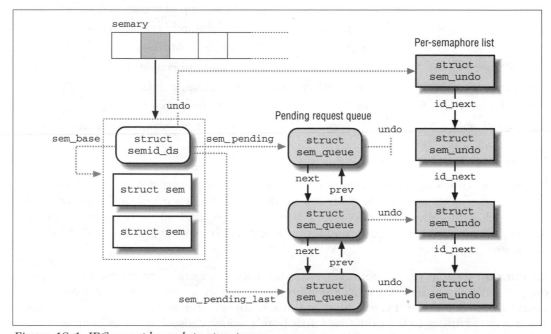

Figure 18-1. IPC semaphore data structures

The index number of the **semary** array represents the slot index *i* mentioned earlier. When a new IPC resource must be allocated, the kernel scans the array and uses the first array element (slot) containing the value **IPC_UNUSED**. The slot index can be easily derived from the IPC identifier by simply masking out its high-order bits (see the earlier section "Using an IPC Resource").

The first locations of the memory area containing the IPC semaphore store a descriptor of type **struct semid_ds**, whose fields are shown in Table 18-8. All other locations in the memory area store several **sem** data structures, one for each primitive semaphore in the IPC semaphore resource. The **sem_base** field of the **semid_ds** structure points to the first **sem** structure in the memory area. The **sem** data structure includes only two fields:

semval
> Value of the semaphore's counter.

sempid
> PID of the last process that accessed the semaphore. This value can be queried by a process through the **semctl()** wrapper function.

Table 18-8. The Fields in the semid_ds Structure

Type	Field	Description
struct ipc_perm	sem_perm	ipc_perm data structure
long	sem_otime	Timestamp of last semop()
long	sem_ctime	Timestamp of last change
struct sem *	sem_base	Pointer to first sem structure
struct sem_queue *	sem_pending	Pending operations
struct sem_queue **	sem_pending_last	Last pending operation
struct sem_undo *	undo	Undo requests
unsigned short	sem_nsems	Number of semaphores in array

Undoable semaphore operations

If a process aborts suddenly, it cannot undo the operations that it started (for instance, release the semaphores it reserved); so by declaring them *undoable* the process lets the kernel return the semaphores to a consistent state and allow other processes to proceed. Processes may require undoable operations by specifying the **SEM_UNDO** flag in the **semop()** function.

Information to help the kernel reverse the undoable operations performed by a given process on a given IPC semaphore resource is stored in a **sem_undo** data structure. It essentially contains the IPC identifier of the semaphore and an array of integers representing the changes to the primitive semaphore's values caused by all undoable operations performed by the process.

A simple example can illustrate how such `sem_undo` elements are used. Consider a process using an IPC semaphore resource with four primitive semaphores and suppose that it invokes the `semop()` function to increment by 1 the first counter and decrement by 2 the second one. If it specifies the `SEM_UNDO` flag, the integer in the first array element in the `sem_undo` data structure is decremented by 1, the integer in the second element is incremented by 2, and the other two integers are left unchanged. Further undoable operations on the IPC semaphore performed by the same process change accordingly the integers stored in the `sem_undo` structure. When the process exits, any nonzero value in that array corresponds to one or more unbalanced operations on the corresponding primitive semaphore; the kernel reverses these operations, simply adding the nonzero value to the corresponding semaphore's counter. In other words, the changes made by the aborted process are backed out while the changes made by other processes are still reflected in the state of the semaphores.

For each process, the kernel keeps track of all semaphore resources handled with undoable operations, so that it can roll them back if the process unexpectedly exits. Furthermore, the kernel has to keep track, for each semaphore, of all its `sem_undo` structures, so that it can quickly access them whenever a process uses `semctl()` to force an explicit value into a primitive semaphore's counter or to destroy an IPC semaphore resource.

The kernel is able to handle these tasks efficiently thanks to two lists, which we denote as the *per-process* and the *per-semaphore* lists. The first one keeps track of all semaphores handled by a given process with undoable operations. The second one keeps track of all processes that are acting on a given semaphore with undoable operations. More precisely:

- The per-process list includes all `sem_undo` data structures corresponding to IPC semaphores on which the process has performed undoable operations. The `semundo` field of the process descriptor points to the first element of the list, while the `proc_next` field of each `sem_undo` data structure points to the next element in the list.

- The per-semaphore list includes all `sem_undo` data structures corresponding to the processes that performed undoable operations on it. The `undo` field of the `semid_ds` data structure points to the first element of the list, while the `id_next` field of each `sem_undo` data structure points to the next element in the list.

The per-process list is used when a process terminates. The `sem_exit()` function, which is invoked by `do_exit()`, walks through the list and reverses the effect of any unbalanced operation for every IPC semaphore touched by the process. By contrast, the per-semaphore list is mainly used when a process invokes the `semctl()` function to force an explicit value into a primitive semaphore. The kernel sets the corresponding element to 0 in the arrays of all `sem_undo` data structures referring to that IPC semaphore resource, since it would no longer make any sense to reverse the effect of previous undoable operations performed on that primitive semaphore. Moreover, the per-semaphore list is also used when an IPC semaphore is destroyed; all related sem_ undo data structures are invalidated by setting the semid field to -1.*

The queue of pending requests

The kernel associates to each IPC semaphore a *queue of pending requests* to identify processes that are waiting on one of the semaphores in the array. The queue is a doubly linked list of sem_queue data structures, whose fields are shown in Table 18-9. The first and last pending requests in the queue are referenced, respectively, by the sem_pending and sem_pending_last fields of the semid_ds structure. This last field allows the list to be handled easily as a FIFO: new pending requests are added to the end of the list so that they will be serviced later. The most important fields of a pending request are nsops, which stores the number of primitive semaphores involved in the pending operation, and sops, which points to an array of integer values describing each single semaphore operation. The sleeper field stores the address of the wait queue containing the sleeping process.

Table 18-9. The Fields in the sem_queue Structure

Type	Field	Description
struct sem_queue *	next	Pointer to next queue element
struct sem_queue **	prev	Pointer to previous queue element
struct wait_queue *	sleeper	Pointer to sleeping process wait queue
struct sem_undo *	undo	Pointer to sem_undo structure
int	pid	Process identifier
int	status	Completion status of operation
struct semid_ds *	sma	Pointer to IPC semaphore descriptor
struct sembuf *	sops	Pointer to array of pending operations
int	nsops	Number of pending operations
int	alter	Flag for altering operations

Figure 18-1 illustrates an IPC semaphore that has three pending requests. Two of them refer to undoable operations, so the undo field of the sem_queue data structure points to the corresponding sem_undo structure; the third pending request has a NULL undo field since the corresponding operation is not undoable.

---

* Notice that they are just invalidated, and not freed, since it would be too costly to remove the data structures from the per-process lists of all processes.

IPC Messages

Processes can communicate with each other by means of IPC messages. Each message generated by a process is sent to an *IPC message queue* where it stays until another process reads it.

A message is composed of a fixed-size *header* and a variable-length *text*; it can be labeled with an integer value (the *message type*), which allows a process to selectively retrieve messages from its message queue.* Once a process has read a message from an IPC message queue, the kernel destroys it; therefore, only one process can receive a given message.

In order to send a message, a process invokes the **msgsnd()** function, passing as parameters:

- The IPC identifier of the destination message queue

- The size of the message text

- The address of a User Mode buffer that contains the message type immediately followed by the message text

To retrieve a message, a process invokes the **msgrcv()** function, passing to it:

- The IPC identifier of the IPC message queue resource

- The pointer to a User Mode buffer to which the message type and message text should be copied

- The size of the message text

- A value *t* that specifies what message should be retrieved

If the value *t* is null, the first message in the queue is returned. If *t* is positive, the first message in the queue with its type equal to *t* is returned. Finally, if *t* is negative, the function returns the first message whose message type is the lowest value less than or equal to the absolute value of *t*.

The data structures associated with IPC message queues are shown in Figure 18-2. A statically allocated array **msgque** includes **MSGMNI** values (usually 128). Like the **semary** array, each element in a **msgque** array can assume the value **IPC_UNUSED**, **IPC_NOID**, or the address of an IPC message queue descriptor.

The message queue descriptor is a **msqid_ds** structure, whose fields are shown in Table 18-10. The most important fields are **msg_first** and **msg_last**, which point to the first and to the last message in the linked list, respectively. The **rwait** field points

---

* As we'll see, the message queue is implemented by means of a linked list. Since messages can be retrieved in an order different from "first in, first out," the name "message queue" is not appropriate. However, new messages are always put at the end of the linked list.

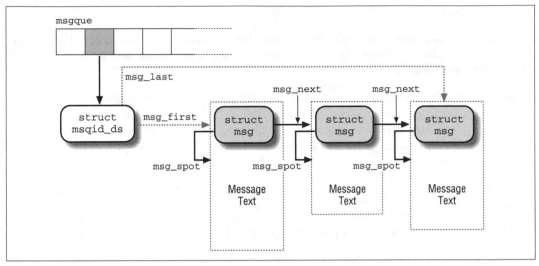

Figure 18-2. IPC message queue data structures

to a wait queue that includes all processes currently waiting for some message in the queue. Conversely, the `wwait` field points to a wait queue that includes all processes currently waiting for some free space in the queue so they can add a new message. The total size of the header and the text of all messages in the queues cannot exceed the value stored in the `msg_qbytes` field; the default maximum size is `MSGMNB`, that is, 16,384 bytes.

Table 18-10. The msqid_ds Structure

Type	Field	Description
struct ipc_perm	msg_perm	ipc_perm data structure
struct msg *	msg_first	First message in queue
struct msg *	msg_last	Last message in queue
long	msg_stime	Time of last msgsnd()
long	msg_rtime	Time of last msgrcv()
long	msg_ctime	Last change time
struct wait_queue *	wwait	Processes waiting for free space
struct wait_queue *	rwait	Processes waiting for messages
unsigned short	msg_cbytes	Current number of bytes in queue
unsigned short	msg_qnum	Number of messages in queue
unsigned short	msg_qbytes	Maximum number of bytes in queue
unsigned short	msg_lspid	PID of last msgsnd()
unsigned short	msg_lrpid	PID of last msgrcv()

Each message is placed into a dynamically allocated memory area. The beginning of this area stores the message header, which is a data structure of type msg; its fields are listed in Table 18-11. The message text is stored in the rest of the memory area. The msg_spot field of the message header contains the starting address of the message text, while the msg_ts field contains the length of the message text; this length cannot be longer than MSGMAX (usually 4056) bytes.

Table 18-11. The msg Structure

Type	Field	Description
struct msg *	msg_next	Next message in queue
long	msg_type	Message type
char *	msg_spot	Message text address
time_t	msg_stime	Time of msgsnd()
short	msg_ts	Message text size

Finally, each message is linked to the next message in the queue through the msg_next field of its message header.

IPC Shared Memory

The most useful IPC mechanism is shared memory, which allows two or more processes to access some common data structures by placing them in a *shared memory segment*. Each process that wants to access the data structures included in a shared memory segment must add to its address space a new memory region (see the section "Memory Regions" in Chapter 7, *Process Address Space*), which maps the page frames associated with the shared memory segment. Such page frames can thus be easily handled by the kernel through demand paging (see the section "Demand Paging" in Chapter 7).

As with semaphores and message queues, the shmget() function is invoked to get the IPC identifier of a shared memory segment, optionally creating it if it does not already exist.

The shmat() function is invoked to "attach" a shared memory segment to a process. It receives as its parameter the identifier of the IPC shared memory resource and tries to add a shared memory region to the address space of the calling process. The calling process can require a specific starting linear address for the memory region, but the address is usually unimportant, and each process accessing the shared memory segment can use a different address in its own address space. The process's page tables are left unchanged by shmat(). We'll describe later what the kernel does when the process tries to access a page belonging to the new memory region.

The shmdt() function is invoked to "detach" a shared memory segment specified by its IPC identifier, that is, to remove the corresponding memory region from the process's address space. Recall that an IPC shared memory resource is persistent: even if no process is using it, the corresponding pages cannot be discarded, although they can be swapped out.

Figure 18-3 illustrates the main data structures used for implementing IPC shared memory. A statically allocated array shm_segs includes SHMMNI values (usually 128). Like the semary and msgque arrays, each element in shm_segs can have the value IPC_UNUSED or IPC_NOID or the address of an IPC shared memory segment descriptor.

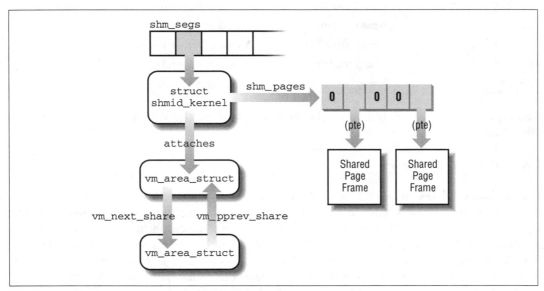

Figure 18-3. IPC shared memory data structures

Each IPC shared memory segment descriptor is a shmid_kernel structure, whose fields are shown in Table 18-12. Some of the fields, which are accessible to User Mode processes, are included in a shmid_ds data structure named u inside the descriptor. Their contents can be accessed by means of the shmctl() function.

The u.shm_segsz and shm_npages fields store the size of the shared memory segment in bytes and in pages, respectively. Although User Mode processes can require a shared memory segment of any length, the length of the allocated segment is a multiple of the page size, since the kernel must map the segment with a memory region.

The shm_pages field points to an array that contains one element for each page of the segment. Each element stores a 32-bit value in the format of a Page Table entry (see the section "Regular Paging" in Chapter 2, *Memory Addressing*). If a page frame is not currently allocated for the page, the element is 0. Otherwise, it is a regular Page Table entry containing the physical address of a page frame or a swapped-out page identifier.

Table 18-12. The Fields in the shmid_kernel Structure

Type	Field	Description
struct ipc_perm	u.shm_perm	ipc_perm data structure
int	u.shm_segsz	Size of shared memory region (bytes)
long	u.shm_atime	Last attach time
long	u.shm_dtime	Last detach time
long	u.shm_ctime	Last change time
unsigned short	u.shm_cpid	PID of creator
unsigned short	u.shm_lpid	PID of last accessing process
unsigned short	u.shm_nattch	Number of current attaches
unsigned long	shm_npages	Size of shared memory region (pages)
unsigned long *	shm_pages	Pointer to array of page frame PTEs
struct vm_area_struct *	attaches	Pointer to VMA descriptor list

In the example illustrated in Figure 18-3, the segment is contained in five pages. Three of them have never been accessed, while the other two pages are stored in RAM.

The **attaches** field points to the first element of a doubly linked list that includes the **vm_area_struct** descriptors of all memory regions associated with the shared memory segment. The list is implemented by means of the **vm_next_share** and **vm_pprev_share** fields of the descriptors. The number of elements in the list is stored in the **u.shm_nattch** field. In Figure 18-3, the shared memory segment has been attached to the address space of two processes.

When mapping IPC shared memory segments, some fields of **vm_area_struct** descriptors have a special meaning:

vm_start *and* **vm_end**
   Delimit the linear address range of the memory region

vm_pte
   Stores the index of the shared memory segment in the **shm_segs** array

vm_ops
   Points to a table of memory region operations called **shm_vm_ops**

Demand paging for IPC shared memory segments

The pages added to a process by **shmat()** are dummy pages; the function adds a new memory region into a process's address space, but it doesn't modify the process's page tables. We can now explain how these pages become usable.

Because the **shmat()** function didn't modify the page tables, a "Page fault" occurs when a process tries to access a location of a shared memory segment. The corresponding exception handler determines that the faulty address is inside the process address space and that the corresponding Page Table entry is null; therefore, it invokes the do_no_page( ) function (see the section "Demand Paging" in Chapter 7). In turn, this function checks whether the nopage method for the memory region is defined. The method is then invoked, and the Page Table entry is set to the address returned from it (see the section "Demand Paging for Memory Mapping" in Chapter 15, *Accessing Regular Files*).

Memory regions used for IPC shared memory always define the nopage method. It is implemented by the shm_nopage( ) function, which performs the following operations:

1. Extracts from the vm_pte field of the memory region descriptor the index of the shm_segs array corresponding to the shared memory segment.

2. Computes the logical page number inside the segment from the vm_start field of the memory region descriptor and the requested address.

3. Accesses the array referenced by the shm_pages field of the shmid_kernel descriptor of the segment and gets the entry corresponding to the page that includes the faulty address. Three cases are considered, depending on the value of the entry:

   — Null entry: no page frame was ever allocated to the page. In this case, allocates a new page frame and stores its Page Table entry in the shm_pages array.

   — Regular entry with Present flag set: the page is already stored in some page frame. Extracts its physical address from the entry in shm_pages.

   — Swapped-out page identifier: the page has been swapped out to disk. Allocates a new page frame, reads the page from disk, copies it into the page frame, and stores the new Page Table entry in the shm_pages array. Actually, the actions performed in this case correspond to the swap-in procedure for pages included in shared memory segments (described later).

4. Increments the usage counter of the page frame allocated or identified in the previous step.

5. Returns the physical address of the page frame.

The do_no_page( ) function sets the entry corresponding to the faulty address in the process's Page Table so that it points to the page frame returned by the method.

Swapping out pages of IPC shared memory segments

The kernel has to be careful when swapping out pages included in shared memory segments. Suppose that two processes P1 and P2 are accessing a page of a shared memory segment. Suppose also that the swap_out( ) function tries to free a page frame assigned to process P1 that is also shared with process P2 (see the section "Page Swap-Out" in Chapter 16, *Swapping: Methods for Freeing Memory*). According to the standard swap-out rules, the shared page should be copied to disk and then released, and a swapped-out page identifier should be written into the corresponding P1's Page Table entry. However, this standard procedure doesn't work, because process P2 could try to access the page through its own page tables: since the corresponding Page Table entry still points to the released page frame, all sort of data corruption could occur.

The `try_to_swap_out()` function (see the section "The try_to_swap_out() Function" in Chapter 16) recognizes this special case by checking whether the memory region includes a `swapout` method. If it is defined, the page frame is not released to the Buddy system; its usage counter is simply decremented by 1, and the corresponding entry in P1's Page Table is cleared. The `swapout` method in `shm_vm_ops` is an empty function: the method must be non-null to let the kernel know the memory is shared, so it must point to some function, even if that function has nothing to do. P2 can safely access the page frame, since it still contains the page of the IPC shared memory.

Shared memory segments are persistent resources, like any IPC resource. This means that page frames of a shared memory segment no longer used by any process are still referenced by the `shm_pages` array. These page frames may be swapped out to disk by means of the `shm_swap()` function, which is periodically invoked by `do_try_to_free_pages()` (see the section "The try_to_free_pages() Function" in Chapter 16). It iteratively scans all descriptors referenced by the `shm_segs` array and, for each descriptor, examines all page frames assigned to each segment. If it determines that the usage counter of some page frame is equal to 1, the corresponding page can be safely swapped out to disk. The swap-out procedure used is similar to that used for non-shared pages, except that the swapped-out page identifier is saved in the `shm_pages` array.

In conclusion, though shared memory pages are in process page tables, they are not handled by the swapping facility like other pages. The swapped-out page identifiers of such pages do not appear in the page table entries but in the `shm_pages` array. When a process attempts to address a swapped-out page, the null page table entry triggers a "Page fault" exception. The kernel retrieves the swapped-out page identifier in the `shm_pages` array and performs the swap-in.

Anticipating Linux 2.4

Static arrays used to represent semaphores and messages have been removed and replaced by dynamic data structures. Larger IPC messages can now be handled.

IPC shared memory regions are implemented in a different way: a new */proc* filesystem, denoted as *sysvipc*, has been introduced. It currently includes only one directory called *shm* containing a virtual file for each IPC shared memory region.

CHAPTER NINETEEN

PROGRAM EXECUTION

The concept of a "process," described in Chapter 3, *Processes*, was used in Unix from the beginning to represent the behavior of groups of running programs that compete for system resources. This final chapter focuses on the relationship between program and process. We'll specifically describe how the kernel sets up the execution context for a process according to the contents of the program file. While it may not seem like a big problem to load a bunch of instructions in memory and point the CPU to them, the kernel has to deal with flexibility in several areas:

Different executable formats
Linux is distinguished by its ability to run binaries that were compiled for other operating systems.

Shared libraries
Many executable files don't contain all the code required to run the program but expect the kernel to load in functions from a library at runtime.

Other information in the execution context
This includes the command-line arguments and environment variables familiar to programmers.

A program is stored on disk as an *executable file*, which includes both the object code of the functions to be executed and the data on which such functions will act. Many functions of the program are service routines available to all programmers; their object code is included in special files called "libraries." Actually, the code of a library function may either be statically copied in the executable file (static libraries), or be linked to the process at run time (shared libraries, since their code can be shared by several independent processes).

When launching a program, the user may supply two kinds of information that affect the way it is executed: command-line arguments and environment variables. *Command-line arguments* are typed in by the user following the executable filename at the shell prompt. *Environment variables*, such as HOME and PATH, are inherited from the shell, but the users may modify the values of any such variables before they launch the program.

In the section "Executable Files" we explain what a program execution context is. In the section "Executable Formats" we mention some of the executable formats supported by Linux and show how Linux can change its "personality" so as to execute programs compiled for other operating systems. Finally, in the section "The exec-like Functions," we describe the system call that allows a process to start executing a new program.

Executable Files

Chapter 1, *Introduction*, defined a process as an "execution context." By this we mean the collection of information needed to carry on a specific computation; it includes the pages accessed, the open files, the hardware register contents, and so on. An *executable file* is a regular file that describes how to initialize a new execution context, i.e., how to start a new computation.

Suppose a user wants to list the files in the current directory: he knows that this result can be simply achieved by typing the filename of the */bin/ls** external command at the shell prompt. The command shell forks a new process, which in turn invokes an execve( ) system call (see the section "The exec-like Functions" later in this chapter), passing as one of its parameters a string including the full pathname for the *ls* executable file, */bin/ls* in this case. The sys_execve( ) service routine finds the corresponding file, checks the executable format, and modifies the execution context of the current process according to the information stored in it. As a result, when the system call terminates, the process starts executing the code stored in the executable file, which performs the directory listing.

When a process starts running a new program, its execution context changes drastically since most of the resources obtained during the process's previous computations are discarded. In the preceding example, when the process starts executing */bin/ls*, it replaces the shell's arguments with new ones passed as parameters in the execve( ) system call and acquires a new shell environment (see the later section "Command-Line Arguments and Shell Environment"); all pages inherited from the parent (and shared with the Copy On Write mechanism) are released, so that the new computation starts

---

* The pathnames of executable files are not fixed in Linux; they depend on the distribution used. Several standard naming schemes such as FHS and FSSTND have been proposed for all Unix systems.

with a fresh User Mode address space; even the privileges of the process could change (see the later section "Process Credentials and Capabilities"). However, the process PID doesn't change, and the new computation inherits from the previous one all open file descriptors that have not been closed automatically while executing the execve() system call.*

Process Credentials and Capabilities

Traditionally, Unix systems associate with each process some *credentials*, which bind the process to a specific user and a specific user group. Credentials are important on multiuser systems because they determine what each process can or cannot do, thus preserving both the integrity of each user's personal data and the stability of the system as a whole.

The use of credentials requires support both in the process data structure and in the resources being protected. One obvious resource is a file. Thus, in the Ext2 filesystem, each file is owned by a specific user and is bound to some group of users. The owner of a file may decide what kind of operations are allowed on that file, distinguishing among herself, the file's user group, and all other users. When some process tries to access a file, the VFS always checks whether the access is legal, according to the permissions established by the file owner and the process credentials.

The process's credentials are stored in several fields of the process descriptor, listed in Table 19-1. These fields contain identifiers of users and user groups in the system, which are usually compared with the corresponding identifiers stored in the inodes of the files being accessed.

Table 19-1. Traditional Process Credentials

Name	Description
uid, gid	User and group real identifiers
euid, egid	User and group effective identifiers
fsuid, fsgid	User and group effective identifiers for file access
groups	Supplementary group identifiers
suid, sgid	User and group saved identifiers

A null UID specifies the root superuser, while a null GID specifies the root supergroup. The kernel always allows a process to do anything whenever the process credential concerned stores a null value. Therefore, process credentials can also be used for checking non-file-related operations, like those referring to system administration

---

* By default, a file already opened by a process stays open after issuing an execve() system call. However, the file will be automatically closed if the process has set the corresponding bit in the close_on_exec field of the files_ struct structure (see Table 12-6 in Chapter 12, *The Virtual Filesystem*); this is done by means of the fcntl() system call.

or hardware manipulation: if the UID stored in some process credential is null, the operation is allowed; otherwise, it is denied.

When a process is created, it always inherits the credentials of its parent. However, these credentials can be modified later, either when the process starts executing a new program or when it issues suitable system calls. Usually, the uid, euid, fsuid, and suid fields of a process contain the same value. However, when the process executes a *setuid program*, that is, an executable file whose *setuid* flag is on, the euid and fsuid fields are set to the identifier of the file's owner. Almost all checks involve one of these two fields: fsuid is used for file-related operations, while euid is used for all other operations. Similar considerations apply to the gid, egid, fsgid, and sgid fields that refer to group identifiers.

As an illustration of how the fsuid field is used, consider the common situation when a user wants to change her password. All passwords are stored in a common file, but she cannot directly edit such file because it is protected. Therefore, she invokes a system program named */usr/bin/passwd*, which has the *setuid* flag set and whose owner is the superuser. When the process forked by the shell executes such a program, its euid and fsuid fields are set to 0, that is, to the PID of the superuser. Now the process can access the file, since, when the kernel perform the access control, it finds a 0 value in fsuid. Of course, the */usr/bin/passwd* program does not allow the user to do anything but change her own password.

Unix's long history teaches the lesson that *setuid* programs are quite dangerous: malicious users could trigger some programming errors (bugs) in the code in such a way to force *setuid* programs to perform operations that were never planned by the program's original designers. Often, the entire system's security can be compromised. In order to minimize such risks, Linux, like all modern Unix systems, allows processes to acquire *setuid* privileges only when necessary, and drop them when they are no longer needed. This feature may turn out to be useful when implementing user applications with several protection levels. The process descriptor includes an suid field, which stores the values of the effective identifiers (euid and fsuid) right after the execution of the *setuid* program. The process can change the effective identifiers by means of the setuid( ), setresuid( ), setfsuid( ), and setreuid( ) system calls.[*]

Table 19-2 shows how these system calls affect the process's credentials. Be warned that, if the calling process does not already have superuser privileges, that is, if its euid field is not null, these system calls can be used only to set values already included in the process's credential fields. For instance, an average user process can force the value 500 into its fsuid field by invoking the setfsuid( ) system call, but only if one of the other credential fields already stores the same value of 500.

---

[*] GID effective credentials can be changed by issuing the corresponding setgid( ), setresgid( ), setfsgid( ), and setregid( ) system calls.

Table 19-2. Semantics of the System Calls that Set Process Credentials

	setuid (e)		setresuid (u,e,s)	setreuid (u,e)	setfsuid (f)
	euid=0	euid≠0			
uid	Set to e	Unchanged	Set to u	Set to u	Unchanged
euid	Set to e	Set to e	Set to e	Set to e	Unchanged
fsuid	Set to e	Set to e	Set to e	Set to e	Set to f
suid	Set to e	Unchanged	Set to s	Set to e	Unchanged

To understand the sometimes complex relationships among the four user ID fields, consider for a moment the effects of the `setuid()` system call. The actions are different depending on whether the calling process's `euid` field is set to 0 (that is, the process has superuser privileges) or to a normal UID.

If the `euid` field is null, the system call sets all credential fields of the calling process (`uid`, `euid`, `fsuid`, and `suid`) to the value of the parameter `e`. A superuser process can thus drop its privileges and become a process owned by a normal user. This happens, for instance, when a user logs in: the system forks a new process with superuser privileges, but the process drops its privileges by invoking the `setuid()` system call and then starts executing the user's login shell program.

If the `euid` field is not null, the system call modifies only the value stored in `euid` and `fsuid`, leaving the other two fields unchanged. This allows a process executing a *setuid* program to have its effective privileges stored in `euid` and `fsuid` set alternately to `uid` (the process acts as the user who launched the executable file) and to `suid` (the process acts as the user who owns the executable file).

Process capabilities

Linux is moving toward another model of process credentials based on the notion of "capabilities." A *capability* is simply a flag that asserts whether the process is allowed to perform a specific operation or a specific class of operations. This model is different from the traditional "superuser versus normal user" model in which a process can either do everything or do nothing, depending on its effective UID. As illustrated in Table 19-3, several capabilities have already been included in the Linux kernel.

Table 19-3. Linux Capabilities

Name	Description
CAP_CHOWN	Ignore restrictions on file and group ownership changes.
CAP_DAC_OVERRIDE	Ignore file access permissions.
CAP_DAC_READ_SEARCH	Ignore file/directory read and search permissions.
CAP_FOWNER	Ignore restrictions on file ownership.
CAP_FSETID	Ignore restrictions on *setuid* and *setgid* flags.

Table 19-3. Linux Capabilities (continued)

Name	Description
CAP_KILL	Ignore restrictions on signal sendings.
CAP_SETGID	Allow *setgid* flag manipulations.
CAP_SETUID	Allow *setuid* flag manipulations.
CAP_SETPCAP	Transfer/remove permitted capabilities to other processes.
CAP_LINUX_IMMUTABLE	Allow modification of append-only and immutable files.
CAP_NET_BIND_SERVICE	Allow binding to TCP/UDP sockets below 1024.
CAP_NET_BROADCAST	Allow network broadcasting and listen to multicast.
CAP_NET_ADMIN	Allow general networking administration.
CAP_NET_RAW	Allow use of RAW and PACKET sockets.
CAP_IPC_LOCK	Allow locking of pages and shared memory segments.
CAP_IPC_OWNER	Skip IPC ownership checks.
CAP_SYS_MODULE	Allow inserting and removing of kernel modules.
CAP_SYS_RAWIO	Allow access to I/O ports through `ioperm()` and `iopl()`.
CAP_SYS_CHROOT	Allow use of `chroot()`.
CAP_SYS_PTRACE	Allow use of `ptrace()` on any process.
CAP_SYS_PACCT	Allow configuration of process accounting.
CAP_SYS_ADMIN	Allow general system administration.
CAP_SYS_BOOT	Allow use of `reboot()`.
CAP_SYS_NICE	Ignore restriction on `nice()`.
CAP_SYS_RESOURCE	Ignore restrictions on several resources usage.
CAP_SYS_TIME	Allow manipulation of system clock and real-time clock.
CAP_SYS_TTY_CONFIG	Allow configuration of tty devices.

The main advantage of capabilities is that, at any time, each program needs a limited number of them. Consequently, even if a malicious user discovers a way to exploit a buggy program, she can illegally perform a limited number of operation types.

Assume, for instance, that a buggy program has only the CAP_SYS_TIME capability. In this case, the malicious user who discovers an exploitation of the bug can succeed only in illegally changing the real-time and the system clock. She won't be able to perform any other kind of privileged operations.

A process can explicitly get and set its capabilities by using, respectively, the `capget()` and `capset()` system calls. However, neither the VFS nor the Ext2 filesystem currently supports the capability model, so there is no way to associate an executable file with the set of capabilities that should be enforced when a process executes that file. Therefore, capabilities are useless for Linux 2.2 end users, although we can easily predict that the situation will change very soon.

In fact, the Linux kernel already takes capabilities into account. Let us consider, for instance, the `nice()` system call, which allows users to change the static priority of a process. In the traditional model, only the superuser can raise a priority: the kernel should thus check whether the `euid` field in the descriptor of the calling process is set to 0. However, the Linux kernel defines a capability called `CAP_SYS_NICE`, which corresponds exactly to this kind of operation. The kernel checks the value of this flag by invoking the `capable()` function and by passing the `CAP_SYS_NICE` value to it.

This approach works thanks to some "compatibility hacks" that have been added to the kernel code: each time a process sets the `euid` and `fsuid` fields to 0 (either by invoking one of the system calls listed in Table 19-2 or by executing a *setuid* program owned by the superuser), the kernel sets all process capabilities, so that all checks will succeed. Similarly, when the process resets the `euid` and `fsuid` fields to the real UID of the process owner, the kernel drops all capabilities.

Command-Line Arguments and Shell Environment

When a user types a command, the program loaded to satisfy the request may receive some *command-line arguments* from the shell. For example, when a user types the command:

```
$ ls -l /usr/bin
```

in order to get a full listing of the files in the */usr/bin* directory, the shell process creates a new process to execute the command. This new process loads the */bin/ls* executable file. In doing so, most of the execution context inherited from the shell is lost, but the three separate arguments `ls`, `-l`, and `/usr/bin` are kept. Generally, the new process may receive any number of arguments.

The conventions for passing the command-line arguments depend on the high-level language used. In the C language, the `main()` function of a program may receive as parameters an integer specifying how many arguments have been passed to the program and the address of an array of pointers to strings. The following prototype formalizes this standard:

```
int main(int argc, char *argv[])
```

Going back to the previous example, when the */bin/ls* program is invoked, `argc` has the value 3, `argv[0]` points to the `ls` string, `argv[1]` points to the `-l` string, and `argv[2]` points to the `/usr/bin` string. The end of the `argv` array is always marked by a null pointer, so `argv[3]` contains `NULL`.

A third optional parameter that may be passed in the C language to the `main()` function is the parameter containing *environment variables*. When the program uses it, `main()` must be declared as follows:

```
int main(int argc, char *argv[], char *envp[])
```

The `envp` parameter points to an array of pointers to environment strings of the form:

    VAR_NAME=something

where **VAR_NAME** represents the name of an environment variable, while the substring following the = delimiter represents the actual value assigned to the variable. The end of the `envp` array is marked by a null pointer, like the `argv` array. Environment variables are used to customize the execution context of a process, to provide general information to a user or other processes, or to allow a process to keep some information across an `execve()` system call.

Command-line arguments and environment strings are placed on the User Mode stack, right before the return address (see the section "Parameter Passing" in Chapter 8, *System Calls*). The bottom locations of the User Mode stack are illustrated in Figure 19-1. Notice that the environment variables are located near the bottom of the stack right after a null long integer.

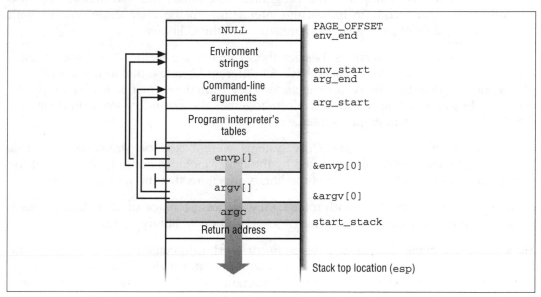

Figure 19-1. The bottom locations of the User Mode stack

Libraries

Each high-level source code file is transformed through several steps into an *object file*, which contains the machine code of the assembly language instructions corresponding to the high-level instructions. An object file cannot be executed, since it does not contain the linear address that corresponds to each reference to a name of a global symbol external to the source code file, such as functions in libraries or other source code files of the same program. The assigning, or *resolution*, of such addresses is performed by the linker, which collects together all the object files of the program and constructs the executable file. The linker also analyzes the library's functions used by the program and glues them into the executable file in a manner described later in this chapter.

Any program, even the most trivial one, makes use of C libraries. Consider, for instance, the following one-line C program:

```
void main(void) { }
```

Although this program does not compute anything, a lot of work is needed to set up the execution environment (see the section "The exec-like Functions" later in this chapter) and to kill the process when the program terminates (see the section "Destroying Processes" in Chapter 3). In particular, when the `main()` function terminates, the C compiler inserts an `exit()` system call in the object code.

We know from Chapter 8 that programs usually invoke system calls through wrapper routines in the C library. This holds for the C compiler too: besides including the code directly generated by compiling the program's statements, any executable file also includes some "glue" code to handle the interactions of the User Mode process with the kernel. Portions of such glue code are stored in the C library.

Many other libraries of functions, besides the C library, are included in Unix systems. A generic Linux system could easily have 50 different libraries. Just to mention a couple of them: the math library *libm* includes basic functions for floating point operations, while the X11 library *libX11* collects together the basic low-level functions for the X11 Window System graphics interface.

All executable files in traditional Unix systems were based on *static libraries*. This means that the executable file produced by the linker includes not only the code of the original program but also the code of the library functions that the program refers to.

Static libraries have one big disadvantage: they eat lots of space on disk. Indeed, each statically linked executable file duplicates some portion of library code.

Modern Unix systems make use of *shared libraries*. The executable file does not contain the library object code, but only a reference to the library name. When the program is loaded in memory for execution, a suitable program called the *program interpreter* takes care of analyzing the library names in the executable file, locating the library in the system's directory tree and making the requested code available to the executing process.

Shared libraries are especially convenient on systems that provide file memory mapping, since they reduce the amount of main memory requested for executing a program. When the program interpreter must link some shared library to a process, it does not copy the object code, but just performs a memory mapping of the relevant portion of the library file into the process's address space. This allows the page frames containing the machine code of the library to be shared among all processes that are using the same code.

Shared libraries also have some disadvantages. The startup time of a dynamically linked program is usually much longer than that of a statically linked one. Moreover, dynamically linked programs are not as portable as statically linked ones, since they may not execute properly in systems that include a different version of the same library.

A user may always require a program to be linked statically. The GCC compiler offers, for instance, the `-static` option, which tells the linker to use the static libraries instead of the shared ones.

Program Segments and Process Memory Regions

The linear address space of a Unix program is traditionally partitioned, from a logical point of view, in several linear address intervals called segments:[*]

Text segment
> Includes the executable code

Data segment
> Contains the initialized data, that is, the static variables and the global variables whose initial values are stored in the executable file (because the program must know their values at startup)

bss segment
> Contains the uninitialized data, that is, all global variables whose initial values are not stored in the executable file (because the program sets the values before referencing them)

Stack segment
> Contains the program stack, which includes the return addresses, parameters, and local variables of the functions being executed

Each `mm_struct` memory descriptor (see the section "The Memory Descriptor" in Chapter 7, *Process Address Space*) includes some fields that identify the role of particular memory regions of the corresponding process:

`start_code, end_code`
> Store the initial and final linear addresses of the memory region that includes the native code of the program, that is, the code in the executable file. Since the text segment includes shared libraries but the executable file does not, the memory region demarcated by these fields is a subset of the text segment.

`start_data, end_data`
> Store the initial and final linear addresses of the memory region that includes the native initialized data of the program, as specified in the executable file. The fields

---

[*] The word "segment" has historical roots, since the first Unix systems implemented each linear address interval with a different segment register. Linux, however, does not rely on the segmentation mechanism of the Intel microprocessors to implement program segments.

identify a memory region that roughly corresponds to the data segment. Actually, start_data should almost always be set to the address of the first page right after end_code, and thus the field is unused. The end_data field is used, though.

start_brk, brk

Store the initial and final linear addresses of the memory region that includes the dynamically allocated memory areas of the process (see the section "Managing the Heap" in Chapter 7). This memory region is sometimes called *heap*.

start_stack

Stores the address right above that of main()'s return address; as illustrated in Figure 19-1, higher addresses are reserved (recall that stacks grow toward lower addresses).

arg_start, arg_end

Store the initial and final addresses of the stack portion containing the command-line arguments.

env_start, env_end

Store the initial and final addresses of the stack portion containing the environment strings.

Notice that shared libraries and file memory mapping have made the classification of the process's address space based on program segments a bit obsolete, since each of the shared libraries is mapped into a different memory region from the ones discussed in the preceding list.

Now we'll describe, by means of a simple example, how the Linux kernel maps shared libraries into the process's address space. We assume as usual that the User Mode address space ranges from 0x00000000 and 0xbfffffff. We consider the */sbin/init* program, which creates and monitors the activity of all the processes that implement the outer layers of the operating system (see the section "Kernel Threads" in Chapter 3). The memory regions of the corresponding *init* process are shown in Table 19-4 (such information can be obtained from the */proc/1/maps* file). Notice that all regions listed are implemented by means of private memory mappings (the letter p in the Permissions column). This is not surprising: these memory regions exist only to provide data to a process; while executing instructions, a process may modify the contents of these memory regions but the files on disk associated with them stay unchanged. This is precisely how private memory mappings act.

Table 19-4. Memory Regions of the init Process

Address Range	Perms	Mapped File
0x08048000–0x0804cfff	r-xp	*/sbin/init* at offset 0
0x0804d000–0x0804dfff	rw-p	*/sbin/init* at offset 0x4000
0x0804e000–0x0804efff	rwxp	Anonymous
0x40000000–0x40005fff	r-xp	*/lib/ld-linux.so.1.9.9* at offset 0

Table 19-4. Memory Regions of the init Process (continued)

Address Range	Perms	Mapped File
0x40006000–0x40006fff	rw-p	*/lib/ld-linux.so.1.9.9* at offset 0x5000
0x40007000–0x40007fff	rw-p	Anonymous
0x4000b000–0x40092fff	r-xp	*/lib/libc.so.5.4.46* at offset 0
0x40093000–0x40098fff	rw-p	*/lib/libc.so.5.4.46* at offset 0x87000
0x40099000–0x400cafff	rw-p	Anonymous
0xbfffd000–0xbfffffff	rwxp	Anonymous

The memory region starting from 0x8048000 is a memory mapping associated with the portion of the */sbin/init* file ranging from byte 0 to byte 20479 (only the start and end of the region are shown in the */proc/1/maps* file, but the region size can easily be derived from them). The permissions specify that the region is executable (it contains object code), read only (it's not writable, because the instructions don't change during a run), and private, so we can guess that the region maps the text segment of the program.

The memory region starting from 0x804d000 is a memory mapping associated with another portion of */sbin/init* ranging from byte 16384 (corresponding to offset 0x4000 shown in Table 19-4) to 20479. Since the permissions specify that the private region may be written, we can conclude that it maps the data segment of the program.

The next one-page memory region starting from 0x0804e000 is anonymous, that is, it is not associated with any file. It is probably associated with the bss segment of *init*.

Similarly, the next three memory regions starting from 0x40000000, 0x40006000, and 0x40007000 correspond to the text segment, the data segment, and the bss segment, respectively, of the */lib/ld-linux.so.1.9.9* program, which actually is the program interpreter for the ELF shared libraries. The program interpreter is never executed alone: it is always memory-mapped inside the address space of a process executing another program.

On this system, the C library happens to be stored in the */lib/libc.so.5.4.46* file. The text segment, data segment, and bss segment of the C library are mapped into the next three memory regions starting from address 0x4000b000. Remember that page frames included in private regions can be shared among several processes with the Copy On Write mechanism, as long as they are not modified. Thus, since the text segment is read only, the page frames containing the executable code of the C library are shared among almost all currently executing processes (all except the statically linked ones).

Finally, the last anonymous memory region from 0xbfffd000 to 0xbfffffff is associated with the User Mode stack. We have already explained in the section "Page Fault Exception Handler" in Chapter 7 how the stack is automatically expanded toward lower addresses whenever necessary.

Execution Tracing

Execution tracing is a technique that allows a program to monitor the execution of another program. The traced program can be executed step-by-step, until a signal is received, or until a system call is invoked. Execution tracing is widely used by debuggers, together with other techniques like the insertion of breakpoints in the debugged program and run-time access to its variables. As usual, we'll focus on how the kernel supports execution tracing rather than discussing how debuggers work.

In Linux, execution tracing is performed through the `ptrace()` system call, which can handle the commands listed in Table 19-5. Processes having the `CAP_SYS_PTRACE` capability flag set are allowed to trace any process in the system except *init*. Conversely, a process *P* with no `CAP_SYS_PTRACE` capability is allowed to trace only processes having the same owner as *P*. Moreover, a process cannot be traced by two processes at the same time.

Table 19-5. The ptrace Commands

Command	Description
PTRACE_TRACEME	Start execution tracing for the current process
PTRACE_ATTACH	Start execution tracing for another process
PTRACE_DETACH	Terminate execution tracing
PTRACE_KILL	Kill the traced process
PTRACE_CONT	Resume execution
PTRACE_SYSCALL	Resume execution until the next system call boundary
PTRACE_SINGLESTEP	Resume execution for a single assembly instruction
PTRACE_PEEKTEXT	Read a 32-bit value from the text segment
PTRACE_PEEKDATA	Read a 32-bit value from the data segment
PTRACE_POKETEXT	Write a 32-bit value into the text segment
PTRACE_POKEDATA	Write a 32-bit value into the data segment
PTRACE_PEEKUSR	Read the CPU's normal and debug registers
PTRACE_POKEUSR	Write the CPU's normal and debug registers
PTRACE_GETREGS	Read privileged CPU's registers
PTRACE_SETREGS	Write privileged CPU's registers
PTRACE_GETFPREGS	Read floating-point registers
PTRACE_SETFPREGS	Write floating-point registers

The `ptrace()` system call modifies the `p_pptr` field in the descriptor of the traced process so that it points to the tracing process; therefore, the tracing process becomes the effective parent of the traced one. When execution tracing terminates, that is, when `ptrace()` is invoked with the `PTRACE_DETACH` command, the system call sets p_pptr to the value of p_opptr, thus restoring the original parent of the traced process (see the section "Parenthood Relationships Among Processes" in Chapter 3).

Several monitored events can be associated with a traced program:

- End of execution of a single assembly instruction
- Entering a system call
- Exiting from a system call
- Receiving a signal

When a monitored event occurs, the traced program is stopped and a SIGCHLD signal is sent to its parent. When the parent wishes to resume the child's execution, it can use one of the PTRACE_CONT, PTRACE_SINGLESTEP, and PTRACE_SYSCALL commands, depending on the kind of event it wants to monitor.

The PTRACE_CONT command just resumes execution: the child will execute until it receives another signal. This kind of tracing is implemented by means of the PF_PTRACED flag in the process descriptor, which is checked by the do_signal() function (see the section "Receiving a Signal" in Chapter 9, *Signals*).

The PTRACE_SINGLESTEP command forces the child process to execute the next assembly language instruction, then stops it again. This kind of tracing is implemented on Intel-based machines by means of the TF trap flag in the eflags register: when it is on, a "Debug" exception is raised right after any assembly language instruction. The corresponding exception handler just clears the flag, forces the current process to stop, and sends a SIGCHLD signal to its parent. Notice that setting the TF flag is not a privileged operation, thus User Mode processes can force single-step execution even without the ptrace() system call. The kernel checks the PF_DTRACE flag in the process descriptor to keep track of whether the child process is being single-stepped through ptrace().

The PTRACE_SYSCALL command causes the traced process to resume execution until a system call is invoked. The process is stopped twice, the first time when the system call starts, and the second time when the system call terminates. This kind of tracing is implemented by means of the PF_TRACESYS flag in the processor descriptor, which is checked in the system_call() assembly language function (see the section "The system_call() Function" in Chapter 8).

A process can also be traced using some debugging features of the Intel Pentium processors. For example, the parent could set the values of the dr0, . . . dr7 debug registers for the child by using the PTRACE_POKEUSR command. When a monitored event occurs, the CPU raises the "Debug" exception; the exception handler can then suspend the traced process and send the SIGCHLD signal to the parent.

Executable Formats

The official Linux executable format is named *ELF* (*Executable and Linking Format*): it was developed by Unix System Laboratories and is quite popular in the Unix world. Several well-known Unix operating systems such as System V Release 4 and Sun's Solaris 2 have adopted ELF as their main executable format.

Older Linux versions supported another format named *a.out* (Assembler OUTput Format); actually, there were several versions of that format floating around the Unix world. It is little used nowadays, since ELF is much more practical.

Linux supports many other different formats for executable files; in this way, it can run programs compiled for other operating systems like MS-DOS EXE programs, or Unix BSD's COFF executables. A few executable formats, like Java or *bash* scripts, are platform-independent.

An executable format is described by an object of type linux_binfmt, which essentially provide three methods:

load_binary
> Sets up a new execution environment for the current process by reading the information stored in an executable file.

load_shlib
> Used to dynamically bind a shared library to an already running process; it is activated by the uselib() system call.

core_dump
> Stores the execution context of the current process in a file named core. This file, whose format depends on the type of executable of the program being executed, is usually created when a process receives a signal whose default action is "dump" (see the section "Actions Performed upon Receiving a Signal" in Chapter 9).

All linux_binfmt objects are included in a simply linked list, and the address of the first element is stored in the formats variable. Elements can be inserted and removed in the list by invoking the register_binfmt() and unregister_binfmt() functions. The register_binfmt() function is executed during system startup for each executable format compiled into the kernel. This function is also executed when a module implementing a new executable format is being loaded, while the unregister_binfmt() function is invoked when the module is unloaded.

The last element in the formats list is always an object describing the executable format for *interpreted scripts*. This format defines only the load_binary method. The corresponding do_load_script() function checks whether the executable file starts with the #! pair of characters. If so, it interprets the rest of the first line as the pathname of another executable file and tries to execute it by passing the name of the script file as a parameter.[*]

Linux allows users to register their own custom executable formats. Each such format may be recognized either by means of a magic number stored in the first 128 bytes of the file, or by a filename extension that identifies the file type. As an example, MS-DOS extensions consist of three characters separated from the filename by a dot: the *.exe* extension identifies executable programs while the *.bat* extension identifies shell scripts.

Each custom format is associated with an interpreter program, which is automatically invoked by the kernel with the original custom executable filename as a parameter. The mechanism is similar to the script's format, but it's more powerful since it doesn't impose any restrictions on the custom format. To register a new format, the user writes into the */proc/sys/fs/binfmt_misc/register* file a string having the following format:

```
:name:type:offset:string:mask:interpreter:
```

where each field has the following meaning:

name
    An identifier for the new format

type
    The type of recognition (M for magic number, E for extension)

offset
    The starting offset of the magic number inside the file

string
    The byte sequence to be matched either in the magic number or in the extension

mask
    String to mask out some bits in string

interpreter
    The full pathname of the program interpreter

As an example, the following command performed by the superuser will enable the kernel to recognize the Microsoft Windows executable format:

```
$ echo ':DOSWin:M:0:MZ:0xff:/usr/local/bin/wine:' > \
    /proc/sys/fs/binfmt_misc/register
```

A Windows executable file has the MZ magic number in the first two bytes, and it will be executed by the */usr/local/bin/wine* program interpreter.

---

[*] It is possible to execute a script file even if it doesn't start with the #! characters, as long as the file is written in the language recognized by the user's shell. In this case, however, the script is interpreted by the shell on which the user types the command, and thus the kernel is not directly involved.

Execution Domains

As mentioned in Chapter 1, a neat feature of Linux is its ability to execute files compiled for other operating systems. Of course, this is possible only if the files include machine code for the same computer architecture on which the kernel is running. Two kinds of support are offered for these "foreign" programs:

- Emulated execution: necessary to execute programs that include system calls that are not POSIX-compliant

- Native execution: valid for programs whose system calls are totally POSIX-compliant

Microsoft MS-DOS and Windows programs are emulated: they cannot be natively executed, since they include APIs that are not recognized by Linux. An emulator like DOSemu or Wine (which appeared in the example at the end of the previous section) is invoked to translate each API call into an emulating wrapper function call, which in turn makes use of the existing Linux system calls. Since emulators are mostly implemented as User Mode applications, we don't discuss them further.

On the other hand, POSIX-compliant programs compiled on operating systems other than Linux can be executed without too much trouble, since POSIX operating systems offer similar APIs. (Actually, the APIs should be identical, although this is not always the case.) Minor differences that the kernel must iron out usually refer to how system calls are invoked or how the various signals are numbered. This information is stored in *execution domain descriptors* of type `exec_domain`.

A process specifies its execution domain by setting the `personality` field of its descriptor and by storing the address of the corresponding `exec_domain` data structure in the `exec_domain` field. A process can change its personality by issuing a suitable system call named `personality()`; typical values assumed by the system call's parameter are listed in Table 19-6. The C library does not include a corresponding wrapper routine, because programmers are not expected to directly change the personality of their programs. Instead, the `personality()` system call should be issued by the glue code that sets up the execution context of the process (see the next section, "The exec-like Functions").

Table 19-6. Main Personalities Supported by the Linux Kernel

Personality	Operating System
PER_LINUX	Standard execution domain
PER_SVR4	System V Release 4
PER_SVR3	System V Release 3
PER_SCOSVR3	SCO Unix version 3.2
PER_WYSEV386	Unix System V/386 Release 3.2.1

Table 19-6. Main Personalities Supported by the Linux Kernel (continued)

Personality	Operating System
PER_ISCR4	Interactive Unix
PER_BSD	BSD Unix
PER_XENIX	Xenix
PER_IRIX32	SGI Irix-5 32 bit
PER_IRIXN32	SGI Irix-6 32 bit
PER_IRIX64	SGI Irix-6 64 bit

The exec-like Functions

Unix systems provide a family of functions that replace the execution context of a process with a new context described by an executable file. The names of such functions start with the prefix **exec** followed by one or two letters; therefore, a generic function in the family is usually referred to as an **exec**-like function.

The **exec**-like functions are listed in Table 19-7; they differ in how the parameters are interpreted.

Table 19-7. The exec-like Functions

Function Name	PATH Search	Command-Line Arguments	Environment Array
execl()	No	List	No
execlp()	Yes	List	No
execle()	No	List	Yes
execv()	No	Array	No
execvp()	Yes	Array	No
execve()	No	Array	Yes

The first parameter of each function denotes the pathname of the file to be executed. The pathname can be absolute or relative to the process's current directory. Moreover, if the name does not include any / characters, the **execlp()** and **execvp()** functions search for the executable file in all directories specified by the **PATH** environment variable.

Besides the first parameter, the **execl()**, **execlp()**, and **execle()** functions include a variable number of additional parameters. Each points to a string describing a command-line argument for the new program; as the l character in the function names suggests, the parameters are organized in a list terminated by a **NULL** value. Usually, the first command-line argument duplicates the executable filename. Conversely, the **execv()**, **execvp()**, and **execve()** functions specify the command-line arguments with a single parameter: as the v character in the function names suggests, the parameter is the address of a vector of pointers to command-line argument strings. The last component of the array must store the NULL value.

The execle() and execve() functions receive as their last parameter the address of an array of pointers to environment strings; as usual, the last component of the array must be NULL. The other functions may access the environment for the new program from the external environ global variable, which is defined in the C library.

All exec()-like functions, with the exception of execve(), are wrapper routines defined in the C library and make use of execve(), which is the only system call offered by Linux to deal with program execution.

The sys_execve() service routine receives the following parameters:

- The address of the executable file pathname (in the User Mode address space).

- The address of a NULL-terminated array (in the User Mode address space) of pointers to strings (again in the User Mode address space); each string represents a command-line argument.

- The address of a NULL-terminated array (in the User Mode address space) of pointers to strings (again in the User Mode address space); each string represents an environment variable in the NAME=value format.

The function copies the executable file pathname into a newly allocated page frame. It then invokes the do_execve() function, passing to it the pointers to the page frame, to the pointer's arrays, and to the location of the Kernel Mode stack where the User Mode register contents are saved. In turn, do_execve() performs the following operations:

1. Statically allocates a linux_binprm data structure, which will be filled with data concerning the new executable file.

2. Invokes open_namei() to get the dentry object, thus the file object and the inode object, associated with the executable file. On failure, returns the proper error code.

3. Invokes the prepare_binprm() function to fill the linux_binprm data structure. This function, in turn, performs the following operations:

   a. Checks whether the permissions of the file allow its execution; if not, returns an error code.

   b. Checks whether the file is being written (that is, whether i_writecount inode's field is not null): if so, returns an error code.

   c. Initializes the e_uid and e_gid fields of the linux_binprm structure, taking into account the values of the *setuid* and *setgid* flags of the executable file. These fields represent the effective user and group IDs, respectively. Also checks process capabilities (a compatibility hack explained in the earlier section "Process Credentials and Capabilities").

    d. Fills the `buf` field of the `linux_binprm` structure with the first 128 bytes of the executable file. These bytes include a magic number and other information suitable for recognizing the format of the executable file.

4. Copies the file pathname, command-line arguments, and environment strings into one or more newly allocated page frames. (Eventually, they will be assigned to the User Mode address space.)

5. Invokes the `search_binary_handler()` function, which scans the `formats` list and tries to apply the `load_binary` method of each element, passing to it the `linux_binprm` data structure. The scan of the `formats` list terminates as soon as a `load_binary` method succeeds in acknowledging the executable format of the file.

6. If the executable file format is not present in the `formats` list, releases all allocated page frames and returns the error code `-ENOEXEC`: Linux cannot recognize the executable file format.

7. Otherwise, returns the code obtained from the `load_binary` method associated with the executable format of the file.

The `load_binary` method corresponding to an executable file format performs the following operations (we assume that the executable file is stored on a filesystem that allows file memory mapping and that it requires one or more shared libraries):

1. Checks some magic numbers stored in the first 128 bytes of the file to identify the executable format. If the magic numbers don't match, returns the error code `-ENOEXEC`.

2. Reads the header of the executable file. This header describes the program's segments and the shared libraries requested.

3. Gets from the executable file the pathname of the program interpreter, which will be used to locate the shared libraries and map them into memory.

4. Gets the dentry object (as well as the inode object and the file object) of the program interpreter.

5. Checks the execution permissions of the program interpreter.

6. Copies the first 128 bytes of the program interpreter into the `buf` field of the `linux_binprm` structure.

7. Performs some consistency checks on the program interpreter type.

8. Invokes the `flush_old_exec()` function to release almost all resources used by the previous computation; in turn, this function performs the following operations.

a. If the table of signal handlers is shared with other processes, allocates a new table and decrements the usage counter of the old one; this is done by invoking the `make_private_signals()` function.

b. Updates the table of signal handlers by resetting each signal to its default action: this is done by invoking the `release_old_signals()` and `flush_signal_handlers()` functions.

c. Invokes the `exec_mmap()` function to release the memory descriptor, all memory regions, and all page frames assigned to the process and to clean up the process's page tables.

d. Sets the `comm` field of the process descriptor with the executable file pathname.

e. Invokes the `flush_thread()` function to clear the values of the floating point registers and debug registers saved in the TSS segment.

f. Invokes the `flush_old_files()` function to close all open files having the corresponding flag in the `files->close_on_exec` field of the process descriptor set (see the section "Files Associated with a Process" in Chapter 12).*

Now we have reached the point of no return: the function cannot restore the previous computation if something goes wrong.

9. Sets up the new personality of the process, that is, the `personality` field in the process descriptor.

10. Invokes the `setup_arg_pages()` function to allocate a new memory region descriptor for the process's User Mode stack and to insert that memory region into the process's address space. `setup_arg_pages()` also assigns the page frames containing the command-line arguments and the environment variable strings to the new memory region.

11. Invokes the `do_mmap()` function to create a new memory region that maps the text segment (that is, the code) of the executable file. The initial linear address of the memory region depends on the executable format, since the program's executable code is usually not relocatable. Therefore, the function assumes that the text segment will be loaded starting from some specific logical address offset (and thus, from some specified linear address). ELF programs are loaded starting from linear address 0x08048000.

12. Invokes the `do_mmap()` function to create a new memory region that maps the data segment of the executable file. Again, the initial linear address of the memory region depends on the executable format, since the executable code expects to find its variables at specified offsets (that is, at specified linear addresses). In an ELF program, the data segment is loaded right after the text segment.

---

* These flags can be read and modified by means of the `fcntl()` system call.

13. Allocates additional memory regions for any other specialized segments of the executable file. Usually, there are none.

14. Invokes a function that loads the program interpreter. If the program interpreter is an ELF executable, the function is named load_elf_interp(). In general, the function performs the operations in steps 11 through 13, but for the program interpreter instead of the file to be executed. The initial addresses of the memory regions that will include the text and data of the program interpreter are specified by the program interpreter itself; however, they are very high (usually above 0x40000000) in order to avoid collisions with the memory regions that map the text and data of the file to be executed (see the earlier section "Program Segments and Process Memory Regions").

15. Sets the exec_domain field in the process descriptor according to the personality of the new program.

16. Determines the new capabilities of the process.

17. Clears the PF_FORKNOEXEC flag in the process descriptor. This flag, which is set when a process is forked and cleared when it executes a new program, is required by the POSIX standard for process accounting.

18. Creates specific program interpreter tables and stores them on the User Mode stack, between the command-line arguments and the array of pointers to environment strings (see Figure 19-1).

19. Sets the values of the start_code, end_code, end_data, start_brk, brk, and start_stack fields of the process's memory descriptor.

20. Invokes the do_mmap() function to create a new anonymous memory region mapping the bss segment of the program. (When the process writes into a variable, it triggers demand paging, thus the allocation of a page frame.) The size of this memory region was computed when the executable program was linked. The initial linear address of the memory region must be specified, since the program's executable code is usually not relocatable. In an ELF program, the bss segment is loaded right after the data segment.

21. Invokes the start_thread() macro to modify the values of the User Mode registers eip and esp saved on the Kernel Mode stack, so that they point to the entry point of the program interpreter and to the top of the new User Mode stack, respectively.

22. If the process is being traced, sends the SIGTRAP signal to it.

23. Returns the value 0 (success).

When the execve() system call terminates and the calling process resumes its execution in User Mode, the execution context is dramatically changed: the code that invoked the system call no longer exists. In this sense, we could say that execve()

never returns on success. Instead, a new program to be executed has been mapped in the address space of the process.

However, the new program cannot yet be executed, since the program interpreter must still take care of loading the shared libraries.*

Although the program interpreter runs in User Mode, we'll briefly sketch out here how it operates. Its first job is to set up a basic execution context for itself, starting from the information stored by the kernel in the User Mode stack between the array of pointers to environment strings and `arg_start`. Then, the program interpreter must examine the program to be executed, in order to identify which shared libraries must be loaded and which functions in each shared library are effectively requested. Next, the interpreter issues several `mmap()` system calls to create memory regions mapping the pages that will hold the library functions (text and data) actually used by the program. Then, the interpreter updates all references to the symbols of the shared library, according to the linear addresses of the library's memory regions. Finally, the program interpreter terminates its execution by jumping at the main entry point of the program to be executed. From now on, the process will execute the code of the executable file and of the shared libraries.

As you may have noticed, executing a program is a complex activity that involves many facets of kernel design such as process abstraction, memory management, system calls, and filesystems. It is the kind of topic that makes you realize what a marvelous piece of work Linux is!

Anticipating Linux 2.4

Linux 2.4 adds a few more personalities: the new kernel is able to execute programs written for SunOS, Sun Solaris, and RISCOS operating systems. The implementation of the `execve()` system call is pretty much the same as in Linux 2.2, though.

---

* Things are much simpler if the executable file is statically linked, that is, if no shared library is requested. The `load_binary` method just maps the text, data, bss, and stack segments of the program into the process memory regions, and then sets the User Mode `eip` register to the entry point of the new program.

SYSTEM STARTUP

This appendix explains what happens right after users have switched on their computers, that is, how a Linux kernel image is copied into memory and executed. In short, we discuss how the kernel, and thus the whole system, is "bootstrapped."

Traditionally, the term *bootstrap* refers to a person who tries to stand up by pulling her own boots. In operating systems, the term denotes bringing at least a portion of the operating system into main memory and having the processor execute it. It also denotes the initialization of kernel data structures, the creation of some user processes, and the transfer of control to one of them.

Computer bootstrapping is a tedious, long task, since initially nearly every hardware device including the RAM is in a random, unpredictable state. Moreover, the bootstrap process is highly dependent on the computer architecture; as usual, we refer to IBM's PC architecture in this appendix.

Prehistoric Age: The BIOS

The moment after a computer is powered on, it is practically useless because the RAM chips contain random data and no operating system is running. To begin the boot, a special hardware circuit raises the logical value of the RESET pin of the CPU. After RESET is thus asserted, some registers of the processor (including `cs` and `eip`) are set to fixed values, and the code found at physical address `0xfffffff0` is executed. This address is mapped by the hardware to some read-only, persistent memory chip, a kind of memory often called ROM (Read-Only Memory). The set of programs stored in ROM is traditionally called BIOS (Basic Input/Output System), since it includes several interrupt-driven low-level procedures used by some operating systems, including Microsoft's MS-DOS, to handle the hardware devices that make up the computer.

Once initialized, Linux does not make any use of BIOS but provides its own device driver for every hardware device on the computer. In fact, the BIOS procedures must be executed in real mode, while the kernel executes in protected mode (see the section "Segmentation in Hardware" in Chapter 2, *Memory Addressing*), so they cannot share functions even if that would be beneficial.

BIOS uses Real Mode addresses because they are the only ones available when the computer is turned on. A Real Mode address is composed of a *seg* segment and an *off* offset; the corresponding physical address is given by *seg**16+*off*. As a result, no Global Descriptor Table, Local Descriptor Table, or paging table is needed by the CPU addressing circuit to translate a logical address into a physical one. Clearly, the code that initializes the GDT, LDT, and paging tables must run in Real Mode.

Linux is forced to use BIOS in the bootstrapping phase, when it must retrieve the kernel image from disk or from some other external device. The BIOS bootstrap procedure essentially performs the following four operations:

1. Executes a series of tests on the computer hardware, in order to establish which devices are present and whether they are working properly. This phase is often called POST (Power-On Self-Test). During this phase, several messages, such as the BIOS version banner, are displayed.

2. Initializes the hardware devices. This phase is crucial in modern PCI-based architectures, since it guarantees that all hardware devices operate without conflicts on the IRQ lines and I/O ports. At the end of this phase, a table of installed PCI devices is displayed.

3. Searches for an operating system to boot. Actually, depending on the BIOS setting, the procedure may try to access (in a predefined, customizable order) the first sector (*boot sector*) of any floppy disk, any hard disk, and any CD-ROM in the system.

4. As soon as a valid device is found, copies the contents of its first sector into RAM, starting from physical address `0x00007c00`, then jumps into that address and executes the code just loaded.

The rest of this appendix takes you from the most primitive starting state to the full glory of a running Linux system.

Ancient Age: The Boot Loader

The *boot loader* is the program invoked by the BIOS to load the image of an operating system kernel into RAM. Let us briefly sketch how boot loaders work in IBM's PC architecture.

In order to boot from a floppy disk, the instructions stored in its first sector are loaded in RAM and executed; these instructions copy all the remaining sectors containing the kernel image into RAM.

Booting from a hard disk is done differently. The first sector of the hard disk, named the Master Boot Record (MBR), includes the partition table[*] and a small program, which loads the first sector of the partition containing the operating system to be started. Some operating systems such as Microsoft Windows 98 identify this partition by means of an *active* flag included in the partition table;[†] following this approach, only the operating system whose kernel image is stored in the active partition can be booted. As we shall see later, Linux is more flexible since it replaces the rudimentary program included in the MBR with a sophisticated program called LILO that allows users to select the operating system to be booted.

Booting Linux from Floppy Disk

The only way to store a Linux kernel on a single floppy disk is to compress the kernel image. As we shall see, compression is done at compile time and decompression by the loader.

If the Linux kernel is loaded from a floppy disk, the boot loader is quite simple. It is coded in the *arch/i386/boot/bootsect.S* assembly language file. When a new kernel image is produced by compiling the kernel source, the executable code yielded by this assembly language file is placed at the beginning of the kernel image file. Thus, it is very easy to produce a bootable floppy containing the Linux kernel. The floppy can be created by copying the kernel image starting from the first sector of the disk. When the BIOS loads the first sector of the floppy disk, it actually copies the code of the boot loader.

The boot loader, which is invoked by the BIOS by jumping to physical address 0x00007c00, performs the following operations:

1. Moves itself from address 0x00007c00 to address 0x00090000.

2. Sets up the Real Mode stack, from address 0x00003ff4. As usual, the stack will grow toward lower addresses.

3. Sets up the disk parameter table, used by the BIOS to handle the floppy device driver.

4. Invokes a BIOS procedure to display a "Loading" message.

5. Invokes a BIOS procedure to load the setup() code of the kernel image from the floppy disk and puts it in RAM starting from address 0x00090200.

6. Invokes a BIOS procedure to load the rest of the kernel image from the floppy disk and puts the image in RAM starting from either low address 0x00010000 (for small kernel images compiled with make zImage) or high address 0x00100000

---

[*] Each partition table entry typically includes the starting and ending sectors of a partition and the kind of operating system that handles it.

[†] The active flag may be set through programs like MS-DOS's FDISK.

(for big kernel images compiled with `make bzImage`). In the following discussion, we will say that the kernel image is "loaded low" or "loaded high" in RAM, respectively. Support for big kernel images was introduced quite recently: while it uses essentially the same booting scheme as the older one, it places data in different physical memory addresses to avoid problems with the ISA hole mentioned in the section "Reserved Page Frames" in Chapter 2.

7. Jumps to the `setup()` code.

Booting Linux from Hard Disk

In most cases, the Linux kernel is loaded from a hard disk, and a two-stage boot loader is required. The most commonly used Linux boot loader on Intel systems is named LILO (LInux LOader); corresponding programs exist for other architectures. LILO may be installed either on the MBR, replacing the small program that loads the boot sector of the active partition, or in the boot sector of a (usually active) disk partition. In both cases, the final result is the same: when the loader is executed at boot time, the user may choose which operating system to load.

The LILO boot loader is broken into two parts, since otherwise it would be too large to fit into the MBR. The MBR or the partition boot sector includes a small boot loader, which is loaded into RAM starting from address 0x00007c00 by the BIOS. This small program moves itself to the address 0x0009a000, sets up the Real Mode stack (ranging from 0x0009b000 to 0x0009a200), and loads the second part of the LILO boot loader into RAM starting from address 0x0009b000. In turn, this latter program reads a map of available operating systems from disk and offers the user a prompt so she can choose one of them. Finally, after the user has chosen the kernel to be loaded (or let a time-out elapse so that LILO chooses a default), the boot loader may either copy the boot sector of the corresponding partition into RAM and execute it or directly copy the kernel image into RAM.

Assuming that a Linux kernel image must be booted, the LILO boot loader, which relies on BIOS routines, performs essentially the same operations as the boot loader integrated into the kernel image described in the previous section about floppy disks. The loader displays the "Loading Linux" message; then it copies the integrated boot loader of the kernel image to address 0x00090000, the `setup()` code to address 0x00090200, and the rest of the kernel image to address 0x00010000 or 0x00100000. Then it jumps to the `setup()` code.

Middle Ages: The setup() Function

The code of the `setup()` assembly language function is placed by the linker immediately after the integrated boot loader of the kernel, that is, at offset 0x200 of the kernel image file. The boot loader can thus easily locate the code and copy it into RAM starting from physical address 0x00090200.

The setup() function must initialize the hardware devices in the computer and set up the environment for the execution of the kernel program. Although the BIOS already initialized most hardware devices, Linux does not rely on it but reinitializes the devices in its own manner to enhance portability and robustness. setup() essentially performs the following operations:

1. Invokes a BIOS procedure to find out the amount of RAM available in the system.

2. Sets the keyboard repeat delay and rate. (When the user keeps a key pressed past a certain amount of time, the keyboard device sends the corresponding keycode over and over to the CPU.)

3. Initializes the video adapter card.

4. Reinitializes the disk controller and determines the hard disk parameters.

5. Checks for an IBM Micro Channel bus (MCA).

6. Checks for a PS/2 pointing device (bus mouse).

7. Checks for Advanced Power Management (APM) BIOS support.

8. If the kernel image was loaded low in RAM (at physical address 0x00010000), moves it to physical address 0x00001000. Conversely, if the kernel image was loaded high in RAM, does not move it. This step is necessary because, in order to be able to store the kernel image on a floppy disk and to save time while booting, the kernel image stored on disk is compressed, and the decompression routine needs some free space to use as a temporary buffer following the kernel image in RAM.

9. Sets up a provisional Interrupt Descriptor Table (IDT) and a provisional Global Descriptor Table (GDT).

10. Resets the floating point unit (FPU), if any.

11. Reprograms the Programmable Interrupt Controller (PIC) and maps the 16 hardware interrupts (IRQ lines) to the range of vectors from 32 to 47. The kernel must perform this step because the BIOS erroneously maps the hardware interrupts in the range from 0 to 15, which is already used for CPU exceptions (see the section "Exceptions" in Chapter 4, *Interrupts and Exceptions*).

12. Switches the CPU from Real Mode to Protected Mode by setting the PE bit in the cr0 status register. As explained in the section "Kernel Page Tables" in Chapter 2, the provisional kernel page tables contained in swapper_pg_dir and pg0 identically map the linear addresses to the same physical addresses. Therefore, the transition from Real Mode to Protected Mode goes smoothly.

13. Jumps to the startup_32() assembly language function.

Renaissance: The startup_32() Functions

There are two different `startup_32()` functions; the one we refer to here is coded in the *arch/i386/boot/compressed/head.S* file. After `setup()` terminates, the function has been moved either to physical address 0x00100000 or to physical address 0x00001000, depending on whether the kernel image was loaded high or low in RAM.

This function performs the following operations:

1. Initializes the segmentation registers and a provisional stack.

2. Fills the area of uninitialized data of the kernel identified by the `_edata` and `_end` symbols with zeros (see the section "Reserved Page Frames" in Chapter 2).

3. Invokes the `decompress_kernel()` function to decompress the kernel image. The "Uncompressing Linux . . . " message is displayed first. After the kernel image has been decompressed, the "OK, booting the kernel." message is shown. If the kernel image was loaded low, the decompressed kernel is placed at physical address 0x00100000. Otherwise, if the kernel image was loaded high, the decompressed kernel is placed in a temporary buffer located after the compressed image. The decompressed image is then moved into its final position, which starts at physical address 0x00100000.

4. Jumps to physical address 0x00100000.

The decompressed kernel image begins with another `startup_32()` function included in the *arch/i386/kernel/head.S* file. Using the same name for both the functions does not create any problems (besides confusing our readers), since both functions are executed by jumping to their initial physical addresses.

The second `startup_32()` function essentially sets up the execution environment for the first Linux process (process 0). The function performs the following operations:

1. Initializes the segmentation registers with their final values.

2. Sets up the Kernel Mode stack for process 0 (see the section "Kernel Threads" in Chapter 3, *Processes*).

3. Invokes `setup_idt()` to fill the IDT with null interrupt handlers (see the section "Preliminary Initialization of the IDT" in Chapter 4).

4. Puts the system parameters obtained from the BIOS and the parameters passed to the operating system into the first page frame (see the section "Reserved Page Frames" in Chapter 2).

5. Identifies the model of the processor.

6. Loads the `gdtr` and `idtr` registers with the addresses of the GDT and IDT tables.

7. Jumps to the `start_kernel()` function.

Modern Age: The start_kernel() Function

The `start_kernel()` function completes the initialization of the Linux kernel. Nearly every kernel component is initialized by this function; we mention just a few of them:

- The page tables are initialized by invoking the `paging_init()` function (see the section "Kernel Page Tables" in Chapter 2).

- The page descriptors are initialized by the `mem_init()` function (see the section "Page Frame Management" in Chapter 6, *Memory Management*).

- The final initialization of the IDT is performed by invoking `trap_init()` (see the section "Exception Handling" in Chapter 4) and `init_IRQ()` (see the section "IRQ Data Structures" in Chapter 4).

- The slab allocator is initialized by the `kmem_cache_init()` and `kmem_cache_sizes_init()` functions (see the section "General and Specific Caches" in Chapter 6).

- The system date and time are initialized by the `time_init()` function (see the section "Real Time Clock" in Chapter 5, *Timing Measurements*).

- The kernel thread for process 1 is created by invoking the `kernel_thread()` function. In turn, this kernel thread creates the other kernel threads and executes the */sbin/init* program, as described in the section "Kernel Threads" in Chapter 3.

Besides the "Linux version 2.2.14 . . . " message, which is displayed right after the beginning of `start_kernel()`, many other messages are displayed in this last phase both by the init functions and by the kernel threads. At the end, the familiar login prompt appears on the console (or in the graphical screen if the X Window System is launched at startup), telling the user that the Linux kernel is up and running.

APPENDIX B

MODULES

As stated in Chapter 1, *Introduction*, *modules* are Linux's recipe for effectively achieving many of the theoretical advantages of microkernels without introducing performance penalties.

To Be (a Module) or Not to Be?

When system programmers want to add a new functionality to the Linux kernel, they are faced with an interesting dilemma: should they write the new code so that it will be compiled as a module, or should they statically link the new code to the kernel?

As a general rule, system programmers tend to implement new code as a module. Because modules can be linked on demand, as we see later, the kernel does not have to be bloated with hundreds of seldom-used programs. Nearly every higher-level component of the Linux kernel—filesystems, device drivers, executable formats, network layers, and so on—can be compiled as a module.

However, some Linux code must necessarily be linked statically, which means that either the corresponding component is included in the kernel, or it is not compiled at all. This happens typically when the component requires a modification to some data structure or function statically linked in the kernel.

As an example, suppose that the component has to introduce new fields into the process descriptor. Linking a module cannot change an already defined data structure like `task_struct` since, even if the module uses its modified version of the data structure, all statically linked code continues to see the old version: data corruption will easily occur. A partial solution to the problem consists of "statically" adding the new fields to the process descriptor, thus making them available to the kernel component, no matter how it has been linked. However, if the kernel component is never used, such extra fields replicated in every process descriptor are a waste of memory. If the new kernel component increases the size of the process descriptor a lot, one would get better system performance by adding the required fields in the data structure only if the component is statically linked to the kernel.

As a second example, consider a kernel component that has to replace statically linked code. It's pretty clear that no such component can be compiled as a module because the kernel cannot change the machine code already in RAM when linking the module. For instance, it is not possible to link a module that changes the way page frames are allocated, since the Buddy system functions are always statically linked to the kernel.

The kernel has two key tasks to perform in managing modules. The first task is making sure the rest of the kernel can reach the module's global symbols, such as the entry point to its main function. A module must also know the addresses of symbols in the kernel and in other modules. So references are resolved once and for all when a module is linked. The second task consists of keeping track of the use of modules, so that no module is unloaded while another module or another part of the kernel is using it. A simple reference count keeps track of each module's usage.

Module Implementation

Modules are stored in the filesystem as ELF object files. The kernel considers only modules that have been loaded into RAM by the */sbin/insmod* program (see the later section, "Linking and Unlinking Modules") and for each of them it allocates a memory area containing the following data:

* A `module` object

* A null-terminated string that represents the name of the module (all modules should have unique names)

* The code that implements the functions of the module

The `module` object describes a module; its fields are shown in Table B-1. A simply linked list collects all `module` objects, where the `next` field of each object points to the next element in the list. The first element of the list is addressed by the `module_list` variable. But actually, the first element of the list is always the same: it is named `kernel_module` and refers to a fictitious module representing the statically linked kernel code.

Table B-1. The module Object

Type	Name	Description
unsigned long	size_of_struct	Size of module object
struct module *	next	Next list element
const char *	name	Pointer to module name
unsigned long	size	Module size
atomic_t	uc.usecount	Module usage counter

Table B-1. The module Object (continued)

Type	Name	Description
unsigned long	flags	Module flags
unsigned int	nsyms	Number of exported symbols
unsigned int	ndeps	Number of referenced modules
struct module_symbol *	syms	Table of exported symbols
struct module_ref *	deps	List of referenced modules
struct module_ref *	refs	List of referencing modules
int (*)(void)	init	Initialization method
void (*)(void)	cleanup	Cleanup method
struct exception_table_entry *	ex_table_start	Start of exception table
struct exception_table_entry *	ex_table_end	End of exception table

The total size of the memory area allocated for the module (including the `module` object and the module name) is contained in the `size` field.

As already mentioned in the section "Dynamic Address Checking: The Fixup Code" in Chapter 8, *System Calls*, each module has its own exception table. The table includes the addresses of the fixup code of the module, if any. The table is copied in RAM when the module is linked, and its starting and ending addresses are stored in the `ex_table_start` and `ex_table_end` fields of the `module` object.

Module Usage Counter

Each module has a usage counter, stored in the `uc.usecount` field of the corresponding `module` object. The counter is incremented when an operation involving the module's functions is started and decremented when the operation terminates. A module can be unlinked only if its usage counter is null.

As an example, suppose that the MS-DOS filesystem layer has been compiled as a module and that the module has been linked at runtime. Initially, the module usage counter is null. If the user mounts an MS-DOS floppy disk, the module usage counter is incremented by 1. Conversely, when the user unmounts the floppy disk, the counter is decremented by 1.

Exporting Symbols

When linking a module, all references to global kernel symbols (variables and functions) in the module's object code must be replaced with suitable addresses. This operation, which is very similar to that performed by the linker while compiling a User Mode program (see the section "Libraries" in Chapter 19, *Program Execution*), is delegated to the */sbin/insmod* external program (described later in the section, "Linking and Unlinking Modules").

A special table is used by the kernel to store the symbols that can be accessed by modules together with their corresponding addresses. This *kernel symbol table* is contained in the __ksymtab section of the kernel code segment, and its starting and ending addresses are identified by two symbols produced by the C compiler: __start__ _ksymtab and __stop___ksymtab. The EXPORT_SYMBOL macro, when used inside the statically linked kernel code, forces the C compiler to add a specified symbol to the table.

Only the kernel symbols actually used by some existing module are included in the table. Should a system programmer need, within some module, to access a kernel symbol that is not already exported, he can simply add the corresponding EXPORT_ SYMBOL macro into the *kernel/ksyms.c* file of the Linux source code.

Linked modules can also export their own symbols, so that other modules can access them. The *module symbol table* is contained in the __ksymtab section of the module code segment. If the module source code includes the EXPORT_NO_SYMBOLS macro, no symbols from that module are added to the table. To export a subset of symbols from the module, the programmer must define the EXPORT_SYMTAB macro before including the *include/linux/module.h* header file. Then he may use the EXPORT_ SYMBOL macro to export a specific symbol. If neither EXPORT_NO_SYMBOLS nor EXPORT_SYMTAB appears in the module source code, all global symbols of the modules are exported.

The symbol table in the __ksymtab section is copied into a memory area when the module is linked, and the address of the area is stored in the syms field of the module object. The symbols exported by the statically linked kernel and all linked-in modules can be retrieved by reading the */proc/ksyms* file or using the query_module() system call (described in the later section, "Linking and Unlinking Modules").

Module Dependency

A module (B) can refer to the symbols exported by another module (A); in this case, we say that B is loaded on top of A, or equivalently that A is used by B. In order to link module B, module A must have already been linked; otherwise, the references to the symbols exported by A cannot be properly linked in B. In short, there is a *dependency* between modules.

The deps field of the module object relative to B points to a list describing all modules that are used by B; in our example, A's module object would appear in that list. The ndeps field stores the number of modules used by B. Conversely, the refs field of A points to a list describing all modules that are loaded on top of A (thus, B's module object will be included when it is loaded). The refs list must be updated dynamically whenever a module is loaded on top of A. In order to ensure that module A is not removed before B, A's usage counter is incremented for each module loaded on top of it.

Beside A and B there could be, of course, another module (C) loaded on top of B, and so on. Stacking modules is an effective way to modularize the kernel source code in order to speed up its development and improve its portability.

Linking and Unlinking Modules

A user can link a module into the running kernel by executing the */sbin/insmod* external program. This program performs the following operations:

1. Reads from the command line the name of the module to be linked.

2. Locates the file containing the module's object code in the system directory tree. The file is usually placed in some subdirectory below */lib/modules*.

3. Computes the size of the memory area needed to store the module code, its name, and the `module` object.

4. Invokes the `create_module()` system call, passing to it the name and size of the new module. The corresponding `sys_create_module()` service routine performs the following operations:

   a. Checks whether the user is allowed to link the module (the current process must have the `CAP_SYS_MODULE` capability). In any situation where one is adding functionality to a kernel, which has access to all data and processes on the system, security is a paramount concern.

   b. Invokes the `find_module()` function to scan the `module_list` list of `module` objects looking for a module with the specified name. If it is found, the module has already been linked, so the system call terminates.

   c. Invokes `vmalloc()` to allocate a memory area for the new module.

   d. Initializes the fields of the `module` object at the beginning of the memory area and copies the name of the module right below the object.

   e. Inserts the `module` object into the list pointed to by `module_list`.

   f. Returns the starting address of the memory area allocated to the module.

5. Invokes the `query_module()` system call with the `QM_MODULES` subcommand to get the name of all already linked modules.

6. Invokes the `query_module()` system call with the `QM_SYMBOL` subcommand repeatedly, to get the kernel symbol table and the symbol tables of all modules that are already linked in.

7. Using the kernel symbol table, the module symbol tables, and the address returned by the `create_module()` system call, relocates the object code included in the module's file. This means replacing all occurrences of external and global symbols with the corresponding logical address offsets.

8. Allocates a memory area in the User Mode address space and loads it with a copy of the `module` object, the module's name, and the module's code relocated for the running kernel. The address fields of the object point to the relocated code. The `init` field is set to the relocated address of the module's `init_module()` function, if the module defines one. (Virtually all modules define a function of that name, which is invoked in the next step to perform any initialization required by the module.) Similarly, the `cleanup` field is set to the relocated address of the module's `cleanup_module()` function, if one is present.

9. Invokes the `init_module()` system call, passing to it the address of the User Mode memory area set up in the previous step. The `sys_init_module()` service routine performs the following operations:

   a. Checks whether the user is allowed to link the module (the current process must have the `CAP_SYS_MODULE` capability).

   b. Invokes `find_module()` to find the proper `module` object in the list to which `module_list` points.

   c. Overwrites the `module` object with the contents of the corresponding object in the User Mode memory area.

   d. Performs a series of sanity checks on the addresses in the `module` object.

   e. Copies the remaining part of the User Mode memory area into the memory area allocated to the module.

   f. Scans the module list and initializes the `ndeps` and `deps` fields of the `module` object.

   g. Sets the module usage counter to 1.

   h. If defined, executes the `init` method of the module to initialize the module's data structures properly. The method is usually implemented by the `init_module()` function defined inside the module.

   i. Sets the module usage counter to 0 and returns.

10. Releases the User Mode memory area and terminates.

In order to unlink a module, a user invokes the */sbin/rmmod* external program, which performs the following operations:

1. From the command line, reads the name of the module to be unlinked.

2. Invokes the `query_module()` system call with the `QM_MODULES` subcommand to get the list of linked modules.

3. Invokes the `query_module()` system call with the `QM_REFS` subcommand several times, to retrieve dependency information on the linked modules. If some module is linked on top of the one to be removed, terminates.

4. Invokes the `delete_module()` system call, passing the module's name to it. The corresponding `sys_delete_module()` service routine performs these operations:

   a. Checks whether the user is allowed to remove the module (the current process must have the `CAP_SYS_MODULE` capability).

   b. Invokes `find_module()` to find the corresponding `module` object in the list to which `module_list` points.

   c. Checks whether both the `refs` field and the `uc.usecount` fields of the `module` object are null; otherwise, returns an error code.

   d. If defined, invokes the `cleanup` method to perform the operations needed to cleanly shut down the module. The method is usually implemented by the `cleanup_module()` function defined inside the module.

   e. Scans the `deps` list of the module and removes the module from the `refs` list of any element found.

   f. Removes the module from the list to which `module_list` points.

   g. Invokes `vfree()` to release the memory area used by the module and returns 0 (success).

Linking Modules on Demand

A module can be automatically linked when the functionality it provides is requested and automatically removed afterward.

For instance, suppose that the MS-DOS filesystem has not been linked, either statically or dynamically. If a user tries to mount an MS-DOS filesystem, the `mount()` system call normally fails by returning an error code, since MS-DOS is not included in the `file_systems` list of registered filesystems. However, if support for automatic linking of modules has been specified when configuring the kernel, Linux makes an attempt to link the MS-DOS module, then scans the list of registered filesystems again. If the module was successfully linked, the `mount()` system call can continue its execution as if the MS-DOS filesystem were present from the beginning.

The modprobe Program

In order to automatically link a module, the kernel creates a kernel thread to execute the */sbin/modprobe* external program,[*] which takes care of possible complications due to module dependencies. The dependencies were already discussed earlier: a module may require one or more other modules, and these in turn may require still other modules. For instance, the MS-DOS module requires another module named *fat* containing

---

[*] This is one of the few examples in which the kernel relies on an external program.

some code common to all filesystems based on a File Allocation Table (FAT). Thus, if it is not already present, the *fat* module must also be automatically linked into the running kernel when the MS-DOS module is requested. Resolving dependencies and finding modules is a type of activity that's best done in User Mode, because it requires locating and accessing module object files in the filesystem.

The */sbin/modprobe* external program is similar to *insmod*, since it links in a module specified on the command line. However, *modprobe* also recursively links in all modules used by the module specified on the command line. For instance, if a user invokes *modprobe* to link the MS-DOS module, the program links the *fat* module, if necessary, followed by the MS-DOS module. Actually, *modprobe* just checks for module dependencies; the actual linking of each module is done by forking a new process and executing *insmod*.

How does *modprobe* know about module dependencies? Another external program named */sbin/depmod* is executed at system startup. It looks at all the modules compiled for the running kernel, which are usually stored inside the */lib/modules* directory. Then it writes all module dependencies to a file named *modules.dep*. The *modprobe* program can thus simply compare the information stored in the file with the list of linked modules produced by the `query_module()` system call.

The request_module() Function

In some cases, the kernel may invoke the `request_module()` function to attempt automatic linking for a module.

Consider again the case of a user trying to mount an MS-DOS filesystem: if the `get_fs_type()` function discovers that the filesystem is not registered, it invokes the `request_module()` function in the hope that MS-DOS has been compiled as a module.

If the `request_module()` function succeeds in linking the requested module, `get_fs_type()` can continue as if the module were always present. Of course, this does not always happen; in our example, the MS-DOS module might not have been compiled at all. In this case, `get_fs_type()` returns an error code.

The `request_module()` function receives the name of the module to be linked as its parameter. It invokes `kernel_thread()` to create a new kernel thread that executes the `exec_modprobe()` function, then it simply waits until that kernel thread terminates.

The `exec_modprobe()` function, in turn, also receives the name of the module to be linked as its parameter. It invokes the `execve()` system call and executes the */sbin/modprobe* external program,* passing the module name to it. In turn, the *modprobe* program actually links the requested module, along with any that it depends on.

---

* The name and path of the program executed by `exec_modprobe()` can be customized by writing into the */proc/sys/kernel/modprobe* file.

Each module automatically linked into the kernel has the MOD_AUTOCLEAN flag in the flags field of the module object set. This flag allows automatic unlinking of the module when it is no longer used.

In order to automatically unlink the module, a system process (like *crond*) periodically executes the *rmmod* external program, passing the *−a* option to it. The latter program executes the delete_module() system call with a NULL parameter. The corresponding service routine scans the list of module objects and removes all unused modules having the MOD_AUTOCLEAN flag set.

SOURCE CODE STRUCTURE

In order to help you to find your way through the files of the source code, we briefly describe the organization of the kernel directory tree. As usual, all pathnames refer to the main directory of the Linux kernel, which is, in most Linux distributions, */usr/src/ linux*.

Linux source code for all supported architectures is contained in about 4500 C and Assembly files stored in about 270 subdirectories; it consists of about 2 million lines of code, which occupy more than 58 megabytes of disk space.

The following list illustrates the directory tree containing the Linux source code. Please notice that only the subdirectories somehow related to the target of this book have been expanded.

init	Kernel initialization code
kernel	Kernel core: processes, timing, program execution, signals, modules, . . .
mm	Memory handling
arch	Platform-dependent code
└ i386	IBM's PC architecture
└ kernel	Kernel core
└ mm	Memory management
└ math-emu	Software emulator for floating point unit
└ lib	Hardware-dependent utility functions
└ boot	Bootstrapping
└ compressed	Compressed kernel handling
└ tools	Programs to build compressed kernel image
└ alpha	Compaq's Alpha architecture
└ s390	IBM's System/390 architecture

└ sparc	Sun's SPARC architecture
└ sparc64	Sun's Ultra-SPARC architecture
└ mips	Silicon Graphics' MIPS architecture
└ ppc	Motorola-IBM's PowerPC-based architectures
└ m68k	Motorola's MC680x0-based architecture
└ arm	Architectures based on ARM processor
fs	Filesystems
└ proc	*/proc* virtual filesystem
└ devpts	*/dev/pts* virtual filesystem
└ ext2	Linux native Ext2 filesystem
└ isofs	ISO9660 filesystem (CD-ROM)
└ nfs	Network File System (NFS)
└ nfsd	Integrated Network filesystem server
└ fat	Common code for FAT-based filesystems
└ msdos	Microsoft's MS-DOS filesystem
└ vfat	Microsoft's Windows filesystem (VFAT)
└ nls	Native Language Support
└ ntfs	Microsoft's Windows NT filesystem
└ smbfs	Microsoft's Windows Server Message Block (SMB) filesystem
└ umsdos	UMSDOS filesystem
└ minix	MINIX filesystem
└ hpfs	IBM's OS/2 filesystem
└ sysv	System V, SCO, Xenix, Coherent, and Version 7 filesystem
└ ncpfs	Novell's Netware Core Protocol (NCP)
└ ufs	Unix BSD, SunOs, FreeBSD, NetBSD, OpenBSD, and NeXTStep filesystem
└ affs	Amiga's Fast File System (FFS)
└ coda	Coda network filesystem
└ hfs	Apple's Macintosh filesystem
└ adfs	Acorn Disc Filing System
└ efs	SGI IRIX's EFS filesystem
└ qnx4	Filesystem for QNX 4 OS
└ romfs	Small read-only filesystem
└ autofs	Directory automounter support
└ lockd	Remote file locking support
net	Networking code

ipc	System V's Interprocess Communication
drivers	Device drivers
└block	Block device drivers
└paride	Support for accessing IDE devices from parallel port
└scsi	SCSI device drivers
└char	Character device drivers
└joystick	Joysticks
└ftape	Tape-streaming devices
└hfmodem	Ham radio devices
└ip2	IntelliPort's multiport serial controllers
└net	Network card devices
└sound	Audio card devices
└video	Video card devices
└cdrom	Proprietary CD-ROM devices (neither ATAPI nor SCSI)
└isdn	ISDN devices
└ap1000	Fujitsu's AP1000 devices
└macintosh	Apple's Macintosh devices
└sgi	Silicon Graphics' devices
└fc4	Fibre Channel devices
└acorn	Acorn's devices
└misc	Miscellaneous devices
└pnp	Plug-and-play support
└usb	Universal Serial Bus (USB) support
└pci	PCI bus support
└sbus	Sun's SPARC SBus support
└nubus	Apple's Macintosh Nubus support
└zorro	Amiga's Zorro bus support
└dio	Hewlett-Packard's HP300 DIO bus support
└tc	Sun's TurboChannel support (not yet finished)
lib	General-purpose kernel functions
include	Header files (*.h*)
└linux	Kernel core
└lockd	Remote file locking
└nfsd	Integrated Network File Server
└sunrpc	Sun's Remote Procedure Call
└byteorder	Byte-swapping functions
└modules	Module support

└ asm-generic	Platform-independent low-level header files
└ asm-i386	IBM's PC architecture
└ asm-alpha	Compaq's Alpha architecture
└ asm-mips	Silicon Graphics' MIPS architecture
└ asm-m68k	Motorola-IBM's Mc680x0-based architectures
└ asm-ppc	Motorola-IBM's PowerPC architecture
└ asm-s390	IBM's System/390 architecture
└ asm-sparc	Sun's SPARC architecture
└ asm-sparc64	Sun's Ultra-SPARC architecture
└ asm-arm	Architectures based on ARM processor
└ net	Networking
└ scsi	SCSI support
└ video	Video card support
└ config	Header files containing the macros that define the kernel configuration
scripts	External programs for building the kernel image
Documentation	Text files with general explanations and hints about kernel components

BIBLIOGRAPHY

This bibliography is broken down by subject area and lists some of the most common and, in the authors' opinions, most useful books and online documentation on the topic of kernels.

Books on Unix Kernels

Bach, M. J. *The Design of the Unix Operating System*. London: Prentice-Hall International, Inc., 1986. A classic book describing the SVR2 kernel.

Goodheart, B. and J. Cox. *The Magic Garden Explained: The Internals of the Unix System V Release 4*. London: Prentice-Hall International, Inc., 1994. An excellent book on the SVR4 kernel.

Leffler, S. J., M. K. McKusick, M. J. Karels, and J. S. Quarterman. *The Design and Implementation of the 4.4 BSD Operating System*. Addison Wesley, 1986. Perhaps the most authoritative book on the 4.4 BSD kernel.

Vahalia, U. *Unix Internals: The New Frontiers*. Upper Saddle River: Prentice-Hall, Inc., 1996. A valuable book that provides plenty of insights on modern Unix kernel design issues. It includes a rich bibliography.

Books on the Linux Kernel

Beck, M., H. Böhme, M. Dziadzka, U. Kunitz, R. Magnus, and D. Verworner. *Linux Kernel Internals (2d ed.)*. Edinburgh Gate: Addison Wesley Longman Limited, 1998. A hardware-independent book covering the Linux 2.0 kernel.

Card, R., E. Dumas, and F. Mével. *The Linux Kernel Book*. New York: John Wiley & Sons, Inc., 1998. Another hardware-independent book covering the Linux 2.0 kernel.

Maxwell, S. *Linux Core Kernel Commentary*. Scottsdale, Ariz.: The Coriolis Group, LLC, 1999. A listing of part of the Linux kernel source code with some interesting comments at the end of the book.

Rubini, A. *Linux Device Drivers*. Sebastopol, Calif.: O'Reilly & Associates, Inc., 1998. A very valuable book somewhat complementary to this one. It gives plenty of information on how to develop drivers for Linux.

Books on PC Architecture and Technical Manuals on Intel 80x86

Intel, *Intel Architecture Software Developer's Manual, vol. 3: System Programming*. 1999. Describes the Intel Pentium microprocessor architecture. It can be downloaded from:

http://developer.intel.com/design/pentiumii/manuals/24319202.pdf

Intel, *MultiProcessor Specification, Version 1.4*. 1997. Describes the Intel multiprocessor architecture specifications. It can be downloaded from:

http://www.intel.com/design/pentium/datashts/242016.htm

Messmer, H. P. *The Indispensable PC Hardware Book (3d ed.)*. Edinburgh Gate: Addison Wesley Longman Limited, 1997. A valuable reference that describes exhaustively the many components of a PC.

Other Online Documentation Sources

Linux source code
The official site for getting kernel source can be found at:

http://www.kernel.org/

Many mirror sites are also available all over the world.

GCC manuals
All distributions of the GNU C compiler should include full documentation for all its features, stored in several info files that can be read with the Emacs program or another info reader. By the way, the information on Extended Inline Assembly is quite hard to follow, since it does not refer to any specific architecture. Some pertinent information about Intel 80x86 GCC's Inline Assembly can be found at:

http://sag-www.ssl.berkeley.edu/~korpela/djgpp_asm.html
http://www.castle.net/~avly/djasm.html

The Linux Documentation Project
> The web site at:

> *http://www.linuxdoc.org*

> contains the home page of the Linux Documentation Project, which, in turn, includes several interesting references to guides, FAQs, and HOWTOs.

Linux kernel development forum
> The newsgroup:

> *comp.os.linux.development.system*

> is dedicated to discussions about development of the Linux system.

The linux-kernel mailing list
> This fascinating mailing list contains much noise as well as a few pertinent comments about the current development version of Linux and about the rationale for including or not including in the kernel some proposals for changes. It is a living laboratory of new ideas that are taking shape. The name of the mailing list is:

> *linux-kernel@vger.kernel.org*

The Linux Kernel online book
> Authored by David A. Rusling, this 200-page book can be viewed at:

> *http://www.linuxdoc.org/LDP/tlk/tlk.html*

> and describes some fundamental aspects of the Linux kernel.

Linux Virtual File System
> The pages at:

> *http://www.atnf.csiro.au/~rgooch/linux/vfs.txt*

> are an introduction to the Linux Virtual File System. The author is Richard Gooch.

SOURCE CODE INDEX

C

INDEX

B

B flag (Segment Descriptor), 39
Bach, Maurice, 2
background (bg) processes, 29
BACKGR_TIMER static timer, 147
bad_area identifier, 217
    faulty address inside address space, 221
    faulty address outside address
        space, 220
bad_pipe_r(), 535
bad_pipe_w(), 535
balancing factor, AVL trees, 201
base field (pipe_inode_info structure), 528
Base field (Segment Descriptor), 38
base time quantum, 281
batch processes, 278
b_blocknr field (buffer head), 400
b_count field (buffer head), 400
b_data field (buffer head), 400
b_dev field (buffer head), 400
b_dev_id field (buffer head), 400
bdflush kernel thread
    kernel_thread() and, 96
    writing dirty buffers to disk, 427
bdflush_max table, 427
bdflush_min table, 427
bdflush_wait task queue, 428
bdf_prm table, 427, 429
BEEP_TIMER static timer, 147
b_end_io field (buffer head), 400, 410, 421
b_flushtime field (buffer head), 400
bforget(), 423
bg_block_bitmap field (Ext2 group
    descriptor), 501
bg_free_blocks_count field (Ext2 group
    descriptor), 501
bg_free_inodes_count field (Ext2 group
    descriptor), 501
bg_inode_bitmap field (Ext2 group
    descriptor), 501
bg_inode_table field (Ext2 group
    descriptor), 501
bg_pad field (Ext2 group descriptor), 501
bg_reserved field (Ext2 group
    descriptor), 501
bg_used_dirs_count field (Ext2 group
    descriptor), 501
bh field (request descriptor), 403

bh_base, grouping bottom halves, 128
bh_cachep slab allocator cache, 417
BH_Dirty flag (b_state field), 401
    brw_page() and, 412
    buffer heads for cached buffers, 420
    make_request() and, 406
BH_Lock flag (b_state field), 401
    buffer heads for cached buffers, 420
    end_request() and, 410
    make_request() and, 406
    mark_buffer_uptodate() and, 413
BH_Protected flag (b_state field), 401
BH_Req flag (b_state field), 401
    ll_rw_block() and, 406
bhtail field (request descriptor), 403
BH_Uptodate flag (b_statc field), 400
    brw_page() and, 412
    end_request() and, 410
    make_request() and, 406
    mark_buffer_uptodate() and, 413
bibliography, 595–597
bind() system call, 380
/bin/swapoff program, 465
/bin/swapon program, 465
BIOS (Basic Input/Output System), 575
    booting Linux from a floppy disk, 577
    bootstrap procedure, 576
    initializing the IDT, 113
bitmap caches, 507–509
bitmaps in buddy system, 166
bitmask mode, 78
BLANK_TIMER static timer, 147
b_list field (buffer head), 400
blk_dev table, 405
blkdev_inode_operations table, 382, 512
blkdev_open()
    activating a swap area, 466
    mounting the root filesystem, 352
    opening a device file, 382
blkdevs table, 381
blk_dev_struct data structure, 404
blksize_size table, 394
block bitmap caches, 507–509
block clustering, 407
block device drivers
    architecture of, 395
    descriptors, 404–407
    high-level, 395
        deferring requests, 402

X

Z

About the Authors

Daniel P. Bovet got a Ph.D. in computer science at UCLA in 1968 and is now full Professor at the University of Rome, "Tor Vergata," Italy. He had to wait over 25 years before being able to teach an operating system course in a proper manner because of the lack of source code for modern, well-designed systems. Now, thanks to cheap PCs and to Linux, Marco and Dan are able to cover all the facets of an operating system from booting to tuning and are able to hand out tough, satisfying homework to their students. (These young guys working at home on their PCs are really spoiled; they never had to fight with punched cards.) In fact, Dan was so fascinated by the accomplishments of Linus Torvalds and his followers that he spent the last few years trying to unravel some of Linux's mysteries. It seemed natural, after all that work, to write a book about what he found.

Marco Cesati got a degree in mathematics in 1992 and a Ph.D. in computer science (University of Rome, "La Sapienza") in 1995. He is now a research assistant in the computer science department of the School of Engineering (University of Rome, "Tor Vergata"). In the past he served as system administrator and Unix programmer for the university (as a Ph.D. student) and for several institutions (as a consultant). During the last three years he has been continuously involved in teaching his students how to change the Linux kernel in strange and funny ways.

Colophon

Our look is the result of reader comments, our own experimentation, and feedback from distribution channels. Distinctive covers complement our distinctive approach to technical topics, breathing personality and life into potentially dry subjects.

The cover image of a man with a bubble is adapted from a 19th-century engraving from the Dover Pictorial Archive. Edie Freeman designed the cover. Emma Colby produced the cover with QuarkXPress 4.1, using the ITC Garamond Condensed font. David Futato designed the interior layout based on a series design by Alicia Cech. Chapter opener images are taken from the Dover Pictorial Archive, the book *Marvels of the New West: A Vivid Portrayal of the Stupendous Marvels in the Vast Wonderland West of the Missouri River* (by William M. Thayer, The Henry Bill Publishing Company, Norwich, CT, 1888), and *The Pioneer History of America: A Popular Account of the Heroes and Adventures* (by Augustus Lynch Mason, A.M., The Jones Brothers Publishing Company, Cincinnati, OH, 1884). Mike Sierra implemented the design in FrameMaker 5.5.6.

Catherine Morris was the production editor, and Norma Emory was the copyeditor for *Understanding the Linux Kernel*. Clairemarie Fisher O'Leary was the proofreader. Jeff Holcomb, Claire Cloutier, and Catherine Morris provided quality control. Judy Hoer and Joe Wizda wrote the index. Linley Dolby, Rachel Wheeler, and Deborah Smith provided production support. The illustrations that appear in the book were produced by Robert Romano using Macromedia FreeHand 8 and Adobe Photoshop 5.

Whenever possible, our books use a durable and flexible lay-flat binding. If the page count exceeds this binding's limit, perfect binding is used.

How to stay in touch with O'Reilly

1. Visit Our Award-Winning Web Site

http://www.oreilly.com/

★ "Top 100 Sites on the Web" —*PC Magazine*
★ "Top 5% Web sites" —*Point Communications*
★ "3-Star site" —*The McKinley Group*

Our web site contains a library of comprehensive product information (including book excerpts and tables of contents), downloadable software, background articles, interviews with technology leaders, links to relevant sites, book cover art, and more. File us in your Bookmarks or Hotlist!

2. Join Our Email Mailing Lists

New Product Releases
To receive automatic email with brief descriptions of all new O'Reilly products as they are released, send email to:
ora-news-subscribe@lists.oreilly.com
Put the following information in the first line of your message (*not* in the Subject field):
subscribe ora-news

O'Reilly Events
If you'd also like us to send information about trade show events, special promotions, and other O'Reilly events, send email to:
ora-news-subscribe@lists.oreilly.com
Put the following information in the first line of your message (*not* in the Subject field):
subscribe ora-events

3. Get Examples from Our Books via FTP

There are two ways to access an archive of example files from our books:

Regular FTP
- ftp to:
ftp.oreilly.com
(login: anonymous
password: your email address)
- Point your web browser to:
ftp://ftp.oreilly.com/

FTPMAIL
- Send an email message to:
ftpmail@online.oreilly.com
(Write "help" in the message body)

4. Contact Us via Email

order@oreilly.com
To place a book or software order online. Good for North American and international customers.

subscriptions@oreilly.com
To place an order for any of our newsletters or periodicals.

books@oreilly.com
General questions about any of our books.

software@oreilly.com
For general questions and product information about our software. Check out O'Reilly Software Online at **http://software.oreilly.com/** for software and technical support information. Registered O'Reilly software users send your questions to: **website-support@oreilly.com**

cs@oreilly.com
For answers to problems regarding your order or our products.

booktech@oreilly.com
For book content technical questions or corrections.

proposals@oreilly.com
To submit new book or software proposals to our editors and product managers.

international@oreilly.com
For information about our international distributors or translation queries. For a list of our distributors outside of North America check out:
http://www.oreilly.com/distributors.html

5. Work with Us

Check out our website for current employment opportunites:
http://jobs.oreilly.com/

O'Reilly & Associates, Inc.
101 Morris Street, Sebastopol, CA 95472 USA
TEL   707-829-0515 or 800-998-9938
       (6am to 5pm PST)
FAX   707-829-0104

International Distributors

http://international.oreilly.com/distributors.html • international@oreilly.com

UK, EUROPE, MIDDLE EAST AND AFRICA (EXCEPT FRANCE, GERMANY, AUSTRIA, SWITZERLAND, LUXEMBOURG, AND LIECHTENSTEIN)

INQUIRIES
O'Reilly UK Limited
4 Castle Street
Farnham
Surrey, GU9 7HS
United Kingdom
Telephone: 44-1252-711776
Fax: 44-1252-734211
Email: information@oreilly.co.uk

ORDERS
Wiley Distribution Services Ltd.
1 Oldlands Way
Bognor Regis
West Sussex PO22 9SA
United Kingdom
Telephone: 44-1243-843294
UK Freephone: 0800-243207
Fax: 44-1243-843302 (Europe/EU orders)
or 44-1243-843274 (Middle East/Africa)
Email: cs-books@wiley.co.uk

FRANCE

INQUIRIES & ORDERS
Éditions O'Reilly
18 rue Séguier
75006 Paris, France
Tel: 33-1-40-51-71-89
Fax: 33-1-40-51-72-26
Email: france@oreilly.fr

GERMANY, SWITZERLAND, AUSTRIA, LUXEMBOURG, AND LIECHTENSTEIN

INQUIRIES & ORDERS
O'Reilly Verlag
Balthasarstr. 81
D-50670 Köln, Germany
Telephone: 49-221-973160-91
Fax: 49-221-973160-8
Email: anfragen@oreilly.de (inquiries)
Email: order@oreilly.de (orders)

CANADA (FRENCH LANGUAGE BOOKS)
Les Éditions Flammarion ltée
375, Avenue Laurier Ouest
Montréal (Québec) H2V 2K3
Tel: 1-514-277-8807
Fax: 1-514-278-2085
Email: info@flammarion.qc.ca

HONG KONG
City Discount Subscription Service, Ltd.
Unit A, 6th Floor, Yan's Tower
27 Wong Chuk Hang Road
Aberdeen, Hong Kong
Tel: 852-2580-3539
Fax: 852-2580-6463
Email: citydis@ppn.com.hk

KOREA
Hanbit Media, Inc.
Chungmu Bldg. 210
Yonnam-dong 568-33
Mapo-gu
Seoul, Korea
Tel: 822-325-0397
Fax: 822-325-9697
Email: hant93@chollian.dacom.co.kr

PHILIPPINES
Global Publishing
G/F Benavides Garden
1186 Benavides Street
Manila, Philippines
Tel: 632-254-8949/632-252-2582
Fax: 632-734-5060/632-252-2733
Email: globalp@pacific.net.ph

TAIWAN
O'Reilly Taiwan
1st Floor, No. 21, Lane 295
Section 1, Fu-Shing South Road
Taipei, 106 Taiwan
Tel: 886-2-27099669
Fax: 886-2-27038802
Email: mori@oreilly.com

INDIA
Shroff Publishers & Distributors Pvt. Ltd.
12, "Roseland", 2nd Floor
180, Waterfield Road, Bandra (West)
Mumbai 400 050
Tel: 91-22-641-1800/643-9910
Fax: 91-22-643-2422
Email: spd@vsnl.com

CHINA
O'Reilly Beijing
SIGMA Building, Suite B809
No. 49 Zhichun Road
Haidian District
Beijing, China PR 100080
Tel: 86-10-8809-7475
Fax: 86-10-8809-7463
Email: beijing@oreilly.com

JAPAN
O'Reilly Japan, Inc.
Yotsuya Y's Building
7 Banch 6, Honshio-cho
Shinjuku-ku
Tokyo 160-0003 Japan
Tel: 81-3-3356-5227
Fax: 81-3-3356-5261
Email: japan@oreilly.com

SINGAPORE, INDONESIA, MALAYSIA AND THAILAND
TransQuest Publishers Pte Ltd
30 Old Toh Tuck Road #05-02
Sembawang Kimtrans Logistics Centre
Singapore 597654
Tel: 65-4623112
Fax: 65-4625761
Email: wendiw@transquest.com.sg

ALL OTHER COUNTRIES
O'Reilly & Associates, Inc.
101 Morris Street
Sebastopol, CA 95472 USA
Tel: 707-829-0515
Fax: 707-829-0104
Email: order@oreilly.com

AUSTRALIA
Woodslane Pty., Ltd.
7/5 Vuko Place
Warriewood NSW 2102
Australia
Tel: 61-2-9970-5111
Fax: 61-2-9970-5002
Email: info@woodslane.com.au

NEW ZEALAND
Woodslane New Zealand, Ltd.
21 Cooks Street (P.O. Box 575)
Waganui, New Zealand
Tel: 64-6-347-6543
Fax: 64-6-345-4840
Email: info@woodslane.com.au

ARGENTINA
Distribuidora Cuspide
Suipacha 764
1008 Buenos Aires
Argentina
Phone: 54-11-4322-8868
Fax: 54-11-4322-3456
Email: libros@cuspide.com

O'REILLY®

TO ORDER: **800-998-9938** • *order@oreilly.com* • *http://www.oreilly.com/*
OUR PRODUCTS ARE AVAILABLE AT A BOOKSTORE OR SOFTWARE STORE NEAR YOU.
FOR INFORMATION: **800-998-9938** • **707-829-0515** • *info@oreilly.com*